An Economic History of the First German Unification

There is a striking chronological parallel between Germany's transition from a post-Malthusian regime to modern economic growth and the formation of a modern nation-state between the late 1860s and the early 1880s, which culminated in the events of 1871. The central question of this book is whether and how such state formation did in fact contribute to economic development.

Twenty chapters written by leading experts in their respective fields deal with various aspects of the book's main question. Together, they identify three channels by which national unification contributed to Germany's economic development: (1) Creation of a nation-state completed a process of institutional Unification of a large inland area and thereby increased the integration of domestic markets. (2) Unification raised the capacity of the political system with respect to regulating complex domains, such as stock companies, patenting, and social insurance. (3) The emerging political regime of market-preserving federalism promoted the quality of economic institutions. Moreover, a set of chapters dealing with the experience of other European economies apart from Germany during the second half of the nineteenth century highlight additional factors in nineteenth-century economic development, most notably the first wave of modern globalization and economic geography.

Readers interested in the history of state building and the economic history of Germany and of Europe in general during the age of industrialization and globalization and students of the economic effects of political integration and decentralized state growth will all gain much from this book.

Ulrich Pfister obtained his PhD from the University of Zürich, Switzerland, in 1984. Since 1996, he is Professor of Social and Economic History at the University of Münster, Germany. His research covers agricultural history, proto-industrialization, demographic history, and historical national accounts.

Nikolaus Wolf obtained his PhD from Humboldt University Berlin in 2003. After positions at the London School of Economics, Free University Berlin, and the University of Warwick, in 2010 he became Professor of Economics and Economic History at Humboldt University. He works on the economic history of Europe in the 19th and 20th centuries, with a focus on economic geography, trade, borders, and identity.

Routledge Explorations in Economic History

Edited by Lars Magnusson, Uppsala University, Sweden

Institutions and Chinese Economic Development
A Comparative Historical Approach
Li Tan

Port-Cities and their Hinterlands
Migration, Trade and Cultural Exchange from the Early Seventeenth-Century to 1939
Edited by Robert Lee and Paul McNamara

The Economy of Renaissance Italy
Paolo Malanima

The Decline of British Industrial Hegemony
Bengal Industries 1914–46
Indrajit Ray

Industry and Development in Argentina
An Intellectual History, 1914–1980
Marcelo Rougier and Juan Odisio
Translated by James Brennan

The Real Estate Market in the Roman World
Edited by Marta García Morcillo and Cristina Rosillo-López

An Economic History of the First German Unification
State Formation and Economic Development in a European Perspective
Edited by Ulrich Pfister and Nikolaus Wolf

For more information about this series, please visit: www.routledge.com/Routledge-Explorations-in-Economic-History/book-series/SE0347

An Economic History of the First German Unification

State Formation and Economic Development in a European Perspective

Edited by
Ulrich Pfister and Nikolaus Wolf

Routledge
Taylor & Francis Group
LONDON AND NEW YORK

First published 2023
by Routledge
4 Park Square, Milton Park, Abingdon, Oxon OX14 4RN

and by Routledge
605 Third Avenue, New York, NY 10158

Routledge is an imprint of the Taylor & Francis Group, an informa business

British Library Cataloguing-in-Publication Data
A catalogue record for this book is available from the British Library

ISBN: 978-1-032-25483-8 (hbk)
ISBN: 978-1-032-25484-5 (pbk)
ISBN: 978-1-003-28343-0 (ebk)

DOI: 10.4324/9781003283430

Typeset in Bembo
by codeMantra

Contents

Contributors

Thilo N. H. Albers is Postdoctoral Researcher at the Institute of Economic History at Humboldt University, Berlin.

Gerold Ambrosius is Professor Emeritus of Economic and Social History, Universität Siegen.

Charlotte Bartels is Postdoctoral Researcher at DIW Berlin.

Sascha O. Becker is Xiaokai Yang Chair of Business and Economics at Monash University, Melbourne, Australia.

Sebastian Till Braun is Professor of Economics VII: Quantitative Economic History at the University of Bayreuth.

Carsten Burhop is Professor of Constitutional, Social, and Economic History at the University of Bonn.

Francesco Cinnirella, is Associate Professor in the Department of Management, Economics and Quantitative Methods at the University of Bergamo.

Nicholas Crafts is Professor Emeritus of Economics and Economic History at the University of Warwick.

Alexander Donges is Postdoctoral Researcher of Economic History at the University of Mannheim.

Jean-Pierre Dormois is Professor of Contemporary History at the University of Bordeaux.

Giovanni Federico is Professor of Economic History, NYU Abu Dhabi.

Jan-Otmar Hesse is Professor of Economic and Social History at the University of Bayreuth.

Erik Hornung is Professor of Economic History at the University of Cologne.

Wolf-Fabian Hungerland, Economics, is Federal Ministry of Economics and Energy and Research Fellow at the Institute of Economic History at Humboldt University, Berlin.

Tobias A. Jopp is Postdoctoral Researcher of Economic and Social History at the University of Regensburg.

Felix Kersting is Postdoctoral Researcher at the Institute of Economic History at Humboldt University, Berlin.

Markus Lampe is Professor of Economic and Social History at the Vienna University of Economics and Business.

Matthias Morys is Senior Lecturer in Economic History in the Department of Economics at the University of York, Great Britain.

Ulrich Pfister is Professor of Social and Economic History at the University of Münster.

Alfred Reckendrees is Associate Professor for Business History in the Department of Management, Politics and Philosophy at the Centre for Business History, Copenhagen Business School.

Eva-Maria Roelevink is Assistant Professor of Economic History at the University of Mainz.

Michael C. Schneider is Postdoctoral Researcher of Economic History at the University of Düsseldorf.

Max-Stephan Schulze is Professor of Economic History at London School of Economics and Political Science, London.

Felix Selgert is Postdoctoral Researcher of Constitutional, Social, and Economic History at the University of Bonn.

Mark Spoerer is Professor of Economic and Social History at the University of Regensburg.

Jochen Streb is Professor of Economic History at the University of Mannheim.

Nikolaus Wolf is Professor of Economics and Economic History at Humboldt University

Dieter Ziegler is Professor of Economic and Business History at the University of Bochum.

Acknowledgements

This volume is the result of an initiative by the Standing Field Committee on Economic History in the *Verein für Socialpolitik* (German Economic Association). Our aim was to bring together the state of research on the economic history of the first German nation-state on the occasion of the 150th anniversary of the founding of the German Reich in January 1871. An authors' workshop, which was essential for the advancement of this project, took place in Heidelberg on 2–4 March 2020. We thank the Fritz Thyssen Foundation for sponsoring this meeting and the Heidelberg Center for American Studies for its hospitality. We also thank Michael Burda, Timothy Guinnane, Jan-Otmar Hesse, Mark Spoerer, and Adam Tooze for their valuable intellectual contributions at various stages of the project. Finally, we gratefully acknowledge the financial support of the Humboldt University Berlin and the University of Münster for the preparation of the final manuscript.

1 Introduction

Ulrich Pfister, Jan-Otmar Hesse, Mark Spoerer, and Nikolaus Wolf

1 Foundation of the German Empire in 1871 as the dawn of an epoch

The proclamation of the German Empire in January 1871 is considered to be a central event in German history, with repercussions all over Europe. Demands for a nation-state had been voiced during the Napoleonic Wars and gained renewed momentum at the end of the 1850s. Moreover, with the North German Confederation of 1866/67, a federal state was already forming in northern Germany. This state had a federal parliament and a federal constitution from which the Imperial Constitution later emerged.[1] However, the German Empire in 1871 did by no means complete the formation of a German nation-state. From monetary and fiscal policy to education, many policy areas remained fragmented for years. Most federal decision-making routines were not established prior to the 1880s. These were essentially based on the Imperial government and the *Reichstag* (the national parliament) but involved numerous other actors—including the Imperial Offices (ministries of the central government), the member states, the parties, and numerous interest groups—through a network of formal and informal institutions. Furthermore, the Hanseatic cities of Hamburg and Bremen did not join the customs territory of the German Empire until 1888 (Henrich-Franke 2018: 31–36; Chapter 4 of this volume).

However, in a remarkable temporal parallel to the formation of a nation-state, a fundamental structural break in Germany's long-term economic development occurred (see Chapter 5 of this volume). The period lasting from the 1810s to around 1870 can be described as the post-Malthusian era, following a variant of unified growth theory (Galor and Weil 2000; Galor 2011); strong population growth was accompanied by an expanding economy, but nearly stagnant values of real output per capita and real wages. This was related to the spread of new labour-intensive agricultural techniques, the deepening of market integration, and the interregional division of labour. About a decade after political unification, Germany entered into the modern economic growth phase: On a per capita basis, real economic output expanded more or less steadily at about 1.5 percent per year, a rate similar to that

DOI: 10.4324/9781003283430-1

from the last quarter of the twentieth century to the present. This resulted from a successful struggle for redistribution (chapter 14) and from the fact that technical progress and the continuous improvement of labour's endowment with capital and human capital had become important drivers of growth. The industries of the so-called Second Industrial Revolution that depended on new technologies and skilled workers experienced strong growth during this period, notably chemical engineering, electrical engineering, and mechanical engineering. The increased importance of human capital in the production process was one of several reasons why married couples began to have fewer children. Over time, this so-called first fertility transition caused a slowdown in population growth, which allowed for substantial improvements in material welfare per capita (for overviews, see Burhop 2011; Tilly and Kopsidis 2020; see also Chapter 5 of this volume).

Can we conclude from this striking temporal parallel that political unification was causal to the observed structural break in Germany's growth regime? This book brings together contributions from experts who discuss recent research in specific areas of economic history under this guiding perspective and embeds it in the European context. With this perspective, we reflect on the chronology common in both history and economic history, not only in German but also in European and global history. The rise of global history studies in recent decades has called into question common chronologies, which were quite predominantly derived from European history (Lorenz 2017). At the same time, however, existing terms for particular time periods continue to be used, such as that of a 'long nineteenth century' or a 'First Globalisation', which is set from 1870 to 1914, as in the *Cambridge Economic History of Modern Europe* of 2010. Jürgen Osterhammel (2006: 48) calls periodisation an 'unloved necessity' and quotes Krzysztof Pomian (1984: 162): 'Les périodisations servent à rendre les faits pensables'. For most research in economic history, 1870 marks the beginning of modern economies, not only in Germany but also in Europe and the world. The laying of the transatlantic telegraph cable (1866) as well as the opening of the Suez Canal and the first trans-American railway connection (both in 1869) are important events with global historical dimensions. Influential narratives of economic history in the late nineteenth century take 1870 as their starting points, such as the so-called First Globalisation (O'Rourke and Williamson 1999), the Second Industrial Revolution (Mokyr 1988), the Second Economic Revolution (North 1981: Chapter 13), or the transition to modern economic growth (Galor 2011: Chapter 2), yet typically without reference to political events. The German case in particular raises the question of how the political unification of 1871 mattered for the country's economic development. How important was unification to the fact that Germany, which was rather backward in relation to its western neighbours, was not only able to make the transition to the Second Industrial Revolution at about the same time but also even significantly pushed ahead, similar to the United States? Conversely, to what extent and how did social and economic factors contribute to the political change that culminated in 1871?

The contributions to this volume address these two questions from different angles, which can be grouped under four major headings that correspond to the structure of the book. The first part deals with the interaction between nation-building, economic development, and economic policy in the process that led to the founding of the German Empire. It addresses the dynamics of the German national movement, the intergovernmental coordination of economic policy since the founding of the *Zollverein*, and the emergence of a national economic policy in the course of the founding of the North German Confederation and the Empire, respectively. The second part examines the founding of the nation-state as a potential turning point both in terms of long-term economic development and with regard to central areas of economic policy, such as fiscal and monetary policy. In the third part, the focus is on economic and social developments within the framework of the new nation-state, such as the relations between private companies and politics, the expansion of education, increasing inequality, and the effects of the first wave of modern globalisation. The chapters in the fourth part change perspective and examine the founding of the German Empire from the outside, namely from the viewpoint of developments in Great Britain, France, Italy, and Austria-Hungary. Thus, the book provides a survey of economic development and nation-building in nineteenth-century Germany, embedded in a wider European perspective.

2 Economic background to the formation of the German nation-state

Various approaches have been developed to study the interaction between economic and political integration in the founding of the German nation-state. The first approach focuses on the economic drivers of national unification. In the German case, the founding of the first nation-state was built on inter-governmental cooperation among German states, which intensified during the middle decades of the nineteenth century. The *Zollverein*, founded in 1834, and the German Confederation, which had emerged from the Congress of Vienna (1814/15), constituted the main framework for this process. Not only was the customs union created with the *Zollverein*, but also, among other things, a uniform bill of exchange system (1848), the Postal Union and Telegraph Union Treaties (1850), the General German Commercial Code (1861), and the harmonisation of coinage (1838, 1857) created important institutional foundations for a common market until the 1860s (see Chapter 3 of this volume).

The unification of Germany in the nineteenth century has often been interpreted against the background of the (neo-)functionalist approach, which originated in the analysis of international relations and has been applied, above all, to the process of European integration since 1950 (Sandholtz and Stone Sweet 2012; Wolf 2012). Correspondingly, scholarship writing in this vein has highlighted analogies between the unification of Germany in the nineteenth century and the early stages of European integration (Henderson 1981; Dumke 1984; Voth 2001). According to this approach, increasing economic interdependence between states leads to a growing demand for international coordination standards and supranational economic law. If the first steps towards integration are successful, the dynamics of integration spill over to other policy areas—in Germany's case, from customs policy to coinage and trade law. On the one hand, the consolidation of inter-governmental co-operation encourages the development of epistemic communities of experts who can plan and implement further integration steps. In Germany, the civil servants involved in the administration of the *Zollverein* and legal experts in commercial and business law were of particular relevance to this process. On the other hand, when inter-governmental relations increasingly transcend the preserve of experts and become the focus of political debates, political actors shift their sphere of action from the state level to the inter-governmental level, which corresponds to the national level, and the latter develops into a new political field of its own right. The debates on customs policy that began in the 1840s are a salient example of this development. From such a (neo-)functionalist perspective, the formation of the nation-state appears to be primarily the result of nineteenth-century market integration (on market integration, see Chapter 7).

However, this narrative remains incomplete in several respects. On the one hand, a simple line of causality from economic factors to political developments is not very plausible. Ideational and intellectual currents, cultural forces, and the development of the power constellation since about 1800, not least the antagonism between Prussia and the Habsburg monarchy, were other important factors.[2] These ideational and political factors interacted with each other, but also with socio-economic change itself. On the other hand, the inevitability of developments is often assumed (hindsight bias), which obscures possible alternatives. Recent literature in economics addresses these problems by examining nation-building and identity change with the methods of empirical microeconomics, which works at the actor level (examples include Alesina and Spolaore 1997; Alesina et al. 2019). In the German case, the developments that led to the founding of the nation-state in 1871 can be represented as an interplay of strategic interests of governments (especially Prussia), the national movement as the supporting layer of national identity, and the process of economic integration (Chapter 2 of this volume). Thomas Nipperdey's well-known thesis, according to which Prussia's territorial expansion in the wake of the Congress of Vienna 'became the strongest driving force of Prussian power politics', proves to be fruitful.

3 Impact of nation-building on economic development: four channels

Many chapters of this volume explore how political unification has contributed to the transition to modern economic growth. Not least because of methodological difficulties, which will be discussed in the next section, the findings cannot always achieve the level of robustness that would be desirable. We are often forced to argue on the basis of plausibility. Nevertheless, the results suggest four channels through which nation-building has impacted on economic development.

Channel 1: Identity politics as a factor of economic behaviour. National movements and the political processes leading to the formation of nation-states are primarily the subjects of political history and political science. Research into the rise of nationalism following Anderson (1983) has emphasised the effect of nation-building on shaping individual behaviour, with education, socialisation, and the mass media as the main mediating factors. It is generally accepted that nation-state symbols of the German Empire had considerable integrating effects: the most important German victory in the French-German War in Sedan became a public holiday; many cities erected so-called Bismarck Towers to celebrate the founder of the Empire; the social security system became a national project itself; and Krupp's biggest cannon was referred to as 'fat Bertha', a symbol of the Reich's military power (Weichlein 2004). Even so, the German Empire remained marked by internal tensions and conflicts at its margins. The language policy pursued to assimilate the Polish population, for example, was at best only successful to a limited extent (see Chapter 15 of this volume).

National values may also have conditioned choices at the household level, as Trentman's (2009) study of the relationship between national identity policy and consumption patterns in Great Britain shows. This effect of nation-building has been rarely studied in Germany thus far. Nevertheless, Chapter 2 of this volume shows that the population in areas that were absorbed by Prussia in the 1810s increasingly chose national first names for their children that had less to do with local tradition or Prussian connotations. Border changes and the resulting integration efforts led to the reorganisation and synchronisation of social identities even in the private sphere. The available evidence suggests that behaviour and behavioural expectations were also synchronised in this way, for example during deployment at the front in the context of the war of 1870–71. The formation of a common national identity is likely to have facilitated the supra-regional cooperation between actors and contributed to growth.

While identity politics may have contributed to economic prosperity, we should not neglect its effects in the form of nationalism and Prussian militarism at the turn of the century. Anglo-German fleet rivalry; industrialists' interest in iron ore deposits in France and Belgium; Bernhard von Bülow's claim to a 'place in the sun' (1897), a euphemistic description for a brutal colonial policy—these are frequently mentioned effects of Germany's nationalism in the late nineteenth century, which cannot be separated from the starting phase of identity politics (Smith 1978, 1986, 2020; Kennedy 1980). We believe, however, that neither imperialist ideas nor rearmament made a significant contribution to the economic growth of the 1880s and 1890s, but rather developed from it as a consequence. This area invites further research.

Channel 2: Market integration. In the wake of the founding of the North German Confederation and the Empire, state action in several fields completed the institutional integration that had been underway for several decades and created a unified internal market. This should have reduced trade costs and enabled a deepening of the interregional division of labour. Beyond a static welfare gain, a deepening of the division of labour also increases the degree of specialisation, which favours the accumulation of knowledge related to highly specific activities. Consequently, the creation of a Germany-wide internal market may also have accelerated the pace of technological progress. Important processes of the late 1860s and 1870s that effected institutional integration relate first to the unification of standards governing economic transactions, specifically in the form of the introduction of metric weights and measures (1868/69; Groß 2015; Kramper 2019: 375–86) and the conclusion of a monetary union with the Mark as the common currency (1873; Chapter 9 of this volume). As the *Reichsbank* was, for a long time, the only bank with branches in all parts of the country, the currency reform contributed to the emergence of a Germany-wide money market. The uniform regulation of citizenship, a liberal trade code (the ADHGB, 1861 and 1869), and freedom of establishment (1867) together created a uniform labour market, and in many respects, also a uniform market for services and capital (Chapters 3 and 4). The harmonisation of patent laws (1877) provided foreign inventors with efficient and largely non-discriminatory access to the German market, promoting not only national but also international technology transfer and technological competition (Chapter 10).

With regard to communications infrastructure, organisational standardisation took place at the national level in the cases of postal services and telegraphy (1868), but hardly with respect to the railways, where technical standardisation was nevertheless far advanced (Chapter 7).

Whether and to what extent the completion of institutional integration in the course of nation-state formation also promoted market integration and thus economic development is anything but clear and has not been systematically investigated thus far. Donges and Streb (Chapter 10 of this volume) consider it likely that the unification of patent law accelerated the spread of new technologies. The growth of the transport capacity of the railways, whose expansion is generally regarded as the central driver of German market integration in the nineteenth century, lost momentum after 1873, and the effect of newly built lines on urban growth was weaker during this period than in the first phase of railway construction around the middle of the century (Chapter 7). The only study of market integration that spans the entire nineteenth century, although based only on four grain price series, finds little further increase in the extent of market integration after the early 1850s (Uebele 2011: 234). Wolf (2009: 862–77), who analyses transport data for a wide range of agricultural and industrial goods, shows that domestic markets were still fragmented until 1913 compared to cross-border trade and compared to the interwar period. A similar conclusion applies to the market for patents within Germany before 1914 (Burhop and Wolf 2013). All these findings suggest that market integration remained limited and was possibly more important for economic growth before 1871 than afterward. At the same time, world market integration increased significantly from the 1890s onwards and was arguably more significant for the transition to modern growth than domestic market integration. Nevertheless, market integration undisputedly constituted one channel among others through which nation-state formation impacted on economic growth.

Channel 3: State capacity in a federalist framework. The expansion of state power, especially the ability of a state to collect taxes (fiscal capacity), enforce law and order, and provide other public goods, has been repeatedly cited in recent research as a central reason for the economic success of nation-states. Comparative studies show a positive correlation between indicators of state capacity and long-term economic development. The centralisation of the ability to levy taxes as well as parliamentary control over the budget is considered to be the main foundations for the emergence of effective and powerful states (Dincecco 2015; Dincecco and Katz 2016; for an overview, see Johnson and Koyama 2017). Did the formation of a German nation-state expand state capacity and contribute to the transition to modern economic growth?

Some facts immediately come to mind that contradict the abovementioned empirical literature. In Germany, the formation of the nation-state was accompanied by only limited centralisation of the tax system; at the beginning of the twentieth century, the lion's share of tax revenue still accrued to the member states and municipalities. The overall tax ratio (tax income over national income) rose only very gradually; a certain acceleration can at best be observed at the end of the nineteenth century, but hardly at the time when the Empire was founded. Finally, the Empire remained a semi-parliamentary regime with limited control of the government and state expenditure by the people's representatives. If one focuses on central government finances, the formation of the nation-state did not represent a step towards the expansion of state power, and no effects of fiscal policy on growth consequences can be discerned. The federal design of the fiscal constitution is the most important reason for this negative finding (see Chapter 6 of this volume).

It is possible, however, that the federal structure of the Empire even favoured Germany's transition to modern economic growth. A federal state structure can help maintain the autonomy of markets by decentralising taxation and, to some extent, regulatory competence as well as the collection and use of information (Weingast 1995; Qian and Weingast 1997). In particular, the continued ability of municipalities to levy taxes and use them, for example, for investment in local infrastructure, might have been beneficial. It may have been a strength of the German fiscal regime that the municipalities had considerably more fiscal autonomy than in most other emerging industrialised countries (Chapter 6).

The economic implications of the Empire's federal structure become particularly obvious in comparison with national unification in Italy (see

Chapter 18 of this volume). In both countries, a hegemon—Prussia and Sardinia-Piedmont respectively—played a central role in the political and military conflicts that led to the formation of a nation-state. In Italy, the hegemon also provided the blueprint for the subsequent establishment of national institutions: In a process nicknamed *unificazione a vapore* (unification by steamroller), the constitution and many elements of economic and social law (including the organisation of the school system) were simply transferred from Sardinia-Piedmont to Italy as a whole. In this way, a centralised unitary state was created in a short time. However, this was a weak state: persistent resistance in the south in the form of *brigantaggio* (banditry), for example, prevented the enforcement of law and order throughout the territory. In Germany, by contrast, despite the much stronger demographic and economic weight of the hegemon, new national institutions were created in a federal state structure from the late 1860s onwards in an independent political process. Furthermore, while Prussia was the dominant actor in this process, its influence remained checked by that of smaller states such as Bavaria, Saxony, and Wurttemberg.

The different state structures of Italy and Germany can be related to the argument that efficient federal structures require the existence of decentralised units that effectively provide public goods. Furthermore, such units must be well rooted in their respective regional societies in order to be credible negotiating partners in higher-level—that is, federal—policy processes (Ziblatt 2006: Chapter 1). In Italy, Sardinia-Piedmont was the only state with a constitutional regime after 1848, and national unification simultaneously sealed the demise of patrimonial ruling structures in other parts of the peninsula. In Germany, however, political and institutional reforms took place as a decentralised process from the early nineteenth century onwards: not only Prussia but also the Rhine Confederation states underwent profound reforms at the time of the Napoleonic Wars. In some German states, the revolutions of 1830 and 1848 brought about more fundamental changes than in Prussia, whose monarchy was henceforth under even greater pressure to legitimise limited political participation (Nipperdey 1983: chapters I and III; Fehrenbach 2007). This also led to the development of different approaches to economic law by individual states—illustrated in this volume by the protection of intellectual property (Chapter 10). Given the persistence of the member states throughout the wars of unification, the development of national economic (and other) institutions required the establishment of new political processes on a new level above that of individual member states, including new statistical tools to systematically describe the dynamics of the new federal state across its members (Chapter 8).

The power structure of the member states of the German Empire was by no means static. Rather, the formation of a federal state from the 1860s to the 1880s appears to have been only one element of rising state capacity observable at several levels. Towards the end of this period, urban municipalities began to offer public services, including energy, water, and transport

(Chapter 4 of this volume). In the 1870s, several member states handed over road construction to lower-level public authorities (municipalities and regional administrations). Road construction had accounted for a considerable part of public expenditure around the middle of the century, if one abstracts from the part of the budget destined for the self-preservation of the state (administration, court pensions, debt service, military), and represented a central element of infrastructure development until the advent of railway construction (Borchard 1968: 200–05, 214–15, 260–78; Müller 2000: 272–77). This resulted in a consolidation of the state at the local and regional levels.

However, the member states not only ceded powers to the Empire, the regional administration, and the municipalities but also expanded their commitment to other tasks. One of them was the creation of public railway companies (Chapter 7 of this volume), and another was the increased state penetration of the education system, particularly in Prussia (Chapter 15). In connection with the so-called *Kulturkampf* (1871–78)—a conflict between states and the Catholic church over control of education and civil marriage—the primary school system, which had until then been organised on a decentralised basis, came increasingly under state control. This was also accompanied by an increase in the state's share of funding for primary schools. In addition, in the late 1860s and 1870s, several technical universities were either newly founded or expanded on the basis of older institutions (Aachen, Berlin, Darmstadt, and Munich). Subsequently, university attendance increased sharply, especially in the sciences and engineering. This increase in state capacity for public education is likely to have given Germany a comparative advantage in terms of human capital endowment, contributing to the rapid development of skill- and knowledge-intensive industries during the Second Industrial Revolution and the transition to modern economic growth.

Channel 4: Improving the quality of economic institutions. Economic theory has recently paid greater attention to the quality of institutions. Acemoglu and Robinson (2012) attribute the prosperity gap between less developed and industrialised countries to the dominance of extractive and inclusive institutions, respectively. A similar approach is taken by North et al. (2009), who explore the transformation from limited access orders to open access orders. This process is expected to improve the quality of economic institutions that result in legal security and equal opportunities. There is evidence to suggest that the economic institutions in the German Empire had already reached the quality of growth-promoting institutions in the sense of the theory, even though the elites retained, in many respects, privileged access to economic and political rents (Webb 2015). Four topics discussed in this volume can be related to this argument. The amendment to the Stock Corporation Act of 1884 demonstrably reduced the transaction costs between shareholders as principals and corporate boards as their agents, which generally encouraged a more efficient allocation of capital in joint-stock companies (Chapter 11 of this volume). The development of integrated and sophisticated procedures of political decision-making on the national level thus led to an institutional setting that improved the functioning of capital markets. This may have contributed to the long-term increase in capital intensity in the industrial sector—an important feature of the early phase of modern economic growth.

Second, a similar reasoning applies to the Patent Act of 1877 (Chapter 10). Undoubtedly, it encouraged the emergence of blocking patents and the formation of patent pools, which probably slowed down technological progress and motivated the formation of cartels. Nevertheless, it also created a national market for intellectual property, which, as mentioned above, likely facilitated the diffusion of innovations and intensified technological competition. In addition, the Patent Act of 1877 contained standards specifically tailored to the chemical industry, which fostered technological competition in this industry and stimulated the emergence of industrial research on a large scale. This contributed to the rise of the German chemical industry to international technological leadership in an important, distinctly knowledge-intensive branch of the Second Industrial Revolution (Murmann 2003).

Third, the introduction of compulsory social insurance for workers in the areas of sickness, industrial accidents, old age, and disability in the 1880s is another case in point (Chapter 13 of this volume). This was an important social innovation through which the federal state intervened in insurance markets and organised transfer payments. Whereas the programmes had positive welfare consequences for the insured, they had no impact on the long-term economic development. In particular, there is no support for the argument that the introduction of old-age insurance reduced the relative value of children and thus contributed to the decline in fertility.

Finally, nation-building was accompanied by a major expansion in the quantity and quality of statistical information, an important prerequisite for the design and functioning of economic institutions. The late 1860s saw the emergence of modern standards for conducting censuses, and in 1878/80 the reporting systems for agricultural production and foreign trade, two important fields of state policy, were put on a completely new footing (Chapter 8 of this volume). The provision of detailed and reliable information is an important public good with regard to establishing or modifying economic institutions. However, we still know little about the use of such new types of statistical information in policy processes or about their economic consequences.

In summary, the founding of the nation-state brought about a considerable improvement in the quality of the institutional structure in many fields, favouring sustained economic growth. However, institutional change was by no means driven exclusively by state action. Rather, we see a broader dynamic that also developed independently of the state, with business associations and cooperation among business companies and the cooperative movement (Guinnane 2001) as important foundations of both formal and informal institutions (Chapter 12 of this volume). An older scholarship has considered this pattern of economic institutions in Imperial Germany to be a variant of organised capitalism, as instruments of rule by the economic elite.

By contrast, more recent research shows that many informal institutions were fragile and constantly changing. In addition, there was considerable competition between alternative institutional solutions to issues emerging in the new national economy.

4 Relevance of the European and global perspective

Many statements made in the previous two sections are formulated cautiously and are based on plausible conclusions rather than compelling evidence. This is, in part, due to research gaps. More fundamentally, it is related to methodological challenges facing the analysis of an epochal threshold, especially when the focus is on a single process, such as German nation-building here. In the following, we reflect on these challenges and discuss ways to deal with them. One fruitful avenue will be to add an external perspective on the economic history of German nation-building: Nationalism, state formation, and state growth were phenomena in the nineteenth century that encompassed large parts of Europe and, to some extent, other continents, and national economies developed in close connection with strong globalisation forces (O'Rourke and Williamson 1999). An approach that undertakes country comparisons and takes global economic processes into account thus allows sharpening findings on individual cases, putting them into perspective, and contextualising them. Below, we describe four specific challenges regarding the determination of the economic effects of German nation-building, for which such an external perspective proves to be highly productive.

First, it is in the nature of an epochal threshold that numerous events take place in a relatively short time, and their effects can take time to unfold. This makes it difficult to identify a single shock and study its effects in the sense of a natural experiment. To pick one example: The establishment of the *Reichsbank* in 1875 was undoubtedly a deep institutional break, but it was not until the 1890s that the *Reichsbank* achieved the market power in the money market necessary for effective monetary policy (see Chapter 9 of this volume). It is, therefore, an open question as to when one can expect any consequences of institutional change for the economy.

Second, in connection with a historical threshold, processes of different kinds can also take place simultaneously, making it difficult to clearly attribute economic consequences to one of them. Specifically, not only the institutional change that accompanied the formation of the nation-state is a candidate for explaining Germany's transition to modern economic growth but also the parallel surge of globalisation (Chapter 16 of this volume). After 1865, Germany changed within a few years from being an important grain exporter to a significant grain importer. The increase of grain imports from the Americas and from Russia and Ukraine, which was a general characteristic of the so-called European grain invasion (O'Rourke 1997), accelerated structural change and contributed to the growth of those sectors of the Second Industrial Revolution, in which Germany had a comparative advantage at the end of the nineteenth century. Both globalisation and accelerated industrialisation also had profound effects on economic inequality (Chapter 14 of this volume). The so-called conservative turn of 1878–79 (Nipperdey 1992: 382–408; Ullmann 1995: 68–76; Wehler 1995: 934–38) was accompanied by a clear change in the orientation of, among other things, foreign economic and social policy (see Chapters 13, 16 and 17). Whereas the grain invasion reduced the incomes of landowners, the rapid accumulation of capital in the industrial sector, combined with the growth of large enterprises, gave rise to a new economic elite of industrialists and bankers. Severe distributional conflicts were the result, reflected in the growing strength of political socialism and trade unions. These processes, partly linked to the conservative turn of 1878–79, meant that both the constellation of actors influencing the occurrence and direction of institutional change and the impact of economic policy programmes were different from the late 1870s onwards from what they had been in the late 1860s (Torp 2014; Bräuer et al. 2021).

Third, it is not easy to develop a meaningful comparative perspective for the study of the economic history of national unification in Germany. Nevertheless, with the help of a qualitative comparison of the findings with those of other larger countries, provisional conclusions can be drawn. The comparison of the German experience with Great Britain and Austria-Hungary suggests that growth differences were driven to some extent by the initial resource endowment and economic structure, the size of the domestic market, and the accessibility of international markets (Chapters 19 and 20 of this volume). Economic policy concepts and instruments have also developed similarly in different countries. For example, a comparison of the foreign trade policies of France and Germany in the second half of the nineteenth century shows that despite different political regimes and a different economic structure, the introduction of protective tariffs in both countries proceeded in a certain chronological parallel, through similar political mechanisms, and resulted in similar levels of protection (Chapters 16 and 17). The economic consequences that can be explicitly attributed to institutional change associated with the formation of a German nation-state are thus limited. Many of the economic processes that occurred in the second half of the nineteenth century were primarily driven by globalisation, the growing synchronisation of business cycles, and the formation of cross-border epistemic communities among economic policy experts.

There are two exceptions to this general finding. First, the German-British comparison suggests that different innovation systems—that is, the supply of human capital, which was primarily driven by the expansion of the education system and the regulations on the protection of intellectual property—partly explain why important sectors of the Second Industrial Revolution grew more rapidly in Germany than in Great Britain (Chapters 10, 15, and 20 of this volume). Second, the comparison between Italy and Germany is particularly instructive (Chapter 18): in Italy, national unification around 1860 produced a centralised yet weak state, whereas, in Germany, the establishment of a federal state was part of a general increase in state capacity. It is likely that the different course of nation-state formation in the two countries also partly explains why the Italian economy grew less than the German economy in the decades after 1860.

The fourth and final challenge concerns data availability. Any fundamental political change tends to be accompanied by changes in the recording categories and systems for observing the economy, society, and politics. This also applies to the case of the formation of the German nation-state (Chapter 8). As a result, important data series do not begin until the 1870s and 1880s, or they change their nature during this period, both of which complicate investigations across the epochal threshold around 1870-71. Gathering more and better data for the period before 1870 remains an important task for German economic history research.

5 Conclusion

We began with questioning the commonly used chronology of an epochal threshold around 1870, which is used in many accounts of German and European development. We did so by asking about the economic causes as well as consequences of German nation-building. What are the results of this endeavour? First, a list of the methodological challenges is involved: An epochal threshold is unique, complex in content, and therefore not easy to define in chronological terms. It often changes the data situation as well. This makes it difficult to develop appropriate empirical strategies for identifying and understanding processes occurring in the context of an epochal threshold—in this case, the formation of the German nation-state. Many statements in this book are therefore formulated cautiously and provisionally and are based to a large extent on plausibility.

With this caveat, the chapters in this book also show how the political geography of the early nineteenth century and the process of market integration that began in this period stimulated supra-state integration that ultimately—yet by no means teleologically—led to the founding of a nation-state. The territorial expansion or 'transfer of Prussia to the Rhine' of 1815 had made a German nation-state under Prussian dominance likely, not least because the new boundaries contributed to customs unification and further market integration. In addition, the research presented in this book suggests that the formation of nation-states via four channels of action allowed Germany to enter the first phase of modern economic growth around 1880: via the effect of national identity policy on the behaviour of households and individuals; via market integration; via an increase in state capacity while preserving the autonomy of markets by way of a federal state structure; and, finally, via improvements in the quality and design of economic institutions. These mechanisms favoured, at least selectively, the accumulation of both physical and human capital and intensified competition for technological innovation. In this way, they contributed to the formation of important structural features of modern economic growth, namely technical progress and a continuous increase in the endowment of the labour force with skills, knowledge, and physical capital.

A comparison with other European countries, however, cautions against attributing Germany's strong economic development directly to the founding of the nation-state. Many economic developments of the second half of the nineteenth century were driven by globalisation and the growing synchronisation of business cycles. Finally, the tentative nature of all these conclusions should be emphasised once again. Overcoming the methodological challenges requires further work. By focussing on the economic aspects of German nation-building, the chapters collected in this volume contribute to its understanding, and hopefully stimulate new research.

Notes

1 Overviews of the foundation of the Empire include, among others, Nipperdey (1983: 704–803, 1992: 11–84); Schulze (1985), Ullmann (1995: 14–22); Wehler (1995: 251–331).
2 See, for example, Ziblatt (2006); on the complex processes surrounding national unification in nineteenth-century Germany, see the overviews mentioned in note 1.

References

Acemoglu, D. and Robinson, J. (2012) *Why Nations Fail: The Origins of Power, Prosperity, and Poverty*, New York: Profile Books.

Alesina, A., Guilano, P. and Reich, B. (2019) 'Nation-building and education', *NBER Working Paper* 18839.

Alesina, A. and Spolaore, E. (1997) 'On the number and size of nations', *Quarterly Journal of Economics,* Vol. 4 (112): 1027–56.

Anderson, B. (1983) *Imagined Communities: Reflections on the Origin and Spread of Nationalism*, London: Verso.

Borchard, K. (1968) *Staatsverbrauch und öffentliche Investitionen in Deutschland 1780–1850*, unpublished PhD dissertation, University of Göttingen.

Bräuer, R., Hungerland, W. and Kersting, F. (2021) 'Trade shocks, labour markets and elections in the first globalisation', *IWH Discussion Paper* Vol. 4 (2021).

Burhop, C. (2011) *Wirtschaftsgeschichte des Kaiserreichs 1871–1918*, Göttingen: Vandenhoeck & Ruprecht.

Burhop, C. and Wolf, N. (2013) 'The German market for patents during the "Second Industrialization" 1884–1913: a gravity approach', *Business History Review,* Vol. 1 (87): 69–93.

Dincecco, M. (2015) 'The rise of effective states in Europe', *Journal of Economic History,* Vol. 3 (75): 901–18.

Dincecco, M. and Katz, G. (2016) 'State capacity and long-run economic performance', *Economic Journal,* Vol. 590 (126): 189–218.

Dumke, R. (1984) 'Der Zollverein als Modell ökonomischer Integration', *Geschichte und Gesellschaft* 10, special issue, *Wirtschaftliche und politische Integration in Europa im 19. und 20. Jahrhundert*, pp. 71–101.

Fehrenbach, E. (2007) *Verfassungsstaat und Nationsbildung*, 2nd ed., Munich: Oldenbourg.

Galor, O. (2011) *Unified Growth Theory*, Princeton, NJ: Princeton University Press.

Galor, O. and Weil, D. (2000) 'Population, technology and growth: from the Malthusian regime to the demographic transition and beyond', *American Economic Review*, Vol. 4 (90): 806–28.

Groß, F. (2015) *Integration durch Standardisierung: Maßreformen in Deutschland im 19. Jahrhundert*, Baden-Baden: Nomos.

Guinnane, T. (2001) 'Cooperatives as information machines: German rural credit cooperatives, 1883–1914', *Journal of Economic History*, Vol. 61 (2): 366–89.

Henderson, W. (1981) 'The German Zollverein and the European Economic Community', *Journal of Institutional and Theoretical Economics*, Vol. 3 (137): 491–507.

Henrich-Franke, C. (2018) '"Integrieren durch Regieren": ein Phasenmodell', in G. Ambrosius, C. Henrich-Franke, and C. Neutsch (eds), *Integrieren durch Regieren*, Baden-Baden: Nomos, pp. 15–51.

Johnson, N. and Koyama, M. (2017) 'States and economic growth: capacity and constraints', *Explorations in Economic History*, Vol. 64: 1–20.

Kennedy, P. (1980) *The Rise of the Anglo-German Antagonism, 1860–1914*, London: Allen & Unwin.

Kramper, P. (2019) *The Battle of the Standards: Messen, Zählen und Wiegen in Westeuropa 1660–1914*, Berlin: De Gruyter Oldenbourg.

Lorenz, C. (2017) 'Der letzte Fetisch des Stamms der Historiker: Zeit, Raum und Periodisierung in der Geschichtswissenschaft', in F. Esposito (ed), *Zeitenwandel: Transformationen geschichtlicher Zeitbegriffe nach dem Boom*, Göttingen: Vandenhoeck & Ruprecht, pp. 63–92.

Mokyr, J. (1998) 'The second Industrial Revolution', chapter manuscript for Valeria Castronovo (ed), *Storia dell'economia mondiale*, Vol. 3, *L'età della rivoluzione industriale*, Rome: Laterza. http://citeseerx.ist.psu.edu/viewdoc/download?doi=10.1.1.481.2996&rep=rep1&type=pdf accessed on July 21, 2020.

Müller, U. (2000) *Infrastrukturpolitik in der Industrialisierung: Der Chausseebau in der preußischen Provinz Sachsen und dem Herzogtum Braunschweig vom Ende des 18. Jahrhunderts bis in die siebziger Jahre des 19. Jahrhunderts*, Berlin: Duncker & Humblot.

Murmann, J. (2003) *Knowledge and Competitive Advantage: The Coevolution of Firms, Technology, and National Institutions*, Cambridge: Cambridge University Press.

Nipperdey, T. (1983) *Deutsche Geschichte 1800–1866: Bürgerwelt und starker Staat*, Munich: Beck.

Nipperdey, T. (1992) *Deutsche Geschichte 1866–1918*, Vol. 2, *Machtstaat vor der Demokratie*, Munich: Beck.

North, D. (1981) *Structure and Change in Economic History*, New York: Norton.

North, D., Wallis, J. and Weingast, B. (2009) *Violence and Social Orders: A Conceptual Framework for Interpreting Recorded Human History*, Cambridge: Cambridge University Press.

O'Rourke, K. (1997) 'The European grain invasion, 1870–1913', *Journal of Economic History*, Vol. 4 (57): 775–801.

O'Rourke, K. and Williamson, J. (1999) *Globalization and History: The Evolution of a Nineteenth-Century Atlantic Economy*, Cambridge, MA: MIT Press.

Osterhammel, J. (2006) 'Über die Periodisierung der neueren Geschichte', *Berlin-Brandenburgische Akademie der Wissenschaften, Berichte und Abhandlungen*, Vol. 10: 45–64.

Pomian, K. (1984) *L'ordre du temps*, Paris: Gallimard.

Qian, Y. and Weingast, B. (1997) 'Federalism as a commitment to reserving market incentives', *Journal of Economic Perspectives,* Vol. 4 (11): 83–92.

Sandholtz, W. and Stone Sweet, A. (2012) 'Neo-functionalism and supranational governance', in E. Jones, A. Menon, and S. Weatherill (eds), *Oxford Handbook of the European Union*, Oxford, Oxford University Press, pp. 18–33.

Schulze, H. (1985) *Der Weg zum Nationalstaat: Die Deutsche Nationalbewegung vom 18. Jahrhundert bis zur Reichsgründung,* Munich: Deutscher Taschenbuch Verlag.

Smith, H. (2020) *Germany, a Nation in Its Time: Before, During, and After Nationalism, 1500–2000,* New York: Liveright.

Smith, W. (1978) *The German Colonial Empire,* Chapel Hill: The University of North Carolina Press.

Smith, W. (1986) *The Ideological Origins of Nazi Imperialism,* Oxford: Oxford University Press.

Tilly, R. and Kopsidis, M. (2020) *From Old Regime to Industrial State: A History of German Industrialization from the Eighteenth Century to World War One,* Chicago, IL: University of Chicago Press.

Torp, C. (2014) *Challenges of Globalization: Economy and Politics in Germany 1860–1914,* New York: Berghahn.

Trentmann, F. (2009) *Free Trade Nation: Commerce, Consumption, and Civil Society in Modern Britain,* Oxford: Oxford University Press.

Uebele, M. (2011) 'National and international wheat market integration in the 19th century: evidence from comovement', *Explorations in Economic History,* Vol. 2 (48): 226–42.

Ullmann, H. (1995) *Das Deutsche Kaiserreich 1871–1918,* Frankfurt: Suhrkamp.

Voth, H. (2001) 'The Prussian Zollverein and the bid for economic superiority', in P. Dwyer (ed), *Modern Prussian History, 1830–1947,* Harlow: Taylor and Francis, pp. 109–25.

Webb, S. (2015), 'Becoming an open democratic capitalist society: a two-century historical perspective on Germany's evolving political economy', *Constitutional Political Economy,* Vol. 1 (26): 19–37.

Wehler, H.-U. (1995) *Deutsche Gesellschaftsgeschichte,* Vol. 3: *Von der "Deutschen Doppelrevolution" bis zum Beginn des Ersten Weltkrieges 1849–1914,* München: Beck.

Weichlein, S. (2004) *Nation und Region: Integrationsprozesse im Bismarckreich,* Düsseldorf: Droste.

Weingast, B. (1995) 'The economic role of political institutions: market-preserving federalism and economic development', *Journal of Law, Economics, and Organization,* Vol. 1 (11): 1–31.

Wolf, D. (2012) 'Neo-Funktionalismus', in H. Bieling and M. Lerch (eds), *Theorien der europäischen Integration,* 3rd ed., Wiesbaden: VS, pp. 55–76.

Wolf, N. (2009) 'Was Germany ever united? Evidence from intra- and international trade, 1885–1933', *Journal of Economic History,* Vol. 3 (69): 846–81.

Ziblatt, D. (2006) *Structuring the State: The Formation of Italy and Germany and the Puzzle of Federalism,* Princeton, NJ: Princeton University Press.

Part I

Nation formation and the evolution of economic policy

2 National identity, economic integration, and the rise of Prussia

Felix Kersting and Nikolaus Wolf

1 Introduction

The nineteenth century was the European age of nation-building. Favoured by the American and French revolutions, prepared by new ideas and changes in economic, social, and political structures, we observe the emergence of nation-states all over Europe. Germany is a particularly interesting case. At the time of the French revolution, the country was a patchwork of political entities, characterised by stark differences in economic development, and divided by religious cleavages, which overlapped with ethnolinguistic differences at the fringes. A century later, Germany had developed into one of the most powerful states in Europe, often perceived as a threat by her neighbours. How did this occur?

The extensive literature on the origins of European nation-states and processes of nation-building emphasise two aspects. On the one hand, nations must be considered as constructed or 'imagined communities', shaped by the interests and ideas of political elites and other groups (Anderson 1983). On the other hand, nation-building always took place within a specific framework, set by collective memory and cultural practices with unifying elements such as language or faith (Smith 1991). The more recent economic literature on nation- and identity-building highlights the constructivist aspect. The focus is either on the need (the 'demand') for new social identities (Akerlof and Kranton 2000), the provision (the 'supply') of group identity by rational and strategic actors such as political elites (Alesina and Reich 2015), or their interaction (Shayo 2009). An important issue is whether and how economic integration and structural change have impacted the demand for a change in identity (Gellner 1983; Chen and Li 2009; Chiang et al. 2019). These recent economic approaches have not yet been examined in the context of German nation-building.

In this chapter, we will analyse the development until the foundation of the nation-state in 1871 with a focus on the interplay between three aspects: first, the strategic interests of governments (especially Prussia); second, the national movement as a carrier of national identity; and third, changes in economic integration across Germany. Thus, we do not intend

DOI: 10.4324/9781003283430-3

to offer an encompassing overview but rather concentrate on aspects that economic history can help clarify. We hope to show that the economic literature on nation-building can inspire new empirical analyses and offer new insights. At the same time, we are aware of open research questions in this field, especially regarding the effect of economic integration and structural change on identity formation.

Our starting point is the well-known hypothesis of Thomas Nipperdey: 'The transfer of Prussia to the Rhine is one of the fundamental facts of German history, one of the bases of the foundation of the Empire in 1866/71. [...] This became the strongest driving force of Prussian power politics' (Nipperdey 2013: 91; own translation). We show that this argument of Nipperdey can be more precisely formulated and, partly, empirically validated. We argue that the westward shift to the Rhine motivated the Prussian government to support (temporarily) a new narrative that sought to portray the Prussian king as the defender of the endangered German borderlands, beyond the struggle against Napoleon. While this remained a brief episode, we provide evidence that this sharpened a national identity in the western territories, which carried over to the wars of unification.

Next, the westward shift heralded a new scope of action for the Prussian government, which it only began to grasp and use in the following years. The political control over long stretches of the Rhine enabled Prussia to dictate access to fiscally important colonial goods in southern Germany via cost-effective waterways. We argue that Prussia's control over the Rhine was an essential precondition for the formation of the *Zollverein* in 1834 as a step towards economic integration.

Third, after the crisis of 1840, Prussia's strategic position on the Rhine helped transform German nationalism into a mass phenomenon that remained compatible with a Prussian state. In the following years, Prussia allowed the German national movement to flourish again, that is, in choral societies and nationalist *Turner* associations, organising mass events and spreading national monuments across the country.

Finally, we provide some tentative evidence of a link between structural change and a rising 'demand' for national identity, building on Gellner (1983). Structural change likely contributed to the erosion of existing identities and loyalties. 'The flip-side was a need for orientation, which stimulated the demand for comprehensive concepts to guide action' (Echternkamp 1998: 484; own translation). This area offers a wide scope for further empirical research.

This point leads us to the old question of whether the German Empire was founded 'from above', as a conservative revolution led by Prussia (Schulze 1985: 119–20; Biefang 1994: 389–91; Wehler 2006). Although the German national movement failed to establish a nation-state in 1815, 1830, 1848, and again in 1859, it nevertheless grew larger and stronger over these years. Similar to national movements in other parts of Europe, the interests, organisations, publications, the 'invented traditions', and myths of the German national movement prepared the framework and scope for nation-building, which could then be filled by government actions from above (Ullmann 1995: 14–20). With regard to Prussia, which is the focus of this study, we argue that the government fostered development, which strengthened the 'demand' for a national identity. The state propaganda in Prussia's new western territories around 1815 and the dynamics of the *Zollverein* are two specific examples. The latter is especially of interest, as it depicts how government actions could inadvertently foster national identity and the quest for a nation-state.

We divide the period between 1800 and 1871 into three phases, with a focus on the relationship between Prussia and the national movement. In the first phase up to 1819, the government contributed directly to the strengthening of national identity, although reluctantly and only for a few years. The second phase was characterised by conflicts between the national movement and governments, up to about 1859. Even so, government policies made indirect but important contributions to the consolidation and expansion of the national movement. In the third phase, triggered by the Italian War of Independence in 1859, the Prussian government again adopted a more active role in an attempt to gain supremacy in the German Confederation. Under the leadership of Bismarck, Prussia began to embrace the national movement as a means to increase its influence over Germany.

2 The early national movement until 1819

The foundation of the German Empire on 18 January 1871 eliminated a centuries-old political patchwork in Central Europe. In hindsight, it is tempting to regard the German nation-state under the Prussian leadership as inevitable, along the lines of Treitschke's *Deutsche Geschichte im Neunzehnten Jahrhundert* (published 1879–94). Given the formation of nation-states elsewhere in Europe, one might argue that Germany had followed a broader trend in this respect. However, to understand the formation of the specific German nation-state that emerged in 1871, we need to discuss possible alternatives.

The modern idea of a nation is characterised by the notion of placing one's nation above all other values, notably above loyalty to a ruler or faith (Langewiesche 2000: 17). This idea developed already before the French Revolution, spread increasingly in the German states after 1800 and became a mass phenomenon around 1840 (Hardtwig 1992; Planert 2002). During the Napoleonic Wars, the concept of a German nation along ethnolinguistic lines became dominant. This concept pushed back alternatives, which competed with each other since the late eighteenth century (Sheehan 1993: 1), such as the concept of a democratic-republican nation (formulated in 1758 by Johann Georg Zimmermann), a Prussian monarchist nationalism (put forward by Thomas Abbt in 1761) or an imperial nationalism oriented towards the Holy Roman Empire (propagated in 1765 by Friedrich Carl von Moser) (Jansen 2011). From the beginning, a liberal movement for civil rights and egalitarian ideas developed alongside ideas of a war community and varieties of xenophobia (Planert 2002: 31–32).

The rise of a specifically ethnolinguistic concept of the 'German nation' might partly be attributed to demand-side factors. The experience of territorial changes in many parts of Germany and elsewhere in Europe undermined old loyalties (Schulze 1985: 54). Moreover, the economy began to change in the late eighteenth century, with accelerated population growth accompanied by rapid urbanisation (Pfister 2017). Economic change mobilised people, who left their villages to seek work in the cities. Frequent territorial change and economic change, have probably undermined old loyalties and contributed to the search for a new and territorially more comprehensive identity organised around language to facilitate exchange (Gellner 1983). Moreover, there were important impulses from abroad: The American Declaration of Independence of 1776 and the French Revolution of 1789 exacerbated the crisis of loyalty to the Ancien Régime. They were initially welcomed by many intellectuals on the continent as the beginning of a new era.

Most direct, however, was the experience of war. The coalition wars since 1792 and the subsequent French occupation of large parts of Germany encouraged both the demand for national identity and its supply by intellectuals and actors in governments and administrations. The French occupation led to a growing burden of taxes and military service. In particular, Napoleon's self-coronation as emperor in 1804 and the humiliating defeat of Prussia in 1806 sparked a new kind of German nationalist feeling, which was directed against the French (Planert 2007). Around this time, a patriotic circle was formed in Berlin, which included the publisher Georg Andreas Reimer, as well as Ernst Moritz Arndt, Friedrich Jahn, Friedrich Schleiermacher, and the Prussian officer August von Gneisenau (Bartmuss et al. 2008). Jahn became known in 1811 as the founder of the German gymnastics (*Turner*) movement, which soon spread to other German states and became the organisational backbone of the early national movement (Düding 1984). Ernst Moritz Arndt, professor at Greifswald since 1806, was particularly active in publishing anti-French pamphlets. Probably best known was his poem *Was ist des Deutschen Vaterland?* from 1813, which called for a German nation-state defined by the reach of the German language. Thus, Arndt and others propagated the idea of a nation along ethnolinguistic lines to overcome the many political, social, and religious divisions among the German states in their struggle against the common enemy.

This anti-French German nationalism slowly gained influence also among the Prussian state elite after the defeat of 1806, and this was, at least partly, for strategic reasons. One motive was the mobilisation of the population against the occupation. Since 1807, Gerhard Scharnhorst, together with von Gneisenau and others, reformed the Prussian army to strengthen the relationship between the army and the population, for example by opening the career path of officers to the middle classes. However, the conservative circle around the King was still reluctant to appeal to national sentiment, fearing its revolutionary power. At the end of 1812, Scharnhorst, Gneisenau, Stein, and other reformers convinced the King of Prussia, Friedrich Wilhelm III, to side with

Russia (Treaty of Kalisch, February 1813) and to openly appeal to nationalist ideas. One of the first steps was a royal decree of February 1813 that every man over 20 years of age must wear the national cockade in public as a sign of his patriotism (Hagemann 2019: 165). Around the same time, a call to form voluntary infantry divisions (so-called *Jäger*) became a massive success, against the King's expectations (Mieck 1992: 53). When Prussia declared war on France in March 1813, the King issued the proclamation *An mein Volk*. For the first time, he appealed to the national pride of the 'Germans and Prussians' to fight foreign occupation. This proclamation was not only published in the leading newspaper of Breslau (today's Wrocław), where the King resided in 1813, but also sent to all post offices of Prussia at that time.

The victory at the Battle of Leipzig against France in October 1813 quickly became part of a new German national mythology. Hundreds of celebrations took place on the first anniversary of the battle, between 16 and 18 October 1814, initiated by Jahn, Arndt, and other nationalists with only sporadic support from state officials (Düding 1984: 112–14). In 1815, Karl Hoffmann published an extensive volume listing and describing more than 300 celebrations in the German states, with a preface written by Ernst Moritz Arndt. The book is an early indicator of the spread of the national movement across Germany. The list of subscribers includes 436 names from 132 (mostly smaller) towns and villages. Most subscribers, who often co-organised the local celebrations, came from the middle classes, including not only many Protestant clergymen but also lower-ranking civil servants (Hoffmann 1815: I–X). The majority lived in the central areas of Germany. The rather small number of celebrations in Prussia and their descriptions suggest that they had a more official character and took place under stricter state control. Hence, at least for Prussia, these figures might underestimate the spread of the national movement. Although the list of subscribers may primarily reflect Hoffmann's personal network, a comparison with the gymnastics associations around 1815, as reported by the *Zentralkommission zur Untersuchung hochverräterischer Umtriebe* (Central Commission; see Weber 1970), shows similar patterns, again except for Prussia (see Figure 2.1).

After the Rhineland and Westphalia became part of Prussia at the Congress of Vienna, the Prussian state developed yet another motive for appealing to the national sentiment and shaping a new kind of national identity. The (Protestant) Prussian government faced the challenge of strengthening the legitimacy of their rule in the western territories, especially in the Catholic areas around Trier, Cologne, and Münster. Central to this strategy was a new narrative in which the Prussian King led the German nation against its enemies, established, for example, at traditional homage ceremonies for the new ruler (Kotulla 2010: 591). During the celebrations in Aachen, all citizens were called upon to wear the national cockade (Tschacher 2010: 259). At the celebration in Münster, a theatre play *Der Altar im Walde* was performed as part of the main programme, portraying the Prussian King Friedrich Wilhelm III as the 'new Hermann'. This referred to the older Hermann myth around

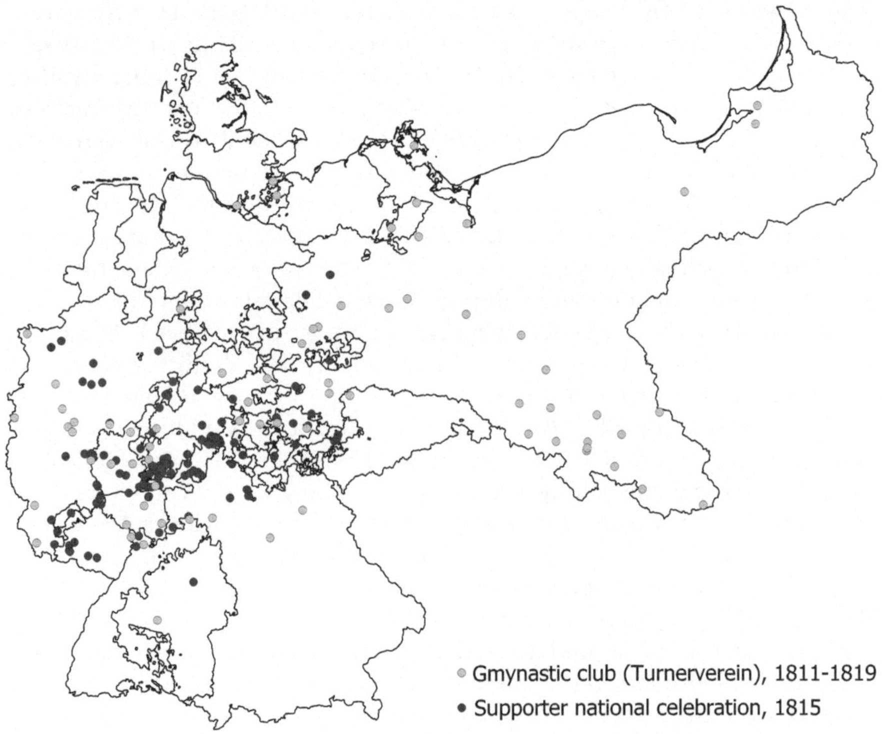

Figure 2.1 Subscribers of Hoffmann (1815) and location of gymnastics associations (ca. 1815).

Source: Authors' figure based on data from Hoffmann (1815) and Untersuchungsbericht über das Turnwesen (1811–19), Mainz 1820.

Arminius, a Germanic chieftain who in AD 9 had won a battle against the Romans. The myth had been (re-)popularised by Arndt and others since 1806 to inspire resistance against the French (Schwengelbeck 2007: 142–144). To a modern observer, these attempts to convey a new identity to the audience seem quite preposterous, yet there is evidence that they may have paid off. Kersting and Wolf (2021) use first names as an indicator of social identity and classify these names based on their philological origin. Parents in the new Prussian cities after 1814 gave their children first names of Germanic origin more often than before and more often compared to parents in other cities not under Prussian rule at the time. Figure 2.2 shows how the proportion of these 'national' first names developed from 1810 onwards in Aachen and Münster (treatment group) compared to Frankfurt a. M., Hanover, Heidelberg, Nuremberg, and Mannheim. For the years after 1814, we observe a substantial increase in these numbers in Aachen and Münster. Moreover, if we only look at the change in the choice of first names by the same parents with at least one child before and after 1814, this effect becomes even more pronounced.[1]

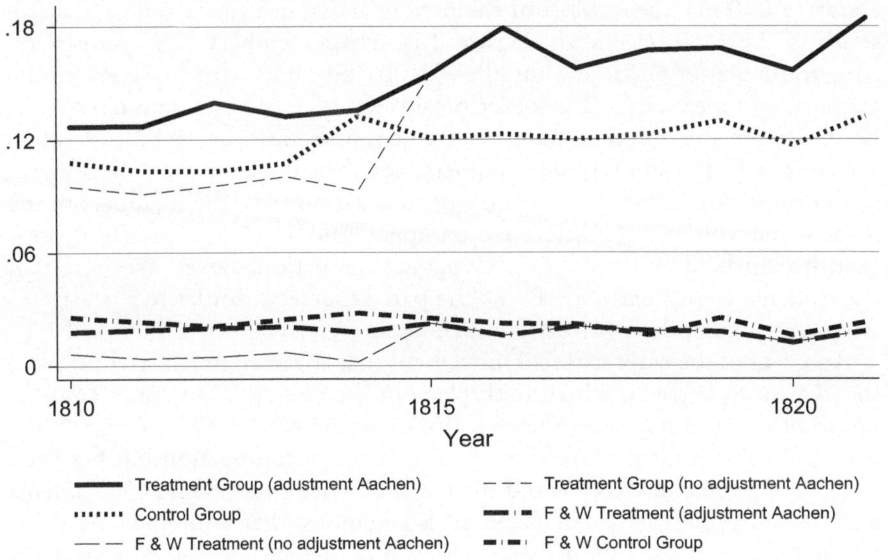

Figure 2.2 National first names in Münster and Aachen compared to a control group, 1810–21 (percentage shares).

Source: Kersting and Wolf (2021).

Moreover, we show that the effect is not driven by changes in the quite prominent frequency of the names Friedrich or Wilhelm (or their female equivalents).

Whether we can consider this as evidence for a change of identities of the parents remains speculative. In addition, we do not know the extent to which any new identities were passed on to the next generation, notably to the children carrying those names. However, the extensive sociological literature on first names points to clear correlations with identities (Lieberson and Bell 1992; Gerhards and Hackenbroch 1997). Kersting and Wolf (2021) provide further evidence on this assumption by comparing the first names of honoured soldiers and active soldiers in the Prussian-French War of 1870–71. Both, overall and within military ranks, soldiers with 'national' first names were awarded significantly more often for bravery in war than other participants in the war. Soldiers with national first names, thus, systematically 'reveal' a type of behaviour that points to a national identity, possibly conveyed to them by their (name-giving) parents through education or the social environment.

During this period, we observe the first rise of nationalist organisations. Most prominent was the gymnastics movement, initiated by Jahn, who in 1810–11 established regular meetings for physical training and nationalist indoctrination. These meetings took place in public and attracted many visitors

(Düding 1984: 50–52). In 1818, there were about 150 gymnastics clubs with about 12,000 members. Most of them were active in Prussia and only a few south of the Main (see again Figure 2.1). Their members were young, urban, and male, often from a middle-class background with students, young artisans, and merchants. The other prominent type of early national organisations were the *Burschenschaften* (student fraternities): In 1818, 14 student fraternities had around 1,000 members, roughly 10 percent of all German students (Schulze 1985: 72). In contrast to the gymnasts, the members of the student fraternities more often had an upper-middle-class, typically Protestant, background and stronger networks at the national level. We note that the students were a particularly mobile part of society, similar to the artisans and merchants in the gymnastics movement.

An event of the early national movement that attracted much attention was the Wartburg Festival, which took place in October 1817 to commemorate both Luther's posting of his theses in 1517 and the Battle of Leipzig in October 1813. The festival marked a turning point in the relationship between the early national movement and the German state elites. Some 450 students and several professors participated in a ceremony that combined religious and national elements with sharp criticism of the authorities. The students burned several symbols of the Ancien Régime and two dozen books by authors critical of either the student fraternities or the gymnasts (for example August von Kotzebue), as well as a version of the French 'Code civil' (Steiger 1967: 109–11).

The governments reacted shortly afterwards with repression against the national movement. The official occasion was the assassination of the poet von Kotzebue, who had previously ridiculed the student fraternities, by a student and gymnast in March 1819. However, after Napoleon's victory and the foundation of the German Confederation in 1815, most governments were keen to suppress the national movement and its revolutionary tendencies. In June 1819, the states of the German Confederation passed the Carlsbad Decrees (*Karlsbader Beschlüsse*), which banned fraternities and gymnastics clubs (*Turnsperre*), introduced press censorship to prevent the dissemination of liberal and national ideas, and established a *Zentralkommission zur Untersuchung hochverräterischer Umtriebe* (Weber 1970) Ernst Moritz Arndt, who had only in 1818 become a professor at the newly founded University of Bonn, was suspended, his writings were confiscated, Jahn was imprisoned, Hoffmann was persecuted and later committed suicide. By the end of 1819, it appeared as if the German national movement was finished.

3 From 1819 to 1859: Social mobilisation, economic integration, and political reaction

Three structural aspects were crucial for the forthcoming decades. First, geographical and social mobility increased again in the wake of Germany's initial phase of industrialisation. This may have contributed to a growing demand for national identity, as suggested by the composition of the early national movement. Changes in transportation, machinery, and power engines were feeding into a growing industry, with a deepening division of labour and integration between markets. To many observers, this undermined the legitimacy of Germany's political patchwork.

A second factor was the expansion of schooling and higher education and the emergence of a public sphere. The number of schools and pupils first expanded in line with population growth, but from the 1840s onwards, the number of pupils in secondary schools increased relative to the population (Fischer et al. 1982: 226). The ability to read and write and the practice of reading spread quickly after 1815. The production of books grew, together with the publication of many new journals and newspapers, and a large expansion of public libraries led to a *Leserevolution* ('reading revolution') (Martino, 1990). This was accompanied by the emergence of a 'bourgeois public sphere' (Jürgen Habermas), which turned the literary public into a political one and fostered the demand for political participation (Wehler 2006: 429–31; Nipperdey 2013: 587–89). The state authorities, not only in Prussia, did their best to curb political demands with strict policing and censorship (Nolte, 2007).

At the same time, however, the governments themselves continued to nurture the underlying technological, institutional, and economic changes. This leads us to the third factor: the formation of the *Zollverein* in 1834, a customs union that abolished the manifold internal barriers to trade, set common external tariffs, and helped coordinate the development of transport infrastructures. The *Zollverein* represented an important step towards the creation of a national institutional structure. A decisive factor in this development was Prussia's 'westward shift' at the Congress of Vienna. After 1815, the Prussian state comprised two separate territories: the old lands, augmented by the northern part of Saxony and former Polish territories in the East, and the Rhineland and Westphalia in the West, separated by the Hessian states (Hesse-Darmstadt and Hesse-Cassel) and the Kingdom of Hanover in-between (Huning and Wolf 2019). Thus, the new Prussian state not only had a long direct border with France but also a strategic interest in strengthening the relations between its eastern and western territories and thus, almost inevitably, in 'growing into' Germany.

Although this territorial order of 1815 initially seemed like a strategic defeat for Prussia, the new borders also brought strategic advantages for Prussia (see Figure 2.3). Prussia had gained control over large stretches of the most important German waterways to the North and Baltic Seas, the Elbe, *and* the Rhine. Access to the sea was of crucial importance because tariffs on (price-inelastic) colonial goods usually accounted for a large part of customs revenues. In Prussia, the share of wine, coffee, tobacco, and sugar in all import duties rose from 45 percent (1822) to 79 percent (1831) (Ohnishi 1973: 119). The Prussian Customs Law of 1818, which abolished internal customs duties and introduced an external customs duty at the state border, represented an important step towards a unified customs policy. Likewise, the Prussian

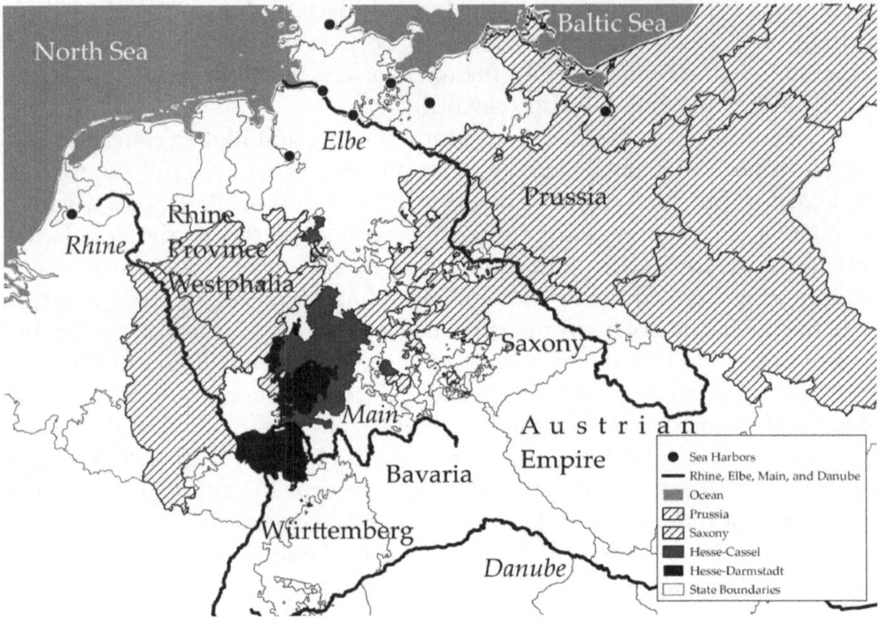

Figure 2.3 German states after 1815.
Source: Huning and Wolf (2019).

government standardised the transit duties that were common at the time. From 1818 onwards, southern German traders had two options: either take detours around Prussia, for example transporting their goods through the mountains of Hesse-Cassel, or accept the combined Prussian duties. The waterways were crucial because land transport was extremely expensive relative to water transport (e.g. Sombart 1902). Huning and Wolf (2019) show that German states whose least expensive transport routes from London led across Prussian territory joined the Prussian customs territory significantly earlier than others did.

Since the appointment of Friedrich von Motz as Minister of Finance in June 1825, Prussia began to exploit its new strategic position to work towards a customs area between the two parts of the state in the east and west. First, a customs union between Hesse-Darmstadt and Prussia in 1828 increased pressure on Bavaria, which attempted to secure access to its exclave, the Bavarian Palatinate. Next, the revolution of 1830 facilitated the liberalisation of the Rhine trade, undermining the land routes via Hesse-Cassel. The recognition of Belgium in the London Protocol of December 1830 meant free access for Prussia to the port of Antwerp through the Scheldt estuary, which ended the supremacy of the Dutch Rhine port of Rotterdam. In March 1831, after years of negotiations, the *Mainzer Rheinschifffahrtsakte* liberalised trade on the Rhine. On 25 August 1831, Hesse-Cassel joined the Prussian Customs Union. It now became almost impossible for southern Germany to bypass Prussian territory. In March 1833, Prussia and the southern states decided to join the Prussian-Hessian customs unions and form the *Zollverein.* The *Zollverein* abolished the manifold internal trade barriers, established common external tariffs, and helped coordinate the development of transport infrastructures (see Chapter 3 of this volume). By 1868, the customs union had expanded to include all German states that would form the German Empire in 1871, except for the north-sea port cities of Hamburg and Bremen.

There was no predetermined path from the *Zollverein* to the nation-state of 1871, but the *Zollverein* helped to prepare the foundation of the German Empire under Prussian dominance in several ways. Membership in the *Zollverein* fostered integration, reducing price differences quite considerably, comparable to the effects of railway construction (Keller and Shiue 2014). The *Zollverein* also helped increase tax revenues for all parties involved (Hahn 1984: 98–99). Less visible, but equally important, was the fact that the *Zollverein* produced a new elite of functionaries who were mobile between the member states. Many of them were to play an important role again in the 1860s (Kreutzmann, 2013). As an institutional framework that united most German states under Prussian dominance and excluded Habsburg, the *Zollverein,* therefore, indicated a possible way forward. In contrast, the role of Austria-Habsburg was increasingly limited to defending the status quo in the German Confederation.

Undoubtedly, the *Zollverein* was also an impulse for the German national movement. As early as April 1819, the *Allgemeiner Deutscher Handels- und Gewerbeverein* was founded, which under the leadership of Friedrich List aimed to promote the unification of the German Confederation in terms of customs policy. The association initially registered rising membership numbers but remained limited to the smaller states in central and southern Germany. This might have been due to List's early focus on protectionist external tariffs, which ran counter to the interests of German trading cities as well as those of factory owners in Saxony or the Rhineland (Hahn 1984: 27–29).

The national movement had an ambivalent stance towards the *Zollverein*—considered a step towards unity but also a threat to liberal ideals. The demand for the unification of customs policy had become louder with the July Revolution and, for instance, at the Hambach Festival, which took place in 1832 in the Bavarian Palatinate. Nevertheless, many activists regarded a unification of customs policy under the reactionary Prussian crown to be unacceptable. The liberal Paul A. Pfizer illustrated these different positions within the national movement in his *Briefwechsel zweier Deutscher* (1832): the two protagonists *Wilhelm* and *Friedrich* agree on the goal of a united German state. However, they differ regarding liberal values: while *Friedrich* does not want to pursue national unification at the expense of democratic ideals, *Wilhelm* is prepared to forego civil liberties in favour of the founding of a nation-state (Etges 2002: 64, Ries 2014: 38). The *Zollverein* helped ensure that *Wilhelm's* position would gradually prevail. In line with Nipperdey, Prussia's 'westward shift' of 1815 played an essential role in this.

In the crisis of 1840, it again became apparent that Prussia's position on the Rhine strengthened the relationship between the national movement and Prussia. In June 1840, Friedrich Wilhelm IV became King of Prussia. He was conservative and deeply religious, with sympathy for a romantic idea of Germany. In July 1840, he allowed Arndt to return to his chair at the University of Bonn. *Turnvater* Jahn was rehabilitated. The King invited the Grimm brothers to Berlin to become members of the Academy of Sciences and to teach at the university. For reasons to be sought outside of Germany, the so-called 'Rhine crisis' began shortly after his accession, with parts of the French press calling for a revision of the 1815 borders. This triggered a wave of anti-French nationalism, especially in the Prussian Rhineland, which spilt over to other German states (Schulze 1985: 82). The *Turnsperre* (ban on gymnastics associations) was lifted in Prussia in 1842. In addition, patriotic singing societies flourished, allowing the national movement to reach larger sections of society than ever before, from artisans to factory owners (Düding 1984: 320). The 'German Rhine' became a central topos of the national movement, for example through the immensely popular Rhine Song of 1840, composed by Nikolaus Becker. Here, as in Schneckenberger's *Wacht am Rhein*, France was considered (again) the enemy and Prussia Germany's gatekeeper.

In the wake of the crisis, the visibility of the national movement reached a new level. Arndt's nationalist song *Was ist des Deutschen Vaterland* from 1813 was sung at all major events of the gymnastics and singing societies, which in turn took place publicly and on a growing scale (Düding 1984: 271). Major monument projects were started, such as the Hermann Monument near Detmold, accompanied by supporters' associations in numerous German cities, or the ceremonial opening of the Valhalla near Regensburg. However, the national movement remained divided regarding the role of democratic rights. Likewise, the question of the political boundaries of a German nation-state remained a contentious issue.

A combination of economic and social change with disappointed political ambitions led to the 1848 revolution in Germany (and elsewhere). Initially triggered by an agrarian crisis, it developed into one of the first industrial crises and led to political unrest (Berger and Spoerer 2001). However, the revolutionaries were divided into more radical democrats and liberal-nationalist constitutionalists. In France, Louis Napoleon came to power with the support of a substantial part of the middle class, which for its part wanted to prevent more radical political change. In the German states, the revolution was initially quite successful. A national parliament met in Frankfurt/Main in May 1848, established a national government as early as June 1848, and even adopted a constitution in March 1849. However, the parliament soon proved to be powerless. The revolution failed mainly for two reasons: first, the military remained under the control of the old elites, and the new national government failed to change this, leading to its resignation after the conflict over Schleswig-Holstein. Second, after calls for national sovereignty in Habsburg, Poland, or Denmark became louder, the divide between democrats and nationalists deepened.

Formally, the constitution of 1849 failed because the Prussian king rejected the idea of a sovereign parliament. However, even the King of Prussia began to accept the project of national unification. After the revolution had ended, alternative ideas of national unification, such as unification under a Prussian monarch, lived on. Prussia's attempts to reform the German Confederation through the *Erfurter Union*, but also the Prussian three-class electoral system introduced in 1850, which weighted votes heavily according to tax payments, should be seen in this context. This electoral system was a concession to the rising bourgeois upper class, as it institutionalised their access to political power. The system was controversial, but it helped prepare a coalition of the Prussian crown with that part of the national movement that preferred national unification to civil rights. Following Pfizer's *Briefwechsel zweier Deutscher, Friedrich* had lost, but *Wilhelm* started to gain influence.

The following years were marked by a return to the political status quo with Prussia and Austria-Habsburg as joint leaders of the German Confederation, and a return to political censorship and repression. Nevertheless, this was a time of dramatic change. The German states fully entered the period of industrialisation, and again fostered all the structural changes and mobilising forces that went along with it. This growth was far more dynamic in the *Zollverein* around Prussia than in the Habsburg Empire. After 1849, the *Zollverein* became an economic powerhouse in Europe, but without political or military power.

4 From 1860 to 1871: National movement and the expansion of Prussia

The late 1850s brought a new dynamic to the question of national unification, triggered by events in Italy and Prussia. The Kingdom of Sardinia attempted, with French support, to unite the regions of Italy against Habsburg. In Prussia, Prince Wilhelm ascended the throne in 1858 and dismissed the conservative cabinet to begin a 'new era'. In the same year, the *Kongress deutscher Volkswirte* (Congress of German Economists) was established in Gotha not only to provide a forum to discuss economic modernisation but also to debate the political unification of Germany (Biefang 1994: 49–50; Hentschel 1975). In 1862, the Kongress publicly called for the transformation of the *Zollverein* into a national political institution with a parliament and administration (Hahn 1984: 162). Several members of the *Zollverein*'s functional elite actively supported these proposals (Kreutzmann 2012: 221–23).

In 1859, the *Nationalverein* was founded in Frankfurt/Main, as the first nationwide organisation that was openly politically oriented, to strive for national unification under Prussian leadership. By 1862, it had developed into a well-structured organisation with around 21.000 members (Biefang

1994: 80). The foundation of the *Nationalverein* and its early political activities were directly related to the war in Italy, where the Kingdom of Sardinia—supported by France—was fighting against Habsburg for the unification of Italy.

While the strategy for national unification remained controversial, even within organisations such as the *Nationalverein*, the national movement flourished again: Singing societies grew, organising events such as the *Deutsche Sängerfest* (German Singers' Festival) in Nuremberg in 1861 with over 20,000 participants. Many performances had a strong nationalist and anti-French character (Klenke 1998: 104–06). The gymnastics movement grew exponentially, beginning in the mid-1850s. The gymnasts were particularly popular in the highly industrialised Saxony and various principalities in central Germany, less so in the border regions in the east, north, and west (Figure 2.4). A statistical examination of membership data shows that it was an urban phenomenon, dominated by members of the lower middle class such as artisans (45 percent), followed by merchants and traders (21 percent) (based on data from Hirth 1865: XXXIX, LIII). The *Leipziger Turnfest* in 1863 was another major event, with around 20,000 participants. It occurred on the 50th

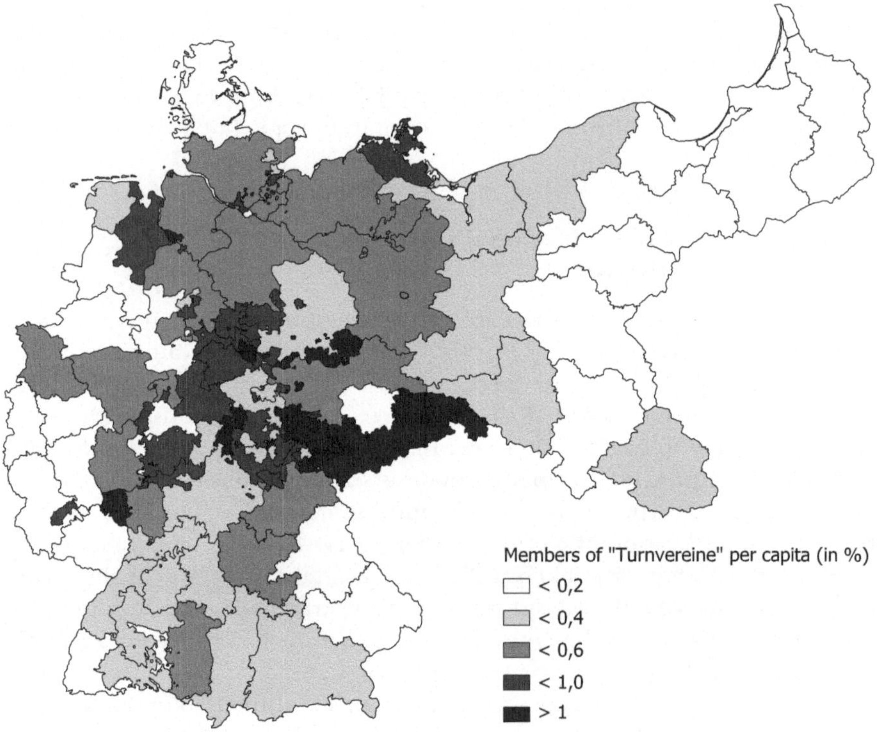

Figure 2.4 Members of gymnastics associations per population (1864).
Source: Authors' figure based on data from Hirth (1865).

anniversary of the Battle of Leipzig, with a young nationalist professor as the keynote speaker, who was convinced of the Prussian mission for Germany: Heinrich von Treitschke.

The growing national movement was able to increasingly influence public opinion. True, it remained undecided about the nature of a nation-state and the way to establish it. However, the public demand for a nation-state could no longer be ignored, not after the success of Italian unification in 1861. Nor could the liberal demand for political participation be pushed aside, as the conflict over the reform of the Prussian army showed. The war over Italy had demonstrated the need to modernise the army. However, the king and his advisors on the one hand, and the increasingly strong liberals in the Prussian parliament on the other, disagreed about the reform and the right of parliament in this regard. After another landslide victory for the liberals in May 1862, the situation came to a head. When King Wilhelm already wanted to resign, the conservatives pushed through the appointment of Otto von Bismarck as Prime Minister and foreign minister, causing outrage among the liberals. Von Rochau wrote in the weekly journal of the *Nationalverein*: 'With the use of this man, the sharpest and last bolt of the reaction by divine rights has been shot' (own translation after Wehler 2006: 271).

However, even though Bismarck was a conservative monarchist, he had realised that the national movements in Europe could hardly be stopped. His goal was to stabilise and increase the power of the Prussian crown in a world of nation-states. As Prussian prime minister, he pursued this goal against the initially strong opposition of all fractions of the German national movement, especially the *Nationalverein*. When Prussia sided with Russia against the Polish uprising of 1863, during the conflict over Schleswig-Holstein in 1864, and particularly during the Austro-Prussian War in June/July 1866, Bismarck's actions led to outrage by the national public.

In hindsight, Bismarck was by no means ignoring public opinion. Rather, he attempted to play *Wilhelm* off against *Friedrich*. In April 1866, shortly before the war with Austria, Bismarck had proposed a reform of the German Confederation under Prussian leadership, suggesting a directly elected national parliament (Biefang 1994: 389–90). The followers of the national movement sharply criticised the proposal, just as the war with Austria. Nevertheless, after Austria's defeat in 1866, the tide turned and many liberals began to support Bismarck. Prussia grew further into Germany through extensive annexations, notably the kingdom of Hanover located between the western and eastern parts of Prussia. The *Nationalverein* split and the right wing of its members joined the National Liberal Party, founded in 1867, which was to be Bismarck's main parliamentary support for the next decade.

The North German Confederation of 1867 anticipated the founding of the German Empire of 1871 in many areas, especially its constitution, which provided the template for that of 1871. The final step towards national unification, that is, the joining of the southern German states to the North German Confederation, was made with a war against France, where Bismarck could fully count on the support of the national movement (Becker 2001: 159). In 1870, when a relative of the Prussian king was offered the Spanish throne, causing outrage in France, Bismarck seized the opportunity to provoke a war with France.

Unlike the war against Austria in 1866, a wave of national emotions carried the war between Germany and France, on both sides of the Rhine. This time, the Prussian army and its German allies could count on many soldiers motivated by fervent nationalism. As mentioned before, we can compare the first names of soldiers that were awarded the Iron Cross in 1870/71 to those of all active war participants as indicated by the loss lists. On average across all ranks, and for each rank separately from general down to ordinary soldiers, honoured soldiers had a national first name significantly more often than average war participants (Kersting and Wolf 2021).

The foundation of the German Empire in 1871 contributed probably to the further strengthening and spread of national identity, even though there are hardly any empirical studies on this. In any case, a reinterpretation of Prussia's role in the history of German national unification began immediately after the war, as is visible in the arts of the period. Anton von Werner was invited to Versailles in January 1871 and commissioned to paint the proclamation of the King of Prussia as German Emperor. In the 1880s, von Werner created two monumental paintings in the Berlin *Ruhmeshalle* (Hall of Fame), a permanent public exhibition on the glory of Prussia that had already started under Wilhelm I: the *Königskrönung Friedrich I. 1701* (coronation of Friedrich I in 1701) and the *Kaiserproklamation zu Versailles, 18. Januar 1871* (Emperor's Proclamation at Versailles in 1871). Next to it, the public could see Georg Bleibtreu's painting *Aufruf 'An mein Volk', 17. März 1813*, remembering the first time that a Prussian king appealed to the 'German' people. After the formation of the German Empire, the Prussian monarchy attempted to return to the narrative of the Napoleonic wars and present the Prussian kings as leaders of the German nation—a narrative that Wilhelm II continued with great success.

5 Conclusion

We presented the emergence of the German nation-state under Prussian leadership in 1871 from the perspective of economic history. We started from the recent economic literature on nation-building and the economics of identity, which examines the interplay of a demand for social identities, driven by structural change, with its supply by strategic actors.

To make this approach more concrete, we adopted Thomas Nipperdey's thesis on Prussia's 'westward shift' as an important impulse for the strategic orientation of Prussian power politics towards the foundation of the Empire in 1871. The foundation of the *Zollverein* in 1834 is a prime example of how such power politics can, in turn, promote structural change and thus influence both the 'supply' of and 'demand' for identity. We also comprehensively addressed the connection between structural change and a 'demand for comprehensive action-guiding concepts' (own translation, Echternkamp 1998). We hope to have demonstrated how questions and methods of economic history can contribute to a better understanding of nation-building. Undoubtedly, major research gaps in this area remain, some of which require extensive empirical groundwork. For example, while we think that structural change contributed to a growing demand for a 'national' identity, further research is necessary to confirm this hypothesis.

Note

1 In Figure 2.2 we show quite a conservative estimate assuming that the responsible administrative offices in Aachen systematically 'frenchised' all first names until the withdrawal of the French troops in January 1814. We, therefore, interpret all French first names for which there was a 'Germanic' equivalent as national (version 'Treatment Group (adjustment Aachen)'). This probably underestimates the increase of national first names in Aachen since 1814. In the version 'Treatment Group (no adjustment Aachen)', we show the development under the opposite assumption that no Frenchisation of German first names took place until 1814.

References

Akerlof, G. and Kranton, R. E. (2000) 'Economics and identity', *Quarterly Journal Economics,* Vol. 115 (3): 715–53.

Alesina, A. and Reich, B. (2015) 'Nation building', *NBER Working Paper* 18839.

Anderson, B. (1983) *Imagined Communities: Reflections on the Origin and Spread of Nationalism*, London: Verso.

Bartmuss, H., Kunze, E. and Ulfkotte, J. (2008) *Turnvater Jahn und sein patriotisches Umfeld: Briefe und Dokumente 1806–1812*, Köln: Böhlau.

Becker, F. (2001) *Bilder von Krieg und Nation: Die Einigungskriege in der bürgerlichen Öffentlichkeit 1864–1913*, München: Oldenbourg.

Berger, H. and Spoerer, M. (2001) 'Economic crises and the European revolutions of 1848', *Journal of Economic History*, Vol. 61 (2): 293–326.

Biefang, A. (1994) *Politisches Bürgertum in Deutschland 1857–1868: Nationale Organisation und Eliten*, Düsseldorf: Droste.

Chen, Y. and Li, S. X. (2009) 'Group identity and social preferences', *American Economic Review*, Vol. 99 (1): 431–57.

Chiang, C. F., Liu, J. T. and Wen, T. W. (2019), 'National identity under economic integration', *Journal of Population Economics*, Vol. 32(2): 351–67.

Düding, D. (1984) *Organisierter gesellschaftlicher Nationalismus in Deutschland (1808–1847): Bedeutung und Funktion der Turner- und Sängervereine für die Deutsche Nationalbewegung*, München: Oldenbourg.

Echternkamp, J. (1998) *Der Aufstieg des deutschen Nationalismus (1770–1840)*, Frankfurt a. M.: Campus.

Etges, A. (2002) 'Von der 'vorgestellten' zur 'realen' Gefühls- und Interessensgemeinschaft? Nation und Nationalismus in Deutschland von 1830 bis 1848', in J. Echternkamp and S. Müller (eds), *Die Politik der Nation: Deutscher Nationalismus in Krieg und Krisen 1760–1960*, München: Oldenbourg, pp. 61–80.

Fischer, W., Krengel, J. and Wietog, J. (1982) *Sozialgeschichtliches Arbeitsbuch I: Materialien zur Statistik des Deutschen Bundes 1815–1870*, München: Beck.

Gellner, E. (1983) *Nations and Nationalism*, Oxford: Blackwell.

Gerhards, J. and Hackenbroch, R. (1997) 'Kulturelle Modernisierung und die Entwicklung der Semantik von Vornamen', *Kölner Zeitschrift für Soziologie und Sozialpsychologie,* Vol. 49 (3): 410–39.

Hagemann, K. (2019) *Umkämpftes Gedächtnis: Die Antinapoleonischen Kriege in der Deutschen Erinnerung*, Paderborn: Schöningh.

Hahn, H. W. (1984) *Geschichte des Deutschen Zollvereins*, Göttingen: Vandenhoeck & Ruprecht.

Hardtwig, W. (1994) *Nationalismus und Bürgerkultur in Deutschland 1500–1914: Ausgewählte Aufsätze*, Göttingen: Vandenhoeck & Ruprecht.

Hentschel, V. (1975) *Die deutschen Freihändler und der volkswirtschaftliche Kongreß 1858 bis 1885*, Stuttgart: Klett.

Hirth, G. (1865) *Statistisches Jahrbuch der Turnvereine Deutschlands*, Leipzig: Keil.

Hoffmann, C. (1815) *Des Teutschen Volkes Feuriger Dank- und Ehrentempel*, Offenbach: Brede'sche Schriften.

Huning, T. R. and Wolf, N. (2019) 'How Britain unified Germany: endogenous trade costs and the formation of a customs union', *CEPR Discussion Paper* 13634.

Jansen, C. (2011) 'The formation of German nationalism, 1740–1850', in H. Walser Smith (ed), *The Oxford Handbook of Modern German History*, Oxford: Oxford University Press, pp. 234–59.

Keller, W. and Shiue, C. H. (2014) 'Endogenous formation of free trade agreements: evidence from the Zollverein's impact on market integration', *Journal of Economic History*, Vol. 74 (4): 1168–1204.

Kersting, F. and Wolf, N. (2021) 'On the origins of national identity: German nationbuilding after Napoleon', *CEPR Discussion Paper* 16314.

Klenke, D. (1998) *Der singende 'deutsche Mann': Gesangvereine und deutsches Nationalbewußtsein von Napoleon bis Hitler*, Münster: Waxmann.

Kotulla, M. (2010) *Deutsches Verfassungsrecht 1806–1918: Eine Dokumentensammlung nebst Einführungen*, Vol. 3, Heidelberg: Springer.

Kreutzmann, M. (2012) *Die höheren Beamten des deutschen Zollvereins: Eine bürokratische Funktionselite zwischen einzelstaatlichen Interessen und zwischenstaatlicher Integration (1834–1871)*, Göttingen: Vandenhoeck & Ruprecht.

Langewiesche, D. (2000) *Nation, Nationalismus, Nationalstaat in Deutschland und Europa*, München: Beck.

Lieberson, S. and Bell, E. O. (1992) 'Children's first names: an empirical study of social taste', *American Journal of Sociology*, Vol. 98 (3): 511–54.

Martino, A. (1990) *Die Deutsche Leihbibliothek: Geschichte einer literarischen Institution (1756–1914)*, Wiesbaden: Harrassowitz.

Mieck, I. (1992) 'Preußen von 1807 bis 1850: Reformen, Restauration und Revolution', in O. Büsch (ed), *Handbuch der Preußischen Geschichte,* Vol. 2, *Das 19. Jahrhundert und große Themen der Geschichte Preußens*, Berlin: de Gruyter, pp. 3–292.

Nipperdey, T. (2013) *Deutsche Geschichte 1800–1866: Bürgerwelt und starker Staat*, München: Beck.

Nolte, J. (2007) *Demagogen und Denunzianten: Denunziation und Verrat als Methode polizeilicher Informationserhebung bei den politischen Verfolgungen im preußischen Vormärz*, Berlin: Duncker & Humblot.

Ohnishi, T. (1973) *Zolltarifpolitik Preußens bis zur Gründung des deutschen Zollvereins: Ein Beitrag zur Finanz- und Außenhandelspolitik Preußens*, Göttingen: Schwartz.

Pfister, U. (2017) The timing and pattern of real wage divergence in pre-industrial Europe: evidence from Germany, c. 1500–1850, *Economic History Review,* Vol. 70 (3): 701–29.

Planert, U. (2002) 'Wann beginnt der 'moderne' deutsche Nationalismus? Plädoyer für eine nationale Sattelzeit', in J. Echternkamp and S. Müller (eds), *Die Politik der Nation. Deutscher Nationalismus in Krieg und Krisen 1760–1960*, München: Oldenbourg, pp. 25–60.

Planert, U. (2007) *Der Mythos vom Befreiungskrieg: Frankreichs Kriege und der deutsche Süden. Alltag—Wahrnehmung—Deutung 1792–1841*, Paderborn: Ferdinand Schöningh.

Ries, K. (2014) 'Antiliberales Gedankengut in den Freiheitskriegen', in E. Grothe and K. Ries (eds), *Liberalismus als Feindbild*, Göttingen: Wallstein, pp. 19–40.

Schulze, H. (1985) *Der Weg zum Nationalstaat: Die Deutsche Nationalbewegung vom 18. Jahrhundert bis zur Reichsgründung*, München: dtv.

Schwengelbeck, M. (2007) *Die Politik des Zeremoniells: Huldigungsfeiern im langen 19. Jahrhundert*, Frankfurt a. M: Campus.

Shayo, M. (2009) 'A model of social identity with an application to political economy: nation, class, and redistribution', *American Political Science Review,* Vol. 103 (2): 147–74.

Sheehan, J. J. (1993) *German History 1770–1866*, Oxford: Oxford University Press.

Smith, A. D. (1991) *National Identity*, Reno: University of Nevada Press.

Sombart, W. (1902) *Der moderne Kapitalismus*, Vol. 1: *Die Genesis des Kapitalismus*, Berlin: Duncker & Humblot.

Steiger, G. (1967) *Aufbruch Urburschenschaft und Wartburgfest*, Leipzig: Urania.

Tschacher, W. (2010) *Königtum als lokale Praxis: Aachen als Feld der kulturellen Realisierung von Herrschaft—Eine Verfassungsgeschichte (ca. 800–1918),* Stuttgart: Steiner.

Ullmann, H. P. (1995) *Das Deutsche Kaiserreich 1871–1918*, Frankfurt: Suhrkamp.

Weber, E. (1970) *Die Mainzer Zentraluntersuchungskommission*, Karlsruhe: Müller.

Wehler, H. U. (2006) *Deutsche Gesellschaftsgeschichte*, Vol. 3: *Von der "Deutschen Doppelrevolution" bis zum Beginn des Ersten Weltkrieges 1849–1914*, München: Beck.

3 Intergovernmental economic cooperation and institutional integration before the founding of the German Empire

Alfred Reckendrees

1 Introduction

'German unity has been created and so has the Emperor', Prussian Chancellor Bismarck proclaimed in an intimate setting on 23 November 1870 (Busch 1879: 25), when the Kingdom of Bavaria agreed to join the new German Confederation founded a week earlier by the North German Confederation and the Grand Duchies of Baden and Hesse. Shortly afterwards, Württemberg joined the agreement and the North German Confederation ratified the unification treaties. Soon after on 3 March 1871, the first election to the parliament (*Reichstag*) took place, which only six weeks later confirmed the Imperial Constitution. The Empire was a constitutional monarchy as well as a federal structure consisting of 25 individual states with different constitutions. The history of its creation, linked to the Prussian-Austrian War of 1866 and the Franco-Prussian War of 1870/71, the hegemonic position of Prussia among the German states, and the role of the Prussian King as German Emperor led historian Hans-Ulrich Wehler (1995: 251–330) to characterise the founding of the Empire as a 'revolution from above' led by Bismarck. However, historian Hans-Peter Ullmann (1995: 20) rightly argued a few years later that founding the Empire 'from above' would hardly have been possible without the 'economic, socio-cultural, and political nation-building that had taken place previously and provided a framework and scope for action'.

The long-standing intergovernmental cooperation and institutional integration, on which the Empire could rely after its foundation, are the subject of this article.[1] Simultaneous integration efforts of commercial and political associations are not considered in this context. Even so, even the intergovernmental perspective reveals that economic integration should not be interpreted as a process determined solely by the ever-present Prussian power politics. Prussia had to compromise and grant far-reaching concessions to other states in order to achieve its economic policy goals. However, striving for hegemony increasingly influenced Prussian attitudes since the beginning of the 1850s. At that time, the forms of institutional cooperation between the states also began to change.

DOI: 10.4324/9781003283430-4

The first steps in the economic integration of the German states can be seen in the founding of the German Customs Union—the *Zollverein*—in 1834, which relieved trade between member states from internal customs duties and imposed common external customs duties. Agreements on a common coinage and monetary system (Dresden Coinage Treaty, 1838) and a bill of exchange system valid in all states of the German Confederation (1849) marked the subsequent stages. Finally, the General Commercial Code for the German Confederation (1861) created a common framework for commercial transactions between companies. If the *Zollverein* was initially the driving force for economic integration, the German Confederation (*Deutscher Bund*, 1815–66) partly took over this function in the 1850s. Nevertheless, neither organisation had suprastate authority; they rather operated through complex interstate treaties and the adoption of jointly developed rules into the respective laws of the member states.

However, it was not only the *Zollverein* and the German Confederation that promoted interstate cooperation. Improvement of infrastructure contributed substantially to institutional integration by motivating agreements on technical standards, norms, and tariffs as well as creating a certain degree of coordination in planning and administration (Ambrosius 2005; Ambrosius and Henrich-Franke 2016). This improvement included the expansion and consolidation of the national and international railway network (Fremdling 1975; Hornung 2015) as well as postal services and the telegraph network which were coordinated in the framework of the German-Austrian Postal Union and the German-Austrian Telegraph Union, both established in 1850 (Reindle 1993; Chapter 7 of this volume). The drivers of this development were by no means primarily the contract-signing governments, but rather networks of experts who, in laborious processes of understanding and rapprochement, elaborated common principles of negotiation and practice, and thereby built up trust amongst each other. They did not merely implement the political goals of 'their' state but also increasingly functioned as administrators of a common suprastate interest. It was only the new customs union between the North German Confederation (*Norddeutscher Bund*, 1867) and the other member states that bore the traits of a suprastate organisation.[2]

The following analysis of the economic integration of the German states builds on the concepts of political economy used by Fritz Scharpf in the context of European integration. He distinguishes between two forms of political integration 'aimed at enlarging the economic space beyond existing national boundaries' (Scharpf 1999: 45), 'negative integration', which is the elimination of existing trade restrictions (e.g. mutual abolition of customs duties), and 'positive integration', which denotes the enforcement of economic policy and regulatory competences for suprastate organisations. The latter can include market creating regulations (e.g. standards and norms to remove non-tariff barriers) and market-correcting regulations (e.g. labour protection). Negative and positive integration can be achieved through supranational law or intergovernmental policy, in this case with intergovernmental policy concepts dominating from the early 1830s until the founding of the North German Confederation in 1867. The approach is compatible with a historical-institutionalist perspective emphasising path dependencies and the performativity of institutionally supported integration processes, in that once established institutional arrangements do not determine future decisions, but influence possible solutions to future problems and thus reduce contingency (cf. Kreutzmann 2013: 193). The functional perspective taken in this chapter does not imply that unification was inevitable and that there were no alternatives to the course of events. Instead, the approach adopted here serves to identify the institutional preconditions for the founding of the Empire.

Section 2 outlines the founding and functioning of the *Zollverein*; Section 3 examines the monetary system, exchange law, and trade law—three policy areas that are particularly relevant for economic integration. I discuss the transition from a more cooperative (but not coequal) to a more power-based process of integration in the 1850s in Section 4. Using the example of the *Zollverein*, Section 5 turns to the functional elites that played a decisive role in shaping the integration process; in Section 6, I summarise the findings. Unfortunately, it is not possible to address the manifold parallels to the widening and deepening of European integration, which has been discussed since the beginning of the 1950s (Viner 1950; Fischer 1960; Henderson 1981; Baldwin 2006).

2 The customs union

With the implementation of the German Customs Union on 1 January 1834, an internal market was created with uniform external customs duties for initially 18 German states, including Bavaria, Hesse-Darmstadt, Electoral Hesse (Hesse-Kassel), Prussia, Saxony, the Thuringian states, and Württemberg. In 1835, Baden and Nassau joined the union; in 1836, the free city of Frankfurt, followed in 1841 by Brunswick and some smaller principalities; in 1842, the Grand Duchy of Luxembourg and, finally, in 1854, the Kingdom of Hanover (Figure 3.1; for historical accounts see Fischer 1864; Weber 1869; Henderson 1939 [1984]; Hahn 1984a).

In retrospect, the founding of the *Zollverein* appears to many scholars as a step towards the political unification of the German states, as it contributed to their economic and administrative integration. However, it was certainly not a 'brilliantly designed' instrument of the Prussian state, 'cloaked with a liberal intergovernmental General Congress' for the creation of the Empire as Kathleen Hancock argues (2009: 61).[3] It is true that around 1830 Prussia was the leading power in the German Confederation alongside Austria and, with its prosperous provinces of the Rhineland, Westphalia, and Saxony, its economic heavyweight. However, even though Prussia had abolished the existing customs duties and excises within its own territory in 1819 (1821), traffic between its own western and eastern provinces was hindered by customs borders. One of the core concerns of Prussian policy was, therefore, to

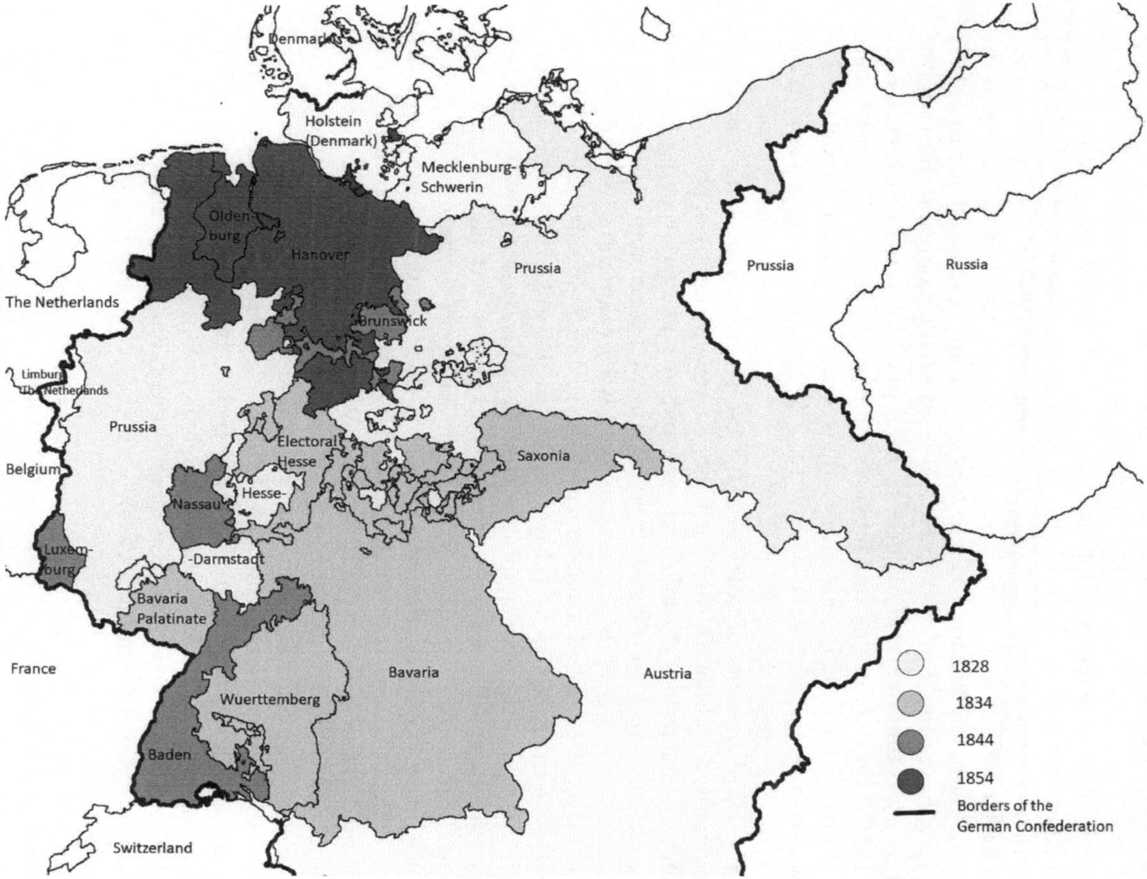

Figure 3.1 The German Customs Union and the German Confederation in 1854.
Source: © IEG Mainz. Edited by the author.

enable the free movement of goods between its eastern and western provinces through customs unions with Hesse-Darmstadt and Electoral Hesse. A corresponding treaty, however, could only be concluded with Hesse-Darmstadt in February 1828. The independence of the Kingdom of Belgium (1830) had an accelerating and compromise-promoting effect on further customs union negotiations. Against this background, the Mainz Convention (1831) became possible, which exempted shipping trade on the Rhine from all transit duties and levies (Strauch 2007) and hence significantly reduced the trade costs for Prussian companies. At the same time, the Prussian-Hessian customs union had the effect of a 'barrier' to the access of South German states to the North Sea ports. Electoral Hesse, whose customs revenues fell particularly sharply due to the shift of the Prussian transit trade from its territory to the Rhine, was thus prepared to agree to a customs union with Prussia as early as 1831. Those states that had previously joined the Bavarian-Württemberg Customs Union (1828) were also ready to enter a common customs union just two years later (cf. Feuerstein 2013: 379–80; Ploeckl 2015; Huning and Wolf 2019).

The fiscal interests of governments were probably a stronger motive for most states to relinquish their tariff border sovereignty as opposed to trade policy considerations. Prussia was prepared to make far-reaching financial concessions, which were based on political as well as economic motives. Rolf Dumke (1984) argues that in view of the July Revolution in Paris and Brussels (1830), Prussia had a fundamental interest in politically stabilising the smaller German monarchies. Membership in the *Zollverein* would improve their position as the very significant customs collection costs were considerably reduced and the revenues distribution key was extremely favourable to them. In principle, the union reduced the length of the external borders at which controls were conducted and customs duties could be levied, and thus their collection costs. The smaller states lying between other member states benefited the most, but so did Bavaria and Württemberg. The treaty between Prussia and Hesse-Darmstadt had already stipulated the joint coverage of the costs of border control and customs collection as well as the distribution of revenues in proportion to the size of the population; this principle became the basis for all subsequent treaties. For Baden, Bavaria, and Württemberg, the number of inhabitants of the relatively populous provinces of Rhineland and Westphalia served as the basis for assessment. For Saxony and the Thuringian states, it was the number of the less populous eastern Prussian provinces (Dumke 1984: 87–88, 98).

Apart from Prussia, all states increased their net revenues through membership in the *Zollverein* (cf. Bienengräber 1868: 14–16; Hahn 1984a: 98–101). Their most important source was a small group of imported goods; for example, 30 and 12 percent of revenues in 1847–49 resulted from the import and transit of coffee and tobacco (and tobacco products), whereas industrial products were of relatively minor importance (Kühne 1846: 25–26). Nevertheless, persistent excise duties on beer and malt, brandy, wine, and tobacco created the potential for conflict. Saxony and the Thuringian Customs Union adopted the Prussian rates; the others levied their own excise duties. As these were often levied at the source (for example, the Bavarian beer tax was determined based on the volume of the brewing kettles), the states often reacted to imports from other *Zollverein* states with additional duties. A compromise was found in that the right to levy own excise duties was granted, but the Prussian rates for wine, spirits, and tobacco and the Bavarian rates for beer and malt defined the taxation limit. Additional levies required the consent of the states concerned and were limited to precisely these products. Wolfram Fischer (1960: 77–78) argues that this made the introduction of new excise duties virtually impossible, as otherwise cheap products from other *Zollverein* states would have entered the market. A state monopoly on salt and playing cards, which Prussia did not want to give up and Hanover did not want to introduce, created similar problems.

The *Zollverein*, founded in 1834 through coordinated bilateral and multilateral treaties, remained an intergovernmental organisation without suprastate powers until the founding of the North German Confederation and the reorganisation of the *Zollverein* in 1867, which then acquired features of a suprastate organisation (Kreutzmann 2013). Especially in the initial years, the *Zollverein* functioned astonishingly 'smoothly'. All decisions had to be consensual after the participating states had initially adopted the Prussian customs rates and administrative principles upon signing the treaty and agreed on a common customs weight, the *Zollverein* Zentner of 50 kilograms.[4] Within this structure, 'harmonisation and standardisation could only be achieved through concerted parallel legislation of the individual states' (Fischer 1960: 71–75, 87; Wadle 1985: 104). However, from the very beginning, the states strove to make the union work; for example, the first general assembly in 1836 already adopted a common customs law.

The customs administration remained organised on a national basis but was oriented towards Prussian standards. An exchange of supervisors in the local customs offices and the central customs directorates, the station controllers, and *Zollverein* representatives facilitated coordination and established a system of mutual control. Decisions were made during the annual general conference, in which initially Bavaria, Hesse-Darmstadt, Electoral Hesse, Prussia, Saxony, and Württemberg as well as the Thuringian Customs Union had seats and voting rights, whereas the other states were only indirectly represented. In the conference, delegates of the represented states, high officials or ministers, deliberated on all customs union issues (customs tariff, accounting of revenues, customs legislation and regulations, complaints by customs union members). Due to the unanimity principle, bilateral and multilateral consultations among the governments were required before each General Assembly. Controversial issues were not submitted to the General Assembly and motions that could not reach consensus were deferred (Hahn 1984a: 79–81). Foreign trade and shipping treaties were negotiated by the respective border states—usually Prussia, which had a stronger negotiating position than Baden vis-à-vis France, for example, due to its economic power—and then submitted to the General Assembly for approval. Although the right of veto hindered fast decisions, it was considered indispensable, since it was expected that state governments would not implement majority decisions that they had not agreed to. Moreover, any veto only had a suspensive effect because the customs union treaties were limited in time (Henderson 1981: 495; Feuerstein 2013: 377). The first treaty had a duration of eight years, the subsequent treaties extended over 12 years. When a treaty expired, Prussia could threaten to terminate it and, in fear of the massive financial losses that most of the member states had to face, could generally push through the desired overall package (Hahn 1984a: 103–08).

The creation of a large duty-free internal market with uniform external tariffs was a case of 'negative integration'; the participating states did not require surrendering any regulatory or economic policy competence. However, the deepening of the internal market also required the removal of non-tariff barriers to trade. For example, almost every state had its weights, lengths and gauges, and currency, which complicated cross-border trade and hindered integration. A similar challenge arose from the difference in the principles of commercial and economic law (Wadle 1985: 105, 114).

The harmonisation of the different coinage, measurement, and weight systems of the German states had been a subject of repeated consultations within the German Confederation since the beginning of the 1820s, but no progress was made (Müller 2005: 435–37). Under the Prussian-Hessian treaty of March 1833, the customs union members provided for agreements on standardising the system of weights and measures, coinage regulations, the tax and duty system, or the 'protection of inventions'. 'Positive integration', however, proved to be a more arduous task than the abolition of existing customs borders since it affected the states' regulatory competences and in many cases required a certain degree of agreement on economic policy views. Nevertheless, the positions of the states differed across policy areas, as did the finally achieved progress in harmonisation. The harmonisation of the monetary system and trade law, which were of principal importance for a common internal market, are outlined in the following section as examples.

3 Monetary cooperation and the harmonisation of commercial law

When the *Zollverein* was founded, there were 34 states and four free cities with minting sovereignty and their own currency in the territory that would come to form the German Empire. The northern states used the (silver) Taler, but the proportion of silver differed across currencies. In the southern states, the (silver) guilder (Gulden) dominated; here, too, different coin weights applied. In addition, there was the (silver) Mark in the Hanseatic cities of Hamburg and Lübeck, and the (gold) Taler in Bremen. Twelve distinct coinage systems made interstate trade and accounting a difficult task for exporting companies. Although the economic weight of Prussia and its currency forced some smaller states to adopt the Prussian coinage foot, a real facilitation of payment transactions only came with the so-called Dresden Coinage Treaty, which was agreed upon among the *Zollverein* states in 1838, after the South German states had harmonised their coinage system a year earlier.

Political conflicts hardly played any role in this context, especially since the Mint Treaty did not interfere with the sovereignty of the states. The precious metal-based exchange rates remained unchanged and were only set to a different coinage base. The Cologne Mark (233.855 grams of silver), from which 14 Taler and 24 ½ Gulden were to be minted, now served as a common reference point for the various Taler and Gulden currencies.[5] Smaller states that were not members of the *Zollverein* joined the coinage union; only the states bordering the North Sea and the Baltic Sea did not participate. In principle, the treaty interfered with the states' sovereignty of coinage only to the extent that they committed themselves to limiting the issuance of coins, such as pfennigs, kreuzers, heller, groschen, and other small coins (cf. Sprenger 1981: 44–53; Wadle 1985: 115–18; Tilly 2003: 85–89).

Two decades later, the Vienna Coinage Treaty (1857), which had been negotiated within the framework of the German Confederation since 1854, was to deepen monetary integration further. Now Austria also joined the common coin regime. To make this possible, the unit of weight of the Cologne Mark was replaced by the 'customs pound' of 500 grams, from which either 30 Taler, 45 (Austrian) Gulden or 52 ½ South German Gulden could be minted. However, since Austria was unable to implement the necessary financial stabilisation measures and did not agree to the convertibility of paper money (Hahn 1984a: 157), it effectively remained outside the common currency area. In addition, a common Taler coin equivalent in value to the Prussian Taler (*Zollvereinstaler*) was introduced, significantly expanding the use of the Prussian Taler as a means of payment and unit of account, whereas the regional coins that remained valid continued to lose importance in trade (Müller 2005: 435–37).

In the nineteenth century, the bill of exchange, the cashless settlement of transactions through a written payment obligation, was mainly used to settle larger business transactions in interregional trade. In Prussia, for example, the financial volume of bills of exchange in 1865 was estimated at three times the amount of metal money in circulation and four times the amount of circulating Prussian banknotes. However, since almost 60 different bill of exchange regulations were in force in the German states in the 1830s, which constituted 'an increasingly troublesome obstacle to trade [...] if the drawer, drawee and endorser' came from different jurisdictions (Wischermann 2004: 110–11), the harmonisation of the bill of exchange regulations was on the agenda of the *Zollverein* at an early stage.

As early as 1836, Württemberg had also proposed the drafting of a common commercial law, well aware that very different economic ideas would clash in this matter. When Prussia, Saxony, and Brunswick were working on a new bill of exchange law ten years later, Württemberg once again proposed 'to establish a common commercial and bill of exchange law, or at least a common bill of exchange law for the entire *Zollverein* for the time being' (Wadle 1985: 126). The concern was that there would be no room for joint negotiations for several years once the states had passed similar laws of their own. This time the other member states took up the proposal. The bill of exchange regulations were to define the rights of debtors and creditors and the uniform handling of transactions not only for the *Zollverein* but also for as many German states as possible. Of particular interest were the Kingdom of Hanover and the trading centres of Hamburg and Bremen, through which large parts of imports and exports were handled. A draft for a General German Bill of Exchange Order was available in 1847. Passed by the Frankfurt National Assembly in 1848, most German states adopted the order as their own law and it was apparently accepted in business transactions across the German states. It was the only resolution of the National Assembly that was to retain legal force. The standardisation was further advanced between 1858 and 1861 within the framework of the German Confederation; it was implemented by most states by 1865 and also became the law of the North German Confederation in 1869 (Pannwitz 1999).

In 1849, the National Assembly also received a draft for a general commercial code for Germany, which was not dealt with. Subsequently, smaller German states, especially Saxony and Bavaria, intensified their efforts to unify the German states economically. In this context, the German Confederation was to serve as a 'mediator of an economic unification of Germany' (Müller 2005: 407) and the *Zollverein* was to form the basis for a 'customs and trade unity' that would also include Austria, a perspective in which Saxony and Bavaria were particularly interested due to their customs borders. Subsequently, a commission of the Confederation formulated a 'Revised Draft of an Agreement between the German Federal States for the Promotion of Trade and Transport' for the Dresden Conference (1851), which aimed at facilitating trade, customs, and transport throughout the Confederation, including standardisation of business and trade taxes (Hahn 1984a: 140–51, 2002; Müller 2005: 407–10).

However, tensions between liberal and protectionist states stood in the way of the unification of commercial law. Even in Prussia, two different codes regulated business transactions, the Code de Commerce in the Rhine Province and the General Land Law in the other provinces. An agreement in the *Zollverein* to which Württemberg submitted a proposal for a common commercial code in 1854 (Baums 1982: 42; Wadle 1985: 127) was furthermore hindered by political conflicts that had been straining the relations between Hesse-Darmstadt and South German states and Prussia since the *Zollverein* Crisis (1851, for the background, see Section 4). The changing political dynamics in the *Zollverein*, now determined by the relationship between the hegemonic powers of Austria and Prussia, will be dealt with in the next section. Firstly, market-creating regulations in trade law will be discussed.

The Bavarian-Saxon initiative of 1851 did not produce any immediate result, but five years later, it brought about intensive efforts towards the standardisation of commercial law and related areas. After the *Zollverein* Crisis had subsided, Bavaria reintroduced the proposal to the German Confederation in 1856. The assembly decided—after Prussia had pushed through the liberal 'principle of free agreement' for the law book in advance—to appoint a committee consisting of senior civil servants (lawyers) and merchants (a list of members in Müller 2005: 580–82) that should draft a General Commercial Code for the German States (*Allgemeines Deutsches Handelsgesetzbuch* or ADHGB), the work of which was based on a draft of the Prussian Commercial Code published at the beginning of 1857. In 1861, after 589 meetings, the draft for the ADHGB was completed (meanwhile the standardisation of the bill of exchange regulations was also further advanced). In addition to the obvious economic motives, many participants saw the commercial code in the context of the idea of German unity. The committee on trade policy linked the presentation of the draft with the wish to 'gain a basis for the further advancement of legal unity in the German nation' (Müller 2005: 414). After its adoption by the Federal Assembly, 39 states incorporated the ADHGB into their own law, and the North German Confederation adopted it in 1869. It remained in force in the German Empire until 1897 and in Austria until 1918 (cf. Goldschmidt 1862; Müller 2005: 414–17; Fleckner 2009; Oestmann 2018: 365–66).[6] The ADHGB standardised the norms of commercial activities for single merchants, partnerships, limited partnerships, and joint-stock companies. The 'firm' became a legal entity to be registered in the commercial register, regardless of its organisational form and the acting person. Where specific regulations existed in the ADHGB, they were considered superior to civil law provisions.

The agreements on the ADHGB and the bill of exchange law indicate the extent to which 'positive integration' was possible in the middle of the nineteenth century. Further attempts to deepen economic integration through market-creating regulation failed due to opposing economic policy views. While liberal positions dominated in Prussia, most states adhered to the protection of domestic trade and existing economic structures. Against this background, the states could not agree on an interpretation of freedom of trade. In this political constellation, free movement of goods and money marked the limit of what was possible and this was the key factor for trade and industry, too. Only during the 1860s, did 'one state after another adopt a liberal trade constitution' (Ambrosius 2001: 74).

A similar fundamental conflict, only briefly touched upon here, concerned patent protection. In Prussia, its critics feared an impediment to the free movement of goods, whereas Saxony and the South German states advocated strong patent protection. As a compromise, the *Zollverein* states agreed on certain principles of mutual recognition in 1842: If a patent holder held a patent in a customs union state, only they would receive the right to apply for a corresponding patent in another customs union state. Protection applied only to the manufacturing of a product, whereas trade, import, and distribution of similar goods remained permitted for everyone. Moreover, the products had to be inventions or substantial improvements to existing products. Baden, Bavaria, Hanover, Saxony, Prussia, and Württemberg implemented these rules by 1847 (Donges and Selgert 2019: 60–66). Further efforts to establish a patent law of the German Confederation, a patent office, and a patent journal failed due to the controversial economic policy positions.[7] The next section will discuss the changing political dynamics in the 1850s.

4 The transition from cooperative integration to power politics

In the 1830s, Prussia had often made considerable concessions to persuade other states to join the *Zollverein*. These included the sharing of customs collection costs and distribution of revenues based on population size. In addition, to assert its interests as effectively as possible, Prussia only negotiated with individual states, which moreover had to initiate the negotiations formally. Integration research has deduced from this a 'domino theory' emphasising the 'demand' of the smaller states for membership. The larger the *Zollverein* became, the more useful it was. The budgets of most states benefited immensely from the *Zollverein* and became financially dependent on it. Prussia's customs revenues, by contrast, fell (Hahn 1984a: 96–102, 1984b: 56). However, economic historian Florian Ploeckl (2015) shows that economic calculations also explain the logic of negotiations from the Prussian perspective and that Prussia was able to obtain considerable concessions from states for which the *Zollverein* was particularly advantageous, for example, the Thuringian Union and Saxony (see also Feuerstein 2013: 378–82). Accordingly, the agreement between Prussia, Württemberg, and Bavaria also motivated Baden to join; and when Nassau joined the union in 1835 seeing itself in an isolated position, Frankfurt followed immediately because it wanted to maintain free access to the Rhine. In addition, the city received four and a half times more revenue than usual due to its economic importance (Henderson 1939 [1984]: 120; Hahn 1984a: 83–87). The accessions of Brunswick (1841) and Luxembourg (1842) followed a similar logic. Prussia clearly had a leading role, but the economically most powerful German state profited less from customs revenues compared to the duty-free movement of goods between its distant provinces and the generally increased economic activity through the *Zollverein*, the effects of which are likely to have varied across regions (Lee 1988). Although assessments of the magnitude of the economic consequences of the *Zollverein* differ, researchers agree that the *Zollverein* generated positive macroeconomic effects and deepened market integration (Dumke 1981; Shiue 2005; Keller and Shiue 2014).

In the mid-1840s, only Austria and the (free-trading) North German states, especially Hanover, Hamburg, and Bremen, which benefited from their advantageous location on the North Sea, were not members of the *Zollverein*.

Within the *Zollverein,* there were disputes at the time about protective tariffs between the more protectionist southern governments and the more free-trade-oriented Prussian state. In addition, there were protectionist efforts to integrate Austria into the *Zollverein* in order to enforce a 'protective tariff regime' jointly. However, Austria was determined to stick to its particularly prohibitive customs system rather than even negotiate a trade treaty. Moreover, Prussia and Austria largely agreed on the policy of the German Confederation so that the southern governments could not exploit conflicting ambitions between Prussia and Austria (Fischer 1864: 401–07; Henderson 1939 [1984]: 153–57, 176–77; Hahn 1984a, 138–39).

The revolutionary years of 1848–49 changed the political landscape. On the one hand, the crisis-ridden economic situation after the revolution revived interest in protective tariffs and the integration of Austria; on the other hand, Prussia began the pursuit of a Small German Confederation (excluding Austria) under its leadership in the early 1850s. Efforts at economic integration were now increasingly overlaid by a political hegemony conflict. The German-Austrian agreements in 1850 on the Postal Union and the Telegraphic Union illustrate continued cooperation on economically relevant issues (cf. Chapter 7 of this volume). However, going forward, institutional integration took a different form.

While Austria aimed to strengthen its position by proposing a Central European Customs Union (Henderson 1939 [1984]: 137–48; Hahn 2002; Hagen 2015), Prussia sought further political integration of the German states without Austria, which is why it blocked any discussion of a Central European Customs Union and was only willing to sign a trade treaty with Austria. Given this situation, the Prussian government entered into secret negotiations on Hanover's accession to the *Zollverein*, provoking the *Zollverein* Crisis, as Hanover's accession would change the strategic positions within the *Zollverein.* The agreement with Hanover secured the free movement of goods between Prussia's western and eastern provinces independently of other *Zollverein* states. Prussia was, therefore, prepared to compensate financially for Hanover's accession on 1 January 1854, for example by granting the kingdom a share of *Zollverein* revenues at 75 percent higher than the normal rate and by lowering customs tariffs for colonial goods (Ploeckl 2015: 296). The possibilities for the Hessian states, Saxony, Württemberg, and Bavaria to exert joint pressure on Prussia was minimised by the treaty with Hanover; and Prussia's unilateral action and the favourable treatment of Hanover angered them. Towards the end of 1851, when the mid-German states started discussing possibilities of their own customs union with Austria, Prussia surprisingly exercised its right to terminate the expiring customs union treaties at the end of 1853. Now the states had to either accept the treaty with Hanover or leave the *Zollverein,* which no one seriously considered. A trade treaty with Austria (1853), which was to become part of the new *Zollverein* treaty, eased the political process. Austria lifted most of its import bans and the contracting parties granted each other most-favoured-nation treatments as well as various preferential tariffs; some tariffs were even abolished. Negotiations on a Central European Customs Union were to begin in 1860, but this turned out to be a tactical concession: In the face of the strong opposition of *Zollverein* states who continued to seek close cooperation with Austria in order to contain Prussia, Prussia concluded a trade agreement with France in 1862. This new treaty provided, among other things, for most-favoured-nation treatment and reduced tax rates, which effectively negated the agreements reached with Austria a few years earlier, leading to a second crisis of the *Zollverein*, in which Prussia once again successfully asserted its position against the goals of other states (Fischer 1864; Weber 1869; Henderson 1939 [1984]; Hahn 1984a).

Against the background of these conflicts, it can be explained that, within the German Confederation, the possibilities of harmonising commercial law or the bill of exchange law were greater than in the *Zollverein*, where any further integration had to appear as a strengthening of the Small German proposition.

5 Expert networks as carriers of institutional integration

From the very beginning, specialist officials played an important role in the expansion of the *Zollverein*. They served as *Zollverein* representatives or as station controllers, the latter being responsible for monitoring customs clearance per the treaties as well as payment of revenues. Particularly the *Zollverein* representatives expanded their area of responsibility over time. The representatives at the General Conferences were senior civil servants who usually took on this role for a long time. Although the *Zollverein* did not have its own administration but only a small Central Bureau of the member states for the settlement of revenues, the higher officials developed an interest in maintaining and expanding their scope of work in the course of their cooperation in the committees and conferences. For example, the idea of compiling common trade statistics for the *Zollverein* arose within the Central Bureau, although it took until 1864 for the statistics for 1861 to be produced.[8] As Martin Kreutzmann's meticulous analysis shows, an overall culture emerged in the *Zollverein* administration that 'elevated the common interest of the *Zollverein* states to the basis of binding patterns of thought and action'. He, therefore, speaks of the 'German Customs Union's higher officials' rather than state representatives (Kreutzmann 2012a: 231). Through various examples, Kreutzmann shows that the officials and the administrative rationality and ethics they developed were possibly even decisive for the expansion and preservation of the *Zollverein*. Especially during the *Zollverein* Crisis of 1851, continued interstate cooperation depended on pragmatist and economically driven approaches. Rudolph Delbrück, who represented Prussia at the General Conferences for many years, wrote in his memoirs that none of the representatives wanted the *Zollverein* to disintegrate: 'The majority of them had worked in *Zollverein* affairs from the beginning of their careers, the *Zollverein* had become a part of their own lives'. He also portrayed the collegial relationship and the 'satisfaction when stone after stone was removed from the way' (Delbrück quoted in Kreutzmann 2012a: 180).

Similar specialised and highly qualified experts were active in the field of jurisprudence, in coinage and monetary affairs or transport and communications. Especially in the field of railway traffic, postal services, or telegraphy, growing cross-border traffic induced numerous efforts to unify standards and norms, in which technical and administrative experts were involved to an increasing extent. This did not lead to integrated technical systems just as yet, but apparently to networks considering and beginning to prepare them (Ambrosius and Henrich-Franke 2016: 41–62). The relationship between professionalisation and an inherent logic of administration has been studied quite well at the level of individual states. In addition, the *Zollverein* officials formed a similar functional elite over time (Hahn 1982: 233–35; Kreutzmann 2012a, 2012b) that was, in fact, given the opportunity to shape policy. The legal experts and merchants involved in the ADHGB may have also developed a shared overarching interest in coordination and integration in the course of their four years of commission work, which may have generated a similar logic of its own as described in Delbrück's memoirs.[9]

6 Conclusion

The founding of the German Customs Union in 1834 meant a new quality of cooperation among a larger group of German states. It extended beyond duty-free domestic trade and a common customs border, when the coinage and monetary system was standardised in 1838 to the extent that a single monetary unit of account facilitated business transactions. The bill of exchange regulation adopted in 1849 was implemented as law by almost all German states. The *Zollverein* was thus on its way to becoming a single market. The institutional cooperation of the states strengthened existing impulses for industrial investment, for example in transportation infrastructure, facilitated trade between the states, and contributed to the expansion of production. It deepened market integration and generated positive macroeconomic effects, which would have varied regionally. In any case, the states were able to increase their customs revenues dramatically, one of the most important sources of state financing in the mid-nineteenth century.

Institutional integration since the early 1830s, accompanied by accelerated industrialisation—including the expansion of transport and communications infrastructure as important push factors—and rising economic growth, created a self-reinforcing development pattern associated with strong barriers to exit. Given the unpredictable new political constellations and changing alliances, the 'functional' perspective underlying this article should not be interpreted to mean that economic and institutional integration was an inevitable process. The persistence of the *Zollverein* under these conditions of political instability and conflict is, in fact, remarkable. The institutional arrangement established in 1833 could probably produce this continuity because the cooperation of the *Zollverein* officials, which originally served the purpose of mutual control, had a sustained effect. Although the shared practices of the higher officials and their joint management of challenges did not create a suprastate organisation, it did create an expert network that had made supranational interest its paradigm of thought and action, and contributed significantly to sustaining the *Zollverein* in times of crisis. It is worth remembering that even when Prussia went to war with Austria (and *Zollverein* states on its side) in 1866, the customs union functioned smoothly: regardless of the acts of war, customs duties were levied jointly; revenues were distributed and paid out as per the statutes.

The political arena in which governments and increasingly professionalised civil servants operated was initially the *Zollverein*, in which Prussia played a leading role, even though many integration initiatives came from smaller states. The revolution of 1848–49 and its aftermath changed the political structure, resulting in a lasting conflict between Prussia and Austria over the leading role in the German Confederation. Austria pressed for admission to the *Zollverein* and was supported by states with a protectionist orientation. Prussia, on the other hand, expanded its own position of power without consulting its partners to an extent that it dominated the policy of the *Zollverein* over time and, in fact, undermined the veto rights of the other states. Under these conditions, deeper institutional integration through the *Zollverein* was no longer conceivable. Smaller states, therefore, pushed ahead with institutional cooperation in the 'arena' of the German Confederation, where the Prussian-Austrian conflict gave them greater room for manoeuvre. The ADHGB, characterised above all by its Prussian drafts, was the most important result of this process. 'Positive integration' did not succeed in other relevant areas.

The German Empire of 1871 was able to complement the internal market by building on proposals already negotiated in the German Confederation as well as on the established institutions of the *Zollverein*. The persistence of the *formal* institutions emerging in intergovernmental cooperation cannot be explained by the set of rules alone; rather, cooperatively generated *informal* institutions, such as supranational interest as a common paradigm of thought and action among higher officials, and their constant efforts to complement 'negative integration' with 'positive integration', reinforced a path-dependent yet not determined process.

Notes

1 'Institutions' are understood in the sense of Douglass C. North (1990) as formal and informal rules of a society and are to be distinguished from 'organisations'.
2 For example, the new Zollverein had a customs parliament, cf. Kreutzmann (2013); for the territory of the North German Confederation, cf. https://www.ieg-maps.uni-mainz.de/mapsp/mapd867.htm.
3 For a contrasting view see Nipperdey (1984: 360–61).
4 The Zollverein Zentner was to be used in trade between member states from 1839 onward; it was also used as a freight weight in the Association of German Railway Administrations (1847) and as a postal weight in the German-Austrian Postal Union (1850).

5 A common *Vereinsmünze* (Customs Union Coin) with a value of two Taler or three and a half Gulden was hardly used in commercial transactions due to its high value and weight.

6 Only Schaumburg-Lippe, Denmark (on behalf of Holstein and Lauenburg) and The Netherlands (on behalf of Luxembourg and Limburg) did not adopt the ADHGB; for a similar Commission for Civil and Criminal Law (1859), cf. Müller (2005: 421–31).

7 The Patent Act of 1877 and the Imperial Patent Office adopted ideas that had their origins in the commissions of the German Confederation (Müller 2005: 501–11).

8 Cf. Verhandlungen (1843: 177–80); Protokolle über die Berathungen in Betreff der zur Herstellung einer Gewerbestatistik der Zollvereinsstaaten erforderlichen Erhebungen (22. 8. 1854), Geheimes Preußisches Staatsarchiv I. Ha Rep. 120 a V Fach 1 Nr. 2 Bd. 6 .

9 To the best of my knowledge, there is no corresponding study on the preparation of the ADHGB, yet Oestmann (2018) describes the emergence of an experts network and its contribution to the unification of maritime law using the example of the Lübeck court.

References

Ambrosius, G. (2001) *Staat und Wirtschaftsordnung: Eine Einführung in Theorie und Geschichte*, Stuttgart: Steiner.

Ambrosius, G. (2005) *Regulativer Wettbewerb und koordinative Standardisierung zwischen Staaten: Theoretische Annahmen und historische Beispiele*, Stuttgart: Steiner.

Ambrosius, G. and Henrich-Franke, C. (2016) *Integration of Infrastructures in Europe in Historical Comparison*, Cham: Springer.

Baldwin, R. E. (2006) 'Multilateralising regionalism: spaghetti bowls as building blocs on the path to global free trade', *World Economy*, Vol. 29 (11): 1451–518.

Baums, T. (1982) *Entwurf eines allgemeinen Handelsgesetzbuches für Deutschland (1848/49): Text und Materialien*, Heidelberg: Recht und Wirtschaft.

Bienengräber, A. (1868) *Statistik des Verkehrs und Verbrauchs im Zollverein für die Jahre 1842–1864*, Berlin: Duncker.

Busch, M. (1879) *Graf Bismarck und seine Leute während des Kriegs mit Frankreich: Nach Tagebuchblättern, Vol. 2*, Leipzig: Grunow.

Donges, A. and Selgert, F. (2019) 'Do legal differences matter? A comparison of German patent law regimes before 1877', *Jahrbuch für Wirtschaftsgeschichte/Economic History Yearbook*, Vol. 60 (1): 57–92.

Dumke, R. H. (1981) 'Die wirtschaftlichen Folgen des Zollvereins', in W. Abelshauser and D. Petzina (eds), *Deutsche Wirtschaftsgeschichte im Industriezeitalter*, Königstein/Taunus: Athenäum, pp. 241–73.

Dumke, R. H. (1984) 'Der Deutsche Zollverein als Modell ökonomischer Integration', *Geschichte und Gesellschaft*, Vol. 10, special issue: *Wirtschaftliche und politische Integration in Europa im 19. und 20. Jahrhundert*, pp. 71–101.

Feuerstein, S. (2013) 'From the Zollverein to the economics of regionalism', *Jahrbücher fur Nationalökonomie und Statistik*, Vol. 233 (3): 367–88.

Fischer, G. (1864) 'Ueber das Wesen und die Bedingungen eines Zollvereins: die Idee eines deutschen Zollvereins und ihre Ausführung geschichtlich entwickelt', *Jahrbücher für Nationalökonomie und Statistik*, Vol. 2: 317–85, 397–432.

Fischer, W. (1960) 'The German Zollverein: a case study in customs unions', *Kyklos*, Vol. 13 (1): 65–89.

Fleckner, A. M. (2009) *Allgemeines Deutsches Handelsgesetzbuch*, http://hwbeup2009.mpipriv.de/index.php/Allgemeines_Deutsches_Handelsgesetzbuch

Fremdling, R. (1975) *Eisenbahnen und deutsches Wirtschaftswachstum 1840–1879: Ein Beitrag zur Entwicklungstheorie und zur Theorie der Infrastruktur*, Dortmund: Gesellschaft für Westfälische Wirtschaftsgeschichte.

Goldschmidt, L. (1862) 'Der Abschluß und die Einführung des allgemeinen Deutschen Handelsgesetzbuchs', *Zeitschrift für das gesammte Handelsrecht*, Vol. 5: 204–27, 515–84.

Hagen, T. J. (2015) *Österreichs Mitteleuropa 1850–1866: Die Wirtschafts-, Währungs-und Verkehrsunion des Karl Ludwig Freiherrn von Bruck*, Husum: Matthiesen.

Hahn, H.-W. (1982) *Wirtschaftliche Integration im 19. Jahrhundert: Die hessischen Staaten und der deutsche Zollverein*, Göttingen: Vandenhoeck & Ruprecht.

Hahn, H.-W. (1984a) *Geschichte des Deutschen Zollvereins*, Göttingen: Vandenhoeck & Ruprecht.

Hahn, H.-W. (1984b), Hegemonie und Integration: Voraussetzungen und Folgen der preußischen Führungsrolle im Deutschen Zollverein, *Geschichte und Gesellschaft*, Vol. 10, special issue: *Wirtschaftliche und politische Integration in Europa im 19. und 20. Jahrhundert*, pp. 45–70.

Hahn, H.-W. (2002) 'Die Dresdner Konferenz: Chance eines handelspolitischen Neubeginns in Deutschland?', in J. Flöter and G. Wartenberg (eds), *Die Dresdener Konferenz 1850/51: Föderalisierung des Deutschen Bundes versus Machtinteressen der Einzelstaaten*, Leipzig: Leipziger Universitätsverlag, pp. 219–38.

Hancock, K. (2009) *Regional integration: Choosing plutocracy*, New York: Palgrave Macmillan.

Henderson, W. O. (1981) 'The German Zollverein and the European economic community', *Zeitschrift für die gesamte Staatswissenschaft/Journal of Institutional and Theoretical Economics*, Vol. 3: 491–507.

Henderson, W. O. (1939 [1984]) *The Zollverein*, 3rd ed., London: Cass.

Hornung, E. (2015) 'Railroads and growth in Prussia', *Journal of the European Economic Association*, Vol. 13 (4): 699–736.

Huning, T. and Wolf, N. (2019) 'How Britain unified Germany: endogenous trade costs and the formation of a customs union', *CEPR Discussion Paper* DP13634.

Keller, W. and Shiue, C. H. (2014) 'Endogenous formation of free trade agreements: evidence from the Zollverein's impact on market integration', *Journal of Economic History*, Vol. 74 (4): 1168–1204.

Kreutzmann, M. (2012a) *Die höheren Beamten des Deutschen Zollvereins: Eine bürokratische Funktionselite zwischen einzelstaatlichen Interessen und zwischenstaatlicher Integration (1834–1871)*, Göttingen: Vandenhoeck & Ruprecht.

Kreutzmann, M. (2012b) 'Die höheren Verwaltungsbeamten des Deutschen Zollvereins: eine nationale Funktionselite?', in H.-W. Hahn and M. Kreutzmann (eds), *Der deutsche Zollverein: Ökonomie und Nation im 19. Jahrhundert*, Köln: Böhlau, pp. 195–226.

Kreutzmann, M. (2013) 'Der Deutsche Zollverein von 1834: von der intergouvernementalen Staatenverbindung zur suprastaatlichen Organisation?', *Journal of European Integration History*, Vol. 19 (2): 189–206.

Kühne, L. S. B. (1846) *Der Deutsche Zollverein während der Jahre 1834 bis 1845*, Berlin: Decker.

Lee, W. R. (1988) 'Economic development and the state in nineteenth-century Germany', *The Economic History Review*, Vol. 41: 346–67.

Müller, J. (2005) *Deutscher Bund und deutsche Nation 1848–1866*, Göttingen: Vandenhoeck & Ruprecht.

Nipperdey, T. (1984) *Deutsche Geschichte 1800–1866: Bürgerwelt und starker Staat*, München: Beck.

North, D. C. (1990) *Institutions, Institutional Change, and Economic Performance*, Cambridge: Cambridge University Press.

Oestmann, P. (2018) 'Court records as sources for the history of commercial law: the Oberappellationsgericht Lübeck as a commercial court (1820–1879)', in H. Pihlajamäki et al. (eds), *Understanding the Sources of Early Modern and Modern Commercial Law*, Leiden: Brill Nijhoff, pp. 364–86.

Pannwitz, K. v. (1999) *Die Entstehung der allgemeinen deutschen Wechselordnung: Ein Beitrag zur Geschichte der Vereinheitlichung des deutschen Zivilrechts im 19. Jahrhundert*, Frankfurt a. M.: Lang.

Ploeckl, F. (2015) 'The Zollverein and the sequence of a customs union', *Australian Economic History Review*, Vol. 55 (3): 277–300.

Reindl, J. (1993) *Der Deutsch-Österreichische Telegraphenverein und die Entwicklung des deutschen Telegraphenwesens, 1850–1871: Eine Fallstudie zur administrativ-technischen Kooperation deutscher Staaten vor der Gründung des Deutschen Reiches*, Frankfurt a. M.: Lang.

Scharpf, F. W. (1999) *Governing in Europe: Effective and Democratic?* Oxford: Oxford University Press.

Shiue, C. H. (2005) 'From political fragmentation towards a customs union: border effects of the German Zollverein, 1815 to 1855', *European Review of Economic History*, Vol. 9 (2): 129–62.

Sprenger, B. (1981) 'Währungswesen und Währungspolitik in Deutschland von 1834 bis 1875', *Kölner Vorträge und Abhandlungen zur Sozial- und Wirtschaftsgeschichte*, Vol. 33, University of Cologne: Institute of Social and Economic History.

Strauch, D. (2007) 'Die Entwicklung des Rheinschifffahrtsrechts zwischen 1815 und 1868', in C. von Looz-Corswarem and G. Mölich (ed), *Der Rhein als Verkehrsweg: Politik, Recht und Wirtschaft seit dem 18. Jahrhundert*, Bottrop: Pomp, pp. 61–92.

Tilly, R. H. (2003) *Geld und Kredit in der Wirtschaftsgeschichte*, Vol. 4, Stuttgart: Steiner.

Ullmann, H.-P. (1995) *Das Deutsche Kaiserreich: 1871–1918*, Frankfurt a. M.: Suhrkamp.

Verhandlungen der sechsten General-Konferenz in Zollvereins-Angelegenheiten (1843), Berlin: Decker.

Viner, J. (1950) *The Customs Union Issue*, New York: Carnegie Endowment for International Peace.

Wadle, E. (1985) 'Der Zollverein und die deutsche Rechtseinheit', *Zeitschrift der Savigny-Stiftung für Rechtsgeschichte/Germanistische Abteilung*, Vol. 102 (1): 99–129.

Weber, W. S. (1869) *Der deutsche Zollverein: Geschichte seiner Entstehung und Entwickelung*, Leipzig: Veit.

Wehler, H.-U. (1995) *Deutsche Gesellschaftsgeschichte*, Vol. 3: *Von der "Deutschen Doppelrevolution" bis zum Beginn des Ersten Weltkrieges 1849–1914*, München: Beck.

Wischermann, C. (2004) 'Die Institutionelle Revolution in Deutschland (1800–1870)', in C. Wischermann and A. Nieberding (eds), *Die institutionelle Revolution: Eine Einführung in die deutsche Wirtschaftsgeschichte des 19. und frühen 20.* Jahrhunderts, Stuttgart: Steiner, pp. 51–153.

4 Politics, administration, and market governance in a federalist environment

The German Empire in the 1870s and 1880s

Gerold Ambrosius

1 Introduction

The founding of the German Empire in 1871 marked a significant break in the relationship between the German states. With the establishment of central state authorities and agencies, a federal state was created not only in a vertical sense but also in a horizontal sense, so that the member states had to realign their relations with each other. In addition, a common economic area with a shared institutional framework was created. Finally, the founding of the nation-state promoted the development of parties, interest organisations, and the media as well as the formation of public opinion. The resulting political mobilisation posed major challenges to the new political order. At the same time, the rapid industrialisation of economy and society placed growing demands on Germany's political-administrative system, which was still in the process of being established. The emerging polity had to rapidly develop its capacity and potential to regulate markets through appropriate legislation and to influence them through public enterprises.

Against this background, the present chapter deals with three topics. Section 2 characterises the state organisation and economic order that emerged from the founding of the German Empire. Section 3 describes the legal capacity and the potential of policy-making that the political-administrative system developed in the wake of national unification. Finally, Section 4 examines the ways in which the federal government of the Empire and the member states made use of these new capacities and potential to shape and govern markets.

2 State structure and economic order

2.1 State structure

Vertical relations between the Empire and the member states. In 1871, twenty-five more or less sovereign states joined to form an overarching federal structure. Their political regimes and economic institutions were similar, but not

DOI: 10.4324/9781003283430-5

identical in every respect (Huber 1988; Holste 2003). Each state (*Bundesstaat*) sought to shape the future common order in its own favour and many fundamental questions remained unresolved. With respect to the vertical relations between the Empire and the member states, the question of whether the Imperial Constitution implied a confederation or a federal state has never been definitively answered. Most contemporary experts in constitutional law saw the Empire as a federal state that did not allow the member states to be completely deprived of their powers. Moreover, the political system of the Empire evolved over time, so that constitutional norms and constitutional reality quickly diverged (Henrich-Franke 2018). Nevertheless, on the eve of the First World War, four decades after its foundation, the German Empire was still far from being a centralised nation-state.

Horizontal relations between the member states. As far as horizontal relations between the member states were concerned, it was not clear from the Imperial Constitution whether these relations were to be cooperative or competitive. If the Empire is seen merely as a framework for managing conflicts between the member states, one emphasises the horizontal element in the state structure, which also implies a potential of institutional competition between the member states. A doctrine shared by many, but not all contemporary experts on constitutional law held that the principle of legal equality applied to the member states. This was mainly justified by the character of the Empire as a confederation of originally sovereign states. However, numerous provisions in the Imperial Constitution deviated from the principle of legal equality among the members of the federation. For example, not all states had the same number of votes in the *Bundesrat*, which was composed of representatives of the member states. Prussia had seventeen votes, while several small states had only one vote. Overall, the competences of the member states were based only to a limited extent on the principle of legal equality by constitutional law. In this respect, the German Empire was characterised by asymmetrical federalism (Lehmbruch 2018).

2.2 Economic institutions

Common economic area. The first and most important impact of national unification on economic institutions relates to the creation of a common economic area in which goods, services, labour, and capital could move freely (Ambrosius 2018: 73–75). With the founding of the *Zollverein* in 1834 and its subsequent expansion, tariffs on trade between German states were abolished and replaced with a unified system of external tariffs (see Chapter 3 of this volume). Non-tariff barriers to trade were also non-existent because the country-of-origin principle was widely accepted. Whereas the customs union thus ensured the free movement of goods within the Empire, regulations of products and production processes could differ between member states, which could result in differences in the competitive position of individual regions.

The situation was similar for trade in services. Non-discrimination against citizens from other member states was secured by Article 3 of the Imperial Constitution. A law enacted by the North German Confederation (*Norddeutscher Bund*) in 1867 guaranteed the free movement of persons and freedom of establishment. The Trade Regulation Act (*Gewerbeordnung*) of 1869 took a more differentiated approach to the various types of economic activity. For example, the licensing requirements for so-called standing trades (*stehende Gewerbebetriebe*), as opposed to itinerant trade, were standardised, among other things through licencing procedures for pharmacists, doctors, and so on that were valid throughout the Empire (Article 29). For some professions, state-specific regulations were still permitted; however, these were not allowed to discriminate against citizens of other member states. As with goods, the free movement of services between the member states was guaranteed.

There were no barriers to labour migration. Being a citizen of the Empire and of a member state formed an inseparable unit, the latter being the precondition for the former. However, the importance of citizenship in a state was reduced by the so-called principle of joint inhabitant rights (*gemeinsames Indigenat*; Article 3 of the Imperial Constitution). Under this principle, every German citizen living in any state of the Empire enjoyed the same rights as citizens originating from that particular state in terms of free choice of residence, freedom of trade, access to public office, and so on. Freedom of movement and choice of residence became individually enforceable rights.

There were also no significant obstacles to the movement of capital. Every German residing in any member state could make transfers to another state without restriction and make investments there, including the purchase of real estate. The Imperial Constitution also transferred authority over monetary matters to the Empire, and in 1873 a common currency, the Mark, was introduced. Finally, in 1870 and 1884 laws were passed that placed the regulation of capital markets on a unified basis (see Chapter 11 of this volume).

Common economic order. The creation of a common market was another major consequence of national unification. The constitutions of the North German Confederation of 1867 and of the German Empire of 1871 did not explicitly address the economic order. They devoted only a few statements to the organisation of markets, ownership of the means of production, and market interventions by political authorities. The same applies to the constitutions of the member states, which, however, mostly date from the first half of the century.

Things are different with the trade regulation acts of individual states, particularly the one enacted by Prussia in 1845, and the North German Confederation of 1869, which was adopted by the southern German states in 1872 as the *Reichsgewerbeordnung* (RGO). On the one hand, the RGO represents 'one of the first major legal codifications of the second half of the nineteenth century, on the other hand [it is] one of the most important documents of economic liberalism in Germany' (Kaufhold 1984: 215). After decades of controversy, the RGO finally established freedom of trade (*Gewerbefreiheit*), albeit not unconditionally. Article 1 stipulated: 'The operation of a trade is permitted to everyone, unless exceptions or restrictions are prescribed or permitted by this law'. Freedom of trade was intended to keep markets free from government interference. However, it was not intended to protect markets from distortive practices by economic actors themselves—except for restrictions related to former feudal privileges or guilds. According to the liberal paradigm, freedom of trade was sufficient to guarantee free agency, free market access, and thus unrestricted competition. This opinion was expressed in an exemplary manner by the Imperial Court (*Reichsgericht*), which played a decisive role in the further development of the institutional framework of the German economy, in a judgement of 1880: following the principle of freedom of trade, everything was permitted that was not expressly prohibited by law. Accordingly, the principle of freedom of trade found its limit only in the principle of public safety and order. If particular economic activities led to socially unacceptable grievances, these had to be remedied by a special law (Kaufhold 1984: 233).

Freedom of trade meant not only freedom of access to a particular activity but also the freedom to choose the way in which it was practised in terms of product design and production methods, scale and scope, number of employees, and location. A limit was again set by the common weal. The public administration was entitled to prohibit 'the further use of a production facility [...] at any time in the event of preponderant disadvantages and dangers for the common weal', whereby 'compensation had to be paid for the proven damage' (Article 51 RGO). There were also special regulations for individual trades that aimed at ensuring public safety and order but did not intervene directly in plant management or business administration (Kaufhold 1984: 217).

Competition as such, that is, as a principle of order and coordination, was not explicitly protected, but conduct that abused 'economic freedom' to the detriment of the consumer was prohibited (Ambrosius 1981). Laws on the so-called legal protection of trade (*gewerblicher Rechtsschutz*) were thus less concerned with protecting competition and more with that of the objects affected by abuse. Market behaviour as such remained without control; specifically, so-called 'unfair competition' was not sanctioned. The older trade and industrial law had assigned this task to the corporations of craftsmen and merchants under the supervision of political authorities (regulated self-regulation; Wischermann and Nieberding 2004: 126–35). With the introduction of freedom of trade, these earlier mechanisms for the supervision of market behaviour fell away for the first time being (Deter 2015).

The trade regulation acts of German states before 1871 and the German Empire correspond to a European trend according to which freedom of trade spread from west to east and from north to south. Nevertheless, the RGO was comparatively liberal compared to regulations in other European countries (Ambrosius and Henrich-Franke 2020: 38–48).

3 The evolution of legal capacity and the potential for policy-making

This section draws on an extended literature to examine the evolution of the political and administrative system of the new Empire during the first two decades of its existence in view of its legal capacity and the potential for policy-making in the economic realm (Huber 1988; Nipperdey 1992; Wehler 1995; Henrich-Franke 2012; Ambrosius et al. 2015, 2018; Hähnel 2017; Höfer 2017; Liedloff 2017). The contemporary political and administrative system included the legislatures of the federal state and the member states, the executive branch at all levels—including the provincial and municipal levels—and, with some limitations, public enterprises. The 'state' or the 'public sector' increasingly acted as consumer, investor, entrepreneur and administrator. Legislatures produced a growing number of norms that set standards for a wide range of economic activities. In the following, the focus is on the legislative, administrative, and entrepreneurial activities of political authorities. For this, they needed financial, physical, and human resources as well as the competence of law-making. This refers to all levels of the federal structure of the German Empire, that is, the central, member state and municipal levels (Jeserich et al. 1984).

3.1 The first half of the 1870s

The office of the Imperial Chancellor (*Reichskanzleramt*), the *Reichstag*—the Parliament whose members were elected by universal male suffrage—and the *Bundesrat* were state organs of the Empire provided for in the constitution and came into being immediately after the establishment of the new federal state. Otherwise, the establishment of new authorities or administrative units was limited. The office of the Imperial Chancellor, which played a pivotal role in policy-making at the level of Empire, underwent moderate internal differentiation in the first years after 1871 but this could not replace the executive capacities of independent Imperial offices or ministries. However, these were not created at first because an expansion of the administration at the top level of the Empire corresponded neither to liberal nor federalist ideals of political order. Additionally, the office of the Imperial Chancellor could rely on the Prussian ministries—Bismarck served as both Chancellor of the German Empire and Prime Minister of Prussia. The *Reichstag* began its work effectively. In the first years of the existence of the Empire, more laws were passed on an annual average than in the following decades. The *Bundesrat* took longer to develop its hybrid role as both a central and federal organ of the Empire. Some member states modernised their administrations; however, it is difficult to assess whether this resulted in an increase in their capacity. Others retained the structure of their governments with their manageable bureaucracies for the time being.

The horizontal relations between the state organs at the Imperial level were rather weak in the beginning. Almost all decisions were taken within the office of the Imperial Chancellor and thus ultimately by Bismarck. A mutual relationship of trust that could have intensified the cooperation between the organs at the federal level hardly developed. Among the member states, the intergovernmental cooperation from the period before 1867/71 essentially continued. As during the era of the German Confederation (*Deutscher Bund*, 1815–1866), bilateral relations were conducted through the foreign ministries and the member states' plenipotentiaries within the *Bundesrat* in Berlin. Soon, however, only Prussia, Bavaria, Württemberg, and Saxony maintained missions in other member states, suggesting a weakening or breaking up of horizontal relations. Therefore, this phase has been characterised as a form of intergovernmentalism under Prussian hegemony. Nevertheless, inter-state contacts at the administrative levels intensified and private organisations, such as the Association of German Railway Administrations, continued to cooperate. However, regional and local administrations remained too heterogeneous for cooperation to develop at the national level (Henrich-Franke 2018: 22).

Vertical relations between the organs of the Empire and the member states—government as well as administration—had to be built from scratch. The Chancellor of the Empire and Prime Minister of the dominant state—Bismarck—showed an authoritarian style of leadership combined with a high ability to mediate conflict. The member states were extremely sensitive to a loss of competence or sovereignty despite their willingness to compromise. The current state of scholarship does not allow a firm conclusion on whether this constellation had a negative effect on the performance of the political and administrative system of the young Empire.

While the policy process that characterised the early Empire does not appear effective, this did not cause serious strain. This was because the demands on the political and administrative systems were still low. The standardisation of norms took place in domains in which the German states had already established common legal frameworks, enacted similar laws, or concluded private-law agreements before the late 1860s. In addition, initially vague laws had to pass legislative assemblies to be filled out with specific regulations. A new, expanded need for market guidance by state authorities was only beginning to emerge in the 1870s.

3.2 The second half of the 1870s

At the national level of the Empire, the second half of the 1870s saw a strong expansion of government, suggesting an 'institutional take-off' of the Empire (Henrich-Franke 2018: 27). New Imperial Offices (*Reichsämter*) were created, among others for justice, finance, home affairs, railways, postal services, and other specialised government agencies such as the Imperial Health Office and the Reichsbank emerged. All these organisations soon became involved in the formulation and implementation of public policy, sometimes in competition with the office of the Imperial Chancellor. However, they too stayed dependent on the ministries of Prussia, as their administrative staff remained small in number. The organisation of the central government now covered all relevant subject areas of public policy; however, the development of a national political arena followed a specific course of political integration in each subject area to create effective federal institutions. The creation of the Imperial Offices enhanced the capacity of political and administrative system. This was urgently needed in view of the growing demands on politics, which increasingly overburdened the office of the Imperial Chancellor. The same was true for the *Reichstag*, whose operational capacity was hampered by the small size of the support staff of the deputies and by under-staffing in the public administration. Nevertheless, the process of legislation grew more effective during this phase.

The policy process also gained strength during this phase because the member states gradually came to terms with their changed role. They no longer acted only as governments formulating and implementing policies at the member state level but also as so-called 'allied governments' at the federal level in the *Bundesrat*. However, policy-making at the level of the Empire still required a great deal of coordination during this phase, because a number of small states continued to be involved in decision-making in the new federal system.

In the municipalities, the transition from the traditional focus on maintaining public order to providing public services continued at an accelerated pace. This occurred against the background of a changing perception of the economic role of political authorities in the 1870s. Member states began to nationalise railways or create their own railway companies to be able to intervene in the transport sector. Likewise, municipalities began to establish and expand public enterprises in the gas and water industries, and later in the electricity and other sectors. The economic role of municipalities thus expanded considerably, at least in the utilities sector.

Horizontal relationships between the office of the Imperial Chancellor and the Imperial Offices were close, partly because Bismarck adhered to the principle of 'double countersignature'. At first, this practice hardly affected the scope of action of the Imperial Offices, because the federal administration was still small, so that close personal contacts were frequent and channels of communication were short. Nevertheless, coordination between the office of the Imperial Chancellor and the Imperial Offices was an issue. This also applies to the relationship between these two state organs and the *Reichstag* and the *Bundesrat*. Bismarck's central role in decision-making often played a pivotal role in mitigating these deficiencies in political coordination. New forms of coordination and cooperation developed between the governments of the member states in the *Bundesrat* itself, and also on the basis of contacts surrounding proceedings in the *Bundesrat*. Relationships between member state governments were now closer than during the period before national unification, which was characterised by intergovernmental policy coordination. The greater the need for coordination, the more inadequate were the formally prescribed forms of coordination.

In the vertical dimension, political coordination between the Imperial government and the member state was slow to develop, which limited the capacity of the political and administrative system. Progress resulted from the endeavours of the new Imperial Offices to establish contact with the member states, and the *Reichstag* also began establishing ties with them. The missions or member states' plenipotentiaries within the *Bundesrat* still played an important role during this phase. While this was not exactly conducive to the efficiency of political coordination, it was apparently still necessary at this stage of integration.

The looming loss of influence of the office of the Imperial Chancellor and the Chancellor himself, as well as the establishment and cautious expansion of the Imperial Offices, reflected changes in quantitative and qualitative aspects of law-making and policy formulation. Political authorities became involved in more and more policy areas, whereas designing new market interventions became more complex owing to a growing body of existing legislation and associated administrative regulations. A major goal of new legislation at the federal level remained the harmonisation of the old, pre-1871 law of the German states within the larger framework of the Empire. Simultaneously, however, the political and administrative system was confronted with new social, economic, and technical phenomena. This challenge had to be faced by the federal government and the governments of the member states alike, because the latter were involved in the creation of new laws and also responsible for their implementation (Mußgang 1984).

3.3 The 1880s and early 1890s

From the early 1880s, a development asserted itself that was to lead to a federal state with well-connected constituent elements in the following years and decades. At the federal level, no new Imperial Offices were created, but the existing ones were expanded and additional subordinate agencies were established. The *Reichstag* filled its role as a legislative body increasingly professionally, routinely, and more efficiently. In contrast, the *Bundesrat* seemed to lose importance in the political process. However, this only applied to the plenary session and the committees. More or less informal forums or formats of cooperation between the member states emerged, which to a certain extent replaced negotiations in the committees and in the plenary session. An important innovation was also the establishment of committees that brought together representatives of the *Reichstag*, member states, and external experts, thus combining horizontal and vertical coordination of policy formulation. These committees served to draft laws before they entered the formal legislative process. This led to 'an informal complementary structure to the constitutional state organs' (Henrich-Franke 2018: 32), which significantly improved the capacity of the political and administrative system to formulate policies on social and economic issues.

At least as important as the expansion of the imperial administration was the continued modernisation of the administrations of the member states.

As the proliferation and increasing complexity of public tasks progressively overburdened the governments of the small states, 'hegemonic federalism'—which was now no longer only associated with Prussia—played a stabilising function that removed restrictions on state growth: small states took over certain legal provisions from larger member states, especially Prussia, or transferred administrative tasks to them.

The degree of horizontal cooperation and coordination increased at all levels of government in the 1880s. At the level of the Empire, the time when all the threads ran together in the office of the Imperial Chancellor finally came to an end. The Imperial Offices began to emancipate themselves from the office of the Imperial Chancellor and also from the ministries of Prussia, without Bismarck losing control altogether. Simultaneously, the relations between the *Reichstag* and the Imperial Offices intensified. Since the resources of the *Reichstag* were limited, it had to draw on the growing expertise of the Imperial Offices to master the increasingly complex legislative process. Conversely, the Imperial Offices now contacted the Reichstag at an early stage in the preparation of new laws, because the political dimension of policy formulation was becoming increasingly obvious. In this respect, one can speak of the 'parliamentarisation' of the Imperial government.

At the level of the member states, governments, administrations and parliaments also worked more closely together to coordinate their position vis-à-vis the Imperial government, to inform each other about legislative projects, and to exchange experiences regarding the implementation of laws and regulations. Coordination was particularly relevant for aggregating regional interests with regard to the work of the above-mentioned commissions at the Imperial level. Small states largely withdrew from policies that overstretched their financial and administrative capacities, thus relieving the political and administrative system. Legislation and policy-making were thus increasingly concentrated on Prussia and the medium-sized states. The development of a well-functioning federal state was probably also promoted by the fact that some policy areas remained the responsibility of the member states. The norms pertaining to such an area could either converge in institutional competition without coordination or differ permanently between member states.

In vertical direction, patterns of cooperation and coordination seem to have depended on the characteristics of the relationships between government agencies at different administrative levels. Examples include financial reform and the regulation of private insurance (Höfer 2017; Liedloff 2017). In general, there was a tendency for vertical coordination to take place primarily between the Imperial administration and the administrations of member states. The former remained dependent on the expertise of the latter. The emerging federalism in the realm of public administration thus developed in both horizontal and vertical directions. The Reichstag was only gradually involved in the expansion of vertical relations in these years.

The social, economic, and technical developments that took place in the 1880s put pressure on the political and administrative system at all levels of government. Demands for regulation and for public services called for an expansion of state action. At the same time, the complexity of the areas to be regulated by state legislation increased. The transition from a liberal state to a modern state that regulated markets and provided public services was finally taking place. Administrative regulations, which were outside a formal legislative process, came to play an important role in policy implementation because norms often took the form of enabling legislation. This contributed to an increase in the influence of public administration and experts both inside and outside state bureaucracies.

4 Market governance

How did the political authorities use the growing capacities and potentials of the political-administrative system to govern markets? Two channels can be distinguished: regulation by public law and micro-level intervention through public enterprise. What follows, in turn, examines these two channels used by public authorities to frame and influence the operation of markets.

4.1 Regulation by public law

Regulation is defined as a specific intervention of the state in the economy, primarily in the management of private companies in specific branches or sectors of economic activity, which goes beyond the general institutional framework (Kaufer 1975). Specifically, regulation is about setting coordinative and regulatory standards through public law (Werle 1997). Coordinative standards are intended to generate positive externalities. For example, the standardisation of signals should facilitate cross-border railway traffic. Regulatory standards, by contrast, are intended to prevent or mitigate negative externalities. For example, the prohibition of certain (potentially harmful) additives in the production of butter is intended to prevent consumers from being deceived and butter producers from gaining an advantage through the use of such substances (Hierholzer 2010). However, the two types of standards cannot be clearly distinguished in all cases.

Coordinative standardisation. Numerous laws and administrative regulations promulgated by the Imperial government intended the setting of coordinative standards. They included norms on technical, administrative, or tariff standards for weights and measures, for postal services, the telegraph system, and the railways. In the case of the railways, coordination initially took the form of private-law agreements in the Association of German Railway Administrations (*Verein deutscher Eisenbahnverwaltungen*), which were then transformed into public-law regulations of the Empire. These included operating regulations (1874), signalling regulations (1875), regulations for the construction and equipment of main railways (1878), the obligation to transport mail (1871/75), and railway police regulations (1885; Henrich-Franke 2012). The example of railway regulation also shows that cooperation in coordinative standardisation between the member states reached its limits when it led to unequal burdens. This danger existed because the sector consisted of both private railway companies, and also included public railway administrations whose revenues were of great importance for the state budgets (Ambrosius and Henrich-Franke 2015).

Other laws, such as those dealing with money, credit, and banking, also set coordinative or so-called transactional standards, specifically for bills of exchange and cheque transactions, bank deposits, or the stock exchange. These included the Bill of Exchange Regulation (1869), the Bank Act (1875) and the Bank Deposit Act (1896), and so on (Pohl 1982; see also Chapter 11 of this volume). Finally, even before the founding of the German Empire, the German states had promoted coordinative standardisation within the framework of international treaties and organisations, such as the German-Austrian Postal Association and the Telegraph Association of 1850 (Reindl 1994; Benz 2013; see also Chapter 7 of this volume). From the 1870s onwards, international treaties were concluded and international organisations developed in increasing numbers, so that coordinative standardisation at the national level was intertwined with that at the international level (Ambrosius and Henrich-Franke 2013). If these were private-law agreements between private actors—a clear demarcation between private, mixed, and state organisations is often not possible at the international level—the soft law thus created had to be converted into hard law by the Reichstag if desired. Examples include medical and veterinary standards.

Few conflicts arose in connection with the harmonisation of coordinative standards both within member states and at the level of the Empire because all actors expected benefits from it—economic stakeholders as well as political and societal actors. This was obvious when a technical system such as the railways was unified. But also when an economic sector such as the financial industry was given a harmonised institutional framework, unification meant that business was made easier, which ultimately benefited everyone. Nevertheless, conflicts of interest could arise, as member states whose standards were adopted by the Empire had lower adaptation costs, so that member states sometimes strove to impose their own standards on all others (Groß 2015). Overall, the regulation of coordinative standards was a relatively swift process and did not absorb too much capacity, as there was little resistance to overcome. Here, cooperative federalism became particularly prominent.

Regulatory standardisation. Regulatory standardisation addressed grievances about products and production processes, which were increasingly scandalised by the press. One area concerned food and consumption goods, as the industrialisation of food processing led to the increasing use of additives that were harmful to health (Hähnel 2017: 88–103). Another area was occupational health and safety: factory work was apparently becoming more and more dangerous, at least the number of serious accidents at work increased because safety regulations were lacking or not properly observed (Ayass 1996/2005).

The protection of children and adolescents remained insufficiently regulated or existing regulation was circumvented (Ambrosius 2018: 77–91).

This resulted partly from the fact that implementation and sanctioning practices varied between member states. The rivalry between private companies and between member states of the Empire was much more pronounced here compared to the harmonisation of coordinative standards, because regulatory standardisation affected competitive, that is, economic and social, advantages and disadvantages. Saxony, for example, resisted a uniform improvement of child protection because child labour gave the Saxon textile industry a competitive advantage. Not all member states supported improved labour protection for women. Prussia was reluctant to enforce stricter meat inspection because it hoped that its own standards, which were less strict than those set by other member states, would give its meat industry a competitive advantage (Ambrosius (2005: 79–82). Notwithstanding these examples, the interests of governments and private companies were not always identical with regard to regulative standards. Labour protection is a case in point: Baden had a particularly progressive system of factory inspection that was criticised by its own companies, but which other states wanted to adopt (Bocks 1978).

In all these cases, the liberal market model followed at the time of the founding of the Empire led to outcomes that were progressively less accepted by society. The business community demanded identical regulatory standards throughout the Empire, in order to create equal market conditions everywhere. This could be achieved either by harmonising existing member state law or by creating new Imperial law. If a regional business community could not obtain deregulation in a member state with comparatively intensive regulation, it would strive for a uniform level of regulation on the level of the Empire as a second-best solution. From the point of view of social reform, consumer protection, or public health, it was also advisable to campaign for Imperial legislation if higher regulative standards could not be achieved in member states (Hähnel 2017).

Contemporary debates on the creation of regulatory standards in a federal state followed two approaches. One school advocated a model of competitive federalism. Institutional competition between member states was to serve as a mechanism for identifying the optimal characteristics of regulative standards. Competition in the sphere of legal norms was seen as an attribute of a market order, which was now conceived in more political-economic, rather than liberal terms. Another school followed a model of institutional convergence. It emphasised the positive welfare effects of equal market conditions throughout the Empire, which could only be achieved through the creation of a unified institutional framework at the federal level.

Overall, there was a fairly broad consensus that the level of regulation should be raised rather than lowered. Probably a majority of the relevant actors in business and politics were also in favour of a harmonisation or unification of the relevant legislation. This consensus was based on the emerging view that Germany should not only be regarded as a common political territory but also as a common social and economic space. Globalisation also led to an increasing perception of institutional competition at the international level. With the massive expansion of cross-border trade, the question arose more urgently as to whether the regulatory framework tended to favour or disadvantage the German economy in international markets.

4.2 The intervention through public enterprise

In addition to regulation under public law, political authorities at all levels increasingly used public undertakings to govern markets. This form of control mainly applied to the infrastructural markets of water supply and disposal, the energy sector (gas, electricity), postal and telegraph services, and local and long-distance public transport (Ziegler 1996; Stier 1999; Hesse 2002; Ambrosius 2019). At the local level, municipal slaughterhouses served to control the meat market, and municipal savings banks formed an important segment of the money and capital market. Municipal waste collection services dominated the waste disposal market.

There were two forms of public enterprise. The first related to undertakings under public law (*Regiebetrieb*), the second to a company organised under private law in the form of a joint-stock company or a limited liability company (from 1892). The second variant usually also included a concession granted under private law. Public undertakings were particularly common at the state and municipal levels. At the turn of the twentieth century, a good 10 percent of the total labour force was working in public enterprises, which generated a good 13 percent of the net domestic product. If enterprises with mixed public and private ownership are also taken into account, the shares were slightly higher (Ambrosius 2012). A similar expansion of public undertakings can also be observed in other European countries, especially at the municipal level. Almost everywhere, local authorities expanded their political and administrative capacities through the instrument of the public enterprise (Toninelli 2000; Kühl 2001; Millward 2005).

The motives for the operational or entrepreneurial involvement of local authorities in economic ventures were manifold; however, above all they followed from the paradigm of what was later called *Daseinsvorsorge*, which refers to public services that secure the material basis of the livelihood of the population. The provision of fresh water, gas, electricity, public transport, postal services, and communications was increasingly seen as basic inputs of production and as elementary consumer goods that private companies were unable to provide to the full extent (Ambrosius 1984: 26–50). In this situation of perceived market failure, local authorities felt compelled to intervene to ensure an adequate supply. Thus, they took a diversion, via microeconomic forms of organisation in order to pursue public welfare (Stern and Püttner 1965).

Two further reasons also contributed to the rise of public enterprise. First, it was not possible to regulate the provision of utilities under public law—pertinent legislation was not enacted until the 1930s (Ambrosius 1995). Second, local authorities had negative experiences with private companies. They failed to secure the desired quality and quantity of services through contractual relations with private suppliers. Long-term concession contracts were inevitably incomplete and simply not suited to regulate the complicated relations between a private company and a public authority in a manner that satisfied both parties. It was not uncommon that private concession-holders failed to fulfil the obligations they had entered into, so that the municipalities appealed to the courts when the concession contracts expired (Stern and Püttner 1965: 73–87). The public enterprise, like public regulation, was an instrument of the political-administrative system. Even if it was very close to the market, it nevertheless expanded its capacity.

5 Conclusion

In the course of the nineteenth century, the German lands evolved from a loose confederation of states to a federal state with closely interconnected constituent elements. In organisational terms, the founding of the North German Confederation in 1867 and the German Empire in 1871 created federalist institutions, but the political integration of the new polity only took place in the following decades. In the beginning, there were twenty-five largely independent political entities that had yet to develop their role as member states within the federal framework of the Empire. They had their own political institutions and jurisdictions, responsibilities, and specific economic and social profiles. The member states thus had specific interests that determined the behaviour of their governments, especially in a situation characterised by increasing political and economic integration. They engaged in both cooperative and competitive relations with the organs of the Empire and with each other. If the German Empire was a nation-state, it was one with a distinctly federal structure in which the member states continued to hold sovereign rights in a number of domains and led distinct lives of their own.

The constitutions of the Empire and the member states as well as the Imperial Trade Regulation Act provided for a loose institutional framework rather than a detailed order for the economy of the new polity. At least they created a common economic area, guaranteed private property, and established freedom of trade. However, private property and freedom of trade were not protected by constitutional law or concepts of economic policy: private property could be expropriated and governments could establish public undertakings. Freedom of trade was intended to protect markets from state intervention, but not from distortions resulting from oligopolies or cartels. Nevertheless, this did not imply that the state had to abstain from market governance. Contemporaries involved in political decision-making and most experts did not follow a consistent concept of economic order. Rather, they followed a paradigm according to which the state should pragmatically assume more responsibility when markets led to socially undesirable outcomes.

Public policy should create the institutional framework of markets, safeguard market operation, and, if necessary, also correct market outcomes.

In the 1870s and 1880s, the legal capacity and potential for policy-making of the political and administrative system expanded considerably. At the Imperial level, new authorities with their own administrative apparatus emerged. The member states continued on their path of political and administrative reform. Public administration in the municipalities evolved beyond its earlier focus on public order towards providing diverse public services. Within the new federal framework, many areas of economic and social policy saw the development of multi-layered structures and processes of cooperation and coordination. All of this increased state capacity in the sense that economic and social issues could be identified, processed, and solved more quickly and efficiently. The development and expansion of the political and administrative system resulted, at least in part, from rising demand for guidance and state intervention, as society became increasingly sensitive to perceived market failures. The scope of state legislation was thus expanded considerably. Moreover, the complexity of public policy increased as laws and related administrative regulations became more detailed and implementation required extended bureaucratic procedures. On the whole, it is likely that the common market and the gradually emerging common legal order, which resulted from the increase in the legal capacity and potential for policy-making of the political and administrative system, had a positive impact on economic development in the medium and long term.

When it came to unifying coordinative standards, policy processes proceeded smoothly and quickly. Mostly, though not always, these were in the interest of producers and consumers alike, so that there was rarely any opposition from individual member states. Regulation by public law (hard law) in this area could partly build on private-law agreements (soft law) already reached in non-governmental organisations. On the one hand, the regulation of coordinative standards promoted economic integration by rendering technical systems compatible, aligning conditions of the production of goods, and facilitating business transactions. On the other hand, the setting of coordinative standards was also a consequence of economic integration, because the more interconnected the German economy became, the more urgently business associations called for coordinative standards. Since coordinative standards primarily serve to generate positive externalities, this form of public-law regulation may have promoted economic development.

By contrast, it was much more difficult to unify regulatory standards. There were conflicting interests between producers and consumers, and also between different economic sectors and branches. Consequently, both the Imperial government and the individual member states pursued specific strategies depending on the social and economic circumstances they faced. Given this situation, policy formulation was more challenging than in the case of coordinative standards. The fact that the scope and the extent of regulation increased over time and that the level of regulation shifted from member states to the Empire shows that this challenge was met. This was the result of growing political pressure, which became manifest with the increased scandalisation of grievances about products and production processes. Additionally, it was a consequence of the political and economic integration of the German Empire, which for a growing part of the population represented not only a common political territory but also a common economic and social space in which universal standards of safety and protection were to prevail. Regional business communities demanded identical regulatory standards throughout the Empire if no advantage could be gained from a low level of regulation in a particular member state. The widening of the scope and the increasing intensity of regulation from the 1870s reversed the trend of liberalisation and deregulation that had prevailed in the decades before. Whether this promoted or hindered economic development is a matter of speculation.

The increasing willingness of political authorities to govern markets was also expressed in the rise of public enterprise. Member states became involved in the operation of railways and later in the supply of electrical energy; municipalities increasingly provided transport services and became active in the utilities sector. For cities and municipalities in particular, operating public undertakings formed a substitute for the lack of regulatory options in order to control local and regional markets. The rise of public enterprise also stemmed from the experience that long-term concession contracts were inevitably incomplete and not suited to regulate the complicated relations between a private company and a public authority in a way that satisfied both parties.

References

Ambrosius, G. (1981) 'Die Entwicklung des Wettbewerbs als wirtschaftspolitisch relevante Norm und Ordnungsprinzip in Deutschland seit dem Ende des 19. Jahrhunderts', *Jahrbuch für Sozialwissenschaft*, Vol. 32 (2): 154–201.

Ambrosius, G. (1984) *Der Staat als Unternehmer: Öffentliche Wirtschaft und Kapitalismus seit dem 19. Jahrhundert*, Göttingen: Vandenhoeck & Ruprecht.

Ambrosius, G. (1995) 'Kommunalwirtschaft im Spannungsfeld von Autonomisierung/Privatisierung und Bindung/Regulierung (vom 19. Jahrhundert bis zu den 1930er Jahren)', in J. Wysocki (ed), *Kommunalisierung im Spannungsfeld von Regulierung und Deregulierung im 19. und 20. Jahrhundert*, Berlin: Duncker & Humblot, pp. 141–63.

Ambrosius, G. (2005) *Regulativer Wettbewerb und koordinative Standardisierung zwischen Staaten: Theoretische Annahmen und historische Beispiele*, Stuttgart: Steiner.

Ambrosius, G. (2012) *Hybride Eigentums- und Verfügungsrechte: Öffentlich-private Kooperationen in systematisch-theoretischer und historisch-empirischer Perspektive*, Berlin: BWV.

Ambrosius, G. (2018) 'Die horizontale Dimension: kompetitive und kooperative Koordination zwischen den Gliedstaaten beim Arbeitsschutz, bei Steuern und bei Eisenbahnen', in G. Ambrosius, C. Henrich-Franke and C. Neutsch (eds), *Integrieren durch Regieren*, Baden-Baden: Nomos, pp. 55–125.

Ambrosius, G. (2019) 'Geschichte der öffentlichen Wirtschaft', in H. Mühlenkamp, F. Schulz-Nieswandt, M. Krajewski and L. Theuvsen (eds), *Öffentliche Wirtschaft: Handbuch für Wissenschaft und Praxis*, Baden-Baden: Nomos, pp. 25–54.

Ambrosius, G. and Henrich-Franke, C. (2013) *Integration von Infrastrukturen in Europa im historischen Vergleich*, Vol. 1, Baden-Baden: Nomos.

Ambrosius, G. and Henrich-Franke, C. (2015) 'Regulierung und Steuerung von Infrastrukturen in föderalen Systemen: Eisenbahnen im Deutschen Reich von 1871 und in der Europäischen Union heute', in G. Ambrosius, C. Henrich-Franke and C. Neutsch (eds), *Föderale Systeme: Kaiserreich—Donaumonarchie—Europäische Union*, Baden-Baden: Nomos, pp. 249–78.

Ambrosius, G. and Henrich-Franke, C. (2020) *Diversität, Transformation, Kontinuität: Europa 1800–1870*, Stuttgart: Kohlhammer.

Ambrosius, G., Henrich-Franke, C. and Neutsch, C. (2015) *Föderale Systeme: Kaiserreich—Donaumonarchie—Europäische Union*, Baden-Baden: Nomos.

Ambrosius, G., Henrich-Franke, C. and Neutsch, C. (eds) (2018) *Integrieren durch Regieren*, Baden-Baden: Nomos.

Ayass, W. (1996/2005) 'Einleitung', in K. E. Born, H. Henning and F. Tennstedt (eds), *Quellensammlung zur Geschichte der deutschen Sozialpolitik 1867–1914*, Darmstadt: Wissenschaftliche Buchgesellschaft, I. Abteilung, Vol. 3, pp. XVI–XLIII, II. Abteilung, Vol. 3, pp. XIX–LII, III. Abteilung, Vol. 3, pp. XIX–XLIV.

Benz, A. (2013) *Integration von Infrastrukturen in Europa im historischen Vergleich*, Vol. 3, *Post*, Baden-Baden: Nomos.

Bocks, W. (1978) *Die badische Fabrikinspektion: Arbeiterschutz, Arbeiterverhältnisse und Arbeiterbewegung in Baden 1879 bis 1914*, Freiburg: Alber.

Deter, G. (2015) *Zwischen Gilde und Gewerbefreiheit*, 2 vols., Stuttgart: Steiner.

Groß, F. (2015) *Integration durch Standardisierung: Maßreformen in Deutschland im 19. Jahrhundert*, Baden-Baden: Nomos.

Hähnel, P. L. (2017) *Föderale Interessenvermittlung im Deutschen Kaiserreich am Beispiel der Nahrungsmittelregulierung*, Baden-Baden: Nomos.

Henrich-Franke, C. (2012) *Gescheiterte Integration im Vergleich: Der Verkehr: Ein Problemsektor gemeinsamer Rechtsetzung im Deutschen Reich (1871–1879) und der Europäischen Wirtschaftsgemeinschaft (1958–1972)*, Stuttgart: Steiner.

Henrich-Franke, C. (2018) 'Integrieren durch Regieren: ein Phasenmodell', in G. Ambrosius, C. Henrich-Franke and C. Neutsch (eds), *Integrieren durch Regieren*, Baden-Baden: Nomos, pp. 15–54.

Hesse, J.-O. (2002) *Im Netz der Kommunikation: Die Reichs-, Post- und Telegraphenverwaltung 1876–1914*, München: Beck.

Hierholzer, V. (2010) *Nahrungsmittel und Norm: Regulierung von Nahrungsmittelqualität in der Industrialisierung 1871–1914*, Göttingen: Vandenhoeck & Ruprecht.

Höfer, P. (2017) *Einzelstaatliche Einflussnahme auf die Finanzpolitik im Deutschen Kaiserreich*, Baden-Baden: Nomos.

Holste, H. (2003) *Der deutsche Bundesstaat im Wandel (1867–1933)*, Berlin: Duncker & Humblot.

Huber, E. R. (1988) *Deutsche Verfassungsgeschichte seit 1789: Bismarck und das Reich*, Vol. 3, Stuttgart: Kohlhammer.

Jeserich, K. G. A., Pohl, H. and von Unruh, G.-C. (1984) *Deutsche Verwaltungsgeschichte,* Vol. 3, *Das Deutsche Reich bis zum Ende der Monarchie*, Stuttgart: Deutsche Verlagsanstalt.

Kaufer, E. (1975) *Theorie der öffentlichen Regulierung*, München: Vahlen.

Kaufhold, K. H. (1984) 'Wirtschaftsverwaltung', in K. G. A. Jeserich, H. Pohl and G.-C. von Unruh (eds), *Deutsche Verwaltungsgeschichte,* Vol. 3, *Das Deutsche Reich bis zum Ende der Monarchie*, Stuttgart: Deutsche Verlagsanstalt, pp. 207–50.

Kühl, U. (2001) *Der Munizipalsozialismus in Europa/Le socialisme municipal en Europe*, Berlin: De Gruyter.

Lehmbruch, G. (2018) 'Die Entwicklunspfade des deutschen Bundestaates: Weichenstellungen und Krisen', in G. Ambrosius, C. Henrich-Franke and C. Neutsch (eds), *Föderale Systeme: Kaiserreich—Donaumonarchie—Europäische Union*, Baden-Baden: Nomos, pp. 327–70.

Liedloff, J. (2017) *Föderale Mitwirkung an den Unfallversicherungsgesetzen im Kaiserreich (1884–1911)*, Baden-Baden: Nomos.

Millward, R. (2005) *Private and Public Enterprise in Europe: Energy, Telecommunication and Transport, 1830–1990*, Cambridge: Cambridge University Press.

Mußgang, R. (1984) 'Die Ausführung der Reichsgesetze durch die Länder und die Reichsaufsicht', in K. G. A. Jeserich, H. Pohl and Georg-Christoph von Unruh (eds), *Deutsche Verwaltungsgeschichte*, Vol. 3, *Das Deutsche Reich bis zum Ende der Monarchie*, Stuttgart: Deutsche Verlagsanstalt, pp. 186–207.

Nipperdey, T. (1992) *Deutsche Geschichte 1866–1918*, München: Beck.

Pohl, M. (1982) *Festigung und Ausdehnung des deutschen Bankenwesens zwischen 1870 und 1914*, in M. Pohl und H. Pohl (eds), *Deutsche Bankengeschichte*, Vol. 2, Frankfurt a. M.: Knapp, pp. 258–61.

Reindl, J. (1994) 'Der 'Deutsch-Österreichische Telegraphenverein' und die Entwicklung des Telegraphenwesens zwischen 1850 und 1871', *Archiv für deutsche Postgeschichte*, Vol. 3: 30–45.

Stern, K. and Püttner, G. (1965) *Die Gemeindewirtschaft: Recht und Realität*, Stuttgart: Kohlhammer.

Stier, B. (1999) *Staat und Strom: Die politische Steuerung des Elektrizitätssystems in Deutschland 1890–1950*, Upstadt-Weiher: Regionalkultur.

Toninelli, P. M. (2000) *The Rise and Fall of State-Owned Enterprises in the Western World: Comparative Perspectives in Business History*, Cambridge: Cambridge University Press.

Wehler, H. A. (1995) *Deutsche Gesellschaftsgeschichte*, Vol. 3: *Von der "Deutschen Doppelrevolution" bis zum Beginn des Ersten Weltkrieges 1849–1914*, München: Beck.

Werle, R. (1997) 'Technische Standardisierung im deregulierenden Europa', *Jahrbuch für Neue Politische Ökonomie*, Vol. 16 (1): 54–90.

Wischermann, C. and Nieberding, A. (2004) *Die institutionelle Revolution: Eine Einführung in die deutsche Wirtschaftsgeschichte des 19. und frühen 20. Jahrhunderts*, Stuttgart: Steiner.

Ziegler, D. (1996) *Eisenbahnen und Staat im Zeitalter der Industrialisierung: Die Eisenbahnpolitik der deutschen Staaten im Vergleich*, Stuttgart: Steiner.

Part II

The formation of the nation-state as a structural and institutional turning point

5 Germany's transition from a post-Malthusian to a modern growth regime, 1860s to 1880s

Ulrich Pfister

1 Introduction

Between the late 1860s and the 1880s and in close chronological parallel to the formation of a modern nation-state, the German economy experienced a profound structural break. Harvest fluctuations lost their influence on business cycles, and a transition to a pattern of development that can be described as a modern growth regime took place. The parallel between this structural break and the change in the political system immediately raises the question of whether and how the formation of a nation-state promoted Germany's transition to modern economic growth. However, what follows will not pursue this issue. Rather, this chapter aims to describe the main features of the structural break in the growth regime that occurred between the 1860s and the 1880s. In addition, it draws attention to forces that possibly aided Germany's transition to modern economic growth apart from institutional changes associated with state formation, the most important being the first wave of modern globalisation that unfolded at approximately the same time.

The chapter begins with a description of the change in the growth regime, specifically the transition from the post-Malthusian era to modern economic growth (Section 2). This is followed by a demonstration that, in the late 1860s, the agricultural sector largely lost its influence on aggregate business cycles (Section 3). Section 4 deals with the consequences of the first wave of modern globalisation for long-term economic development. The text ends with a short conclusion.

2 From the post-Malthusian era to the modern growth regime

On a per capita basis, real net national product (NNP) expanded at an annual rate of 1.5 percent from 1880 to 1913, which is similar to the rate of economic growth prevailing since approximately 1980. Prior to the first appearance of growth rates that would later prove to be characteristic of the modern age, there was a prolonged period of gradual acceleration of growth, hereinafter referred to as the post-Malthusian era. At the current, still very rudimentary

DOI: 10.4324/9781003283430-7

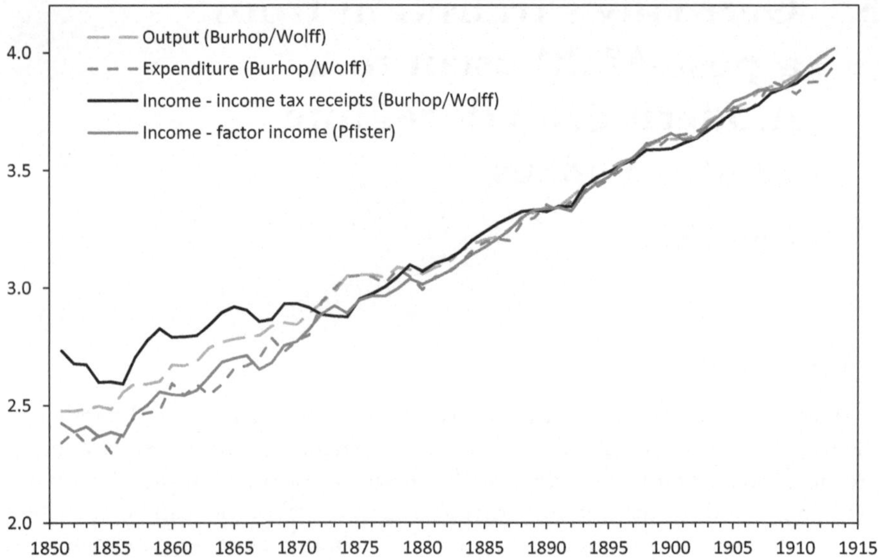

Figure 5.1 Real net national product, 1851–1913 (natural logarithm of billions of Marks, prices of 1913).

Sources: Burhop and Wolff (2005: 634, 651–52); Pfister (2020: Online Appendix SA2, column T).

state of knowledge, the growth rate of the real NNP per capita was approximately 0.3–0.5 percent from 1820 to 1850 and in the range of 0.6 to 1.1 percent from 1851 to 1880 (Pfister 2020: 517). Given the great uncertainty regarding the likely true rates of aggregate economic growth between approximately 1820 and 1880, the overall economic development during this period can be characterised from two contrasting perspectives. One is based on Rostow's concept of take-off into sustained growth; the other adopts the Crafts-Harley view of British industrialisation. Against the background of recent research, the latter view seems more plausible.

Following an opinion widely shared by earlier scholarship, which is referred to here as the take-off view, Germany made a rapid transition from pre-modern stagnation and poverty to sustained economic growth around the middle of the nineteenth century (Rostow 1956; Abel 1978). The period between the late 1830s and the first half of the 1870s was marked by the first phase of industrialisation, during which cotton manufacture and heavy industries clustered around railway construction—coal mining, iron smelting, and iron processing—expanded at annual rates of 7–8 percent; transport services of the railway network, measured in ton-kilometres, even increased by 15.1 percent p.a. between 1850 and 1879 (Fremdling 1975: 21; Spree 1979: 231–34).

Nevertheless, it would be wrong to conclude from the rapid expansion of early industrial leading sectors that the aggregate economy experienced high growth rates as well. The frequently used output-side reconstruction of the real NNP, which has also been endorsed by the Maddison project database,[1] expanded at an annual rate of 1.7 percent per capita in 1851–80. This is consistent with the view of a rapid take-off into sustainable economic growth during this period. However, different estimates of the NNP diverge considerably up to the 1870s (see Figure 5.1); the series based on income tax receipts shows a trend growth rate of only 0.6 percent per year and per capita. Burhop and Wolff (2005) argue that this latter series is probably the most trustworthy: It is the only one consistent with a stable ratio of government expenditure to NNP, whereas the other three series shown in Figure 5.1 imply that the unification wars around 1870 were fought with a lower government expenditure to NNP ratio than in 1850, which is not plausible. Especially the estimate of the output side NNP is subject to numerous issues related to index construction. The growth rate of value added in agriculture is also probably too high (Pfister 2019: 46–49). Burhop and Wolff (2005: 635–39, 652), therefore, construct a compromise estimate that weights the series derived from income tax receipts with 0.5 and the other three series with 0.167 each. On a per capita basis, this series expanded at an annual rate of 1.1 percent from 1851 to 1880. This figure can be regarded as the upper limit of the likely true rate of economic growth in the period in question (cf. Pfister 2020: 513–14).

It seems, therefore, that economic growth in Germany accelerated only gradually between approximately 1820 and 1880, in line with the view of Crafts and Harley (1992) concerning economic growth during the Industrial Revolution in Britain. The main explanation for the contrast between this finding and the rapid expansion of the leading sectors of the first phase of industrialisation is the small size of the latter. Their locations were confined to a few districts—industrialisation was initially a regional rather than a national phenomenon (Fremdling and Tilly 1979; Pollard 1991)—and their demand for labour was still modest. As late as 1875, half of the total workforce was still active in agriculture, and workers in modern industrial sectors (metal production, iron processing, chemicals, and cotton processing) accounted for only 21 percent of the workforce in manufacturing that year (Hoffmann 1965: 196–97, 205; Kirchhain 1977: 73). Thus, the modern sector was initially small, so that its rapid growth from the late 1830s exerted only a very gradual impact on the dynamics of the aggregate economy during the first phase of industrialisation.

The evolution in the growth regime in the nineteenth century can be characterised in some more detail by looking at real wages outside agriculture (Figure 5.2). In 1880, the daily or weekly labour income, calculated in constant prices, was similar to that of 1820. The increase after the mid-1850s merely compensated for the decline that had occurred since the 1820s in the

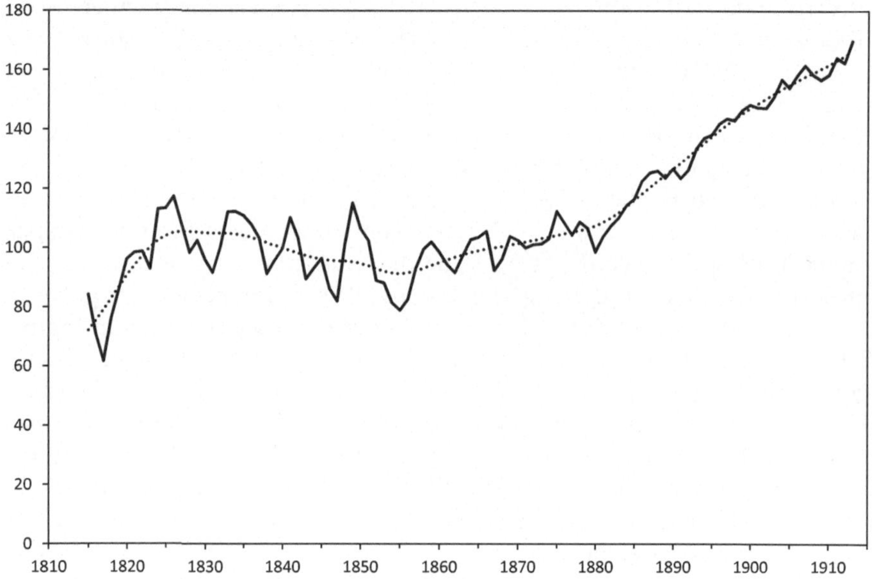

Figure 5.2 The real wage, 1815–1913 (Index, 1871 = 100).

Source: Pfister (2018: 587); data series in GESIS ZA8709, Table A.03. Until 1850, data are day wages of unskilled urban construction workers, and from 1850 annual wages in industry and urban crafts. Until 1850, the annual price of Allen's basket of consumer goods serves as a deflator, thereafter a Fisher index of consumer prices.

Note: The dotted graph represents the trend obtained with HP filter (λ = 100).

wake of a drop in the annual mean temperature, serious crop failures, and an ample supply of labour following the high rates of natural increase around 1820 (Rapp 2000: 138–40; Luterbacher et al. 2004; Fertig et al. 2018: 20–23). Only from about 1880 did a sustained increase in real wages set in.

Another key element in locating a structural break around 1880 is the change in the time series properties of the real wage. The tests reported in Table 5.A1 in the Appendix show that the real wage was stationary from 1820 to 1880. Stationarity means that the real wage series returned to its long-term equilibrium value after each shock. Due to climatic conditions, food availability was good in the 1820s, and thus living standards were relatively high, whereas severe crop failures in the later 1840s and 1850s depressed material welfare. The stationarity of real wages means that these were random external shocks that had no medium-term impact on labour productivity. By contrast, from 1880 to 1913, the real wage was no longer stationary. Shocks now had a permanent effect on material welfare; the forces underlying the data generation process of the real wage series had changed fundamentally around 1880.[2]

This result should be seen in conjunction with two other facts. First, from the end of the 1820s at the latest, population growth followed a stationary trend. Over the entire period between 1815 and 1870, the population grew at an annual rate of 0.8 percent, which was equivalent to a doubling of the pace of demographic expansion compared to the eighteenth century. Second, from the late 1810s onwards, the mortality rate reacted only weakly to downswings in the real wage, which mainly resulted from crop failures (Fertig 2018: 19; Pfister and Fertig 2020). These two findings combined imply that after the Napoleonic Wars, unlike before, population growth no longer led to a decline in material welfare and a high vulnerability with respect to subsistence crises. Rather, a continuous increase in the level of technology enabled the acceleration of population growth without serious negative consequences for the standard of living. This finding justifies characterising the period between the late 1810s and the 1870s as a post-Malthusian regime of economic growth.

In order to characterise the development of the German economy during this period in more detail, it is worth considering the implications of the behaviour of real wages and population. If the real wage remains constant (more precisely: stationary) and the population develops along a stationary trend, there will be a linear relationship between the level of technology and population. Thus, from the 1810s to the 1870s, a pattern of scale-dependent technical progress prevailed, in which the technical level increased in line with population growth, thus compensating for the fall in the marginal product of labour induced by population growth. Such a situation is broadly consistent with unified growth theory. Together with the persistence of the positive relationship between income and birth rate, the relationship between population and the level of technology constitutes a basic feature of the post-Malthusian growth regime (Galor and Weil 2000: 808–09, 824–25; Galor 2011: 17–30, 165–66; see also Kremer 1993).

In historical situations, technological progress occurring as an externality of population growth manifests itself mainly in two ways, namely Smithian growth and Boserupian growth. For Adam Smith, the size of the market determines the extent of the division of labour, and population growth increases market size. Deepening the division of labour improves the allocation of factors of production and thus increases total factor productivity. The specialisation of the labour force leads to steeper learning curves, which in turn promotes technological progress. In nineteenth-century Germany, the construction of paved roads and railways, the creation of a customs union with the Zollverein of 1834, and the integration of monetary and commercial law were all processes that promoted market integration. Thus, they supported the post-Malthusian growth regime by pushing back the limits of Smithian growth (Kelly 1997; Hornung 2015; Uebele and Gallardo Albarrán 2015; Keller and Shiue 2016; see also Chapters 3 and 7 of this volume).

Boserupian growth is based on the idea that an increase in population through the expansion of the labour supply improves the application of labour-intensive agricultural innovations and facilitates the diffusion of innovations through shorter distances between the more numerous settlements. In the case of nineteenth-century Germany, the first phase of agricultural modernisation in the form of the spread of all-year-round stall-feeding and the cultivation of fodder crops and potatoes can be associated with a pattern of Boserupian growth. Potato cultivation, in particular, not only increased the amount of energy usable by humans per acre but also diversified the harvest risk, which may partly explain the decline in the severity of food shortages from the 1810s (Boserup 1965; Achilles 1993; Nunn and Qian 2011; Uebele and Grünebaum 2014).

Related to Boserupian growth is the concept of directed technological progress. Profits from research and development depend on the number of potential users of the new technology. Therefore, innovators focus their efforts to develop new technologies primarily on increasing the productivity of the relatively abundant factor of production. This argument explains why technological progress during early industrialisation was primarily labour-augmenting (Harrod-neutral), whereas in the twentieth century, it was human capital-augmenting. In this view, the acceleration of population growth at the beginning of the nineteenth century laid the foundation for directed technological progress of the labour-augmenting type. In fact, the behaviour of the land rent suggests a transition to labour-augmenting technological progress at the beginning of the nineteenth century (Acemoglu 2009: 56–64; Crafts 2011: 157–58; Bracht and Pfister 2020: 252–57, 277, 280–81).

Economic development in 1880–1913 followed a completely different regime. First, the variety of branches characterised by an industrial mode of production increased. Although the industrial complex based on coal mining and iron processing remained prominent, chemicals and electrical and mechanical engineering either emerged as new industries or gained considerable importance. In all three branches, Germany had a strong comparative advantage at the beginning of the twentieth century (see Chapter 16 of this volume). In textile manufacture, stages of production other than mechanical spinning and branches other than cotton processing were increasingly industrialised after the 1870s; domestic industries declined significantly in the last decades of the nineteenth century (Schäfer 2016: 383–91). Whereas the first phase of industrialisation in the 1840s to the 1870s was concentrated in a few leading sectors, the industrial base broadened significantly during the era of the second industrial revolution.

Second, new forces driving economic growth emerged. The aforementioned finding shown in Appendix Table 5.A1 that the behaviour of real wages in 1880–1913 reflected a more complex process of data generation than in the first part of the nineteenth century mirrors this fact. On the one hand, capital deepening now assumed a major role in economic growth; as late as 1850–70, the capital-labour ratio in industry had risen at an annual rate of only 0.6 percent; after a strong surge in the first half of the 1870s, the capital-labour ratio in manufacturing followed a trend growth rate of

3.3 percent per annum in 1880–1913 (Hoffmann 1965: 204–06; Burhop and Wolff 2005: 652–53). On the other hand, human capital gained significant importance in the production process. Sectors that became important during the second phase of industrialisation, especially the chemical industry and electrical engineering, were human capital intensive, as shown by the high number of patents in these branches. Technological progress was now directed less towards the more efficient use of labour as a production factor and more towards the valorisation of human capital. The increased relevance of the latter factor of production is reflected in the fact that in Prussia around 1900, taxable income at the district level was related both to the frequency of valuable patents obtained in the preceding decades and the secondary school enrolment rate in 1871 (Murmann 2003; Streb et al. 2006: 357–63; Cinnirella and Streb 2017; see also Chapter 15 of this volume). Compared with the post-Malthusian era, improvements in the resource endowment of labour, that is, the driving force of economic growth emphasised by the Solow model, thus gained significantly in relevance for the development of the German economy.

Finally, the transition to the modern growth regime is marked by the onset of the first fertility transition. On a national level, marital fertility began to decline around 1895; depending on the indicator used and the region under consideration, the onset of the fertility decline can be traced back to the 1880s (Knodel 1974: 39, 58–64; Galloway et al. 1994: 142). Studies undertaken in the framework of unified growth theory, in particular, have emphasised the development of parents' preference for the quality vs. quantity of children (in the sense of health and education) as an important variable in long-term economic growth (Kremer 1993; Galor and Weil 2000; Galor 2011: ch. 5). Given the low relevance of human capital in the production process during the post-Malthusian era, parents had little reason to invest income gains in improving the quality of their children. The above-mentioned increase in population growth after 1800 is consistent with this idea. However, given the increased importance of human capital in the production process during the second industrial revolution, parents began to invest in their children's education, valuing child quality rather than the quantity of children. With a given budget and infant and child mortality rates, they had to reduce their birth rate for this purpose. Specifically, in Prussia, around 1900, an interaction effect between the number of patents filed by companies and the literacy rate on marital fertility can be seen at the district level: the more innovations required human capital on the local level, the more an expansion of education contributed to a reduction of fertility (Cinnirella and Streb 2017: 222–23). Although population growth accelerated again to 1.3 percent per annum in 1880–1913 because of a concomitant decline in mortality, the reduction in the birth rate provided an important basis for a growth pattern in which an expansion of economic output was only partially offset by population growth and instead led to a sustained increase in real per capita income.

The bottom line is that around 1880, the German economy experienced a transition from a post-Malthusian to a modern growth regime. The institutional change associated with the formation of the nation-state and the concomitant gain in state capacity is a possible explanation for this structural break. In addition, the following two sections show that other forces were at work during the 1860s and 1870s that might also have contributed to a change in the growth regime.

3 From agricultural to industrial business cycles

Not only the growth regime but also the cyclical pattern of the German economy changed during the era of modern state formation, and the two processes may have been interrelated.

Uebele and Ritschl (2009) identify business cycles using indices of stock prices. This is based on the idea that with efficient capital markets stock prices reflect discounted future income flows. Consequently, stock prices fluctuate in parallel with the relative prices of new and existing capital goods as well as with investment and output. There are two issues with this approach, however. First, it can be argued that by no means do all sectors and industries cover their capital requirements via the capital market and that individual economic sectors have their own short-term dynamics; thus, fluctuations in share price indices may be representative only of a sub-sector of the economy. During the period under review, for example, agriculture, construction, and textile production were sectors or industries not financed via the capital market and possibly exhibited different short-term dynamics than the industries connected to capital markets. Second, share price indices are only available from 1870 onwards; thus, it is not possible to examine economic fluctuations during earlier periods.

The two issues can be solved using the marriage rate as an indicator of business cycles. In analogy to prices of securities, it can be argued that at least in historical times, decisions to marry were based on expectations concerning discounted future income flows from all factors of production owned by the future household (labour, capital, and land). This assumption relies on the fact that in the dominant neo-local marriage pattern, the establishment of a new household was associated with costs and possibly debt. Moreover, couples wishing to marry had to consider the expenses associated with parenthood. Empirically, the turning points of the Ronge stock price index cycles and cycles of the marriage rate in the period 1870–1913 correspond well (Pfister 2018: 589–92). On the one hand, this finding justifies the use of the marriage rate as an indicator of aggregate business cycles. On the other hand, it implies that the short-term economic dynamics from 1870 onwards were largely driven by modern, capital market-based industries.

If one extends the period under study back to the 1820s, a correlation between cycles of marriage rates and inverted cycles of food prices emerges, reflecting fluctuations in domestic agricultural production (Figure 5.3). This

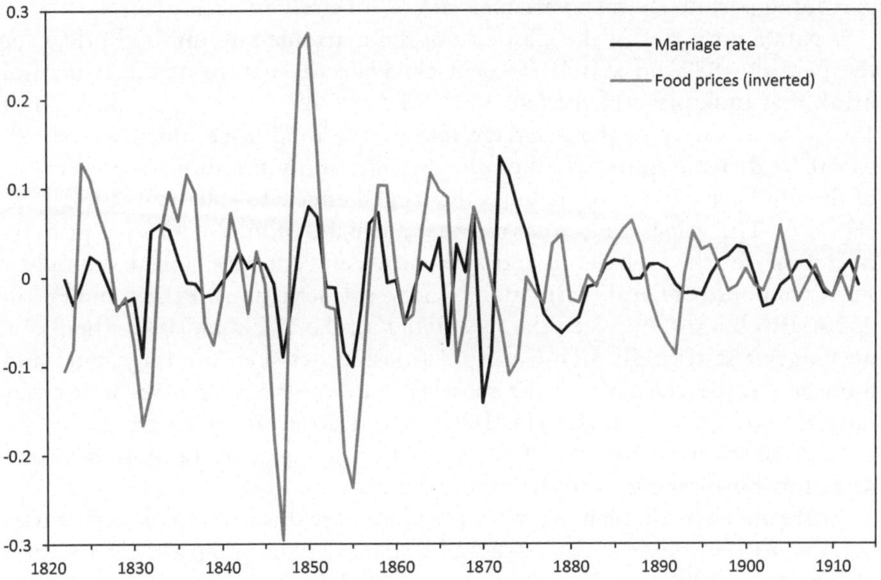

Figure 5.3 Deviation of the marriage rate and food prices from trend, 1822–1913.

Sources: Own calculation based on the following data series: Marriage rate: until 1870 Fertig et al. (2018: 31–33), from 1870 Hoffmann (1965: Table II/1, 172–74). Food price index: until 1889 Pfister (2018: 582, GESIS ZA8710, Table A.02.03), from 1870 Hoffmann (1965: Table II/148, 598–601); the index was extended back to 1822 on the basis of constant weights from 1848 to 1822.

Note: Values of both variables are in natural logarithms so that the vertical scale can be read as a proportional deviation from the medium-term trend. The medium-term trend was determined using the HP filter with $\lambda = 100$.

pattern seems to last until the mid-1860s. During this period, the turning points in the cycles of the marriage rate also tally poorly with other business cycle dating schemes, which are mainly based on indicators from non-agricultural economic sectors (Spree 1979: 237; Sarferaz and Uebele 2009: 381; Pfister 2018: 592). Thus, until the 1860s, the short-term dynamics of the German economy were, to a considerable extent, characterised by weather-related fluctuations in agricultural output (Spree 1979: 236).

The visual impression in Figure 5.3 can be confirmed by an analysis of the relationship between the marriage rate and the food price index. Figure 5.A1 in the Appendix performs a structural break test for this relationship. In 1867, a structural break occurred with an error probability of less than 1 percent; however, it cannot be excluded that a structural break occurred as early as the late 1850s. Particularly, 1867 is a highly plausible candidate for a structural break in that the marriage rate and food prices rose significantly in that year (Figure 5.3; food price cycles inverted); during the preceding period, the two variables moved inversely to each other.

Separate estimates of the elasticity of the marriage rate on food prices for the periods 1822–66 and 1875–1913 elucidate the nature of the structural break that took place in the late 1860s (Table 5.A2 in the Appendix). Until 1866, the elasticity of the marriage rate on the food price index was −0.25 to −0.41, depending on whether one considers only the simultaneous effect of the food price index or includes the lagged effects to calculate cumulative elasticity. The values are similar to other estimates of the Malthusian preventive check for the eighteenth and early nineteen centuries, and they imply a strong response of family formation to harvest fluctuations (Pfister and Fertig 2020). By contrast, between the second half of the 1870s and 1913, there was no longer a statistically significant relationship between marriage rates and food prices; the elasticity of the marriage rate on the food price index was only −0.06. Clearly, in the late 1860s, a transition occurred from a cyclical pattern strongly influenced by fluctuations in agricultural output to one driven by business cycles in the modern sectors.

There are two complementary explanations for this finding. The first uses Sen's (1981) entitlement approach and emphasises the progress of structural change (Bass 1991: 27, 272). In an economy dominated by the agricultural sector, a negative harvest shock reduces not only the supply but also the demand for agricultural products. Harvest failures reduce the demand for harvesters and threshers, which in turn reduces the income of lower-class households dependent on wage labour and decreases their capability to demand food. By contrast, in an industrial economy, where households of the lower class gain their income from work in the non-agricultural sectors, which are little affected by fluctuations in domestic agricultural production, real incomes and thus consumption will develop much more steadily. In this view, the disappearance of the link between marriage rates and food prices, perhaps from the late 1850s onwards, and certainly after 1867, reflects the fact that non-agricultural incomes increased in the course of the first phase of industrialisation and the associated structural change. As a result, fluctuations in agricultural production lost their relevance for the income expectations of the population at large.

The second statement refers to the so-called European grain invasion after the end of the US Civil War (1861–65) in the context of the first wave of modern globalisation, which is discussed in more detail in the following section. The integration of transatlantic grain markets had the effect of significantly reducing the volatility of food prices. Specifically, the average deviation of the price index shown in Figure 5.3 from the trend fell from 9.4 percent in the period 1822–66 to 2.7 percent in 1875–1913 (standard deviation of absolute values). This also reduced the weight of fluctuations in food prices in household income expectations.

The findings of this section suggest the hypothesis that the transition from a cyclical pattern of aggregate economic activity dominated by harvest fluctuations to one driven by business cycles in the modern sectors potentially contributed to the transition from the post-Malthusian to the modern growth regime described in the previous section. The smoothing of consumption caused by structural changes in the course of industrialisation and the international integration of grain markets reduced the risk of income expectations. This is shown not least by the reduction in the mean distance from the trend in real wages from 3.3 percent in 1822–66 to 2.0 percent in 1875–1913 (series of Figure 5.3; standard deviation of absolute values). The smoothing of income fluctuations also increased the risk-adjusted return on household investment in human capital, shifting parental preferences from quantity to quality in children. This stimulated investment in human capital and favoured the onset of the first fertility transition. Accordingly, the change in the pattern of the aggregate business cycle possibly aided the transition to modern economic growth.

4 Globalisation shock and factor incomes

In the late 1860s and 1870s, Germany experienced a globalisation shock that permanently changed the extent and nature of its integration into the world economy and thus, together with the change in the cyclical pattern of aggregate economic activity, to which it was partly related, created favourable conditions for the transition to a modern growth regime.

Between 1865 and 1879, the degree of openness measured as the ratio of imports and exports to NNP increased from 20.0 to 38.5 percent.[3] At the same time, the commodity structure of foreign trade changed permanently: Until the mid-1860s, Germany was one of the most important agricultural exporters; it probably exported an average of approximately 3 percent of the grain harvest. From the end of the 1860s onwards, export surpluses disappeared, and from 1873 onwards, increasing shares of grain consumption were covered by imports, at an order of magnitude of approximately 8 percent already by 1880 (Grant 2005: 220). Germany, like other economies in the Old World, was thus strongly affected by the so-called European grain invasion, which began at the end of the US Civil War (1861–65): By the mid-1860s, the technical, institutional, and political conditions were obviously in place to integrate the landlocked areas in the interior of the American continent into the world economy. This changed in a lasting way both what was happening in grain markets and the pattern of comparative advantage of all economies (O'Rourke 1997).

The integration of grain markets between Germany and overseas territories that were subject to different weather conditions than cereal farmers in the Old World helped to dampen fluctuations in consumption. The finding that a structural break from an agricultural to an industrial business cycle pattern most likely occurred in 1867 (Figure 5.A1) is consistent with the onset of the European grain invasion in the years following the end of the US Civil War.

In addition, the European grain invasion caused a strong shift in factor incomes, which in turn pushed the long-term development of the German

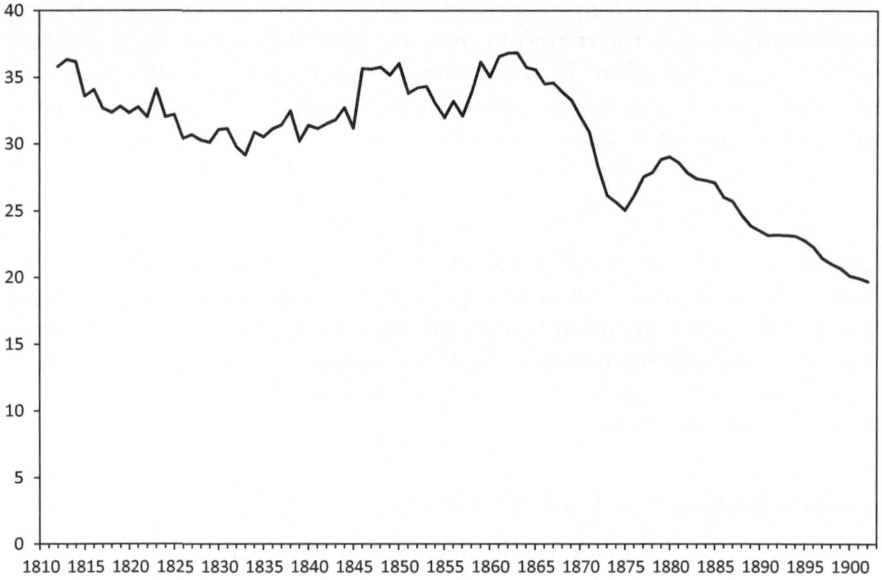

Figure 5.4 The rent-wage ratio in Germany, 1812–1902 (days of work per hectare of land).

Source: Bracht and Pfister (2020: 277).

Note: Land rent is measured in grams of silver per hectare on five noble estates in Westphalia; the non-agricultural wage is the nominal wage in grams of silver per day underlying the real wage series in Figure 5.2.

economy in a new direction. Figure 5.4 shows the development of the ratio of rents and non-agricultural wages in the nineteenth century and thus the relation of rents of the two production factors land and labour (hereinafter r-w ratio). This ratio indicates the marginal rate of technical substitution between the two factors of production, and the scale accordingly has an intuitive meaning: it indicates how much labour substitutes for a unit of land. A value of the r-w ratio of 35 then means that the product of one hectare of land can be substituted by 35 working days.

The r-w ratio reached its maximum in 1861–63; the US-American Civil War thus emerges as an important turning point in German economic history. After a fall that lasted from the end of the Napoleonic Wars into the early 1830s, probably due to the favourable climatic conditions during this period mentioned above, the r-w ratio rose significantly between the early 1830s and the early 1860s. This development was probably related to population growth and the growing market integration with Great Britain resulting from the dismantling of the Corn Laws (O'Rourke and Williamson 1999: 83). It reflects the intensification of land use in the course of the first agricultural modernisation and Smithian growth in the post-Malthusian era.

Between the end of the US Civil War and 1900, by contrast, the r-w ratio fell by 43 percent. Thus, the European grain invasion led to an enormous shift in income away from landowners and towards households earning their living from non-agricultural wage labour. The young nation-state was burdened with distributional conflicts between globalisation winners and losers right from the start (Torp 2014; O'Rourke and Williamson 1999: 54–64).

From an economic point of view, the European grain invasion brought about a strong reduction in the shortage of land on the old continent. In 1865, it took 35 days of work to substitute the products of one hectare of land, whereas in 1900, 20 days were sufficient. The first wave of modern globalisation thus brought about a new potential for structural change, specifically in the form of a reduction in the proportion of people employed in agriculture. It supported the broadening of the industrial base of the German economy mentioned above in connection with the transition to the modern growth regime and facilitated the valorisation of the comparative advantage in terms of human capital endowment.

5 Conclusion

In close chronological parallel to the formation of a nation-state, Germany's long-term economic development experienced a profound structural break in several respects between the late 1860s and the 1880s. Above all, there was a transition from a post-Malthusian to a modern growth regime. Under the first regime, which prevailed between the late 1810s and the 1870s, the technological level rose mainly in line with population growth. The first agricultural modernisation and Smithian growth via market integration, which was promoted by the improvement of transport infrastructure and institutional change, are the most important feature of this scale-dependent phase of economic growth. The rapid expansion of the modern industrial sector, which began in the late 1830s and 1840s, was closely linked to the process of market integration through the strong weight of railway construction in fixed capital formation and was initially confined to a few leading sectors. As these were still relatively small and concentrated in a few regions, the rate of aggregate economic growth accelerated only gradually.

After the deep crisis of the 1870s, the German economy expanded in real terms and on a per capita basis from 1880 to 1913 at a rate similar to the one recorded since 1980. This transition to a regime of modern economic growth was accompanied by a significant broadening of the industrial base. The increase in capital intensity and the development of human capital-intensive branches such as chemicals and electrical engineering contributed to the acceleration of the pace of economic growth. The increase in returns on human capital prompted parents to attribute greater importance to the quality of their children than to their quantity. This is one of the causal factors among several others that led to the decline in the birth rate that began in the 1890s at the latest. In the long run, the fertility decline contributed to a smaller proportion of the increase in aggregate output being absorbed by demographic expansion compared with the nineteenth century, which was also conducive to economic growth on a per capita basis.

The striking temporal parallel between the transition from a post-Malthusian to a modern growth regime and the formation of Germany's first nation-state suggests the hypothesis that the increase in state power and the accompanying institutional change were causally connected with Germany's transition to modern economic growth. This hypothesis is too complex to be explored in the framework of this chapter. Moreover, there were other factors that potentially contributed to a change in the growth regime of the German economy as well. The first relates to the globalisation shock of the late 1860s and 1870s. It not only led to a stronger integration of Germany into the world economy but also to the transformation from an exporter of agricultural products to a major importer of grain. This increased the potential for structural change and thus contributed to the broadening of the industrial base of the German economy in the transition to the second phase of industrialisation and the modern growth regime.

The second factor, which was closely linked to the first wave of modern globalisation, involved a transition from a cyclical pattern dominated by agricultural output—that is, by harvest fluctuations—to one driven by the modern industrial sector. Specifically, it is highly probable that in 1867 food prices lost their influence on the marriage rate, approximately three years after the so-called European grain invasion, which started mainly in the United States, began to make itself felt in German factor incomes. Moreover, the volatility of the marriage rate also declined both as a result of international grain market integration and structural change, which made labour incomes less dependent on harvest outcomes. Insofar as the marriage rate reflects expectations regarding discounted future income flows, a decrease in its volatility implies, ceteris paribus, an increase in the risk-adjusted return on investment in human capital. The change in the cyclical pattern of the German economy thus probably fostered the emergence of an important precondition for the transition to the modern growth regime, namely a growing appreciation by parents for the quality of their children.

Three fundamental, partially interrelated changes—the transition from a post-Malthusian to a modern growth regime, the first wave of modern globalisation in conjunction with the European grain invasion, and the shift from an agrarian to an industrial economic pattern—thus occurred in a relatively short period between the late 1860s and early 1880s. The extent to which this profound structural break in German economic history was also related to the formation of a modern nation-state, which also occurred during this period, is an important research question for understanding the economic consequences of political change.

Appendix

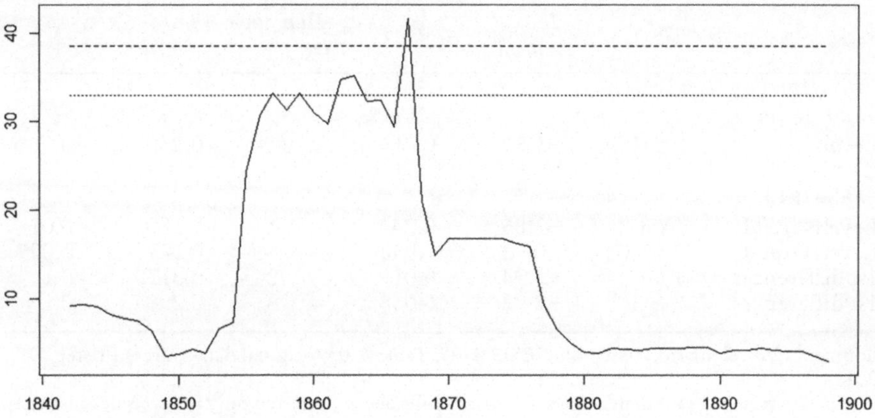

Figure 5.A1 F-test for structural break in the relationship between marriage rate and food prices.

Sources: See Figure 5.3.

Note: The test is based on the following model (autoregressive distributed lag regression following Cuddington and Dagher 2015):

$$m_t = \gamma_0 + \nu_{p0} p_t + \sum_{l=1}^{L} \nu_{p,l} p_{t-l} + \sum_{l=1}^{L} \nu_{m,l} m_{t-l} + \sum_{i=1}^{4} \gamma_i T_i + u_t$$

where m is the marriage rate, p the natural logarithm of the food price index, and u *is* an i.i.d. random shock, all in year t. L denotes the number of lags. T are dummy variables for the years 1870, 1871, 1872, and 1873, respectively, and they control for the fact that the Franco-Prussian War of 1870/71 led to a postponement of marriages to the following years (see Figure 5.3). γ and ν are estimation parameters. Standard information criteria for the number of lags suggest $L = 3$. Following Lütkepohl (2007: 318–320), a lag-augmented structural break test is carried out in which the number of lags is increased by 1 to $L = 4$. The broken line denotes a structural break at $p < 0.01$, the dotted line at $p < 0.05$.

Appendix tables

Table 5.A1 Unit root and stationarity tests of the real wage, 1820–1913

	ADF			*KPSS*		
	Lag	*Test statistic*	*p*	*Truncation lag*	*Test statistic*	*p*
1820–1913						
Levels+trend	8 (AIC)	−0.97	0.939	6	0.341	<0.01
1st differences	2 (SC)	−6.85	<0.01	2	0.100	>0.1
1st differences	9 (AIC)	−3.05	0.036	6	0.240	>0.1

(Continued)

	ADF			KPSS		
	Lag	*Test statistic*	*p*	*Truncation lag*	*Test statistic*	*p*
1820–1879						
Levels	2 (AIC)	−3.50	0.013	1	0.250	>0.1
1880–1913						
Levels+trend	1 (SC)	−2.85	0.242	1	0.288	<0.01
Levels+trend	7 (AIC)	−0.72	0.958	4	0.173	0.027
1st differences	1 (SC)	−4.24	<0.01	2	0.317	>0.1
1st differences	7 (AIC)	−2.92	0.058	8	0.298	>0.1

Source: Own calculation based on GESIS 8709, Table A.03 (original data sources Pfister 2017, 2018).
Note: The real wage is taken in logs. The first differences are tested only in levels because they do not show a trend.

Table 5.A2 Elasticity of marriage rate (m) on food prices (p), first differences (OLS regression coefficients, standard error in parentheses)

	1822–1866		*1875–1913*	
constant	6.4E-05	(5.2E-05)	−4.0E-06	(2.2E-05)
Δm-1	−0.3171^{+}	(0.1774)	0.6819⋆	(0.1914)
Δm-2	−0.1311	(0.1771)	−0.2669	(0.1654)
Δp	−0.0020⋆	(0.0006)	−0.0005	(0.007)
Δp-1	−0.0011^{+}	(0.0006)	0.0006	(0.0007)
Δp-2	−0.0001	(0.0007)	−0.0006	(0.0007)
R^2 adj.	0.345		0.214	
DW	1.93		2.05	
Implied instantaneous elasticity	−0.25		−0.06	
Implied cumulative elasticity	−0.41		−0.06	

Sources: See Figure 5.3.
Notes: ⋆$p < 0.05$, $^{+} < 0.1$ The model is the same as the one underlying Figure 5.A1. Since the food price index may not be (trend) stationary in the second period,[4] the model underlying Figure 5.A1 is transformed into first differences. The point elasticity of the marriage rate on the food price index is obtained by dividing the regression coefficients by the mean value of the marriage rate. The implied instantaneous elasticity is derived from the coefficient Δp, the implied cumulative elasticity from the sum of the coefficients for Δp, $\Delta p-1$, and $\Delta p-2$.

Notes

1 https://www.rug.nl/ggdc/historicaldevelopment/maddison/releases/; cf. Bolt and van Zanden (2014).
2 Although the period 1880–1913 is short for tests on time series properties, one always finds a unit root when the period is extended backward in time.
3 Trade data from Lampe and Wolf (2015); data for net national product from Pfister (2020). See also Chapter 16 of this volume.
4 KPSS tests for different lags reject the null hypothesis of trend stationarity with an error probability of less than 5 percent.

References

Abel, W. (1978) *Agrarkrisen und Agrarkonjunktur: Eine Geschichte der Land- und Ernährungswirtschaft Mitteleuropas seit dem hohen Mittelalter*, 3rd ed., Hamburg: Parey.

Acemoglu, D. (2009) *Introduction to Modern Economic Growth*, Princeton, NJ: Princeton University Press.

Achilles, W. (1993) *Deutsche Agrargeschichte im Zeitalter der Reformen und Industrialisierung*, Stuttgart: Ulmer.

Bass, H. (1991) *Hungerkrisen in Preußen während der ersten Hälfte des 19. Jahrhunderts*, St. Katharinen: Scripta-Mercaturae.

Bolt, J. and van Zanden, J. L. (2014) 'The Maddison Project: collaborative research on historical national accounts', *Economic History Review*, Vol. 67 (3): 627–51.

Boserup, E. (1965) *The Conditions of Agricultural Growth: The Economics of Agrarian Change under Population Pressure*, London: Earthscan.

Bracht, J. and Pfister, U. (2020) *Landpacht, Marktgesellschaft und Agrarentwicklung: Fünf Adelsgüter zwischen Rhein und Weser, 16.–19. Jahrhundert*, Stuttgart: Steiner.

Burhop, C. and Wolff, G. (2005) 'A compromise estimate of German net national product, 1851–1913 and its implications for growth and business cycles', *Journal of Economic History*, Vol. 65 (3): 613–57.

Cinnirella, F. and Streb, J. (2017) 'The role of human capital and innovation in economic development: evidence from post-Malthusian Prussia', *Journal of Economic Growth*, Vol. 22 (2): 193–227.

Crafts, N. F. R. (2011) 'Explaining the first Industrial Revolution: two views', *European Review of Economic History*, Vol. 15 (1): 153–68.

Crafts, N. F. R. and C. K. Harley (1992) 'Output growth and the British Industrial Revolution: a restatement of the Crafts-Harley view', *Economic History Review*, Vol. 45 (4): 703–30.

Cuddington, J. T. and Dagher, L. (2015) 'Estimating short and long-run demand elasticities: a primer with energy-sector applications', *Energy Journal*, Vol. 36 (1): 185–209.

Fertig, G., Schlöder, C., Gehrmann, R., Langfeldt, C., and Pfister, U. (2018) 'Das postmalthusianische Zeitalter: die Bevölkerungsentwicklung in Deutschland, 1815–1871', *Vierteljahrschrift für Sozial- und Wirtschaftsgeschichte*, Vol. 105 (1): 6–33.

Fremdling, R. (1975) *Eisenbahnen und deutsches Wirtschaftswachstum 1840–1879: Ein Beitrag zur Entwicklungstheorie und zur Theorie der Infrastruktur*, Dortmund: Gesellschaft für Westfälische Wirtschaftsgeschichte.

Fremdling, R. and Tilly, R. (eds) (1979) *Industrialisierung und Raum. Studien zur regionalen Differenzierung im Deutschland des 19. Jahrhunderts*, Stuttgart: Klett-Cotta.

Galloway, P., Hammel, E., and Lee, R. (1994) 'Fertility decline in Prussia, 1875–1910: a pooled cross-section time series analysis', *Population Studies*, Vol. 48 (1): 135–58.

Galor, O. (2011) *Unified Growth Theory*, Princeton, NJ: Princeton University Press.

Galor, O. and Weil, D. (2000) 'Population, technology and growth: from the Malthusian regime to the demographic transition and beyond', *American Economic Review*, Vol. 90 (4): 806–28.

Grant, O. (2005) *Migration and Inequality in Germany 1870–1913*, Oxford: Clarendon Press.

Hoffmann, W. (1965) *Das Wachstum der deutschen Wirtschaft seit der Mitte des 19. Jahrhunderts*, Berlin: Springer.

Hornung, E. (2015) 'Railroads and growth in Prussia', *Journal of the European Economic Association*, Vol. 13 (4): 699–736.

Keller, W. and Shiue, C. (2016) 'Market integration as a mechanism of growth', *CEPR Discussion Paper* 11627.

Kelly, M. (1997) 'The dynamics of Smithian growth', *Quarterly Journal of Economics,* Vol. 112 (3): 939–64.

Kirchhain, G. (1977) *Das Wachstum der deutschen Baumwollindustrie im 19. Jahrhundert: Eine historische Modellstudie zur empirischen Wachstumsforschung*, New York: Arno.

Knodel, J. (1974) *The Decline of Fertility in Germany, 1870–1939*, Princeton, NJ: Princeton University Press.

Kremer, M. (1993) 'Population growth and technological change: one million BC to 1990', *Quarterly Journal of Economics,* Vol. 108 (3): 681–716.

Lampe, M. and Wolf, N. (2015) 'Binnenhandel und Außenhandel', in T. Rahlf (ed.), *Deutschland in Daten: Zeitreihen zur Historischen Statistik*, Bonn: BPB, pp. 276–91.

Luterbacher, J., Dietrich, D., Xoplaki, E., Grosejan, M., and Wanner, H. (2004) 'European seasonal and annual temperature variability, trends and extremes', *Science,* Vol. 303: 1499–1503.

Lütkepohl, H. (2007) *New Introduction to Multiple Time Series Analysis*, Berlin: Springer.

Murmann, J. (2003) *Knowledge and Competitive Advantage: The Coevolution of Firms, Technology, and National Institutions*, Cambridge: Cambridge University Press.

Nunn, N. and Qian, N. (2011) 'The potato's contribution to population and industrialization: evidence from a historical experiment', *Quarterly Journal of Economics,* Vol. 126 (2): 593–650.

O'Rourke, K. (1997) 'The European grain invasion, 1870–1913', *Journal of Economic History,* Vol. 57 (4): 775–801.

O'Rourke, K. and Williamson, J. (1999) *Globalization and History: The Evolution of a Nineteenth-century Atlantic Economy*, Cambridge, MA: MIT Press.

Pfister, U. (2017) 'The timing and pattern of real wage divergence in pre-industrial Europe: evidence from Germany, c. 1500–1850', *Economic History Review,* Vol. 70 (3): 701–29.

Pfister, U. (2018) 'Real wages in Germany during the first phase of industrialization, 1850–1889', *Jahrbuch für Wirtschaftsgeschichte,* Vol. 59 (2): 567–96.

Pfister, U. (2019) 'Langfristiges Agrarwachstum in Deutschland, ca. 1500–1880: ein Überblick', *Zeitschrift für Agrargeschichte und Agrarsoziologie,* Vol. 67 (2): 37–68.

Pfister, U. (2020) 'The Crafts-Harley view of German industrialization: an independent estimate of the income side of net national product, 1851–1913', *European Review of Economic History,* Vol. 24 (3): 502–21.

Pfister, U. and Fertig, G. (2020) 'From Malthusian disequilibrium to the post-Malthusian era: the evolution of the preventive and positive checks in Germany, 1730-1870', *Demography,* Vol. 57 (3): 1145–70.

Pollard, S. (1991) 'Regional markets and national development', in M. Berg (ed.), *Markets and Manufactures in Early Industrial Europe*, London: Routledge, pp. 29–56.

Rapp, J. (2000) *Konzeption, Problematik und Ergebnisse klimatologischer Trendanalysen für Europa und Deutschland*, Offenbach/Main: Deutscher Wetterdienst.

Rostow, W. (1956) 'The take-off into sustained growth', *Economic Journal,* Vol. 66 (261): 25–48.

Sarferaz, S. and Uebele, M. (2009) 'Tracking down the business cycle: a dynamic factor model for Germany 1820–1913', *Explorations in Economic History,* Vol. 46 (3): 368–87.

Schäfer, M. (2016) *Eine andere Industrialisierung: Die Transformation der sächsischen Textilexportgewerbe, 1790–1890*, Stuttgart: Steiner.

Sen, A. (1981) *Poverty and Famines: An Essay on Entitlement and Deprivation*, Oxford: Clarendon Press.

Spree, R. (1979) 'Veränderung der Muster zyklischen Wachstums der deutschen Wirtschaft von der Früh- zur Hochindustrialisierung', *Geschichte und Gesellschaft*, Vol. 5: 228–50.

Streb, J., Baten, J., and Yin, S. (2006) 'Technological and geographical knowledge spillover in the German empire 1877–1913', *Economic History Review*, Vol. 59 (2): 347–73.

Torp. C. (2014) *The Challenges of Globalization: Economy and Politics in Germany, 1860–1914*, New York: Berghahn.

Uebele, M. and Gallardo Albarrán, D. (2015) 'Paving the way to modernity: Prussian roads and grain market integration in Westphalia, 1821–1855', *Scandinavian Economic History Review*, Vol. 63 (1): 69–92.

Uebele, M. and Grünebaum, T. (2014) 'Food security, harvest shocks and the potato as secondary crop in Saxony, 1792–1811', in G. Kollmer-von Oheimb-Loup, S. Lehmann and J. Streb (eds), *Chancen und Risiken internationaler Integration: Mikro- und makroökonomische Folgen der Internationalisierung*, Ostfildern: Jan Thorbecke, pp. 31–59.

Uebele, M. and Ritschl, A. (2009) 'Stock markets and business cycle comovement in Germany before World War I: evidence from spectral analysis', *Journal of Macroeconomics*, Vol. 31 (1): 35–57.

6 Fiscal regime, nation-building, and state capacity

Interactions among public finances, national unification, and economic development

Mark Spoerer

1 Introduction

The discussion on the rise of Europe since the early modern period has been increasingly conducted from an internationally comparative perspective since the turn of the millennium. The focus is no longer only on the so-called Little Divergence between different regions of Europe but also on the Great Divergence between Europe and regions like India and China (see, among others, Pomeranz 2000; Vries 2013; Brandt et al. 2014; Broadberry et al. 2018). In this context, the role of the state in economic and political development plays an important role under the catchword of state capacity. In a comparative analysis of European states from 1750 to 1913, Mark Dincecco, a political scientist working in the field of history, examined how effective states could be formed. He argues that during this period there was a long-term relationship between state capacity, that is, 'the fiscal and administrative power of states', and economic growth (Dincecco 2015; quote from Dincecco and Katz 2016: 189). Dincecco emphasises two elements that were mainly formed in the nineteenth century: the centralisation of state finances and the restriction of government power. The former allowed the state to expand its tax base and generate more tax revenue, which ultimately expanded its political-military room for manoeuvre. The latter, through parliamentary budget control, including a right of veto—'taxation with representation' (Besley and Persson 2013: 106)—had led to tax revenues being used appropriately in this sense. Only Prussia was included among the 11 states examined by Dincecco; the German Empire was excluded, as it was only founded at the end of his period of study. There is also the question to what extent the factors emphasised by Dincecco contributed to nation-building in the German case, namely, the unification of the Empire in 1871 and the rise of Germany as a great power. On the eve of the First World War, Germany was undoubtedly an effective state. It had strong economic growth, stable institutions, and, along with France and Russia, was one of the three central continental European powers, also and especially from a military perspective. This article examines the interactions between public finances on the one hand and the founding of

DOI: 10.4324/9781003283430-8

the German Empire on the other, as well as the rise of Germany as a major economic and political power, in terms of nation-building and state capacity from the mid-nineteenth century to the eve of the First World War. The focus is on the German fiscal regime, which is the institutional ensemble of public expenditure, revenue, and debt.

The next section provides a predominantly descriptive empirical review of public finances before the founding of the Empire and their development afterwards. Section 3 addresses a subject which has been long discussed in international research, namely, the extent to which the fiscal regime contributed to the formation of the nation-states (nation-building) and their institutional consolidation (e.g. O'Brien and Hunt 1999). In reversing the causal direction, section 4 investigates the extent to which the state was able to expand its fiscal and thus political scope of action through appropriate rationalisation and reform of public finances (state capacity). Finally, Section 5 considers the extent to which public finances contributed to Germany's belated industrialisation and, more generally, to the economic growth that gained momentum from the 1860s onwards.

Ultimately, I will argue that owing to the pronounced fiscal federalism that dominated the German Empire's public finances until the beginning of the First World War, none of the three causal mechanisms was particularly important. Neither did public finances contribute to nation-building or in any significant way to the subsequent political or economic dynamism of the Empire, nor was the Empire able to make them more efficient in its own sense and thus gain state capacity. There is no convincing evidence (yet) of a sustained positive influence of public finances on industrialisation and economic growth. Perhaps this critical verdict will provoke further research that may in some cases result in different conclusions.

2 Basic features of public finances in Germany from the mid-nineteenth century to the First World War

The founding of the Empire on 18 January 1871 united 25 formally independent states that hitherto had their own fiscal regimes that had developed over centuries. The same applied to Alsace-Lorraine, which was administered directly by the Empire. Owing to similar political, economic, and cultural characteristics on the one hand and geographical proximity on the other, the systems of public revenue and expenditure in Germany were structurally quite similar. However, they were legally and fiscally completely independent of each other. Harmonisation of any kind, such as already existed regarding the monetary system, had not taken place in the area of public finances. The only exception was customs duties, which were levied uniformly at the external borders of the *Zollverein*, which had come into operation in 1834. Even double taxation agreements did not exist between German states until 1869 (for the agreement concluded between Prussia and Saxony, see Bräunig 2016: 61; see also Clauss 1888: 149, 172, 195–96).

In the mid-nineteenth century, the public revenues of the member states of the German Confederation had a rather heterogeneous structure. Following the French model, the southern German states in particular relied heavily on object taxes (especially land, building, and trade taxes), while subject taxes (class, head, and rudimentary income taxes) played a greater role in most territories of the rest of Germany. An income tax in the modern sense was introduced in England, the other reference model, in 1842. In Germany, it was first introduced in 1878 by Saxony, the most industrialised German territorial state at that time, and then by Baden in 1884 and Prussia in 1891 (Schremmer 1989: 443; Ullmann 2009: 144–45). In addition to the aforementioned direct taxes, there were a large number of indirect taxes, which included not only external customs duties but also many excise duties that were applied in very different ways. A general turnover tax was not introduced until 1918.

The distribution of tasks between the newly founded Empire and member states was quite typical for a federal state. The Empire was responsible for defence, international relations, and the administration of the *Reichsland* Alsace-Lorraine, which was annexed in 1871. It operated a number of public government enterprises like the *Reichspost* and the railways in Alsace-Lorraine. The other railway companies were still in private or member-state ownership at that time (see Chapter 7 of this volume). In continuation of earlier intergovernmental treaties (like the *Zollverein* in 1833, various coinage treaties in 1837, 1839, and 1857, the General German Commercial Code in 1861, etc.), a large number of harmonisation measures were pending in such diverse economically relevant areas as the legal, monetary, and patent system, among others. The reorganisation of public finances in the federal state was another area of reform.

At the founding of the Empire, most German states faced the problem of economic growth primarily taking place in the secondary sector, in contrast to the very static tax system which tended to focus on taxing the average expected (i.e. not the actual) income from agriculture, business, and real estate ownership. For the sake of both tax fairness and fiscal reasons, many German states tried to adapt their system of public revenue to the growing economic power and to make greater use of the new sources of income. The direct taxes, especially the income tax, which were reorganised or newly created for this purpose, soon proved to be profitable and were therefore not to be handed over to the Empire. Instead, in continuity with the practice in the *Zollverein* and the North German Confederation (1867–71), the latter was awarded customs duties. These were to remain the main source of revenue for the Empire until the First World War. Second, most of the member states ceded a variety of (indirect) taxes on the consumption of salt, tobacco, brandy, sugar, and beer to the Empire (with special arrangements for Baden, Württemberg, and Bavaria). These taxes were standardised by the Empire (partially already within the framework of the North German Confederation) in order to avoid compensatory and transitional levies at the internal borders, which would hinder traffic and competition. Third, the Empire had a few less significant transport taxes, and fourth, surpluses of public government enterprises, such as the *Reichspost* and the railway in Alsace-Lorraine. The Empire did not have its own financial administration; even customs duties were collected at its borders by the respective member states and transferred to Berlin after the deduction of collection costs (Ullmann 2005: 59–60, 73). The main expenditures of the Empire were by far the army and the navy, followed by expenditures for the administration of its enterprises (Schremmer 1989: 473–475).

3 Fiscal regime and nation-building

For the question to what extent the fiscal regime could contribute to nation-building, a look at the financial equalisation between the Empire and member states, which is very idiosyncratic from today's perspective, is instructive. The Imperial Constitution of 1871 stipulated that if the Empire could not finance its tasks from its own resources, the member states had to pay so-called matriculation contributions (as they had already done in the Holy Roman Empire, which had ceased to exist in 1806, albeit to a much lesser extent), which were apportioned to the member states on a per capita basis (i.e. without regard to the ability to pay). In 1879, when the Empire raised tariffs that protected farmers and some industrial branches, but not consumers, the member states feared that this could expand the Empire's financial leeway to an unwanted extent (see Chapters 16 and 17 of this volume). Therefore, the *Reichstag* enforced a clause in the law, named after the Centre MP Franckenstein, which obliged the Empire to transfer customs and tobacco tax revenues initially exceeding a fixed amount of (1880) 130 million Mark (increased to 143 million Mark in 1896 and 180 million Mark in 1897; repealed in 1904) to the member states on a per capita basis (von Kruedener 1987). The member states first paid the customs and excise revenues to the Empire, which, from 1880 to 1904, transferred the sum exceeding the respective maximum amount of customs and tobacco tax revenues back to the member states and then requested matriculation contributions in the event of a remaining budgetary deficit. These back-and-forth transactions made budget planning considerably more difficult for the member states. Renowned public finance economists of different generations, like Adolph Wagner (1835–1917) and Wilhelm Gerloff (1880–1954), therefore pleaded for a thorough reform of Imperial finances (Wagner 1887, 1908; Gerloff 1909). However, the Imperial financial reforms, especially from 1906 onwards, did not fundamentally change the structural imbalances between the Empire and the member states, although the need for action increased from the end of the 1890s onwards, especially as a result of the policy of high armament (naval bills, etc.). Accordingly, they were considered half-hearted by many public finance experts. Only the fiscal reforms of 1919/20, implemented under the impression of the lost war and the need to pay reparations, were to bring about a fundamental change in the German fiscal regime (Ullmann 2005: 101–03).

From a perspective committed to the common good, it was easy to call for the reform of the finances of the Empire and of the cumbersome fiscal equalisation system. However, reforms were opposed by the fiscal and partly also political interests of the member states. Whereas the above-mentioned financial reasons were arguments for ceding most indirect taxes to the Empire, there were weighty individual fiscal interests in keeping direct taxes with the member states. By the early 1870s, many member states had supplemented the originally very inflexible property taxes with other direct taxes that taxed so-called 'non-funded' types of income, that is, income not based on land, business, or real estate ownership. This included corporate and speculative profits, the income of the self-employed and employees, etc. Consequently, member states were now in a better position to let public revenues participate in the rapidly growing prosperity. With income tax, which almost all member states introduced starting in 1878, they gained an unexpectedly rich source of revenue. The member states did not want to cede this very revenue-elastic tax (i.e. tax revenues grew at least proportionally with income) to the Empire.

In the case of Prussia, which accounted for almost two-thirds of the Empire in terms of territory and population, another political motive was important. In contrast to indirect taxes, it is easy to provide income and wealth taxes with progressive elements with which redistribution goals can be realised. This was not in the interest of the wealthy elites, especially as they had disproportionately strong influence in the Prussian lower house—and consequently on tax law as well—owing to the three-class electoral system introduced in 1848/49 which continued to exist until 1918. The more direct taxes a voter paid, the more likely it was for his vote to count more than those of low-income voters. In contrast, as the seats in the *Reichstag* were determined by universal and equal (male) suffrage (one man, one vote), it would have been much easier for social reformers at the Empire level to implement distributional policy goals with the help of income tax than in Prussia. This was one of the reasons all attempts to introduce an Imperial income tax or even to transfer the income taxes of the member states to the Empire failed until 1919 (Hallerberg 2002; Ziblatt 2008).

Although the increasing financial needs of the Empire in the context of naval armament led to the introduction of direct taxes shortly before the First World War, particularly the capital gains tax and the military contribution (a wealth tax) in 1913, the tax revenues of the municipalities increased even more (Spoerer 2004: 116–18). The Empire being, as Bismarck put it before the *Reichstag* in 1879, a 'troublesome boarder of the member states', had no alternative but to become increasingly indebted by issuing government bonds (Witt 1970; Schremmer 1989: 468–70).

Table 6.1 shows the development of public debt of the Empire and of Prussia, the largest member state by far. After the Napoleonic wars, most German states had high public debt and it took decades to reduce it to a moderate level. As the example of Prussia shows, they succeeded. It was only in the second half of the century that more new debt was issued than old debt was repaid, both

Table 6.1 Public debt of Prussia and the German Empire from 1794 to 1913

	Prussia			*German Empire*		
	million M	*M per capita*	*Debt ratio in percent*	*million M*	*M per capita*	*Debt ratio in percent*
1794	144	16.8				
1807	160	32.7				
1815	863	83.7	42.5			
1820	652	58.5	27.9			
1848	475	29.4	10.8			
1866	870	44.4	14.7			
1872	1,248	50.3	14.2	39	0.9	0.4
1882	2,686	97.0	26.7	488	10.7	4.9
1892	6,240	204.0	48.2	1,806	35.9	14.0
1902	6,721	189.0	38.0	2,934	50.8	16.6
1910	9,421	236.0	36.3			
1913				5,017	74.9	16.6

Sources: Prussia until 1902: Schremmer (1989: 454), Prussia 1910, public debt: Heckel (1911: 500), population and net national product (NNP): Hoffmann and Müller (1959: 87), German Empire, public debt: Kaiserliches Statistisches Amt (1880–1914), population and NNP: Hoffmann (1965: 173–74, 825–26).
Notes: Debt ratio = debt/net national product (NNP) at market prices; M: Mark.

at the state and municipality levels (not included in Table 6.1 for the lack of complete data). The main reason were the economic opportunities offered to existing (mining, iron, and steel production) or new (utilities, railways) public enterprises. Thus, unlike at the beginning of the nineteenth century, the function of public loans was not to fill gaps between ordinary revenues and expenditures but rather to finance potentially profitable investment projects.

For the Empire, the situation was different. As the inflow of matriculation contributions was matched by the outflow of remittances, the Empire was often a net payer to the member states, particularly in 1888–98 and 1912–19 (Schremmer 1989: 480–81). Therefore, it lacked the proper means to maintain the army and build up a navy that would be second only to the British. As seen in Table 6.1, the Empire's debt increased drastically. On the eve of the First World War, the total public debt in Germany was 29.5 billion Marks, of which 5 billion pertained to the Empire, 17 billion to the member states, and 8 billion to the municipalities (Schremmer 1989: 470; about 10 percent higher figures are reported by Ullmann 2005: 71). The debt ratio (calculated here as public debt/gross domestic product) was around 52 percent, which is not far from the Maastricht criterion of 60 percent set by the European Union (as there is no reliable estimate for the GDP in 1913, the figure for the gross national income—56.6 billion Marks—is used here; Ritschl and Spoerer 1997: 51).

The description of fiscal equalisation shows that a decidedly strong fiscal federalism prevailed in the German Empire (see also Hefeker 2001). No contribution of the fiscal regime to nation-building of any kind can be discerned. Niall Ferguson (1994; 1998: 135–42) took Bismarck's assessment, which is mostly accepted in the literature, to the extreme by arguing that it was the Empire's weak financial position that made an arms race against Germany's main adversaries (France, Russia, and Great Britain) futile in the long run and thus prompted the Imperial military to launch a pre-emptive strike in the summer of 1914. In contrast, Blankart (2007: 51–54) critically examined the common interpretation à la Bismarck. He interprets the fact that the Empire could regularly overdraw its budget and take on debt as an expression of a soft budgetary constraint. In principle, it hardly had to impose a financial constraint on itself, as it could always count on either being supported by the member states or otherwise taking on further debt. However, this interpretation, which has hardly found any support so far, can be countered by the fact that it argues purely from a fiscal perspective and leaves out considerable political frictions that manifested, for example, in the *Reichstag* debates on taking on further debt, and in the press (Teschemacher 1915; Witt 1970).

4 Fiscal regime and state capacity

There is no doubt that the German Empire was one of the fastest growing economies in the world in the last three decades before the First World War. Calculated over all three levels of government, it achieved a comparatively high public sector share, which, according to Schremmer's calculations was slightly above the corresponding values of England (not: Great Britain) and France in the last two decades before the First World War (Schremmer 1989: 362).[1] Table 6.2, in which tax revenues of all three levels of government (with gaps in municipal tax revenues) are added and related to national income, shows this for Prussia.

Figure 6.1 shows this correlation graphically for Prussia and Württemberg. The profits of public companies are also taken into account. In connection

Table 6.2 Tax load ratio in Prussia from 1857 to 1913

	Total tax revenues in million Mark	*National income in million Mark*	*Tax load ratio in percent*
1857	243	4,874	5.0
1869	417	7,849	5.3
1876	556	9,422	5.9
1883	647	10,237	6.3
1895	1,005	14,793	6.8
1902	1,431	17,691	8.1
1913	2,853	30,184	9.5

Sources: Calculated based on data from Spoerer (2004: 108–09) and Hoffmann and Müller (1959: 86–87).

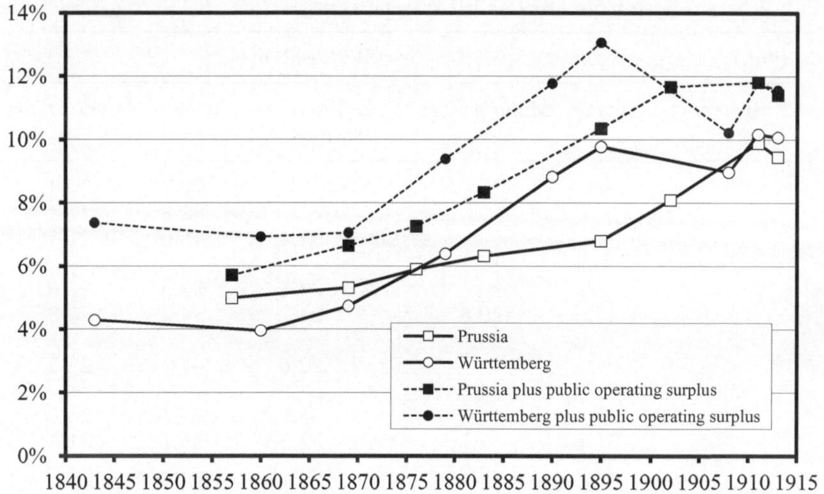

Figure 6.1 Tax load ratios in Prussia and Württemberg from 1843 to 1913 (in percent of national income).

Source: Spoerer (2004: 109, 112, 115).

Notes: All levels of government including *Zollverein*, North German Confederation and Empire. Municipalities include municipal associations.

with the discussion of Prussian railway tariffs, Rainer Fremdling pointed out that their fiscally motivated setting, which was far above the costs, acted like a sales tax (Fremdling 1980: 38; see also Hallerberg 2002). In principle, this applies to all public enterprises: If their profits are higher than their costs, including depreciation and imputed entrepreneurial wages, they can be understood as 'indirect indirect taxes'. In Figure 6.1, the two dotted graphs, therefore illustrate, in addition to the classical tax load ratio, the quotient of taxes plus these 'indirect-indirect taxes' to national income. In Prussia, they played a significant role in the 1880s and early 1890s until the effects of Miquel's tax reforms from 1892 onwards, and can be mainly attributed to the profits of the Prussian railways. Overall, however, the graph reflects the gentle rise in the state share in an overall growing economy as described by Wagner's 'law': as a strongly growing extractive force of a strengthening state in the sense of state capacity.

This impression is reinforced when one realises how small the fiscal importance of the Empire was in quantitative terms (Table 6.3). The effects of the transition from individual statehood to the North German Confederation (1867) or the Empire (1871) differed between Prussia and Württemberg, which is also the result of the high operating surpluses of the Prussian railways that are not recorded in Table 6.3. Despite the fluctuations in the shares of the member states and the Empire, it is clear that the dynamic on

Table 6.3 Shares of different government levels in total tax revenues in Prussia and Württemberg from 1819 to 1913 (in percent)

	Prussia			*Württemberg*		
	Zollverein/ *Reich*	*State*	*Municipalities*	Zollverein/ *Reich*	*State*	*Municipalities*
1819					79.7	20.4
1831					82.8	17.2
1843				32.4	46.0	21.6
1857	21.2	60.4	18.4			
1860				24.1	53.3	22.6
1869	33.8	45.6	20.6	24.7	54.4	20.8
1876	35.6	35.2	29.1			
1879				22.6	47.9	29.5
1883	34.9	30.8	34.2			
1890				35.9	37.7	26.3
1895	44.5	22.8	32.7	32.3	36.1	31.6
1902	39.1	22.4	38.6			
1908				31.1	32.8	36.2
1911	40.1	20.3	39.6	`35.2	32.4	32.4
1913	37.7	20.4	41.9			

Source: Calculated based on data from Spoerer (2004: 109, 117–18).

Table 6.4 Share of total tax revenues of the administrative levels subordinate to the central government (in percent)

State	*Fiscal year*	*Share*
Switzerland	1900	65.3
United States	1902	62.8
Prussia	1911	59.9
Germany	1907	56.6
Great Britain	1904/05	40.2
Italy	1906/07	29.5
France	1902	21.1

Sources: Ritzmann-Blickentorfer (1996: 959); Prussia: Spoerer (2004: 109); all others: Denkschriftenband (1908, Vol. I: 439, 662; Vol. II: 37–38, 97, 143–44, 436).

the revenue side (the mirror image applies to expenditure as well) was at the municipal level, which was able to expand its share significantly after the foundation of the Empire.

Before the First World War, Switzerland and the United States, both of which were decidedly federal states, were the only two developed states in the world in which the share of public finances accounted for by the subordinate levels of government was as significant as in Germany (Table 6.4). This emphasises that the Empire was a federal state with comparatively weak fiscal centralisation.

5 Fiscal regime, industrialisation, and economic growth

Economic history has long examined the extent to which the fiscal regime promoted German industrialisation, either directly or through other channels, and thus contributed to the strong economic growth since the 1880s at the latest. Eckart Schremmer argued that German fiscal regimes have generally been favourable towards industrialisation (Schremmer 1985; 1987; 1989: 484–89; for Prussia, see also Lee 1975: 153–78). Object taxes, which formed the backbone of tax revenues in almost all German states until the late nineteenth century, had been created in times when agriculture accounted for the largest share of value-added and economic growth was hardly visible. In a static society, it may have made sense to subject direct taxes to a system of repartition with revenue ceilings and fixed sectoral shares, as was the case in Württemberg, for example. However, for a dynamic society, increasingly driven by a burgeoning manufacturing sector, the traditional tax system was outdated. The new trade taxes that many German states introduced in the 1810s and 1820s taxed businesses according to visible characteristics (type of industry, number of employees, etc.). However, these were only loosely correlated with productivity and/or profitability. Most national business taxes (such as those in Prussia and Württemberg) were regressive and rewarded the substitution of labour for capital.

Therefore, it has been argued that tax systems weighed more heavily on the agricultural sector than on the manufacturing sector and within the latter, favoured capital-intensive enterprises. Whereas this was certainly beneficial for manufacturing and industrialisation in the narrow sense of the term, it is not clear a priori whether it was really beneficial for the German economy as a whole. By international standards, the share of manufacturing in the total German output was unusually high. Before the First World War, no European economy had such a high share of manufacturing as Germany, at 44 percent (Maddison 1992: 248–49; Mitchell 1993: 912–17). It was not without reason that Germany was still characterised as being over-industrialised in the late twentieth century. In this respect, it is not immediately apparent to what extent an intended or unintended fiscal sparing of the manufacturing sector made macroeconomic sense.

Moreover, it is not entirely clear, whether, in this race between sectoral economic performance and taxation, the tax system really burdened agricultural production more than manufacturing and services (Spoerer 2004: 98). After 1815, every major Prussian tax reform (except the 1861 land tax reform) shifted the tax burden westward and thus to the more industrialised provinces. To assess whether taxes fell more on the agricultural sector than on manufacturing, regional value-added data broken down by sector would be necessary. However, such data are not available. It is therefore not clear which forces prevailed in terms of actual taxation: the political influence of aristocracy with its large agricultural estates (cf. e.g. for Prussia Hallerberg 2002) or the economic dynamism of industrial entrepreneurs. The former tried to shift the tax burden onto the booming industrial sector through reforms, whereas the latter managed to dilute the effective tax burden through growth.

For Württemberg, which is well documented in terms of data, the available information allows a comparison between sectoral economic growth and tax burden. If local taxes are included, it becomes clear that they placed an additional burden on manufacturing and thus possibly overcompensated for the effects of state taxes that were strongly oriented towards agriculture. The analysis of the combined effects of state and local taxes at best confirms the hypothesis that the Württemberg tax system favoured manufacturing in the second quarter of the nineteenth century, prior to the industrialisation of the state. After the middle of the century, the state and municipal tax system succeeded in keeping up with the economic power of booming trade. It is therefore questionable whether the tax system in Württemberg actually favoured manufacturing (Spoerer 2010: 123–25). Whether this finding is transferable to other member states cannot be determined at this stage. In any case, it underlines the importance of including municipal finances in the analysis.

If one insists on establishing a connection between the fiscal regime and state capacity, industrialisation, or economic growth, it is perhaps the growth of municipal finances that is relevant here. The rapid socioeconomic structural change that Germany experienced from around the middle of the nineteenth century in the context of industrialisation led to considerable challenges for municipal finances. First, the strong population growth and the accompanying urbanisation should be mentioned here. Whereas in 1852 (1871) there were only 2 (8) cities with more than 100,000 inhabitants in Germany, by 1910, there were already 48 (Guinnane 2003: 51). This led to challenges for the school system and public infrastructure such as street lighting, water, gas and electricity supply, and local public transport. Many of these tasks required the construction of local networks whose cost structure had the character of a natural monopoly, that is, it would have been economically inefficient to build a competing parallel network. It is therefore not surprising that the public sector did not only want to keep this business from private monopolists for regulatory reasons (or at least not entrust it to private enterprise without regulation), but also because it served as a convenient source of income for itself (cf. Chapter 4 of this volume).

These new tasks and expenses arose to a disproportionate extent in the municipalities, many of which were experiencing rapid urbanisation. The pronounced German fiscal federalism allowed for the disproportionate increase in municipal taxes in the second half of the nineteenth century, as shown in Table 6.3. It was perhaps economically helpful that German municipalities received a large share of tax revenues directly and could spend them on infrastructural measures that helped the local economy to a much greater extent than in other, more centralised countries (except the US). This can be seen as a strength of the German fiscal regime. Under certain circumstances, this brought about positive competition, which was not possible in states with strong central finances. The existence of tax competition has been empirically shown for the greater Berlin area (Spoerer 2004: 190–92). Beyond that, however, the link between strong municipal finances and economic growth must remain speculation.

6 Conclusion

The preceding discussion has shown that the sufficient conditions for an effective state elaborated by Dincecco did not exist in the case of the German Empire, or existed only to a limited extent. To what extent the *Reichstag* had complete de facto parliamentary control, including the right of veto, over Imperial finances is not entirely clear, as the discussion on hard vs. soft budget constraint shows. Although the centralisation of public finances was constantly urged by many experts, often with the same arguments as Dincecco, it clearly did not take place. Rather, it was the municipalities that were able to increase their share of public finances at the expense of the member states and the Empire. If Prussia, the largest member state, had no interest in ceding lucrative tax revenues to the Empire, it is understandable that the pronounced fiscal federalism continued to exist. Only under the impression of the lost war and because of the need to mobilise resources for the payment of reparations to be paid by the Empire, did its finance minister Matthias Erzberger push through a far-reaching centralisation of the finances of the Empire in 1919/20, almost in a rush. The conclusion is that the German fiscal regime had no decisive influence on the founding of the Empire (nation-building) or on the economic or political consolidation of the Empire (state capacity).

Accordingly, an interaction with the accelerating industrialisation after the founding of the Empire and especially after 1879 can at best only be grasped in an outline. Rising incomes allowed greater leeway for tax skimming, so that the tax ratio doubled in the second half of the nineteenth century from originally about five to about ten percent. To what extent public finances, or even just the tax system, had an impact on economic growth is not really tangible, particularly given the precarious data situation for municipal finances. Public spending on utilities and transport infrastructure was certainly sensible, but assessing whether the extent was adequate is beyond today's research capabilities. The same applies to the effects of changes in the tax system on economic incentives, which may perhaps be determined by future microeconom(etr)ic studies at the level of individual states or municipalities.

Note

1 Schremmer points to the many uncertainties in his database; however, at least the magnitudes for Prussia and the Empire match the tax load ratios in Spoerer (2004: 115).

References

Besley, T. and Persson, T. (2013) 'Taxation and development', in M. Auerbach et al. (eds), *Handbook of Public Economics*, Amsterdam: Elsevier, Vol. 5, pp. 51–110.

Blankart, C. B. (2007) *Föderalismus in Deutschland und in Europa*, Baden-Baden: Nomos.

Bräunig, C. (2016) *Herbert Dorn (1887–1957): Pionier und Wegbereiter im internationalen Steuerrecht*, Tübingen: Mohr Siebeck.

Brandt, L., Ma, D. and Rawski, T. G. (2014) 'From divergence to convergence: reevaluating the history behind China's economic boom', *Journal of Economic Literature*, Vol. 52 (2): 45–123.

Broadberry, St., Guan, H., Li, D. D. (2018) 'China, Europe, and the Great Divergence: a study in historical national accounting, 980–1850', *Journal of Economic History*, Vol. 78 (4): 955–1000.

Clauss, Th. (1888) 'Das Reichsgesetz vom 13. Mai 1870 wegen Beseitigung der Doppelbesteuerung unter vergleichender Berücksichtigung des schweizer Bundesrechtes', *Finanz-Archiv*, Vol. 5 (1): 139–97.

Dincecco, M. (2015) 'The rise of effective states in Europe', *Journal of Economic History*, Vol. 75 (3): 901–18.

Dincecco, M. and Katz, G. (2016) 'State capacity and long-run economic performance', *Economic Journal*, Vol. 126 (590): 189–218.

Ferguson, N. (1994) 'Public finance and national security: the domestic origins of the First World War revisited', *Past and Present*, Vol. 142: 141–68.

Ferguson, N. (1998) *The Pity of War*, London: Allen Lane.

Fremdling, R. (1980) 'Freight rates and state budget: the role of the national Prussian railways 1880–1913', *Journal of European Economic History*, Vol. 9 (1): 21–39.

Gerloff, W. (1909) 'Beiträge zur Reichsfinanzreform', *Jahrbücher für Nationalökonomie und Statistik*, Vol. 37 (4): 433–68.

Guinnane, T. W. (2003) 'Population and the economy in Germany, 1800–1990', in S. Ogilvie and R. Overy (eds), *Germany: A New Social and Economic History Since 1800*, London: Arnold, pp. 35–70.

Hallerberg, M. S. (2002) 'On the political economy of taxation in Prussia', *Jahrbuch für Wirtschaftsgeschichte*, Vol. 43 (2): 11–33.

Heckel, Max von (1911) *Lehrbuch der Finanzwissenschaft*, Vol. 2, Leipzig: Hirschfeld.

Hefeker, C. (2001) 'The agony of central power: fiscal federalism in the German Reich', *European Review of Economic History*, Vol. 5 (1): 119–41.

Hoffmann, W. (1965) *Das Wachstum der deutschen Wirtschaft seit der Mitte des 19. Jahrhunderts*, Berlin: Springer.

Hoffmann, W. G. and Müller, J. H. (1959) *Das deutsche Volkseinkommen 1851–1957*, Tübingen: Mohr.

Kaiserliches Statistisches Amt (ed) (1880–1914) *Statistisches Jahrbuch für das Deutsche Reich*, Berlin: Puttkammer & Mühlbrecht.

Lee, W. R. (1975) 'Tax structure and economic growth in Germany (1750–1850)', *Journal of European Economic History*, Vol. 4 (1): 153–78.

Maddison, Angus (1992) *Dynamic Forces in Capitalist Development: A Long-Run Comparative View*, Oxford: Oxford University Press.

Mitchell, B. R. (1993) *International Historical Statistics: Europe 1750–1988*, 3rd. edition, New York: Stockdon.

O'Brien, P. K. and Hunt, P. (1999) 'Excises and the rise of the fiscal state in England, 1586–1688', in W. M. Ormrod, M. Bonney and R. Bonney (eds), *Crises,*

Revolutions and Self-Sustained Growth: Essays in European Fiscal History, 1130–1830, Stamford: Paul Watkins Publishing, pp. 414–26.

Pomeranz, K. (2000) *The Great Divergence: China, Europe, and the Making of the Modern World Economy*, Princeton, NJ: Princeton University Press.

Reichsschatzamt (ed) (1908) *Denkschriftenband zur Begründung des Entwurfs eines Gesetzes betreffend Änderungen im Finanzwesen*, Berlin: Guttentag.

Ritschl, A. and Spoerer, M. (1997) 'Das Bruttosozialprodukt in Deutschland nach den amtlichen Volkseinkommens- und Sozialproduktsstatistiken 1901–1995', *Jahrbuch für Wirtschaftsgeschichte*, Vol. 38 (2): 27–54.

Ritzmann-Blickentorfer, H. (ed) (1996) *Historische Statistik der Schweiz*, Zürich: Chronos.

Schremmer, E. (1985) 'Föderativer Staatsverbund, öffentliche Finanzen und Industrialisierung in Deutschland', in H. Kiesewetter and R. Fremdling (eds), *Staat, Region und Industrialisierung*, Ostfildern: Scripta Mercaturae, pp. 3–65.

Schremmer, E. (1987) 'Die badische Gewerbesteuer und die Kapitalbildung in gewerblichen Anlagen und Vorräten in Baden und Deutschland, 1815 bis 1913', *Vierteljahrschrift für Sozial- und Wirtschaftsgeschichte*, Vol. 74 (1): 18–61.

Schremmer, E. (1989) 'Taxation and public finance: Britain, France, and Germany', in *Cambridge Economic History of Europe*, Vol. 8, Cambridge: Cambridge University Press, pp. 315–494.

Spoerer, M. (2004) *Steuerlast, Steuerinzidenz und Steuerwettbewerb: Verteilungswirkungen der Besteuerung in Preußen und Württemberg (1815–1913)*, Berlin: Akademie.

Spoerer, M. (2010), 'The evolution of public finances in nineteenth-century Germany', in J. L. Cardoso and P. Lains (eds), *Paying for the Liberal State: The Rise of Public Finance in Nineteenth Century Europe*, Cambridge: Cambridge University Press, pp. 103–31.

Teschemacher, H. (1915) *Reichsfinanzreform und Innere Reichspolitik 1906–1913: Ein geschichtliches Vorspiel zu den Ideen von 1914*, Berlin: Springer.

Ullmann, H.-P. (2005) *Der deutsche Steuerstaat: Geschichte der öffentlichen Finanzen vom 18. Jahrhundert bis heute*, München: Beck.

Ullmann, H.-P. (2009) *Staat und Schulden: Die Geschichte der öffentlichen Finanzen in Deutschland seit dem 18. Jahrhundert*, Göttingen: Vandenhoeck & Ruprecht.

Von Kruedener, J. (1987) 'The Franckenstein paradox in the intergovernmental fiscal relations of Imperial Germany', in P.-C. Witt (ed), *Wealth and Taxation in Central Europe: The History and Sociology of Public Finance*, New York: Berg, pp. 111–23.

Vries, P. H. H. (2013) *Escaping Poverty: The Origins of Modern Economic Growth*, Göttingen: Vandenhoeck & Ruprecht.

Wagner, A. (1879) 'Ueber die schwebenden deutschen Finanzfragen', *Zeitschrift für die gesamte Staatswissenschaft*, Vol. 35 (1): 68–114.

Wagner, A. (1908) *Die Reichsfinanznot und die Pflichten des deutschen Volks wie seiner politischen Parteien: Ein Mahnwort eines alten Mannes*, Berlin: Puttkammer & Mühlbrecht.

Witt, P.-C. (1970) *Die Finanzpolitik des Deutschen Reiches von 1903 bis 1913: Eine Studie zur Innenpolitik des Wilhelminischen Deutschland*, Lübeck: Matthiesen.

Ziblatt, D. (2008) 'Does landholding inequality block democratization? A test of the 'bread and democracy' thesis and the case of Prussia', *World Politics*, Vol. 60 (4): 610–41.

7 Nation-state formation and market integration

Postal service, telegraph system, and railways

Sebastian Till Braun and Jan-Otmar Hesse

The founding of the German Empire in 1871 not only concluded a process of political unification but also created an economic area. Although this German economic area continued to exhibit institutional and organisational disruptions and price differences, it also eliminated numerous administrative and technical barriers to trade. This chapter discusses the extent to which the administrative and technical unification in the fields of communications and transport achieved by the founding of the nation-state created a more significant economic area that paved the way for modern economic growth by accelerating structural change and eliminating frictions in trade. We examine the period from about 1840 to 1890, drawing mainly on findings from the extant literature. In a brief introductory section, we first outline the broad developmental trends in market integration in Germany in the decades before the founding of the German Empire. In the second section, we trace the administrative unification process for communications and transport from the middle of the nineteenth century and describe the structure of institutions that emerged in the course of the founding of the Empire. Finally, we attempt to identify the effects that the founding of the nation-state had on communication and transport.

1 Market integration in the nineteenth century

The process of globalisation in the nineteenth century was characterised by the increasing integration of the goods markets both within and across countries. Whereas at least some German cities like Hamburg and Königsberg were already closely integrated into the international goods markets by the middle of the century (Uebele 2011),[1] the integration of the German internal market, which will be the subject of this chapter, lagged behind that of many other countries at the end of the nineteenth century (Jacks 2005). Based on trade data for agricultural and various industrial goods, Nikolaus Wolf (2009) concludes that the process of internal market integration remained incomplete in the nineteenth century. Cultural and especially language barriers, administrative differences, and topography continued to form de facto trade

DOI: 10.4324/9781003283430-9

barriers within the internal market of the German Empire on the eve of World War I. The progress in market integration to be considered in the following section must be seen against the background of this incomplete result.

One of the key drivers of internal market integration was the abolition of customs duties, which was gradually implemented from the Restoration period onwards. The founding of a customs union—the *Zollverein*—in 1834 and its subsequent expansion represented an essential step towards creating a uniform and free internal market in the later German Empire. Many historians believe that the *Zollverein* helped the option of so-called Lesser Germany (*kleindeutsche Lösung*) to the founding of the nation-state achieve a breakthrough (see Chapter 3 of this volume). This argument, however, does not refer to the effects of market integration, but rather to the institutional course set by the founding of the *Zollverein*, which comprised a common customs parliament, a statistical authority, and a financial administration for the distribution of customs revenues among the member states (Hahn 1984). Recent studies in the field of economic history have sought to quantify the effects that the establishment of the *Zollverein* had on market integration by studying commodity price convergence. Keller and Shiue (2014) show that from 1820 to 1880, bilateral grain price gaps among 40 German cities declined by about 70 percent. Membership in the *Zollverein* reduced regional differences in grain prices by almost a third.

The methodological difficulties in interpreting commodity price convergence as market integration are well known (Federico 2012). It may also be debated whether the integration of grain markets is a meaningful measure for the economic effects of customs policy during a period of industrialisation in which a considerable proportion of grain was exported (Wehler 1987: 137–39, 644–45). The importance of the founding of the *Zollverein* for market integration has been demonstrated using various methods (Ploeckl 2013) and will not be disputed here.

The difficulty of precisely determining the integration effect that emanated from the customs union lies not least in the parallel development of a transport and communications infrastructure that also promoted the integration of markets, but whose precise effects have not yet been fully elucidated, if only because the multiplicity of different small-scale networks and regulations makes a conclusive analysis difficult. Starting as early as in the first half of the nineteenth century—and thus before the age of the German railways—the development of the road network promoted the integration of grain markets (Uebele and Gallardo Alberrán 2015). The contribution of the railways to the reduction of regional price differences may have been even more significant and may have even exceeded the contribution of the *Zollverein* (Keller and Shiue 2020).[2] Thus, the remainder of this chapter focuses on the economic consequences of the development of a transport and communications infrastructure and of the unification of the related services in the context of the foundation of the German nation-state.

2 Administrative unification of communication and transport

The rise of nation-states in the nineteenth century was paralleled by the development of large, uniform transport and communications networks across Europe. The creation of the German network was in itself a project related to nation-building, which is evident from the construction of the large canals and the militarily significant railway lines on the border with France. Network creation was an early project of internationalisation, because from the very beginning, the path to success could only be achieved through multilateral cooperation. This was especially true for the territory of the German Confederation, which was characterised by relatively small states. As early as 1866, the coordination and integration of transport and communications networks were thus discussed at length in the parliament of the German Confederation; these discussions have rightly been interpreted as early forms of international cooperation in these fields, even if they ultimately led to the founding of a German nation-state, which excluded Austria (Weichlein 2004). From the middle of the century onward, therefore, there had already been numerous mergers and instances of cooperation. What follows addresses the reorganisation of postal, telegraph, and railway services to contextualise the institutional turning point as marked by the foundation of the German Empire.

In the early nineteenth century, there were still 31 independent postal administrations in the German Confederation, which merged into 17 by 1850. In the first half of the century, some territories had ceded their sovereign postal administration to the noble family of Thurn and Taxis, which had established itself as a dominant provider of postal services to the Holy Roman Empire from the sixteenth century onward (Behringer 1990). Thus, with the outbreak of the German-Austrian War in 1866, there were only 14 independent postal administrations left in the territory of the later German Empire, namely Prussia, Saxony, Mecklenburg-Schwerin, Mecklenburg-Strelitz, Oldenburg, Brunswick, Lübeck, Bremen, Hamburg, Württemberg, Baden, Bavaria, and the Thurn and Taxis administration based in Frankfurt am Main. The franchise of the latter on the territory of the later German Empire extended to the Hessian duchies, various Thuringian dominions, the two principalities of Lippe, and the Hanseatic cities (Schilly 1983; Grillmeyer 2005). The transport of mail and parcels across national borders was organised through different treaty systems containing detailed provisions on postal traffic, where the distribution of revenue between two states always played a major role. These bilateral treaties were in effect for the medium term of 10 or 20 years. Prussia, probably the best studied in this area, concluded numerous such treaties across Europe (Hesse 1997).

For the territory of the German Confederation, the German-Austrian Postal Union Treaty was concluded in 1850. This multilateral treaty system, in which the member countries agreed on standards and fee-splitting, considerably simplified the postal services. However, inter-regional mail traffic was still subject to a basic fee based on distance, which was divided between the contracting parties for each individual letter and parcel. The contracting parties could not agree upon the distribution of the common revenues among member countries, such as, according to the model of the *Zollverein* of 1834 (Stephan 1859). This proved even more difficult than arriving at an agreement regarding the distribution of revenues in the *Zollverein*, as the revenues accrued when a letter was posted in a local post office and would then have had to be transferred from there to a centralised office. With a few exceptions (Prussia was one of them), the distance-based postage system applied to domestic traffic, and the territories united in the Postal Union initially even demanded transit fees from the other members if, for example, a letter had to be transported from Prussia to Austria via the territory of Bavaria (Benz 2013). This led to complex organisational processes because the mail had to be shipped to a specialised border office *(Auslandspostamt)* and handed over to the neighbouring border post office, typically causing the items to take detours.

The wars accompanying unification since 1866 resolved this complicated situation within a few years. After defeating its opponents in the Prussian-Austrian War (1866), Prussia appropriated the Saxon postal administration without compensation and integrated it into the Prussian postal administration. The military occupation of Frankfurt in the autumn of 1866 was paralleled by the occupation of the Thurn and Taxis headquarters and the subsequent takeover of the postal administration. Heinrich Stephan, the young postal officer who carried out this takeover, exuberantly compared it to the Prussian victory in the battle of Königgrätz (in a letter to the Prussian Post Office from September 20, 1866, quoted following Dallmeier 1990: 241). These events were major and long-overdue components of modernisation in the field of communications. The member states of the North German Confederation, including Prussia, transferred postal sovereignty to the new federal administration on 1 January 1868. The latter introduced a distance-independent uniform postage rate in the new territory, modelled on Rowland Hill's Penny Post reforms in Britain (1840), with surpluses from postal traffic going to the federal budget. When the Empire was founded in 1871, only the postal administrations of Bavaria and Württemberg remained independent, whereas that of Baden was integrated into the new postal administration of Imperial Germany in 1872. The Imperial Postal Service (*Reichspostverwaltung)* was in charge of the entire German Empire, except the territories of the kingdoms of Bavaria and Württemberg; contemporary administrative language designed the territory under the authority of the Imperial Postal Services as *Reichspostgebiet* (Imperial Postal Territory). The independence of the Bavarian and Württemberg postal administrations was related to their internal organisation and financial independence from the Imperial budget. At the same time, the tariff structure was identical to that of the *Reichspost*, and the Imperial Constitution expressly stipulated that only the *Reichspost* administration was to represent the German Empire externally in postal matters (Schilly 1984; Hesse 2001). The founding of the Empire saw a considerable step forward in the field of communications, which included a steadily growing share of parcels and samples. Until the 1850s, the postal service was a sovereign institution meant for exchanging messages, especially local ones, subsidised by a distance-based tariff at the expense of cross-border communication and ultimately considered a source of income for princely budgets. From 1868 onwards, a national communication system emerged that was operated primarily to promote the economy (Stephan 1859: 381). This system was not yet fully unified; parcels were still predominantly priced according to distance, and national postal administrations in Saxony, for example, occasionally resisted subordination to a Prussian-dominated Imperial Postal Administration. Nevertheless, this standardisation led to a huge increase in the performance of postal traffic, as the following section shows.

The development of telegraphy in the territory of the German Confederation followed a very similar course only in terms of results. In 1868, it was centralised as a federal administration under the decisive influence of the Prussian administration. In 1876, it was merged with the postal administration to form the *Reichs-Post- und Telegraphenverwaltung* (Imperial Postal and Telegraph Administration) in a national organisation, which was finally placed on an equal footing with the other imperial offices in 1880 with the designation *Reichspostamt* (Imperial Post Office; Hesse 2001). However, the history of the development of telegraphy is closely linked to its strategic military importance, which is why it was often—as in Prussia, for example—initially subordinate to the War Ministry. This responsibility was concerned on the one hand with the strategic importance of the lines in the event of war, and on the other with state control of communications. With the transfer of the system to civilian use from 1850 onwards, Prussia and the other states were able to follow the example of the postal service; at the same time as the German-Austrian Postal Union Treaty was signed in 1850, a German-Austrian Telegraph Union was also founded in the German Confederation. In contrast to the postal service, this association was concerned with administrative issues and technical standards (Reindl 1993). As different federal states used different technological systems and, in some cases, other telegraphic languages, it was quite common before the founding of the German Empire for telegrams to be stopped at state borders, written down, and handed over to the telegraph official of the neighbouring state, who then fed it back into their own telegraph system. Not least due to the great importance of telegraphy in the Austro-German and Franco-Prussian Wars (Kaufmann 1996), the military's influence in the telegraph administration, which in Prussia had been formally subordinate to the Ministry of Trade and Commerce since 1850, remained strong until the founding of the German Empire. The telegraph offices had indeed been largely merged with the post offices since the 1850s. However, the administrative leadership of the two authorities remained strictly separate until 1876. Traditionally, a high-ranking military officer headed the Prussian telegraph administration. It was only in the course of the reorganisation of the

Empire's domestic administration, which was connected by the chancellor's political shift from liberalism to conservatism that the two authorities were finally merged in 1876, with the much larger postal administration dominating (Hesse 2001: 56–57).

In addition to the importance of the military in telegraph administration, two other important differences from postal administration should be highlighted: First, telegraphy was a contemporary cutting-edge technology, a highly dynamic area in the nascent electrical industry in which different companies competed for technological leadership. Siemens & Halske developed into a de facto monopoly supplier of telegraph equipment, not only for the Prussian telegraph administration, but also in Russia and Bavaria, only initially competing with equipment provided by Morse (Bähr 2016). The technological standardisation that was important for the erection of networks in the future was, in many cases, not achieved through telegraph contracts but by the monopolisation of the supplier. A similar process took place with respect to telegraph cables, for which Felten & Guilleaume, a company based in Cologne, rose to the position of the dominant supplier (Wessel 1983). Second, immediately after its introduction in the 1840s, telegraphy paved the way to a global market in which competition for the first connection between England and the USA played a central role. The first functioning cable connection in 1857 initially lasted only a few days. It was not until 1866 that the connection was installed permanently, with a consortium of British banks and industrial companies using Siemens' deep-sea cable patent to lay a cable from the Siemens factory in England—a key event, as it were, in the so-called first wave of globalisation (Holtorf 2013).

Whereas the integration of postal communications was about the administrative unification of a personnel-intensive and cumbersome organisational structure characterised by numerous local patriotic resistances, telegraphy meant the establishment of a technical communications network based on a new and dynamic technology that was conceived from the very beginning as a global infrastructure to which the German networks were to be directly connected. Pragmatic interests in speedy communication links were mixed with imperial needs, especially England's, to control global communication (Müller 2016). However, despite all the differences in the emergence of these communication networks and their economic structures, they were always overlapping communication systems based on the division of labour. Their effect on the German economy's long-term, structural economic change can therefore only be assessed if both networks are considered simultaneously, and even ultimately only if the link with a third communication network, the railways, is taken into account.

The history of the railway networks in Germany has been examined and narrated independently of the history of post and telegraphy. Given the importance of railways as a leading sector for German industrialisation, this certainly made sense (Fremdling 1985). However, for the question that is examined here, of whether the administrative integration of infrastructure had long-term impacts on Germany's economic development, the separation cannot be maintained. The railways not only assumed a central function for logistics in the key sectors of the German economy by transporting bulk goods such as coal, steel products, and grain but also, via the railway mail service, for the delivery of numerous small commercial products and consumer goods, as well as letter post itself (Sautter 1951). There were close links between the telegraph and railway networks. The railways used telegraphs, especially in the pioneering phase of the often single-track lines, to coordinate train traffic, so that they had built up a dense network, which, in Prussia, for example, had also been available for public use since the 1850s. It was not until the monopoly legislation after the founding of the German Empire that this public use of railway telegraphs was restricted: Only telegrams from passengers could be carried. The economic imbalance in the state telegraphy had made this step necessary.

The administrative integration of national railway systems is widely known, and its history has often been told (Fremdling 1985; Heinze and Kill 1988; Ziegler 1996). A short version will suffice for our purpose here. The railways first emerged as small island networks more or less simultaneously in different states, either at the initiative of local governments or by industrial interest groups. These island networks grew together in the 1840s, with state- and privately-owned railway companies coexisting, a very liberal system from today's perspective. At the time of the founding of the German Empire, there were 63 railway companies. In the course of the founding of the Empire, Bismarck tried, as is well known, to nationalise and centralise the multitude of different railway administrations in a national railway system. The takeover of Alsace-Lorraine after the Franco-Prussian War offered the opportunity to transfer the railways there to Imperial ownership. For that purpose, the *Reichseisenbahnamt* (Imperial Railway Office) was founded in 1873 as the supreme administrative authority. According to Bismarck's plans, the other railway administrations were to be merged into this authority. However, his plans did not succeed, as even the Prussian railway administration opposed them (Weichlein 2004: 60). Thus, there was an astonishing coexistence of state and private railway companies in the German Empire, which were transferred into state ownership in the two decades after the founding of the German Empire.

The *Königlich Preußische Staatsbahn* (Royal Prussian State Railways) was a decisive player here. Created by the determined state railways policy under Minister of Trade August von der Heydt, the company grew by taking over private railways and later, during the Prussian expansion, also by incorporating, for example, the railway networks of Hanover and Nassau. After the founding of the German Empire, the large private railway corporations that still existed, such as the important *Köln-Mindener Eisenbahn-Gesellschaft*, which operated several long-distance lines in north-western Germany, were taken over by the Prussian State Railways. Whereas at the time of the founding of the German Empire, only a third of the Prussian railway network was operated by the state, the Prussian State Railways controlled over 90 percent of all railway lines there at the end of the Bismarck era. After further nationalisation and takeovers, the administration of the Prussian railways, which was by then subordinate to the Ministry of Public Works, merged with the Hessian administration to form the Prussian-Hessian Railway Administration, which, before the First World War, was by far the largest company in the German Empire. With around 400,000 employees, it was ahead of the Imperial Postal Administration, which had over 270,000 employees. The route network of the Prussian-Hessian railways alone covered almost 30,000 km on the eve of the First World War, just one-tenth less than today's route network of *Deutsche Bahn*, which is responsible for a much larger area.

In contrast to the postal service and telegraphy, the founding of the German Empire did not lead to the rapid and comprehensive integration of the railway networks. As late as the 1890s, there were still countless reports from rail travellers complaining about the poor organisation of rail transport, which was caused by changing and often non-transparent responsibilities (Weichlein 2004: 47). Post and telegraphy were in state hands everywhere. When the Empire was founded, ultimately, only competing national sovereign rights had to be overcome or, at most, recalcitrant regional administrations had to be integrated into the Imperial administration. In contrast, the network integration of rail transport touched upon a process of organisational standardisation that was not completed until the *Reichsbahn* was founded in 1920. Naturally, major friction in the field of freight and passenger transport by rail remained even after the foundation of the Empire. Nevertheless, the 1870s, with the fundamental regulatory decision in favour of the state railway monopoly, were of decisive importance for the further development of the German railway system (Ziegler 1996: 279–81).

3 Economic effects of network formation

It is a basic principle of modern information economics that the enlargement of an information network leads to a disproportionate increase in utility, because not only the newly added users of the network experience an increase in utility, but also all existing users in the network because of the larger number of possible connections (Varian et al. 2004). Such 'positive network externalities' can only take effect if the network itself is frictionless and barrier-free, which can neither be claimed for the railway network nor for post and telegraphy after the founding of the Empire, as shown above. The network externalities, which theoretically should have resulted from the massive expansion of the communications networks after the founding of the Empire, are for this reason alone by no means necessarily present. Above all, however, they are not at all easy to prove. The difficulty here lies primarily in the fact that the period between the 1850s and 1890s was, in many ways, a dynamic time. Emigration and internal migration turned the entire country upside down; a quarter of the population no longer lived where it had been born in 1890. In previously predominantly rural regions, breathtakingly fast-growing industrial regions sprang up, primarily in the Ruhr area. Within just two decades, industrial employment had replaced agricultural employment in terms of volume and importance. Urbanisation changed the everyday lives of large sections of the population. This list could be continued. How can the aspect of network formation be filtered out from the multitude of these effects, all of which also influenced the structure and use of communication and transport networks? The patchy data complicates the question further. In this respect, the results discussed below must remain provisional.

For railway construction, several empirical studies show that connection to the railway network had a considerable positive effect on the city or region in question. The methodological challenge of these studies is to distinguish correlation from causality (Fishlow 1965). For example, a positive correlation between rail access and regional economic development may be evidence of the positive impact of rail. However, such a correlation may also result from the fact that large and rapidly growing cities and regions were connected to the railway network first. The railway connection would then be a consequence—and not a cause—of economic growth. To overcome this problem of reverse causality, Erik Hornung, in a recent study of Prussia, exploits the fact that the railway network first connected important cities (e.g. in Prussia Berlin with Potsdam and Magdeburg or Berlin with Hamburg). These cities were mostly connected by direct routes because of the high construction costs and the state of railway technology. Consequently, less important cities that lay along this direct route between two nodes were also connected to the network. Hornung shows that annual population growth in cities that were connected to the Prussian railway network this way—'by chance', so to speak—was one to two percentage points higher than in comparable cities without a railway connection (Hornung 2015). However, the study only quantifies the effect until 1871 and not thereafter.

In a recent study of Württemberg, Sebastian Braun and Richard Franke (2022) conclude that railway access increased population growth by 0.3–0.4 percentage points per year between 1843 and 1871 relative to non-connected communities. Therefore, the effect appears much smaller in Württemberg than in the larger Prussian network. The marked differences between the results may indicate the importance of positive network externalities, which were less pronounced in the smaller Württemberg network. However, they could also indicate that rural and less densely populated communities, the focus of Braun and Franke's analysis, benefited less from the railway than urban regions. Braun and Franke (2022) show that the growth-enhancing effect of the railways was significantly larger in initially more populous and industrial parishes. Thus, the railways reinforced regional disparities (Voigt 1953; Huber 1979). Consistent with the results for Württemberg, Büchel and Kyburz (2020) recently demonstrated that Switzerland's mostly rural railway communities grew only moderately faster than did comparable communities without a railway connection.

However, the modernisation thrust of the railway should by no means be underestimated. Braun and Franke (2022) conclude that by 1895, the number of industrial workers in Württemberg's railway communities was almost a fifth higher than in communities without railway access. The employment effect was particularly pronounced in the textile and machine building industries. Here, the railway connection increased the number of employees by more than 50 percent. The railway accelerated the transition from an agrarian to an industrial society.

It would now be worth considering ways to include in these regional studies the potential network effects created by the foundation of the Empire. First, the growth effects of the railway before and after 1871 could be compared. Table 7.1 shows the impact of railway access on annual population growth for different periods. Between 1855 and 1871, municipalities that received access to the railway until 1854 grew on average 0.51 percentage points faster than municipalities without a railway connection. The yearly growth impulse dropped slightly to 0.43 percentage points in 1871–90 after the Empire's founding, and then rose significantly around the turn of the century (to 0.81 percentage points in 1890–1910). Thus, in the two decades following 1871, no major additional growth impulse was visible, at least for Württemberg. However, such impulses could be far more pronounced in other regions, namely in areas that were integrated into the Prussian railway network during the founding of the Empire, Hanover or Saxony, for example. Württemberg could serve as an ex-negativo case study. The growth effects were probably smaller than in Prussia because the positive network externalities did not materialise to the same degree.

However, the observations for Württemberg coincide with the development of passenger and freight traffic on German railways as a whole (see Table 7.2). After strong demand impulses emanated again from the railways during the *Gründerboom* (Founders' Boom), the percentage growth in transport volume weakened noticeably after the *Gründerkrise* (Founders' Crisis) in 1873 (Fremdling 1985). Freight transport prices hardly fell after 1880

Table 7.1 Growth effect of the connection to the Württemberg railway in 1845–54

Period	*Annual growth effects (Population, in percentage points)*
1843–1855	0.32
1855–1871	0.51
1871–1880	0.46
1880–1890	0.41
1890–1900	0.69
1900–1910	0.92

Source: Own calculation based on data from Braun and Franke (2022); winner versus runners-up sample, see Braun and Franke (2022) for details. Estimates are based on a panel regression model with time and community fixed effects.

Table 7.2 Average annual growth rates of traffic on German railways 1850–1910

Time period	*Passenger transport (passenger kilometres)*	*Freight (ton-kilometres)*
1850–1860	8.3%	18.7%
1860–1870	9.9%	13.4%
1870–1873	8.6%	19.6%
1873–1880	1.9%	3.8%
1880–1890	5.6%	5.5%
1890–1900	6.0%	4.6%
1900–1910	5.8%	4.1%

Source: Own calculation based on Fremdling (1985).

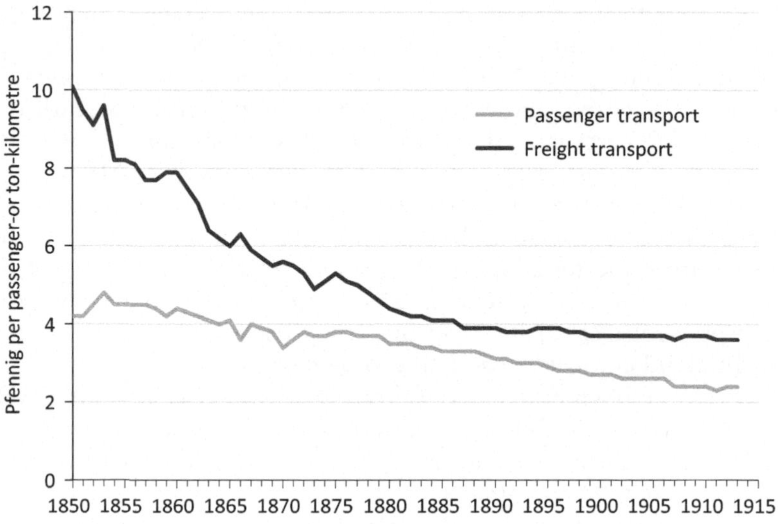

Figure 7.1 Railway transport rates, 1850–1913.
Source: Own presentation based on Fremdling (1985).

(Figure 7.1). The railways lost their status as a leading sector. It is, therefore, difficult to extract from these macroeconomic figures a significant growth impulse from the founding of the Empire. However, these considerations do not involve a counterfactual comparison. It thus remains unclear how the growth effects of the railways would have developed without the founding of the Empire.

The difficulties in efficiently merging the national railway administrations may explain why the founding of the German Empire did not increase the railway's growth-enhancing effect. As we have seen, this administrative integration was far more successful in the cases of post and telegraphy. However, comparable analyses of the growth impulses are yet to be carried out

(Lampe and Ploeckl 2014; Ploeckl 2016). In the following section, we try to draw a comparison based on the available statistical data on the density and efficiency of the communication networks, between the regions that were quickly incorporated into the Prussian network and should therefore have benefited more from 'positive network externalities' and the networks that remained independent. The analysis must remain tentative as it does not consider the numerous parallel driving forces that changed communications behaviour (industrialisation, migration, education, etc.). Comparison is also complicated by the fact that the borders of the postal districts often changed several times in the course of the founding of the Empire. The figures, therefore, often refer to different geographical units.

Table 7.3 compares the development of postal services and telecommunications using the summary measures of network density (inhabitants per post office) and performance (letters and telegrams per inhabitant, inhabitants per telephone connection) between Prussia (1860/61) and the *Reichspostgebiet*

Table 7.3 Development of postal and telegraph services in Prussia/*Reichspostgebiet*, Bavaria, and Württemberg

	1860/1861	*1876/1883*	*1895*	*1910*
Prussia/Reichspostgebiet				
Inhabitants per sq.km	63	77	100	125
Inhabitants per post office	8492	5218	1544	1615
Letters per inhabitant	7.6	17	42	99
Telegrams per inhabitant	0.02	0.25	0.61	0.94
Inhabitants per telephone connection			468	96
Bavaria				
Inhabitants per sq.km	62	70	77	91
Inhabitants per post office	4999	3649	2707	2174
Letters per inhabitant	6.65	21.7	43.9	104.68
Telegrams per inhabitant	0.06	0.39	0.66	0.84
Inhabitants per telephone connection		19217	753	116
Württemberg				
Inhabitants per sq.km	88	96	107	112
Inhabitants per post office	6124	3778	3130	1861
Letters per inhabitant	5.34	15.24	52.11	122.72
Telegrams per inhabitant	0.07	0.72	1.07	1.08
Inhabitants per telephone connection			505	56

Sources: Prussia: Jahrbuch für die amtliche Statistik des Preußischen Staates 1 (1863); Reichspostgebiet: Hesse (2001: 444–47); Bavaria: Königlich Bayerisches Statistisches Bureau: Verzeichnis der Gemeinden des Königreichs Bayern mit ihrer Bevölkerung im Dezember 1861 (1863); Zeitschrift des Königlich-Bayerischen Statistischen Bureaus 3 (1871); Statistisches Jahrbuch für das Königreich Bayern (1894, 1897, 1911); Württemberg: Württembergische Jahrbücher für vaterländische Geschichte, Geographie, Statistik und Topographie (1861); Württembergische Jahrbücher für Statistik und Landeskunde (1876, 1895); Statistisches Handbuch für das Königreich Württemberg, years 1910 and 1911 (1912).

(1876–1910) and the post and telegraph administrations of Württemberg and Bavaria. As mentioned above (Section 2), the *Reichspostgebiet* encompassed the territory under the authority of the Imperial Postal Administration and is considered Prussia's successor for this comparison. The two southern German kingdoms showed a higher initial level of development of postal and telecommunication services. This difference is probably partly because of the much denser population; the eastern areas of Prussia, in particular, were very sparsely populated and had correspondingly poorer postal services, which pushed the average figures for Prussia down before the founding of the Empire. Even after 1871, the *Reichspostgebiet* showed a much greater heterogeneity and variance than did the other two areas. The regions with rapidly growing populations were primarily located in the *Reichspostgebiet*, so that the average population density there increased much faster than in Bavaria and Württemberg. Against this background, however, it is all the more striking that the network of post offices and telegraph stations in Prussia grew even faster so that the communications network there had already caught up with the Bavarian network in terms of network density and performance in the 1890s and had overtaken the Württemberg network. These summary data speak for a clear positive network effect of the integration into the Imperial Postal Administration after the founding of the Empire.

This positive effect should have been particularly pronounced in regions that experienced a transition from an independent postal administration to the *Reichspostverwaltung* as a result of the founding of the Empire, namely the areas served by the Thurn and Taxis and Baden. This can be explored based on the statistics by the regional offices (*Oberpostdirektionen*) within the Imperial Postal Administration that are not exactly congruent with the territories of pre-unification authorities. After 1867, the former Thurn and Taxis franchises were reorganised into the regional offices of Darmstadt, Frankfurt am Main, and Kassel, and were incorporated first into the Prussian postal service and later into the organisation of the *Reichspost*. Postal and telegraph services in Baden were reorganised after 1872 into the regional offices of Karlsruhe and Konstanz. According to our hypothesis, these districts should have benefited from the transfer to the larger network. They should have shown a visibly faster increase in performance than comparable Prussian regions, which were part of the larger network from the beginning. For this purpose, we used Prussian regions comparable to the Baden and Hessian regions in terms of population density and development as a benchmark (Table 7.4).

A comparison of the figures shows that the two regional offices in Baden had a much denser network of post offices than did the comparable Prussian regions when the Empire was founded. At the same time, the former Hessian territories tended to be less well equipped, which may have been the result of the poor economic situation of the Thurn and Taxis postal administration after the loss of large postal districts since 1848 (Grillmeyer 2005: 404). The regional offices of Baden maintained a lead until the First World War but were not able to expand it significantly. The district of Konstanz had a very

Table 7.4 Regional postal and telegraph services (*Oberpostdirektionen*, OPD) Baden, Hesse and Prussia in comparison

	1841/49/51	*1876*	*1895*	*1910*
formerly Prussian OPD				
Arnsberg-Dortmund				
Inhabitants per sq.km	75	112	197	311
Inhabitants per post office	5223	4287	1742	2333
Letters per inhabitant	3.24	22	40	70
Telegrams per inhabitant		0.23	0.44	0.48
Inhabitants per telephone connection			861	109
Merseburg-Halle				
Inhabitants per sq.km	73	86	110	127
Inhabitants per post office	9645	5677	1467	1297
Letters per inhabitant	1.79	14	37	66
Telegrams per inhabitant		0.18	0.44	0.43
Inhabitants per telephone connection			824	129
Liegnitz (Silesia)				
Inhabitants per sq.km	68	72	78	86
Inhabitants per post office	11658	4516	1830	1410
Letters per inhabitant	1.77	13	33	63
Telegrams per inhabitant		0.14	0.39	0.49
Inhabitants per telephone connection			1520	160
formerly Baden OPD				
Karlsruhe				
Inhabitants per sq.km		121	154	199
Inhabitants per post office	8143	3150	1148	1539
Letters per inhabitant	6.80	20	43	91
Telegrams per inhabitant		0.35	0.75	0.81
Inhabitants per telephone connection			479	88
Constance				
Inhabitants per sq.km		76	81	94
Inhabitants per post office	8143	2561	1072	868
Letters per inhabitant	6.80	15	38	66
Telegrams per inhabitant		0.2	0.5	0.6
Inhabitants per telephone connection			2470	133
formerly Hessian OPD				
Darmstadt				
Inhabitants per sq.km	101	111	136	167
Inhabitants per post office	11847	5108	1119	1297
Letters per inhabitant		17	38	76
Telegrams per inhabitant		0.21	0.49	0.51
Inhabitants per telephone connection			891	113
Kassel				
Inhabitants per sq.km	78	75	79	93
Inhabitants per post office	8296	4756	1573	773
Letters per inhabitant		12	32	73
Telegrams per inhabitant		0.14	0.43	0.51
Inhabitants per telephone connection			1029	129

Sources: Reichspostgebiet: Hesse (2001: 444–47); for figures prior to the founding of the Reich for Prussia 1851: Reden (1854); for Baden 1841: Inhabitants: Fischer et.al. (1982: 40); Baden and Hesse: Dallmeier (1990: 56). The numbers for Darmstadt and Kassel refer to the Grand Duchy of Hesse-Darmstadt and the Electorate of Hesse-Kassel in 1849. The districts are not completely congruent with the respective regional offices (*Oberpostdirektionen*) of the Imperial Postal Administration.

well-developed postal network and a relatively poorly-developed telephone system. However, the Hessian districts (with the particular case of Frankfurt am Main being disregarded here) seemed to have benefited disproportionately from the integration into the *Reichspostgebiet.* They started from a much worse initial situation and by 1910 reached a level that, in some cases, even exceeded the comparable Prussian districts. The rural regional offices (that is, Kassel and Konstanz) seemed to have especially benefited from the integration into the Prussian postal administration. However, this does not prove the existence of positive effects of network integration. First, the selected districts may have benefited from their favourable transport location. Second, the network expansion may have been because of industrial settlements, which we have not accounted for in our analysis. Third, the social profile of the respective districts may have possibly influenced the communications activities of the inhabitants.

4 Conclusion

In this chapter, we took as our starting point the question of whether market integration and the organisational unification of railways, postal services, and telegraphy, which was implemented in parallel with the founding of the Empire, contributed to the transition to modern economic growth and thus to the Empire's economic prosperity. Despite the limitations of the evidence gathered, we reckon that—if there was such a contribution to growth—it was at least not visibly enhanced by the founding of the Empire. In the railway sector, the contribution to growth was probably stronger before, rather than after the founding of the Empire. The railway's growth-enhancing effect was stronger in central and urban regions than in the rural peripheries. In the case of postal services and telegraphy, we observed a convergence in the statistical indicators after the foundation of the Empire, with rural regions benefiting more than urban ones. However, it was not possible to investigate how this contributed towards economic growth. The fundamental convergence of the technical infrastructure, which was undoubtedly brought about by the founding of the Empire, did not level out economic heterogeneity. The opposite may have been true. At least the railway network exacerbated regional disparities by drawing economic activity to those German regions that were characterised by a higher level of industrial development, to begin with.

Notes

1 In addition to Hamburg and Königsberg, the study also covers Cologne and Munich.

2 The *Zollverein* and the expansion of the transport system had a reciprocal influence on each other. Thus, when the German railway network was expanded, the cities located within the *Zollverein* were probably connected first.

References

Bähr, J. (2016) *Werner von Siemens 1816–1892: Eine Biografie*, München: Beck.

Behringer, W. (1990) *Thurn und Taxis: Die Geschichte ihrer Post und ihrer Unternehmen*, München: Pieper.

Benz, A. (2013) *Integration von Infrastrukturen in Europa im historischen Vergleich*, Vol. 3, *Post*, Baden-Baden: Nomos.

Braun, S. T. and Franke, R. (2022) 'Railways, growth, and industrialization in a developing German economy, 1829–1910', *Journal of Economic History*, Vol. 82 (4): 1183–1221.

Büchel, K. and Kyburz, S. (2020) 'Fast track to growth? railway access, population growth and local displacement in 19th century Switzerland', *Journal of Economic Geography*, Vol. 20 (1): 155–95.

Dallmeier, M. (1990) (ed) *500 Jahre Post—Thurn und Taxis: Ausstellung anläßlich der 500jährigen Wiederkehr der Anfänge der Post in Mitteleuropa, 1490–1990*, Regensburg: Fürst Thurn und Taxis Zentralarchiv.

Federico, G. (2012) 'How much do we know about market integration in Europe?', *Economic History Review*, Vol. 65 (2): 470–97.

Fischer, W. et al. (eds) (1982) *Sozialgeschichtliches Arbeitsbuch*, Vol. 1, *Materialien zur Statistik des Deutschen Bundes*, München: Beck.

Fishlow, A. (1965) *American Railroads and the Transformation of the Ante-bellum Economy*, Cambridge, MA: Harvard University Press.

Fremdling, R. (1985) *Eisenbahnen und deutsches Wirtschaftswachstum 1840–1879: Ein Beitrag zur Entwicklungstheorie und zur Theorie der Infrastruktur*, Dortmund: Gesellschaft für westfälische Wirtschaftsgeschichte.

Grillmeyer, S. (2005) *Habsburgs Diener in Post und Politik: Das Haus Thurn und Taxis zwischen 1745 und 1867*, Mainz: von Zabern.

Hahn, H.-W. (1984) *Geschichte des Deutschen Zollvereins*, Göttingen: Vandenhoeck & Ruprecht.

Heinze, W. G. and Kill, H. (1988) 'The development of the German railway system', in R. Mayntz and T. P. Hughes (eds), *The Development of Large Technical Systems*, Boulder: Westview, pp. 105–34.

Herrmann, K. (1981) *Thurn und Taxis-Post und die Eisenbahnen: Vom Aufkommen der Eisenbahnen bis zur Aufhebung der Thurn und Taxis-Post im Jahre 1867*, Kallmünz: Lassleben.

Hesse, J.-O. (1997) 'Weltpostverein: Stephans Rolle beim Aufbau internationaler Kommunikationsnetze', in K. Beyrer (ed), *Kommunikation im Kaiserreich: Der Generalpostmeister Heinrich von Stephan*, Heidelberg: Braus, pp. 77–82.

Hesse, J.-O. (2001) *Im Netz der Kommunikation: Die Reichs-, Post- und Telegraphenverwaltung 1876–1914*, München: Beck.

Holtorf, C. (2013) *Der erste Draht zur Neuen Welt: Die Verlegung des transatlantischen Telegrafenkabels*, Göttingen: Wallstein.

Hornung, E. (2015) 'Railroads and growth in Prussia', *Journal of the European Economic Association*, Vol. 13 (4): 699–736.

Huber, Paul (1979), 'Regionale Expansion und Entleerung im Deutschland des neunzehnten Jahrhunderts: eine Folge der Eisenbahnentwicklung?', in R. Fremdling and R. H. Tilly (eds), *Industrialisierung und Raum: Studien zur regionalen Differenzierung im Deutschland des 19. Jahrhunderts*, Stuttgart: Klett-Cotta, pp. 27–55.

Jacks, D. S. (2005) 'Intra- and international commodity market integration in the Atlantic economy, 1800–1913', *Explorations in Economic History*, Vol. 42 (3): 381–413.

Kaufmann, S. (1996) *Kommunikationstechnik und Kriegführung 1815–1945: Stufen telemedialer Rüstung*, München: Fink.

Keller, W. and Shiue, C. H. (2014) 'Endogenous formation of free trade agreements: evidence from the Zollverein's impact on market integration', *Journal of Economic History*, Vol. 74 (4): 1168–204.

Keller, W. and Shiue, C. H. (2020) 'Market integration and institutional change', *Review of World Economics*, Vol. 156 (2): 251–85.

Lampe, M. and Ploeckl, F. (2014) 'Spanning the globe: the rise of global communications systems and the first globalisation', *Australian Economic History Review*, Vol. 54 (3): 242–61.

Müller, S. (2016) *Wiring the World: The Social and Cultural Creation of Global Telegraph Networks*, New York: Columbia University Press.

Ploeckl, F. (2013) 'The internal impact of a customs union: Baden and the Zollverein', *Explorations in Economic History*, Vol. 50 (3): 387–404.

Ploeckl, F. (2016) 'Uniform service, uniform productivity? Regional efficiency of the Imperial German postal, telegraph, and telephone service', *Australian Economic History Review*, Vol. 56 (2): 221–43.

Reden, F. W. von (1854) *Erwerbs- und Verkehrs-Statistik des Königstaats Preußen*, Darmstadt: Jonghaus.

Reindl, J. (1993) *Der Deutsch-Österreichische Telegraphenverein und die Entwicklung des deutschen Telegraphenwesens 1850–1871: Eine Fallstudie zur administrativ-technischen Kooperation deutscher Staaten vor der Gründung des Deutschen Reiches*, Frankfurt a. M.: Lang.

Sautter, K. (1951) *Geschichte der Deutschen Reichspost (1871 bis 1945)*, Frankfurt a. M.: Bundesdruckerei.

Schilly, E. (1983) 'Nachrichtenwesen', in K. Jeserich (ed), *Deutsche Verwaltungsgeschichte*, Vol. 2, *Vom Reichsdeputationshauptschluss bis zur Auflösung des Deutschen Bundes*, Stuttgart: Deutsche Verlagsanstalt, pp. 257–85.

Schilly, E. (1984) 'Nachrichtenwesen', in K. Jeserich (ed), *Deutsche Verwaltungsgeschichte*, Vol. 3, *Das Deutsche Reich bis zum Ende der Monarchie*, Stuttgart: Deutsche Verlagsanstalt, pp. 386–406.

Stephan, H. von (1859) *Geschichte der Preussischen Post von ihrem Ursprunge bis auf die Gegenwart*, reprint Glashütten im Taunus: Auvermann, 1976.

Uebele, M. (2011) 'National and international market integration in the 19th century: evidence from comovement', *Explorations in Economic History*, Vol. 48 (2): 226–42.

Uebele, M. and Gallardo Albarrán, D. (2015) 'Paving the way to modernity: Prussian roads and grain market integration in Westphalia, 1821–1855', *Scandinavian Economic History Review*, Vol. 63 (1): 69–92.

Varian, H. R., Farrell, J., and Shapiro, C. (2004) *The Economics of Information Technology: An Introduction*, Cambridge: Cambridge University Press.

Voigt, F. (1953) 'Verkehr und Industrialisierung', *Zeitschrift für die gesamte Staatswissenschaft/Journal of Institutional and Theoretical Economics*, Vol. 109 (2): 193–239.

Wehler, H.-U. (1987) *Deutsche Gesellschaftsgeschichte*, Vol. 2, *Von der Reformära bis zur industriellen und politischen Deutschen Doppelrevolution 1815–1845/49*, München: Beck.

Weichlein, S. (2004) *Nation und Region: Integrationsprozesse im Bismarckreich*, Düsseldorf: Droste.

Wessel, H. A. (1983) *Die Entwicklung des elektrischen Nachrichtenwesens in Deutschland und die rheinische Industrie von den Anfängen bis zum Ausbruch des Ersten Weltkrieges*, Wiesbaden: Steiner.

Wolf, N. (2009) 'Was Germany ever united? Evidence from intra- and international trade, 1885–1933', *Journal of Economic History*, Vol. 69 (3): 846–81.

Ziegler, D. (1996) *Eisenbahnen und Staat im Zeitalter der Industrialisierung: Die Eisenbahnpolitik der deutschen Staaten im Vergleich*, Stuttgart: Steiner.

8 The changing capacity for self-description

The creation of a national statistical service

Michael C. Schneider

1 Introduction

Most German states that united to form the German Empire in 1871 already had statistical offices that documented economic, demographic, social, political, and cultural processes with varying degrees of accuracy in their publications. The new Imperial Statistical Office that was established in 1872, shortly after the founding of the Empire, did not replace the existing statistical offices of the individual states, but coordinated the work of the statistical offices of the member states in Empire-wide surveys, such as the censuses, and was responsible for collecting information that related to the Empire as a whole, such as external trade statistics. The data contained in the several hundred volumes of the *Statistik des Deutschen Reichs*—the principal publication of the Imperial Statistical Office—served as a basis for political decision-making during the era of the German Empire (even though this remains poorly researched) and form an important basis for economic and social historical research today. In order to be able to conduct such research in a meaningful way, knowledge of the conditions under which these figures came into being is extremely important. The figures by no means reflect the reality of the time in accordance with today's research interests, but rather the categorisations and also the methods of recording must be placed in their historical background. Moreover, statistical categories and methods of data collection evolved over time, and this impact on census results to a considerable extent (Speich Chassè 2013; Brückweh 2015; Göderle 2016; Haas et al. 2019).

This chapter begins by examining the condition of official statistics in German states during the decades preceding national unification (Section 2). The analysis will concentrate on Prussia, whose statistical service is the best-studied among all German states. It will also shed light on a central figure among German statisticians, namely, Ernst Engel, who headed the statistical office first of Saxony, then from 1860 until the early 1880s of Prussia. Sections 3 and 4 turn to the challenges for official statistics that resulted from the foundation of the German Empire. On the one hand, we will explore the relationship between the reporting systems of the member states and the federal level that was added with the founding of the Imperial Statistical Office. To

DOI: 10.4324/9781003283430-10

what extent did the Empire dominate, and to what extent did member states maintain their autonomy in matters relating to official statistics? In contrast to the well-researched Italian case (see, e.g., Patriarca 1996), scholarship on this question is barely developed with regard to Germany, so only tentative answers can be given. On the other hand, we will address the question of what the emerging nation-state wanted to know about its economic and demographic development in statistical terms, and what it actually did find out. The structure of the extensive material produced by the *Reichsstatistik*—the national reporting system managed by the Imperial Statistical Office—the categories that it applied, and the data-collection methods that were followed were all the result of complex decision-making processes among the statisticians involved, and these could also have turned out differently from the way they actually did turn out. To show how this worked in practice, section 5 will examine in detail how the combined factory and occupational censuses of 1882, 1895 and 1907 were designed.

It is important to stress that the statistical offices by no means merely executed requests from actors in politics, public administration, and the emerging field of social science. Rather, already before the foundation of the Empire, a professional self-image of statisticians emerged, which meant that the content and method of statistical surveys were discussed and decided on within the statistical offices. This epistemic community (cf. Weingart 2003: 127–41) of official statisticians was not confined to Germany alone: Since the middle of the nineteenth century, statisticians in most European countries engaged in an intense exchange of information across borders and, following Conrad et al. (2007: 34), can therefore be understood as a transnational social formation. Specifically, many heads of German statistical offices followed the efforts of their European and U.S. colleagues very closely when it came to professionalising statistical surveys. Statisticians from Germany often participated in international statistical congresses, at which far-reaching recommendations concerning statistical practice were adopted (Horstmann 2020). Section 6 will show in more detail how the profession of German statisticians was embedded in a transnational epistemic community.

What the German Empire knew about itself in statistical terms is not easy to answer either, albeit for another reason: The ways in which public authorities, business companies, social scientists, political parties and the wider public made use of the massive output of the *Reichsstatistik* remains barely studied. Likewise, there is only tentative evidence concerning the process by which the procedures of collecting statistical information became standardised across the different parts of Germany. Less research has been carried out on the factory censuses (*Betriebsstättenzählungen*), which are of particular interest from the point of view of economic history, than on population or medical statistics. What we know suggests that the process of standardisation took a very long time and little more than the beginnings were achieved in the 1870s and 1880s. Nevertheless, the *Reichsstatistik* that developed after 1871 laid the foundations of a statistical practice that made it possible, after the First

World War in the Weimar Republic, to conceive of the national economy as a system whose mechanics could be understood and described in principle (cf. Tooze 2001). Such a systematic approach had not been formulated earlier, mainly because a coherent concept of national accounts was still lacking at the time of national unification (Tooze 2001; Lepenies 2013).

2 Statistical offices in German states before the foundation of the Reich

As early as the last third of the eighteenth century, a statistical practice had emerged in some parts of Europe that no longer merely collected data relating to a particular context, such as tax lists or crop yields. Rather, such information was progressively detached from their original context and transformed to an independent system of knowledge generation. This practice drew on approaches by British economists writing a century earlier, such as William Petty's 'political arithmetic' (Slack 2004). From the end of the eighteenth century onwards, policy-makers in many European states made increasingly ready use of this growing body of statistical information (Behrisch 2004, 2016; Desrosières 2005). However, this was not a straightforward process. In Bavaria, for instance, a household census undertaken in 1771 remained without consequence. It was not until around 1800 that a political discourse developed that did not stop at the mere recording of population data and crop yields, but embedded these data in a perspective of Bavaria's potential for economic development (Denzel 1998; Behrisch 2016: 193–316).

Against the background of a tradition of collecting economic and demographic data, Prussia established a statistical office in 1805/10, which until 1934 was responsible for the statistical recording of vital events, education, the development of trade and industry and similar topics (Behre 1905; Hoffmann 2012: 43–60). Some other states, such as Bavaria, founded their statistical offices similarly early (Zahn 1911: 849–53), whereas Saxony, for example, organised the collection of statistical information on the basis of a private association for a long time. Only in 1850 did it create a statistical office, with statistician Ernst Engel serving as its first director (Weber 2003).

Thus, during the first half of the nineteenth century, most of the German states, in line with a general trend throughout Europe and the United States, established statistical services. While they differed with respect to their organisation and their responsibilities, they shared a common orientation towards the interest of the respective state in obtaining information on population and economic development (Desrosières 2005; Lee 2006). Collecting statistical information was meant to strengthen a state's capacity to act—knowledge of one's own economy could, for example, help in intergovernmental trade treaty negotiations (Weber 2003: 80; Hoffmann 2012: 227).

Apart from enabling specific applications of knowledge based on statistical information, the Prussian Statistical Bureau, in the last decade before the foundation of the German Empire, also shared a pan-European statistical enthusiasm that expected a comprehensive statistical recording of all conceivable and countable phenomena to be able to unravel hitherto hidden laws underlying the economy and society (Porter 1986: 18–39; Schneider 2013). This also explains the wide range of topics covered by Prussian statistics: In the middle of the nineteenth century, statistical surveys related to physical geography; weather and water level reports; various categories of population statistics, including denominational data and information on physical disabilities; the distribution of land ownership; agriculture and forestry; mining and metallurgy; and industry and crafts. Data were collected on construction activity, trade, transport, insurance, prices and consumption of individual foodstuffs. Information was collected on public welfare and poor relief, crime statistics, and health and medical statistics. Both regular and irregular surveys were carried out on churches, education, the arts, sciences, and the military. Despite its length, this enumeration remains far from complete—ultimately, the sheer countability of the objects in all these fields seems to have been the decisive criterion to justify their observation. By no means were all topics surveyed with the same intensity and regularity; rather, quite a few surveys took place irregularly or even only locally, so that it is hardly possible to provide a systematic picture in a limited space (Engel 1863). All surveys followed the ideal of complete coverage. Until the twentieth century, thinking in terms of samples and probabilities, and mathematical–statistical thinking in general, remained alien to German official statistics (Krüger et al. 1987).

The industrial and occupational censuses (*Gewerbezählungen*) that the statistical services of some German states compiled at irregular intervals in the course of the first two-thirds of the nineteenth century were often extraordinarily detailed, but, as has been shown for the Prussian case, they exhibited such profound methodological deficiencies in many respects that their informative value must have been limited even for the state interest at the time (cf. Hoffmann 2012). Within the framework of the *Zollverein*—the customs union formed in 1834 (see Chapter 3)—the first comprehensive occupational census took place in 1846, and the interest of the participating states was primarily directed towards an assessment of the effects of the newly imposed tariff rates. On this occasion, the statistical office of Prussia already identified some of the problems that were to occupy industry and occupational censuses for many decades to come. The most important one referred to the distinction between main and secondary employment, which, if not done carefully, could easily lead to double counting. A further occupational census was carried out in 1861 for the whole of the *Zollverein*; this and other industrial and occupational censuses carried out by individual states formed the background experience on which industrial and occupational censuses during the era of the Empire were based (Hoffmann 2012: 200–30).

Population statistics constituted another central element of official statistics (Lee 2002). For some time before the founding of the German Empire, there was considerable pressure to standardise the design of population censuses, because since its founding in 1834, the *Zollverein* had distributed customs revenues among its member states according to the size of their population. Thus, from the 1840s onwards, the *Zollverein* conferences also debated methodological issues related to census-taking, without always reaching an agreement. In a sense, the statistics conferences held after the founding of the Empire followed from these *Zollverein* conferences (Viebahn 1858–68; Schneider 2013: 192). During the 1860s, the statistical office of Prussia in particular developed various methods to make population censuses more reliable. Specifically, it no longer relied on compilations by lower-level administrative authorities but collected the questionnaires filled out by respondents individually and analysed them in-house, which was not only more expensive but also more reliable (Schneider 2013: 239–82). Such was the methodological experience against which German statisticians discussed the options for an Empire-wide statistical reporting system around 1871.

3 The reorganisation of official statistics in the context of the foundation of the German Reich

At the time of the foundation of the German Empire, both the population statistics and the industrial and occupation censuses of the German states had already reached a considerable level of development. Nevertheless, methods of data collection were by no means uniform, despite all attempts at coordination. Moreover, the question arose as to how far the established categories used in occupational censuses could still do justice to the rapidly changing circumstances. Statisticians thus faced a dilemma: If they retained outdated categories of occupational classifications, they would be unable to track structural change. Some occupations disappeared, while others emerged and were not captured by the existing categories. But if the classification scheme was modified from one census to the next, results could not be compared over time (Hoffmann 2012: 216–17). This problem plagued industrial and occupational census-taking until the end of the Empire and beyond.

These and other methodological issues, together with the non-uniformity of the individual state statistics, prompted the *Zollverein* Federal Council in 1869 to set up a commission to place the statistical services of the federation on a new footing (Fürst 1972: 15). This so-called *Kommission zur weiteren Ausbildung der Statistik des Zollvereins* (Commission for the Further Development of the Statistics of the Customs Union) drew on the experience that the various statistical offices of the various German states had gathered in the preceding decades. It brought together a number of statisticians from public authorities as well as university professors and other experts who were mobilised on a case-by-case basis and met 81 times until 1871 (Zahn 1911: 833). This commission laid the foundations for the statistical reporting system of the future Empire. It addressed detailed recommendations to the *Bundesrat* (the chamber of representatives of the member states), first of the North German Confederation, then of the Empire. It thus defined the course of action to be taken in many domains of the emerging *Reichsstatistik*, including demographic and economic statistics (Fürst 1972: 15). At around the same time, Ernst Engel formulated a detailed critique of contemporary economic statistics and pleaded for a fundamental reform that aimed at a comprehensive inventory of all economic activities (Engel 1870). With such programmatic writings and his successful modernisation of the work of the statistical office of Prussia, Engel not only had an impact on the development official statistics in other German states and the emerging nation-state but also offered important suggestions to German economists such as Gustav Schmoller and Lujo Brentano. It is no coincidence that Engel was also one of the founding members of the *Verein für Socialpolitik*, the association of German economists (Grimmer-Solem 2003).

Because it was in many respects easier to count the population than to record economic activities in their entirety and complexity, the Commission was fairly quick to agree on procedures for conducting future population censuses. It could also build on well-established coordination mechanisms among the members of the *Zollverein* in this domain. But there were also methodological challenges, in the face of which the statisticians capitulated for the time being. One of them related to emigration, which individual member states had already attempted to record. Distinguishing between temporary and permanent emigration and recording the seaport from which migrants left for other continents proved to be particularly difficult. Nevertheless, the Commission recommended that the reporting schemes that were in place in individual member states be continued in order to gain further experience (Kaiserliches Statistisches Amt 1873: 98). This recommendation followed the long-standing practice in official statistics of drawing conclusions for future improvements from the observation of one's own practice, which was always perceived as deficient.

Another task of the Commission was to redesign foreign trade statistics. Although cross-border merchandise trade had already been recorded during the decades of the existence of the *Zollverein*, only trade that was subject to tariffs and only the quantities of goods, not their value, had been recorded (Torp 2014: 14; see also Chapter 16 of this volume). The Commission was well aware of these deficits, and others, in the foreign trade statistics. It diagnosed that both legislators and the business community would be interested in a reliable recording of cross-border merchandise trade in its entirety. This would make it possible to observe changes not only in trade flows in relation to trading partners but also 'in the conditions of income and consumption' (Kaiserliches Statistisches Amt 1873: 126). At the same time, there was also an interest in obtaining information on the competitiveness of the German economy in comparison with its trading partners (Kaiserliches Statistisches Amt 1873: 126 130). For the time being, however, the work of the Commission ended with vain recommendations. Until the end of the 1870s, German foreign trade statistics continued to suffer from the same deficits as in the years before the founding of the Empire. A greater problem was apparently also that of misdeclarations, for example when the actual country of origin was not disclosed, but only the country from which the goods were imported (cf. Torp 2014: 15–16). However, this still seemed better than dispensing with foreign trade statistics altogether, which would have meant leaving the community of states that produced such statistics (Kaiserliches Statistisches Amt 1873: 130).

With a law on the 'Statistics of merchandise trade of the German customs area with foreign countries', enacted in 1880, all cross-border trade in goods, including trade not subject to tariffs, was recorded at last. In addition, the value of trade was determined as well, so that these statistics became much more meaningful. However, for a considerable time, the value of traded goods was still estimated by a rather crude procedure. It was not until after the turn of the century that more realistic data were collected for the value of exports, and only after the First World War for the values of imports as well. Of course, foreign trade statistics also followed the general tendency in official statistics to break down the information on a given category into more and more subcategories, so that the data on trade became increasingly fine-grained (cf. Torp 2014: 16–17).

The importance of agriculture in the German economy in the first period after unification is reflected in the extensive occupation of the Commission with the agricultural statistics. On the one hand, the statisticians were able to draw on experience gained in member states over many decades, since agricultural statistics, along with population statistics, were among the early building blocks of the recording of economic activity in the eighteenth century (Behrisch 2016). On the other hand, the Commission noted considerable deficits in existing reporting schemes, which were deemed incomplete and inconsistent. With respect to crop yields, for example, 'hardly more than superficial assumptions' could be made. The Commission, therefore, made detailed proposals on how to remedy the situation with more clearly formulated survey forms (Kaiserliches Statistisches Amt 1873: 116). In fact, agricultural statistics developed into one of the most important branches of official statistics after 1871, which was also possible because the agricultural elites were more willing to cooperate—at least before the First World War—than the industrial elites when it came to industrial output statistics (cf. Tooze 2001: 58).

Finally, the Commission endorsed Engel's recommendation to separate the industrial census from the occupation census, which was oriented along the lines of the population census, and to concentrate on information relating to the plant or factory level. The work of the Commission apparently focused on the development of a robust and sustainable classification scheme that would also take into account the increasing differentiation of manufacturing branches. The new classification kept to both the classifications used in earlier censuses and the categorisation recommended by the International Statistical Congress of 1857 (Kaiserliches Statistisches Amt 1873: 340). The main challenges were, on the one hand, the 'progress in the division of labour', which required ever finer distinctions between individual branches of economic activity, and, on the other hand, the close interdependence among neighbouring branches of industry, which presented the enumerators with great difficulties in the process of data collection (Kaiserliches Statistisches Amt 1873: 340).

The statisticians demanded, for example, that not only the number of enterprises in a particular branch be counted but also that detailed information be collected on the method of production (with or without machines, with or without apprentices), on export ratio and many other criteria, since this would give the desired statistics their proper meaning (Kaiserliches Statistisches Amt 1873: 341). The statisticians were aware of the fact that only a small proportion of these far-reaching questions would actually be answered truthfully by the plant owners, just as they were aware of the changes in the division of labour and the increase in the number of large companies, that is, of the shifts in the economic structure that were already evident around 1870 (Kaiserliches Statistisches Amt 1873: 343; Horstmann 2020: 215).

The extent to which the recommendations of the Commission were followed by the later *Reichsstatistik* cannot be determined given the present state of research. In any case, the recommendation to conduct industrial and occupational censuses at short intervals in five years, one year after the population census, was not followed. In 1875, the first comprehensive industrial and occupational census of the Empire took place, parallel to the population census at the beginning of December of the same year. Further industrial and occupational censuses were then taken in 1882, 1895, and 1907. Data were collected in the summer, so that the results are not readily comparable with those of the 1875 census because of the seasonal variation in the level of economic activity. In summary, the commission's achievement was to provide an inventory of German statistics and to make recommendations for their development in the future. The extent to which these recommendations were followed and how they affected the practice of the *Reichsstatistik* remains to be explored.[1]

4 The establishment of the imperial statistical office and its responsibilities

The activities of the Imperial Statistical Office (*Kaiserliches Statistisches Amt*, KSA), founded in 1872, and the gradual expansion of its responsibilities have not yet been studied as well as those of the major statistical offices of German states before the foundation of the Empire. However, the source material subsisting in archives of member states makes it clear that the poorly staffed KSA, which initially consisted of only a director and a few civil servants, depended crucially on the statistical services of the member states to fulfil its tasks (see, e.g., Kiesewetter 1991: 156). The responsibility of the KSA related mainly to parts of demographic statistics—above all, the compilation and aggregation of the results of the population censuses supplied by the Länder; this was a task that the KSA had taken over from the Central Bureau of the *Zollverein*. In addition, the KSA produced foreign trade statistics and, from the late 1870s, it was in charge of other reporting systems as well, such as agricultural statistics (Zahn 1911: 833; Fürst 1972: 16). It was also the task of the KSA to contribute to the standardisation of the statistics collected in the individual states. However, due to the federal structure of the Empire (Nipperdey 1992: 85–109), the KSA had no right to impose instructions on the statistical offices of the member states, for example regarding the formulation of questionnaires for surveys or the regulations guiding the processing of data. Therefore, the statisticians of the KSA and of the statistical offices of member states endeavoured to reach an agreement on such issues in regular conferences.

By no means was this mechanism of coordination always successful. Statistics relating to causes of death, which were important for an effective public health policy, provide an example. In this case, a uniform classification scheme was not achieved until 1905, and recording causes of death continued to show strong regional differences for a considerable time (Leidinger et al. 1997). There were also methodological disputes between the Empire and the individual states in the realm of population and occupational censuses. The final design of a census and the form of its publication were always the result of a process of political negotiation in which the interests of individual states were brought to a common denominator that often involved compromise. And by no means was the largest single state, Prussia, always able to prevail on individual issues (Schneider 2013: 358, 393).

A major challenge for data users today resides in the fact that the uniform appearance of the published statistical information from the era of the German Empire sometimes conceals quite different practices of data collection prevailing in individual states. However, the extent to which the federal structure of *Reichsstatistik* affected the results and consistency of statistical information has not yet been systematically studied (for tentative evidence, see Tooze 2001: 61–62). Provisional evidence, such as staff size, suggests a gradual increase in the weight of the KSA relative to the statistical offices of member states. The quality and proficiency of the work done in the KSA also increased because it was able to offer much more attractive salaries than, for example, the Prussian statistical office (Schneider 2013: 197).

5 The occupational and industrial censuses of 1882, 1895 and 1907

The foregoing has established that the federal structure of the official statistics of the German Empire had an effect on both the structure and the methodology of economic and population statistics reflecting a complex process of negation between the statistical offices of the member states and the Empire. At the same time, uniformity of data collection was doubtful in more than one case. A further factor affecting the quality of economic statistics was the fact that it is more difficult to obtain information from firms relating to the value and quantity of output and the conditions of production than, say, information on vital events. Even in the industrial census of 1907, statisticians encountered staunch resistance from firms, which tried hard not to disclose any more information than absolutely necessary to outsiders, and they probably succeeded to a large extent (Tooze 2001: 56).

Despite such difficulties, the KSA organised three comprehensive surveys, in each case linking an occupational census with an industrial census (*Berufs- und Betriebszählung*). The resulting censuses of 1882, 1895, and 1907, which have already been mentioned several times, provide a wealth of information on the structure of the national economy and employment relationships that is still intensively used by researchers in economic and social history today.[2] However, the contexts in which they were compiled, the structure of the occupational categories, and the validity of their results have only been partially studied. While there is research relating to occupational censuses, industrial censuses still need to be investigated in more detail (Schneider 2013: 343–422).

Adam Tooze (2001: 40–75) argues that the *Reichsstatistik* was less and less able adequately to capture changing economic realities the longer the Empire existed. One of his central assumptions is that official statistics adhered to a picture of the German economy that was dominated by agriculture and handicrafts, and overlooked (or wished to overlook) the fact that in reality a highly dynamic industrial economy had emerged, which also included huge business companies. According to Tooze, only during the First World War did it become apparent that the information supplied by the Imperial Statistical Office was no longer adequate to meet wartime requirements, so that the government ministries began to compile data on their own. What follows examines this hypothesis using the first occupational and industrial census of 1882 as an example. What expectations did politicians have of this census, and what expectations did the statisticians themselves have?

The complicated history of the 1882 occupational census provides a good illustration of the expectations and factors that influenced the evolution of official statistics in the German Empire. The initial impetus came from the Imperial Office of the Interior. The first impulse came from the Imperial Office of the Interior, which was actually only interested in better information on the structure of farms and on employment conditions in the countryside.[3] However, confronted with this wish, the KSA, together with the statistical offices of the member states, considered it of little use to conduct such a census without a general occupational census that would also cover industrial employment. From the point of view of the statisticians, this was necessary because many industrial workers were still engaged in agriculture as a secondary occupation. It was therefore relevant to know the exact extent of secondary employment in agriculture in relation to industrial employment to produce meaningful information on employment in agriculture. Because such an undertaking seemed to be very complicated, the statisticians tried to delay the project and combine it with the census that was due in 1885. However, after the Emperor and the Imperial government had announced a comprehensive social insurance programme at the end of 1881, the need for comprehensive occupational statistics became more pressing (cf. chapter 13 of this volume). Calculating the cost of the accident insurance programme, for instance, required information on the occupational structure of the workforce (cf. Schneider 2013: 351–422).

The statistical offices of the German states had already gained experience with questions on occupation that had been included in population censuses. Consequently, they had also become familiar with methodological pitfalls, for example when it came to distinguishing between main and secondary employment. In Prussia, for example, this issue led to the decision not to publish the data on occupations collected in the context of the 1875 census. Statisticians also briefly considered evaluating the responses regarding occupation from the 1880 census, but this project was quickly abandoned in view of the inadequacy of the survey material.[4]

The organisation of the new occupational and industrial census, which was carried out in June 1882 under severe time constraints, was apparently largely unproblematic. This was perhaps because the problems of assigning occupational titles, the definition of a household, and similar issues were only addressed in connection with the evaluation of the census results. This is evident from the fact that in some member states a significant portion of census cards was corrected by the regional statistical authorities. Above all, the distinction between main and secondary occupations was not as clear to the population as statisticians had hoped—frequently, respondents listed several occupations without weighting them. Consequently, corrections carried out by the statistical offices were to a certain extent arbitrary, and the statisticians were well aware of this. A further shortcoming related to the incomplete coverage of unpaid work of family members, especially in agriculture, but also in restaurants, for instance (Hoffmann 1965: 183). Despite all these issues, the results pertaining to the national level were published rapidly (Kaiserliches Statistisches Amt 1884).

The conditions surrounding the occupational and industrial census of 1882 do not tally well with Tooze's hypothesis that the *Reichsstatistik* was biased toward a backward-looking perspective of the German economy and society. It is also unlikely that the census introduced such a bias by asking about the occupation in which respondents were originally trained, rather than the occupation actually practised at the time of the survey, as Tooze (2001: 52) surmises. In fact, the questions on occupation were designed to ask about current employment (Schneider 2013: 376). This is consistent with the experience of statisticians that it made no sense to ask about past events because answers were unreliable. The design of the occupational and industrial census of 1882 was built on learning processes that official statistics had gone through since their institutionalisation at the beginning of the nineteenth century.

The next occupational and industrial census was initiated in 1894 by Imperial Chancellor von Caprivi. Contemporary debates on whether Germany should still be considered an 'agrarian state' or rather an 'industrial state', given the rapid rise of modern industrial branches and concomitant structural change, may also have played a role (cf. Barkin 1970; Wehler 1995: 618–20). The KSA prepared an occupational and industrial census for 1895 in cooperation with the statistical offices of the member states. Naturally, the experience gained in 1882 was drawn upon, and all-too-detailed questions, for instance, on the occupational status of widows, were avoided, since even at great expense only pseudo-accuracy could have been achieved. This was one of the most important learning effects experienced by contemporary statisticians: It was possible to overload a census with too many and too detailed questions in such a way that even the quality of the results for simpler questions suffered. The differentiation of occupations resulting from the dynamics of the industrial sector was taken into account through a significant increase in the number of occupational categories, 207, compared with 153 in 1882. The several thousand individual occupations declared by respondents were assigned to these occupational categories. The mistake of not systematically asking about children under 14 in 1882 (who were often forgotten by the respondents) was also avoided in 1895.

The last occupational and industrial census of 1907 followed the now-established pattern. A new element was the apparent pressure exerted by the KSA to take over both the organisation of the census and the analysis of the survey material, which met with obstinate resistance from the statistical offices of the member states. Until the outbreak of the First World War, this latent conflict between the two levels of authority had still remained unresolved.

6 Integration of national statistics into a transnational context: the role of international statistical congresses

Well before the founding of the Imperial Statistical Office, the field of official statistics had become integrated into a transnational context. German statisticians observed statistical practices abroad, both in Europe and the United States, and across all domains of statistics. Early on, Ernst Engel referred to other European nations when discussing deficiencies in the Prussian population and industrial statistics (Schneider 2013: 225). A transnational orientation was obviously useful in areas that could benefit from cooperation, such as foreign trade statistics, but it can also be observed in other fields, such as population statistics.

Existing scholarship credits the International Statistical Congresses, which were held more or less regularly since 1853, with a strong influence on the design of national statistics (e.g. Osterhammel 2010: 58). However, it seems doubtful whether this is true with regard to the design and organisation of large national censuses. In well-studied cases, such as population statistics, scepticism seems appropriate. On the one hand, the resolutions of the congresses were non-binding recommendations to which the member states were not obliged to adhere. On the other hand, the German example shows how difficult it was to establish a certain uniformity of statistical procedures within the same territory, so that a uniform alignment with principles developed at the transnational level seems unlikely (cf. Randeraad 2010). Early on, the congresses also urged the international standardisation of industrial censuses, but this did not materialise (Horstmann 2020: 130). To be sure, statisticians engaged in transnational exchange and, even more so, closely observed each other and compared their own practice with that of their colleagues in other countries. How the transnational character of the statistical profession influenced the development of official statistics on the national level, however, still requires further examination.

7 Conclusion

On what basis did official statistics in the new nation-state develop after 1871? And what direction did demographic and economic statistics take in the years that followed? The *Reichsstatistik* evolved naturally from the official statistics that had developed in the German states since the beginning of the nineteenth century. Most states had statistical offices that collected and published data on a wide range of topics relating to their respective economies and societies. Over the decades preceding national unification, statistical practice became increasingly professionalised. In Prussia, this happened in particular after Ernst Engel became director of the statistical office there in 1860. For a long time, however, occupational and industrial statistics still suffered from considerable weaknesses, which severely limited their value. At the same time, long before the founding of the Empire, there were efforts to coordinate the official statistics of the German states better, in order to improve the comparability of results, especially in the area of population censuses.

The newly founded German Empire took up these trends. The great importance that decision-makers attached to strengthening the national coordination of official statistics is reflected in the establishment of an Imperial Statistical Office as early as 1872. The Commission for the Further Development of the Statistics of the Customs Union, which had been set up in 1869, had already conducted preparatory work by delineating the field to be covered by official statistics on the national level and by defining the distribution of responsibilities between the Imperial Statistical Office and the statistical offices of the member states. It was clear that even after the establishment of a statistical authority on the level of the Empire, the statistical offices of the individual states would continue to exist.

Since its establishment, the Imperial Statistical Office coordinated the major censuses, especially the population censuses, but it always had to take into account the interests of the individual states, whose statistical offices also organised the surveys and carried out the analysis of the data. The evidence suggests that the official statistics of Imperial Germany were permeated with federal elements. A national 'statistical view' seems to have emerged only slowly and not in all areas at the same time. A strong federal element is also evident from the negotiations in which the Empire and the member states laid down the layout of the occupational and industrial censuses of 1882, 1895, and 1907. The history of these three censuses also testifies to the growing ability of official statistics to track the economic dynamics of the early Empire.

Much research remains to be done on the motives and expectations that public authorities, interest groups, and not least the statisticians themselves associated with the occupational and industrial censuses. Similarly, the robustness of these data also needs to be examined in greater detail. One of the most important questions for future research concerns the ways in which statistical data entered contemporary debates on social and economic issues and related legislation. Only when we know how the use of statistical data fed into the decision-making by governments and parliaments will it be possible to assess the extent to which official statistics have contributed to nation-building.

Notes

1 Horstmann (2020: 215–16) has recently suggested that the extent to which the recommendations of the Commission have been followed should not be overestimated.
2 Examples include Kaufhold (1987); Lehmann (2010); Ritter and Tenfelde (1992).
3 One can only speculate about the reasons of the Ministry for demanding such information. In any case, the proposals of the Commission for the Further Development of the Statistics of the Customs Union of 1870/71 do not seem to have played a role here.
4 The original survey material—that is, the questionnaires established on an individual basis—is no longer available in the case of Prussia for any population and occupational census, so that it is not possible to determine to what extent, for example, the information provided by persons interviewed has been corrected and adjusted in the statistical offices.

References

Barkin, K. D. (1970) *The Controversy over German Industrialization, 1890–1902*, Chicago, IL: University of Chicago Press.

Behre, O. (1905) *Geschichte der Statistik in Brandenburg-Preußen bis zur Gründung des Königlichen Statistischen Bureaus*, Berlin: Heymann.

Behrisch, L. (2004) ''Politische Zahlen': Statistik und die Rationalisierung der Herrschaft im späten Ancien Régime', *Zeitschrift für Historische Forschung*, Vol. 31: 551–77.

Behrisch, L. (2016) *Die Berechnung der Glückseligkeit: Statistik und Politik in Deutschland und Frankreich im späten Ancien Régime*, Ostfildern: Thorbecke.

Brückweh, K. (2015) *Menschen zählen: Wissensproduktion durch britische Volkszählungen und Umfragen vom 19. Jahrhundert bis ins digitale Zeitalter*, Berlin: De Gruyter Oldenbourg.

Conrad, S., Eckert, A. and Freitag, U. (eds) (2007) *Globalgeschichte: Theorien, Ansätze, Themen*, Frankfurt a. M.: Campus.

Denzel, M. A. (1998) *Professionen und Professionisten: Die Dachsbergsche Volksbeschreibung im Kurfürstentum Bayern (1771–1781)*, Stuttgart: Steiner.

Desrosières, A. (2005) *Die Politik der großen Zahlen: Eine Geschichte der statistischen Denkweise*, Berlin: Springer.

Engel, E. (1863) 'Die Statistik im Dienste der Verwaltung mit besonderer Berücksichtigung der im Preußischen Staate bestehenden Einrichtungen', *Zeitschrift des Königlich Preußischen Statistischen Bureaus*, Vol. 3: 269 –308.

Engel, E. (1870) 'Die Nothwendigkeit einer Reform der volkswirthschaftlichen Statistik insbesondere der Gewerbestatistik im Gebiet des Zollvereins sowie in allen übrigen Staaten von Europa (Teil 1)', *Zeitschrift des Kgl. Preußischen Statistischen Bureaus*, Vol. 10: 142–232.

Fürst, G. (1972) '100 Jahre Reichs- und Bundesstatistik', *Allgemeines Statistisches Archiv*, Vol. 56: 336–63.

Göderle, W. (2016) *Zensus und Ethnizität: Zur Herstellung von Wissen über soziale Wirklichkeiten im Habsburgerreich zwischen 1848 und 1910*, Göttingen: Wallstein.

Grimmer-Solem, E. (2003) *The Rise of Historical Economics and Social Reform in Germany 1864–1894*, Oxford: Oxford University Press.

Haas, S., Schneider, M. C. and Bilo, N. (eds) (2019) *Die Zählung der Welt: Kulturgeschichte der Statistik vom 18. bis 20. Jahrhundert*, Stuttgart: Steiner.

Hoffmann, F. (2012) *'Ein den thatsächlichen Verhältnissen entsprechendes Bild nicht zu gewinnen': Quellenkritische Untersuchungen zur preußischen Gewerbestatistik zwischen Wiener Kongress und Reichsgründung*, Stuttgart: Steiner.

Hoffmann, W. (1965) *Das Wachstum der deutschen Wirtschaft seit der Mitte des 19. Jahrhunderts*, Berlin: Springer.

Horstmann, J. (2020) *Halbamtliche Wissenschaft: Internationale Statistikkongresse und preußische Professorenbürokraten*, Paderborn: Ferdinand Schöningh.

Kaiserliches Statistisches Amt (ed) (1873) *Statistik des Deutschen Reichs*, Vol. 1, Berlin: Königlich Preußisches Statistisches Bureau.

Kaiserliches Statistisches Amt (ed) (1884) *Berufsstatistik nach der allgemeinen Berufszählung vom 5. Juni 1882: 1. Berufsstatistik des Reichs und der kleineren Verwaltungsbezirke*, Berlin: Puttkammer & Mühlbrecht.

Kaufhold, K. (1987) 'Erwerbstätigkeit und soziale Schichtung im Deutschen Reich um 1900: Quantitative Aspekte nach den Berufszählungen von 1895 und 1907', in H. Henning et al. (eds), *Wirtschafts- und sozialgeschichtliche Forschungen und Probleme: Karl Erich Born zur Vollendung des 65. Lebensjahres*, St. Katharinen: Scripta Mercaturae, pp. 175–224.

Kiesewetter, H. (1991) 'Quellen zur historischen Statistik des Königreichs Sachsen im Industriezeitalter (1750–1914)', in W. Fischer and A. Kunz (eds), *Grundlagen der historischen Statistik von Deutschland: Quellen, Methoden, Forschungsziele*, Opladen: Westdeutscher Verlag, pp. 145–74.

Krüger, L., Daston, L. J. and Heidelberger, M. (eds) (1987) *The Probabilistic Revolution: Ideas in History*, Cambridge, MA: MIT Press.

Lee, R. (2002) 'Official statistics, demography and population policy in Germany, 1872–1933', in R. Mackensen (ed), *Bevölkerungslehre und Bevölkerungspolitik vor 1933*, Opladen: Westdeutscher Verlag, pp. 253–72.

Lee, R. (2006) 'Defining population by statistics 1850–1939: German practice within a European context', in R. Mackensen (ed), *Bevölkerungsforschung und Politik in Deutschland im 20. Jahrhundert*, Wiesbaden: Springer, pp. 89–117.

Lehmann, S. (2010) 'The German elections in the 1870s: why Germany turned from Liberalism to protectionism', *Journal of Economic History*, Vol. 70 (1): 146–78.

Leidinger, B., Lee, R. and Marschalck, P. (1997) 'Enforced convergence: political change and cause-of-death registration in the Hansestadt Bremen, 1860–1914', *Continuity and Change*, Vol. 12 (2): 221–46.

Lepenies, P. (2013) *Die Macht der einen Zahl: Eine politische Geschichte des Bruttoinlandsprodukts*, Berlin: Suhrkamp.

Nipperdey, T. (1992) *Deutsche Geschichte 1866–1918: Machtstaat vor der Demokratie*, Munich: Beck.

Osterhammel, J. (2010) *Die Verwandlung der Welt*, 5th ed., Munich: Beck.

Patriarca, S. (1996) *Numbers and Nationhood: Writing Statistics in Nineteenth-Century Italy*, New York: Cambridge University Press.

Porter, T. (1986) *The Rise of Statistical Thinking 1820–1900*, Princeton: Princeton University Press.

Randeraad, N. (2010) *States and Statistics in the Nineteenth Century: Europe by Numbers*, Manchester: Manchester University Press.

Ritter, G. and Tenfelde, K. (1992) *Arbeiter im Deutschen Kaiserreich 1871 bis 1914*, Bonn: Dietz.

Schneider, M. C. (2013) *Wissensproduktion im Staat: Das königlich preußische statistische Bureau 1860–1914*, Frankfurt a. M.: Campus.

Speich Chassé, D. (2013) *Die Erfindung des Bruttosozialprodukts: Globale Ungleichheit in der Wissensgeschichte der Ökonomie*, Göttingen: Vandenhoeck & Ruprecht.

Slack, P. (2004) 'Government and information in seventeenth-century England', *Past & Present*, Vol. 184: 33–68.

Tooze, J. A. (2001) *Statistics and the German State, 1900–1945: The Making of Modern Economic Knowledge*, Cambridge: Cambridge University Press.

Torp. C. (2014) *The Challenges of Globalization: Economy and Politics in Germany, 1860–1914*, New York: Berghahn.

von Viebahn, G. (1858–1868) *Statistik des zollvereinten und nördlichen Deutschlands*, 3 Vols., Berlin: Reimer.

Weber, D. (2003) *Die sächsische Landesstatistik im 19. Jahrhundert: Institutionalisierung and Professionalisierung*, Stuttgart: Franz Steiner.

Wehler, H. (1995) *Deutsche Gesellschaftsgeschichte*, Vol. 3: *Von der 'Deutschen Doppelrevolution' bis zum Beginn des Ersten Weltkrieges 1849–1914*, Munich: Beck.

Weingart, P. (2003) *Wissenschaftssoziologie*, Bielefeld: Transcript.

Zahn, F. (1911) 'Die amtliche Statistik in den einzelnen Staaten', in J. Conrad, L. Elster, W. Lexis and E. Loening (eds), *Handwörterbuch der Staatswissenschaften*, 3rd ed., Jena: Fischer.

9 The gold standard and the *Reichsbank*

The transformation of the monetary regime

Matthias Morys

1 Introduction

The founding of the German Empire represents an important turning point in German political history and arguably constitutes one of the key events of the nineteenth century. However, how important was 1871 for German economic history? It *facilitated* the transition to the gold standard (1873) and *enabled the foundation* of the *Reichsbank*, the central bank of the new state (1875). The founding of the German Empire is thus closely related to two key events in nineteenth-century German monetary history and hence constitutes an important turning point.

Nevertheless, the relevance of the founding of the German Empire should not be overstated. With respect to the gold standard, a widely shared opinion holds that the founding of the Empire constituted a turning point in not only Germany's monetary regime but also international monetary history. According to this view, the German monetary reform of 1871/73 was the tipping point that allowed the gold standard inspired by England to become the global monetary standard. By contrast, we argue that the German states were as much involved as any other European country in the contemporary debate of the 1860s on the respective advantages and disadvantages of using gold or silver. The choice of currency standard has implications transcending an individual economy; thus, the obvious choice for members of the emerging federal state was to transfer competence in monetary affairs to the Empire. Therefore, the new institutional structures *facilitated* the transition to the gold standard. However, the latter likely would have occurred even without national unification, as simultaneous developments in many other European countries show.

Similarly, founding the *Reichsbank* in 1875 was merely the prelude to the unification of German monetary policy. Initially, 32 other banks of note issue continued to exist and pursued their own interest rate policies. Only through a quarter-century-long process was the *Reichsbank* able to gradually implement a uniform monetary policy throughout the Empire. This was not only a success of the *Reichsbank* as an institution but also reflects the increasing integration of initially quite heterogeneous money markets in different parts of the country.

DOI: 10.4324/9781003283430-11

The remainder of this chapter is structured as follows. Sections 2 and 3 discuss the transition to the gold standard in 1871/73 and the founding of the *Reichsbank* in 1875, respectively. Section 4 explores the *Reichsbank's* monetary policy and how successful both the gold standard and *Reichsbank* were. Section 5 concludes the chapter and addresses the question whether the founding of the Empire represents a turning point in German monetary history.

Much of the terrain explored in this chapter remains thinly covered by the existing scholarship. Extant research has mainly focused on the coinage reform of 1871/73 and the monetary policy of the *Reichsbank* under the classical gold standard. As both topics have important international ramifications, scholarly interest in them has remained alive both in Germany and elsewhere. However, many important topics relating to the *Reichsbank's* history prior to 1914 remain neglected. For example, there is no research of note on the *Reichsbank* as a commercial bank. Similarly, the question of interest rate convergence and money market integration in the far-flung German Empire has received insufficient attention.

2 Introduction of the gold standard in 1873

2.1 International background: emergence of the classical gold standard in the 1870s

The emergence of the classical gold standard is a key event in monetary history. For the first time, all major industrialised countries linked their currencies to gold alone, ending the three-tiered global monetary system of the 1850s and 1860s, in which gold served as the currency anchor in some countries, silver in others, and a combination of both elsewhere. In this context, 'currency anchor' means that other forms of currency, such as banknotes and book money, might exist, but they can always be converted into the precious metal forming the anchor (legal obligation of the central bank to exchange banknotes for coins). Such a system implies that countries using the same currency anchor share a fixed exchange rate.

In the case of bimetallism, the anchor function is assigned to gold and silver simultaneously. At first glance, such a regime is extremely attractive, as it allows gold, which has a higher value-to-weight ratio than silver, to be used for large transactions, and silver for everyday payments. However, who guarantees that the price ratio between both metals, as codified in the coinage laws (15.5 to 1 under the important French legislation of 1803), corresponds to the price ratio on bullion markets? It was precisely this discrepancy between mint (or official) and market ratios that became the Achilles' heel of bimetallism. There is agreement that, within certain limits, a large bimetallic currency area can have a stabilising effect on the price ratio on bullion markets (Oppers 2000). However, dispute exists regarding where these limits are: how big does a shock on the precious metal markets need to be to transform a bimetallic system into a de facto monometallic one? These two perspectives—bimetallism as a self-stabilising system or an unstable system balancing on a knife's edge—were already irreconcilably opposed in the nineteenth century (Fisher 1894), and have not been reconciled to date (Flandreau 1996; Oppers 1996; Meissner 2015; Morys 2019; Wiegand 2019).

The emergence of the classical gold standard is usually dated to 1873 (Eichengreen 2008: 15–19; Meissner 2005). In July 1873, the German Empire enacted its Coinage Act, which represented the final break with the silver currencies of the member states and introduced the gold standard. Two months later, France stopped silver coinage by private individuals and thus initiated the transition to a so-called 'limping gold standard'. Germany and France henceforth belonged to the same metallic standard that England had used since 1717 and codified into law in 1821. With these three large European economies on the same standard, the dice were cast in favour of gold. Subsequently, network effects resulting from international trade and capital movements made the gold standard even more attractive.

Certainty among historians ends here, however, as the precise reasons behind the decisions of German and French authorities are less clear, owing to three main issues. First, did France's decision depend on the German coinage law passed two months prior? Second, were both governments acting under external impulses or did their decisions follow from a more fundamental desire to introduce the gold standard? At first glance, an external impulse appears likely in the case of France: Germany's transition to gold would release a considerable amount of German silver coins, an inflow of which might endanger the stability of French bimetallism. However, external forces might also have prevailed in the case of Germany. Since the late 1860s many German experts, adhered to the view that a transition to gold was not a question of principle but of timing. Third, what explains why other states (located primarily in Scandinavia) had already switched to the gold standard in the early 1870s (i.e. before Germany and France)? Does this fact—largely overlooked by existing scholarship—suggest that decisions to introduce the gold standard reflected structural developments that led the world, as it were with an invisible hand, towards gold monometallism?

The pre-conditions leading to the formation of the classical gold standard emerged earlier and were of a more general nature than the special interests of only one or two European states (Morys 2012). The enormous gold discoveries in California (1848) and Australia (1851) were the starting point, gradually shifting coin circulation in European economies from silver to gold. This gave rise to a pan-European movement demanding a transition to the gold standard. For the first time, sufficient gold appeared to be available to contemplate such a step. At the International Monetary Conference of 1867, the vast majority of countries spoke out in favour of adopting the gold standard. Notably, this was at a time when there was not yet any indication of the subsequent decline in the price of silver relative to gold. Germany and France only followed the general course of development shared by all countries that were on the silver or bimetallic standard in the 1860s (Morys 2012). The emergence of the classical gold standard was not an idiosyncratic process in which an incidental event—such as France's desire for revenge after the Franco-Prussian War of 1870 (Flandreau 1996)—caused a fundamental transformation of the world monetary system. Rather, the immense gold discoveries after 1848 set in motion a process that lasted approximately 25 years, gradually changing the world monetary system and eventually resulting in the emergence of the classical gold standard.

2.2 Germany's transition to the gold standard in 1873

From this perspective, the young German Empire has a significantly reduced role in the formation of the classical gold standard. The German states before 1871 and the German Empire afterwards represented only one player among many. Moreover, Germany was not the dominant player, either on its own or in conjunction with France. Within the German context, the reparation payments from France, which are occasionally mentioned in this context (Kindleberger 1984: 428; Friedman 1990), were likely not a significant factor in the German decision. After all, many other silver-currency countries, such as the Netherlands or the Scandinavian states, introduced the gold standard without such an addition to their reserves (Wiegand 2019: 11).

To view the founding of the Empire as a necessary condition for Germany's transition to the gold standard, one would need to emphasise institutional factors. Delegating coinage rules and monetary policy to the level of the Empire created an institutional framework in which a transition to gold could be decided quickly. A comparison with the Italian unification ten years earlier also shows a coinage policy that offered itself as a natural field of activity for the new state and quickly led to an intensive discussion regarding the preferred currency anchor (Fratianni and Spinelli 1997; Morys 2006: 67–88). However, such a perspective neglects two important aspects. First, the North German Confederation of 1867 already had the right to legislate on coinage and currency matters (Borchardt 1975). The Imperial Constitution of 16 April 1871 only transferred the competences of the southern German states in this regard to the level of the Empire. Second, in the 1850s and 1860s, coinage and currency policy became an issue that, owing to international implications, could not be easily settled at the individual-state level, and thus constituted a driving force for Germany's national unification. Institutional change was to some extent endogenous; economic challenges drove political integration, and the newly founded Empire could meet these challenges more aptly than the individual member states before 1871.

An analysis of the proceedings of the first national conventions of the chambers of commerce held in 1861, 1865, and 1868 helps shed light on the intellectual background against which the transition to gold took place in Germany.[1] While the treaties of Dresden (1838) and Vienna (1857) made progress towards harmonising coinage standards among German states, they fell short of unifying them. Consequently, in the 1860s, the issues of the currency anchor—gold, silver, or bimetallism—and of the weight (and shape) of individual coins—how many coins were to be minted from one pound of gold or silver—arose simultaneously. The partial adoption of the French system promised to solve both problems simultaneously. France had gold coins that were used in all states of the Latin Monetary Union (Belgium, France, Italy, and Switzerland), and their coinage was based on the modern system of metric units. Adopting the coinage system of the Latin Monetary Union made it possible to unify coinage among the German states and, at the same time, intensify the connection with a trading area that was more significant than Great Britain from the viewpoint of the German states. However, complete adoption of the French currency system was ruled out because of its bimetallic character, which was often derided as an 'alternating standard' at conventions of the German chambers of commerce: gold today and silver tomorrow. Hence, selective adoption presented a conceivable policy option: introduce the gold standard as practiced by France with respect to gold coins but disregard the system's bimetallic element.

The discussions at the conventions of the chambers of commerce in 1861, 1865, and 1868 culminated in the demand that the German Confederation or (after 1867) North German Confederation should hold legislative powers over coinage and currency matters. They argued that coinage and currency reform required cooperation and could not be pursued at the level of the individual member states. Accordingly, responsibility in monetary affairs was transferred to the North German Confederation in 1867 and then extended to all German states by the Imperial Constitution of 1871. This course of events supports the thesis that the Empire's formation played a facilitating role in the transition to the gold standard, rather than genuinely constituting a necessary condition. The transition to the gold standard would in all likelihood have occurred regardless, as simultaneous developments in several other European countries demonstrate.

3 Establishment of the Reichsbank and emergence of a unified monetary policy

3.1 Foundation of the Reichsbank in 1875

Establishing the *Reichsbank*—and the associated paper money reform—proved to be more difficult than transitioning to the gold standard and could only be tackled after the coinage and currency reform of July 1873. The coinage and currency reform required intensive cooperation between finance ministries, central banks, and mints; however, the actual costs were small.

The reforms of the banks of note issue and of paper money were an altogether different matter. The German states had little experience with using paper money, and the population was sceptical about banknotes and state paper. For example, in 1820, the widely read *Brockhaus Encyclopaedia* stated,

'The very notion of paper money sounds so terrible to many ears that they are frightened at the mere mentioning of it' (quoted from Deutsche Bundesbank 1963: VIII). However, over the course of the nineteenth century, the German states developed a keen interest in banks of note issue, which seemed as useful for both financing their own budgets as facilitating trade and industry. Sixteen banks were founded in the boom years between 1853 and 1856, and 20 more opened their doors before the founding of the German Empire (Sprenger 1981). These banks' spheres of activity overlapped in many cases, but not necessarily, with the territories of the individual German states. Some of these banks had a purely private ownership structure, while others were characterised by varying degrees of state involvement.

Even before the Empire was founded, the banks of note issue were perceived as insufficiently regulated and requiring reform. Furthermore, the individual states were anxious to preserve spheres of influence and sources of revenue; thus, they provided strong backing for the banks of note issue located in their own territory. Therefore, as a first step, it was only possible to agree in July 1873 to withdraw from circulation the state paper of the member states and low-value banknotes with denominations below 100 Marks (Sprenger 2001: 181). Both measures facilitated fiscal consolidation and were intended to strengthen confidence in the banks of note issue.

Meanwhile, the all-important question of which institution(s) would henceforth be allowed to issue banknotes was so controversially debated that the draft version of the intended piece of legislation remained completely silent on the matter. It simply did not mention an Imperial Bank at all (Bopp 1954: 34). The central bank issue quickly became the object of a conflict between advocates of centralism and advocates of federalism, a tension typical of the Empire's early years. Through the Banking Act of 14 March 1875, the centralists achieved the establishment of the *Reichsbank*, a central bank responsible for regulating the circulation of money throughout the Empire. Nevertheless, the federalists succeeded in preserving the note-issuing rights of the existing banks of note issue. This was a typical compromise of the 1870s, as it corresponded to the constellation of political power at the time. Moreover, as we explain below, it had a certain economic logic. At the time, the German money market was so poorly integrated that it could exist with—or even benefit from—different interest rate policies.

Thus, the plurality of banks of note issue was thus preserved—and with it their right to an independent interest rate policy implemented by setting discount rates. In total, 32 institutions carried on into the new era. Central bank oligopolies were by no means unusual in European comparison and were mostly an expression of a historical legacy of federalism. In 1861, Italy began with six such banks, and during the gradual expansion of the Greek national territory between 1864 and 1913, for banks in the newly-acquired territory, their note-issuing rights were left untouched (Fratianni and Spinelli 1997; Lazaretou 2014). Only the large number of banks of note issue was specific to the German case; however, this can easily be explained by the Empire's large number of member states.

The *Reichsbank* emerged from the *Preußische Bank* and took over its assets and liabilities as of 1 January 1876, and took its place alongside the existing banks of note issue. In many respects, creating a new central bank for the Empire as a whole was actually rebranding an existing organisation (Borchardt 1975). In the 1860s, the *Preußische Bank* already accounted for two-thirds of German banknotes in circulation and issued the only banknotes accepted in all states of the German Confederation. In some crises of the 1850s and 1860s, the Prussian Bank seems to have functioned as a central bank (Lichter 1999: 222–23; Otto 2002: 357–79). If the *Reichsbank* had not been founded, the Prussian Bank would likely have eventually acquired a position similar to that of the later *Reichsbank* on the basis of its market power. From the Prussian perspective, founding the *Reichsbank* offered the opportunity for a new institution that could be present throughout the territory of the Empire and thus gain greater acceptance.

3.2 Functions of the Reichsbank and gradual emergence of a uniform monetary policy

According to section 12 of the Banking Act, the *Reichsbank* had the threefold responsibility of regulating money circulation throughout the territory of the Reich, facilitating payment settlements, and supporting capital utilisation. We also find such formulations in the regulations of other central banks founded at around the same time (Morys 2014); however, they should not be misunderstood as a plan of action. We know little about the role of the *Reichsbank* as a commercial bank, and the 'utilisation of capital' (i.e. the granting of long-term loans) is at odds with the role of a central bank with its short-term assets and liabilities.

The truly decisive point was that the *Reichsbank* tied the German currency to the gold standard. As the only bank in the Empire, it was obliged to exchange currency from paper money into gold and from gold into paper money (Sprenger 2001: 182–85). It alone anchored the Mark in the gold standard. All banks of note issue had to cover at least one-third of the notes they issued with gold and silver coins, *Reichskassenscheine* (a type of state paper), gold bars, or foreign gold coins. For the remainder (i.e. a maximum of two-thirds of the banknotes in circulation), they had to hold discounted bills of exchange with a maximum maturity of three months. However, only the *Reichsbank* was obliged to buy gold bullion at a fixed price of 1,392 Marks for one pound of fine gold against the issue of its own notes. It was precisely this exchange obligation that ensured the approximate identity of the nominal value of coins and banknotes and the intrinsic value of gold coins.

These cover requirements made the discount rate (i.e. the annualised percentage deduction when selling a bill of exchange to the *Reichsbank* before maturity) the *Reichsbank*'s most important policy instrument. A challenge arose from the fact that the *Reichsbank* was competing in the money market with the other 32 banks of note issue, as they were trying to secure a larger market share by offering lower discount rates. In this situation, the *Reichsbank* not only had to fear for its own business but also could not be certain that its own discount rate would be the key rate of the German money market.

Despite recent work on the topic, especially by Mandeng (2019), our knowledge remains incomplete regarding how the interest rates of the *Reichsbank* and the other banks of note issue related to each other. However, a very general answer can be developed on the basis of older works (e.g. Bopp 1954). Until the 1890s, the dispersion of interest rates was considerable, with the official discount rate of the *Reichsbank* constituting the upper limit. For example, in 1881, *The Economist* stated:

> The rate of discount in Germany appears to differ much in different parts of the country. In the East of Germany 6 to 8 percent appears to be wanted for bills which may be done at 4 percent at the date elsewhere.
>
> (quoted in Mandeng 2019: 31)

The large interest rate differential reflected the young Empire's great economic heterogeneity. Regions in the thinly populated and mostly agrarian East had much higher interest rates than did the industrial West. In this situation, the other banks of note issue exploited their information advantage, namely the possibility of finding a market-clearing interest rate for their much smaller sphere of influence. However, such strong interest rate dispersion across the Empire could only persist because money market integration was still low in the 1870s and 1880s (for a similar finding for Norway, see Klovland and Oksendal 2017).

The many small banks of note issue benefited from continued market segmentation. After a certain hesitation phase (1875–80), the *Reichsbank* realised that it needed to push ahead with money market integration if it wanted to achieve a uniform monetary policy. Starting in 1880, it made use of a strategy similar to that of its competitors. It abandoned a uniform *Reichsbank* discount rate and introduced a so-called 'preferential discount rate' (Bopp 1954: 47–49). The preferential discount rate was far more variable than the official discount rate and was often 100 basis points (or more) below it. It was used for bills of exchange of higher quality, a minimum amount of 3,000 Marks, and a remaining time to maturity of at least six weeks. Bills of this type were not particularly numerous; however, they related to large transactions, and thus precisely to the market segment that determined the so-called 'Berlin stock exchange discount rate' (the key discount rate for commercial transactions). During some years, the *Reichsbank* conducted more than half of its transactions—in terms of volume, not number of bills—on the money market at the preferential rate (Bopp 1954: 49). With this instrument, the *Reichsbank* succeeded step-by-step in capturing larger parts of the discount market and imposing its own interest rate throughout the Empire. The price for this was, of course, that the preferential discount rate was often only a few basis points above the Berlin stock exchange discount rate.

Unfortunately, this process has not been quantitatively researched. The *Reichsbank* made two attempts to impose its own interest rate on the banks of note issue, first in 1887 in a convention with the latter and then by law in 1899 (Mandeng 2019: 38, 81). The first attempt failed, seemingly because money market integration had not sufficiently progressed, allowing the other central banks to escape from the harmonising impulse of the *Reichsbank*. However, the second attempt succeeded, and starting in 1899, the banks of note issue mostly followed the *Reichsbank* discount rate.

3.3 Foundation of the Reichsbank: turning point or evolutionary step?

The gradual emergence of a key interest rate suggests that the founding of the *Reichsbank* was not so much a turning point as an evolutionary step—albeit an important one—in the development of monetary policy in Germany. Such an evolutionary view is supported by some regulations of the Banking Act of 1875. The law set a maximum for each bank's uncovered note circulation. The *Reichsbank* was allowed 250 million Marks, whereas the other 32 banks of note issue together were allowed only 135 million Marks. These quotas were of great practical importance. For example, in the initial phase of the *Reichsbank*, approximately one-third of its banknotes circulated uncovered (Sprenger 2001: 186). Furthermore, according to section 9 of the Banking Act, the quotas of banks that ceased to issue banknotes fell to the *Reichsbank*. This favoured the rise of the *Reichsbank*, as can be seen from the composition of circulating banknotes. The *Reichsbank*'s share of the total issue, which had already amounted to 77 percent in 1876, reached 88 and 94 percent in 1900 and 1913, respectively (Sprenger 1982: 137).

The rise of the *Reichsbank* was paralleled by a sharp decline in the number of private and state banks of note issue. Out of 32 banks, 15 ceased issuing as soon as 1875 and became purely commercial banks. This first wave of closures involved mostly small banks that were aware they would be unable to compete with the coming branch offices of the *Reichsbank* at their own places of business. However, the more the *Reichsbank* sought monetary sovereignty, the more difficult it became for the other banks to defend their niche. Nine of them fell victim to this development during the period of preferential discount rates (1880–98), this time including larger banks such as the *Hannoversche Bank*. The banking crisis of 1901 did the rest, and after 1906, only four banks of note issue other than the *Reichsbank* remained: the *Bayerische Notenbank*, *Sächsische Bank*, *Badische Bank*, and *Württembergische Notenbank* (Mandeng 2019: 41). No research has yet been conducted on why exactly these four banks were able to hold on (until 1934); however, it is likely that the governments of the strong southern German states, eager for a certain level of independence, played a role.

Other developments helped the *Reichsbank* establish itself as a true central bank. The *Reichsbank's* role as a lender-of-last-resort remains little known, with only the financial crisis of 1901 receiving some attention (Bopp 1954: 202). At that time, the *Reichsbank* appears to have fulfilled its obligation as the last source of credit in a series of bank collapses, while the fourth and fifth largest banks of note issue, the *Frankfurter Bank* and *Bank für Süddeutschland*, ceased operations (Mandeng 2019: 41). The banking crisis of 1901 appears *prima facie* similar to the cases of Belgium and Italy, where banking crises offered the emerging central bank an opportunity to strengthen its own position (Bonelli 1991; Buyst and Maas 2008).

An important instrument for the ascendency of the *Reichsbank* to money market dominance was the establishment of a nationwide network of branch offices offering payment and clearing services. The number of *Reichsbank* branches rose from 182 in 1876 to 487 in 1914, making the *Reichsbank* the only bank with a presence throughout Germany. By the First World War, the number of customers had increased eightfold and the turnover on these accounts increased twentyfold (Burhop 2011: 124). Beyond strengthening the *Reichsbank*'s position in the money market, the operation of a network of payment services also benefitted its management of reserves. In contrast to banknotes, current account balances did not need to be covered by gold, and the increasing reliance on cashless payment reduced the demand for gold coins. From a monetary policy perspective, the rapid growth of current account holdings and the relative decline of cash holdings made it easier to comply with the Banking Act's reserve requirements.

4 The monetary policy of the Reichsbank, the classical gold standard, and price level stability

4.1 The monetary policy of the Reichsbank and the classical gold standard

The monetary policy of the *Reichsbank* was never limited to discount rate policy, and beginning in 1898, open market policy (buying and selling securities on the open market) and foreign exchange policy (buying and selling foreign assets with the aim of influencing the exchange rate) appear to have played a greater role (Bopp 1954: 202–04). However, a comparative study of central bank balance sheets suggests that at least foreign exchange policy played only a subordinate role (Bazot et al. 2019). Thus, for good reason, existing scholarship analyses the monetary policy of central banks before the First World War through their discount rate policy (Bloomfield 1959; Morys 2013).

Quantitative research conducted over the last 20 years has established that the *Reichsbank*'s monetary policy was very successful in international comparison (Bordo and McDonald 2005; Morys 2013). In particular, the *Reichsbank* is seen as a good example of meeting the external constraints imposed by the rules of the gold standard without unduly burdening the domestic economy. In a system of fixed exchange rates with free movement of capital, a small open economy is forced to follow the global interest rate, implying that, in principle, it loses its monetary autonomy (so-called 'macroeconomic trilemma'; Obstfeld et al. 2005). However, neither on a theoretical nor an empirical level is it clear how binding this constraint actually is.

In the case of the classical gold standard, scholarship relating to the macroeconomic trilemma has its roots in the classical discussion regarding the 'rules of the game' which goes back to Keynes: how rigid or how flexible were these rules? (Nurkse 1944; Bloomfield 1959). The *Reichsbank* appears to have been able to manage the tension between the external and domestic constraints of the gold standard. It maintained exchange rates very close to gold parity (i.e. the exchange rate between two gold currencies defined by the intrinsic value of their coin). Exchange rates showed similarly narrow fluctuations around gold parity only in England, France, and the Netherlands. Moreover, the *Reichsbank* was one of the few central banks that always allowed banknotes to be exchanged for gold without delay and in unlimited amounts (Morys 2013: 211). The continued adherence to both rules made Germany's use of the gold standard credible in the eyes of market participants, and Germany became one of five core countries on the classical gold standard alongside England, France, Belgium, and the Netherlands.

This credibility created considerable leeway with respect to monetary policy (Bordo and McDonald 2005), and the *Reichsbank* was not forced to always counteract gold outflows by raising the discount rate. In an effort to shield the domestic economy from the vicissitudes of international capital markets, it left the discount rate at a low level and sterilised the gold outflow (i.e. expanded the domestic component of the money supply to counteract the gold outflow). Specifically, it increased the volume of discounting, although the rules of the gold standard actually require the exact opposite. Thus, the conflict between internal and external stability inherent in this system of fixed exchange rates was minimised. Recent research by Bazot et al. (2019) shows that only the five core states of the gold standard were actually in this privileged position.

Germany appears to have enjoyed this greater monetary autonomy partly because it evolved over time from an interest rate follower to an interest rate setter—at least within continental Europe. Thiemeyer's (2009: 82–94) assertion that the transition to gold was part of Germany's strategy to play a leading role in European monetary policy is probably overdrawn. Nevertheless, over time, the *Reichsbank* came to play a leading role among the central banks of mainland Europe. For example, Morys (2013: 214–15) shows that the discount rate decisions of the central banks of Italy, the Netherlands, Austria-Hungary, and the Scandinavian states can be better explained by the interest rate policy of the *Reichsbank* than by that of the Bank of England.

The *Reichsbank* acquired this privileged role partly because the Mark was increasingly perceived as an important currency; it became a leading currency under the classical gold standard after the British pound and alongside the French franc (Lindert 1969; Flandreau and Jobst 2005). From the turn of the twentieth century, foreign assets accounted for an increasingly large share of reserves, pushing central banks to decide the currency in which they wanted to invest their foreign exchange reserves. For example, in 1913, the Austro-Hungarian Bank held 60.2 percent of its currency reserves in Marks (Morys 2006: 18). The Mark also became the currency for many European loans (Feis 1931; Austrian National Bank et al. 2014), albeit rarely on its own and typically alongside the Pound, the Franc, and gold itself, that is, subscription to the bond and interest payment could be made in any of the four currencies.

German capital exporters played an important role in this process, as they wanted to hold foreign investments in their own currency. Capital exports increased so much in the late nineteenth century that Germany became the third most important capital exporter after England and France (Daudin et al. 2010). Germany's share of global foreign investment was 12.8 percent in 1913, against 41.8 and 19.8 percent for Great Britain and France, respectively, of which just over half was invested in Europe (53.3 percent). Admittedly, this was not solely a consequence of the *Reichsbank's* good monetary policy. A high level of capital exports reflects a strong real economy in which a high savings rate led, among other things, to foreign investment. Nevertheless, monetary policy was part of a virtuous cycle in which the monetary and real economies supported each other.

4.2 Price level stability and perception of the gold standard by the population and politicians

Introducing the gold standard was also intended to ensure price level stability. Although the price level remained stable in the long run, there were nevertheless considerable annual price changes and long phases of inflation and deflation. Prices showed a tendency to rise between 1850 and 1875, fell between 1875 and 1895, and then rose again between 1895 and 1913—all as a more or less direct consequence of the discovery of gold deposits in California (1848), Australia (1851), South Africa (1888), and Alaska (1896). The longer the period we choose to examine, the more stable the price level appears. In an overall view of the period from 1871 to 1913, the average annual inflation rate reached only 0.5 percent. However, during the first decade following national unification, the cost of living rose by 15.5 percent between 1871 and 1874, only to fall by 14.9 percent by 1880. Thus, while there was price level stability between 1871 and 1880, the average absolute annual price change was a full 4.5 percent. Under the gold standard, prices fluctuated far more than the average inflation rate would suggest (Sprenger 2001: 189–91; Burhop 2011: 135–36).

To date, no systematic research has examined how the population of the Empire perceived the gold standard and the *Reichsbank*.[2] Several indications suggest that people were aware that they benefitted from the gold standard, even if in an unspecified manner. For example, in 1878, Bismarck refused to attend the First Bimetallic Conference on the grounds that no one should doubt Germany's adherence to the recently introduced gold standard. Three years later, a small delegation was sent to the Second Bimetallic Conference—for purely domestic political reasons—but with the clear instruction from Bismarck not to engage in meaningful negotiation (Reti 1998). When the *Reichsbank*'s monetary policy came under serious criticism for the first time in 1907 in the context of the American banking crisis, a commission was set up with the aim of regaining lost confidence (Bopp 1954: 206). In the same year, silver lost its legal tender status (it had previously retained this status up to a certain amount), and two years later, 'Imperial currency' was officially renamed 'gold currency' (Sprenger 2001: 187–88). Although these might all constitute isolated measures, they could also have been small steps on the way to anchoring the gold currency more firmly in the consciousness of the population.

5 Conclusion

In this chapter, we have established that the gold standard and the *Reichsbank* were successful institutions of the German Empire. The gold standard brought price and exchange rate stability, and Germany rose to become one of the core countries of the classical gold standard. This is evidenced by Germany's interest rate leadership with respect to the economies of the European mainland. The *Reichsbank*, which at the beginning of the period under study still had to ward off competition from several private and state banks of note issue, became an important central bank alongside the much older institutions of the Bank of England (1694) and the Bank of France (1803).

Can we conclude from this that the foundation of the Empire was an important turning point in German monetary history? In particular, the close chronological parallels between the founding of the Empire, transition to the gold standard (1873), and founding of the *Reichsbank* (1875) seem to support such a view. Nevertheless, the evidence reviewed in this chapter points to an evolutionary development of the monetary regime of Germany. A unified monetary policy did not emerge immediately in 1875, but resulted from the gradual convergence of the interest rates of various banks of note issue, in a process drawn out over 25 years in which the *Reichsbank* skilfully exploited the opportunities created by the Bank Act of 1875. Similarly, the creation of the German Empire facilitated the adoption of the gold standard; however, this important step would have likely also occurred without political unification. Most other European states also introduced the gold standard at approximately the same time—sometimes earlier, sometimes later.

Rather, the transition to the gold standard and founding of the *Reichsbank* can be interpreted from a perspective that reverses the direction of causality. Germans perceived a common currency and unified monetary policy as being in their economic interest in the 1850s and 1860s. Both objectives could be achieved more easily in a federation, rather than on the individual-state level; thus, they became an economic force behind political integration. The founding of the German Empire in 1871 was, therefore, to some extent, endogenous to economic motivations.

The adoption of the gold standard and founding of the *Reichsbank* took place at the beginning of a 40-year period of economic expansion that made the German Reich one of the three major industrialised nations alongside Great Britain and the United States. This stands in some analogy to the monetary reform of 1948 and founding of the *Bank deutscher Länder* (1948, since 1957 *Bundesbank*), which—at least in public discourse—are often seen as the starting point of the German economic miracle of the 1950s and 1960s. The second major episode of German monetary history is widely considered a key element in the economic history of the Federal Republic of Germany. By contrast, little is known about this first episode, and it has many research gaps. Thus, correcting this imbalance is a task for future research.

Notes

1 The proceedings have been published as Verhandlungen des ersten deutschen Handelstages zu Heidelberg. Heidelberg 1861; Verhandlungen des dritten deutschen Handelstages zu Frankfurt am Main. Frankfurt a. M. 1865; Verhandlungen des vierten deutschen Handelstages zu Berlin. Berlin 1868. For an analysis, see Morys (2019).
2 The only exception is the research on the discussion of gold monometallism versus bimetallism in the 1880s and 1890s; see Thiemeyer (2009: 140–46 and 199–201).

References

Austrian National Bank, Bank of Greece, Bulgarian National Bank and National Bank of Romania (eds) (2014) *South-Eastern European Monetary and Economic Statistics from the Nineteenth Century to World War II*, Vienna: Austrian National Bank.

Bazot, G., Monnet, E. and Morys, M. (2019) 'Taming the global financial cycle: central banks and the sterilization of capital flows in the first era of globalization (1891–1913)', *CEPR Discussion Paper 13895.*

Bloomfield, A. I. (1959) *Monetary Policy under the International Gold Standard, 1880–1915*, New York: Federal Reserve Bank of New York.

Bonelli, F. (ed) (1991) *La Banca d'Italia dal 1894 al 1913: Momenti della formazione di una banca centrale*, Rome: Banca d'Italia.

Bopp, K. R. (1954) 'Die Tätigkeit der Reichsbank von 1876 bis 1914', *Weltwirtschaftliches Archiv*, Vol. 72 (1): 34–59, (2): 179–222.

Borchardt, K. (1975) 'Währung und Wirtschaft (von der Reichsgründung bis zum 1. Weltkrieg)', in Deutsche Bundesbank (ed), *Währung und Wirtschaft in Deutschland 1876–1975*, Frankfurt a. M.: Knapp, pp. 3–55.

Bordo, M. D. and McDonald, R. (2005) 'Interest rate interactions in the classical gold standard, 1880–1914: was there any monetary independence?' *Journal of Monetary Economics*, Vol. 52 (2): 307–27.

Burhop, C. (2011) *Wirtschaftsgeschichte des deutschen Kaiserreichs, 1871–1918*, Göttingen: Vandenhoeck & Ruprecht.

Buyst, E. and Maas, I. (2008) 'Central banking in nineteenth-century Belgium: was the NBB a lender of last resort?', *Financial History Review*, Vol. 15 (2): 153–73.

Daudin, G., Morys, M. and O'Rourke, K. (2010) 'Globalization 1870–1914', in S. Broadberry and K. O'Rourke (eds), *An Economic History of Modern Europe*, Vol. 2, Cambridge: Cambridge University Press, pp. 5–29.

Deutsche Bundesbank (ed) (1963) *Deutsches Papiergeld 1772–1870*, Munich: Giesecke & Devrient.

Eichengreen, B. (2008) *Globalizing Capital: A History of the International Monetary System*, 2nd ed., Princeton: Princeton University Press.

Feis, H. (1931) *Europe: The World's Banker 1870–1914*, New Haven: Yale University Press.

Fisher, I. (1894) 'The mechanics of bimetallism', *Economic Journal*, Vol. 4 (15): 527–37.

Flandreau, M. (1996) 'The French crime of 1873: an essay on the emergence of the international gold standard, 1870–1880', *Journal of Economic History*, Vol. 56 (4): 862–97.

Flandreau, M. and Jobst, C. (2005) 'The ties that divide: a network analysis of the international monetary system, 1890–1910', *Journal of Economic History*, Vol. 65 (4): 977–1007.

Fratianni, M. and Spinelli, F. (1997) *A Monetary History* of *Italy*, Cambridge: Cambridge University Press.

Friedman, M. (1990) 'Bimetallism revisited', *Journal of Economic Perspectives*, Vol. 4 (4): 85–104.

Kindleberger, C. (1984) *A Financial History of Western Europe*, London: Allen & Unwin.

Klovland, J. T. and Oksendal, L. F. (2017) 'The decentralised central bank: bank rate autonomy and capital market integration in Norway, 1858–1892', *European Review of Economic History*, Vol. 21 (3): 259–79.

Lazaretou, S. (2014) 'Greece: from 1833 to 1949', in Oesterreichische Nationalbank, Bank of Greece, Bulgarian National Bank and National Bank of Romania (eds), *South-East European Monetary and Economic Statistics from the Nineteenth Century to World War II*, Vienna: Austrian National Bank, pp. 101–70.

Lichter, J. (1999) *Preußische Notenbankpolitik in der Formationsphase des Zentralbanksystems 1844–1857*, Berlin: Duncker & Humblot.

Lindert, P. H. (1969) *Key Currencies and Gold, 1900–1913, Princeton:* Princeton University, Department of Economics, *International Finance Section.*

Mandeng, O. J. (2019) *Central Bank Reform, Spatial Diversity and Monetary Policy in Germany, 1876–1890*, Ph.D. thesis, London School of Economics and Political Science.

Meissner, C. (2005) 'A new world order: explaining the international diffusion of the gold standard, 1870–1913', *Journal of International Economics*, Vol. 66 (2): 385–406.

Meissner C. (2015) 'The limits of bimetallism', in O. Humpage (ed), *Federal Reserve Policy Seen Through the Lens of Economic History: Essays to Commemorate the Federal Reserve System's Centennial*, Cambridge: Cambridge University Press, pp. 194–216.

Morys, M. (2006) *The classical gold standard in the European periphery: a case study of Austria-Hungary and Italy, 1870–1913*, Ph.D. thesis, London School of Economics and Political Science.

Morys, M. (2012) 'The emergence of the classical gold standard', *Centre for Historical Economics and Related Research at York Discussion Papers* 12/01.

Morys, M. (2013) 'Discount rate policy under the classical gold standard: core versus periphery (1870s–1914)', *Explorations in Economic History*, Vol. 50 (2): 205–26.
Morys, M. (2014) 'South-Eastern European monetary history in a pan-European perspective, 1841–1939', in Austrian National Bank, Bank of Greece, Bulgarian National Bank and National Bank of Romania (eds), *South-Eastern European Monetary and Economic Statistics from the Nineteenth Century to World War II*, Vienna: Austrian National Bank, pp. 25–53.
Morys, M. (2019) 'Der weltweite Übergang zum klassischen Goldstandard in den 1870er Jahren: reiner Zufall oder tiefere Kräfte?', in G. Schulz (ed), *Ordnung und Chaos: Trends und Brüche in der Wirtschafts- und Sozialgeschichte*, Stuttgart: Steiner, pp. 95–112.
Nurske, D. (1944) *International Currency Experience: Lessons of the Interwar Period*, Geneva: League of Nations.
Obstfeld, M., Shambaugh, J. C. and Taylor, A. M. (2005) 'The trilemma in history: tradeoffs among exchange rates, monetary policies, and capital mobility', *Review of Economics and Statistics*, Vol. 87 (3): 423–38.
Oppers, S. E. (1996) 'Was the worldwide shift to gold inevitable? an analysis of the end of bimetallism', *Journal of Monetary Economics*, Vol. 37 (1): 143–62.
Oppers, S. E. (2000) 'A model of the bimetallic system', *Journal of Monetary Economics*, Vol. 46 (2): 517–33.
Otto, F. (2002) Die Entstehung eines nationalen Geldes: Integrationsprozesse der deutschen Währungen im 19. Jahrhundert, Berlin: Duncker & Humblot.
Reti, S. P. (1998) *Silver and Gold: The Political Economy of International Monetary Conferences, 1867–1892*, Westport: Greenwood.
Sprenger, B. (1981) 'Währungswesen und Währungspolitik in Deutschland von 1834 bis 1875', *Kölner Vorträge und Abhandlungen zur Sozial- und Wirtschaftsgeschichte* 33.
Sprenger, B. (1982) 'Geldmengenänderungen in Deutschland im Zeitalter der Industrialisierung (1835 bis 1913)', *Kölner Vorträge und Abhandlungen zur Sozial- und Wirtschaftsgeschichte* 36.
Sprenger, B. (2001) *Das Geld der Deutschen*, Paderborn: Schöningh.
Thiemeyer, G. (2009) *Internationalismus und Diplomatie: Währungspolitische Kooperation im europäischen Staatensystem 1865–1900*, Berlin: De Gruyter.
Wiegand, J. (2019) 'Destabilizing the global monetary system: Germany's adoption of the gold standard in the early 1870s', *International Monetary Fund Working Paper* 19/32.

10 Patent law and technical progress

Alexander Donges and Jochen Streb

1 Introduction

In contrast to the industrial pioneers England, France, and the United States, the newly founded German Empire had no national patent law that allowed inventors to efficiently protect their innovations against unauthorised imitation. Murmann (2003: 29) considers this lack of patent protection as an important reason for the rapid rise of the German chemical industry. Without paying royalties, German entrepreneurs could imitate innovative synthetic dyes developed in France and Britain and sell these products on the unprotected German market. Starting in the 1860s, many companies were founded in the German chemical industry. These companies engaged in fierce price competition, and only those market participants able to quickly reduce their production costs survived. The winners of this German selection process could then also successfully compete with foreign rivals. In Murmann's view, the latter did not achieve comparable efficiency gains because they had become comfortable in their patent-protected domestic monopoly. Kiesewetter (1992: 170) notes a comparable development in the mechanical engineering industry. Foreign competitors regarded German machine builders as 'the most notorious pirates' in Europe (Richter and Streb 2011). Schiff (1971) makes a similar argument in claiming that Switzerland and the Netherlands owe their rapid industrialisation to the absence of their own patent laws.

However, comparisons with these two neighbouring states of the German Empire must not lead to the conclusion that the German Patent Law of 25 May 1877 was the first modern patent system introduced on German soil (Reichsgesetzblatt 1877: 501–10). Just as in Italy, where a national patent law replaced the older patent laws of the formerly independent Italian principalities in 1864, patent systems had existed in most German territories since the beginning of the nineteenth century (Nuvolari and Vasta 2019). Therefore, unlike in Switzerland, for example, the institutional change was more gradual. However, for German companies, the unification of domestic patent law created a considerable advantage. Beginning in 1877, it was sufficient to acquire a single patent to obtain patent protection throughout the German

DOI: 10.4324/9781003283430-12

Empire, while before harmonisation, patent protection had to be applied for separately in each German state.

To assess how the introduction of the German Patent Law affected technical progress—Seckelmann (2006: 1) calls this law a 'reaction accelerator'—it is necessary to find a measure that allows innovation activities to be compared over time and across regions. In Section 2, we briefly discuss whether patent statistics meet this requirement. In Section 3, we explain the diversity of German patent systems prior to the introduction of the German Patent Law. In this way, we establish the prerequisites for Section 4, in which we discuss the effects of the German Patent Law on the structure of patentees and their inventions. Our discussion shows that the introduction of the German Patent Law had other economic effects beyond promoting innovation and growth. In particular, we argue in Section 5 that the introduction of a nationwide patent system facilitated restraints on competition. Section 6 concludes.

2 The quantification of technical progress

Measuring technical progress by using patent statistics is not a generally accepted practice. As Figure 10.1 illustrates, patents describe only a subset of all innovations created in a society, either because patent law does not allow certain innovations to be patented or because some inventors prefer to protect their innovations from imitation by keeping them secret instead of filing a patent. To provide empirical evidence for the supposed differences between patents and innovations, Moser (2012) uses data on products exhibited at World's Fairs hosted since 1851. According to Moser, these exhibits reveal a more comprehensive picture of innovation activity than do patents. Based on

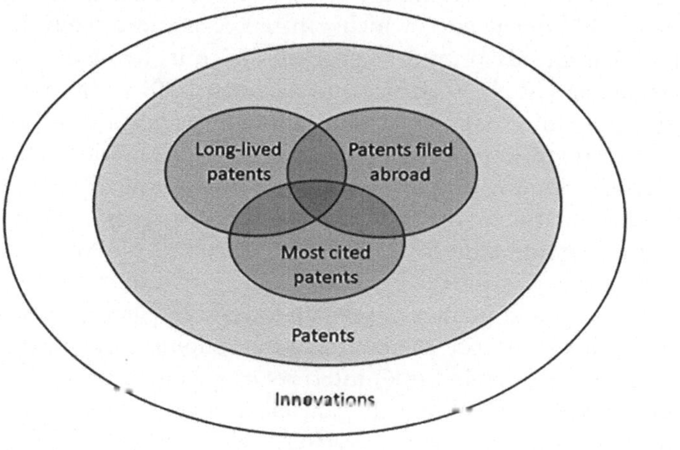

Figure 10.1 Innovations, patents, and valuable patents.
Source: Streb (2016: 450).

her observation that only a small proportion of exhibits were patented, Moser concludes that, in the nineteenth century, most inventors still refrained from protecting their innovations by filing patents. However, Domini (2020) criticises Moser's use of World's Fair exhibits as a proxy for innovation, arguing that, at World's Fairs, firms primarily advertised finished goods they wanted to export, but rarely the innovative machines and processes used to produce them. This controversy illustrates the difficulties in quantifying innovation. Since alternative innovation proxies are often not available or also have their weaknesses, researchers still have little choice but to rely on patent statistics. A notable advantage is that patent data are collected systematically and usually include extensive information, such as the name and location of the patentee and the intended field of application of the invention.

Merely counting the number of patents cannot account for differences with respect to the technological and economic impact of patented innovations. Some patents protect ground-breaking basic innovations, such as Nicolaus Otto's four-stroke engine (granted by the Imperial Patent Office in 1877 under patent number 532), while many others concern less significant inventions, such as the 'device for cutting boiled eggs' (patent number 27,632), patented in 1883. Recent research has established three different methods to address this problem and identify the valuable patents within a set of all patents (Streb 2016: 448–53). In empirical studies that analyse patenting activities after 1945, it has become common practice to measure the value of patents by the frequency with which they are cited in subsequent patents (cf. Jaffe and Trajtenberg 2002). However, since citing important precursor patents was not common before World War II, we must use one of the two other methods, when analysing historical patent statistics.

First, it can make sense to focus on innovations that a patentee also patented in foreign countries. Establishing such international patent families involves considerable additional cost, which a patentee is more likely to bear if an innovation has already proved its profitability in its home market (Cantwell 1989; Degner and Streb 2013; Sáiz and Amengual 2018). Second, whenever a patent system requires regular patent renewal by paying an additional fee, it is possible to distinguish patents with respect to their duration (Sullivan 1994). In the German Empire, such a renewal fee was due annually, and the price increased as the duration of the patent increased, starting with an initial fee of 50 Marks at the beginning of the second year, and up to 700 Marks at the beginning of the fifteenth year, the longest possible patent term. This fee structure prompted most patent holders to give up low-profit patents early so that only about 10 percent of all patents granted in the Empire reached a lifespan of ten years or more. Streb et al. (2006) interpret patents maintained for at least ten years as the subset of economically valuable innovations during this period.

In the following, we employ various patent statistics. Considering the qualifications discussed above, we assume that these statistics allow us to analyse the development of technical progress in the German Empire and its predecessor states with sufficient accuracy.

3 German patent systems in the period before 1877

Prior to the introduction of the nationwide German Patent Law, several different patent systems existed across the German states. The state governments gradually introduced these patent systems during the first half of the nineteenth century (Donges and Selgert 2019a). This development reflects the general reform process and professionalisation of the bureaucracy at the time.

The Prussian patent system was based on a royal decree issued in 1815 (Donges and Selgert 2020). Unlike England and other European countries that used registration systems without sophisticated novelty examinations (Mokyr 2009), the Prussian patent system required every invention to be reviewed by a technical commission. Based on this examination, officials in the Prussian Ministry of the Interior (later in the Ministry of Trade) had the final decision on patent approval (Heggen 1975: 31–32). In practice, this procedure set very high hurdles for obtaining a Prussian patent, as the responsible civil servants could only rarely be convinced of an invention's novelty. This restrictive approach, which stood in sharp contrast to the patent policies of other countries, was enforced by advocates of economic liberalism, who had a strong influence on the Prussian government. These liberals understood patents primarily as an instrument to restrict competition, while the outnumbered supporters of a more active industrial policy wanted to encourage innovation by granting patents more generously. In this respect, the low number of patents per capita in comparison to other countries is not a proof of Prussia's technological backwardness, but rather reflects the specific design of its patent system.

According to older literature, the Prussian patent system hampered innovation due to its restrictive patent policy (Heggen 1975); however, recent research questions this view. In this context, it is worth noting that Prussian patent fees were very low, compared to those of other countries. Since the mid-nineteenth century, patent fees amounted to only 1 to 2.5 Thalers in Prussia, enabling even inventors with limited financial resources to file for a patent (Donges and Selgert 2019a: 77). Donges and Selgert (2020) argue that the Prussian patent system fostered innovation through the interaction of two different channels: low fees encouraged patent applications and restrained patent-granting maintained competition between innovators. In combination with other factors, such as its excellent education system, the design of the patent system might have been an important reason for Prussia's technological catching-up in the mid-nineteenth century.

Other German states were inspired by the Prussian example and soon introduced their own patent systems (Donges and Selgert 2019a: 61–62). The Kingdom of Bavaria integrated rules on granting patents into trade law in 1825, the government of the Grand Duchy of Baden issued a patent decree in 1827, and the Kingdoms of Württemberg and Saxony followed with their own legislation in 1828. Other medium-sized states started to regulate the granting of patents later: the Kingdom of Hanover in 1847, Electorate of Hesse in 1852, and Grand Duchy of Hesse in 1858. Some smaller German

Table 10.1 Average yearly number of patents granted per million inhabitants

	Novelty examination		*Registration system*	
	Prussia	*Baden*	*Bavaria*[a]	*Saxony*[b]
1840–49	4.1	3.1	19.1	10.9
1850–59	3.8	11.7	11.7	42.0
1860–69	3.6	27.6	20.0	70.0
1870–77	8.3	73.7	32.1	104.8

Data source: Donges and Selgert (2019a, p. 70).

a Bavaria used a registration system with formal novelty examination between 1853 and 1861

b Saxony used technical novelty examinations before 1853.

principalities did not establish specific patent laws; however, in administrative practice, they adhered to the principles set by their larger neighbouring states when granting patents. Other states, including the three Hanseatic cities, did not grant patents at all. Donges and Selgert (2019a) show that, prior to 1877, the German patent systems differed regarding the application and approval process, treatment of foreign inventors, and level of patent fees.

These legal differences may explain the large geographical variation in the number of patents granted per capita (Table 10.1). The most astonishing contrast is between Prussia and Bavaria. While Prussia granted only 3.6 patents per million inhabitants and year in the 1860s, Bavaria granted 20, although at that time, Bavaria was economically underdeveloped when compared to Prussia. This example illustrates that the number of patents granted is not a meaningful proxy for innovation when comparing countries that have different patent laws.

Prior to the founding of the German Empire, there were attempts to harmonise the various patent systems in the *Zollverein* (the German customs union); however, these had only limited success. In 1842, the *Zollverein* states signed a joint agreement on patenting, but it did not include mutual patent recognition by the member states. As in the period before, inventors had to apply for separate patents in each member state to protect their inventions in the entire territory of the *Zollverein*. An aggravating factor was that a patent application could be approved in one state but still rejected in another. One reason for the failure to achieve more far-reaching harmonisation was that the Prussian proponents of a restrictive patent policy were unable to compromise with the patent-friendly representatives of Saxony and the southern German states.

Therefore, the *Zollverein* agreement of 1842 was limited to rules primarily aimed at preventing the erosion of free trade through the use of patents (Donges and Selgert 2019a: 71–72). Unlike modern patent law, a member state's patent on an innovative product, such as a novel cotton yarn, did not forbid a competitor from importing this product from other states and distributing it within the geographical scope of the patent. Only manufacturing a product innovation within the territory of the patent was prohibited. Comprehensive production and sale monopolies applied only to machinery and machinery-like products. This differentiation had far-reaching consequences for patenting strategies in the *Zollverein*. From 1842 onward, firms filed mainly patents for machines and production methods. Patents for other end products were of less importance. It is conceivable that this patenting practice strengthened inter-firm competition, particularly in the emerging chemical industry. Since patents only protected the innovative process needed to manufacture a new chemical product but not the product itself, competitors were motivated to circumvent patent protection by discovering alternative production methods. No such incentives existed in Britain and other industrialised countries where not only new production methods but also new chemical products could be patented. Therefore, the innovative drive of German chemical companies quickly surpassed that of their foreign competitors (Murmann 2003: 29).

In the Constitution of the North German Confederation of 1867, Prussia insisted that granting patents become a federal competence. Bismarck hoped that this centralisation would make it possible to fully abolish patent protection within the Confederation. However, an attempt to do so failed as early as 1868, owing to opposition from business people (Seckelmann 2015: 49). In 1871, the Constitution of the German Empire adopted the provisions of the North German Confederation. Article 4 lists patents on inventions and the protection of intellectual property among numerous economic and legal affairs that were to be subject to the supervision and legislation of the Empire (Bundesgesetzblatt des Deutschen Bundes No. 16 1871: 65). Hereby the Constitution of 1871 also followed on from the draft constitution of the Frankfurt National Assembly of 1849, which had already proposed the nationwide unification of the patent system (Stenographischer Bericht über die Verhandlungen der deutschen constituierenden Nationalversammlung zu Frankfurt am Main Vol. 8, 1849: 5756). However, the fundamental conflict between advocates of a patent-friendly legislation in the southern German states and Prussian patent-critics continued even after the German Empire was founded. The attempts to reach a compromise among the federal states succeeded only during the *Gründerkrise*—the economic downturn of the mid-1870s—which strengthened the preference for more state intervention in the economy among Prussian government officials. Moreover, foreign countries pushed the German Empire to reform its patent law and adapt it to international practice (Seckelmann 2006: 155–79), arguing that foreign inventors should be granted similar legal protections in Germany as German inventors already had abroad.

Finally, the German Patent Law of 25 May 1877 harmonised the German patent system and transferred the granting of patents to a central authority, the Imperial Patent Office, as stipulated in the Imperial Constitution. Although more than six years passed between the adoption of the Constitution and the patent law, the process of legal harmonisation took even longer in other areas. For example, civil law was only unified when the nationwide German Civil

Code was introduced in 1900. Low costs are a possible explanation for the comparatively rapid harmonisation of patent law. The Imperial Patent Office dispensed with decentralised structures; thus, the old patent authorities of the federal states, which had existed before 1877 could be easily dissolved. The insights gained in the previous discussions between the member states of the *Zollverein* also facilitated the unification of the patent systems.

4 Economic consequences of patent law harmonisation

In many respects, the German Patent Law incorporated elements that had already been common patenting practices prior to 1877. Paragraph 1 of the German Patent Law, for example, explicitly excludes 'inventions of foodstuffs, beverages, pharmaceuticals, as well as of substances produced by chemical means, unless the inventions concern a specific process to produce the objects' from patent protection, thus confirming the previous practice in the *Zollverein*. With regard to other legal characteristics, the harmonisation of German patent laws led many states to considerable discontinuities, owing to the differences that existed before 1877. In the following, we consider three essential features that changed in 1877 as a result of introducing the German Patent Law and discuss the potential economic effects of these changes.

4.1 Implementation of novelty examinations

Although the German Patent Law of 1877 did not fully incorporate the Prussian patent system, it did adopt one of its essential characteristics: the technical novelty examination of patent applications. Therefore, the unification of patent law marked a turning point, especially for Bavaria and Saxony. Before 1877, these states had a registration system without comprehensive technical novelty examination of patent applications, which was similar to the French model at that time (Seckelmann 2006: 79–86; Donges and Selgert 2019a: 73). By contrast, not only Prussia but also the other medium-sized German states applied novelty examinations.

From the perspective of a patent applicant, a registration system had both advantages and disadvantages compared to a novelty examination. It obviously would have been straightforward to apply successfully for a patent under a registration system. However, patents previously examined for novelty were more valuable on average, as it would be easier to enforce these patents in court in the case of litigation with imitators, when compared to patents that a technical commission had not yet officially determined to be novel (Khan and Sokoloff 2006). The 'seal of quality' associated with novelty examinations may have also promoted trade in patents because it reduced information asymmetries between buyers and sellers of patents. According to Burhop (2010), approximately 8 percent of all patents granted in the German Empire changed owner at least once. Moreover, Burhop (2010) has found evidence for an increasing division of labour between individual professional inventors and companies. The former focused on the development of new technical solutions, which were then patented and sold to interested companies with manufacturing and distribution capacities to produce and sell these innovations on a large scale.

However, novelty examinations made patent applications more expensive than would be the case under a registration system. Inexperienced applicants often relied on the services of patent agents who could be commissioned to formulate promising patent specifications, although the employment of patent agents distinctly increased patent application costs (Feldhaus 1915; Donges and Selgert 2021). The effects of novelty examinations on inexperienced individual inventors or smaller companies were therefore ambiguous. Although the additional expenses associated with introducing novelty examinations considerably increased the financial hurdles for successful patent applications, inventors with little financial means could still strongly benefit from the decline in transaction costs and the associated development of a market for patents. These inventors were often unable to make their inventions suitable for mass production and selling the patent to financially strong companies was a rational alternative.

Patents whose novelty had been approved by a patent authority not only helped to create a market for innovations but also made it easier to raise capital to expand production capacity or finance follow-up innovations. Information asymmetries, which occur between inventors and investors, make it particularly difficult for young companies to obtain access to venture capital. The basic problem is that investors are unable to accurately assess the prospects for success of an entrepreneurial innovation project from the outside. There is an undeniable risk that, once entrepreneurs receive external funding, they will waste it on an utopian project or even disappear altogether. Studies on providing venture capital in the twenty-first century suggest that companies can reduce investor uncertainty by acquiring patents, because investors interpret patents as a positive signal of the probability an innovation will be successful (Bessler and Bittelmeyer 2008). Patents indicate not only that the patent authority considers the invention to be sufficiently new and economically exploitable but also the patentee's previous financial and intellectual commitment. According to Lehmann-Hasemeyer and Streb (2016), patents already fulfilled this signalling function in the nineteenth century.

Lehmann-Hasemeyer and Streb (2016) noticed that companies with patents were disproportionately represented on the Berlin stock exchange. Although only a small number of German firms owned any patents at all, more than 40 percent of the 474 corporations that went public on the Berlin stock exchange between 1892 and 1913 had filed at least one patent before or after their IPO. Furthermore, almost 20 percent held at least one long-lasting and thus particularly valuable patent. The finding that patenting increased on average after the IPO justifies the deduction that going public helped companies to attract the capital they needed to realise their planned innovation projects. The Berlin stock exchange provided this capital without charging any particular risk premium; on the contrary, corporations that acquired a particularly high number of patents after their IPO recorded above-average subscription proceeds. Obviously, investors did not shy away from providing capital for innovative and riskier companies, but rather preferred buying their shares. Accordingly, against this background, it might be necessary to reassess the role of universal banks during German industrialisation (cf. Gerschenkron 1962). Universal banks may have refused to provide loans to finance firms' innovations themselves, but instead acted as 'gatekeepers', organising IPOs of innovative corporations and thus helping them to raise equity capital.

While private individuals filed the majority of patents in the first half of the nineteenth century, over the long term, their relative importance declined to the benefit of larger companies, whose share increased from about 30 percent in 1877 to over 50 percent at the beginning of the twentieth century (Figure 10.2; Nicholas 2010, 2011; Donges and Selgert 2021). This development was driven by more than the nationwide introduction of novelty examinations favouring financially strong inventors. Another factor was the liberalisation of the German stock-corporation law, which explains the rising number of stock corporations that filed patents following the 1870s (Donges

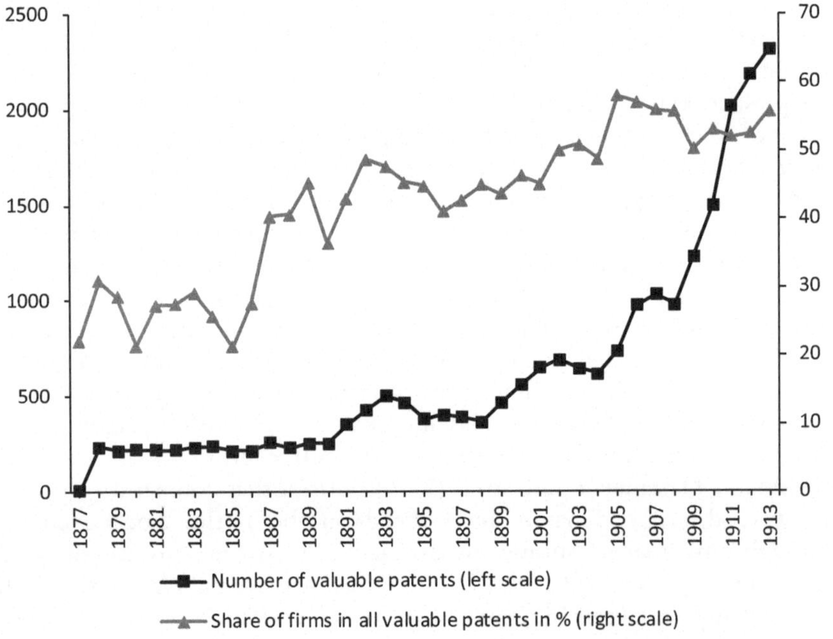

Figure 10.2 Valuable (long-lived) patents granted to domestic patentees, 1877–1913.

Note: The left scale shows the number of valuable (long-lived) patents granted to domestic firms and individuals in the respective year; the right scale shows the percentage of all valuable patents granted to firms in the respective year; see Streb et al. (2006) for the data source and definition of valuable patents.

and Selgert 2021). Economies of scale and increasing capital intensity in research and development (R&D) also played a role, especially in the chemical and electrical engineering industries, the leading sectors of the 'second industrial revolution'. In these industries, large firms with their own R&D and patent departments drove technical progress forward (Maestrejuan 2013). For example, in the mid-1890s, among the ten German companies with the most long-lived patents, there were no fewer than eight from the chemical industry (Bayer, BASF, Hoechst, Cassella, AGFA, Leonhardt & Co., Merck, and Schering) and two from the electrical engineering industry (Siemens & Halske and Felten & Guilleaume; Degner 2009). To analyse whether performance bonuses enhanced the innovativeness of employed inventors of these companies, Burhop and Lübbers (2010) investigate employment contracts of scientists who worked in the R&D departments of Bayer, BASF, and Siemens & Halske at the time. They show that a high proportion of performance-related bonuses in total compensation was positively correlated with the number of long-lived patents owned by the respective companies. In addition, individual experience might have played a role, as the number of patents increased with the average length of the scientists' employment.

Figure 10.3 underlines the outstanding patenting activities in the leading industries of the second industrial revolution. Since the 1880s, the chemical industry was the most innovative German industry, accounting for up to 30 percent of the total number of valuable patents granted to domestic patentees. The decline of this figure to approximately 15 percent after the turn of the century should not obscure the fact that the absolute number of valuable patents related to chemical innovations continued to rise in the early twentieth century. The chemical industry's relative loss was partly due to the disproportionate increase in valuable patents in electrical engineering. Scientific instruments also accounted for a considerable share of all valuable patents. These instruments included microscopes or precise measuring and testing equipment, which were, in turn, required to develop new innovations in all high-tech sectors of that time. In contrast, the share of valuable patents related to steam engines and railways decreased in line with this trend. This development symbolises the declining relevance of the technologies of the first industrial revolution.

Labuske and Streb (2008) argue that the increasing international competitiveness of the German mechanical engineering industry can be explained by the high level of innovation in this sector. Recent findings by Hungerland and Wolf (2020) also suggest a positive correlation between domestic patenting activities and the export success of German industries. On the eve of the First World War, German companies revealed comparative advantages especially in the areas of synthetic dyes and fertilisers. Other technically sophisticated German products, such as electrical apparatus, measuring instruments, and telescopes, were also highly competitive in the international market. In all these areas, an above-average number of valuable patents had been granted in the decades before.

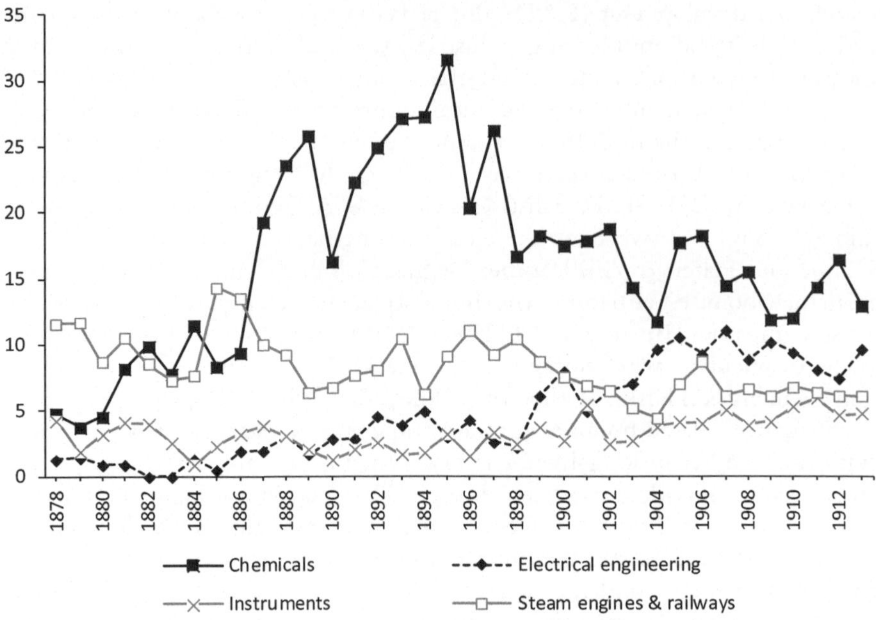

Figure 10.3 Valuable patents by selected technology groups (in %), 1878–1913.

Note: The figure shows the percentage share of all valuable (long-lived) patents granted to domestic patentees (companies or individuals) in the respective year for selected technology groups. The technology groups include all patents for the following technology classes (as defined by the Imperial Patent Office): chemical industry: 12 (chemical processes), 16 (fertilisers), 22 (dyestuffs); electrical engineering: 21 (electrical engineering); instruments: 42 (instruments); steam engines and railways: 13 (steam boilers), 14 (steam engines), 20 (railways), 24 (firing installations). See Streb et al. (2006) for the data source and definition of valuable patents and technology classes.

After 1877, it is possible to compare patenting activities in different German regions, which were by then all part of the same patent system. As Figure 10.4 shows, patenting activities were not evenly distributed but spatially concentrated, with centres in the Upper Rhine, Neckar basin, regions around Frankfurt and Cologne, Ruhr area, Saxony, and Berlin and its surrounding cities. Cinnirella and Streb (2017) show that differences in human capital endowment provide a possible explanation for these regional disparities, while Donges et al. (2022) highlight the role of institutional differences. The fact that patenting activities were concentrated along waterways and in population centres is in line with Sokoloff's (1988) observations in the US. Streb et al. (2006: 368) note that, in the German Empire, administrative districts with a particularly large number of long-lived patents were characterised by innovative clusters of technologically and economically related industrial sectors (Streb et al. 2007; Streb 2019). They conclude that the localised exchange of

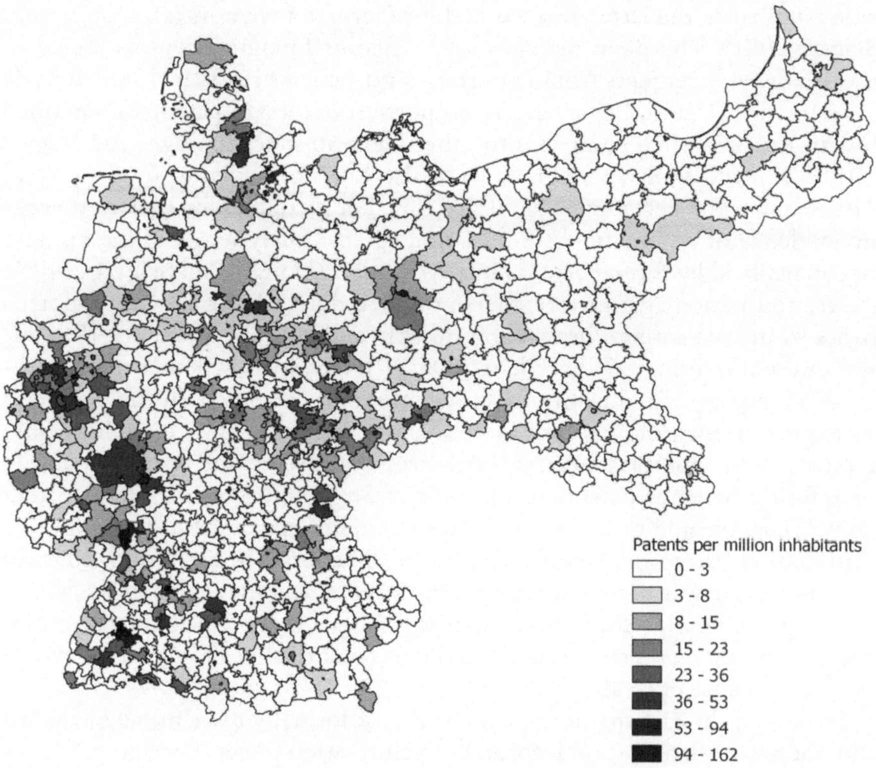

Figure 10.4 Mean number of patents per million inhabitants in 1890, 1900, and 1910.
Source: Donges et al. (2022).
Note: The figure shows the mean number of valuable (long-lived) patents as defined by Streb et al. (2006) per million inhabitants, based on data from 1890, 1900, and 1910, for which census population data is available at the county level. The map does not include Alsace-Lorraine.

knowledge between firms from different industries was an important driver of regional innovation.

4.2 Discrimination against foreigners

The introduction of the German Patent Law ended the period of systematic discrimination against foreign patent applicants, which had been common in some states of the *Zollverein* (Donges and Selgert 2019a). This was particularly true for Prussia, where foreigners, with some exceptions, were not allowed to own patents until the mid-nineteenth century. Foreign inventors could install local patent agents as intermediaries, who applied in Prussia for the patent in their own name, and thus became its formal owner if it was granted. This practice was associated with high costs and risks. In particular, conflicts of interest between foreign inventors and German patent agents could not be ruled out, since the latter also worked for German inventors (cf. Donges and Selgert 2021). The open discrimination against foreign inventors ended in the 1860s for foreigners from countries with which Prussia had signed trade agreements. Overall, however, the proportion of foreign patentees remained low in Prussia, when compared to other German states (Donges and Selgert 2019a: 85). In Saxony, foreigners were also long forbidden to own a patent. Other states pursued more liberal policies. For example, for Baden, there is no evidence of systematic discrimination against foreigners, and the number of patents held by foreigners was relatively high (Donges and Selgert 2019b).

Discrimination against foreigners provided domestic firms with opportunities to imitate foreign innovation quickly and cheaply, a practice that was not unusual internationally (Khan 2005: 57). However, whether the domestic economy benefited from such discrimination depended on the degree of its export orientation, because there was a risk that foreign countries would retaliate with appropriate countermeasures, such as levying protective duties or refusing to grant patents to inventors from countries with unfair patent laws. Thus, the additional profits in the domestic market resulting from discrimination had to be weighed against possible losses in foreign markets. In this respect, it was more appropriate for large economies, such as Prussia to discriminate against foreigners, than for the southern German states with small domestic markets. The latter could not risk the loss of important export markets because of retaliation.

However, the fact that foreigners were not formally discriminated against did not mean there was no informal discrimination either. Foreign patentees could be placed at a disadvantage during the application process or in legal patent disputes (Mai and Stoyanow 2014; Webster et al. 2014). One example of informal discrimination is the Kingdom of Württemberg, although this state's government pursued a relatively liberal patent policy on the surface. Lehmann-Hasemeyer and Streb (2020) show that Württemberg's patent authority systematically charged inventors from other *Zollverein* states comparatively high patent fees, despite the government's commitment to treating foreigners the same as domestic patentees being stipulated in the 1842 *Zollverein* agreement.

After the unification of the German patent system, the open and systematic discrimination against foreigners ended. From now on, foreigners were entitled to apply for and own patents in the German Empire in the same way as domestic patentees. Anything else would have hardly made sense in the globalised world of the second half of the nineteenth century, when export-oriented German companies hoped for fair treatment abroad. Consequently, in 1903, the German Empire joined the Paris Convention of 1883, in which the participating states agreed to treat domestic and foreign patentees equally (Seckelmann 2006: 226–28). However, the formal equal treatment of domestic and foreign patentees did not imply that informal discrimination was also abandoned. For example, Richter and Streb (2011) show that the German

Patent Office delayed patent applications by foreigners in the period between World Wars I and II to provide domestic companies with time to adapt their own patent strategies.

Nevertheless, there is no doubt that the improved legal framework led to a rapid increase in foreign patenting in Germany after 1877. The share of foreign patentees in all newly granted long-lived patents tripled from 10 percent in 1877 to more than 30 percent in the mid-1880s (Degner and Streb 2013: 23). Between 1877 and 1914, this ratio averaged 27 percent, which was significantly higher than in the US, where foreigners held only slightly more than 10 percent of all patents in the 1910s (Cantwell 1989: 23). As Figure 10.5 illustrates, American inventors comprised by far the largest group of foreign patentees in the German Empire, followed by the British and French. Obviously, the most advanced industrialised countries were also the largest exporters of innovative technical knowledge to Germany. This technology transfer took place via patent specifications, in which the details of inventions were described. German firms could legally use this information. They could either copy the foreign technology after the patent protection had expired or, even before that date, use the technical insights revealed by the patent specifications for their own follow-up innovations. This kind of technology transfer may have become increasingly important with growing technological complexity.

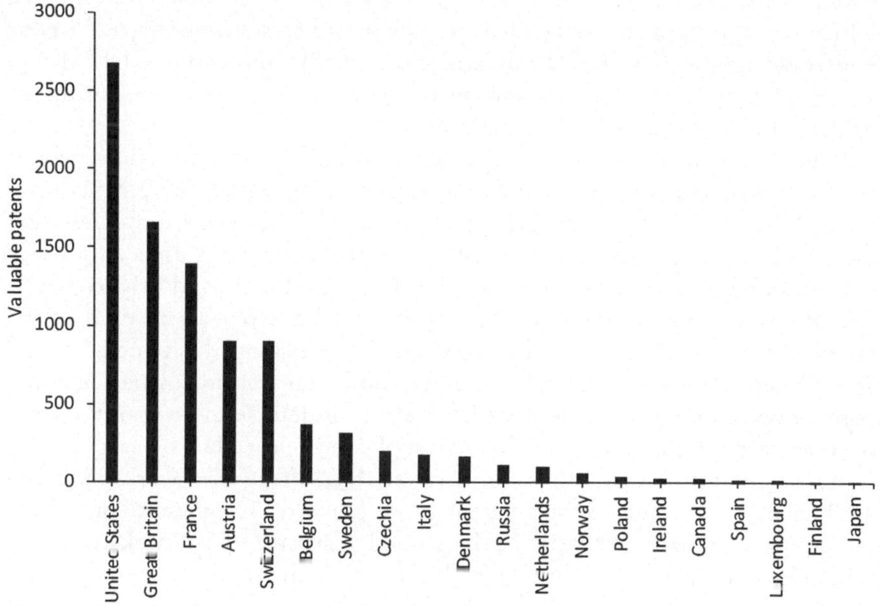

Figure 10.5 Valuable patents of foreigners in Germany, 1877–1914, by country of origin.

Source: Degner and Streb (2013: 24).

Trade economists frequently use the gravity model that assumes that the bilateral foreign trade volume of two countries is largely determined by both the size of their economies and their geographical distance. Since foreigners primarily applied for patents in Germany when they wanted to export there, foreign patentees and exports to Germany should show a similar geographical and sectoral pattern. Figure 10.5 suggests that this assumption is true. Most foreign owners of German patents came from the leading economies of that time, but often also from neighbouring (and German-speaking) countries. Burhop and Wolf (2013) show that distance also played a role in international patent trade. When holding all other factors constant, the frequency of patent transfers decreased with increasing distance between the buyer and seller of a German patent.

4.3 Patent fees and patent terms

The introduction of the German Patent Law also led to a standardisation of patent fees and terms. Before 1877, it is difficult to make inter-state comparisons, because the fees in each German state comprised different components, which also changed over time (Donges and Selgert 2019a: 76–80). To further complicate worse, we must account for state-specific maximum patent terms. If we take a five-year patent from 1850 as an example, the usual patent fees ranged from 1 to 2.5 Thalers in Prussia and up to 34 Thalers in Baden. Compared to the estimated average annual income of craftspeople and workers, which was approximately 104 Thalers, such patent fees were not prohibitively expensive, as was the case in England in the eighteenth century (cf. Mokyr 2009). However, with the exception of Prussia, these fees were hardly affordable for inventors with low incomes.

When comparing patent fees charged before 1877, we also must account for large differences in the size of the territories in which the patents were valid. Some small states charged low fees in absolute terms, but these fees were still very expensive relative to the size of the territory, especially when compared with the low fees demanded in Prussia (Donges and Selgert 2019a: 77). If an inventor wanted to acquire a patent for five years in each of the larger states of the *Zollverein*, the estimated total fees ranged between 123 and 160 Thalers. This estimate still does not include transaction costs, such as the costs of obtaining information, which were considerable in view of the large number of different patent systems and application procedures.

According to the German Patent Law of 1877, a fee of 50 Marks (equal to 17 Thalers) was required for a patent to be granted. The patent could then be renewed annually, whereby in the second year a fee of 50 Marks was due, which increased continuously by 50 Marks for each additional year. Thus, a patent with a term of five years costed 550 Marks, which corresponded to 183 Thalers. In this respect, the patent fee for a nationwide patent after 1877 was only slightly higher than the total fee of up to 160 Thalers which an inventor would have had to pay before 1877 for comprehensive patent protection in all larger *Zollverein* states. Considering that the new nationwide patent law also covered the smallest states (e.g. the Thuringian states), which were not included in our estimation of total fees for the *Zollverein*, we can assume that the costs for 'full coverage' were similar under both patent regimes. However, in contrast to the situation prior to 1877, a single patent application was now sufficient, which considerably reduced the transaction costs of obtaining full coverage. In addition to the nationwide introduction of novelty examinations mentioned above, decreasing transaction costs might have contributed to developing an integrated market for patents in the German Empire.

However, it was primarily professional inventors and large companies, who would have sought to protect their innovations in all relevant states of the *Zollverein* anyway, that profited from the introduction of a nationwide patent. For individual inventors or small firms, for whom it had previously been sufficient to obtain a patent in their home state only, the patent fees increased massively. This was particularly true for inventors from Prussia, who had benefited from extremely low fees before 1877. The observation that the creation of a nationwide patent law mainly favoured financially strong inventors also helps to explain the relative increase in firm patents at the expense of patents filed by individuals (Figure 10.2).

5 Competition and innovation

Compared to before 1877, the German Patent Law made it much easier to create barriers to market entry by means of patents. This was particularly true for companies that had the financial means to protect their inventions over a long period of time, as the German Patent Law allowed a maximum patent term of 15 years. Before 1877, the maximum patent term had been much shorter, especially in Prussia, where patents were generally granted for only three years and rarely extended (Donges and Selgert 2019a: 80–83). Moreover, large companies quickly realised that they could block innovation by their competitors effectively by accumulating as many patents as possible. A quote from Carl Duisberg, who was a member of the board of directors of the chemical company Farbenfabriken vorm. Friedr. Bayer & Co AG starting in 1900 (and later even the head of the board; Plumpe 2016), illustrates this strategic behaviour:

> We could not lose any time. According to the patent legislation, it was crucial to be the first applicant. [...] Therefore, it was common practice, whenever we discovered a new [chemical] reaction, to write down a patent application immediately including all theoretical possibilities and send it to the patent office in Berlin at the very same day.
>
> (Duisberg 1933: 134)

In the light of this statement, we should interpret the high number of long-lived patents held by large German companies in the second industrial revolution not only as an indicator of their successful innovation activities but also as evidence for their strategy to restrain competition by blocking patents. The fact that patents can be a measure of both innovativeness and competitive constraints makes it more difficult to test the hypothesis that large companies are more innovative than small and medium-sized enterprises, as put forward by Schumpeter (1942: 132) in one of his later contributions.

According to von Hippel (2002: 87), the fear of paralysing legal disputes related to the validity of blocking patents was also an important reason for cartel agreements between large and innovative German chemical companies. A similar development can be observed in the electrical engineering industry. For example, Pahlow (2015: 119) points to the 'Patent Interest Group for Incandescent Lamps' (*Patentinteressengemeinschaft wegen Glühlampen*) founded by General Electric, AEG, Siemens & Halske, and Deutsche Gasglühlicht AG. This cartel aimed to end patent disputes and divide the markets among its members. In summary, patents may have led to competition restraints in three different ways. First, patents granted temporary production and sales monopolies; second, blocking patents hindered technologically related innovations of competitors; and third, patents promoted the creation of patent pools and cartel agreements. The resulting decrease in competition may have negatively affected innovation and economic growth and, consequently, diminished the positive effects induced by the German patent law harmonisation.

6 Conclusion

In economic history textbooks on the German Empire, scholars either completely ignore the harmonisation of patent law or succinctly characterise it as another possible driver of technical progress (cf. Tilly 1990; Burhop 2011). In this chapter, we have explained that introducing the German Patent Law had complex and ambiguous consequences with regard to technical progress. While it is correct to assume that the German Patent Law opened efficient and mostly non-discriminatory access to the German market for foreign inventors for the first time in history, thus promoting technology transfer and international competition, the new German patent system also enabled new types of market barriers, such as blocking patents and patent pools. Furthermore, these restrictive practices encouraged more far-reaching cartel agreements in many sectors, which might have slowed down technical progress. Newly available databases on German patent activities offer a sound basis to evaluate and quantify the net effect of the German Patent Law of 1877 on innovation. More research is also needed to determine the extent to which private inventors were pushed back in favour of large companies, and how this development affected technological change in Germany.

References

Bessler, W. and Bittelmeyer, C. (2008) 'Patents and the performance of technology firms: evidence from initial public offerings in Germany', *Financial Markets and Portfolio Management*, Vol. 22 (4): 323–56.

Burhop, C. (2010) 'The transfer of patents in Imperial Germany', *Journal of Economic History*, Vol. 70 (4): 921–39.

Burhop, C. (2011) *Wirtschaftsgeschichte des Kaiserreichs 1871–1918*, Göttingen: Vandenhoeck & Ruprecht.

Burhop, C. and Lübbers, T. (2010) 'Incentives and innovation? R&D management in Germany's chemical and electrical engineering industries around 1900', *Explorations in Economic History*, Vol. 47 (1): 100–11.

Burhop, C. and Wolf, N. (2013) 'The German market for patents during the 'Second Industrialization,' 1884–1913: a gravity approach,' *Business History Review*, Vol. 87 (1): 69–93.

Cantwell, J. (1989) *Technological Innovation and Multinational Corporations*, Oxford: Blackwell.

Cinnirella, F. and Streb, J. (2017) 'The role of human capital and innovation in economic development: evidence from post-Malthusian Prussia', *Journal of Economic Growth*, Vol. 22 (2): 193–227.

Degner, H. (2009) 'Schumpeterian German firms before and after World War I: the innovative few and the non-innovative many', *Zeitschrift für Unternehmensgeschichte*, Vol. 54 (1): 50–72.

Degner, H. and Streb, J. (2013) 'Foreign patenting in Germany, 1877–1932', in P.-Y. Donzé and S. Nishimura (eds), *Organizing Global Technology Flows: Institutions, Actors, and Processes*, New York: Routledge, pp. 17–38.

Domini, G. (2020) 'Exhibitions, patents, and innovation in the early twentieth century: evidence from the Turin 1911 international exhibition', *European Review of Economic History*, Vol. 24 (3): 578–600.

Donges, A. and Selgert, F. (2019a) 'Do legal differences matter? A comparison of German patent law regimes before 1877', *Jahrbuch für Wirtschaftsgeschichte*, Vol. 60 (1): 57–92.

Donges, A. and Selgert, F. (2019b) 'Technology transfer via foreign patents in Germany, 1843–1877', *Economic History Review*, Vol. 72 (1): 182–208.

Donges, A. and Selgert, F. (2020) 'The consequences of radical patent regime change', mimeo.

Donges, A. and Selgert, F. (2021) 'The social background of Prussian inventors and entrepreneurs during the First Industrial Revolution', *Zeitschrift für Unternehmensgeschichte/Journal of Business History*, Vol. 66(1): 1–41.

Donges, A., Meier, J.-M. and Silva, R. (2022) 'The impact of institutions on innovation', *Management Science*, article preview online.

Duisberg, C. (1933) *Meine Lebenserinnerungen*, Leipzig: Reclam.

Feldhaus, F. M. (1915) 'Die Preisliste eines Patentanwalts von 1871', *Geschichtsblätter für Technik, Industrie und Gewerbe*, Vol. 2: 158–65.

Gerschenkron, A. (1962) *Economic Backwardness in Historical Perspective*, Cambridge: Belknap.

Heggen, A. (1975) *Erfindungsschutz und Industrialisierung in Preußen: 1793–1877*, Göttingen: Vandenhoeck & Ruprecht.

von Hippel, W. (2002) 'Auf dem Weg zum Weltunternehmen (1865–1900)', in W. Abelshauser (ed), *Die BASF. Eine Unternehmensgeschichte*, München: Beck, pp. 17–116.

Hungerland, W.-F. and Wolf, N. (2020) 'The panopticum of Germany's foreign trade, 1880–1913', Institute of Economic History, School of Business and Economics, Humboldt-University of Berlin, mimeo.

Jaffe, A. and Trajtenberg, M. (2002) *Patents, Citations, and Innovations: A Window on the Knowledge Economy*, Cambridge, MA: MIT Press.

Khan, B. Z. (2005) *The Democratization of Invention: Patents and Copyrights in American Economic Development*, Cambridge: Cambridge University Press.

Khan, B. Z. and Sokoloff, K. L. (2006) 'Institutions and technological innovation during early economic growth: evidence from the great inventors of the United States, 1790–1930', in T. S. Eicher and C. García-Peñalosa (eds), *Institutions, Development, and Economic Growth*, Cambridge, MA: MIT Press, pp. 123–58.

Kiesewetter, H. (1992) 'Beasts or Beagles? Amerikanische Unternehmen in Deutschland', in H. Pohl (ed), *Der Einfluss ausländischer Unternehmen auf die deutsche Wirtschaft vom Spätmittelalter bis zur Gegenwart*, Stuttgart: Steiner, pp. 165–96.

Labuske, K. and Streb, J. (2008) 'Technological creativity and cheap labour? Explaining the growing international competitiveness of German mechanical engineering before World War I', *German Economic Review*, Vol. 9 (1): 65–86.

Lehmann-Hasemeyer, S. and Streb, J. (2016) 'The Berlin stock exchange in Imperial Germany: a market for new technology?', *American Economic Review*, Vol. 106 (11): 3558–76.

Lehmann-Hasemeyer, S. and Streb, J. (2020) 'Discrimination against foreigners: the Wuerttemberg patent law in administrative practice', *Journal of Economic History*, Vol. 80 (4): 1071–1100.

Maestrejuan, A. R. (2013) 'Managing invention: setting the boundaries of ownership', in S. Arapostathis and G. Dutfield (eds), *Knowledge Management and Intellectual Property*, Cheltenham: Edward Elgar, pp. 44–61.

Mai, J. and Stoyanow, A. (2014) 'Home country bias in the legal system: empirical evidence from the intellectual property rights protection in Canada', *York University Department of Economics Working Paper* 2014/2.

Mokyr, J. (2009) 'Intellectual property rights, the industrial revolution, and the beginning of modern economic growth', *American Economic Review*, Vol .99 (2): 349–55.

Moser, P. (2012) 'Innovation without patents: evidence from world's fairs', *Journal of Law and Economics*, Vol. 55 (1): 43–74.

Murmann, J. P. (2003) *Knowledge and Competitive Advantage: The Coevolution of Firms, Technology, and National Institutions*, Cambridge: Cambridge University Press.

Nicholas, T. (2010) 'The role of independent invention in US technological development, 1880–1930', *Journal of Economic History*, Vol. 70 (1): 57–82.

Nicholas, T. (2011) 'Independent invention during the rise of the corporate economy in Britain and Japan', *Economic History Review*, Vol. 64 (3): 995–1023.

Nuvolari, A. and Vasta, M. (2019) 'Patenting the Risorgimento: economic integration and the formation of the Italian patent system (1855–1872)', *Jahrbuch für Wirtschaftsgeschichte*, Vol. 60 (1): 93–122.

Pahlow, L. (2015) 'Das Patent als Waffe im Wirtschaftskampf: Patentrecht und Kartellrecht in der Weimarer Republik', in M. Otto and D. Klippel (eds), *Geschichte des deutschen Patentrechts*, Tübingen: Mohr Siebeck, pp. 109–27.

Plumpe, W. (2016) *Carl Duisberg 1861–1935: Anatomie eines Industriellen*, München: Beck.

Richter, R. and Streb, J. (2011) 'Catching-up and falling behind: knowledge spillover from American to German machine tool makers', *Journal of Economic History*, Vol. 71 (4): 1006–31.

Sáiz, P. and Amengual, R. (2018) 'Do patents enable disclosure? Strategic innovation management of the four-stroke engine', *Industrial & Corporate Change*, Vol. 27 (6): 975–97.

Schiff, E. (1971) *Industrialization without National Patents*, Princeton: Princeton University Press.

Schumpeter, J. A. (1942) *Capitalism, Socialism, and Democracy*, New York: Routledge.

Seckelmann, M. (2006) *Industrialisierung, Internationalisierung und Patentrecht im Deutschen Reich, 1871–1914*, Frankfurt a. M.: Klostermann.

Seckelmann, M. (2015) 'Das Patentrecht als 'Reaktionsbeschleuniger': die Entwicklung des Patentrechts im zweiten deutschen Kaiserreich (1871–1914)', in M. Otto and D. Klippel (eds), *Geschichte des deutschen Patentrechts*, Tübingen: Mohr Siebeck, pp. 37–70.

Sokoloff, K. L. (1988) 'Inventive activity in early industrial America: evidence from patent records, 1790–1846', *Journal of Economic History*, Vol. 48 (4): 813–50.

Streb, J. (2016) 'The cliometric study of innovations', in C. Diebolt and M. Haupert (eds), *Handbook of Cliometrics*, Heidelberg: Springer, pp. 447–68.

Streb, J. (2019) 'Persistenz im Schumpeterschen Wettbewerb', in G. Schulz (ed), *Ordnung und Chaos: Trends und Brüche in der Wirtschafts- und Sozialgeschichte*, Stuttgart: Steiner, pp. 135–52.

Streb, J., Baten, J. and Yin, S. (2006) 'Technological and geographical knowledge spillover in the German Empire 1877–1918', *Economic History Review*, Vol. 59 (2): 71–106.

Streb, J., Wallusch, J. and Yin, S. (2007) 'Knowledge spill-over from new to old industries: the case of German synthetic dyes and textiles 1878–1913', *Explorations in Economic History*, Vol. 44 (2): 203–23.

Sullivan, R. J. (1994) 'Estimates of the value of patent rights in Great Britain and Ireland, 1852–1976', *Economica*, Vol. 61 (1): 37–58.

Tilly, R. H. (1990) *Vom Zollverein zum Industriestaat: Die wirtschaftlich-soziale Entwicklung Deutschlands 1834 bis 1914*, München: Deutscher Taschenbuch Verlag.

Webster, E., Jensen, P. H. and Palangkaraya, A. (2014) 'Patent examination outcomes and the national treatment principle', *RAND Journal of Economics*, Vol. 45 (2): 449–69.

Part III

Economic development and economic institutions in early Imperial Germany

11 Stock exchanges, banks, and the panic of 1873

Carsten Burhop and Felix Selgert

1 Introduction

According to Article 4 of the Imperial Constitution, the founding of the German Empire transferred legislative authority in the areas of trade, banking, and commercial law to the new central authorities. However, these powers were not initially used with regard to the banks and financial markets dealt with here: The Banking Act of 1875 dealt only with banks of issue; it was not until the Mortgage Bank Act of 1899 and the Banking Act of 1934 that the activities of commercial banks were defined and regulated. The amendment of the most important part of business law for the development of banks and capital markets, the Stock Corporation Act, had already been negotiated and implemented in the North German Confederation before the foundation of the Empire; it was merely expanded to the southern German states with the founding of the Empire. It was not until 1884, as a result of the 1873 panic, often referred to as *Gründerkrise* in German historiography, that a new regulation was introduced, which, however, had long-term effects on the structure of the German variety of capitalism. Furthermore, the regulation of commodity and securities exchanges remained in the hands of the federal states until the Stock Exchange Act was passed in 1896.

At the institutional level, the foundation of the Empire thus had little impact on the development of capital markets and commercial banks. By contrast, at the level of the monetary system, clear and immediate effects quickly became apparent. The sharp expansion of the money supply by almost 30 percent in 1871 and 1872, as well as the monetary contraction of the years 1873–77, is attributed to the reparations, coinage, and central-banking policies of the young nation-state (Tilly 1972: 350–54; Chapter 9 of this volume). Expansion and contraction of the money supply went hand in hand with boom and bust. But not everything was lost in the great crash of 1873. Rather, some of the banks that emerged during the early 1870s had a long-term impact on German economic development, and some regulations enacted after the crash permanently reordered the financial sector. Accordingly, this article first outlines the structures and changes in the German banking and financial markets in the decades surrounding the founding of the Empire

DOI: 10.4324/9781003283430-14

and discusses the influence of banks and stock exchanges on economic development. Subsequently, the causes as well as the course and consequences of boom and bust are discussed. Finally, we turn to the question of whether capital-market institutions were created after the panic of 1873 in the course of a 'second founding of the Empire' that influenced the economic development of the Empire in the long term.

2 Structural history of finance capital

Shortly before the outbreak of the First World War, the banking lobbyist Jakob Riesser stated,

> it is the most urgent and noblest duty of banks and bankers to strive, at least within their sphere of activity and according to their powers, to close the profit and loss account of the capitalist economic order with a balance in favour of economic progress.
>
> (Riesser 1912: 7)

The contribution of banks to economic growth, and in particular of universal banks, was also emphasised four decades later by the economic historian Alexander Gerschenkron and has been an evergreen of economic history research ever since (Fohlin 1999; Guinnane 2002: 96–115). For him, banks were 'specific instruments of industrialization in a backward country'. In particular, German banks,

> [...] accompanied an industrial enterprise from the cradle to the grave, from establishment to liquidation throughout all the vicissitudes of its existence. Through the device of formally short-term, but in reality, long-term current account credits and through development of the institution of the supervisory boards to the position of most powerful controlling bodies within corporate organization, the banks acquired a formidable degree of ascendancy over industrial enterprises, which extend far beyond the sphere of financial control into the entrepreneurial and managerial decisions.
>
> (Gerschenkron 1962: 14)

According to Gerschenkron, the great need for capital in a country with few large assets for a catch-up industrialisation based on mining, heavy industry, mechanical engineering, large-scale chemicals, and electrical engineering could be promoted by the skilful allocation of capital. For this purpose, the large universal banks, which cultivated relationship banking, were primarily necessary until the late nineteenth century (Gerschenkron 1962: 14–15, 21).

In contrast to Riesser and Gerschenkron, who tended to attribute a causal link between real economic growth and the financial sector, especially the banks, Richard Ehrenberg, in his stage model formulated in 1883, saw in the financial sector a lagging element leading to speculative excesses: at the beginning, according to Ehrenberg, there were technical inventions, followed by an upswing in large-scale industry, which was accompanied by freedom of trade and commerce. In stage three, there was an increased need for large amounts of capital, which was accompanied by a shift towards free incorporation in stock corporation law. The fourth stage would then see an increase in the number of joint-stock companies, which would lead to the fifth and final stage of the model: the upswing in stock market speculation (Ehrenberg 1883: 127).

In Germany, private bankers had indeed been acting as universal banks in railway financing since the 1830s (Tilly 1966; Guinnane 2002: 96–100). However, since the financing volume often exceeded the capacity of a single banker, several bankers quickly worked together in syndicates. From the late 1840s onwards, these consortia evolved into credit banks organised as corporations (AG) or limited partnerships with tradeable shares (KGaA)—on the one hand, to stabilise cooperation, and, on the other, to limit risks (Tilly 1986: 118–21, 1989: 191–92, 1998: 13).[1] Of the six major banks that were to dominate German banking until the years before the First World War, four—*Discontogesellschaft, Darmstädter Bank für Handel und Industrie, Berliner Handelsgesellschaft* and *Schaaffhausen'sche Bankverein*—date back to this railway age of the 1840s and 1850s (Riesser 1912: 50–67, 385–421). This period also saw the establishment of a division of labour and risk in German banking: while the newly formed joint-stock banks concentrated on long-term infrastructure and industrial financing, the central banks, in particular the Prussian Bank and later the *Reichsbank*, took on the task of supplying banks and the economy with means of payment and processing payment transactions (Tilly 1986: 122–23, 1989: 192–93, 195–96, 1998: 17).

The extent, period, and mechanisms of a causal influence of the financial sector on economic development have long been disputed (Fohlin 2012, Chapters 8 and 9). Nevertheless, according to recent results using German data, a causal influence of financial intermediation by joint-stock banks on the growth of output, capital endowment, and total factor productivity of industry is observed from the 1850s to 1870s. From the 1880s onwards, however, the joint-stock banks lost their causal influence on industrial development. Instead, from the 1870s onwards, we observe a close interplay between banks and stock exchanges in the field of industrial finance, because the banks supported company start-ups, initial public offerings (IPOs), and seasoned equity offerings (SEOs) (Burhop 2006, 2011: 170–72, 176–78; Feldenkirchen 1979a, 1979b, 1982a, 1982b).

The financial system thus adapted to the transformed framework and competitive conditions of the 1870s. In fact, banks could only play a causal role in economic growth because they were relatively large compared to their customers and because the small number of large banks resulted in market power and the ability to coordinate. They had the power to enable industrial *take-off* with low interest rates, and later to achieve oligopoly profits through high interest rates (De Rin and Hellmann 2002). However, intense competition from the numerous joint-stock credit banks created during the founding period and competition from corporate finance in deregulated stock markets undermined the banks' pro-growth position.

How market power in the banking market developed between 1860 and 1880 can only be assessed incompletely. The number of joint-stock banks increased significantly during 1870–73, and market concentration in this segment declined. Between 1857 and 1872, the Herfindahl index of capitalisation of the joint-stock banks fell from about 0.15 to about 0.02. At the peak of the boom, one thus observes an almost perfect competitive setting. By 1882, the Herfindahl index value had doubled, i.e., the intensity of competition remained very high after the crash. Measured by the market share of the three largest joint-stock banks, there was no significant change in terms of market power until the First World War (Burhop 2002: 112). However, the struggle for market share intensified not only because of numerous newly founded joint-stock banks. Another important pillar of the German banking system, the savings banks, increased their number from 618 in 1860 to 1,407 two decades later, especially in the course of the 1860s, but also still after the foundation of the German Empire (Hoffmann 1969: 566). The number of cooperative credit institutions also grew rapidly, but relatively evenly, from around 300 in 1860 to approximately 2,500 in 1880 (Guinnane 2002: 89). Savings banks and cooperative banks thus emerged in numerous towns, districts, and municipalities, either in competition with existing financial institutions or by opening up entirely new markets.

Furthermore, it can be empirically established that the struggle for market shares took place in a growing market and that, through banks, savings banks, and insurance companies, via securities markets and from public-sector budget surpluses, it was possible to finance domestic net investment in the years around the early years of the Empire (Hoffmann 1965: 812).[2] Financial intermediation worked—across all institutional reforms and monetary and real economic crises. In the course of the years 1860–64, net investments of around two billion Marks were financed; in the following five years (1865–69), two and a half billion Marks; in the five-year period 1870–74, 8.4 billion Marks; and in the following five years (1875–79), as much as 3.4 billion Marks. Intermediation services tended to grow after the founding of the Empire, and they even increased faster than the economic value added (Burhop 2011: 168). On average, funds from the public sector were the most important source of financing. However, strong fluctuations can be observed here, caused by war financing, recycling of French reparation payments, and nationalisation of the railways. In contrast, insurance companies hardly contributed at all to investment financing. Parallel to the expansion and contraction of the money supply, the joint-stock banks in particular experienced an explosive rise in importance after the foundation of the Empire until 1872, followed by a temporary decline. In the medium term, however, as can be seen in Figure 11.1, joint-stock banks, savings banks, and real-estate financiers developed evenly and

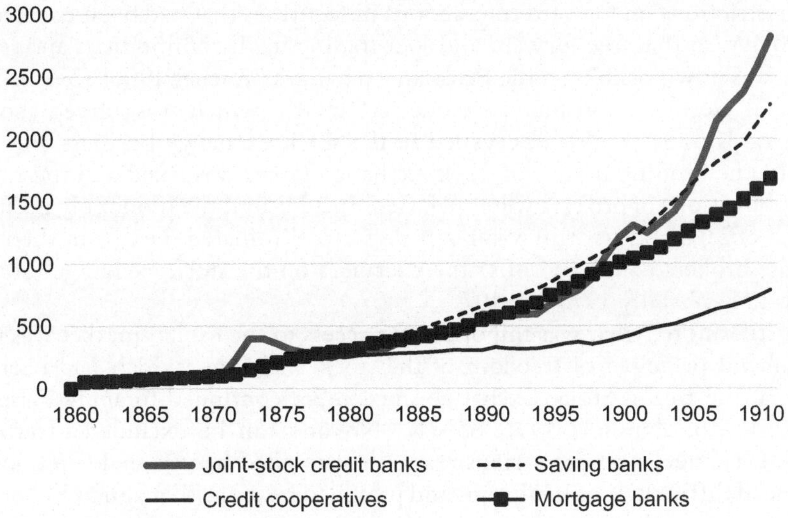

Figure 11.1 Index of the balance-sheet total development of banking groups 1860–1910 (1870 = 100)

Source: Own calculation with data from Burhop (2002: 128), Deutsche Bundesbank (1976: 56–66), Hoffmann (1965: 736, 739, 743–45).

in lockstep until the turn of the century. Only shortly before the turn of the century did the joint-stock banks set out on a growth spurt that was not followed by the other segments of the lending industry. However, this upswing of the joint-stock banks, which is much discussed in the literature, can hardly be linked to developments in the period of the foundation of the Empire.

Like the relevance of banks, the importance of securities markets for the net financing of private enterprises fluctuated. During the 1860s, private railway companies were the focus of interest; after 1870, industrial and bank corporations joined them. The liquidation of many joint-stock banks and the nationalisation of some railway companies heralded the temporary decline of securities exchanges as an important source of financing for businesses (Burhop et al. 2018). It was not until the second half of the 1880s, after legislators and the self-regulatory forces of financial market participants had established better institutions, that the stock exchange business revived and a successful dualism of financial markets and banks developed in Germany (Fohlin 2007, Chapter 7; Burhop et al. 2018).

3 The deregulation of capital market institutions before the foundation of the Empire

One important prerequisite for the increasing importance of banks and stock exchanges in the 1870s is to be found in their deregulation. The prelude to this was inconspicuous: On 1 July 1860, the Prussian government lifted several restrictions on forward transactions in securities that had been enacted in the 1840s, so that free forward and spot trading in all commodities and securities was now possible on the Prussian exchanges (Wiener 1906: 13–14). The General German Commercial Code (ADHGB), which was agreed shortly afterwards in 1861, also intervened in the stock-exchange business. For example, the binding nature of stock-exchange prices was fixed and the rights and obligations of brokers were specified. In addition, the monopoly position of the official and sworn broker was de facto eliminated, i.e., from then on, private brokers could also offer their services on the stock exchange (Struck 1881: 211–17; Tilly 1975: 91–107).

Furthermore, what was important for access to the capital market was that the liberal principle of freedom of the stock exchange, which had been in force at the Berlin Stock Exchange since 1825, continued to apply (Wiener 1906: 14–15; Zänsdorf 1937: 63–71). 'No one can be excluded [from the stock exchange] without serious reasons'—provided he was male and not in financial difficulties or bankrupt, and provided he was either a member of the cooperation of the Berlin merchants or had paid the stock-exchange admission fee (Wiener 1906: 12–13). The admission of trading articles was handled even more liberally: The admission of securities or products to be traded on the exchange remained unregulated. An unregulated primary market and a barely regulated secondary market for securities thus formed the legal background of the Prussian stock exchanges.

Initially, however, and in the most important federal states, the primary market for securities was strictly limited by corporate law by means of a compulsory state licence to incorporate. Only in well-founded cases did the authorities approve the formation of corporations, so that the number of such companies in Germany remained very small. The highlight and closing point of the deregulation phase was consequently the liberalisation and standardisation of the regulations on corporations and limited partnerships with tradeable shares, passed in the early summer of 1870 (Schubert 1981). With this amendment, the transition from the concession system to the normative system generally took place on 11 June 1870 in the states of the North German Confederation—the other states followed after the founding of the German Empire on 16 April 1871—with the exception of banks of issue and railway corporations (Weigt 2005: 25). Henceforth, one had a legal right to form a corporation if one met the standards required by law. Until then, governments had stuck to the concession system for three main reasons. First, fundamental legal policy considerations militated against the creation of legal entities. Second, it was feared that the economic power of corporations, i.e., the emergence of monopoly capitalism, would reduce general prosperity. Third, the 'protection of the public and the creditors of the company against fraud and unsoundness' was considered.[3] These reasons, according to the legislator, had in the meantime become obsolete, because numerous other legal entities could come into being without a concession, because these could be used for the monopoly capitalist accumulation of large fortunes, and because confidence in the soundness of state-licensed joint-stock companies would promote swindling and fraud instead of reducing it.

The collaboration of many small capitalists into a large corporation was regarded by researchers as particularly important for Germany, because there were only a few very wealthy individuals who could have founded a capital-intensive company from their own assets. The limited liability, the ease of individual liquidation thanks to the admission of bearer shares and the relatively comprehensive publicity ensured the willingness to participate in corporations. In addition to these advantages, but only after the crash of 1873, the disadvantages, especially those related to corporate governance, were also clearly identified. The shared and limited risk combined with the high liquidity of the shares significantly reduced the monitoring incentives for shareholders. On the other hand, the incentives for the management and supervisory boards resulting from bonuses may have been insufficient to link them closely to the long-term objectives of the company. The focus on short-term bonus, share price, and dividend targets pushed the long-term corporate welfare into the background. Moreover, incorporation was often the ultimate purpose of the corporation, and the founding oligarchy often controlled the general meeting and supervisory board during the first years of life of new corporations (van der Borght 1883: 7–15; Bayer und Burhop 2009).

4 Banks and stock exchanges between boom and bust (1870–79)

At the beginning of the 1870s, the room for manoeuvre on the primary and secondary market for shares was used first and foremost by numerous, newly founded joint-stock credit banks, which in turn entered the start-up business and set up further banks, as well as transforming existing industrial enterprises into joint-stock companies in order to sell their share certificates on the stock exchange quickly (Blume 1914; Burhop 2004). However, the prerequisite for the boom was not only the liberalisation of important capital market institutions that took place before the foundation of the German Empire. The founding of the nation-state, the expansion of the money supply that accompanied the monetary reforms, the French reparations payments, the catch-up in private and public consumption after the war-induced interruption, the continued expansion of the German railway network, as well as the urbanisation accelerated by freedom of movement and settlement and the real-estate speculation resulting from it are all named as promoting factors (Kindleberger 1990: 312–14; Blume 1914: 13, 26; Weigt 2005: 7–9, 12–13; Baltzer 2007: 1, 4–7).

The payment and use of French reparations had direct relevance for the development of the financial sector (Soetbeer 1874: 3–11). However, the potentially manifold effects of the French reparation payments have not yet been comprehensively analysed, so that the impact of the transfer on the economy can only be speculated on. In her explanation of the *Gründerboom*, Anja Weigt (2005: 10–11) assumes that between four and 4.8 billion Marks[4] flowed into Germany and that these were used to pay off the debts of the states, to repay the war bonds, and to expand the railways. In particular, the repayment of public debt resulted in investment pressure for the previous owners of government securities, the extent of which is quantified very differently in the literature.[5] In fact, in the preliminary peace of Versailles, as well as in the Frankfurt peace treaty, the payment of war reparations within about three years had been agreed upon. Since France was able to raise the necessary funds surprisingly fast by issuing two bonds, the last installment flowed to Germany as early as September 1873 (Baltzer 2007: 4–7).

In fact, in 1870 and 1871, Germany initially saw a significant increase of about one billion Marks in the public debt because the war against France had to be financed. In the following two years, the states and the central government repaid an almost identical amount of about 1.1 billion Marks of their securitised debt (Hoffmann 1965: 789). It is unknown to what extent investors reallocated their portfolios in favour of domestic equities. What is known, on the other hand, is that investors in the main German financial centres subscribed to at least 520 million Marks worth of those French bonds, the proceeds of which were used to finance the reparations. Moreover, it is known that the German state used the French payments not only for debt repayment but also for construction projects, the procurement of military goods, the creation of a war chest, and the establishment of a veterans' pension fund (Monroe 1919: 269, 274). The first two measures strengthened aggregate demand and withdrew funds from the monetary cycle, respectively. The Imperial Disability Fund, established in May 1873, invested some 560 million Marks in fixed-interest German securities by February 1874, thus tightening the supply of safe investments for other capital-market participants during the financial-market panic (Kähler 1897: 40–41).

What is certain is that investment opportunities expanded after 1870 because numerous corporations had been founded and their shares listed on the stock exchange. In total, 928 corporations with a share capital of around 2.8 billion Marks were founded in Germany between 1871 and 1873 (Metzler 1911: 129). Since many of the companies were reorganisations of existing enterprises into the legal form of a corporation, the nominal value of the shares did not at all correspond to the increase in economic capital.[6] The economic capital of existing corporations grew, however, through capital increases amounting to a nominal total of almost 900 million Marks and through the issue of bonds to an amount that could not be precisely specified, but was presumably substantial. While the issuance of bonds was primarily carried out by railway companies, the new formations were concentrated in other industries. These included 162 commercial companies, mainly banks, 119 food and beverage companies, 109 mining and metallurgical companies, 84 construction companies, and 77 mechanical-engineering factories.[7] Although not all corporations had been listed on the stock exchange, IPOs were numerous.

In Berlin alone, which developed into the most important financial centre in Germany after 1870, 251 IPOs were recorded in the founding years (Burhop et al. 2018: 21).

In addition to the attraction of a broader investment spectrum, transaction cost-reducing trading facilitations on the secondary market probably also contributed to the boom. For example, the bank of the *Berliner Kassenverein* developed into the clearing house of the Berlin stock exchange in the years around 1870 (Bank des Berliner Kassen-Vereins 1900: 34–35).

Stock-exchange turnover data are not available, but the number of stock exchange visitors (who could trade on the floor) and brokers at the Berlin Stock Exchange can be used as indicators of the increasing liquidity of the secondary market (Buchner 2019: 452–55, 466). The number of stock-exchange visitors had already been rising since the mid-1860s, and it reached a local maximum of 2,858 visitors in 1874, which was only reached again in 1883 and then permanently exceeded. The trend was relatively steady between 1865 and 1872, with an increase from 1,452 to 2,142 stock-exchange visitors. In 1873 alone, however, the number of stock-exchange visitors increased by a third. Particularly striking was the increase in the number of visitors to the exchange who were neither members of the Berlin merchant community nor carried out large transactions. In 1871, only 657 of these 'retail investors' were registered at the stock exchange, in 1872 already 748, and in 1873 even 1,418. At the same time, the number of sworn, official brokers increased from 37 to 110. Thus, after the foundation of the Empire, a hitherto undreamed-of dynamism developed on the primary and secondary market for shares (Blume 1914: 78–79).

The competitive conditions in the banking market changed, above all, as a result of the establishment of numerous credit banks in the legal form of a corporation. The number of incorporated credit banks rose from 12 to 31 as early as the 1860s—especially from 1867 onwards. By 1872, a further 124 credit banks had been added, including *Deutsche Bank* and *Dresdner Bank*, two of the six major banks that were still considered to have a formative influence on German economic history in the years before the First World War. *Commerzbank*, which was to join the ranks of Berlin's major banks after the turn of the century, also saw the light of day in 1870.[8] However, the true rise of *Dresdner Bank* and *Commerzbank* only began after the opening of branches in Berlin, and *Deutsche Bank's* triumphant advance was only heralded by its departure from its originally formulated goal of being the bank funding German foreign trade.

The emergence of Berlin as a new German financial centre in the wake of the founding of the Empire and the opportunities for expansion offered by the boom were successfully exploited by these three institutions, if one takes a long-term perspective. On the other hand, from 1873 onwards, numerous other banks rapidly exited the market in large but declining numbers, so that by 1879 a stock of 77 credit banks had been established (Burhop 2002: 127). The total assets of the incorporated banks, which had increased in the course of the 1860s from around 300 to approximately 500 million Marks, subsequently quadrupled in the start-up boom to 2.1 billion Marks by 1872. From 1873 onwards, the balance-sheet total fell again, reaching a low of 1.3 billion Marks in 1878. If we break down the growth of the years 1869–72 into the main areas of lending, we find that around 45 percent of the growth can be attributed to current account overdrafts, 15 percent to bill discounting and around 30 percent to securities business. In the downturn, current-account overdraft business then fell by 45 percent, and securities business by 35 percent. By contrast, bill-discounting business remained stable (Burhop 2002: 128). Despite these high rates of contraction, the volume of business remained just above the level of 1871, even at the low point of the crisis. Thus, only the exaggeration of 1872 was corrected. From a structural point of view, however, two effects of the panic of 1873 become apparent: the importance of securities business—whether in the form of a report and Lombard loans or in the form of own purchases of securities—declined permanently (Burhop 2002: 118–21). Moreover, starting in the late 1870s, the maturity transformation of the joint-stock banks steadily increased, i.e., there was a move away from the established system of converting equity into short-term loans and towards the maturity transformation of modern banking—henceforth, sight and savings deposits were increasingly converted into loans instead of equity (Burhop 2002: 123).

The timing and cause of the panic of 1873 are still disputed. Two speeches in which the national liberal member of parliament Eduard Lasker denounced speculation and corruption in the Prussian railway system in February 1873, the Vienna stock market crisis beginning in May, the conclusion of payment of the French reparations in September 1873, the beginning of the New York stock market crisis in the same month and the collapse of a major Berlin real-estate financier, the *Vereinsbank Quistorp & Co.* in October 1873, are named as the triggering factors (Kindleberger 1990: 314–16; Weigt 2005: 40). In fact, the historical stock-price index reached a local maximum as early as November 1872, followed by a steady decline in prices and a sharp collapse in September 1873, after which prices continued to fall until reaching a turning point in 1879 (Weigt 2005: 83–84, 87). It was not until 1890 that the price peak marked in 1872 was again surpassed, albeit only briefly. It was not permanently surpassed until after the turn of the century. However, the overall performance of the stock market was better than the prices would suggest because investors realised a large part of the return through dividend payments (Weigt 2005: 92, 111). From a long-term perspective, the 1870s actually mark an important transition period because stock prices tended to fall between 1840 and 1880 amid sharp fluctuations, whereas they tended to rise between 1880 and the Great War as variance declined (Weigt 2005: 118).

However, the crisis did not manifest itself in the first place in falling share prices and a lack of dividends, but in numerous corporate bankruptcies. The number of bankruptcies, which had reached a low in 1872, rose every year thereafter until 1880 (Pohl 1991: 46). Companies were also increasingly forced to withdraw from the stock market. In particular, corporations that had been set up after the 1870 amendment fell with particular frequency. Within this group, joint-stock banks were particularly vulnerable to bankruptcy. In fact, of the firms that had gone public on the Berlin Stock Exchange between 1870 and 1873, some 40 percent went bankrupt or into liquidation within five years (Baltzer 2007: 44, 47–48, 50, 52–53, 63; Burhop et al. 2018: 23). Small firms, in particular, were exposed to a significant risk of bankruptcy, so that the exclusion of such corporations from the stock market was a relevant regulatory instrument (Burhop et al. 2018: 25–26).

5 Re-regulation of capital market institutions after the panic of 1873

Shortly after the start of the panic, the operators of the Berlin Stock Exchange reacted to the grievances on the stock market and created a stock-exchange commission in August 1874 (Burhop 2015). Rules of procedure, which were not enacted until January 1876, stipulated that this body had to decide on the inclusion of new securities in the official price list (Gebhardt 1928: 55–56). With a similar objective, namely to improve product quality in the primary market for securities, an expert commission of the Exchange Board had already been charged a few months earlier with deciding on the introduction of securities into non-official trading. From January 1882 onwards, it was also stipulated that inclusion in the official price list was only possible if shares with a nominal value of at least one million Marks were to be issued and if a prospectus containing all valuation-relevant information was published in Berlin newspapers and by posting on the stock exchange. The publication of a prospectus was now also mandatory for securities that were to be listed in the non-official part of the market. Only when there was evidence of regular and substantial trading in the security could an official listing be permitted (Gebhardt 1928: 56, 111). Small companies that were particularly susceptible to bankruptcy were thus excluded from the Berlin Stock Exchange, and the transparency requirements for all other newcomers to the exchange were raised significantly (Lotz 1890: 69; Gebhardt 1928: 110).

The crisis of 1873 also led to reform considerations with regard to stock-corporation law (Schubert and Hommelhoff 1985: 8–41). Although the bust built up immediate pressure for reform, the amendment of stock-corporation law was delayed until 1884 (Franks et al. 2006). The amendment undertook a significant re-regulation of corporate law in several areas (Selgert 2021). First, it reformed the incorporation procedure, which had been barely specified in 1870. The purpose of the amendment was to ensure that share capital was paid in, to make the incorporation process more transparent to shareholders, and to make founders liable under criminal and civil law for violations of the incorporation rules. To this end, the amendment set the face value of shares at 1,000 Marks and made the shareholder liable for its full payment. In order to make the formation process itself more transparent, the amendment introduced a definition of the term 'founder' and established a mandatory disclosure of the founding process.

Second, the 1884 corporate law strengthened the position of shareholders by declaring decisions on capital increases, the approval of the balance sheet and the appointment of auditors, as well as the approval of amendments to the articles of association, to be inalienable rights of the general meeting. In addition, the amendment strengthened shareholders' claims against the supervisory board and the management board, which could now be asserted by a simple majority of votes. This not only increased the civil liability of the latter two bodies. Violations of the duty of care by the supervisory board and the management board were now also subject to more stringent criminal prosecution and could be punished with heavy fines and prison sentences of several years. Third, the amendment restricted the management powers of the supervisory board and tightened the supervisory duties of this body. Fourth, the amendment established shareholder control of the company by creating extensive minority and individual rights. These allowed individual shareholders, for example, to challenge decisions of the general meeting that were contrary to the articles of association or the law, to request an appeal of the general meeting, to postpone the balance-sheet negotiations, or to demand a special audit and, as a consequence, to claim damages from the supervisory board and the management board.

There is evidence in the literature that the strengthening of shareholder rights has led to more stable governance structures. For example, in the pre-reform period, a clear correlation can be observed between the profits of the corporation and the compensation of the board of directors. This should have provided an incentive for the board to work towards high profits, and thus high dividends. On the other hand, such an incentive system is very expensive and, since the workload of the board cannot be observed, inefficient. After the 1884 reform, the link between profits and remuneration of the board of directors decreased, i.e., pecuniary incentives were substituted by better institutions (Bayer and Burhop 2009).

The stock-exchange regulations of 1882 and the provisions of the 1884 corporate law in regard to the founding process also seem to have contributed to the stabilisation of the financial market: Compared to the 1870s, the survival probability of newly listed corporations on the Berlin Stock Exchange was about 61 percent higher in the period 1882–96 (Burhop et al. 2018). The increasing reserves that became mandatory under the 1884 act probably also contributed to the new stability of corporations well beyond the formation phase.[9] Although German industrial corporations were already converting more than 10 percent of their profits into equity before the formal obligation to build up reserves in 1884, the reform provisions now forced them to do so even in years of weak profits. As a result, the ratio of reserves to share capital at German corporations in the 1880s always exceeded 10 percent (as required by law). In the late 1880s, the reserve ratio even rose to over 14 percent, reaching 20 percent by the end of the 1890s. The reserve requirement seems to have been particularly important in the case of large banks. Here the conversion of profits into equity fluctuated much more before 1884 and remained mostly below the level of industrial corporations even after the reform. The growing internal financing of commercial enterprises also reduced their dependence on banks and volatile stock markets. In addition to growing competition among banks for financing mandates from industrial clients, this may have been another factor in the loss of a causal influence of financial intermediation on industrial economic development.[10]

6 Conclusion

After the founding of the Empire in 1871, libertarian capital-market institutions combined with money and optimism first created a boom and then a crisis of financial capitalism. The founding of numerous incorporated banks and other corporations, the issuance of their shares, especially on the Berlin Stock Exchange, and the rapid trading of the securities on the trading floor characterised the years 1872 and 1873, in particular. In the panic that began in the course of 1873, numerous banks and real-estate companies fell, and the fictitious values they represented dissolved.

Nevertheless, the 1870s marked a break in capital-market development in Germany, because both the self-governing bodies of business and the legislature drew lessons from the institutional deficits revealed in the crisis, implementing important reforms in corporate law and stock-exchange regulations. The corporate law of 1884, the Stock Exchange Regulations of 1882, and the Stock Exchange Act of 1896, respectively, established a stable core of capital-market institutions that were able to develop their effectiveness after the 'second foundation of the Empire'. In addition, the 1870s saw the final breakthrough of corporations, and the credit banks organised in this legal form. Three institutions founded in these years—the *Deutsche Bank*, the *Dresdner Bank,* and the *Commerzbank*—occupied the key positions of the 'Deutschland AG' for more than a hundred years from the 1880s onwards. An important component of this 'Deutschland AG', the networking of the business elite through supervisory board mandates, was only created by the massive rise in importance of the corporation as a legal form for large companies. Nevertheless, the more intense competition resulting from more numerous market participants probably meant that the incorporated banks lost their causal role in industrial economic growth from the 1880s onwards. From then on, banks accompanied growth but did not create it.

Notes

1 Guinnane et al. (2007) discuss the characteristics of different legal types.
2 For better comparability, all amounts were converted into Marks.
3 Deutscher Reichstag (1870, Vol. 13: 645–60, here p. 649).
4 At an exchange rate of 1.25 francs per Mark.

5 Gömmel (1992: 154) cites a capital market impact of between two and 2.4 billion Marks. Baltzer (2007: 70) puts the 'investment pressure' at only 333 million Marks.
6 Forty to sixty percent of the newly founded corporations were reorganisations (Baltzer 2007: 28–29; Burhop 2011: 23).
7 Deutsches Reich (1884: 390–96).
8 Riesser (1912: 385–421). On the *Deutsche Bank*, see Plumpe (2020: 2–66); and on the *Commerzbank*, see Ziegler (2020: 23–73).
9 The amendment stipulated that five percent of the profit be initially allocated to a reserve fund until it reached ten percent of the share capital.
10 The figures are based on a sample of 47 industrial stock corporations and nine major banks listed in Berlin, collected from Saling's stock-exchange securities.

References

Baltzer, M. (2007) *Der Berliner Kapitalmarkt nach der Reichsgründung 1871: Gründerzeit, internationale Finanzmarktintegration und der Einfluss der Makroökonomie*, Münster: LIT.

Bank des Berliner Kassen-Vereins (1900) *Die Bank des Berliner Kassen-Vereins 1850-1900: memorandum on 1 October 1900*, Berlin.

Bayer, C. and Burhop, C. (2009) 'Corporate governance and incentive contracts: empirical evidence from a legal reform', *Explorations in Economic History*, Vol. 46 (4): 464–81.

Blume, H. (1914) *Gründungszeit und Gründungskrach mit Beziehung auf das deutsche Bankwesen*, Danzig: Kafemann.

Buchner, M. (2019) *Die Spielregeln der Börse: Institutionen, Kultur und die Grundlagen des Wertpapierhandels in Berlin und London, ca. 1860–1914*, Tübingen: Mohr Siebeck.

Burhop, C. (2002) 'Die Entwicklung der deutschen Aktienkreditbanken von 1848 bis 1913: Quantifizierungsversuche', *Bankhistorisches Archiv*, Vol. 28 (2): 103–28.

Burhop, C. (2004) *Die Kreditbanken in der Gründerzeit*, Stuttgart: Steiner.

Burhop, C. (2006) 'Did banks cause the German industrialization?', *Explorations in Economic History*, Vol. 43 (1): 39–63.

Burhop, C. (2011) *Wirtschaftsgeschichte des Kaiserreichs 1871–1918*, Göttingen: Vandenhoeck & Ruprecht.

Burhop, C. (2015) 'Regulierung und Selbstregulierung am Berliner Aktienmarkt', *Zeitschrift für Neuere Rechtsgeschichte*, Vol. 37 (1): 32–49.

Burhop, C., Chambers, D. and Cheffins, B. (2018) 'The rise and fall of the German IP market, 1870–1938', *Jahrbuch für Wirtschaftsgeschichte*, Vol. 59 (1): 9–37.

De Rin, M. and Hellmann, T. (2002) 'Banks as catalysts for industrialization', *Journal of Financial Intermediation*, Vol. 11 (3): 366–97.

Deutsche Bundesbank (1976) *Deutsches Geld- und Bankwesen in Zahlen 1876–1975*, Frankfurt a. M.: Knapp.

Deutscher Reichstag (1870) *Verhandlungen des Reichstags des Norddeutschen Bundes: Drucksachen*, Berlin: Sittenfeld.

Deutsches Reich (1884) *Gesetz betreffend die Kommanditgesellschaften auf Aktien und die Aktiengesellschaften*, Berlin: Sittenfeld.

Ehrenberg, R. (1883) *Die Fondsspekulation und die Gesetzgebung*, Berlin: Springer.

Feldenkirchen, W. (1979a) 'Kapitalbeschaffung in der Eisen- und Stahlindustrie des Ruhrgebiets 1879–1914', *Zeitschrift für Unternehmensgeschichte*, Vol. 24 (1): 39–81.

Feldenkirchen, W. (1979b) 'Banken und Stahlindustrie im Ruhrgebiet: zur Entwicklung ihrer Beziehungen 1873–1914', *Bankhistorisches Archiv*, Vol. 5 (2): 26–51.

Feldenkirchen, W. (1982a) 'Zur Kapitalbeschaffung und Kapitalverwendung bei Aktiengesellschaften des deutschen Maschinenbaus im 19. und beginnenden 20. Jahrhundert', *Vierteljahrschrift für Sozial- und Wirtschaftsgeschichte,* Vol. 69 (1): 38–74.

Feldenkirchen, W. (1982b) 'Kölner Banken und die Entwicklung des Ruhrgebiets', *Zeitschrift für Unternehmensgeschichte,* Vol. 27 (1): 81–106.

Fohlin, C. (1999) 'Universal banking in pre-World War I Germany: model or myth?', *Explorations in Economic History,* Vol. 36 (3): 305–43.

Fohlin, C. (2007) *Finance Capitalism and Germany's Rise to Industrial Power,* Cambridge: Cambridge University Press.

Fohlin, C. (2012) *Mobilizing Money: How the World's Richest Nations Financed Industrial Growth,* Cambridge: Cambridge University Press.

Franks, J, Mayer, C. and Wagner, H. (2006) 'The origins of the German Corporation. Finance, ownership, and control', *Review of Finance,* Vol. 10 (4): 537–585.

Gebhard, H. (1928) *Die Berliner Börse von den Anfängen bis 1896,* Berlin: Prager.

Gerschenkron, A. (1962) 'Economic Backwardness in Historical Perspective', in A. Gerschenkron, *Economic Backwardness in Historical Perspective,* Cambridge, MA: Belknap, pp. 5–30.

Guinnane, T. W. (2002) 'Delegated monitors, large and small: Germany's banking system, 1800–1914', *Journal of Economic Literature,* Vol. 40 (1): 73–124.

Guinnane, T. W., Harris, R., Lamoreaux, N. R. and Rosenthal, J.-L. (2007) 'Putting the corporation in its place', *Enterprise & Society,* Vol. 8 (3): 687–729.

Hoffmann, W. G. (1965) *Das Wachstum der deutschen Wirtschaft seit der Mitte des 19. Jahrhunderts,* Berlin: Springer.

Hoffmann, W. (1969) 'Die Entwicklung der Sparkassen im Rahmen des Wachstums der deutschen Wirtschaft (1850–1967)', *Zeitschrift für die gesamte Staatswissenschaft,* Vol. 125 (4): 561–605.

Kähler, W. (1897) 'Die Bedeutung des Reichsinvalidenfonds für den preußischen Kommunalkredit', *Jahrbücher für Nationalökonomie und Statistik,* Vol. 68: 737–52.

Kindleberger, C. P. (1990) *Historical Economics: Arts or Science?* New York: Harvester Wheatsheaf.

Lotz, W. (1890) *Die Technik des deutschen Emissionsgeschäfts,* Leipzig: Duncker & Humblot.

Metzler, L. (1911) *Studien zur Geschichte des deutschen Effektenbankenwesens,* Leipzig: Poeschel.

Plumpe, W. (2020) 'Im Zeitalter der ersten Globalisierung 1870–1914', in W. Plumpe et al. (eds), *Deutsche Bank: Die globale Hausbank 1870–2020,* Berlin: Propyläen, pp. 1–231.

Pohl, M. (1991) 'Die Überlebenschancen von Unternehmensgründungen in der Zeit von 1870 bis 1918', in H. Pohl (ed), *Überlebenschancen von Unternehmensgründungen,* Stuttgart: Steiner, pp. 29–47.

Riesser, J. (1912) *Die deutschen Großbanken und ihre Konzentration,* 4th ed., Jena: Fischer.

Schubert, W. (1981) 'Die Abschaffung des Konzessionssystems durch die Aktienrechtsnovelle von 1870', *Zeitschrift für Unternehmens- und Gesellschaftsrecht,* Vol. 10 (2): 285–317.

Schubert, W. and Hommelhoff, P. (1985) *Hundert Jahre modernes Aktienrecht: Eine Sammlung von Texten und Quellen zur Aktienrechtsreform 1884 mit zwei Einführungen,* Berlin: De Gruyter.

Selgert, F. (2021) *Macht und Kontrolle im Unternehmen: Die politische Ökonomie des Aktionärsschutzes im Deutschen Reich, 1870–1937*, Göttingen: Vandenhoeck & Ruprecht.

Soetbeer, A. (1874) *Die fünf Milliarden*, Berlin: Habel.

Struck, E. (1881) *Die Effektenbörse: Eine Vergleichung deutscher und englischer Zustände*, Leipzig: Duncker & Humblot.

Tilly, R. H. (1966) *Financial Institutions and Industrialization in the Rhineland 1815–1870*, Madison: University of Wisconsin Press.

Tilly, R. H. (1972) 'Zeitreihen zum Geldumlauf in Deutschland 1870–1913', *Jahrbücher für Nationalökonomie und Statistik*, Vol. 187 (4): 330–63.

Tilly, R. H. (1986) 'German banking, 1850–1914: development assistance for the strong', *Journal of European Economic History*, Vol. 15 (1): 113–52.

Tilly, R. H. (1989) 'Banking institutions in historical and comparative perspective', *Journal of Institutional and Theoretical Economics*, Vol. 145 (1): 189–209.

Tilly, R. H. (1998) 'Universal banking in historical perspective', *Journal of Institutional and Theoretical Economics*, Vol. 154 (1): 7–32.

Tilly, W. M. (1975) *Die amtliche Kursnotierung an den Wertpapierbörsen*, Baden-Baden: Nomos.

Van der Borght, R. (1883) *Statistische Studien über die Bewährung der Aktiengesellschaften*, Jena: Fischer.

Weigt, A. (2005) *Der deutsche Kapitalmarkt vor dem Ersten Weltkrieg: Gründerboom, Gründerkrise und Effizienz des deutschen Aktienmarktes bis 1914*, Frankfurt a. M.: Knapp.

Wiener, F. A. (1906) *Die Börse: Eine Studie über die Entwicklung des Rechts und der Verfassung der deutschen, insbesondere der Berliner Börse und der hauptsächlichsten Börsen des Auslandes*, Berlin: Puttkammer & Mühlbrecht.

Zänsdorf, K. (1937) *Verfassung und Organisation der deutschen Börsen im Lichte der rechtsgeschichtlichen Entwicklung*, Würzburg: Triltsch.

Ziegler, D. (2020) 'Die Commerzbank 1870 bis 1945: Entwicklung und Behauptung als Filialgroßbank', in S. Paul et al. (eds), *Hundertfünfzig Jahre Commerzbank 1870–2020*, Munich: Siedler, pp. 23–218.

12 How organised was capitalism in the Empire? Lobby associations, cartels, and interlocking directorates

Eva-Maria Roelevink and Dieter Ziegler

1 Introduction

Former accounts of the history of industrialisation in Germany saw the founding of the Empire and the great depression of the 1870s as the beginning of a new phase of industrialisation, which they described as 'mature capitalism'. Whether this characterisation is appropriate or not shall not be discussed here, but the question of the changes in the economic order brought about by the founding of the nation-state is obvious. Did the founding of the Empire promote economic power in the form of lobby associations, cartels, and personal linkages between several big industrial concerns and between banks and industrial undertakings, and was the 'anarchy' of the market even tamed by 'organisation'?

These questions are not new. They already caused considerable research efforts in the 1970s. As a further development of a concept first used by the Austrian Marxist Rudolf Hilferding during the First World War, which would be able to overcome the 'anarchy of the market', 'organised capitalism' was revived at the German *Historikertag* 1972 by some young historians who saw themselves methodologically as social scientists (Winkler 1974: 7). It was meant as an offer for discussion to GDR historiography and its unquestioned 'monopoly capitalism' theory.[1] The young—but already largely established—'savages' were thus directed against the prevailing primacy of (domestic) politics in West German historiography (Nolte 2002: 53–68) and intended to present an 'appropriate system of coordinates' for historical analysis (Wehler 1974: 36) with their research on organised capitalism and its conceptual complement, the interventionist state. Hence, there was no lack of criticism. Superficially, the conceptual framework was denounced (Hentschel 1978: 12; critical: Kocka 1984: 615–17); more decisive for the resistance in the conservative majority of West German historians, however, was probably the fact that the advocates of the concept of organised capitalism (Kocka 1974: 24–26, 1984: 615–17) were prepared to take a serious look at the findings of their colleagues on the other side of the Iron Curtain (Nussbaum 1976; Baudis and Nussbahn 1978). They were in no way interested in delegitimising the political system of the Federal Republic. Rather, the firm belief in the

DOI: 10.4324/9781003283430-15

modernisation theorem was just reaching its peak, so that Hilferding's ideas were rather to be understood as an early variant of the then widely received model of a 'planned economy of the modern capitalist type' by the British economist Andrew Shonfield (1965, see also Köster 2015). Yet, since it soon became apparent that steering in capitalism was not all that far off, and since there was a lack of possibilities for empirical verification due to the restrictive access to archives by West German large companies and banks, as well as by the GDR authorities, the discussion quickly died out and the concept of organised capitalism disappeared into oblivion, at the latest with the end of the Cold War. Nevertheless, the questions of how organised German capitalism was in the Empire and what significance the founding of the nation-state had still arise. Today, however, primary sources are available to answer these questions to an extent that could not even be dreamed of in the 1970s.

This article looks at three features of 'organised capitalism' in the light of current research: lobby associations, cartels, and networks of interlocking directorates. However, instead of pursuing the question of the polyvalent interdependence of state and economy, as was still the case in the 1970s, research on the organisation and organisational performance within the economy itself has now become the focus of attention. In the meantime, this has also become clear: Whether the founding of the Empire was causal for the development of the characteristics of organised capitalism or even acted as a catalyst is highly doubtful. Firstly, counterfactually, a similar regulatory framework (corporation law, banking and stock exchange legislation, competition law) would also be conceivable in Prussia without the German Empire; and secondly, numerous policy areas of the 'intervention state' were matters for the individual states, which jealously guarded that the Empire did not dispute their competences.

2 Lobby associations

Research on lobby associations reached its peak in the 1960s and 1970s. It was not unusual for reference to be made to the work of the political scientist Theodor Eschenburg, who had already published a small booklet in the 1950s with the strikingly formulated question of a 'rule of the lobby associations', which was widely received at the time (Eschenburg 1955). However, as historical research on lobby associations was soon able to prove, the boundaries and relations between these associations and the state were already much more fluid in the German Empire than Eschenburg had stated; and the shaping of association interests was also a complex and multifaceted process.

There are arguments for and against the assumption that the founding of the Empire had a major impact on the development of lobbying: On the other hand, the associations of the Empire did not arise from a spontaneous impulse, but from a tradition. Local federations of industrialists had already been founded in the early nineteenth century (Fischer 1973: 139–40), especially in southern and central Germany. In Prussia, in turn, the chambers of commerce remained more pronounced as forms of representation under public law (Fischer 1964; Ullmann 1980: 300–05). The supra-regional German Association of Commerce (*Deutscher Handelstag*, DHT), founded in 1861, was also a kind of continuation of the Prussian Association of Commerce and was thus part of this tradition (Gehlen 2013). However, an economic-policy orientation of the DHT only emerged much later; initially, the meetings were a bourgeois festive event and hardly served to influence current economic policy (Schäfer 1973: 120–24).

The foundation of the German Empire in 1871 meant a change in the sphere of action of the lobby associations, which had hitherto been organised regionally and by sector. Decisions regarding economic policy shifted to Berlin. The entrepreneurs reacted to this. This might be an argument in favour of understanding the foundation of the German Empire at least as a catalyst on the way to a modern (economic) association system (Ullmann 1988: 113). In addition, the founding of the Empire fixed the participation of the political parties and the *Reichstag* (the national parliament) in political decision-making. There was no future for the rule of lobby associations, even if they initially claimed their own right to representation—and thus at least an equal status to the political parties (Nipperdey 1961: 264). Finally, however, the founding of the Empire also provided a tangible occasion for increased cooperation. For example, the Association of South German Cotton Industrialists (*Verein süddeutscher Baumwollindustrieller*) was founded in 1870 because the textile industrialists feared that the annexation of Alsace-Lorraine would increase domestic competition. This motivated an increased cooperation in the interest of lasting customs protection (Böhme 1972: 307–08; Blaich 1979: 5–6).

Initially, the Empire consistently continued the liberal trade policy pursued by Prussia since 1860. However, the interests of the associations were diverse, and the concert of expressed interests and demands was by no means harmonious: the free-trade policy had strong supporters, for example in numerous chambers of commerce, the DHT, the German Agricultural Council (*Deutscher Landwirtschaftsrat*) and, not least, in the ministerial bureaucracy. However, the opponents of free trade, the textile industry in southern Germany, the heavy industry associations in the coal and steel regions of the Rhine and Ruhr, Saar, and Oder, formed a counterweight that, although not unified, could be taken seriously.

Nevertheless, it was not possible at first to draw the—still economically important and politically influential—group of agrarians into the ranks of the protectionists (Blaich 1979: 7–9). It was not until the great depression and the 'grain invasion' of the 1870s that the advocates of protectionism gained strength. In 1876, the *Central Association of German Industrialists* (CDI) was founded and quickly achieved its founding goal (Burhop 2011: 110). However, it was not solely responsible for the turnaround in customs policy in 1879. For in the meantime the situation of German agriculture had also worsened dramatically since due to freight cost reductions in transatlantic cargo shipping, the spread of steamships washed US grain onto European markets in large quantities and at low prices (O'Rourke and Williamson 1999: 29–31). In this situation, which threatened the very existence of the large grain-producing estates in eastern Prussia, their representatives felt compelled to strengthen the phalanx of supporters of protective tariffs. Together, the CDI and the agrarians now concentrated on Chancellor Otto von Bismarck, in particular—and not just on lobbying through the tortuous channels of the ministerial bureaucracy. And indeed, Bismarck swayed to the side of the protectionists, figuring that customs revenues could reduce the financial dependence of the Empire on the federal states. In 1879, the project of a turnaround in customs policy was pushed through by the goal-oriented—but not fundamentally interest-congruent—alliance of Rye, Iron, and Bismarck (Torp 2005: 163–67; Bührer 2013: 189–194).

It was to prove decisive for the organisation of industrial interests that the CDI did not remain in its embryonic organisational state after the turn towards protectionism; rather, it considerably expanded its sphere of activity and thus began to develop its own institutional logic. In 1879, the earmarking of the foundation could be abandoned, and the CDI could be given a renewed claim, namely the 'safeguarding of the industrial and economic interests of the country'. It was only with this step that the CDI completed its transformation from a protectionist lobby organisation to an umbrella association of industry (Kaelble 1967: 3–9). Nevertheless, the efficiency of lobbying was repeatedly hampered by internal conflicts. Strong internal sub-groups formed within the CDI; central groups here were the agro-industrialists (which should not be confused with the Farmers' Federation), the syndicate directors, and the industrialists of medium-sized companies. None of these groups was able single-handedly to determine the line of the CDI (Kaelble 1967: 62–94; critical: Mielke 1976: 90). The CDI's line was mainly the result of a negotiation process between these groups, and thus a temporary compromise, which explains the federation's zigzag course, especially in its cooperation with, and demarcation from, other federations (Kaelble 1967: 110).

In 1890, Bismarck was dismissed as Imperial Chancellor, and his successor, Leo von Caprivi, partially reversed his predecessor's tariff increases (Torp 2005: 179). The agrarians mobilised against this, effectively spreading the word that the new government's trade policy favoured only industry, so that cracks in the alliance of rye and iron began to break open in public. Under the pressure of collapsing grain prices (O'Rourke 1997: 775–801), the agrarians founded the Farmers' Federation (BdL) in 1893. Although the Federation quickly developed into a mass organisation, it was dominated by East Elbian big landowners, the politically influential junkers, who played a decisive role in Caprivi's downfall (Puhle 1967: 45–47). The BdL was the most powerful and influential German interest group (Torp 2005: 226). Under this pressure, Caprivi's successor, Chlodwig zu Hohenlohe-Schillingsfürst, once again focused trade policy more strongly on the interests of agriculture, admittedly without disregarding the industries interested in protective tariffs.

Barely 20 years after the founding of the CDI, a competing federation of industrialists, the *Bund der Industriellen* (BDI), was founded in 1895,[2] which developed into the second umbrella organisation of industry, because the conflicts of interests within the industrial economy intensified, and several industries no longer saw their interests represented by the CDI. In this respect, the BDI founded itself programmatically as a counter-draft to the CDI (Ullmann 1979: 27–33). But even the BDI was by no means an efficient umbrella organisation. As early as 1897, membership figures stagnated; strong sub-associations, a narrow financial base, and the regionally uneven distribution of members in the territory of the Empire limited its legitimacy, causing considerable problems in the establishment of an institutional and powerful association framework.

In 1909, the Hansa-Bund, a third intersectoral interest group, was formed with the declared aim of fighting the Prussian junkers and the junker-dominated policy of the BdL (Mielke 1976: 9–10, Kollmer 1979). The initiative for this new association had come from the big banks and the wholesale trade. However, internal power struggles also blocked this association until the oppositional minority left in 1911 and the Hansa-Bund was finally able to pursue its original objective (Mielke 1976: 83–91).

3 Cartels

In the 1960s and 1970s, research on industrial lobby associations was mainly interested in the influence of said associations on politics, but the inward shaping of interests in the context of the differentiating association system was neglected. This is a research gap that still exists. Broader organisational histories, aimed at the interconnectedness within the economy, are still lacking (Plumpe 1990: 659–60). This can certainly be attributed to the neglect of a parallel development closely intertwined with the formation of lobby associations, which is actually quite astonishing for imperial Germany—seen, after all, as the 'land of cartels'. Although cartels and lobby associations were consistently mentioned together in the model of organised capitalism, their relationship was not empirically explored further but merely simplistically described as 'concentration' (Maschke 1964: 5–6). This resulted in research that was strongly focused on individual associations. By contrast, there is no comparably well-founded cartel research on a robust empirical basis. Yet, there are good reasons to assume that lobby associations and cartels entered into a developed and successful symbiosis, at least in parts of the economy. In heavy industry, for example, protective tariff interests were closely linked to cartelisation (Webb 1980). This was because high domestic prices to finance dumping for plant utilisation on the export markets presupposed the regulation of production quantities and prices, which had to take place beyond the individual interest of a company. The lobby groups, especially the well-organised associations of heavy industry, served as a kind of showcase and communicator for the cartels, which self-organised dumping among themselves under the umbrella of the protective tariff through export premiums and the like. Their most important task was to influence economic policy, as research on trade associations has rightly emphasised. However, the associations also ensured that the cartels had room for self-regulation and warded off state influence.

Cartels regulating prices and production quantities, as well as syndicates that additionally took over the sales organisation of certain product groups, were privately founded organisations of largely similar industrial interests that bound their members firmly to certain rules of conduct by means of contracts 'originally by arbitrary regulation and with the aim of largely dominating the market' (Tschierschky 1930: 3). According to the leading cartel lobbyist and business lawyer Siegfried Tschierschky, the cartels gained their power through organised joint action. Of greatest importance for the spread of the cartels was the fact that there was no legal containment, so that they were able to sail below the regulatory-legal umbrella, thus being able to develop their power through increasing organisation. The repeatedly cited decision of the Imperial Court of 1897 (see Nörr 1994: 8–14, Schröter 1994: 462), which recognised contractual cartel agreements as lawful within the framework of contractual freedom, was preceded by a fundamental decision on the cartel issue. As early as 1890, the Imperial Court had held that cartels did not harm the principle of free enterprise.[3] Significantly, in both cases, the Court did not hear a case about a powerful cartel in the coal or iron and steel industry, but about smaller cartels that had not formed a comprehensive organisation. The large cartels, on the other hand, quickly developed their own legal practices, which were integrated into the cartel agreements via clauses, thus becoming binding for the members. They stipulated, for example, that cartel disputes were to be heard in private arbitration courts and not in ordinary courts. The cartels had moved away from the initial 'arbitrariness' and created comprehensive cartel organisations. Therefore, their actual 'activity' never came into the full 'light of day'. The 'cartel manipulations'—and thus the considerable damage to consumers—could rather be hidden continuously and with the help of the lobby associations behind the 'trade secrets', as the miners' unionist Otto Hue criticised as early as 1906 (Hue 1906: 64).

There is still a great deal of ambiguity in research about the extent and effect of cartelisation (detailed, and from an international perspective: Levenstein and Salant 2007). One of the harshest critics of the revival of the theory of organised capitalism assessed the significance of cartelisation in the Empire as follows: 'The number of cartels was large, the share of cartelised total production probably quite high. The effectiveness and success, however, were low' (Hentschel 1978: 101). The last sentence is particularly controversial (Jovović 2012: 237). If 'effectiveness and success' were based on market power, such as a market dominance of the cartels of over 80 or even 85 percent of the production of an industry at the national level, their economic significance was probably indeed low. Even the Rhenish-Westphalian Coal Syndicate (*Rheinisch-Westfälisches Kohlen-Syndikat*, RWKS) cannot be considered successful under these conditions. But if one identifies success as the 'organised restriction of competition' (Schröter 2011: 202), then the assessment is different. To measure its effect solely in terms of the national economy seems naïve in the face of contemporary entrepreneurial decisions. After all, participation in a cartel meant nothing else but a considerable reduction of individual entrepreneurial freedom, which was all the stronger the more functions the cartel or syndicate integrated. However, what the quid pro quo consisted of, in particular whether there were other quid pro quos besides the high cartel prices, is as controversially discussed as the effects of market power (Burhop 2011: 157, see also Lübbers 2008; Bittner 2005; Schröter 2013).

The first wave of cartel foundations began in the 1870s.[4] But here, too, there was a predecessor tradition with the guilds. The founding of the German Empire thus had an indirect rather than a direct effect on the development of cartels (Isay 1930: 7–15; see also Barnikel 1972: 1–4; Jovović 2012: 239–40). The Great Depression after the foundation of the Empire ensured that cartels were initially regarded as 'children of necessity' (*Kinder der Not*; Jovović 2012: 249–52). For when the necessity was over, many cartels dissolved again. However, in the second wave of cartelisation, from the 1890s onwards, it became clear that cartels were by no means merely instruments for overcoming crises. Rather, they developed a self-regulating relevance and considerable persistence (Schröter: 1994: 459–60). The rail cartel *Vereinigte Stahlwerke* (United Steelworks), founded in 1873, proved to be very durable and, in the 1890s, formed the starting point for agrarians and social democrats to criticise cartels in fundamentally opposing ways, but in the same direction. The discussion of the rail cartel in the *Reichstag* was significant for the cartel debate in the Empire as a whole, because it reached the wider public for the first time. The leading social democrat and *Reichstag* deputy August Bebel used the discussion on the rail cartel to draw attention to the coal syndicate, which in his view was far more dangerous (Blaich 1973: 67–69). A more far-reaching discussion of cartels by the 'intervention state' did not begin until about 20 years after the founding of the Empire.

The RWKS, which was founded in Essen in 1893 and controlled over 85 percent of the coal production in the Ruhr coalfield, but only in the Ruhr coalfield, was considered dangerous not only by the Social Democrats but also by many other contemporaries. Founded to 'exclude unhealthy competition on the coal market for the future' (Syndikatsvertrag 1893; see Anonymous 1933), the syndicate soon went beyond setting production quotas and centralised price determination and also centralised the sales organisation for its members (Böse 2018: 2). This was necessary because the syndicate, although it covered the largest coalfield in the Empire, did not have monopoly power on the coal markets. The political discussion was dominated by the question of price-fixing. The organisation of sales, on the other hand, was unclear. This area of responsibility formed the actual core of the syndicate and its enduring power and was therefore successfully kept out of the public debate (Roelevink 2015: 69–75).

While the history of the RWKS in the early twentieth century can be considered quite well-researched, almost nothing is known about other cartels, particularly those outside the heavy industry, such as the sugar cartel and the spirit syndicate (Liefmann 1972: 77). However, they are of great importance for the question of the economic order in the German Empire. The "agrarians" had a positive attitude towards these cartels of the agricultural sideline business, while they sharply criticised the cartels of the coal and steel industries as consumers (Blaich 1973: 104). Thus, in the case of both the sugar cartel and the spirit syndicate, the agrarians profited not only from the protective tariff but also, as producers, from cartelisation (Morgenroth 1907: 27). It is noteworthy in this context that the potash syndicate was also among the cartels supported by the agrarians, but not for protective tariff motives. The agricultural lobby associations, especially the BdL, made every effort to support the potash syndicate as consumers of potash fertiliser, because the syndicate used the high revenues from the export business to subsidise fertiliser prices at home thanks to its world-market monopoly. That is why the BdL even had an indirect stake in the potash syndicate.[5] In contrast to the heavy industrial cartels, especially the coal syndicates, which had also formed in the other coalfields following the example of the RWKS, the potash syndicate was predominantly viewed positively due to the participation of the Prussian state (Blaich 1973: 161–75; Mette 1997: 54–59). This was because the Prussian state ended up being the guarantor of fertiliser price subsidies, which—at least according to theory—increased average land productivity, thus allowing agricultural prices to fall (Büschenfeld 1997: 293). From the point of view of some potash mines, however, this also reduced the value of the syndicate for their own company, so that the syndicate would probably have been dissolved in 1910 if the pressure of the BdL had not prompted the imperial government to prevent the dissolution of the syndicate by legal means (Mette 1997: 138–43).

4 Networks of interlocking directorates

For Hilferding (1968: 414), the power of the lobby associations and the cartels had a third dimension with the 'intimate connection of industrial and bank capital', but this was discussed rather marginally in the historiographical debate of the 1970s. In a more advanced stage of organised capitalism, Hilferding expected the control of the real economy to be taken over by the merger of the (great) banks into a 'central bank' as a private-sector planning authority (Hilferding 1968: 243, 322). The observable background to this thesis at the beginning of the twentieth century was the high number of votes at the general meetings of joint-stock companies, cast by bank representatives, which indicated a close capital linkage between banks and industry, as well as a close personnel linkage between big industry and great banks, as shown in the composition of the supervisory boards. The social cohesion and exclusivity of the bourgeois elites were admittedly not a German peculiarity.

One only has to think of the so-called old-boy networks of public schools or amongst Oxbridge graduates in Britain or the graduates of the *grandes écoles* in France (Stanworth and Giddens 1974, Scott and Griff 1984, Bourdieu 1989). But German corporate law institutionalised this personal intertwining in a way that was hardly observable in any other country around 1900.

The starting point for this development was the amendment to the (Prussian) Stock Corporation Law of 1870, which, since Prussia had in the meantime become part of the North German Confederation, was also binding for many North German states and applied to all German states after the founding of the Empire. The new Stock Corporation Act not only abolished the obligation to obtain a licence when founding joint-stock companies but also privatised state supervision by prescribing the formation of a 'supervisory board' to which this task fell. In practice, however, the supervisory board, which initially usually consisted of the 'founders' and a few major shareholders, did not limit itself to supervising the 'management', but very often—contrary to the legislator's intention—interfered directly in the management of the company, as a result of which its control was no longer guaranteed due to the lack of a supervisory body. The legislator did recognise the problem and attempted to solve it in 1884 through an amendment of the law by more clearly delineating the functions of the supervisory board and the executive board (Assmann 1992: 44; Lutter 2007: 392; Burhop 2006: 1–3; see also the contribution by Burhop and Selgert in this volume). But the more stock corporations with widely spread shareholdings were founded, and the larger, more complex and thus also more confusing they became for a supervisory board, the weaker and the more insignificant the board's control function became.

At the turn of the twentieth century, the supervisory board took on a different function in large companies that were not owned by one or a few families (such as *Krupp* or *Siemens*) but were in free float (such as *AEG*, *Gelsenkirchener Bergwerks-AG* or the Berlin great banks). In these companies, the board functioned as an information exchange of a few dozen 'big linkers': persons with numerous supervisory-board mandates in companies of big industry or banks, who met again and again as supervisory-board members in changing constellations (fundamentally on this, see Ziegler 1984; Pappi et al. 1987). There were no upper limits on the mandates per person or the number of members per supervisory board. At the beginning of the twentieth century, some individuals held up to 40 mandates (with an increasing tendency; calculation by the authors based on information taken from *Handbuch der deutschen Aktiengesellschaften 1906*), so that it must have been clear to every informed observer, including Hilferding, that these individuals, who as a rule managed a company in their main profession, would hardly have the time to control the executive boards of the companies on whose supervisory boards they sat, as the legislator had intended.

The people with the most supervisory-board mandates in the Empire included only comparatively few industrialists, among whom, moreover, were comparatively few managers (calculation by the authors). When accepting supervisory-board mandates at the beginning of the twentieth century (Krenn 2012: 138–54), the members of the executive boards of industrial joint-stock companies almost always had to obtain the approval of their own supervisory board, which was not always granted, because the importance of supervisory-board mandates in other companies had not yet been recognised, and the expense associated with holding the mandate was considered too high in relation to the benefit for one's own company (Ziegler 1997: 40). One of the few exceptions was the general manager of the largest coal company in the Ruhr area, Emil Kirdorf, who, not coincidentally, was also the most influential personality in this most important of all German cartels, as chairman of the supervisory board of the RWKS (Roelevink 2017). The other industrialists among the 'big linkers' were owner-entrepreneurs, in many cases even members of industrial dynasties, such as Hugo Stinnes, Isidor Loewe and Peter Klöckner.

By far the largest group among the big linkers at the end of the Empire were the bankers and bank directors with a total of about 80 percent. This finding is in line with a contemporary study from 1906, when bank representatives accounted for almost 30 percent of 1,000 German stock corporations with a total of 6,783 supervisory board positions (Eulenburg 1906: 95, Windolf 2006). According to this, bank representatives must have held more than 2,000 mandates, whereby the eight German great banks together hardly had more than 30 board members. Consequently, a large number of mandates must have been concentrated among the individual bank representatives, which then explains their high share among the big linkers. The owner-entrepreneurs (private bankers) and the managers (as representatives of the great banks) were still almost on an equal footing. The directors of the larger provincial banks followed closely behind. In fact, the board members (as well as the unlimited partners in the case of the *Kommanditgesellschaften auf Aktien*) of the eight Berlin great banks together held 650 mandates in 1906, with *Dresdner Bank* and *Disconto-Gesellschaft* leading the way with 123 and 122 mandates, respectively (Ziegler 2020: 42).

Hilferding and many bank critics after him interpreted the close bank-industry relationship as a symptom of the 'power of the banks' over the industrial sector. For Hilferding (1968: 321–22), this already sowed the seeds for the future central bank. For provided that the banks cooperated in their domination strategy, they could pursue industrial policy and thus establish a planning authority within an otherwise 'anarchic' market.

Recent research, however, assesses the great importance of private bankers and bank directors in the supervisory boards of (big) companies differently. It explains the finding firstly by a special feature of German stock-corporation law, the so-called proxy voting right. According to this, it was permitted to have the voting right for the general meeting of a joint-stock company transferred if the shareholder did not want to participate himself and agreed to the transfer of voting rights. By the banks exercising the voting right for the shares held in their custody accounts, the missing major shareholder was created artificially, as it were, which the representatives of the banking federation justified by saying that this prevented a minority of shareholders from pushing through resolutions to the detriment of the company or the shareholders who did not attend the general meeting (Hartmann 1924/25, Solmssen 1930).

So far, the finding can still be reconciled with the 'banking power' thesis. However, the second explanation for the close bank-industry linkage is no longer valid, for the motivation of the banks, as creditors, to place a representative on the supervisory board of a non-bank was not the claim to pursue an industrial policy but to reduce the information asymmetry that basically exists between creditor and debtor. In this respect, the bank representatives on the supervisory board did have control, but their interest was limited to the creditworthiness of a significant credit customer. For through its supervisory-board mandate, a creditor bank received insider information that allowed it better to assess the risks of its exposure (Da Rin 1996: 29–33, critically Fohlin 2007: 192). This was also in the interest of the debtor. By reducing the uncertainty about the creditworthiness of its debtor through the information gained on the supervisory board, the bank was able to take higher risks or limit the risk premium on the interest rate on the loan more than would have been possible without this exclusive information. However, it was not at all in the debtor's interest for a bank to have a monopoly on this information, as the bank could also use this advantage for its own benefit. However, if several banks had this information, because representatives of different banks on the supervisory board were given access to it, it was in principle possible to play the banks off against each other and negotiate better conditions than under monopoly conditions (Ziegler 2020: 34).

The rapid growth in the number of bankers and bank managers on the supervisory boards of non-banks after the turn of the century, therefore, had two causes. First, there was an increase in the number of public limited companies where it was worthwhile for one or more banks to seek a seat on the supervisory board and, if necessary, even to enforce co-optation by means of the proxy voting right. Secondly, non-banks increasingly succeeded in freeing themselves from the monopoly of a single bank by appointing several representatives of different banks to their supervisory boards. This was also the experience of Emil Kirdorf, who had been able to free his company from the monopoly of one of the Berlin's great banks, the *Disconto-Gesellschaft*, as a creditor at the beginning of the twentieth century. Therefore, in response to Gustav Schmoller's anti-cartel and anti-bank statements, he could claim with a clear conscience that never before had 'the influence of the great banks in the big industry of Rhineland and Westphalia [been] as small as it is at present' (Verein für Socialpolitik 1906: 285).

This explains why so many bank managers, especially of the major Berlin banks, sat on the supervisory boards of big companies, but not why almost as many private bankers were co-opted there. As creditors, their houses were too weakly capitalised for big industry. Only a few private bankers had been able to force their way onto the supervisory board of a joint-stock company through the proxy voting right. In their case, too, it was the non-bankers' interest in the person. For precisely because private bankers hardly represented their own interests as creditors with their activities as supervisory-board members, they were extremely valuable as a corrective to the more interest-driven great bank managers. They sat on the supervisory boards primarily as information dealers, and this was precisely their interest in accepting such mandates. The more mandates they held, the larger the pool of information was in which the boards of non-banks were interested (Ziegler and Wixforth 1997).

As research into banking history, which has been based on bank archives for around 25 years, has been able to show, the personal linkages between banks and industry during the last peacetime years of the Empire cannot be taken as an indication of bank dominance over the industrial sector. An attempt at control via proxy voting would also have been futile. For if the banks had tried to use their block votes at the general meetings to become a private-sector planning authority, the state could have taken away the basis for this with the stroke of a pen—by abolishing the proxy voting right.

5 Conclusion

In his 'History of Capitalism', Jürgen Kocka (2013: 89–90) continued to speak of 'organised capitalism' with regard to cartels and banks—not explicitly, but probably essentially in relation to, the Wilhelmine Empire, to which he attributed a 'profound change in the form of capitalism'. At the same time, however, he also emphasised that the principle of competition, 'despite all alliances and monopolistic tendencies [...], had continued to be valid even between the giant companies'. Furthermore, he saw the 'intensive networking of industrial and bank capital' as a characteristic of this epoch. However, he also emphasised that 'contrary to what is often assumed, there can be no question of the domination of one side over the other'.

But is what then remains really sufficient to speak of an organised state of the market-based economic order of the Empire? At first glance it seems so. The lobby associations were indeed able to achieve spectacular successes. The protective tariffs in particular would not have been pushed through so quickly without the intensive lobbying of the CDI and other protectionists. However, an examination of the associations' practices shows that the interests were often very different, so that the formulation of a common position took time and often turned out to be lukewarm in the end. The great importance of the politically conservative heavy industry within the CDI, which was close to the monarchy, has often been discussed. But it was precisely their (often uncompromising) policy of interests that provoked the withdrawal of politically liberal-minded companies and less protectionist-oriented industries, which significantly weakened the CDI's clout. In this respect, the founding of BDI and *Hansa-Bund* is precisely not a sign of efficiently organised interest politics. The BdL must be assessed somewhat differently. After its comparatively late founding, it even contributed significantly to the downfall of a chancellor who was not exactly an agriculturalist; at least after that, no government dared openly to oppose the BdL and the interests it articulated. Agriculture may have been an efficiently organised sector in terms of interest politics, but—because of its dwindling importance in the national economy of the Empire, and also because of the tenacity of the feudal ruling structures in the countryside—it was a capitalist sector only to a limited extent.

The lobby associations were much more successful than in their lobbying when shielding the activities of the cartels from the state and the public. For as much as the trade associations tried to influence the state and its policies, third parties could basically be kept out of the affairs of the cartels. The reason for this secrecy, however, was less the organisation of the cartelised markets than the upstream negotiations within the cartels. The cartels were by no means as powerful as many contemporaries and, after them, numerous historians assumed. Many cartels broke up, and those that existed for longer than a business cycle often only narrowly escaped dissolution. The idea of competition among the cartel members did not disappear, but shifted from the markets to the inside of the cartels—and this was difficult for the contemporary public to recognise and understand. Even among themselves, the cartels were anything but cooperative. The hard-coal syndicates, for example, never managed to enter into serious negotiations with the lignite syndicates about a division of the (energy) markets. And the lignite syndicates had no reason to do so once they had started to produce electricity from the lignite extracted from open-cast mines. A cartel did not give up a competitive advantage, even in the interest of the organisation.

The same applies to bank-industry relations. They were the result of a disproportionately more capital-intensive first industrial leading sector complex of railways and heavy industry around the middle of the nineteenth century, compared to the textile industry in Great Britain, with a simultaneously underdeveloped financial market. Already during this period, a close connection developed between individual bankers and many companies in these growth industries—again in comparison to the industrial pioneer country of Great Britain. In the imperial period, with the breakthrough of the joint-stock commercial bank and the spread of free-floating industrial joint-stock companies, also known as managerial capitalism, this relationship deepened and took on a more institutionalised form. After the turn of the century, when many non-banks resisted their house bank's claim to sole representation, they could count on the fact that the house banks' competitors were only waiting for the opportunity to force their way into the business. A demarcation of spheres of interest in the interest of a higher order of the markets did not exist here either.

This finding speaks to the critique that Gerald Feldman already put forward during the revival of organised capitalism in the 1970s. While Feldman

(1974: 350–51) welcomed in principle the attempts to 'establish a conceptual framework for historical analysis', he saw the emergence of 'industrial organisation' and 'state intervention' as the result of 'the secular Central European tradition going back to mercantilist absolutism' and the 'belated but all the more massive breakthrough of industrialisation'. Today, almost fifty years later, it would probably no longer be formulated in this way. But the economic order of the Empire was not a change in the form of capitalism, but the specifically German manifestation of a market economy that was characterised by path dependencies, successful survival strategies of pre-modern elites and successful adaptation strategies to secure international competitiveness.

Notes

1 The orthodox attitude of GDR research, based on Lenin's theory of state-monopoly capitalism of 1917, was viewed critically by West German (neo-) Marxists, who were unable to enter into a constructive dialogue on their theory of 'late capitalism' either with the Marxists in the GDR or with the 'bourgeois' historians politically close to social democracy. On this line of thought, cf., among others, Mandel (1972); Theorie des Monopols (1975); and contributions of Jörg Huffschmidt, Robert Katzenstein, Elmar Altvater, and Thomas Hagelstange. Cf. on this, from a historiographical perspective, Wellhöner (1989: 32–34).

2 As late as 1913 it was called the 'Bund der Unzulänglichen' (federation of the deficients), according to the *Frankfurter Zeitung*; the paper was close to heavy industry, especially Emil Kirdorf; cf. (Ullmann 1976: 9).

3 Against the background of this decision, the decision of the Imperial Court of 1897 is even, cautiously but clearly, a weakening of the freedom of contract; cf. Blaich (1973: 43–45).

4 Liefmann (1927: 24–29) dates the founding of the first modern cartels, for salt, bismuth and tinplate, to the 1860s; it was only after the founding of the German Empire that more cartels were formed. However, public and also academic discussion of cartels began much later: The first public mention of a cartel was made in 1879 in connection with rail-rolling mill exports in the *Reichstag*; and the seminal work by Kleinwächter did not appear until 1883.

5 In 1908, an 'agricultural consortium' acquired the potash fields of *Gewerkschaft Burbach*; cf. Mette (1997: 127–30).

References

Anonymous (1933) *Die Syndikatsverträge des Rheinisch-Westfälischen Kohlensyndikats*, Essen.

Assmann, H. (1992) *Aktiengesetz: Großkommentar*, Vol. 1: *Einleitung*, Berlin: De Gruyter.

Barnikel, H. (1972) 'Kartelle in Deutschland: Entwicklung, theoretische Ansätze und rechtliche Regelungen', in H. Barnikel (ed), *Theorie und Praxis der Kartelle*, Darmstadt: Wissenschaftliche Buchgesellschaft, pp. 1–64.

Baudis, D. and Nussbaum, H. (1978) *Wirtschaft und Staat in Deutschland vom Ende des 19. Jahrhundert bis 1918/19*, Berlin/Ost: Akademie.

Bittner, T. (2005) 'An event study of the Rhenish-Westphalian Coal Syndicate', *European Review of Economic History*, Vol. 9 (3): 337–64.

Blaich, F. (1973) *Kartell- und Monopolpolitik im kaiserlichen Deutschland: Das Problem der Marktmacht im deutschen Reichstag zwischen 1879 und 1914*, Düsseldorf: Droste.

Blaich, F. (1979) *Staat und Verbände in Deutschland zwischen 1871 und 1945*, Wiesbaden: Steiner.

Böhme, H. (1972) *Deutschlands Wege zur Großmacht: Die deutsche Handelspolitik 1848–1881*, 2nd. ed. Köln: Kiepenheuer & Witsch.

Böse, C. (2018) *Kartellpolitik im Kaiserreich: Das Kohlensyndikat und die Absatzorganisation im Ruhrbergbau 1893–1919*, Berlin: De Gruyter.

Bourdieu, P. (1989), *La noblesse d'État: Grandes écoles et esprit de corps*, Paris : Edition de Minuit.

Bührer, W. (2013) 'Die Unternehmerverbände und Otto von Bismarck', in M. Epkenhans and U. v. Hehl (eds), *Otto von Bismarck und die Wirtschaft*, Paderborn u. a.: Schöningh, pp. 185–200.

Burhop, C. (2006) 'Banken, Aufsichtsräte und Corporate Governance im Deutschen Reich (1871–1913)', *Bankhistorisches Archiv*, Vol. 32 (1): 1–25.

Burhop, C. (2011) *Wirtschaftsgeschichte des Kaiserreichs 1871–1918*, Göttingen: Vandenhoeck & Ruprecht.

Büschenfeld, J. (1997) *Flüsse und Kloaken: Umweltfragen im Zeitalter der Industrialisierung, (1870–1918)*, Stuttgart: Klett-Cotta.

Da Rin, M. (1996) 'Understanding the development of the German Kreditbanken, 1850–1914: an approach from the economics of information', *Financial History Review*, Vol. 3 (1): 29–47.

Eschenburg, T. (1955) *Herrschaft der Verbände?* Stuttgart: Deutsche Verlagsanstalt.

Eulenburg, F. (1906) 'Die Aufsichtsräte der deutschen Aktiengesellschaften', *Jahrbücher für Nationalökonomie und Statistik*, Vol. 32: 92–109.

Feldman, G. (1974) 'Der deutsche Organisierte Kapitalismus während der Kriegs- und Inflationsjahre 1914–1923', in H. A. Winkler (ed), *Organisierter Kapitalismus: Voraussetzungen und Anfänge*, Göttingen: Vandenhoeck & Ruprecht, pp. 150–72.

Fischer, W. (1964) *Unternehmerschaft, Selbstverwaltung und Staat: Die Handelskammern in der deutschen Wirtschafts- und Staatsverfassung des 19. Jahrhunderts*, Berlin: Duncker & Humblot.

Fischer, W. (1973) 'Staatsverwaltung und Interessenverbände im Deutschen Reich 1871–1914' [1967], in H. Varain (ed), *Interessenverbände in Deutschland*, Köln: Kiepenheuer & Witsch, pp. 139–62.

Fohlin, C. (2007) *Finance Capitalism and Germany's Rise to Industrial Power*, Cambridge: Cambridge University Press.

Gehlen, B. (2013), *Der Deutsche Handelstag und die Regulierung der deutschen Wirtschaft 1861 bis 1914*, unpublished habilitation thesis, University of Bonn.

Handbuch der deutschen Aktiengesellschaften 1906 (1907), Berlin: Börsen- und Finanzliteratur.

Hartmann, W. (1924/25) 'Das Stimmrecht der Depotaktie', *Bankarchiv*, Vol. 24: 486–91.

Hentschel, V. (1978) *Wirtschaft und Wirtschaftspolitik im wilhelminischen Deutschland: Organisierter Kapitalismus und Interventionsstaat?* Stuttgart: Klett-Cotta.

Hilferding, R. (1968) *Das Finanzkapital*, Frankfurt a. M.: Europäische Verlagsanstalt.

Hue, O. (1906) 'Bemerkungen zur Kartellenquete', *Sozialistische Monatshefte*, Vol. 10 (1): 57–64.

Isay, R. (1930) 'Die Entwicklung der deutschen und ausländischen Kartellgesetzgebungen', *Zeitschrift für ausländisches und internationales Privatrecht*, Vol.4 (1): 1–47.

Jovović, T. (2012) 'Deutschland und die Kartelle: eine unendliche Geschichte', *Jahrbuch für Wirtschaftsgeschichte,* Vol. 53 (1): 237–73.

Kaelble, H. (1967) *Industrielle Interessenpolitik in der Wilhelminischen Gesellschaft: Centralverband Deutscher Industrieller 1895–1914*, Berlin: De Gruyter.

Kocka, J. (1974) 'Organisierter Kapitalismus oder Staatsmonopolistischer Kapitalismus? Begriffliche Vorbemerkungen', in H. Winkler (ed), *Organisierter Kapitalismus: Voraussetzungen und Anfänge*, Göttingen: Vandenhoeck & Ruprecht, pp. 36–57.

Kocka, J. (1984) 'Organisierter Kapitalismus im Kaiserreich?' *Historische Zeitschrift,* Vol. 230: 165–84.

Kocka, J. (2013) *Geschichte des Kapitalismus*, München: Beck.

Kollmer, G. (1979) *Dokumentation zur Organisationsgeschichte des Hansa-Bundes*, Wiesbaden: Steiner.

Köster, R. (2015) 'Grenzen der Prognostik: Andrew Shonfields nüchterner Blick in den Bauch des 'modernen Kapitalismus' (1965)', *Zeithistorische Forschungen*, Online-Ausgabe, Vol. 12 (3), 520–25.

Krenn, C. (2012) *Alle Macht den Banken? Zur Struktur personaler Netzwerke deutscher Unternehmen am Beginn des 20. Jahrhunderts*, Wiesbaden: Springer VS.

Levenstein, M. and Salant, S. (eds) (2007) *Cartels*, Vols. 1 and 2, Cheltenham: Edward Elgar.

Liefmann, R. (1927), *Kartelle, Konzerne und Trusts*, 7th ed., Stuttgart: Moritz.

Liefmann, R. (1972) 'Kartelle' [1923], in H. H. Barnikel (ed), Th*eorie und Praxis der Kartelle*, Darmstadt: Wissenschaftliche Buchgesellschaft, pp. 67–108.

Lübbers, T. (2009) 'Is cartelization profitable? A case study of the Rhenish Westphalian Coal Syndicate, 1893–1913', *Preprints of the Max Planck Institute for Research on Collective Goods.*

Lutter, M. (2007) 'Der Aufsichtsrat im Wandel der Zeit: Von seinen Anfängen bis heute', in W. Bayer and M. Habersack (eds), *Aktienrecht im Wandel der Zeit: Grundsatzfragen des Aktienrechts*, Vol. 2, Tübingen: Mohr Siebeck, pp. 389–429.

Mandel, E. (1972) *Der Spätkapitalismus: Versuch einer marxistischen Erklärung*, Frankfurt a. M.: Suhrkamp.

Maschke, E. (1964) *Grundzüge der deutschen Kartellgeschichte bis 1914*, Dortmund: Gesellschaft für Westfälische Wirtschaftsgeschichte.

Mette, T. (1997) *Kali-Industrie, Kali-Staat und Kali-Junker: Recht und Wirtschaft am Beispiel des Reichskaligesetzes vom 25. Mai 1910*, St. Katharinen: Scripta Mercaturae.

Mielke, S. (1976) *Der Hansa-Bund für Gewerbe, Handel und Industrie 1909-1914: Der gescheiterte Versuch einer antifeudalen Sammlungspolitik*, Göttingen: Vandenhoeck & Ruprecht.

Morgenroth, W. (1907) *Die Exportpolitik der Kartelle: Untersuchungen über die handelspolitische Bedeutung des Kartellwesens*, Leipzig: Duncker & Humblot.

Nipperdey, T. (1961) 'Interessenverbände und Parteien in Deutschland vor dem Ersten Weltkrieg', *Politische Vierteljahrsschrift,* Vol. 2 (3): 262–80.

Nolte, P. (2002) 'Historische Sozialwissenschaft', in J. Eibach and G. Lottes (eds), *Kompass der Geschichtswissenschaft*, Göttingen, Vandenhoeck & Ruprecht: pp. 53–68.

Nussbaum, H. (1976) 'Zur Diskussion um den historischen Platz des Staatsmonopolistischen Kapitalismus in der neueren marxistisch-leninistischen Literatur', *Jahrbuch für Wirtschaftsgeschichte,* Vol. 17 (1): 69–94.

O'Rourke, K. (1997) 'The European grain invasion, 1870–1913', *Journal of Economic History,* Vol. 57 (4): 775–801.

O'Rourke, K. and Williamson, J. (1999) *Globalization and History: The Evolution of a nineteenth-Century Atlantic Economy*, Cambridge, MA: MIT Press.

Pappi, F. et al. (1987) 'Die Struktur der Unternehmensverflechtungen in der Bundesrepublik', *Kölner Zeitschrift für Soziologie und Sozialpsychologie*, Vol. 39: 669–92.

Plumpe, W. (1990) 'Unternehmerverbände und industrielle Interessenpolitik', in W. Köllmann et al. (eds), *Das Ruhrgebiet im Industriezeitalter*, vol. 1., Düsseldorf: Schwann, pp. 655–727.

Puhle, H. (1967) *Agrarische Interessenpolitik und preußischer Konservatismus im wilhelminischen Reich (1893–1914)*, Hannover: Literatur und Zeitgeschehen.

Roelevink, E. (2015) *Organisierte Intransparenz: Das Kohlensyndikat und der Niederländische Markt, 1915–1932*, München: Beck.

Roelevink, E. (2017) 'Die Handlungskompetenz eines Managers: der Aufstieg Emil Kirdorfs und die Gelsenkirchener Bergwerks-AG, 1873–1903/04', *Vierteljahrschrift für Sozial- und Wirtschaftsgeschichte*, Vol. 104 (3): 376–411.

Schäfer, D. (1973) 'Der Deutsche Handelstag auf dem Weg zum wirtschaftlichen Verband' [1966], in H. Varain (ed.), *Interessenverbände in Deutschland*, Köln: Kiepenheuer & Witsch, pp. 120–38.

Schröter, H. (1994) 'Kartellierung und Dekartellierung 1890–1990', *Vierteljahrschrift für Sozial- und Wirtschaftsgeschichte*, Vol. 81 (4): 457–93.

Schröter, H. (2011) 'Das Kartellverbot und andere Ungereimtheiten: Neue Ansätze in der internationalen Kartellforschung', in M. Müller, H. R. Schmidt and L. Tissot (eds), *Regulierte Märkte: Zünfte und Kartelle / Marchés régulés: Corporations et cartels*, Zürich: Chronos, pp. 199–213.

Schröter, H. (2013) 'Cartels revisited: an overview on fresh questions, new methods, and surprising results', *Revue Économique*, Vol. 64 (6): 989–1010.

Scott, J. and Griff, C. (1984) *Directors of Industry: the British Corporate Network 1904–1976*, Cambridge: Polity Press.

Shonfield, A. (1965) *Modern Capitalism: The Changing Balance of Public and Private Power*, Oxford: Oxford University Press.

Solmssen, G. (1930) *Entwicklungstendenzen und weltwirtschaftliche Aufgaben der deutschen Großbanken*, Berlin: De Gruyter.

Stanworth, P. and Giddens, A. (1974) 'An economic elite: a demographic profile of company chairmen', in P. Stanworth, and A. Giddens (eds), *Elites and Power in British Society*, Cambridge: Cambridge University Press.

Torp, C. (2005) *Die Herausforderung der Globalisierung: Wirtschaft und Politik in Deutschland, 1860–1914*, Göttingen: Vandenhoeck & Ruprecht. English edition (2014) *The Challenges of Globalization: Economy and Politics in Germany, 1860–1914*, New York: Berghahn.

Tschierschky, S. (1930) *Kartellpolitik*, Berlin: Heymann.

Ullmann, H. (1978) *Bibliographie zur Geschichte der deutschen Parteien und Interessenverbände*, Göttingen: Vandenhoeck & Ruprecht.

Ullmann, H. (1980) 'Zur Rolle industrieller Interessenorganisationen in Preußen und Deutschland bis zum Ersten Weltkrieg', *Geschichte und Gesellschaft*, Vol. 6 (special issue): 300–23.

Ullmann, H. (1988) *Interessenverbände in Deutschland*, Frankfurt a. M.: Suhrkamp.

Verein für Socialpolitik (1906) *Verhandlungen der Generalversammlung in Mannheim im September 1905, Verhandlungen des Vereins für Socialpolitik*, Vol. 116, Leipzig: Duncker & Humblot.

Webb, S. B. (1980) 'Cartels, technology, and growth in the German steel industry, 1879 to 1914', *The Journal of Economic History,* Vol. 40 (2): 309–30.

Wehler, H. U. (1974) 'Der Aufstieg des Organisierten Kapitalismus und Interventionsstaates in Deutschland', in H. A. Winkler (ed), *Organisierter Kapitalismus: Voraussetzungen und Anfänge,* Göttingen: Vandenhoeck & Ruprecht, pp. 36–57.

Wellhöner, V. (1989) *Großbanken und Großindustrie im Kaiserreich,* Göttingen: Vandenhoeck & Ruprecht.

Windolf, P. (2006) 'Unternehmensverflechtungen im organisierten Kapitalismus: Deutschland und USA im Vergleich 1896–1938', *Zeitschrift für Unternehmensgeschichte,* Vol. 51 (2): 191–222.

Winkler, H. A. (1974) 'Einleitende Bemerkungen zu Hilferdings Theorie des Organisierten Kapitalismus', in H. A. Winkler (ed), *Organisierter Kapitalismus: Voraussetzungen und Anfänge,* Göttingen: Vandenhoeck & Ruprecht, pp. 9–18.

Ziegler, D. (1997) 'Kontinuität und Diskontinuität der deutschen Wirtschaftselite 1900 bis 1938', in D. Ziegler (ed), *Großbürger und Unternehmer,* Göttingen: Vandenhoeck & Ruprecht, pp. 31–53.

Ziegler, D. (2020) ''Bankenmacht', 'Verwaltungsherrschaft', 'Aktionärsdemokratie'? Zum Problem der Kontrolle der Geschäftsleitung in deutschen Aktiengesellschaften 1870–1931', *Zeitschrift für Unternehmensgeschichte,* Vol. 61 (1): 25–56.

Ziegler, D. and Wixforth, H. (1997) 'Deutsche Privatbanken und Privatbankiers im 20. Jahrhundert', *Geschichte und Gesellschaft,* Vol. 23 (2): 205–35.

Ziegler, R. (1984) 'Das Netzwerk der Personen- und Kapitalverflechtungen deutscher und österreichischer Wirtschaftsunternehmen', *Kölner Zeitschrift für Soziologie und Sozialpsychologie,* Vol. 36 (3): 585–614.

13 Social insurance and its consequences for workers' living conditions

Tobias A. Jopp and Jochen Streb

1 Introduction

The introduction of compulsory social insurance for broad sections of the population under Imperial Chancellor Otto von Bismarck in the form of health insurance (1883), accident insurance (1884), and invalidity and old-age insurance (1889) was arguably one of the most important institutional innovations in the Empire, giving the German welfare state its specific character up until now (Ritter 2010: 1–21). Germany was the first Western industrialised country that comprehensively protected its people against the existential risks of illness, invalidity, old age, and death. Comparable insurance mechanisms or social insurance systems on a small scale had already existed in many individual German states before the foundation of the German Empire in 1871. However, the founding of the Empire was a catalyst for the rapid harmonisation of state-specific rules and practices and—as paradoxical as this may sound in connection with Bismarck's authoritarian regime—promoted the democratisation of access to social benefits through the strong expansion of the number of people insured. Had the Empire not been founded, German states would probably have expanded their specific social security systems anyway, possibly inspired by the example of already existing insurers such as the miners' associations (see below). However, in this counterfactual situation, it would have taken much longer for all German states to achieve the same comprehensive standard. That is why the German social insurance system would then not have served as an early model for other governments. Many foreign states have followed the example of Germany, which is why the social insurance system of German design became the core of a prevalent international welfare state paradigm.[1] It comprises compulsory insurance for all target groups of social legislation, the insurance principle,[2] co-financing by employees and employers, and the use of the pay-as-you-go system as a standard financing technique (Kuhnle and Sander 2010: 70–73; Ritter 2010: 87–102).

What exactly is social about social insurance—beyond the fact that it is meant to cover the whole population (Zweifel and Eisen 2003: 1–4)? In our view, it is the communitarisation of individual risks. Social insurance agencies

DOI: 10.4324/9781003283430-16

charge their insurance contributions based on income and not according to individual risk. This contrasts sharply with private insurers that calculate an individual's contribution according to his or her risk profile, which is why, for example, a higher individual risk of disease leads to higher premiums regardless of income. The social insurance agencies' approach reflects the governmental objective to redistribute from higher to lower incomes. This form of redistribution only works in conjunction with compulsory membership and a large and heterogeneous group of insured persons (Riley 1997; Gorsky 1998; Emery and Emery 1999; Murray 2003, 2011; Hennock 2007: 141–50, 166–81; Harris 2012). A special feature of the pay-as-you-go system is that it also allows transferring income from the younger working generation to the older generation of pensioners. Unlike in the decades after the Second World War, when redistribution interests stood at the centre of the German social insurance system's modernisation, redistribution was not an important political reason for establishing social insurance in the Empire, though (Jopp 2013: 24–33).

Why did the intervention of the central government into protection against life risks, which is closely linked to the name of Bismarck, take place in the 1880s, and, thus, earlier than elsewhere (Ullmann 1979: 575; Kuhnle and Sander 2010: 65)? Politicians might have pursued the social objective to fight the impoverishment of workers and the 'ravages of capitalism' (Cutler and Johnson 2004: 91) by guaranteeing workers' subsistence income (Hennock 2007). This social motive, which suggests that Bismarck and his advisers sympathised with the working class, is dominated by power considerations leading to the political exploitation of social insurance (Ullmann 1979: 575), because Bismarck used the social insurance system to alienate workers from their own political and welfare organisations. As insured workers now had something to lose, namely their acquired insurance claims, they should have had a higher stake in the political stability of the still-young nation-state.[3] Seen in this light, social insurance was above all an instrument of power meant to subdue workers, thereby supplementing the ineffective Socialist Act of 1878 (Ritter 2010: 61–87). The introduction of social insurance not only pacified the working class but also promised to reduce the political influence that the Catholic Church traditionally gained through its charity work. Social insurance was therefore also a weapon in the dispute between the state and the Catholic Church (the so-called *Kulturkampf*) (Manow 2009; Kuhnle and Sander 2010: 66). In sum, the introduction of social insurance can be understood as an attempt to establish (central) state capacity by claiming comprehensive regulatory competence in an elementary area of life. Bismarck's objective of containing any political centrifugal forces that threatened the existence of the newly founded Empire thus appears to be a necessary precondition for the rapid introduction of a comprehensive social insurance system. Still, a change of perspective is possible: Instead of only asking who should be kept under control by the social insurance system, we could also explore who other than the central government had a legitimate interest in its implementation. Many sources refer to the businessmen who expected that the social insurance system helped to maintain the working capacity of their employees (Ullmann 1979; Reckendrees 2020).

In this chapter, we discuss whether the introduction of social insurance promoted social and economic progress in the German Empire. Our main hypothesis is that Bismarck's social insurance system was a powerful social innovation that paved the way for the modern welfare state with all its advantages and disadvantages. Social insurance not only improved workers' living conditions considerably but also created systemic path dependencies that confront our society today with difficult problems, especially that of a rapidly ageing population. It is precisely these interactions between social security and demographic development that have come into the focus of economic and social historical research most recently. On the one hand, scholars explore whether the introduction of social insurance has accelerated the demographic transition in Germany. On the other hand, they analyse whether an ageing population will undermine the existing social insurance system.

Our article is structured as follows. In the second section, we elaborate on how German people dealt with social insecurity before the foundation of the Empire. In the third section, we present the main stylised facts about the development of Bismarck's social insurance between its introduction in the 1880s and the First World War. The fourth section discusses recent research in economic history that examines the relationship between social insurance and demographic changes. In the fifth section, we conclude.

2 The predecessors of Bismarck's social insurance system

In (historical) research on the welfare state, the term 'mixed economy of welfare' describes a society's combination of different forms of individual and collective measures of protection against the vicissitudes of life (Harris and Bridgen 2007: 1). In Germany, as in many other Western countries, this mix has undergone considerable change since the Middle Ages. We observe that collective forms of social security became more and more important, first organised on a cooperative basis by guilds and brotherhoods and later initiated by governments in the form of social insurance or comparable programmes (Frerich and Frey 1993: 6–28; Wagner-Braun 2002: 28–37; Hardach 2003; Harris and Bridgen 2007; on self-regulation, see Collin 2011; Collin et al. 2011; Tennstedt 2011; Ayaß 2012).

In contrast to what is often propagated, Bismarck's social insurance system was not a social innovation born out of nothing that radically broke all prevailing traditions. Rather, it was based on various older collective social security measures which, taken together, anticipated the essential features of Bismarck's social insurance system. In contrast to the latter, however, these predecessors covered only a small part of the total population. One of these forerunners was the commercial relief funds dating back to the Prussian Trade and Industry Code of 1845 and its successor laws. The commercial relief funds combined elements of compulsory and voluntary membership as well as private and state initiatives and served as local health insurance funds that provided moderate sick pay and took over the costs for medicine. The support of invalids and surviving dependents did not play a major role yet (Frevert 1984; Wagner-Braun 2002: 42–73; Tennstedt 2011). Apart from Prussia, such commercial relief funds existed in other German states as well. At the time of the foundation of the Empire, the number of commercial relief funds totalled about 8,000 and the number of their members was about one million (Wagner-Braun 2002: 58).

We also want to highlight the long tradition of occupational benefit schemes in mining (since around 1260), shipping (since around 1500), and the railway sector (since 1839), which offered a much wider range of benefits than the commercial relief funds (Montz 2010; Guinnane and Streb 2011; Sulzer 2012; Jopp 2013). Among these occupation-specific mutual associations, the ones of the (Prussian) miners (so-called *Knappschaften*) served as the major model for the design of Bismarck's social insurance system (Tampke 1982: 80). The roots of the miners' mutual associations can be traced back to the thirteenth century and the Harz Mountains and to the fifteenth century and the Ore Mountains. Here, the miners created associations for the cultivation of religious customs and the mutual financial support in case of need and were already familiar with the obligation to pay regular contributions in form of the so-called *Büchsenpfennig* (Jopp 2013: 49).

In eighteenth-century Prussia, the miners' collective security system developed parallel to the rise of the local mining industry. Originally founded as cooperative organisations, the miners' associations changed during the absolutist era to organisations under the direct management of the Prussian authorities who sought to tightly control the working class. The predominant function of miners' associations was now the preservation of miners' ability to work by alleviating the financial consequences of illness and industrial accidents (Jopp 2013: 50). The liberal reforms of the Prussian mining law between 1851 and 1865 once again significantly changed the shape of the miners' associations. Membership became compulsory again and the self-management by the two sides of the industry was reinstated. In addition, the insurance principle was formally introduced. The range of benefits included daily sick pay and death benefits, the coverage of costs of consultations, hospital stays and medication, lifelong invalidity and widow's pensions, and orphan's pensions up to the age of 14 (Jopp 2013: 51–67). In 1871, the Empire's foundation year, there were 91 miners' associations in Prussia alone with a total of about 227,000 actively contributing members and about 48,300 pensioners corresponding to 87 percent of all German miners that were organised in mutual associations (Jopp 2013: 93, 97). There is no doubt that the first full-fledged social insurance system on German soil existed since 1854, the year in which the Prussian miners' social security act was passed. However, this social insurance system was still limited to one industry.

3 Stylised facts on Bismarck's social insurance system between 1883 and 1913

The predecessors of Bismarck's universal social insurance system not only provided an example of how to design such a system but also served as practical cornerstones for the organisational setup of the new health, invalidity, and old-age insurance. Some of the older systems, such as the miners' associations, even continued to exist parallel to Bismarck's social insurance system. From 1883 onwards, they operated as supplementary insurance funds (*Zuschusskassen*) that had the purpose of providing a mark-up on the benefits provided by Bismarck's national system.

The new health insurance act (1883, in force from December 1, 1884) acknowledged seven different types of funds as carriers of the new health insurance. Some of them had already existed before the foundation of the Empire, such as the relief and auxiliary funds, albeit not in the numbers now required. That is why many additional health insurance funds had to be established during the Empire (Frerich and Frey 1993: 97–99, 101–03). Their numbers increased from almost 19,000 in 1885 covering 4.5 million industrial workers and so-called company officials[4] to about 23,000 in 1911 with over 16 million members (Hennock 2007: 163–64; Jopp 2013: 93, 97). In these two reference years, the insured employees accounted for 21 and 45 percent of the working population, respectively (see Figure 13.1). The health insurance funds' total expenditures, two-thirds of which were financed by contributions from the insured and one-third by employers, rose from about 50 to 450 million Marks (see Figure 13.2) corresponding to an increase in per

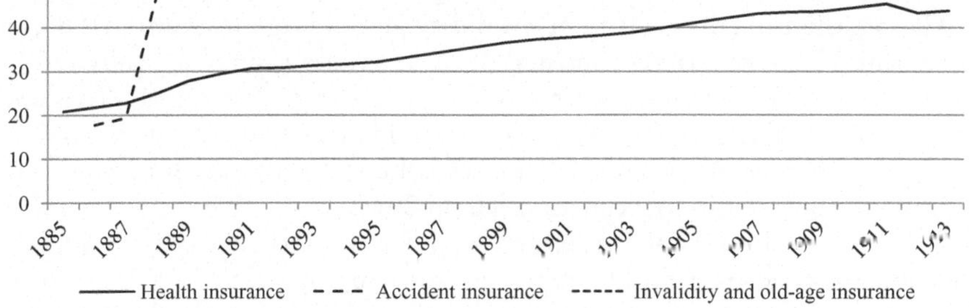

Figure 13.1 Insured as a percentage of the working population, 1885–1913.
Sources: Khoudour-Castéras (2008: 234–37) and Sniegs (1998: 210).

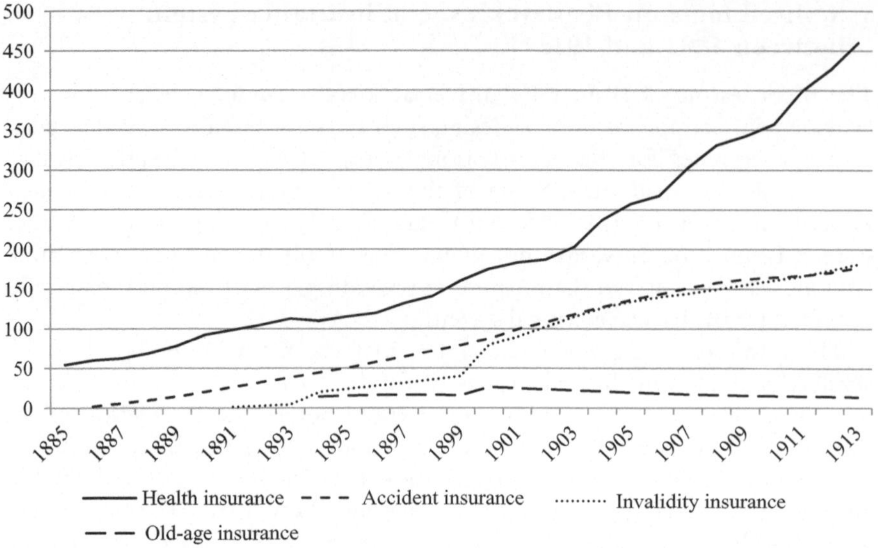

Figure 13.2 Total nominal expenditure of the three traditional branches of social insurance, 1885–1913 (in million Marks).

Sources: Khoudour-Castéras (2008: 234–37).

capita expenditures from about 13 to 34 Marks. Daily sick pay was among the most important benefits amounting to 50 percent of the local daily wage, and payable from the third day of sickness on and for a maximum of 13 (from 1903: 26) weeks. Coverage of costs for medical treatment and medicines was another main benefit (Frerich and Frey 1993: 102). In some cases, the health insurance funds also financed medical expenses for family members. The nominal daily sick pay rose from one Mark in 1885 to just under 1.50 Marks in 1910; total expenditure per case of illness increased from 30 to 67 Marks over the same period. This increase was driven by two developments: nominal wages rose due to high industrialisation, and diagnostic and treatment options expanded because of medical progress.

The organisational structure of invalidity and old-age insurance (1889, in force from January 1, 1891) consisted of 31 new state insurance funds and 11 special funds which originated from the predecessor systems (Frerich and Frey 1993: 99–101, 106–07). The latter included three large miners' associations and a merger of several smaller ones, all of which took on new tasks in addition to their traditional functions (Jopp 2013: 72–74). The new invalidity and old-age insurance spent a larger proportion of its revenue, which was contributed in equal parts by employers and employees, for invalidity pensions intended to maintain a worker's remaining working capacity (Scheubel 2013: 83–90). Only a smaller part was devoted to the relatively meagre old-age pensions to which a worker was entitled from the age of 70 onwards (see Figure 13.2). The Empire increased each individual pension by a fixed supplement of 50 Marks per year. However, even the invalidity pension was on average only 17 percent of the wage and therefore, much smaller than the invalidity pension of 30 percent or more that was provided by the miners' occupation-specific insurance scheme at the same time (Sniegs 1998: 146; Kaschke 2000; Jopp 2013: 138). In the new invalidity and old age insurance, the share of insured persons amounted to about 50 percent of the working population and was therefore considerably larger than that of the health insurance scheme. This is because, in addition to industrial workers and company officials with annual earnings of up to 2,000 Marks, agricultural workers and domestic servants were also included (see Figure 13.1).

The accident insurance (1884, in force since October 1, 1885) is the only one of the three pillars of Bismarck's social insurance system that cannot be traced back to predecessor systems. The employers' liability insurance associations (*Berufsgenossenschaften*), which became responsible for managing accident insurance funds, were truly new organisations that represented all companies in the same branch of industry (Frerich and Frey 1993: 95–97, 103–06). The introduction of accident insurance must be seen as a political reaction to the unpopular Imperial Liability Act of 1871, which required workers who were claiming compensation for an accident at work to prove the fault of their employer in court. With the Accident Insurance Act, the Imperial Liability Act became obsolete. From now on, every worker affected by an accident at work was entitled to compensation regardless of the question of guilt. Figure 13.2 shows how the total expenditure on accident insurance expanded in the German Empire. In comparison to invalidity and old-age insurance, accident insurance's invalidity pensions were very generous. Workers who were completely unable to work after an accident at work received a pension that amounted to two-thirds of their last earnings. Pensions were payable from the fourteenth week of work incapacity onwards; for the first thirteen weeks, support was provided by health insurance. The observation that costs per accident fell from 240 (1887) to between 130 (1904) and 150 (1913) Marks suggests that the proportion of fatal and other serious accidents decreased over time (cf. Khoudour-Castéras 2008: 235). In contrast to the other pillars of Bismarck's social insurance system, accident insurance was fully financed by the employers. Its coverage grew rapidly to more than 75 percent of the working population, and since 1908, almost all employees had accident insurance (see Figure 13.1).

4 Economic and social effects of Bismarck's social insurance system

In this section, we discuss six research questions that have been addressed by economic historians in recent years. Most of the approaches have in common the attempt to prove, with the help of quantitative methods, that the demographic changes in the German Empire were caused (or, at least, intensified) by the introduction of Bismarck's social insurance system.

We begin with research projects that understand social security as a direct determinant of the demographic development in Germany and beyond. Population growth can be broken down into two components: first, the birth surplus as the balance of the (unadjusted) birth and death rates; and, second, the migration balance as the difference between cross-border immigration and emigration. The introduction of social insurance might have had short- and long-term effects on mortality (subsection 4.1), fertility (subsection 4.2), and emigration (subsection 4.3). All these changes contributed to the demographic transition. Recall that it also took place in European countries which had not established a social insurance system. In general, the demographic transition is defined as the shift from a reproductive regime with persistently high mortality and birth rates to a reproductive regime with persistently low mortality and fertility. In the latter reproductive regime, societies tend to age in the long term (Rothenbacher 2002; Guinnane 2011; Galor 2012). Figure 13.3 illustrates the demographic transition for the German case, which is characterised by the fact that mortality began to fall earlier than fertility.

Scholars also explore accident insurance's impact on accident frequency (Section 4.4), highlight the problems that an aging population creates for a pay-as-you-go pension system (Section 4.5), and ask whether social insurance affected private savings (Section 4.6).

Figure 13.3 The demographic transition in Germany, 1815–1940 (within the borders of 1871).

Sources: 1815–71: Fertig et al. (2018: 31–33). 1872–1940: Rothenbacher (2002: Appendix Table D4).

4.1 Has health insurance reduced mortality?

From 1871, mortality began to fall steadily in Germany to 11 deaths per 1,000 inhabitants in the 1930s (see Figure 13.3); accordingly, life expectancy at birth increased from 35.5 to 60 years for men, and from 38.5 to 63 years for women (Rothenbacher 2002). The introduction of compulsory health insurance is only one factor among a range that may have contributed to the decline in mortality. Other possible causes were the increase in real wages enabling workers to consume a healthier diet, the construction of a public water supply and sanitation system, and medical progress, making it possible to diagnose and treat ever more diseases effectively (Spree 1981; Bauernschuster et al. 2020). Identifying a causal effect of health insurance on mortality decline in the German Empire is therefore not an easy task.

Based on historical data for Prussia, Stefan Bauernschuster et al. (2020) compare trends in the mortality of industrial workers and civil servants, who were not covered by Bismarck's social insurance system, before and after the introduction of health insurance for workers. If this institutional reform had a causal effect on mortality, then these two trends should differ more after 1884 than before. The authors observe that, between 1884 and 1900, death rates fell more sharply among insured workers than among civil servants. According to their calculations, one-third of the difference can be explained by the introduction of health insurance. They distinguish three channels of impact. First, insured workers had far more frequent contact with doctors and other medical staff from whom they learned how to protect themselves against infectious diseases by following simple hygiene rules. This transfer of knowledge reduced the spread of airborne diseases such as tuberculosis; infections spread via drinking water could only be contained by improvements to the sanitary infrastructure. Second, the democratisation of access to health services such as medical consultations and medicines improved the general health status of broad sections of the population and, thereby, decreased both their morbidity and mortality. Third, this health effect has been strengthened by the increasing stationary treatment of workers in hospitals, as this service was now also financed by health insurance (Spree 1995).

4.2 Has invalidity and old-age insurance reduced fertility?

In the nineteenth century, most people still relied primarily on their own families to protect themselves against the elementary risks of life. Having many children was associated with the hope of being provided for in the event of illness and invalidity as well as during old age; children thus fulfilled an insurance function. Figure 13.3 shows that from the turn of the century onwards, the birth rate in Germany began to fall steadily and was roughly halved by 1940. This observation raises the question of whether the introduction of Bismarck's social insurance system persuaded people to abandon this traditional form of risk provision.

Robert Fenge and Beatrice Scheubel pursue precisely this question (Scheubel 2013; Fenge and Scheubel 2017). Under the assumption that raising children always entails a loss of earnings from work, the introduction of a pay-as-you-go pension scheme would leave people exposed to two opposing incentives. On the one hand, the demand for children may increase because the disposable annual income decreases due to the compulsory payment of contributions to the old-age insurance, and thus the opportunity costs of having children also fall. On the other hand, the demand for children may decline because the comparatively low (implicit) interest on contributions reduces the lifetime income of the insured, who try to compensate for this by working overtime. To answer the question of which of these two effects predominated in the German Empire, the authors compare the development in 23 German states and provinces in the two reference years, 1895 and 1907. They conclude that approximately 15 percent of the decline in fertility during the period under review can be explained by the introduction of Bismarck's invalidity and old-age insurance.

In their study, Timothy Guinnane and Jochen Streb (2021) account for the demographic effects of all three branches of social insurance. Especially, they consider that the pillars of social insurance not only influenced fertility but also the propensity to marry. If an employed person (whether man or woman) became a member of the new social insurance system, the incentive for couples to marry increased because families were financially better protected in the event of an accident or sickness than before. As the birth rate was positively correlated with the frequency of marriage, there existed a further indirect channel of impact between the social insurance system and fertility. The authors also consider that certain occupational groups such as miners had their own social insurance system already before the 1880s (see Section 2). Other occupational groups such as farmworkers or servants were only partially integrated into Bismarck's social insurance system, or, like farmers and other self-employed persons, were not integrated into it at all. If we assume that the social insurance system provided a massive incentive to have fewer children, fertility in mining-dominated counties must have fallen long before 1883, whereas no observable effects should have occurred after 1883. In their empirical approach, Guinnane and Streb (2021) compare the annual demographic development in 450 Prussian counties before and after the introduction of social insurance for the period, 1880 to 1895. Unlike Fenge and Scheubel (2017), they find no significant influence of social insurance on fertility, which is consistent with the fact that the German Empire was not a forerunner but a laggard in the Western European fertility decline (Guinnane 2011: 591).

4.3 Has social insurance influenced cross-border migration?

Figure 13.4 illustrates the development of the German emigration rate. We observe emigration peaks in the years 1854, 1872, and 1881 with almost four, three, and five emigrants per 1,000 inhabitants, respectively. By far the most important destination country during these waves of emigration from Germany was the United States. The secular decline in transatlantic emigration from the Empire since the 1880s is usually attributed to the rapid German industrialisation process, which narrowed the wage gap with the United States, and the effects of falling fertility in Germany, which reduced the pressure to emigrate. David Khoudour-Castéras (2008) rejects these traditional explanations and argues that the drying up of emigration flows can best be explained by the introduction of Bismarck's social insurance system. He argues that while the income opportunities in the United States were much better, social security was much worse than in the German Empire; the latter even more so after the introduction of the social insurance system. The German workers' insurance claims represented an indirect 'social security wage' that we should add to their real wages if we do not want to make a mistake when comparing trans-Atlantic wage trends. Khoudour-Castéras (2008) calculates the 'social security wage' as the sum of per-capita expenditures in all three branches of social insurance. He shows that when this figure is included, the wage gap between Germany and the United States was smaller after 1883 and also shrank more rapidly.

The level of the 'social security wage' calculated by Khoudour-Castéras amounted to only about 4 percent of the direct real wage on average. Whether German people who considered emigrating noticed this small implicit increase in real wage and let it persuade them to stay in their country of birth remains questionable. According to Khoudour-Castéras, Germans were particularly risk-averse and therefore preferred the existential safety that

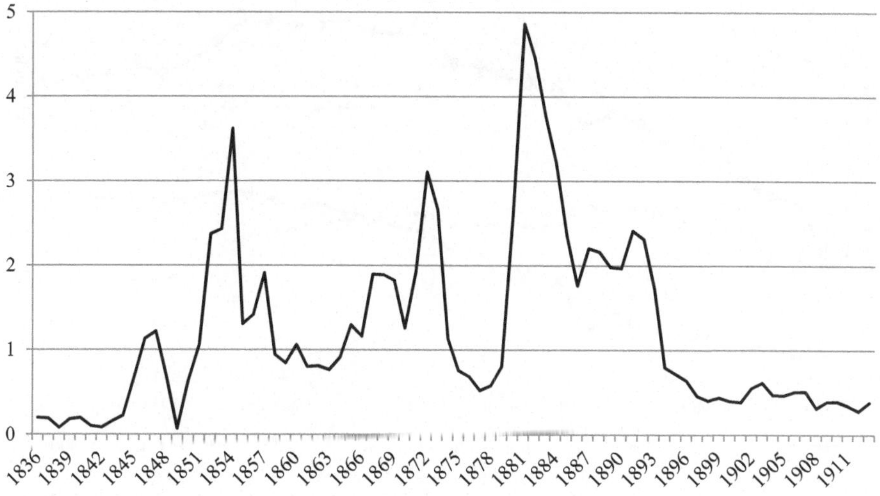

Figure 13.4 Emigrants per 1,000 inhabitants, 1836–1913 (within the borders of 1871).
Sources: Population: See Figure 13.1; Emigration: Khoudour-Castéras (2008: 214).

Bismarck's social insurance system provided over the better career options in the United States. Given the longer-term reversal of migration flows, the question arises whether Bismarck's social insurance system has attracted immigrants. However, an empirical study that would answer this question for the case of the German Empire is not yet available.

4.4 Has accident insurance contributed to more occupational safety?

Even though the Accident Insurance Act of 1884 was aimed at the financial compensation for occurring work accidents, it also allowed the newly-founded employers' liability insurance associations to issue accident prevention regulations for their member companies. Figure 13.5 illustrates the development of the accident rates (accidents per 1,000 employees) averaged across all employers' liability insurance associations with respect to the three accident categories, 'minor' (incapacity to work is between 14 weeks and six months), 'serious' (incapacity to work is more than six months), and 'fatal'. We see that the incidence of fatal accidents and serious accidents only began to decline sustainably at the beginning of the twentieth century. Guinnane and Streb (2015) conclude from this observation that the employers' liability insurance associations initially felt little incentive to enforce accident prevention regulations; or to put it more pointedly, it cost the companies less to allow for accidents and compensate them afterwards than to invest in accident prevention (Guinnane and Streb 2015).

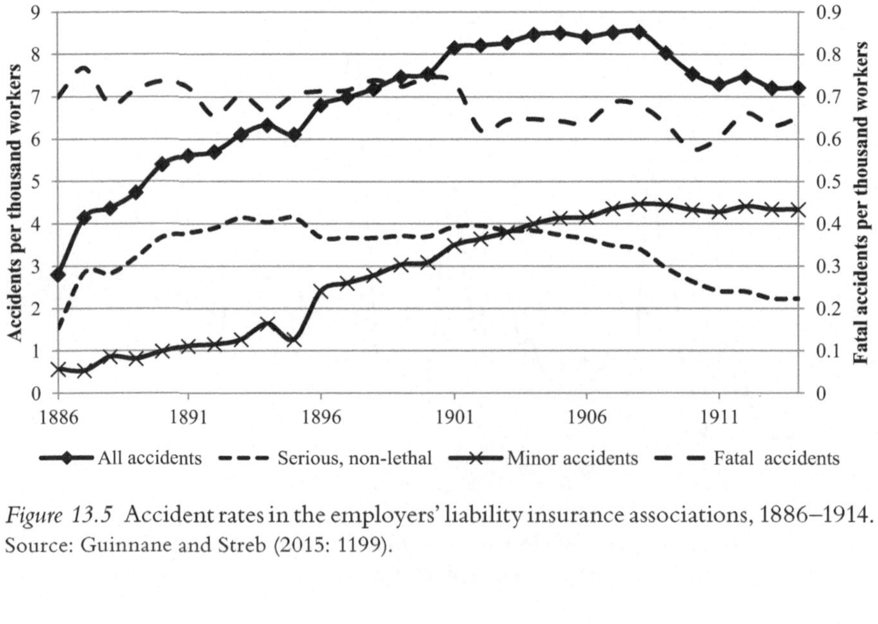

Figure 13.5 Accident rates in the employers' liability insurance associations, 1886–1914. Source: Guinnane and Streb (2015: 1199).

The authors identified the reason for this incentive structure in the accident insurance's tariff regulations. The contribution that a company had to pay depended on its size and its accident risk. While the size of a company was measured by its individual wage and salary bill, its accident risk was not calculated with the help of company-specific accident statistics. Instead, the employers' liability insurance associations assigned to each company a more general risk figure that summarised the past accidents in a large number of similar companies and could therefore hardly be influenced by an isolated change in behaviour of an individual company.

According to Guinnane and Streb (2015), this procedure had two side effects. On the one hand, entrepreneurs might have felt compelled to increase mechanisation because the substitution of labour by capital could reduce an individual company's wage and salary bill and thus its contribution to the employers' liability insurance association. On the other hand, there was no incentive to invest in company-specific accident prevention measures which would only have paid off if the company could have expected a noticeable reduction in the risk figure that the employers' liability insurance association assigned to it. Instead, companies with inadequate accident protection were able to pass on most of the costs of accident regulation to companies that had been assigned the same risk figure even though they recorded considerably fewer accidents. This mismanagement may explain why accident rates rose after the introduction of accident insurance.

The Imperial Insurance Office (*Reichsversicherungsamt*), the responsible regulatory authority, finally succeeded in convincing the employers' liability insurance associations to differentiate the risk figures they assigned to the companies. This made it easier for an individual company to reduce its own financial contribution through successful accident prevention. The timing of the decline in fatal and very serious accidents coincides with these reforms, which took place around the turn of the century.

4.5 How fair was the intergenerational contract in pension insurance?

In the last fifty years, a rapidly ageing population has been putting the German pay-as-you-go pension insurance system under enormous financial pressure because fewer and fewer contributors are available to support more and more pensioners. If in an ageing society, the government aims at keeping both the contribution rate and the pension level stable over time, unpopular measures are inevitable. The logic of the pay-as-you-go system implies that the ratio of pensioners to contributors has to be repeatedly brought back to an acceptable level by raising the retirement age bit by bit. Alternatively, the government might support the pension scheme with a continuously growing, tax-financed subsidy which is alien to the social insurance system (Jopp 2016: 983–84).

In the German Empire, such problems did not seem to play a role yet. Both the German society as a whole and the insured group of employees were still far away from biological ageing; and the ratio of pensioners to contributors as a measure of social ageing was still low, with up to a maximum of six pensioners that had to be financed by 100 contributors (see Figure 13.6; Jopp 2016: 980–81). However, Tobias A. Jopp (2013) shows that the miners' invalidity insurance was already exposed to ageing in the nineteenth century because of sectoral saturation effects. That is why the managers of the miners' invalidity insurance already had to deal with problems that would not occur in Bismarck's universal pension insurance until many decades later. This applies in particular to the long-term decline in implicit rates of return.

While the implicit rate of return of a funded pension scheme corresponds to the market interest rate at which the capital stock of the pension fund is invested, the implicit rate of return in a pay-as-you-go system corresponds to the growth rate of the insured wage and salary bill (Breyer 2000: 386–89). Many economists have pointed out that in an ageing society, the mechanics of the pay-as-you-go system are eroding the intergenerational contract between contributors and pensioners because the long-term decline in implicit rates of return is unavoidable (Jopp 2016: 990). Jopp (2016) illustrates that the Prussian miners' mutual associations (*Knappschaften*) were already confronted with this unpleasant development. Figure 13.6 shows that the average ratio of pensioners to contributors in the Prussian miners' associations was increasing in the late nineteenth century towards more problematic levels. If we include pensions for widows and orphans into the calculation, the burden with pensioners was sometimes even as high as 40 pensioners per 100 contributors. To

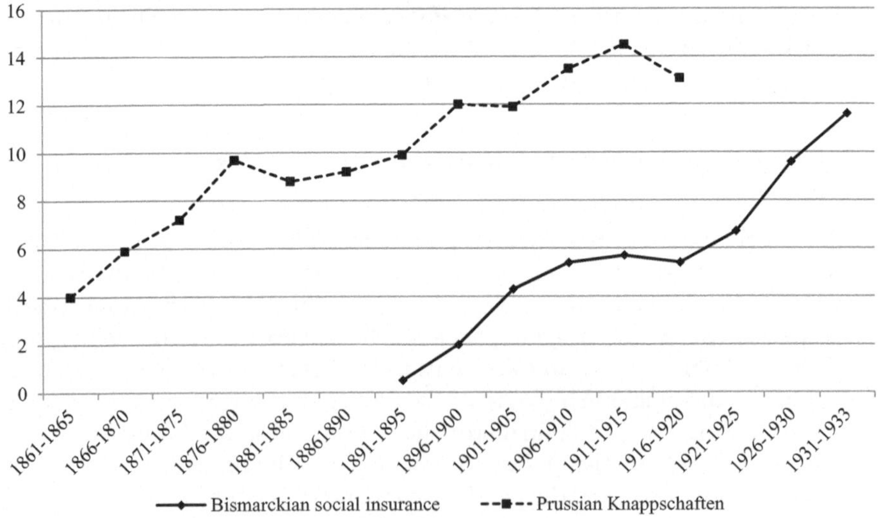

Figure 13.6 Invalidity pensioners per 100 contributors (1861–1933).
Sources: Sniegs (1998: 210, 215–17); Jopp (2013: 112).

put this number into perspective, note that the number of pensions that had to be financed by 100 contributors in the Federal German pension fund was 46 in 2006 (Jopp 2013: 114–15). The miners' associations of the nineteenth century reacted with a combination of increases in contribution rates and reductions in pension levels with the result that the average implicit rate of return in the miners' invalidity pension scheme fell significantly over time: from 14 percent for the retirement cohort of 1860–64 to only about 3 percent for the cohort of 1895–99. The unspoken promise of intergenerational fairness, which demands that all generations that participate in a pay-as-you-go system should be subject to the same financial burdens and benefits, could not be kept at the expense of later generations (Jopp 2016: 986–87).

4.6 Has social insurance reduced the level of private savings?

In addition to having many children, saving was the second most important form of individual protection against the vicissitudes of life before 1883. We observe the establishment of savings banks since the late eighteenth century, starting in northern Germany. They were founded to give poorer people an opportunity to save small amounts of money in interest-bearing investments and thus gradually build up a capital stock for bad times (Proettel 2020: 28–29). Bismarck and his advisers, however, believed that workers usually neglected their financial needs in old age and therefore tended to save too little. That is why the introduction of social insurance as a compulsory saving mechanism seemed justified despite the existence of savings banks.

Starting from the hypothesis that the introduction of compulsory contributions to Bismarck's social insurance system has crowded out private savings, Sibylle Lehmann-Hasemeyer and Jochen Streb (2018) find empirical evidence that this paternalistic, never-questioned argument holds true. Using the example of the Prussian savings banks in the period from 1874 to 1904, they show that in counties with an above-average proportion of newly insured occupational groups, savings activities were comparatively low and continued to decline. In their view, the first observation demonstrates the crowding-out effect of social insurance. The second observation speaks for learning effects on the part of the insured who, over time, learned through their own experience that the promised benefits of the social insurance system took place. The authors conclude that workers reduced their private risk provision in the form of savings parallel to their growing confidence in Bismarck's social insurance system.

Lehmann-Hasemeyer and Streb (2018) argue that the additional savings deposits that would have been built up in a counterfactual situation when Bismarck's social insurance had not existed would have been significantly below the monetary value of the insurance claims (especially from pensions) that the insured were accumulating in historical reality. In other words, without social insurance, people would have saved more but this extra amount would not have been enough to guarantee their minimum subsistence level in crisis times and old age. Apart from the fact that many people simply could not save more because they needed their meagre income to purchase essential goods in the present, the insufficient propensity to save can also be explained by the fact that people systematically underestimated their increasing life expectancy and thus their financial needs in old age. In this respect, Bismarck's paternalistic argument works in two ways.

5 Conclusion

What was innovative about Bismarck's social insurance system? From an organisational point of view, there was not much new. An industry-specific type of social insurance system had already existed for the group of miners since 1854; some of the main characteristics that define social insurance can even be traced back further into the past and also to other predecessors. From a quantitative perspective though, Bismarck democratised the access to social insurance to a very considerable degree. Even though the coverage of the three branches of social insurance still varied enormously, and total expenditures amounted to only about 1.5 percent of total economic output in 1913 (while today's figures come to about 30 percent) (Jopp 2013: 130), the impressive expansion of insured persons represents a remarkable social innovation of the German Empire. It was this new quantitative dimension that gave Bismarck's social insurance system the international visibility it needed to spread beyond Germany. Bismarck's social insurance system was the birth of a new type of welfare state that has remained a persistent topic of political and public discourse.

We have shown that the introduction of social insurance can be justified economically with the phenomenon of individual 'under-saving'. Individuals profited in two ways from social insurance; it not only alleviated the financial consequences of elementary vicissitudes of life but also reduced the probability of these events (such as sickness or accidents at work) through prevention. At the macroeconomic level, the introduction of social insurance has contributed to long-term demographic changes such as the ageing of societies that present modern economies with difficult challenges. There is still scientific disagreement about the impact on fertility. With regard to the decline in mortality, however, the view is that Bismarck's social insurance system has accelerated it through several channels.

Notes

1 The British-type welfare state, connected with the name of William Beveridge, emerged after the Second World War as the second major international welfare state paradigm (Boyer 2019).

2 This means that the insurance benefits depend on the occurrence of the insured event (causality principle) and on the payment of premiums (equivalence principle).

3 At the same time, workers' contributions compensated for the lack of financing power of the German central government.

4 In the early German Empire, employees in private commercial enterprises, who had supervisory functions, were usually called company officials. They were covered by social insurance as long as their daily salary did not exceed 6.60 Marks. The unusual term 'company official' can be explained by the fact that in the early years of Prussian mining, for example, foremen with supervisory function were in fact state officials. In the course of the liberal reform of the mining law (1851–65), they became employees of the private companies and came to be called company officials. The social class of the white-collar workers (to which the company officials belong) has been forming since the late nineteenth century. Their existence was formally recognised under social law with the introduction of white-collar workers' insurance in 1911.

References

Ayaß, W. (2012) 'Regulierte Selbstregulierung in den Berufsgenossenschaften der gesetzlichen Unfallversicherung', in P. Collin et al. (eds), *Regulierte Selbstregulierung im frühen Interventions- und Sozialstaat,* Frankfurt a. M.: Klostermann, pp. 123–43.

Bauernschuster, S., Driva, A. and Hornung, E. (2020) 'Bismarck's health insurance and the mortality decline', *Journal of the European Economic Association*, Vol. 18 (5): 2561–607.

Boyer, G. R. (2019) *The Winding Road to the Welfare State: Economic Insecurity and Social Welfare policy in Britain,* Princeton, NJ: Princeton University Press.

Breyer, F. (2000) 'Kapitaldeckungs- versus Umlageverfahren', *Perspektiven der Wirtschaftspolitik*, Vol. 1 (4): 383–405.

Collin, P. (2011) 'Optionen und Kontinuitäten regulierter Selbstregulierung in der frühen Kranken- und Altersversicherung', *Zeitschrift des Max-Planck-Instituts für Europäische Rechtsgeschichte,* Vol. 18: 186–212.

Collin, P. et al. (eds) (2011) *Selbstregulierung im 19. Jahrhundert: zwischen Autonomie und staatlichen Steuerungsansprüchen,* Frankfurt a. M.: Klostermann.

Cutler, D. M. and Johnson, R. (2004) 'The birth and growth of the social insurance state: explaining old age and medical insurance across countries', *Public Choice,* Vol. 120 (1): 87–121.

Emery, G. and Emery, J. C. H. (1999) *A Young Man's Benefit: The Independent Order of Odd Fellows and Sickness Insurance in the United States and Canada, 1860–1929,* Montreal et al.: McGill-Queen's University Press.

Fenge, R. and Scheubel, B. (2017) 'Pensions and fertility: back to the roots', *Journal of Population Economics,* Vol. 30: 93–139.

Fertig, G. et al. (2018) 'Das postmalthusianische Zeitalter: die Bevölkerungsentwicklung in Deutschland, 1815–1871', *Vierteljahrschrift für Sozial- und Wirtschaftsgeschichte,* Vol. 105 (1): 6–33.

Frerich, J. and Frey, M. (1993) *Handbuch der Geschichte der Sozialpolitik in Deutschland. Band 1: Von der vorindustriellen Zeit bis zum Ende des Ersten Weltkriegs*, Munich: Oldenbourg.

Frevert, U. (1984) *Krankheit als politisches Problem 1770–1880: Soziale Unterschichten in Preußen zwischen medizinischer Polizei und staatlicher Sozialversicherung*, Göttingen: Vandenhoeck & Ruprecht.

Galor, O. (2012) 'The demographic transition: causes and consequences', *Cliometrica,* Vol. 6 (1): 1–28.

Gorsky, M. (1998) 'The growth and distribution of English friendly societies in the early nineteenth century', *Economic History Review,* Vol. 51 (3): 489–511.

Guinnane, T. W. (2011) 'The historical fertility transition: a guide for economists', *Journal of Economic Literature,* Vol. 49 (3): 589–614.

Guinnane, T. W. and Streb, J. (2011) 'Moral hazard in a mutual health insurance system: German Knappschaften, 1867–1914', *Journal of Economic History,* Vol. 71 (1): 70–104.

Guinnane, T. W. and Streb, J. (2015) 'Incentives that (could have) saved lives: government regulation of accident insurance associations in Germany, 1884–1914', *Journal of Economic History,* Vol. 75 (4): 1196–1227.

Guinnane, T. W. and Streb, J. (2021) 'The introduction of Bismarck's social security system and its effects on marriage and fertility in Prussia', *Population and Development Review,* Vol. 47 (3): 749–80.

Hardach, G. (2003) 'Optionen der Altersvorsorge im 19. und 20. Jahrhundert in Deutschland', *Zeitschrift für Unternehmensgeschichte,* Vol. 48: 5–28.

Harris, B. (2012) *Welfare and Old Age in Europe and North America: The Development of Social Insurance,* London: Routledge.

Harris, B. and Bridgen, P. (2007) *Charity and Mutual Aid in Europe and North America Since 1800,* New York: Taylor & Francis.

Hennock, E. P. (2007) *The Origin of the Welfare State in England and Germany, 1850–1914,* Cambridge: Cambridge University Press.

Jopp, T. A. (2013) *Insurance, Fund Size, and Concentration: Prussian Miners' Knappschaften in the Nineteenth and Early Twentieth Centuries and Their Quest for Optimal Scale,* Berlin: Akademie.

Jopp, T. A. (2016) 'After us, the deluge: German miners' experience with pay-as-you-go pensions and the intergenerational contract before the great inflation', *Economic History Review,* Vol. 69 (3): 972–98.

Kaschke, L. (2000) 'Nichts als Bettelgelder? Wert und Wertschätzung der Alters- und Invalidenrenten im Kaiserreich', *Historische Zeitschrift,* Vol. 270 (1): 345–88.

Khoudour-Castéras, D. (2008) 'Welfare state and labor mobility: the impact of Bismarck's social legislation on German emigration before World War I', *Journal of Economic History,* Vol. 68 (1): 211–43.

Kuhnle, S. and Sander, A. (2010) 'The emergence of the western welfare state', in F. G. Castles et al. (eds), *The Oxford Handbook of the Welfare State,* Oxford: Oxford University Press, pp. 61–80.

Lehmann-Hasemeyer, S. and Streb, J. (2018) 'Does social security crowd out private savings? The case of Bismarck's system of social insurance', *European Review of Economic History,* Vol. 22 (3): 298–321.

Manow, P. (2009) *Religion und Sozialstaat: Die konfessionellen Grundlagen europäischer Wohlfahrtsregime,* Frankfurt a. M.: Campus.

Montz, M. (2010) 'Vergessener Vorreiter der Sozialversicherung? Betriebliche soziale Sicherung bei den preußischen Eisenbahnen, 1838–1914', in C. Bartels (ed), *Beiträge zur Tagung 'Vergangenheit und Zukunft sozialer Sicherungssysteme am Beispiel der Bundesknappschaft und ihrer Nachfolger' im Deutschen Bergbau-Museum Bochum 8. und 9. Oktober 2009,* Bochum: Deutsches Bergbau-Museum, pp. 109–42.

Murray, J. E. (2003) 'Social insurance claims as morbidity estimates: sickness or absence?', *The Journal of the Society for the Social History of Medicine,* Vol. 16: 225–45.

Murray, J. E. (2011) 'Asymmetric information and countermeasures in early twentieth-century American short-term disability microinsurance', *Journal of Risk and Insurance*, Vol. 78 (1): 117–38.

Proettel, T. (2020), *Die Stellung der Sparkassen im Markt für gewerbliche Finanzierungen: Untersuchungen über das Kreditgeschäft der Sparkassen während der Industrialisierung*, Ostfildern: Thorbecke.

Reckendrees, A. (2020) 'Why did German early industrial capitalists suggest workers' pensions, arbitration boards, and minimum wages?', *Jahrbuch für Wirtschaftsgeschichte*, Vol. 61 (2): 351–76.

Riley, J. C. (1997) *Sick, Not Dead: The Health of British Working Men during the Mortality Decline*, Baltimore, MD: Johns Hopkins University Press.

Ritter, G. A. (2010) *Der Sozialstaat: Entstehung und Entwicklung im internationalen Vergleich*, 3rd ed., Munich: Oldenbourg.

Rothenbacher, F. (2002) *The European population 1850–1945*, Houndmills: Palgrave Macmillan.

Scheubel, B. (2013) *Bismarck's Institutions: A Historical Perspective on the Social Security Hypothesis*, Tübingen: Mohr Siebeck.

Sniegs, M. (1998) *Statistik als Steuerungsinstrument in der historischen Entwicklung der Invaliditäts- und Altersversicherung 1891–1911*, PhD dissertation, University ofBremen.

Spree, R. (1981) *Soziale Ungleichheit vor Krankheit und Tod*, Göttingen: Vandenhoeck & Ruprecht.

Spree, R. (1995) 'Krankenhausentwicklung und Sozialpolitik in Deutschland während des 19. Jahrhunderts', *Historische Zeitschrift*, Vol. 260: 75–105.

Sulzer, M. (2012) *Soziale Sicherungssysteme in der Seeschifffahrt: Von der berufsständischen Armenfürsorge zur See-Sozialversicherung*, Bremen: Hauschild.

Tampke, J. (1982) 'Bismarcks Sozialgesetzgebung: ein wirklicher Durchbruch?', in W. J. Mommsen and W. Mock (eds), *Die Entstehung des Wohlfahrtsstaates in Großbritannien und Deutschland 1850–1950*, Stuttgart: Klett-Cotta, pp. 79–91.

Tennstedt, F. (2011) 'Die Hilfs- und Unterstützungskassen in Preußen: Selbstregulierung der sozialen Vorsorge für den Krankheitsfall', in P. Collin et al. (eds), *Selbstregulierung im 19. Jahrhundert —zwischen Autonomie und staatlichen Steuerungsansprüchen*, Frankfurt a. M.: Klostermann, pp. 275–92.

Ullmann, H.-P. (1979) 'Industrielle Interessen und die Entstehung der deutschen Sozialversicherung 1880–1889', *Historische Zeitschrift*, Vol. 229: 574–610.

Wagner-Braun, Margarethe (2002) *Zur Bedeutung berufsständischer Krankenkassen innerhalb der privaten Krankenversicherung in Deutschland bis zum Zweiten Weltkrieg: Die Selbsthilfeeinrichtungen der katholischen Geistlichen*, Stuttgart: Steiner.

Zweifel, P. and Eisen, R. (2003) *Versicherungsökonomie*, 2nd ed., Berlin: Springer.

14 Inequality and its drivers in Germany, 1840–1914

Thilo N. H. Albers and Charlotte Bartels

1 Introduction

Globalisation and industrialisation brought fundamental changes to the distribution of income and wealth. From the mid-nineteenth century to the eve of World War I, cities expanded and industrialisation provided individuals with new opportunities to earn income, invest capital, and become rich from the returns generated by their investments. For broad segments of the population, including workers, the living standards rose. A new entrepreneurial elite replaced the old feudal one. This transformation of the economy coincided with a rise in economic inequality, which itself brought about drastic changes to the social and political landscape. Organisational innovations such as trade unions emerged, aiming to reduce inequalities. Similarly, policy innovations such as the social legislation of the newly founded Empire were a response to the widening economic disparities between social classes. Studying inequality in the nineteenth century thus improves our understanding of both the contemporary political change surrounding the formation of the nation-state and the foundations of social policy that are still relevant today.

In this chapter, we focus on economic inequality in the narrow sense, that is, on the structure of factor incomes and the distribution of income and wealth. Inequality had many facets in the nineteenth and early twentieth century, many of which have been studied elsewhere. They range from differences in gender-specific literacy rates in England (de Pleijt et al. 2019) to inequality in physical stature in the United States and France (Crayen and Baten 2010) and inequality with respect to land ownership and education in Prussia (Cinnirella and Hornung 2016). Earlier work on Germany by Hartmut Kaelble (1983) takes a multidimensional approach towards social inequality including, amongst others, housing, health, and income.

Our focus on the economic dimension of inequality builds on recent advances in the literature. With his studies on the long-term evolution of income and wealth distributions and capital accumulation, Thomas Piketty has placed this type of research on a new methodological and empirical foundation. Specifically, he synthesises the insights of several generations of researchers, encompassing the Historical School, theorists such as Kuznets and

DOI: 10.4324/9781003283430-17

Solow, macroeconomic wealth accountants such as Goldsmith, and most recent approaches such as those from Atkinson (cf. Piketty and Saez 2003; Piketty 2014; Piketty and Zucman 2014). Building on this synthesis, numerous researchers have further refined the relevant methodologies and produced new historical data sets for a wide range of countries. These international efforts have rendered it possible to compare economic inequality over time and across countries.

Based on tax statistics and as part of these efforts, we have constructed a series of the share of total income and the share of total wealth held by the top 1 percent of the population in Germany (Bartels 2019; Albers et al. 2020). Figures 14.1 and 14.2 display their evolution from the late nineteenth century until today. Such a long-run perspective offers two distinct advantages. First, we can identify episodes of rising, stagnating, and falling inequality. Second, by comparing these episodes, we can gauge the relative magnitude of changes, and thus, their economic significance. Figure 14.1 shows the top percentile's share in total income. Between 1871 and the turn of the century, it rose from 16 to 19 percent and then stagnated until 1914. Considering that this share has fluctuated in the narrow corridor between 10 and 19 percent over the past 140 years, the increase by three percentage points appears

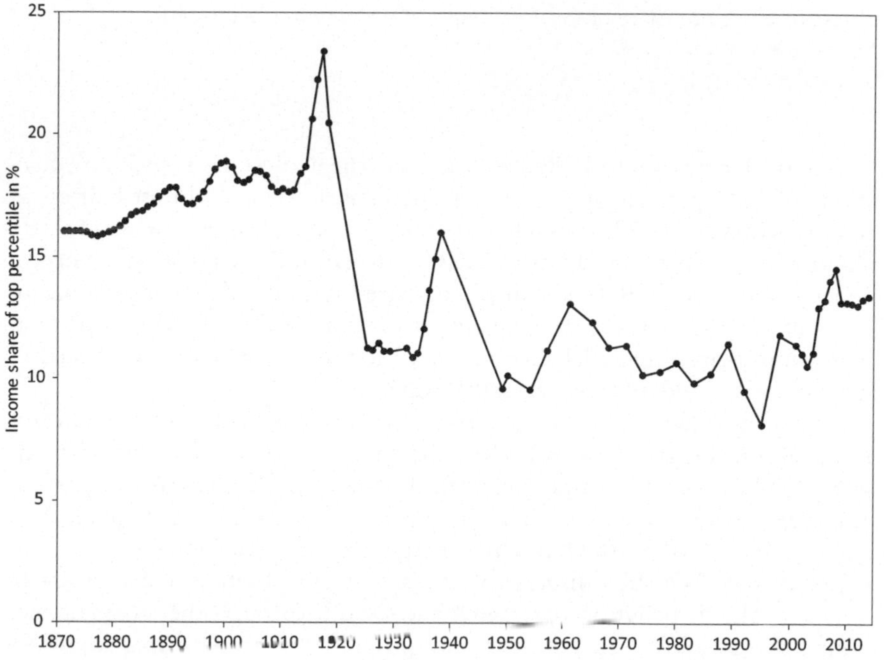

Figure 14.1 Income share of top 1 percent in Germany in the long run.
Source: Bartels (2019).

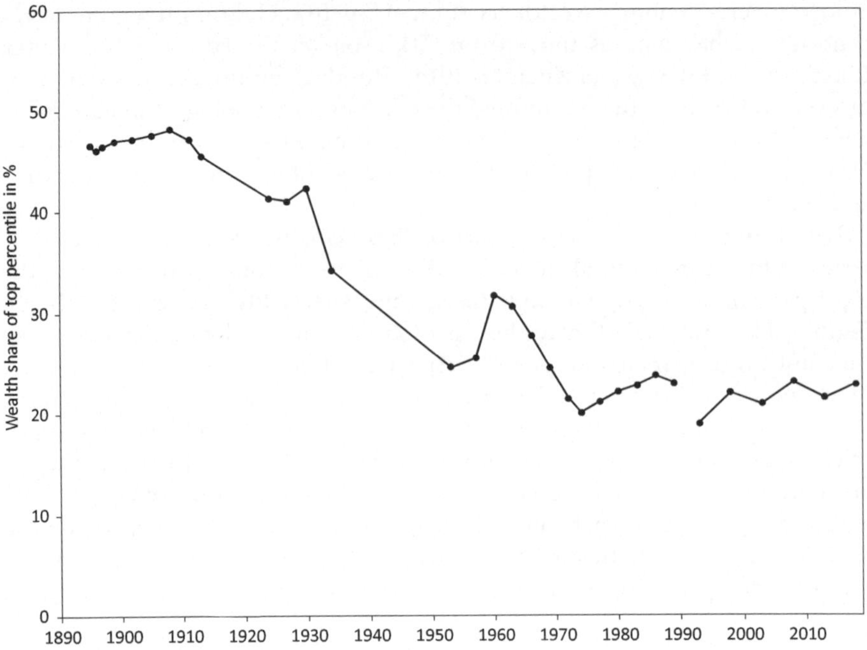

Figure 14.2 Wealth share of top 1 percent in Germany in the long run.
Source: Albers et al. (2020).

economically meaningful. Figure 14.2 traces the evolution of wealth inequality. In 1914, 1 percent of the German population owned almost half of the total private wealth. This high level of wealth concentration remained virtually unchanged between 1895 and 1914, mirroring the stagnation of income concentration from 1900 onwards. Compared with more recent periods, the levels of income and wealth inequality prevailing during the era of the German Empire are unparalleled. However, they do not appear exceptional by international standards (Bartels 2019; Albers et al. 2020).

Two stylised facts thus emerge. First, economic inequality was at its historical peak on the eve of World War I. Secondly, income inequality virtually stagnated between 1900 and 1914 even though it had been increasing before. What explains these patterns regarding levels and changes of inequality? To explore them further, the following section provides additional national and regional data. We then discuss the impact of globalisation and industrialisation on the distribution of income and wealth through the lenses of economic theory and descriptive statistics, providing potential explanations for the rise of inequality until 1900 and its high level. After a brief analysis of the new economic elite, the final section turns to the political consequences of economic inequality. Our political economy perspective also addresses the potential relevance of the formation of the nation-state for the stagnation of inequality from 1900 onwards.

2 The evolution of inequality

How did inequality evolve from the beginning of industrialisation until the eve of World War I? The German series for top-income and top-wealth shares displayed in Figures 14.1 and 14.2 begins only after the founding of the Empire. However, the first phase of industrialisation in Germany is usually considered to have taken place in 1840–70. This period is relevant for the analysis of inequality, even if one was only interested in the final decades of the nineteenth century. First, globalisation and industrialisation were presumably important forces shaping inequality trends in the last quarter of the century. However, they were well-advanced at this stage. To analyse their relevance, an assessment of inequality trends prior to the 1870s is indispensable. Second, extending the period under consideration backwards enables us to gauge the degree to which the formation of the nation-state represents a rupture in the evolution of inequality. Although the data available are scarcer than after the Empire's foundation, there are three ways to investigate inequality trends before 1871. First, recent research provides new insights into inequality before the onset of industrialisation. Second, one can employ alternative, less data-intensive inequality measures. Third, one can draw on regional data, contrasting rural and urban areas. We explore these avenues below.

Based on economic theory, we could expect pre-industrial economies to be marked by high levels of inequality. Apart from land, there were no factors of production that yielded significant returns on capital. Since the typical worker did not work for much more than the subsistence wage, one can conjecture that land ownership concentration and the level of inequality were high. Contemporaries such as Gustav Schmoller and other members of the Historical School conducted empirical studies on pre-industrial inequality. Alfani et al. (2022) built on these attempts, extended the existing data, and documented the evolution of inequality between 1300 and 1850. Confirming the theoretical priors from above, the authors documented high levels of inequality. Moreover, urban areas appear to have been more unequal than rural ones.

To trace the development of inequality during the first phase of industrialisation, we rely on two alternative distributional measures. We construct these measures based on recent estimates of wages and the net national product (Pfister 2017, 2018, 2019, 2020). The so-called Williamson index shown in Figure 14.3 captures the ratio of national income per capita y to the wage of an urban construction worker w. The index rises if wage growth does not keep up with average income growth, signalling a rise in economic inequality. Moreover, we can derive another indicator from the income side of the national accounts, namely the factorial distribution of income. It documents

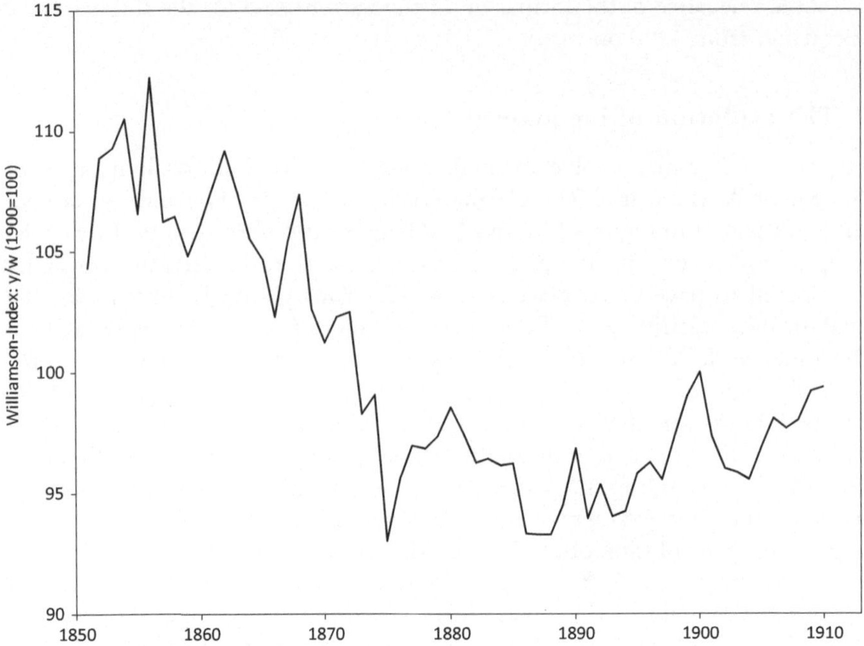

Figure 14.3 The Williamson index.
Source: Pfister (2018, 2020).

the relative remuneration of the production factors land, capital, and labour. While capital shares and personal income inequality typically correlate, the strength of this relationship is neither undisputed nor time-invariant (cf. Bengtsson and Waldenström 2018). Our focus thus lies on the importance of income from land relative to other types of capital (Figure 14.4).

The trajectory of the Williamson index can be divided into two periods. The index falls from 1860 to the mid-1870s and then, after fluctuating for a decade without trend, shows a marked increase towards the end of the century. How can we explain the fact that the Williamson index falls so sharply in the 1860s? An important factor was probably the so-called grain invasion (cf. Chapter 5 of this volume). As grain markets became increasingly integrated internationally, the income of landowners fell. This is also reflected in Figure 14.4. The share of the income from land in the national income fell, while the share of other capital incomes rose. Since wages remained relatively stable during the first phase of industrialisation from 1840 to 1870 (Pfister 2018), urban workers gained relative to the landed gentry. However, this trend of falling inequality reversed in the second phase of industrialisation, beginning in 1870. While wages began to increase (Pfister 2018), capital income apparently grew even faster. This appears to be the most plausible interpretation for the rise in the Williamson index. We will discuss the

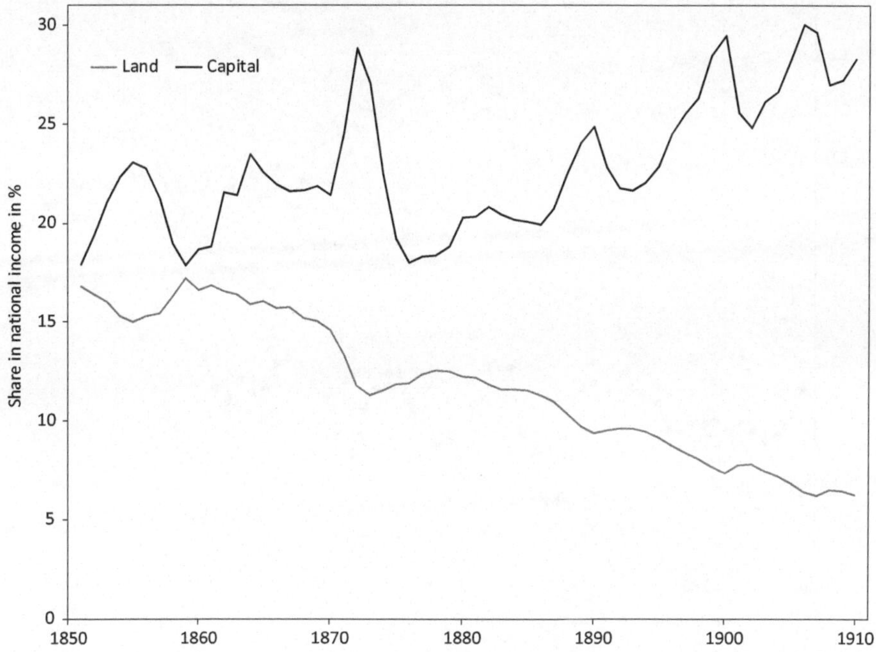

Figure 14.4 Factor shares of land and capital in Net National Product.
Source: Pfister (2020).

inequality pattern prevailing during this second phase of industrialisation in detail below.

So far, we have looked at Germany as one unit. Since data for the analysis of the personal income distribution are available at the state level (Tilly 2010; Bartels 2019), we can also examine regional differences. At the expense of national representativeness, the sub-national data allows us to extend the period under study backwards, improve our understanding of the role of regional trends in the national distribution, and identify differences in the level and evolution of inequality between urban and rural areas.

Figures 14.5 and 14.6 show estimates for two inequality measures across German states. Tabulated tax data allow us to calculate the Pareto coefficient and the income share of a given population group, such as the top 1 percent. The decline of the Pareto coefficient, depicted in Figure 14.5, indicates rising inequality. In Prussia and Bremen, which collected income taxes earlier than other German states, trends differed considerably during the first phase of industrialisation. While the decline of the Prussian Pareto coefficient indicates that inequality rose in the largest state of pre-unified Germany, the constant coefficient in the merchant city of Bremen implies a stable level. At first, this evidence seems inconsistent with the discussion above. After all, the Williamson index indicates a decrease in inequality.

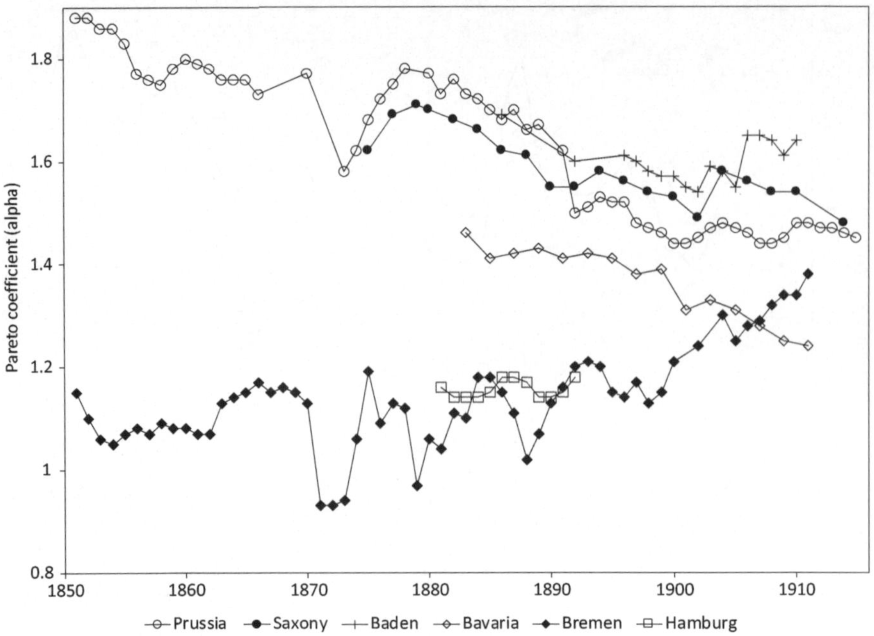

Figure 14.5 Regional estimates of income inequality: Pareto α coefficients.
Source: Grumbach (1957).

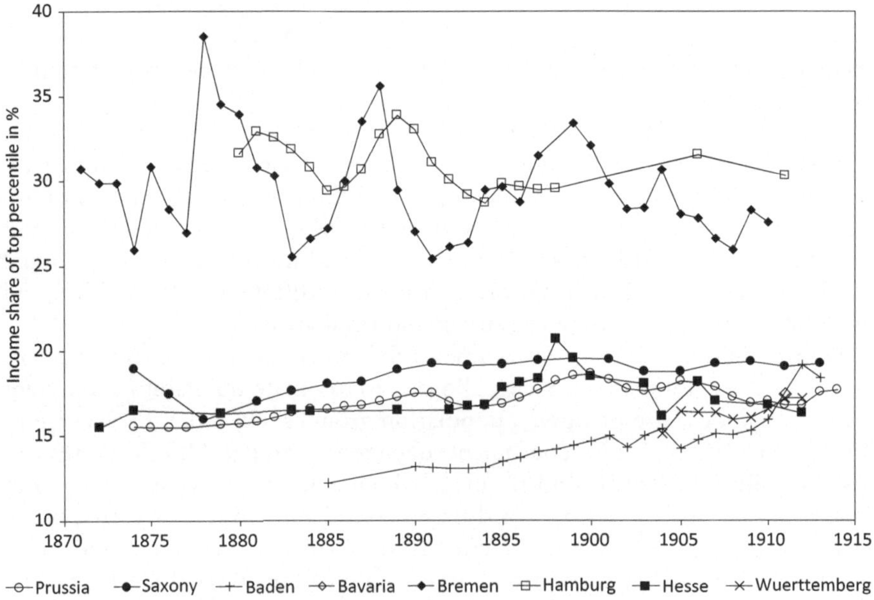

Figure 14.6 Income share of top 1 percent in German states.
Source: Bartels (2019).

Without going into the large number of inequality measures in depth at this point (cf. Cowell 2011), the contrasting trends illustrate that different measures emphasise different aspects of the distribution and do not necessarily exhibit the same trend. The Pareto coefficient is based on tax-paying households only, whose share in the population continuously changed over the nineteenth century. This is particularly true for Prussia where several tax reforms took place (Spoerer 2004: 39–102). The Williamson index, on the other hand, is based on a comparison of the average wage of an urban construction worker and national income per capita. It omits, at least in the denominator, the wages of agricultural workers, which fell relative to those in non-agricultural sectors during the grain invasion (Pfister 2019: 233–34). The supposed contradiction between these two measures thus originates in their respective inequality definitions rather than in limited data quality. Overall, it is not clear whether inequality rose or fell during the first phase of industrialisation relative to its pre-industrial level. It is also possible that two processes neutralised each other: Globalisation lowered inequality through the relative decline of land rents. Conversely, industrialisation increased inequality.

The picture is much clearer for the second phase of German industrialisation, which began around 1870. This is partly due to better data, which allow us to calculate the more familiar and easily interpretable measure of the top percentile's income share for several states (Figure 14.6). The level of inequality was higher in more industrial states such as Prussia and Saxony than in the more agrarian ones such as Baden and Württemberg. The city-states of Hamburg and Bremen exhibited much higher levels of inequality than all other states. The evidence thus suggests that urbanisation and inequality were positively correlated. Moreover, inequality in all but the city-states was higher in 1900 than it had been in 1871. From 1900 onwards, the rise in inequality slows down, especially in the industrial states of Saxony and Prussia. For Prussia, which comprised about 62 percent of the population of the German Empire on the eve of World War I (Kaiserliches Statistisches Amt 1914: 1), neither the Pareto coefficient nor the top percentile's income share exhibited a clear trend during this period.

In sum, the evidence presented so far suggests that the evolution of inequality between the mid-nineteenth century and World War I can be divided into three periods (cf. Kaelble 1983, 2017 for a similar periodisation). During the first period up to the 1870s, there is uncertainty about its course. Due to a relative decrease in land incomes, the Williamson index suggests falling inequality. In contrast, estimates of the Pareto coefficient indicate rising or at least constant inequality. In the second period, from about 1870 to about 1900, a clear rise in inequality is evident. It coincides with strongly increasing levels of globalisation and industrialisation. As we discuss below, these two forces were likely to affect inequality more than the concurrent formation of the nation-state. In the third period, from the turn of the century to World War I, both income and wealth inequality stagnate. We find that this stagnation occurred at a high level, unparalleled in the remainder of the twentieth and the early twenty-first centuries.[1]

In addition to this periodisation, two findings emerge that are important for the following discussion. First, cities showed significantly higher income inequality than rural regions. Second, the analysis of the functional income distribution over time shows that land income lost importance relative to income from other types of capital.

3 Globalisation, industrialisation, and inequality

The evolution of economic inequality from the mid-nineteenth century until World War I is best understood against the background of radical structural change. Focusing on the period 1871–1910, Table 14.1 summarises its key parameters. National income per capita grew by more than 40 percent in real terms. The share of industry, transport, banking, insurance, and trade in aggregate output rose by more than 50 percent, while the share of agriculture shrank by almost half. The urbanisation rate doubled from 24 to 48 percent. Meanwhile, import and export volumes grew by more than 250 percent. What role did globalisation and industrialisation play in the rise of inequality? Since convincing causal empirical evidence on this question is

Table 14.1 Structural change in the German Empire

	1870/1871	*1910*	*Growth (%)*
Growth and sectoral change			
Net national product (1990 $) per capita	1959	3383	42%
Share of agriculture	40%	23%	−43 %
Share of industry, crafts, banks, insurance, and transport	36%	56%	56%
Globalisation			
Export volume (1913 = 100)	20.3	77.5	282%
Import volume (1913 = 100)	23.5	88.3	276%
Income inequality			
Top 1% income share	16%	18%	13%
Top 10% income share	37%	39%	8%
Key variables of two sector models			
Urbanisation rate	24%	48%	100%
Urban–rural wage ratio (day labourers)	1.12	1.14	2%
Net value added (1913 Marks) per agricultural worker	672	982	46%
Firm concentration	22.8%	45.6%	100%

Sources: Net national product: Pfister (2020); shares of national income by sector: Dumke (1987: 104); trade volumes: Hoffmann (1965: 533–37); income inequality: Bartels (2019); urbanisation rate—defined as the share of population in municipalities with more than 5,000 inhabitants: Köllmann (1969); wage ratio of day labourers (five-year averages): own calculation based on Pfister (2018, 2019) extrapolating with Hoffmann (1965: 493); net value added per worker in agriculture: Grant (2005: 236); firm concentration—measured as the share of workers in firms with more than 50 employees in 1875 and 1907: Bartels et al. (2021).

scarce, we approach this question by bringing together economic theory and descriptive data.

The Heckscher-Ohlin model provides a framework through which we can explore the effect of globalisation on inequality in the nineteenth century (cf. O'Rourke and Williamson 1999). In this model, countries specialise in goods that require mainly the factor with which they are relatively well-endowed. The nineteenth-century world was divided into the 'New World' (North and South America) and the 'Old World' (Europe). In the New World, there was relatively more land, while European countries were relatively labour-abundant. Therefore, the Old World specialised in the production of labour-intensive goods, whereas the New World specialised in land-intensive food production. According to the Stolper–Samuelson theorem, specialisation causes the return of the relatively abundant factor to increase relative to that of the other factor. Such stylised division of the nineteenth-century world economy implies that wages in Europe must have risen relative to land rents.

Is this key prediction of the Heckscher-Ohlin model for the Old World borne out by the data? Indeed, the empirical evidence for Europe as a whole and Germany in particular points to a rising ratio of wages to land rents. This decreasing inequality between workers and landowners is also consistent with the role of the grain invasion (O'Rourke and Williamson 1999: 57–92; Chapter 5 in this volume). Yet, the model can only partly account for the observed evolution of inequality. First, the model focuses on trade, and thus, does not allow us to gauge the effects of industrialisation. Second, wage-land rent ratios leave one of the three classical factors of production aside: capital.

Although there is little causal empirical evidence on the effect of industrialisation on inequality, existing scholarship on the German Empire univocally suggests a positive relationship (Kaelble 1983; Dumke 1987, 1991; Grant 2005). This unanimity originates in both theoretical and empirical insights. Theoretically, industrialisation should have led to a reallocation of capital to more productive, and thus, more profitable uses. Empirically, the data presented earlier in this chapter suggest that the transition from an agricultural economy with a low rate of urbanisation to an industrial and more urbanised economy was associated with higher inequality. Two-sector models elucidate the precise mechanisms through which urbanisation and changes in the productivity of capital affect inequality (Dumke 1987, 1991). In particular, we discuss three models: (i) the Lewis model highlighting the role of surplus labour, (ii) the Kuznets model emphasising the difference between urban and rural areas, and (iii) the Krugman model placing economies of scale at the heart of spatial inequality.

The Lewis model of economic development assumes an agricultural rural sector and a modern industrial urban sector (Lewis 1954). At the beginning of industrialisation, there is a reservoir of underemployed workers in the agricultural sector (surplus labour). The migration of these workers to the city initially pushes wages in the industrial sector down to subsistence levels, while owners of capital reap high returns and reinvest them. This creates not only growth but also higher inequality. When the reservoir of underemployed labour is depleted, wages grow in line with productivity, leading to the reduction of the imbalance of factor incomes from capital and labour.[2]

Three metrics from Table 14.1 elucidate the empirical relevance of the Lewis model. First, the urbanisation rate doubled during this period. Thus, consistent with the Lewis model, there was indeed substantial migration from rural areas to cities. The second indicator pertains to the reservoir of surplus labour. The associated underemployment in agriculture can only be measured indirectly, for example, by contrasting productivity changes with technological progress. Net value added in agriculture increased by nearly 50 percent between 1871 and 1910—roughly equal to the increase in national income per capita. However, because the rate of technical progress was much higher in industry than in agriculture, at least part of this productivity growth must have been due to the decline of underemployment in agriculture (Dumke 1987: 106; Grant 2005: 204–07, 236, 249). The third indicator is the rural-urban wage gap. Urban wages exceeded their rural counterparts by 12 and 14 percent in 1871 and 1914, respectively. One could argue that such a temporary increase in the gap is consistent with the model[3] since it predicts that wages rise once the rural labour pool is depleted. The depletion of surplus labour is also reflected in Berlin's net migration. It fell sharply from 1890 onwards and even became negative from 1905 (Grant 2005: 64). Urban real wages rose in response after they had remained stagnant for a long time (Pfister 2018). In sum, key aspects of the Lewis model are consistent with the data.

The Kuznets model provides further insights into the mechanical role of the urban–rural divide (Kuznets 1955). Like the Lewis model, it has two sectors—a modern (urban) one and an agricultural (rural) one. The national income distribution results from aggregating the two distributions. Based on empirical observations, Kuznets assumes that incomes are both higher on average and more unequally distributed in the modern sector. At the beginning of industrialisation, only a small part of the population lives in this sector. According to the Kuznets model, the urbanisation that accompanies industrialisation will lead to more inequality. The underlying mechanism is that the increasing share of the high-income urban sector in the national distribution drives up the overall variance of incomes. Does the German data agree with the key components of the Kuznets model? Indeed, there was a significant urban–rural wage differential (Table 14.1). Moreover, income was more unequally distributed in urban and industrial areas than in rural areas (Figures 14.5 and 14.6; Spoerer 2004: 46–83). Despite its many critics, the underlying mechanism for the upward slope of the Kuznets curve is convincing and, in the case of Germany, consistent with the data.

Finally, the Krugman (1991) model provides important insights even though its focus and typical applications pertain to regional inequality (cf. Crafts and Wolf 2014). A key ingredient of the Krugman model is the plausible assumption that the returns to scale are constant in the agricultural sector, whereas they are increasing in the urban industrial sector. In such a world, the doubling of factor inputs (capital and labour) in the industrial sector leads to more than twice the output. Correspondingly, the incomes of workers and capital owners increase faster in the urban industrial sector than in the rural agricultural sector. A corollary is that regional polarisation leads to higher personal income inequality at the national level. Did industrialisation lead to returns to scale in Imperial Germany? Indeed, Table 14.1 documents an increase in firm concentration in Prussia (proxied by firm size). It doubled between 1875 and 1907. In line with the Krugman model, there was also rising regional inequality—the wage differential between rural and urban areas increased, even if to a limited degree. Another implication of the Krugman model extends beyond industrialisation. Globalisation could have led to more inequality in a world where economies of scale matter. As international markets allowed for better exploitation of economies of scale, they led to a greater spatial polarisation of economic activity.

Combining the insights of the theoretical models on globalisation and industrialisation helps to rationalise the evolution of inequality from 1850 to 1914. The effects of globalisation on capital owners depend on the type of their capital. The grain invasion led to losses for landowners relative to urban workers as per the Heckscher-Ohlin model. This should have had an inequality-reducing effect. On the other hand, in line with the Krugman model, owners of industrial capital should have benefited disproportionately from the opening of markets, implying an inequality-increasing effect of globalisation. Migration to cities is likely to have increased national inequality in accordance with both the Lewis model and the Kuznets model. As surplus labour was progressively absorbed by emerging industries, and migration to cities decreased, the ratio of wages to capital incomes stabilised, and inequality ceased to increase. However, to improve our understanding of this stagnation from 1900 onwards, it is essential to take the political and the institutional framework into account (Section 5).

4 A new economic elite

Both our description of the functional income distribution and the discussion of theoretical models indicate that the importance of land rents decreased relative to that of other capital. This process is also reflected in the composition of the economic elite in the German Empire. Relying on wealth and income tax returns from 1908, civil servant Rudolf Martin compiled a millionaires list for Prussia (Gajek 2014).[4] In the following, we focus on the 100 richest millionaires and break them down into landowners, bankers and financiers, merchants, and entrepreneurs. We further distinguish landowners based on whether coal deposits were unearthed on their land during industrialisation (Table 14.2). By this historical coincidence, some of them were able to convert 'old money' into 'new money' by building mines on their property.

Table 14.2 The 100 richest Prussians according to the origin of their wealth (1908)

Origin of assets	*Number*	*Share of wealth among the top 100*	*Return on capital*	*Share of nobility*
Landowners	15	12%	4.12%	93%
Landowners with coal	8	18%	5.20%	100%
Bankers & financiers	22	22%	5.29%	82%
Merchants	10	7%	5.99%	50%
Industrial entrepreneurs	45	40%	6.44%	47%

Source: Albers et al. (2020). The return on capital is calculated as the quotient of income and wealth.

Around a quarter of the 100 richest Prussians belonged to the group of landowners. The landowners with coal deposits made up the richest group of the top 100: although only eight belonged to this subgroup, they owned 18 percent of the net wealth of the top 100. The richest and probably most well-known among them was Prince Henckel von Donnersmarck. The 15 landowners without coal deposits, including political and military figures such as the Duke of Ratibor, owned only 12 percent of the wealth among the top 100. Whether with or without coal deposits, the fact that the land-owning class embodied 'old money' is also indicated by their social status. All its members, except for the Jewish landowner Julius Schöttler from Breslau, belonged to the nobility.

Bankers and financiers made up roughly another quarter of the hundred richest Prussians. Their share of wealth corresponded exactly to their relative frequency among the top 100, namely, 22 percent. This group was part of both the old and the new elite. Banks like Metzler and Oppenheim, whose names appear in the list of the 100 richest Prussians, had existed for more than three and two centuries, respectively. While their pre-industrial core business was often limited to issuing and trading government bonds (Tilly 1980: 34), industrialisation created new opportunities for more productive investments, and correspondingly, higher profits. This certainly also applied to the ten merchants on the list. Among them, for example, was James Simon of Berlin, whose family had become rich from trading cotton (Martin 1913: 141). Merchants and financiers were clearly among the profiteers of industrialisation but often had accumulated sizable fortunes before its onset.

The group of industrial entrepreneurs embodies the 'new money'. Its two richest representatives were Bertha Krupp von Bohlen und Halbach and August Thyssen, but Martin's list also includes other important dynasties such as Siemens. With 45 households, entrepreneurs made up the most important group among the richest hundred Prussians in 1908.

What can the snapshot of the economic elite in 1908 tell us about the transformation of the economic elite during the nineteenth century? Since there were few opportunities for profitable investments of wealth other than land at the beginning of the century, it is plausible to assume that the pre-industrial elite comprised mainly landowners. This had changed by the early twentieth century because the returns to land and industrial capital differed substantially. In 1908, the average rate of return for entrepreneurs was 2.3 percentage points higher than that of feudal landowners (Table 14.2). We can gauge the transformative power of such differences by calculating the time that it would take for wealth to double: With a rate of return of 6.4 percent, entrepreneurs would double their wealth every 11 years, while landowners with a rate of return of 4.1 percent would require 17 years to do so.[5] A social marker points to the transformation of the elite beyond such calculations. Compared to the old elite, the frequency of noble titles among entrepreneurs was low.

Consistent with the data on factor incomes of land and capital, the individual-level data on the richest Prussians suggest that the transformation of the economic elite was well-advanced by the beginning of the twentieth century. The maturity of the transformation process may have played a role in the limited dynamics of wealth concentration between 1895 and 1914 (Figure 14.2). Of course, this new elite also began to exert political influence, including through the coalition-building with old elites (the so-called 'marriage of iron and rye', cf. chapter 16 of this volume). However, the changing distribution of wealth and income had far more political consequences than this coalition.

5 The political economy of inequality in the Empire

We now know that inequality rose between 1870 and 1900, that a new elite of industrial entrepreneurs had replaced large parts of the landowning elite, and that the level of inequality was very high on the eve of World War I. The final part of this chapter turns to the political consequences of these developments. We also explore how political change, coupled with institutional innovations in the wake of the formation of the nation-state, might have in turn limited further increases in economic inequality from the turn of the century onwards.

The Prussian three-class franchise provides a good example of the close connection between economic and political power in the nineteenth century (Becker and Hornung 2020). In stark contrast to the national electoral law for the Reichstag, the electoral law for the Prussian House of Representatives weighted votes according to the direct tax burden paid by the constituents. As a result, widening economic disparities translated into political inequality. For example, from 1886 to 1894, the Krupps alone held about one-third of all votes in their constituency (Hardtwig 1990). Becker and Hornung (2020) demonstrate that the three-class franchise biased political decision-making far beyond such extreme cases, that is, by supporting more liberal policies rather than policies that allowed the old elites to capture rents. In addition to this intra-elite bias favouring business, the comparison of Prussian and Reichstag elections highlights the political consequences of inequality:

While the social democrats had been represented in the Reichstag since the founding of the German Empire, they did not make it into the Prussian House of Representatives until 1908 (Becker and Hornung 2020: 1). In contrast to our discussion on economic inequality, the relevance of the creation of the nation-state is thus obvious in the political domain. It created a platform for the Social Democratic Party that had not existed at the level of its largest territorial state.

The close connection between the increase in economic inequality and the rise of social democracy is evident from both electoral data and contemporary debates. The social democrats' vote share in Reichstag elections rose from 3.2 percent in 1871 to 32.6 percent in 1912 (Kaiserliches Statistisches Amt 1880: 140, 1915: 340). Indeed, a recent study suggests a positive relationship between industrialisation, inequality, and the strength of the social democrats (Bartels et al. 2021). Contemporary political and academic debates provide further testimony. First, the so-called revisionism debate within the Social Democratic Party between the reformers around Bernstein and the socialists around Kautsky was a major dispute about the party's future. It revolved around the impact of capital accumulation and concentration on inequality and poverty as well as the political implications of this process (Bartels et al. 2021). Second, a group of academics around Schmoller and Sombart began to devote themselves to the study of inequality. Among them, Adolph Wagner (1904) analysed the long-term evolution of inequality using Prussian tax data (Dumke 1987: 2). Although this group was often mocked as academic socialists (*Kathedersozialisten*), they were by no means isolated. Prussian civil servants also published studies on inequality in the journal of the Prussian statistical office (Biedermann 1918).

The 'social question' also occupied an important place in the legislation of the young Empire. Bismarck tried to counter social democratic ideas with a 'carrot and stick' policy mix. On the one hand, he sought to repress the movement through the anti-socialist laws of 1878. On the other hand, Bismarck complemented these laws with a carrot through the establishment of compulsory social insurance, which aimed to improve the workers' economic situation and appease them. With the introduction of health insurance (1883), accident insurance (1884), and pension insurance (1889), the state provided compulsory insurance for a significant share of its citizens for the first time. State-level legislation on the property and income taxation also increasingly took social welfare aspects such as individual earning capacity, marital status, and the number of children into account (Bartels 2014: 29–44).

So far, we have analysed the effect of economic inequality on politics. But how did the rise of the social democrats and their ideas affect inequality? At no time before World War I were the social democrats involved in the government of the Empire. Nevertheless, the labour movement played an important political role for two reasons. First, the new social insurance schemes led to a minimum level of support for many at the bottom of the income distribution. Second, tax policy became an equalising element, even if only to a limited degree (Kaelble 2017: 27).

Alongside these political innovations, trade unions, most of which formed part of the social democratic movement, became an equalising force in the German Empire. Having benefited from the founding of the nation-state and the anti-socialist laws (Ritter 1989: 302), they organised strikes that led to an improvement in working conditions and wages. In light of historical scholarship and modern labour market models, their actions were likely sufficiently strong to affect the income distribution (Kaelble and Volkmann 1986; Mortensen and Pissarides 1994). While existing research does not allow us to conclude the precise magnitude of their importance in mitigating inequality, it is safe to assume that trade unions contributed to the stability of economic inequality during the one-and-a-half decades preceding World War I (cf. Kaelble 2017: 31).

The evolution of inequality thus exerted influence on politics and institutions in the German Empire, but it was also affected by political developments themselves. Undoubtedly, the increase in economic inequality up to 1900 popularised and strengthened the social democratic movement. One can also link Bismarck's social legislation—the beginnings of social policy at the federal level in Germany—to both the high levels of inequality and the rise of the social democratic movement. While political and academic discourses raised the public's awareness of inequality, new legislation and trade union activity were proximate forces mitigating inequality. Although evidence of their quantitative importance is scarce, it seems likely that they contributed to the stability of inequality after 1900. The process of nation-building and the creation of the German Empire mattered in that they provided a framework for social legislation and a platform for the social democratic movement.

6 Conclusion

The development of economic inequality from 1850 to the eve of World War I can be divided into three periods. Before 1871, there is uncertainty about the evolution of inequality. Two opposing processes were crucial during this period. The grain invasion after the American Civil War led to falling returns from land and this reduced inequality. In contrast, three effects of industrialisation tended to increase inequality: Surplus labour (Lewis), urban–rural wage differentials as urbanisation increased (Kuznets), and higher returns to scale in the growing industrial sector relative to agriculture (Krugman). Even if the empirical evidence is insufficient to draw firm conclusions, it does not seem implausible that the effects of globalisation and industrialisation balanced each other out during this first phase.

In the second period from 1871 to 1900, we observe a clear increase in inequality. The three aforementioned mechanisms of industrialisation dominated. In addition, expanding international markets facilitated the exploitation of economies of scale. This phase also saw the rise of the social democratic movement, which in turn led to political responses to inequality. This was greatly aided by the founding of the nation-state. In contrast to the

Prussian three-class franchise, the Empire's universal male suffrage created a national platform for the Social Democratic Party. In addition, the trade union movement also gained strength.

During the third period, from 1900 to 1914, inequality stagnated at a high level. Wages rose due to the depletion of surplus labour reservoirs, decreasing migration to cities, and the growing power of trade unions. Estimating the quantitative importance of each of these factors is an avenue for future research. Overall, the evidence for Germany suggests that the transition from a feudal to an industrial economy increased inequality. However, this transformation, in turn, led to the birth of the welfare state, which sought to prevent further increases in inequality.

Notes

1 This chimes with existing scholarship (cf. Dumke 1991; Grant 2005; Dell 2008).
2 See also Allen (2009) and Grant (2005, chapter 5) for summaries of the Lewis model. Allen (2009) himself questions the role of surplus labour for the British case. Instead, he models two phases of industrialisation, the former of which he calls 'Engels' Pause', using an adaptation of the Solow model. Allen's analysis emphasises the balance of capital accumulation and technical progress as the main mechanism rather than surplus labour.
3 One should, however, not attach too much significance to small changes. Pfister (2019: 231) discusses the data problems in such calculations, especially the role of non-monetary compensation.
4 Kaelble (1985) and Augustine (1991) employ these data in a social history context.
5 The corresponding formula is $\textit{doubling time} = \frac{LN(2)}{LN(1 + \textit{rate of return})}$

References

Albers, T. N. H., Bartels, C. and Schularick, M. (2020) 'The distribution of wealth in Germany, 1895–2018', *ECONtribute Working Paper.*

Alfani, G., Gierok, V. and Schaff, F. (2022) 'Economic inequality in preindustrial Germany, ca. 1300–1850', *Journal of Economic History,* Vol. 82 (1): 87–125.

Allen, R. C. (2009) 'Engels' pause: technical change, capital accumulation, and inequality in the British industrial revolution', *Explorations in Economic History,* Vol. 46 (4): 418–35.

Augustine, D. L. (1991) 'Arriving in the upper class: the wealthy business elite of Wilhelmine Germany', in D. Blackbourn and R. J. Evans (eds), *The German Bourgeoisie,* London: Routledge, pp. 46–86.

Bartels, C. (2014) *Versicherung und Anreize im deutschen Wohlfahrtsstaat,* Wiesbaden: Springer Gabler.

Bartels, C. (2019) 'Top incomes in Germany, 1871–2014', *Journal of Economic History,* Vol. 79 (3): 669–707.

Bartels, C., Kersting, F. and Wolf, N. (2021) 'Testing Marx. Income inequality, concentration, and socialism in late 19th century Germany', *Stone Center Working Paper Series,* No. 32.

Becker, S. O. and Hornung, E. (2020) 'The political economy of the Prussian three-class franchise', *Journal of Economic History,* Vol. 80 (4): 1143–88.

Bengtsson, E. and Waldenström, D. (2018) 'Capital shares and income inequality: evidence from the long run', *Journal of Economic History,* Vol. 78 (3): 712–43.

Biedermann, E. (1918) 'Die Einkommens- und Vermögensverhältnisse der preussischen Bevölkerung im Zeitraum 1895–1914 und ihre Übertragungsmöglichkeit auf das deutsche Reich', *Zeitschrift des Königlich Preussischen Statistischen Landesamts,* Vol. 58: 60–86.

Cinnirella, F. and Hornung, E. (2016) 'Landownership concentration and the expansion of education', *Journal of Development Economics,* Vol. 121: 135–52.

Cowell, F. A. (2011) *Measuring Inequality*, Oxford: Oxford University Press.

Crafts, N. and Wolf, N. (2014) 'The location of the UK cotton textiles industry in 1838: a quantitative analysis', *Journal of Economic History,* Vol. 74 (4): 1103–39.

Crayen, D. and Baten, J. (2010) 'New evidence and new methods to measure human capital inequality before and during the industrial revolution. France and the US in the seventeenth to nineteenth centuries', *Economic History Review,* Vol. 63 (2): 452–78.

Dell, F. (2008) *L'Allemagne inégale: inégalités de revenus et de patrimoine en Allemagne, dynamique d'accumulation du capital et taxation de Bismarck à Schröder 1870–2005*, PhD dissertation, École des hautes études en sciences sociales Paris.

de Pleijt, A., Nuvolari, A. and Weisdorf, J. (2019) 'Human capital formation during the first industrial revolution: evidence from the use of steam engines', *Journal of the European Economic Association,* Vol. 18 (2): 829–89.

Dumke, R. H. (1987) *Economic Inequality and Industrialization in Germany, 1850–1913,* PhD dissertation, University of Münster.

Dumke, R. H. (1991) 'Income inequality and industrialization in Germany, 1850–1913: the Kuznets hypothesis re-examined', in Y. S. Brenner, H. Kaelble and M. Thomas (eds), *Income Distribution in Historical Perspective*, Cambridge: Cambridge University Press, pp. 117–48.

Gajek, E. M. (2014) 'Sichtbarmachung von Reichtum: das Jahrbuch des Vermögens und Einkommens der Millionäre in Preußen', *Archiv für Sozialgeschichte,* Vol. 54: 79–108.

Grant, O. (2005) *Migration and Inequality in Germany, 1870–1913*, Oxford: Clarendon Press.

Grumbach, F. (1957), *Statistische Untersuchungen über die Entwicklung der Einkommensverteilung in Deutschland*, PhD dissertation, University of Münster.

Hardtwig, W. (1990) 'Großstadt und Bürgerlichkeit in der politischen Ordnung des Kaiserreichs', in L. Gall (ed), *Stadt und Bürgertum im 19. Jahrhundert*, München: Oldenbourg, pp. 19–64.

Hoffmann, W. G. (1965) *Das Wachstum der deutschen Volkswirtschaft seit der Mitte des 19. Jahrhunderts*, Berlin: Springer.

Kaelble, H. (1983) *Industrialisierung und soziale Ungleichheit: Europa im 19. Jahrhundert. Eine Bilanz*, Göttingen: Vandenhoeck & Ruprecht.

Kaelble, H. (1985) 'Wie feudal waren die deutschen Unternehmer im Kaiserreich? Ein Zwischenbericht', in R. H. Tilly (ed), *Beiträge zur quantitativen vergleichenden Unternehmensgeschichte*, Stuttgart: Klett-Cotta, pp. 148–74.

Kaelble, H. (2017) *Mehr Reichtum, mehr Armut. Soziale Ungleichheit in Europa vom 20. Jahrhundert bis zur Gegenwart*, Frankfurt a. M.: Campus.

Kaelble, H. and Volkmann, H. (1986) 'Streiks und Einkommensverteilung im späten Kaiserreich', in J. Bergmann, J. Brockstedt, H. Kaelble, H.-J. Rupieper, P. Steinbach and H. Volkmann (eds), *Arbeit, Mobilität, Partizipation, Protest*, Opladen: Westdeutscher Verlag, pp. 159–98.

Kaiserliches Statistisches Amt (various years): *Statistisches Jahrbuch für das deutsche Reich*, Berlin: Putkammer & Mühlbrecht.

Köllmann, W. (1969) 'The process of urbanization in Germany at the height of the industrialization period', *Journal of Contemporary History*, Vol. 4 (3): 59–76.

Krugman, P. (1991) 'Increasing returns and economic geography', *Journal of Political Economy*, Vol. 99 (3): 483–99.

Kuznets, S. (1955) 'Economic growth and income inequality', *American Economic Review*, Vol. 45 (1): 1–28.

Lewis, W. A. (1954) 'Economic development with unlimited supplies of labour', *Manchester School*, Vol. 22 (2): 139–91.

Martin, Rudolf (1912) *Jahrbuch des Vermögens und Einkommens der Millionäre in Preußen*, Berlin: W. Herlet.

Mortensen, D. T. and Pissarides, C. A. (1994) 'Job creation and job destruction in the theory of unemployment', *Review of Economic Studies*, Vol. 61 (3): 397–415.

O'Rourke, K. H. and Williamson, J. G. (1999) *Globalisation and History: The Evolution of a Nineteenth-Century Atlantic Economy*, Cambridge, MA: MIT.

Pfister, U. (2017) 'The timing and pattern of real wage divergence in pre-industrial Europe. Evidence from Germany, c. 1500–1850', *Economic History Review*, Vol. 70: 701–29.

Pfister, U. (2018) 'Real wages in Germany during the first phase of industrialization, 1850–1889', *Jahrbuch für Wirtschaftsgeschichte/Economic History Yearbook*, Vol. 59 (2): 567–96.

Pfister, U. (2019) 'The inequality of pay in pre-modern Germany, late 15th century to 1889', *Jahrbuch für Wirtschaftsgeschichte/Economic History Yearbook*, Vol. 60 (1): 209–43.

Pfister, U. (2020) 'The Crafts-Harley view of German industrialization: an independent estimate of the income side of net national product, 1851–1913', *European Review of Economic History*, Vol. 70 (3): 502–21.

Piketty, T. (2014) *Capital in the 21st Century*, Cambridge, MA: Harvard University Press.

Piketty, T. and Saez, E. (2003) 'Income inequality in the United States, 1913–1998', *Quarterly Journal of Economics*, Vol. 118 (1): 1–41.

Piketty, T. and Zucman, G. (2014) 'Capital is back: wealth-income ratios in rich countries 1700–2010', *Quarterly Journal of Economics*, Vol. 129 (3): 1255–310.

Ritter, G. A. (1989) 'Die Sozialdemokratie im deutschen Kaiserreich in sozialgeschichtlicher Perspektive', *Historische Zeitschrift*, Vol. 249 (1): 295–362.

Spoerer, M. (2004) *Steuerlast, Steuerinzidenz und Steuerwettbewerb: Verteilungswirkungen der Besteuerung in Preußen und Württemberg (1815–1913)*, Berlin: Akademie-Verlag.

Tilly, R. H. (1980) *Kapital, Staat und sozialer Protest in der deutschen Industrialisierung. Gesammelte Aufsätze*, Göttingen: Vandenhoeck & Ruprecht.

Tilly, R. H. (2010) 'The distribution of personal income in Prussia, 1852 to 1875. An exploratory study', *Jahrbuch für Wirtschaftsgeschichte*, Vol. 51 (1): 175–94.

Wagner, A. (1904) 'Zur Methodik der Statistik des Volkseinkommens und Volksvermögens', *Zeitschrift der Königlich-Preussischen Statistischen Bureaus*, Vol. 44: 41–122.

15 Education systems and human capital accumulation

Sascha O. Becker, Francesco Cinnirella, and Erik Hornung

1 Introduction

The German Empire never established a national education system, and each of the twenty-six states managed its educational affairs. Even today, German education policy is decided at the state level, not the federal level. Unification in 1871 coincided with an ongoing process of centralising educational systems within the German states. Furthermore, unification strengthened the power of the government relative to the church that hitherto wielded substantial influence over education.

This chapter summarises the recent quantitative literature that studies the causes and consequences of the education system and human capital investments during the nineteenth century. This period, during which the internationally backward German states developed into a unified nation at the frontier of industrial development, was a crucial period for the expansion of the education systems of the states. Before the nineteenth century, Germany overall, with its mix of Protestant and Catholic populations, had higher levels of human capital investment as measured by book production than Catholic countries in Europe, but, by the same measure, it lagged behind the more developed Protestant countries such as England, the Netherlands, and also Sweden.[1]

However, Germany had taken the international lead from the early nineteenth century, especially in primary schooling (see Figure 15.1). Primary schools had become the envy of international observers who frequently visited the German lands to study the education system (Lindert, 2004: 89). In the 1880s, Germany was overtaken by France in terms of enrolment rates but still had a substantial lead over England.

Within Germany, there was substantial heterogeneity across states. Whereas some states had achieved universal primary enrolment by the time of unification, states like Prussia and Bavaria had somewhat lower enrolment. However, they were still among the leaders in primary education worldwide. The high level of primary enrolment resulted from a massive educational expansion in the early nineteenth century. The largest of the German states, whose statistical bureau recorded education data at high frequency, Prussia

DOI: 10.4324/9781003283430-18

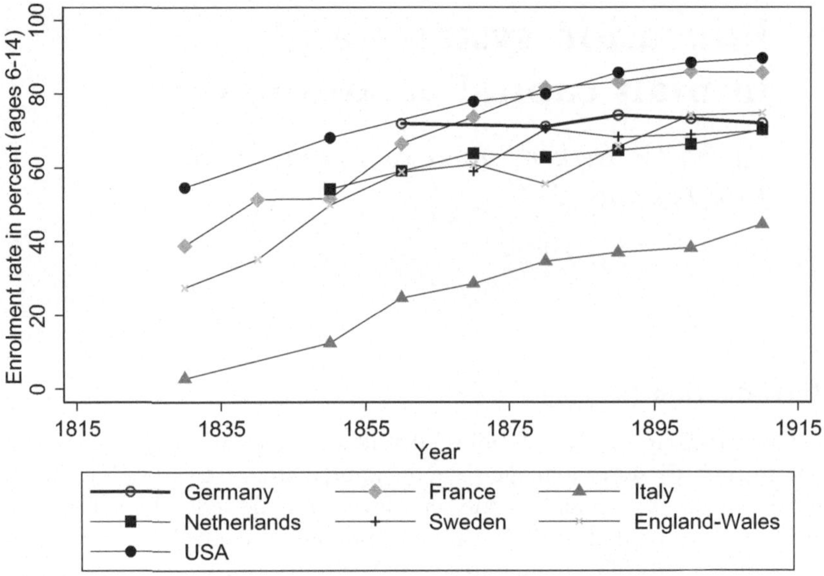

Figure 15.1 Primary school enrolment in international comparison.

Percent of children aged 5–14 enrolled in public and private primary schools (Germany, Sweden, USA only public schooling). Source: Own elaboration based on data from Lindert (2004).

experienced an increase in enrolment rates of 6- to 14-year-old children from 60 to 83 percent in the decades following the Congress of Vienna (see Figure 15.2).[2]

In addition to the fact that the Prussian administration collected detailed data, Prussia is an interesting case because of the massive heterogeneity it accommodated. In the following sections, we introduce literature that exploits this heterogeneity to understand how education shaped many developments during the nineteenth century in Prussia. In section 2, we first summarise literature that presents evidence on the religious roots of regional differences with respect to educational systems and educational attainment. We continue by portraying the institutional changes following the Napoleonic Wars and their consequences on the expansion of educational attainment. The ensuing sectoral shift from agriculture to industry with substantial heterogeneity across the industrialising west and the agricultural east permits to study changes in the returns to and the demand for education. Section 3 will describe the consequences of the expansion of educational systems for the progress of industrialisation, the decline of fertility during the demographic transition, and the secularisation of society at the end of the nineteenth century. The literature summarised here shows how high levels of human capital helped trigger industrialisation via technology adoption and how demographics were affected by altering parents' choices for the quality

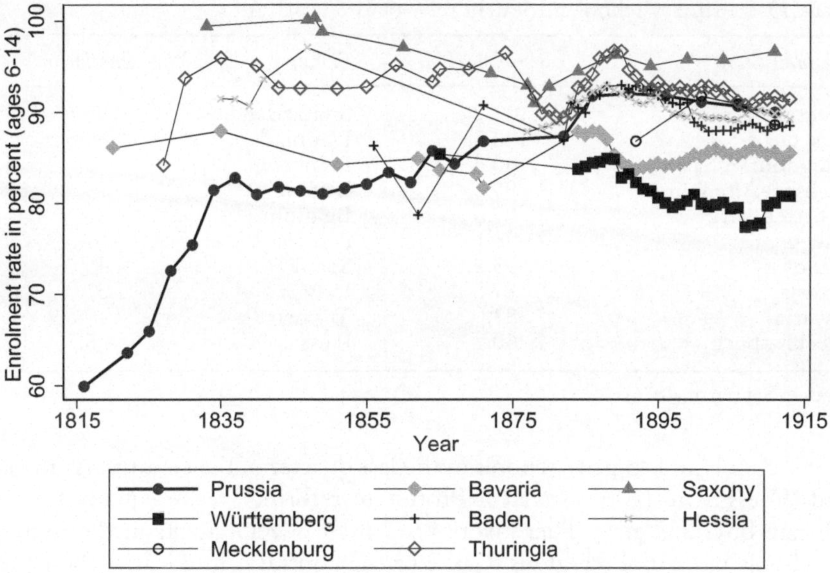

Figure 15.2 Primary school enrolment across states, 1816–1914.

Percent of children aged 6–14 enrolled in public primary schools in the largest German states. Bavaria: Public plus private. Source: Own elaboration based on data from Nath et al. (2016).

and quantity of children. Finally, section 4 will focus on the centralisation of education and the educational policies adopted to Germanise ethnic minorities during the *Kulturkampf* period. An increasing awakening of nationalistic sentiments followed unification. As ethnic differences between the German majority and Slavic minorities became salient, education content was exploited to force assimilation.

2 Origins of high education levels

*Religious origins of heterogeneous preferences for education***.** The German states showing the highest enrolment rates at the national unification were either Protestant or included a sizeable Protestant minority (Table 15.1). Thus, religion may have constituted an essential driver of educational preferences. Before any central state intervention in the schooling sector, education was high on the agenda of Protestant reformers. For instance, Martin Luther encouraged local rulers at his time to establish and maintain Christian schools while at the same time encouraging parents to send their children to school (Luther 1520, 1524, 1530). Indeed, as Green (1979) shows, there was a dramatic increase in the diffusion of schools in Protestant areas. While until 1539, there were only 55 boys' and 4 girls' schools in the 102 towns in the Electorate (Kurfürstentum) of Brandenburg, those numbers went up to 100

Table 15.1 Primary school enrolment rates before unification

German State	*Enrolment*	*Country*	*Enrolment*
Sachsen-Weimar	102.2	Switzerland	95.1
Nassau	100.5	Denmark	89.6
Kingdom of Saxony	100.3	France	76.5
Sachsen-Altenburg	99.1	Britain	76.2
Württemberg	99.0	Belgium	66.5
Baden	98.1	Austria	57.3
Hanover	93.2	Spain	45.3
Prussia	87.5	Italy	31.9
Bavaria	83.0	Turkey	10.5
Mecklenburg	60.7	Russia	5.7

Source: Seyffarth (1876).

boys' schools and 45 girls' schools in the last quarter of the century. As Becker and Woessmann (2008) stressed, Protestant reformers were equally keen to educate boys *and* girls. There were no similar developments in the number of schools in Catholic regions. Quite to the contrary, in Bavaria, the largest Catholic state in Germany, there were still strong objections against schools in the countryside in general as late as 1614 (Gawthrop and Strauss 1984).

While this anecdotal evidence is only suggestive of a Protestant education lead, the first Prussia-wide census statistics on school enrolment, in 1816, confirm a clear Protestant-Catholic gap (Becker and Woessmann 2008). In counties with an all-Protestant population, the share of girls enrolled in public elementary school was 25.9 percent and the share of boys 23.6 percent higher than in counties with an exclusively Catholic population, a substantial difference.[3] These numbers also confirm that the gender gap in education is smaller in Protestant areas, in line with the Protestant quest to also educate girls.

Institutional background of the educational expansion. Historically, education policy was subject to various local conditions and showed vast heterogeneity at the local level. The church strongly shaped lower education, but the states did not intervene in this relationship. In many rural areas, the population was subject to the landed nobility that held power over educational matters. School finance and teacher salaries were obtained from local sources and not determined by state taxes. During the early modern period, primary schooling, therefore, had always been a decentralised matter, subject to vast heterogeneity across and within the German states. Still, already before unification, German primary education was clearly distinguishable from education in other countries, primarily due to its focus on religious-pious content with a second focus on useful knowledge (Kuhlemann 1991: 207; Jeismann 1992).

Our knowledge about education in historical Germany is overwhelmingly determined because much of the research has been undertaken on Prussian schooling, especially primary schooling. Comparatively early, the Prussian

Kings attempted to establish rules for compulsory schooling. In 1717, Frederick William I demanded that parents send their children to school (when available); in 1763, Frederick II confirmed this rule for children aged 5 to 14. The edicts, however, remained unenforced and did not come with any fiscal commitments (Lindert 2003, 2004). Thus, educational attainment in the countryside remained low.

Following the Napoleonic Wars, Prussia was the first state to establish a ministry of culture responsible for matters of religion, education, and health. Soon other German states followed suit and established administrations that worked toward unifying conditions and content of education within the respective state borders (Kesper-Biermann 2013: 26). Wilhelm von Humboldt's new ideals strongly influenced higher education but had less impact on primary education. According to him, universities had the purpose of creating new knowledge, whereas primary schools should disseminate knowledge (Beuttler 2012).

The early reformers of primary education envisioned curricula with a broad general education but failed with the local reality of schooling, especially in the countryside. During the first half of the nineteenth century, the typical curriculum focused exclusively on reciting the catechism, reading, writing, and singing. Progress in enriching the school curriculum with arithmetic and introducing standardised textbooks was made with the Prussian regulations by Ferdinand Stiehl in 1854 (see Table 15.2). In 1872, new legislation transferred school supervision from church to state, improved teacher training, and replaced some religious instruction with natural sciences and physical education in the curriculum. Pure memorising was officially abdicated but remained the norm, especially in the one-room schools of the rural countryside. Following unification, primary education's aims shifted from

Table 15.2 Curricula of Prussian one-room schools

1854–1872		*1872–1921*			
	All Grades		*Lower Grades*	*Middle Grades*	*Higher Grades*
Subject	*Hours/week*	*Subject*	*Hours per week*		
Religion	6	Religion	4	5	5
Reading & Writing	12	German	11	10	8
Chant	3	Chant	1	2	2
Arithmetic	5	Arithmetic & Geometry	4	4	5
		Drawing	-	1	2
		Social Studies	-	6	5
		Gymnastics	-	2	2

Source: Kuhlemann (1991: 453–55).

religious-pious instruction to educating students as loyal German subjects forming a national identity (Kuhlemann 1991: 183, 203). Especially from the late 1880s, instruction in history and language pursued the Germanisation of ethnic minorities and aimed to thwart socialist tendencies.

Figure 15.2 shows the development of primary school enrolment rates across major German states over the nineteenth century. The post-Napoleonic war period is characterised by the first phase of expansion of educational activity as a substantial increase in Prussian primary schooling until 1837 (cf. Schleunes 1979: 317). By then, more than 80 percent of children of primary school age (6–14) regularly attended these schools. The second phase of expansion starting in the 1860s culminated in almost universal enrolment in the 1880s. A concurrent expansion can be observed in secondary and tertiary education (Nath et al. 2016). These developments obscure initially large differences between urban and rural areas and differentially developed regions such as Poznan and Saxony.

In comparison, Figure 15.2 reveals that some states had experienced the first expansion earlier than Prussia. Many had tried to implement compulsory schooling laws during the eighteenth century. Saxony achieved universal enrolment already in the 1830s. Württemberg was arguably the state in which mass schooling developed the earliest and served as a model for other states (Nath et al. 2016: 446).

Unification did not change that there was a Bavarian, a Hessian, a Saxonian, and a Prussian education system. Attempts to pass state-level education legislation (*Unterrichtsgesetz*) failed in Bavaria and Prussia until the early twentieth century due to opposition by the church. In contrast, Württemberg had a primary school law since 1836 and Baden since 1868. However, states did not differ radically in their timing of educational modernisation during the last decades of the nineteenth century. There was a secular trend to improve student-teacher ratios, the number of classes per school, and the curriculum. Nevertheless, heterogeneity remained strong between states and within states, especially between rural and urban schools (Becker and Woessmann, 2009; Becker and Cinnirella, 2020; Kersting et al., 2020).

State involvement in primary schooling remained limited, and contributions toward school finance varied vastly across the states. The government's share in school funding in 1900 was 27 percent in Prussia, 36 percent in Bavaria, 31 in Württemberg, 22 percent in Baden, and 14 in the Kingdom of Saxony (Kuhlemann 1991: 208). Whereas Prussia abolished tuition fees in the constitution of 1850, most other states maintained some form of tuition fees.

The first expansion phase between 1816 and 1837 in Prussia may have been a direct consequence of the reforms implemented during the Napoleonic Wars. Reforms such as the abolition of serfdom and guilds arguably increased incentives for the population to invest in human capital because restrictions on mobility and occupational choice were lifted. Particularly the abolition of serfdom contributed to expanding the demand for education. In the nineteenth century, regions in which serfdom had originally prevailed were characterised by a high concentration of land ownership. Cinnirella and Hornung (2016) show that the concentration of large landownership is negatively related to enrolment rates in early nineteenth-century Prussia. However, the negative relationship vanishes over time and becomes insignificant from 1864. The authors argue that the agricultural reforms related to the abolition of serfdom changed the relationship between the landed nobility and the peasantry. When mobility restrictions were lifted, this altered the incentives for the rural population to invest in their human capital. As the peasants were no longer bound to the land and had freedom of occupational choice, they could reap the benefits of their investment (Ashraf et al., 2018). Indeed, the authors show that a lack of supply of schooling does not drive the low enrolment rates in regions initially characterised by serfdom and, therefore, must come through differences in the demand.

In addition to state expansion and changes in agrarian institutions, educational expansion was most likely driven by industrialisation, improvements in health and life expectancy, and institutional factors such as child labour laws and pension systems. These form the topic of the next section.

3 Education and economic development

Education and industrial development. Unification fell into a period of substantial structural change in Germany. The first phase of industrialisation started with an extensive market integration due to new transport infrastructure, especially railroads and the foundation of the customs union (*Zollverein*) in the 1830s (see Chapters 3 and 7 in this volume). Many workers became employed in mining and centralised textiles, metals, and machine industry factories. Following unification, Germany entered a period of high industrialisation with the expansion of chemicals and electrical engineering, industries where German firms constituted the technological frontier.

During the first period of industrialisation, the adoption of new technologies and production processes from England and Belgium allowed German regions to catch up. According to theories of development by Nelson and Phelps, countries that are further away from the technological frontier can use the advantage of relative backwardness by adopting existing technologies (Nelson and Phelps 1966; see also Gerschenkron 1962 for a broader discussion of relative economic backwardness). This requires that the population has the necessary skills to adopt and implement these technologies. Once closer to the frontier, countries need to generate new technologies themselves and thus require the skills needed for inventive activities.

When production technologies fundamentally change, the working population needs to have a higher level of education to adjust to these changes. It has been widely argued that broad education and mass literacy did not play a role in the Industrial Revolution in England, which shows comparatively low enrolment rates in Figure 15.1. The comparative economic development of Great Britain and Germany is consistent with this theory. However, German regions such as Prussia that were relatively less developed in the early nineteenth century may have benefited from their initial high level of education. Becker et al. (2011) show that Prussian regions whose population had experienced more years of primary schooling also had higher levels of subsequent industrialisation by 1849. However, they show that this result only holds for the non-textile sectors where technological development was arguably more disruptive than textiles.

A similar relationship prevailed during the era of high industrialisation. Higher literacy rates are related to more innovation, especially in Prussian counties' chemistry and electrical engineering industries. Furthermore, Cinnirella and Streb (2017) show that the skills of master artisans exert an independent effect on innovation, whereas secondary schooling is not associated with innovation.[4]

Across Germany, secondary schooling was typically devoted to teaching classical and humanistic content and abstract mathematics in line with cultural values prevailing among the urban bourgeoisie. The high schools (Gymnasium) qualified children of the higher classes for university admittance and a career in the administration or clergy. Therefore, it is not surprising that qualitative research typically argues that secondary education did not contribute to economic development.

Nevertheless, German secondary schools also covered more applied training. Vocational schools, such as the technical schools (*Gewerbeschulen*) and continuation schools, became widespread around unification. While there were approximately 400 such schools in Germany by 1870, this number tripled by 1900.[5] Such schools provided a more technical education that likely was useful for industrial development. Semrad (2015) shows that Bavarian counties with a *Gewerbeschule* as early as 1835 that also remained in place at unification in 1871 had a higher share of the population employed in manufacturing and services in 1882 and saw a larger per capita number of business registrations.

University education also saw a robust increase. Standardised by the number of people in the age group 18–25, the share of people enrolled in universities in Germany doubled from about 3 (per 1000) in 1871 to 6 (per 1000) before the First World War (Diebolt 2005). Moreover, students opting for university education seem to have steered towards programmes in science and mathematics. The share of students studying theology declined from about 25 percent in 1865 to 8 percent in 1910; during the same period, students studying math or science increased from 4 to 14 percent (Figure 15.3).

Education and demographic development. Education is also intimately linked with demographic developments. The trade-off between the number of children and the human capital invested in each child is not only said to be a fundamental trade-off parents face but also a crucial ingredient of unified growth theory, which models the transition from Malthusian stagnation to sustained growth in a unified framework (see Galor 2011, 2012 for an authoritative overview).

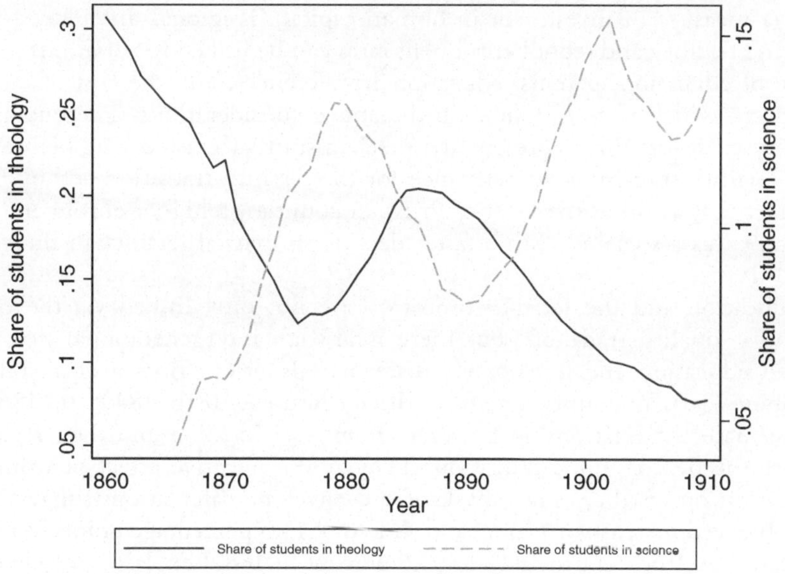

Figure 15.3 University education in selected faculties, 1860–1910.
Share of university students enrolled in theology and faculties of mathematics and science.
Source: Own elaboration based on data from Diebolt (2005).

The concept of the quantity–quality trade-off assumes, on the one hand, that parents benefit from a large number of children, for example, in the form of an increase in domestic labour or support in old age. On the other hand, the endowment of children with human capital in the form of skills, education, and health is associated with direct costs in the form of time spent with children and opportunity costs related to the working time of children. If the individual payoff to human capital increases in the course of economic development—in this case, as a result of the rise of human capital-intensive industries during the era of high industrialisation—the utility gained from the quality of children increases, and parents decide in favour of a smaller number of children who are endowed with more human capital than would be possible for a higher number of offspring. This argument implies that the first fertility transition in the form of a declining birth rate, which began in the 1880s, was closely related to Germany's economic development outlined at the beginning of this section and the expansion of the education sector. Moreover, this relationship was mediated by changes in household decisions regarding the trade-off between the number of children and the endowment of children with human capital.

At the level of Prussian counties, the quantity–quality trade-off can already be observed in the first half of the nineteenth century (Becker et al., 2010, 2012). Specifically, in 1849 there was a robust negative correlation between the number of children per woman (a measure of fertility) and the enrolment rate (a measure of investment in human capital). Regional differences concerning fertility and school enrolment rates can be linked to variations in the price of education, parents' educational preferences, and the cost of raising children, which is consistent with the above considerations. The quantity–quality trade-off thus represented a mechanism that existed long before the first fertility transition. Its relevance for the fertility transition is shown by the fact that again at the level of Prussian counties, a higher enrolment rate in 1849 was associated with a faster decline in marital fertility in the years 1880–1905.

Education and the fertility transition are not only linked via the child quantity–quality trade-off, but there is also an intergenerational link between education and fertility via maternal education. Becker et al. (2013) combine Prussian county data from three censuses—1816, 1849, and 1867—to estimate the relationship between women's education and their fertility before the demographic transition. They find a negative effect of women's education on fertility. Their back-of-the-envelope calculations suggest that the observed increase in average enrolment of 13.5 percentage points in Prussia (from 80.1 percent in 1849 to 93.6 percent in 1882) explains one-quarter of the total decline in the child-woman ratio during the fertility transition period 1875–1910.

This evidence suggests that education interacted with fertility and was thus a factor in the demographic transition during the nineteenth century. The increasing payoff to education during the nineteenth century meant that parents increasingly opted for more education of fewer offspring, in line with the child quantity–quality trade-off. At the same time, more educated parents had fewer children, whereby education affected the fertility decline via two separate channels.

In sum, the expansion of education had a broad range of important repercussions on the economy and society in nineteenth- and early twentieth-century Germany. It fostered economic development and helped spur the demographic transition.

4 Education and nation building

Finally, in this section, we address the role of primary education in Imperial Germany in creating the 'German nation'. After reviewing some related literature, we address aspects of public finance, i.e. the centralisation of the funding of the primary education system and speculate about the role this centralisation reform might have had in nation-building. Subsequently, we discuss how the *Kulturkampf* 'used' the education system to reach its goal of eliminating the authority of the Catholic church. We conclude with a look at the trend of language skills of schoolchildren in Prussia to speculate about the success or failure of the Germanisation policies.

The idea that the education system can play a crucial role in nation-building is old. Dewey (1916: 108–10) argues that 'under the influence of German thought, in particular, education became a civic function, and the civic function was identified with the realisation of the ideal of the national state'. He continues claiming that the purpose of German education was disciplinary training rather than personal development. The contribution of education to modern nation-building has also been emphasised by other countries (e.g. Weber 1976). Regarding the United States, Bandiera et al. (2019) show that compulsory schooling laws were passed significantly earlier in states with a larger share of European migrants. They interpret this result as evidence in favour of the nation-building role of the education system.

More specifically on language policies, Clots-Figueras and Masella (2013) show how the language of instruction can have a significant role in an individual's identity formation. As we shall see, the Prussian government also attempted to push a restrictive language policy that progressively banned Polish as the language of instruction, a move that seems to have backfired.

Kulturkampf and primary education in Prussia. Kulturkampf describes the conflicting relationship between the Prussian (Protestant) government and the Catholic church. On the one hand, the Prussian government feared organised Catholicism and its potential political impact; on the other hand, the Prussian government held the Catholic church responsible for the poor education levels of the Polish-Catholic population in the eastern regions of Prussia. Consequently, laws at the federal level and in Prussia were passed to decrease the Catholic church's power. From an institutional perspective, the Catholic division of the Ministry of Ecclesiastical and Education Affairs was dissolved in July 1871. From the educational perspective, the most important measure undertaken to undermine Catholic power over schools was the School Inspection Law passed in 1872. This law shifted the authority to appoint inspectors from the church to the state and delegated to the state the extent of the inspector's supervisory powers (Schueler 2016). The clear aim of the law was to eliminate the control of the Catholic church over schools. Such measures triggered a strong reaction by the Catholic clergy, who, wherever possible, reacted with noncompliance. Resistance, particularly strong in the province of Westphalia, also took the form of strikes of Catholic industrial workers and boycotts of national holidays (Roerkohl 1992).

The main task of school inspectors was the monitoring of school attendance. They also reported on pupils' school achievements and the effectiveness of teachers' instruction. With the School Inspection Law of 1872, school supervision was secularised through the employment of full-time professional inspectors. By 1873, the implementation of secular school inspectors was restricted to 50 counties due to budget constraints (Schueler 2016). Secular school inspectors were first introduced in east Elbian Polish-speaking Catholic regions. The predominantly Catholic provinces of Rhineland and Westphalia followed suit. The introduction of central school inspectors stopped in 1879 when Adalbert Falck, Minister of Ecclesiastical and Education Affairs, stepped down from office. 1879 is also the year when the *Kulturkampf* practically ended.

The historical literature is critical of the School Inspection Law as it is deemed ineffective (Schueler 2016). Contemporary observers stressed the resistance to the law. Lamberti (1989) concedes that secular school inspectors might have contributed to improving school performance in the Rhineland. Schueler (2016) provides a systematic analysis of the impact of the School Inspection Law of 1872 on education. She finds that in the east-Elbian regions monitoring by the central school inspectors increased primary school enrolment rates by 5.9 percentage points. However, no effect of the Law of 1872 is detected in the western provinces of Rhineland and Westphalia. These effects likely resulted from two mechanisms. On the one hand, secular monitoring contributed to reducing the size of classes. In the period between 1864 and 1886, the number of pupils per teacher decreased by 13 percent due to the school inspection. On the other hand, she also finds evidence consistent with strong resistance against the reform in counties mainly populated by Catholics. She finds that a high share of Catholics in a county mitigates the overall positive effect of centralised secular monitoring on enrolment rates.

In the context of the *Kulturkampf*, education and, in particular, teachers have played a crucial role. In what follows, we analyse the reform that centralised primary education provision in Prussia. In fact, this reform, to a large extent, revolved around the funding and recruitment of school teachers.

Centralisation of primary education. The conflict over school supervision, which took place during the *Kulturkampf*, was part of a longer-term process of centralising primary education under the authority of the Prussian state. Until the 1870s, funding of public primary education in Prussia was mainly local. According to Lindert (2004), Prussian success in attaining high levels of enrolment rates early in the nineteenth century is to be ascribed to the high level of decentralisation of the education system in its first phase. Local school funds came primarily from tuition fees, foundations, schooling societies, municipal taxes, and patronage from the nobility. Decisions about the allocation of school funds were made by the school board (*Schulvorstand*), which consisted of the noble landlord in the estates or the mayor in urban and rural municipalities, the local clergyman, and a few school community members. Notably, the local administration was also responsible for appointing teachers (Glueck 1979).

From 1886, the process of teachers' recruitment started to change. The Prussian government was particularly concerned about those east Elbian provinces that lagged behind in terms of enrolment rates and educational attainment. Thus, in the provinces of Posen and West Prussia, a new regulation moved the authority to hire new teachers from the local to the state level (Lamberti, 1989). This was the first attempt to gain full control of the education system, especially in those regions with a relatively high concentration of Polish people. This partial shift to centralisation in the recruitment of primary school teachers was extended to the whole of Prussia in 1888/89. The centralisation of funding for school teachers operated as follows: the state contributed a fixed sum for each fully employed teacher, which amounted to 500 Marks for the first teacher of each school, 300 Marks for every other teacher, and 100 Marks for supplementary teachers. As a result, state spending on primary education increased from 10 to 35 percent of the total public spending on education in 1886–91. In addition to that, 200,000 Marks were promised for school inspections, and 2 million Marks were destined for the construction of primary schools in these two provinces. Public spending on teachers increased from 14 to 50 percent in the same period (Cinnirella and Schueler 2016).[6]

More generally, in 1888/89, a law to centralise public primary education funding was passed. As mentioned, the new education law not only fixed the level of subsidies for teacher salaries but also abolished school fees and relieved landlords of their burden to fund primary schools. In 1897, the teacher pay law (*Diensteinkommensgesetz*) fixed a minimum wage for all Prussian teachers. Finally, the school law of 1906 created a uniform legal framework for central state funding (Lamberti 1989; Cinnirella and Schueler 2016).

Germanisation through language policy. The Prussian educational system was denominational, with separate schools for Protestant, Catholic, and Jewish children, generally under the supervision of their clergy. In the eastern provinces characterised by large shares of Poles, instruction in the Polish language was tolerated (Clark 2007). The Prussian authorities recognised the cultural identity of the Polish or Slavic-dominated regions. The edict of 1822 formally recognised the importance of language and nationality to Polish-speaking citizens. A regulation of 1842 mandated that the language of school instruction was that of the majority of the students (Lamberti, 1989).

Yet, during the initial era of the German Reich, Bismarck began to promote policies aimed at the 'Germanisation' of ethnic minorities, that is, policies aimed at instilling German culture in the non-ethnic German population. According to Bismarck (and the Chancellors after him), public primary education was supposed to play a vital role in the Germanisation policy. Indeed, several laws were passed that gradually established German as the only language of instruction at school. Polish as a language of instruction in primary school was first banned in 1873 in the provinces of Posen and West Prussia. The only exception was religious instructions, which were permitted to be taught in Polish in lower grades. By the end of 1902, religion was taught to Polish children in the German language in 252 schools. In contrast, Polish continued to be the exclusive language of Catholic religious instructions in 853 schools in the countryside (Lamberti 1989: 139).

As a result of the progressive language ban, organised resistance by the Polish population started to form. In particular, school strikes were organised to demonstrate against the Prussian language policy. The first notable school strike took place in the border town of Wreschen in 1901 as a response to the suppression of Polish as a language of religious instruction in the upper level of catholic schools. The school strike received a nationwide echo through press coverage. The extension of the use of German as a language of religious instruction accelerated in 1906, triggering a series of school strikes. The most famous strike was the one that took place in Posen in 1906, where about 10 percent of the schoolchildren boycotted school attendance after German, as the only language of instruction, had been extended to all schools.

The language of schoolchildren over time. As we have seen, the Prussian government openly conceived the education system as instrumental in forming a national identity and instilling a German culture in non-ethnic German citizens. A systematic and rigorous analysis of whether the *Kulturkampf*, the centralisation of the education system, and the language policy affected the formation of a German identity goes beyond the scope of this chapter. However, we can look at one important outcome of the Germanisation policy: the language spoken by the schoolchildren. The education censuses in Prussia, carried out every five years from 1886, contain data on the number of schoolchildren in different languages. Interestingly, the census also distinguishes between the number of schoolchildren speaking exclusively one language (e.g. only German or only Polish) and speaking two languages (e.g. German and Polish).[7]

Figure 15.4 reports the shares of schoolchildren speaking *only* Polish in the six census years in five east Elbian provinces. From the large differences in levels, we can appreciate the concerns of the Prussian government about the situation in Posen and West Prussia. In 1886 more than half (52 percent) of the schoolchildren in Posen spoke only Polish; in West Prussia, it was about 35 percent.

We can also see that the trend in Posen and West Prussia probably did not correspond to the expectations of the Prussian government. In Figure 15.5, we zoom in on Posen and West Prussia. As is evident, the share of schoolchildren

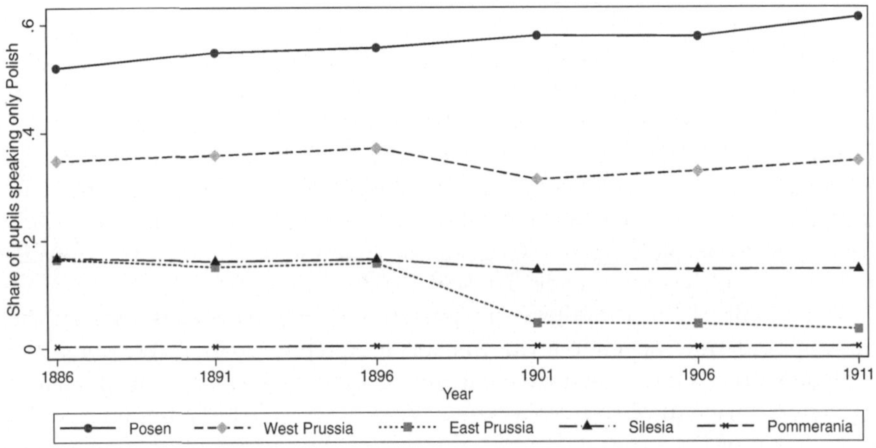

Figure 15.4 Share of schoolchildren speaking only Polish in five Prussian provinces, 1886–1911.

Source: Own elaboration.

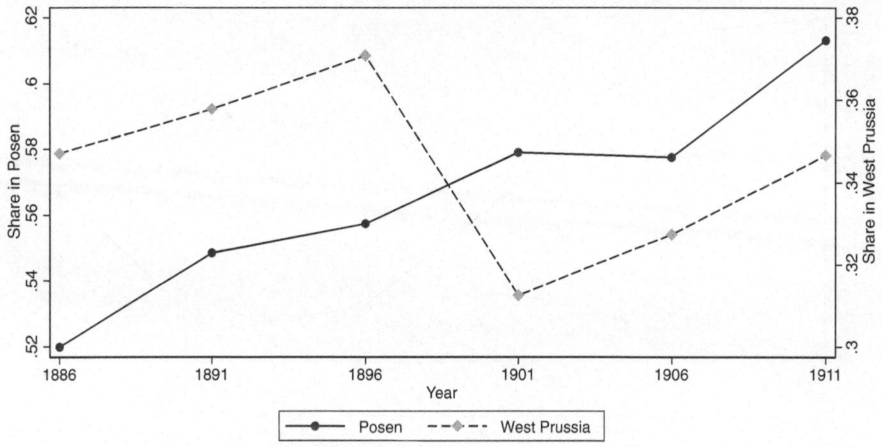

Figure 15.5 Share of schoolchildren speaking only Polish in Posen and West Prussia, 1886–1911.

Source: Own elaboration.

speaking only Polish in Posen increased from 52 percent in 1886 to almost 62 percent in 1911. The trend in West Prussia is not as monotonic as in Posen, but the share increases after 1901, in line with the exacerbation of the language restrictions.

Another metric of the success (or failure) of the Germanisation policy is the share of bilingual schoolchildren, namely speaking *both* German and Polish (Figure 15.6). The first thing to note is the low level of bilingualism in Posen, which from 1886 to 1901 oscillates between 3.5 and 4 percent. There is, however, an increase in the share of bilingual schoolchildren, which seems to coincide with the period in which the language policy became more restrictive. In percentage terms, the increase in the share of bilingualism between 1901 and 1911 was about 35 percent. The trend for the share of schoolchildren speaking only German seems to suggest that the restrictive language policy might have contributed to halting the decline observed in the period 1886–1901.

5 Conclusion

In summary, it has become clear that the recent outburst of new quantitative studies on the causes and consequences of Prussian educational attainment provides valuable insights into our understanding of economic development during the nineteenth century. However, it is similarly straightforward that substantial gaps remain in this area. More research will be necessary to expand our view on German education systems outside of Prussia and outside of primary education. It will be important to verify the above findings for other German states to generalise our findings.

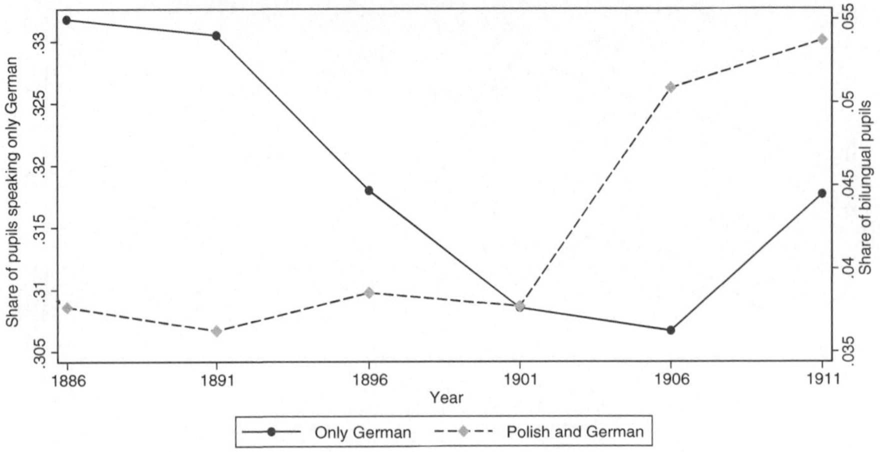

Figure 15.6 Share of schoolchildren speaking both German and Polish, Province of Posen, 1886–1911.

Source: Own elaboration.

Zooming in on unification, we established that the German government saw primary education as a tool to create a national identity and implement its political goals. The School Inspection Law of 1872 was a central element of the *Kulturkampf* against the Catholic church's power in Prussia. The educational reform that mainly centralised the funding and recruitment of primary school teachers and the ban of Polish as an instruction language aimed at assimilating and indoctrinating non-German speaking schoolchildren. Whereas the effectiveness of these policies still needs to be systematically evaluated, Imperial Germany provides a clear example of how the educational system can be instrumental to nation-building.

Notes

1 Baten and van Zanden (2008). A'Hearn et al. (2009: 801) confirm this picture when looking at numeracy levels.
2 Data on secondary schools are much less comprehensive; even the Prussian Statistical Office, often at the forefront of data collection, published disaggregated statistics on secondary schools only until 1864.
3 The Protestant-Catholic enrolment gap is also substantial (>10 percent for both genders) when just focusing on Westphalia and the Rhine Province, the two westernmost provinces of Prussia.
4 It is important to note that there is still little research on the role of technical schooling, which was spreading during the nineteenth century, also in Prussia.
5 According to our own calculations, the number of vocational schools in Prussia increased from 56 to 500, in Bavaria from 98 to 378, in Saxony from 66 to 208, in Württemberg from 27 to 47, and in Baden from 14 to 26.

6 To put these figures in context, overall central spending in 1891 amounted to 27.7 million Marks.
7 The categories are mutually exclusive in the censuses.

References

A'Hearn, B., Baten, J., and Baten, D. (2009) 'Quantifying quantitative literacy: age heaping and the history of human capital', *Journal of Economic History,* Vol. 69 (3): 783–808.

Ashraf, Q. H., Cinnirella, F., Galor, O., Gershman, B. and Hornung, E. (2018) 'Capital-skill complementarity and the emergence of labor emancipation', *CEPR Discussion Paper* 12822.

Bandiera, O., Mohnen, M., Rasul, I. and Viarengo, M. (2019) 'Nation-building through compulsory schooling during the age of mass migration', *Economic Journal,* Vol. 129 (4): 62–109.

Baten, J. and Van Zanden, J. L. (2008) 'Book production and the onset of modern economic growth', *Journal of Economic Growth,* Vol. 13 (3): 217–35.

Becker, S. O. and Cinnirella, F. (2020) 'Prussia disaggregated: the demography of its universe of localities in 1871', *Journal of Demographic Economics,* Vol. 86 (3): 259–90.

Becker, S. O., Cinnirella, F. and Woessmann, L. (2010) 'The trade-off between fertility and education: evidence from before the demographic transition', *Journal of Economic Growth,* Vol. 15 (3): 177–204.

Becker, S. O., Cinnirella, F. and Woessmann, L. (2012) 'The effect of investment in children's education on fertility in 1816 Prussia', *Cliometrica,* Vol. 6 (1): 29–44.

Becker, S. O., Cinnirella, F. and Woessmann, L. (2013) 'Does women's education affect fertility? Evidence from pre-demographic transition Prussia', *European Review of Economic History,* Vol. 17 (1): 24–44.

Becker, S. O., Hornung, E. and Woessmann, L. (2011) 'Education and catch-up in the industrial revolution', *American Economic Journal: Macroeconomics,* Vol. 3 (3): 92–126.

Becker, S. O. and Woessmann, L. (2008) 'Luther and the girls: religious denomination and the female education gap in nineteenth-century Prussia', *Scandinavian Journal of Economics,* Vol. 110 (4): 777–805.

Becker, S. O. and Woessmann, L. (2009) 'Was Weber wrong? A human capital theory of protestant economic history', *Quarterly Journal of Economics,* Vol. 124 (2): 531–96.

Beuttler, F. W. (2012) ''Rendering to the Kaiser': Protestantism, education, and the state in German history', in W. Jeynes and D. W. Robinson (eds), *International Handbook of Protestant Education,* Dordrecht: Springer, pp. 163–93.

Cinnirella, F. and Hornung, E. (2016) 'Landownership concentration and the expansion of education', *Journal of Development Economics,* Vol. 121: 135–52.

Cinnirella, F. and Schueler, R. (2016) 'The cost of decentralization: linguistic polarization and the provision of education', *CESifo Working Paper* 5894.

Cinnirella, F. and Streb, J. (2017) 'The role of human capital and innovation in economic development: evidence from post-Malthusian Prussia', *Journal of Economic Growth,* Vol. 22 (2): 193–227.

Clark, C. (2007) *Iron Kingdom: The Rise and Downfall of Prussia, 1600–1947,* München: Penguin.

Clots-Figueras, I. and Masella, P. (2013) 'Education, language and identity', *Economic Journal,* Vol. 123 (570): F332–57.

Dewey, J. (1916) *Democracy and Education: An Introduction to the Philosophy of Education*, New York: MacMillan.

Diebolt, C. (2005) *Die langfristige Entwicklung des Schulsystems in Deutschland im 19. und 20. Jahrhundert*, Köln: GESIS Datenarchiv.

Eddie, S. A. (2013) *Freedom's Price: Serfdom, Subjection, and Reform in Prussia, 1648–1848*, Oxford: Oxford University Press.

Galor, O. (2011) *Unified Growth Theory*, Princeton, NJ: Princeton University Press.

Galor, O. (2012) 'The demographic transition: causes and consequences', *Cliometrica*, Vol. 6: 494–504.

Gawthrop, R. and Strauss, G. (1984) 'Protestantism and literacy in early modern Germany', *Past and Present*, Vol. 104: 31–55.

Gerschenkron, A. (1962) *Economic Backwardness in Historical Perspective: A Book of Essays*, Cambridge, MA: Harvard University Press.

Glueck, H. (1979) *Die preussisch-polnische Sprachenpolitik: Eine Studie zur Theorie und Methodologie der Forschung über Sprachenpolitik, Sprachbewusstsein und Sozialgeschichte am Beispiel der preussisch-deutschen Politik gegenüber der polnischen Minderheit vor 1914*, Hamburg: Buske.

Green, L. (1979) 'The education of women in the Reformation', *History of Education Quarterly*, Vol. 19 (1): 93–116.

Jeismann, K.-E. (1992) 'Bildungsbewegungen und Bildungspolitik seit der Mitte des 18. Jhs. im Reich und im Deutschen Bund. Wechselwirkungen, Übereinstimmungen und Abweichungen zwischen den deutschen Staaten', in E. Lechner, H. Rumpler and H. Zdarzil (eds), *Zur Geschichte des österreichischen Bildungswesens*, Wien: Verlag der österreichischen Akademie der Wissenschaften, pp. 401–26.

Kersting, F., Wohnsiedler, I. and Wolf, N. (2020) 'Weber revisited: the Protestant ethic and the spirit of nationalism', *Journal of Economic History*, Vol. 80 (3): 710–45.

Kesper-Biermann, S. (2013) 'Kommunikation, Austausch, Transfer: Bildungsräume im 19. Jahrhundert', in E. Möller and J. Wischmeyer (eds), *Transnationale Bildungsräume: Wissenstransfers im Schnittfeld von Kultur, Politik und Religion*, Göttingen: Vandenhoeck & Ruprecht, pp. 21–41.

Kuhlemann, F.-M. (1991) 'Schulen, Hochschulen, Lehrer', in C. Berg (ed), *Handbuch der deutschen Bildungsgeschichte*, Vol. 4, *1870–1918: Von der Reichsgründung bis zum Ende des Ersten Weltkriegs*, München: Beck, pp. 170–370.

Lamberti, M. (1989) *State, Society and the Elementary School in Imperial Germany*, Oxford: Oxford University Press.

Lindert, P. H. (2003) 'Voice and growth: was Churchill right?', *Journal of Economic History*, Vol. 63 (2): 315–50.

Lindert, P. H. (2004) *Growing public: Social Spending and Economic Growth since the Eighteenth Century*, Cambridge: Cambridge University Press.

Luther, M. (1520) 'An den christlichen Adel deutscher Nation von des christlichen Standes Besserung (To the Christian nobility of the German nation concerning the reform of the Christian estate)', in *Dr. Martin Luthers Werke: Kritische Gesamtausgabe*, Vol. 6, Weimar: Hermann Böhlaus Nachfolger, 1888.

Luther, M. (1524) 'An die Ratsherren aller Städte deutschen Landes, dass sie christliche Schulen aufrichten und halten sollen (To the councilmen of all cities in Germany that they establish and maintain Christian schools)', in *Dr. Martin Luthers Werke: Kritische Gesamtausgabe*, Vol. 15, Weimar: Hermann Böhlaus Nachfolger, 1899.

Luther, M. (1530) 'Eine Predigt, dass man Kinder zur Schule halten solle (A Sermon on Keeping Children in School)', in *Dr. Martin Luthers Werke: Kritische Gesamtausgabe*, Vol. 30, part 2, Weimar: Hermann Böhlaus Nachfolger, 1909.

Nath, A., Titze, H., Dartenne, C. M., Kasel, G., Oelerich-Sprung, C., Schmeitzner, K. and Wloch, H. (2016) *Datenhandbuch zur deutschen Bildungsgeschichte: Differenzierung und Integration der niederen Schulen in Deutschland 1800–1945*, Göttingen: Vandenhoeck & Ruprecht.

Nelson, R. R. and Phelps, E. S. (1966) 'Investment in humans, technological diffusion, and economic growth', *The American Economic Review*, Vol. 56 (1): 69–75.

Roerkohl, A. (1992) *Der Kulturkampf in Westfalen*, Münster: Landesbildstelle Westfalen.

Schleunes, K. A. (1979) 'Enlightenment, reform, reaction: the schooling revolution in Prussia', *Central European History*, Vol. 12: 315–42.

Schueler, R. (2016) 'Centralized monitoring, resistance, and reform outcomes: evidence from school inspections in Prussia', *Ifo Working Paper* 223.

Semrad, A. (2015) 'Modern secondary education and economic performance: the introduction of the Gewerbeschule and Realschule in nineteenth-century Bavaria', *Economic History Review*, Vol. 68 (4): 1306–38.

Seyffarth, L. W. (1876) *Allgemeine Chronik des Volksschulwesens*, Vol. 11 (Jahr 1875), Altona: Haendcke & Lehmkuhl.

Weber, E. (1976) *Peasants into Frenchmen: The Modernization of Rural France 1870–1914*, Stanford, CA: Stanford University Press.

16 Globalization and foreign trade

Wolf-Fabian Hungerland and Markus Lampe

1 Introduction

Internal market integration and the transformation of foreign into internal trade through the formation of the *Zollverein*, the German Customs Union, in 1834 played a central role in Germany's unification. Textbooks on Imperial Germany consider the 'protectionist turn' of 1879 as the milestone of a conservative 'second foundation' of the Empire, with a subsequent politically anti-modernist and economically protective orientation (e.g. Wehler 1994). Nevertheless, during the late nineteenth century, the German economy experienced rapid globalization that turned protectionist policies into (incomplete) compensatory measures. We devote most of this chapter to the economic aspects of Germany's globalization experience; however, we also consider its political aspects. We start with a broad perspective on economic globalization during the nineteenth century and show that after the foundation of the Empire, emigration waves weakened in the medium term, whereas capital exports increased strongly. Nevertheless, external trade presented the key element of Germany's international economy, thus shaping multiple opportunities and challenges for the German economy as a whole. We thus discuss it in greater depth using newly available data.

2 Germany in the first era of modern globalization

Trade and trade policy were central to the public perception of the Empire's globalization experience. Economic globalization, however, is a multi-layered process that also involves international migration and capital flows. It can be quantified and traced over time through the importance of international movements of commodities and factors of production (labour and capital) relative to the size of the aggregate economy. We should also expect that globalization is reflected by a convergence of domestic commodity prices and factor remunerations (wages, interest rates) with world market prices (O'Rourke and Williamson 1999).

Between 1834 and 1914, about 5.4 million Germans emigrated, the vast majority of them (4.9 million) to the United States.[1] Emigration was

DOI: 10.4324/9781003283430-19

concentrated in several waves—1846–1857, 1864–1873, and 1880–1893. In each case, between 1 and 1.4 million people left Germany. Business cycles and war in the United States contributed to each wave at least as much as conditions in Germany. In terms of magnitude, the first wave was the most significant, with over 250,000 individuals emigrating in 1854—almost 0.7 percent of population of the *Zollverein*—a figure that was never reached again in absolute or relative terms. The peak of the smaller second wave in 1869 (136,000: 0.35 percent) still occurred before the foundation of the Empire, and the long third wave experienced its first peak in 1881 (221,000: 0.5 percent) and a smaller second peak in 1891 (120,000: 0.2 percent). After 1894, in no single year more than 40,000 people emigrated from the German Empire, although the transport of emigrants remained a successful business for North German shipping companies (Brinkmann 2008). The 1910 US census reported 2.3 million people born in Germany (Chiswick and Hatton 2003) at a time when the Empire counted 64.6 million inhabitants, including about 1.3 million foreign citizens, a good half of them from Austria-Hungary.

The macroeconomic consequences of German emigration are difficult to assess. Data from O'Rourke and Williamson (1999: 19, 126) on international wage convergence suggest that German wages grew faster than the international average, but did not converge on the wages in the main destination country: German wage levels in 1870–1913 were still only about 52 to 54 percent of those in the United States. O'Rourke and Williamson also find that wages rose faster than land rents in Germany, which implies that migration improved the income ratio between labour and land (see also Chapter 5 of this volume). However, the transformation of Germany from a net exporter to net importer of grain—despite agricultural protection—and thus commodity market integration, provides a more significant explanation for this phenomenon than emigration (see Section 3.1). Direct effects of German emigration, such as money remittances, were relatively insignificant as well. Data on postal money orders from the United States to Germany, which were at least partially attributable to emigrants, indeed showed a positive balance for Germany. However, even at their peak in 1910–13, they accounted for less than one percent of the German invisible balance surplus, while income from foreign investments alone compensated for a steadily negative trade balance (Wolf 2022).

Unfortunately, reliable data on the development of German capital exports are only available from 1883 onwards, when the periodical *Der deutsche Ökonomist* started publishing data about foreign securities issued on German stock exchanges. Data on the capital and services and invisible balances indicate that Germany was a net exporter of capital from 1883 onwards, to an extent unprecedented before the foundation of the Empire (Torp 2014; Wolf 2022; see also Schaefer 1995). Torp (2014: 26–30) estimates that in 1913 the German Empire had a net stock in capital investments abroad of about 30 billion Mark, of which two-thirds were portfolio investments in form of foreign securities issued in Germany and about one-third were foreign direct investments by German companies, although the available data on the latter are less reliable. Income from these investments abroad apparently overcompensated the annual outflow of newly invested capital. Kling et al. (2011) find that foreign direct investment was particularly important in the expanding industries of the so-called 'second industrialization', that is, mechanical and electrical engineering and the chemical industry, and were aimed at increasing their presence in foreign markets.

With some faith in the validity of the existing data on foreign trade (see Section 4.1) we can use a measure of openness—defined as the ratio of imports to the gross domestic product—to chart Germany's globalization experience from 1850 to 1918 (Figure 16.1). There were two waves of globalization. The first ran from 1850 until the tariff reform of 1879, with an import boom between 1865 and 1875 that coincided with the economic boom following the founding of the Empire and one of the most pronounced free trade eras in modern history. Between 1865 and 1875, imports increased by nine to 10 percent per year. After the protectionist turn of 1879, the second wave of globalization began, which lasted until the First World War. In view of the uncertainty surrounding the quality of data around the statistical reform of 1880, it cannot be conclusively assessed whether the protectionist turn indeed decreased openness by 8.5 percentage points.

We conclude that Germany's integration into the world economy was not the result of the foundation of the Empire. Instead, a longer-term trend with a globalization spurt before and around 1871 was interrupted by the 'second

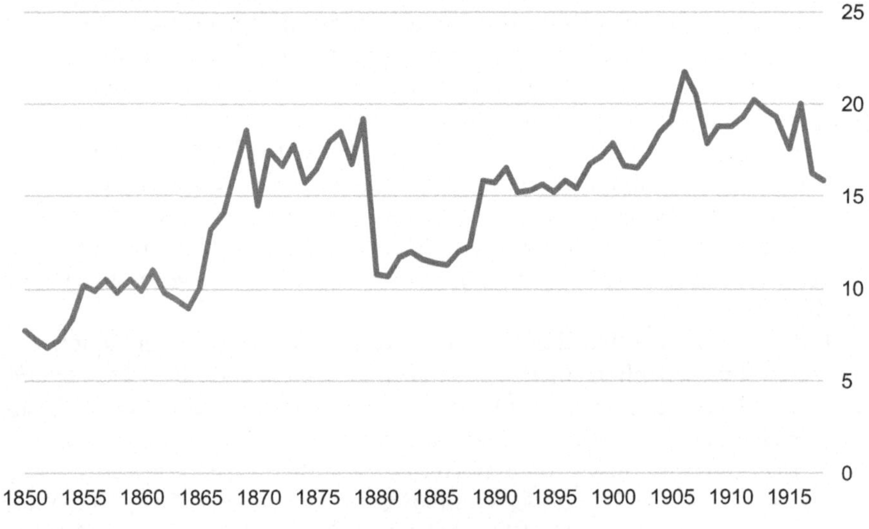

Figure 16.1 Degree of openness as import-to-GDP ratio.

Source: Own elaboration with data from Rahlf (2016); imports updated following Hardach (1977: 33) and Hungerland and Wolf (2022). Import value as percent of GDP, excluding imports of precious metals. All underlying data in current prices.

foundation' of 1878/79. Research using German and foreign grain prices finds that a globalization trend began in the 1830s, deepened after 1856, and was not reverted by the foundation of the Empire or the protectionist turn, although the latter resulted in (slightly) deeper internal market integration in Germany (O'Rourke and Williamson 1999: 44; Uebele 2013). However, in a period of advancing industrialization grain markets can hardly be considered representative of all markets.

If we contrast the degree of openness to international trade discussed above with a measure of the degree of (trade) policy openness, namely, average import duties (Figure 16.2), political fluctuations appear more prominent. Tariff levels decreased almost continuously from the late 1850s until 1877, before the protectionist turn led to an increase that stabilized at the end of the 1880s. This was followed by a slight decline in average import duties until the First World War. This resulted partly, from a combination of rising prices, whereas tariffs, which were specific tariffs, remained more or less constant.

3 German trade policy since 1846

3.1 From a free-trade customs union to a moderately protectionist Empire

German trade policy before the 1860s is generally described from the perspective of its outcome: the Prussia-dominated *Zollverein* became the customs territory of a unified German Empire. Similarly, the initial formation of the

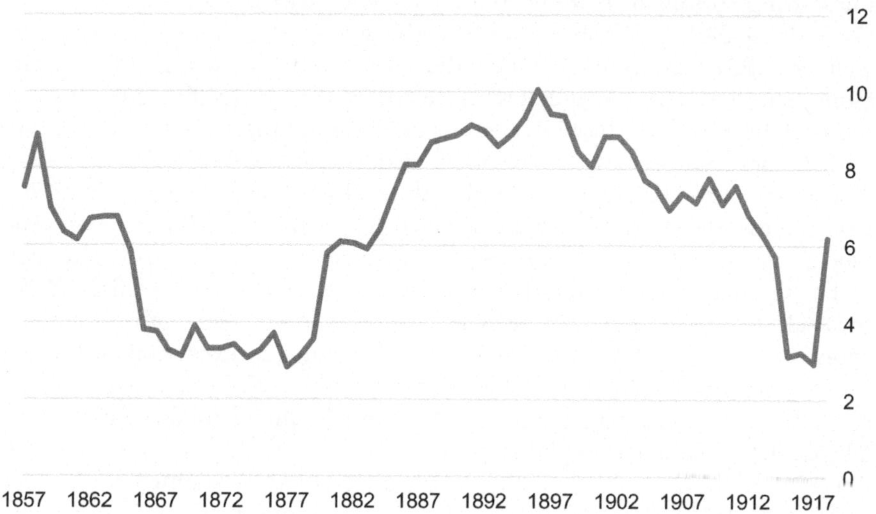

Figure 16.2 Average ad-valorem equivalent of tariff duties, 1857–1918.

Source: Lampe and Sharp (2013); import duty revenues as share of import value. In current prices.

Zollverein in 1834 appears as a result of the unification of tariffs in Prussia in 1818, which after the Congress of Vienna consisted of unconnected Western and Eastern territories. The long borders of Prussia implied high costs of customs collection, which a more connected customs area could significantly decrease. Prussia also controlled the access of most other German states to the North Sea and Baltic ports and possessed the largest internal market in Germany (Huning and Wolf 2019; see also Chapter 2 of this volume). Prussia's *Zollverein* initiative was therefore able to offer more attractive conditions to other states than rival projects of economic integration (Ploeckl 2015). By 1854, the *Zollverein* thus encompassed almost the entire territory of the later German Empire, with the exception of Schleswig, Holstein, the two Mecklenburg principalities, the Hanseatic cities of Hamburg, Bremen, and the territories of Alsace and Lorraine that were French in 1854.

The Prussian customs tariff of 1818, which formed the basis of the *Zollverein* tariff, was comparatively liberal for the period after the Napoleonic Wars, and this continued to be the case for the *Zollverein* tariff (see Table 16.1 below). In particular, it was less protectionist than the customs tariff of Austria, which repeatedly launched alternative initiatives for customs unions. In 1853, Austria and the *Zollverein* established mutual tariff preferences for twelve years and agreed on a clause that stipulated Austria's accession to the *Zollverein* after the expiration of the treaty in 1865.

Prussia, however, which preferred a customs union comprising only Lesser Germany under its leadership, interrupted this process. It took advantage of the momentum to reduce tariffs on manufactures created by the Cobden-Chevalier trade treaty of 1860 between France and Great Britain, the leading trading nations of Europe, and concluded a treaty with France in 1862 (Zorn 1963: 320–22). Prussia then effectively forced this agreement onto the *Zollverein,* threatening to not renew the *Zollverein* treaties due in 1865. In the same year, the treaty concluded with Austria in 1853 was replaced by a simple most-favoured-nation (MFN) agreement that put Austria on equal footing with France and other treaty partners of the *Zollverein* (Torp 2014: 70–81). The Austro-Prussian War of 1866 led to the final break between the *Zollverein* and the Habsburg Monarchy. In 1870, a new liberal *Zollverein* tariff provided, inter alia, for duty-free imports of grain and, from 1873, iron and steel.

The German Empire initially continued the free-trade course of the *Zollverein*. However, the panic of 1873 led to the postponement of the planned abolition of iron and steel tariffs until 1877, with the exception of the pig iron tariff (Torp 2014: 84–87). This phase ended in 1879, when a new, more protectionist customs law was passed that could be understood as a prelude to a broader backlash against the previous liberal economic order (Webb 1974; Tena-Junguito et al. 2012; see also chapter 17 of this volume and Wehler 1994: 41–47). While the relatively moderate iron and steel tariffs were a direct response to the economic crisis, the initially low grain tariffs that were successively increased during the 1880s responded to increased competitive pressure from global market integration and transportation innovations. The pressure was exacerbated by the deflationary tendencies resulting from the introduction of the gold standard in 1873 (see Chapter 9 of this volume). Falling prices aggravated the indebtedness of agricultural estates and made it difficult for heavy industry to service debts contracted to undertake earlier investments (Webb 1974; Aldenhoff-Hübinger 2002; Torp 2014). Heavy industry reacted with increased cartelization, and tariffs supported its strategy of charging higher prices on the domestic market than for exports, as they made reimports unprofitable (Webb 1980; see also Chapter 12 of this volume). Representatives of the agricultural sector later attempted similar strategies without success (Aldenhoff-Hübinger 2002: 56–58).

1879 is also seen as a turning point in the political history of the Empire: Bismarck and the conservatives made trade policy the main issue of the Reichstag elections in July 1878 and were successful with this strategy (Lehmann 2010). The following conservative turn is often referred to as the 'second foundation of the Empire', and the combination of the political interests of traditional agrarian-aristocratic elites and heavy industry, which later profited from naval armament, has been dubbed a 'Coalition of rye and iron'. Classical accounts by Kehr (1930), Gerschenkron (1943) and Wehler (1994) have interpreted this course of events as part of a broader strategy of elites to prevent socio-political modernization. Recent research has cautioned against such sweeping generalizations and has pointed to the instability of the protectionist coalition of agriculture and (heavy) industry beyond the 1880s (Torp 2010).

From the 1880s, other countries also sought to 'take back control', that is, to expand the scope of action for trade policy, through renegotiation of the MFN treaties of the 1860s (Marsh 1999). This resulted in tariff wars, such as the one between Germany and Russia in the early 1890s. When France, which had been a central node in the European trade treaty network since 1860, planned to not extend its treaties upon expiration in 1892, the existing European trade agreement network was in danger to break apart completely. In Germany, Leo von Caprivi, Bismarck's successor since 1890, formed a domestic political alliance that built on export interests to preserve the international treaty network and thus to stabilize tariff levels and planning horizons for export industries. Germany's treaty negotiations with its eastern and southern neighbours subsequently led to slight reductions in grain tariffs for the first time in decades (Altenhoff-Hübinger 2002: 146–54; Torp 2014: Chapter 4). This triggered the reorganization of protectionist interests in agriculture, now dominated by a new, populist mass organization led by representatives of the large landowners, the German Agrarian League (*Bund der Landwirte*; Aldenhoff-Hübinger 2002: 105–12, 150–54). Agricultural interests subsequently obtained a variety of concessions to cushion the effects of the treaties, including protectionist sanitary regulations for livestock and implicit and explicit export subsidies for beet sugar and grain (Hunt 1974; Webb 1974, 1982; Aldenhoff-Hübinger 2002: 118–23, 154, 188–89, 224; Torp 2014: 208–10, 241–51).

Caprivi was replaced already in 1894, and the new government under Hohenlohe-Schillingsfürst promised to renegotiate the Caprivi treaties upon expiration (1904) based on a prior tariff reform. The latter was passed in December 1902 after more than five years of preparation and, after another change in government, went down in history as the Bülow tariff (Torp 2014: 171–74). It was a compromise between the protectionist interests in the German Empire and the export industries, which feared retaliation in the event of excessive tariff increases. Throughout the legislative process, grain tariffs and livestock hygiene laws became the focus of debate; finally, non-negotiable minimum duties were fixed for four key grain types (Aldenhoff-Hübinger 2002: 155–73; Torp 2014: 185–86, 201). Despite this protectionist stance, the existing trade agreements were subsequently renewed, although the key agreement with Russia only came about because the latter needed access to the Berlin Stock Exchange for its government bonds after its defeat in the war against Japan and was forced to accept unfavourable trade treaty outcomes to secure it (Torp 2014: 220–22).

3.2 German trade policy in the European context

Products from agriculture, heavy industry, and initially the textile industry dominated German trade policy debates. These industries made up a significant share of production and employment and formed the basis of influential economic and political elites. However, trade policy outcomes varied considerably: while grain tariffs increased steadily from 1878 to 1906, except for the Caprivi treaties, tariffs on most iron and steel products remained unchanged after 1879 (Webb 1974, 1980, 1982). At the same time, the protectionist turn of 1879 and its support by a cross-industry alliance were by no means unique in Europe (Aldenhoff-Hübinger 2002; see also Chapter 17 of this volume).

Ad valorem equivalents of specific duties, shown in Table 16.1, are useful to place German trade policy in a broader context. Ad valorem equivalents rise when quantity-specific duties increase, and also when prices fall (and vice versa). 1846 is the first year with appropriate data after the foundation of the *Zollverein*; 1859 represents the situation before the Franco-Prussian trade treaty; 1875 is just before the height of the German free trade era; 1890 captures the situation after the protectionist turn of 1879 and the Caprivi treaties; by 1907, the Bülow tariff was in effect.

Over the entire period, Germany was less protectionist than the European average and also than its neighbours France, Austria-Hungary, and Russia. After 1879, German tariff levels converged to an average that included not only protectionist countries such as Portugal, Spain, and France but also the United Kingdom and the Netherlands, which followed a policy of free trade. For grain tariffs, represented by tariffs on wheat, Germany, together with France, led the protective reaction to the 'grain invasion' of Europe (O'Rourke 1997). Tariffs on animal foodstuffs increased only moderately, which was also owing to the fact that protection with respect to this class of goods operated

Table 16.1 European tariff levels in comparison

	1846		*1859*		*1875*		*1890*		*1907*	
	D	*Euro 11*	*D*	*Euro 11*	*D*	*Euro 11*	*D*	*Euro 11*	*D*	*Euro 11*
Grains	19	20	13	10	8	9	28	16	29	21
Wheat	5	18	6	4	0	8	35	11	40	24
Animal foodstuffs	8	9	5	5	2	4	9	7	13	12
Revenue goods (sugar, coffee, and tobacco)	52	89	49	47	35	48	75	103	67	121
Sugar (unrefined and refined)	89	129	91	44	55	56	112	126	88	148
Sugar (domestic tax deducted)	83	n/a	62	n/a	30	n/a	45	n/a	22	n/a
Industrial raw materials (textile fibres: wool, cotton; hides, skins; minerals: coal, iron ore; wood)	4	12	4	3	0	2	1	4	1	5
Iron and steel	43	39	56	29	6	8	18	12	16	12
Textiles: yarns	19	48	16	33	6	10	13	10	11	11
Textiles: cloths	46	48	46	31	12	19	25	22	21	28
Other manufactures (silk, paper, leather, and copper)	9	23	11	20	3	7	9	9	7	12
Mean (all)	22	34	22	22	9	14	21	22	18	24
Mean (revenue goods excluded)	16	29	17	19	5	8	11	11	10	13
	0	0	0	0	0	0	0	0	0	0
Import weighted average tariff	n/a	14	7	10	3	9	9	10	7	9

Sources: Tena-Junguito et al. (2012); Lampe (2020); ongoing work by Lampe and Tena-Junguito. In percent of import value. Ad valorem equivalents of domestic sugar taxes for Germany only based on Teichmann (1955: 315–49), for other countries 'not available' (n/a). Euro 11: Belgium, Denmark, France, Italy (prior to 1861: Piedmont-Sardinia), Netherlands, Norway, Portugal, Spain, Sweden, Switzerland, United Kingdom. The silk industry is listed under 'other manufactures' and not as 'textiles' because the underlying data contains a combined average for yarn and cloths of silk. 'Mean (all)' is based on 19 commodity groups; several of them are shown as aggregates in this table. Import weighted average tariff: as in Figure 16.2.

primarily through hygiene regulations. Specific duties on iron and steel and their ad valorem equivalents remained largely constant after their increase in 1879. The situation was similar for textiles and other manufactures. Tariffs on industrial raw materials remained low, while tariffs on commodities of tropical origin, which were primarily motivated by the fiscal revenue they generated, rose sharply and remained high. Sugar tariffs acquired additional significance, as German agriculture became the world's largest beet sugar producer through modernization efforts in the shadow of tariffs and export subsidies (Aldenhoff-Hübinger 2002). In particular, an input tax levied on sugar beets was reimbursed upon exportation, with the reimbursement assuming a significantly lower sugar extraction rate than actually attained, thus effectively subsidizing exports. In 1891, an explicit export subsidy replaced this implicit practice (Aldenhoff-Hübinger 2002: 119–21, 153). According to Webb (1982), the prohibition of such subsidies in the 1902 Brussels International Sugar Convention ended German support for sugar beet cultivation. Nevertheless, the government continued to impose the maximum tariff rate permitted by the Convention and thus preserved government revenues and protection at least partially (Teichmann 1955: 346–51; Aldenhoff-Hübinger 2002: 160–62, 167).

Overall, the support that tariff policy provided to agriculture and some industrial branches by no means stopped or reversed globalization and market integration. Nevertheless, it resembled the mercantilism of the pre-1818 period (and thus strategic industrial policy) and its effective later successor, the Common Agricultural Policy of the European Economic Community (Wehler 1994: 48–59; Aldenhoff-Hübinger 2002: 171; Plumpe 2019: 272).

3.3 Distributive effects

At the macroeconomic level, it is difficult to evaluate the effects of trade policy. Lehmann and O'Rourke (2011) find, in general, for the late nineteenth century that agricultural tariffs hindered economic growth, that revenue tariffs had little economic effects, and industrial tariffs might have affected growth positively. For Germany, at the industry level, Webb (1980) presents similar findings for the iron and steel tariffs, while Tilly (1990: 113–14) concludes that grain tariffs retarded structural change from agriculture to industry (see Aldenhoff-Hübinger 2002: 183).

The effects of the agrarian tariffs on incomes can be assessed more clearly because contemporaries have collected the relevant data. Aldenhoff-Hübinger (2002: 174–80, 224) demonstrates that owing to implicit export subsidies import duties almost perfectly translated into higher grain prices: the difference between the price of wheat in Berlin and in London was almost exactly equivalent to the German wheat tariff. Consequently, land rents for the large landed estates in eastern Prussia evolved relatively favourably by European standards, although they rose less than wages (O'Rourke 1997: 797; Aldenhoff-Hübinger 2002: 184–85). Whether smaller farms benefitted similarly from protection is the subject of a long-standing debate (Hunt 1974; Webb 1974, 1982). Gerloff (1908; cited by Torp 2014: 260) calculated that higher food prices resulting from the Bülow tariff cost urban households 2 to 3 percent of their real income; Brentano (1925; cited by Wehler 1994: 55) similarly concluded that industrial workers had to work 13–18 days more per year to maintain their standard of living. Wehler (1994: 53) concludes that this put pressure on women from urban households to take up employment. Webb (1982: 324–25) estimates that agricultural protection redistributed 2 to 3 percent of national income from consumers to agricultural producers (see also Burhop 2011: 114).

4 Regional and commodity structure of Germany's foreign trade

4.1 Data

Nobel Prize winner W. Arthur Lewis (1983) stated that 'German trade statistics before 1907 are a booby trap'. Whereas the foreign trade statistics of the German Empire, especially after 1889, offer detailed information in international comparison (see Roeske 1978, 1985). The data documentation is unsatisfactory for the period before 1871, when statistics neither recorded imports or exports completely nor values (only quantities) or trading partners (only border crossings; Dedinger 2015). From about 1858, at least import records can be used—with much effort—for a reconstruction of trade flows between Germany and Europe if they are combined with trade partner statistics and prices from Hamburg, Bremen, and contemporary publications (Lampe 2008). Bondi (1958) did something similar for total imports and exports of the *Zollverein* since 1834, but his figures (which we use in Figure 16.1) should be treated with caution (Borries 1970: 5–6).

After 1871, the data documentation improves only step by step. First, until 1880, the data on the trade of the German customs territory with foreign countries remains incomplete; only the protectionist turn of 1879 ensured complete coverage of imports and exports from 1880 onwards (Torp 2014: 14–16). Second, the territories of the customs area and the Empire were not congruent for a long time; for example, Bremen and Hamburg joined the customs territory only in 1888; until then, these cities appear as foreign territory and commodity traffic between them and the Empire was considered foreign trade, creating a distorted picture (Buchheim 1982). Third, the commodity classification changed over time, making it difficult to compare the data, and thus requires a translation of all product categories into the Standard International Trade Classification (SITC). Hungerland and Altmeppen (2021) standardized all available data, so that additional data from the statistics of Hamburg and Bremen can be used to solve the second problem by applying a generalized version of Buchheim's (1982) quota method to integrate the data for the Hanseatic cities and the German Empire (Hungerland and Wolf

2022: Appendix). The first problem remains unsolved and allows us to take a closer look at the actual foreign trade of the German Empire only from 1880 onwards.

4.2 Intensive and extensive margins

The total value of imports and exports was about seven billion Mark in 1880 and about 21 billion Mark in 1913. While 34 trading partners and 334 SITC five-digit categories appeared in the data in 1880, trade with 86 countries and in 834 five-digit categories was reported in 1913. Thus, trade grew in terms of value and the number of products and trading partners increased. To get a better understanding of German trade growth and the interplay between the geographical and the commodity structure of trade, we can decompose trade into the growth of existing trade relations—the intensive margin—and the emergence or disappearance of trade relations—the extensive margin—for all product-country combinations, so-called Armington varieties (Armington 1969). Hungerland and Wolf (2022) decompose trade growth between 1880 and 1913 into these three margins as follows:

$$\frac{\sum_i V_{it} - \sum_i V_{it-1}}{\sum_i V_{it-1}} = \frac{\sum_{i\in I} V_{it} - \sum_{i\in I} V_{it-1}}{\sum_i V_{it-1}} - \frac{\sum_{i\in I_{t-1}^D} V_{it-1}}{\sum_i V_{it-1}} + \frac{\sum_{i\in I_t^N} V_{it}}{\sum_i V_{it-1}} \quad \text{(eq. 1)}$$

The first term on the right side of Equation 1 describes the intensive margin, which is the growth of trade for all product-country combinations active in both years. I_{t-1}^D is the value of all Armington varieties that disappear between 1880 and 1913, I_t^N is the value of all varieties that emerge in this period. Thus, the last two terms represent the extensive margins of disappearing and newly added goods. Figure 16.3 shows that the emergence of new trade relations contributed strongly to trade growth in the three decades prior to the First World War: the growth of the margin of new goods amounted to 256 percent for imports, and 292 percent for exports. By contrast, total imports expanded by 295 percent and exports only at 261 percent, which is owing to the disappearance of some product-country combinations. Growth at the intensive margin was only a minor driver of growth, and only on the import side, where trade relations intensified by 64 percent. On the export side, trade in existing product-country combination actually fell by 4 percent.

The massive expansion at the extensive margin indicated a rapid expansion of the range of traded products and, strong penetration of new markets.

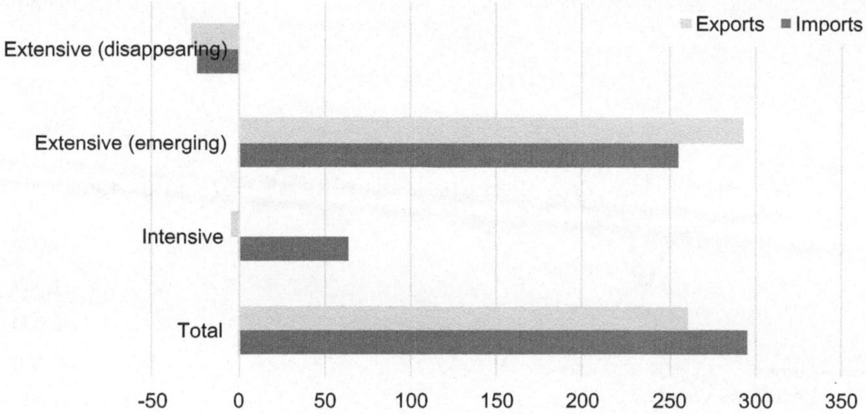

Figure 16.3 Intensive and extensive margins.
Source: Hungerland and Wolf (2022). Growth in percent between 1880 and 1913. For definitions, see text.

For example, books were exported to the United States, furs to Romania, toy vehicles to the United Kingdom, and silk to France. The countries with the greatest growth in new varieties were those which had been the most important trading partners already in 1880: Great Britain, Austria-Hungary, Russia, France, and the Netherlands. Although we cannot observe trade at the firm level, the pattern of aggregate trade corresponds to key insights of 'New New Trade Theory'. The latter predicts that productivity differences at the firm level determine whether and how much firms export (Melitz and Redding 2014). The higher their productivity, the more likely firms are able to absorb the fixed costs of market entry—in addition to variable and value-dependent trade costs. In light of this theory, the strong growth of German trade at the extensive margin points to significant productivity gains among exporting firms, and on the import side, a diversification of import sources.

4.3 Regional structure and comparative advantages

Germany's European neighbours remained its most important trading partners during the first globalization; more than half of German trade took place with other European countries. Nevertheless, German foreign trade diversified, especially with regard to imports: whereas in 1880 around 70 percent of imports still came from Europe, in 1913 the share was down to 55 percent. Exports, on the other hand, actually became somewhat more concentrated: the share of exports going to other European countries rose from 70 to 75 percent over the same period. This led to a contrasting development of the respective trade balances, as Figure 16.4 illustrates: in the thirty years before World War I, the trade balance with Europe turned increasingly positive,

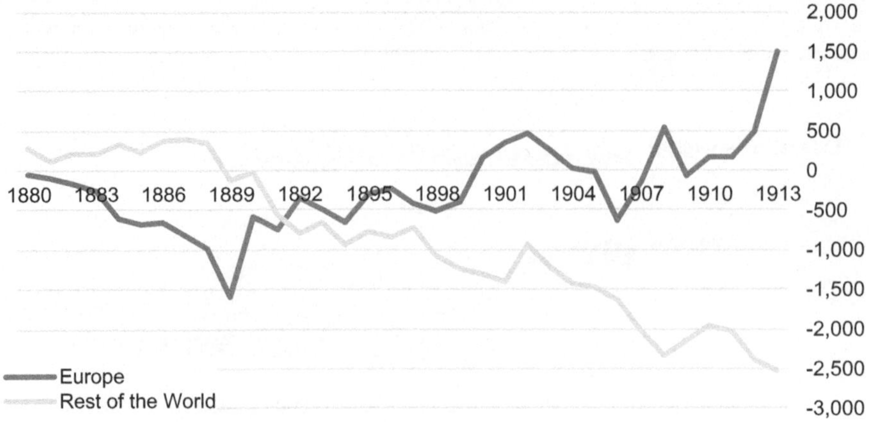

Figure 16.4 Regional trade balances.
Source: Hungerland and Wolf (2022). Million Mark.

while it showed a widening deficit with the rest of the world; trade with the Americas exhibited the largest deficit.

The divergence in regional trade balances was driven by different levels of development among trading partners and significant variation in the supply and demand of different commodities. The economy of the German Empire was characterized by relatively abundant, but comparatively cheap human capital as well as comparatively close cooperation between business and academic research and the resulting strength of the innovation system (Broadberry and Burhop 2007; Labuske and Streb 2008). Before the First World War, industrial production was characterized by small lot sizes and individualized production methods (Buchheim 1982). With the exception of coal, raw materials were scarce and agriculture became increasingly efficient elsewhere, particularly in the Americas. The latter triggered the protectionist trade policies discussed earlier, which however could only slow down the specialization process (Findlay and O'Rourke 2009: Chapter 7).

A particular sector of the economy develops a comparative advantage if production in this sector is subject to relatively low opportunity costs by international standards. This may result, for example, from relatively high labour productivity (Ricardo) or from the relative abundance of a factor of production such as capital, raw materials, labour, or land (Heckscher-Ohlin). If a sector has a comparative advantage, exports of its products are likely to exceed imports. International differences in opportunity costs of production at the sector or branch level lead to different patterns of comparative advantage which then form the basis of international trade.

If we follow the predictions of Ricardo or Heckscher and Ohlin, nineteenth-century Germany developed a comparative advantage in capital-intensive production, specifically in the products of the 'second industrial revolution': chemicals, electrical engineering, and (motor) vehicles. In particular, in the three decades before World War I, exports of chemicals (SITC 5) grew by about 100 percent and those of machinery and transport equipment (SITC 7) by more than 700 percent (Table 16.2). Nevertheless, in 1913 the largest export items also included coal, cotton fabrics, and hides and skins. Nevertheless, according to Table 16.2 imports also grew in sectors in which Germany supposedly had a comparative advantage, namely in industrial and manufactured products (SITC 5–8). Conversely, exports of agricultural products and raw materials increased (SITC sectors 0, 2, and 3).

A simplified version of revealed comparative advantage (RCA) serves to consider sectoral and regional comparative cost advantages in a more differentiated way (Hungerland and Wolf 2022).[2] The RCA index used here uses the difference between normalized net exports in sector or with trade partner i and a normalized net trade balance, weighted with the share of i in total trade:

$$RCA_{it} = \frac{X_{it} - M_{it}}{X_{it} + M_{it}} - \frac{\sum_{it}(X_{it} - M_{it})}{\sum_{it}(X_{it} - M_{it})} \times \frac{X_{it} + M_{it}}{\sum_{it}(X_{it} + M_{it})} \times 100 \qquad \text{(eq. 2)}$$

X denotes exports, M denotes imports and all i-wise indices sum up to zero. A positive RCA index value points to a comparative advantage in sector i, a negative value to a comparative disadvantage.

Figure 16.5 maps the RCA indices for SITC 1-digit sectors (left) and by continents (right). At first glance, panel A shows the expected pattern: Germany showed a comparative advantage in the industry, namely, in chemicals, machinery, and in the broad class of manufactured goods (SITC 6). Comparison between 1880 and 1913 also shows that most advantages became stronger over time. Among SITC 3-digit industries, Germany had especially strong advantages in synthetic dyes (SITC 531), fertilizers (SITC 562),

Table 16.2 Sectoral trade growth

SITC 1-Digit sector		*Imports*	*Exports*
0	Food and live animals	159%	121%
1	Beverages and tobacco	3%	−59%
2	Crude/raw materials, inedible, except fuels	162%	39%
3	Mineral fuels, lubricants, and related materials	141%	431%
4	Animal and vegetable oils, fats, and waxes	36%	−32%
5	Chemicals and related products	50%	102%
6	Manufactured goods classified chiefly by material	114%	140%
7	Machinery and transport equipment	259%	734%
8	Miscellaneous manufactured articles	133%	133%
9	Other commodities and transactions	2542%	44%

Source: Hungerland/Wolf (2022). Growth in percent from 1880 to 1913.

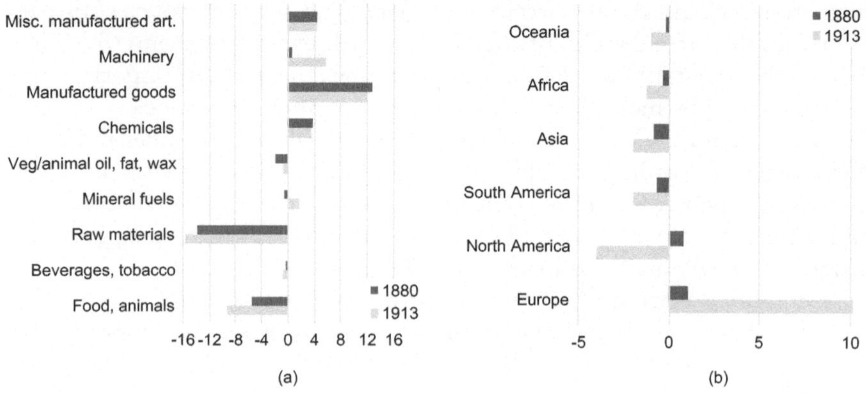

Figure 16.5 Comparative advantage.

Source: Hungerland and Wolf (2022). RCA indices by SITC 1-digit sector. For definitions, see text.

Notes: (a) SITC-1 digit sectors (b) Continents.

railway vehicles and wagons (SITC 791), automobiles (SITC 781) and agricultural machinery (SITC 721). There were comparative advantages in other industries as well, e.g., for sugar (SITC 601, cf. section 3.2.), shoes (SITC 851) or paper and cardboard (SITC 641), and, as mentioned, coal (included in the SITC 1-digit sector mineral fuels).

Panel B of Figure 16.5 depicts Germany's comparative advantage broken down by continent. It becomes clear that advantages only existed in relation to European neighbours, especially the United Kingdom, the Netherlands, Austria-Hungary, Switzerland, France, and Belgium—Germany's main trading partners (the Russian Empire was an important exception). Vis-à-vis the rest of the world, Germany revealed a comparative disadvantage. Differentiating by SITC-1-digit varieties, an even more differentiated picture emerges: with Russia, Germany had its strongest comparative advantage in manufactured goods (SITC 6), but at the same time its largest disadvantage in food and live animals (SITC 0) and raw materials (SITC 3). Thus, Germany's comparative advantage becomes more nuanced the more we look beyond broadly defined sectors, namely, at individual products and trading partners: specialization is clearly visible, and this took place in a highly specific manner across goods and trading partners. Moreover, in many sectors, significant changes are visible over relatively short periods—Germany's comparative advantage was thus often local rather than global, and dynamic (Redding 1999; Deardorff 2004).

4.4 Intra-industry trade

There is a further characteristic of German foreign trade before the First World War that the traditional narrative based on two-factor models (as in

O'Rourke and Williamson 1999) and relative cost differences can only insufficiently explain: reciprocal or intra-industry trade (IIT), that is simultaneous imports and exports in the same product category. Germany also exported goods in which it supposedly had no comparative advantage, and imported goods it should primarily have been exporting according to classical trade theories. Hungerland and Wolf (2022) calculate indices of IIT at the SITC-5-digit level to measure the extent of IIT:

$$IIT_{it} = \frac{(X_{it} + M_{it}) - |X_{it} + M_{it}|}{X_{it} + M_{it}} \times 100 \qquad \text{(eq. 3)}$$

Here, X denotes exports, M imports. The index represents the proportion of IIT in each SITC 5-digit category i. Figure 16.6 reports the IIT indices for 1913, differentiating high-income and all other trading partners as well as manufactures (SITC sectors 6–8) and all other SITC 1-digit sectors. It becomes clear that about one-third of trade with the high-income economies in Europe and North America was intra-industry—in manufactures (share: 35 percent) as well as in all other goods (29 percent). Trade in copper with Portugal, in firewood with France, or in yarns with Austria-Hungary was almost completely intra-industry. By contrast, trade with less developed countries was pronouncedly inter-industry, independent of product category.

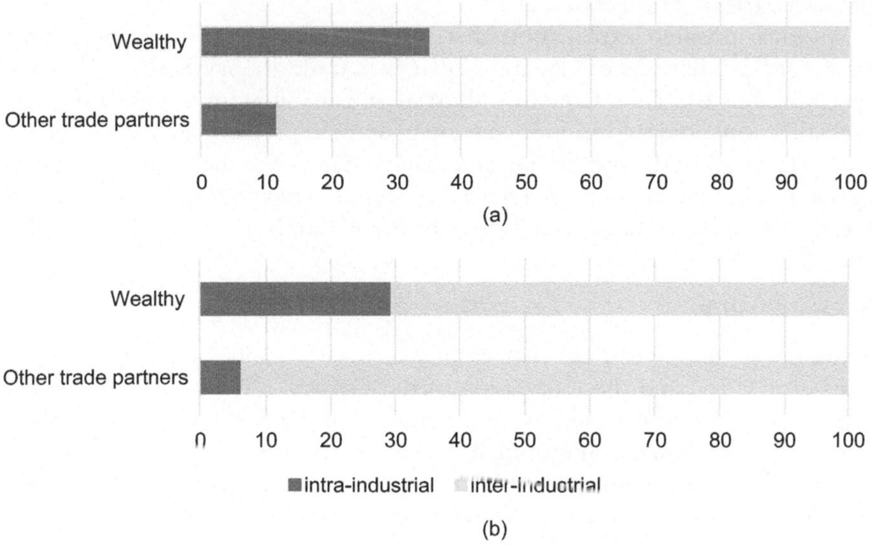

Figure 16.6 Intra-industrial trade in 1913.

Source: Hungerland and Wolf (2022). Percent of total foreign trade. For definitions, see text.

Notes: (a) SITC-1 digit sectors 0 to 4 (b) SITC-1 digit sectors 5–8.

Most traded goods were not homogeneous bulk commodities, but items that differed by manufacturer in specification and quality (Brown 1995). The majority of traded products did not come from high-tech sectors but were conventionally manufactured consumer goods (Buchheim 1986). Trade in such goods is typically characterized not only by differences in factor endowments but also by monopolistic competition, product differentiation, and economies of scale, respectively (Krugman 1979, 1980). Increasing returns to scale occur when falling trade costs increase market size, resulting in more units being sold. This spreads the fixed costs of production—which are often significant in industry—over a larger batch size, causing average unit costs—and with them the price—to fall and sales to increase. In the presence of increasing returns to scale, specialization often takes place within a product category, so that markets with products differentiated by quality, brand, and so on, emerge. That kind of IIT arises mainly between wealthier, i.e. 'larger' economies that resemble each other in preferences, factor endowments, and market size. For example, Brown (1995) documents the pronounced monopolistic competition in high-income export markets for German cotton textiles, a traditional industry characterized by high fixed costs. The IIT observed between Germany and its high-income trading partners matches the consumer capitalism that gradually emerged from the late nineteenth century and fully developed in the mid-twentieth century. The presence of monopolistic competition, product differentiation, and economies of scale suggests that during the first globalization, international trade led to welfare gains in Germany not only through comparative advantage but also by increasing product variety (Hungerland 2018).

Another possible explanation that might reconcile the seemingly contradictory predictions of classical and newer trade theory is that Germany specialized at the same time in industrial and manufactured goods (*between* specialization), and within more narrowly defined product categories outside manufacturing in the production and export of goods at the higher-value end of the product spectrum (*within* specialization). However, showing this for the German Empire remains a subject for future research.

5 Conclusion

From the perspective of the history of globalization and foreign trade, German unification and the foundation of the German Empire in 1871 do not represent a structural break. Since the middle of the nineteenth century, the first wave of globalization unfolded, fuelled by technological progress—most notably the steam engine—and by Europe-wide free trade policy that also encompassed Germany and eliminated the last remnants of mercantilism. The unification of Lesser Germany occurred in the middle of this period; it was preceded by the *Zollverein*, which promoted the economic integration of a similar territory. Besides the formation of the *Zollverein* in 1834 and its reconfiguration in 1865/66, the protectionist turn under Bismarck in 1879 was particularly important for foreign trade. It created modern German trade statistics, which, like the accession of Hamburg and Bremen to the German customs territory in 1889, left its mark on the sources underlying the study of Germany's globalization experience.

The conventional account of the first globalization portrays it as the deepening of the division of labour between a labour and capital-rich Old World and a land-rich New World. While German trade policy since 1879 corresponds to this picture, a pattern of between-sector specialization driven by comparative advantage can only be observed to a limited extent with respect to Germany's foreign trade. Comparative advantages also existed in trade with neighbouring countries in Europe, were often local, and evolved dynamically. Furthermore, an increasing part of German foreign trade occurred in the form of intra-industry trade, driven by monopolistic competition in markets characterized by product differentiation and economies of scale. Such a pattern already foreshadows the second era of globalization from the mid-twentieth century. Thus, with its transition to modern economic growth, the German economy in the late nineteenth century also changed the nature of its integration into the international economy.

Notes

1 All figures in this section—if not indicated otherwise—are from Rahlf (2016).
2 In contrast to Balassa's (1965) RCA index, the Lafay (1992) index used here only requires data from one country and not the disaggregated data of all sectors and trade partners.

References

Aldenhoff-Hübinger, R. (2002) *Agrarpolitik und Protektionismus: Deutschland und Frankreich im Vergleich 1879–1914*, Göttingen: Vandenhoeck & Ruprecht.

Armington, P. (1969) 'A theory of demand for products distinguished by place of production', *International Monetary Fund Staff Papers*, Vol. 16 (1): 159–78.

Balassa, B. (1965) 'Trade liberalisation and revealed comparative advantage', *The Manchester School*, Vol. 33 (2): 99–123.

Bondi, G. (1958) *Deutschlands Aussenhandel 1815–1870*, Berlin: Akademie.

Borries, B. (1970) *Deutschlands Außenhandel 1836–1856: Eine statistische Untersuchung zur Frühindustrialisierung*, Stuttgart: Fischer.

Brentano, L. J. (1925) *Die deutschen Getreidezölle*, Stuttgart: Cotta.

Brinkmann, T. (2008) '"Travelling with Ballin": the impact of American immigration policies on Jewish transmigration within Central Europe, 1880–1914', *International Review of Social History*, Vol. 53 (3): 459–84.

Broadberry, S. and Burhop, C. (2007) 'Comparative productivity in British and German manufacturing before World War II: reconciling direct benchmark estimates and time series projections', *Journal of Economic History*, Vol. 67 (2): 315–49.

Brown, J. C. (1995) 'The imperfect competition and Anglo-German trade rivalry: markets for cotton textiles before 1914', *Journal of Economic History*, Vol. 55 (3): 494–527.

Buchheim, C. (1982) *Deutsche Gewerbeexporte nach England in der zweiten Hälfte des 19. Jahrhunderts*, Ostfildern: Scripta Mercaturae.

Buchheim, C. (1986) 'Germany on the world market at the end of the 19th century: successful supplier of consumer related manufactures', in H. Pohl and B. Rudolph (eds), *German Yearbook on Business History*, Berlin: Springer, pp. 41–55.

Burhop, C. (2011) *Wirtschaftsgeschichte des Kaiserreichs 1871–1918*, Göttingen: Vandenhoeck & Ruprecht.

Chiswick, B. and Hatton, T. (2003) 'International migration and the integration of labor markets', in M. D. Bordo, A. M. Taylor and J. G. Williamson (eds), *Globalization in Historical Perspective*, Chicago: University of Chicago Press, pp. 65–117.

Deardorff, A. V. (2004) 'Local comparative advantage: trade costs and the pattern of trade', *RSIE Discussion Papers* 500.

Dedinger, B. (2015) 'Trade statistics of the Zollverein, 1834–1871', *Revue de l'OFCE*, Vol. 140: 67–85.

Findlay, R. and O' Rourke, K. H. (2009) *Power and Plenty: Trade, War and the World Economy in the Second Millennium*, Princeton, N.J.: Princeton University Press.

Gerloff, W. (1908) 'Verbrauch und Verbrauchsbelastung kleiner und mittlerer Einkommen in Deutschland um die Wende des 19. Jahrhunderts: eine konsum- und finanzstatistische Studie', *Jahrbücher für Nationalökonomie und Statistik*, Vol. 35 (1): 1–44, 145–72.

Gerschenkron, A. (1943) *Bread and Democracy in Germany*, Berkeley: Cornell University Press.

Hardach, G. (1977) *The First World War 1914–1918*, London: University of California Press.

Hungerland, W.-F. (2018) 'The gains from import variety in two globalisations: evidence from Germany', *European Historical Economics Society Working Paper* 120.

Hungerland, W.-F. and Altmeppen, C. (2021) 'What is a product anyway? Applying the standard international trade classification (SITC) to historical data', *Historical Methods*, Vol. 54 (2): 65–79.

Hungerland, W.-F. and Wolf, N. (2022) 'The panopticon of Germany's foreign trade, 1880–1913: new facts on the first globalization', *European Review of Economic History*, Vol. 26 (4): 479–507.

Huning, T. and Wolf, N. (2019) 'How Britain unified Germany: endogenous trade costs and the formation of a customs union, *CEPR Discussion Paper* 13634.

Hunt, J. C. (1974) 'Peasants, grain tariffs and meat quotas: Imperial German protectionism reexamined', *Central European History*, Vol. 7 (4): 311–31.

Kehr, E. (1930) *Schlachtflottenbau und Parteipolitik 1894–1901*, Berlin: Ebering.

Kling, G., Baten, J. and Labuske, K. (2011) 'FDI of German companies during globalization and deglobalization', *Open Economies Review*, Vol. 22 (2): 247–70.

Krugman, P. (1979) 'Increasing returns, monopolistic competition, and international trade', *Journal of International Economics*, Vol. 9 (4): 469–79.

Krugman, P. (1980) 'Scale economies, product differentiation, and the pattern of trade', *American Economic Review*, Vol. 70 (5): 950–59.

Labuske, K. and Streb, J. (2008) 'Technological creativity and cheap labour? Explaining the growing international competitiveness of German mechanical engineering before World War I', *German Economic Review*, Vol. 9 (1): 65–86.

Lafay, G. (1992) 'The measurement of revealed comparative advantage', in M. G. Dagenais and P.-A. Muet (eds), *International Trade Modelling*, London: CRC Press, pp. 209–34.

Lampe, M. (2008) 'Bilateral trade flows in Europe, 1857–1875: a new dataset', *Research in Economic History*, Vol. 26: 81–155.

Lampe, M. (2020) 'European trade policy in the 19th century', *Oxford Research Encyclopedia of Economics and Finance*, https://doi.org/10.1093/acrefore/9780190625979.013.551.

Lampe, M. and Sharp, P. (2013) 'Tariffs and income: a time series analysis for 24 countries', *Cliometrica*, Vol. 7 (2): 207–35.

Lehmann, S. H. (2010) 'The German elections in the 1870s: why Germany turned from liberalism to protectionism', *Journal of Economic History*, Vol. 70 (1): 146–78.

Lehmann, S. H. and O'Rourke, K. H. (2011) 'The structure of protection and growth in the late nineteenth century', *Review of Economics and Statistics*, Vol. 93 (2): 606–16.

Lewis, A. W. (1983) 'The rate of growth of world trade, 1830–1973', in S. Grassman and E. Lundberg (eds), *The World Economic Order: Past and Prospects*, London: Palgrave Macmillan, pp. 11–81.

Marsh, P. T. (1999) *Bargaining on Europe: Britain and the First Common Market, 1860–1892*, New Haven: Yale University Press.

Melitz, M. J. and Redding, S. J. (2014) 'Heterogeneous firms and trade', in G. Gopinath, E. Helpman and K. Rogoff (eds), *Handbook of International Economics Vol. 4*, Amsterdam: Elsevier, pp. 1–54.

O'Rourke, K. H. (1997) 'The European grain invasion, 1870–1913', *Journal of Economic History*, Vol. 57 (4): 775–801.

O'Rourke, K. H. and Williamson, J. G. (1999) *Globalization and History: The Evolution of a Nineteenth-Century Atlantic Economy*, Cambridge, MA: MIT Press.

Ploeckl, F. (2015) 'The Zollverein and the sequence of a customs union', *Australian Economic History Review*, Vol. 55 (3): 277–300.

Plumpe, W. (2019) *Das kalte Herz*, Berlin: Rowohlt.

Rahlf, T. (2016) 'The German time series dataset, 1834–2012', *Jahrbücher für Nationalökonomie und Statistik*, Vol. 236 (1): 129–43.

Redding, S. J. (1999) 'Dynamic comparative advantage and the welfare effects of trade', *Oxford Economic Papers*, Vol. 51 (1): 15–39.

Roeske, U. (1978) 'Die amtliche Statistik des Deutschen Reichs 1872 bis 1939: historische Entwicklung, Organisationsstruktur, Veröffentlichungen', *Jahrbuch für Wirtschaftsgeschichte*, Vol. 19 (4): 85–95.

Roeske, U. (1985) 'Das amtliche Quellenwerk der deutschen Reichsstatistik: eine Übersicht über die Veröffentlichungsreihe 'Statistik des Deutschen Reichs' 1873 bis 1944', *Jahrbuch für Wirtschaftsgeschichte*, Vol. 26 (1): 213–43.

Schaefer, K.-C. (1995) *Deutsche Portfolioinvestitionen im Ausland 1870–1914*, Münster: LIT.

Teichmann, U. (1955) *Die Politik der Agrarpreisstützung: Marktbeeinflussung als Teil des Agrarinterventionismus in Deutschland*, Cologne: Bund.

Tena-Junguito, A., Lampe, M. and Tâmega Fernandes, F. (2012) 'How much trade liberalization was there in the world before and after Cobden-Chevalier?', *Journal of Economic History*, Vol. 72 (3): 708–40.

Tilly, R. (1990) *Vom Zollverein zum Industriestaat: die wirtschaftlich-soziale Entwicklung Deutschlands 1834–1914*, München: DTV.

Torp. C. (2010) 'The 'Coalition of 'rye and iron' under the pressure of globalization: a reinterpretation of Germany's political economy before 1914', *Central European History*, Vol. 43 (4): 401–27.

Torp. C. (2014) *The Challenges of Globalization: Economy and Politics in Germany, 1860–1914*, New York: Berghahn.

Uebele, M. (2013) 'What drives commodity market integration? Evidence from the 1800s', *CESifo Economic Studies*, Vol. 59 (2): 412–42.

Webb, S. B. (1974) 'Tariff protection for the iron industry, cotton textiles, and agriculture in Germany, 1879–1914', *Jahrbücher für Nationalökonomie und Statistik*, Vol. 192 (3–4): 336–57.

Webb, S. B. (1980) 'Tariffs, cartels, technology and growth in the German steel industry, 1879 to 1914', *Journal of Economic History*, Vol. 40 (2): 309–29.

Webb, S. B. (1982) 'Agricultural protection in Wilhelminian Germany: forging an empire with pork and rye', *Journal of Economic History*, Vol. 42 (2): 309–26.

Wehler, H.-U. (1994) *Das Deutsche Kaiserreich 1871–1918*, 7th ed., Göttingen: Vandenhoeck & Ruprecht.

Wolf, N. (2022) 'Zahlungsbilanz', in T. Rahlf (ed), *Deutschland in Daten*, Bonn: Bundeszentrale für politische Bildung, pp. 298–309.

Zorn, W. (1963) 'Wirtschafts- und sozialgeschichtliche Zusammenhänge der Reichsgründungszeit (1850–1879)', *Historische Zeitschrift*, Vol. 197: 318–42.

Part IV

State and economic development in a European perspective

17 Political change and the origins of protectionism

A French–German comparison (1860s to 1890s)

Jean-Pierre Dormois

1 Introduction

The customs tariff sponsored by Chancellor Bismarck and passed by the Reichstag on 12 July 1879 represents a landmark in German and European history. This decision casts perhaps as long a shadow as the infamous Smoot-Hawley Act enacted by the Congress of the United States in June 1930, universally blamed for deepening the incipient depression. Although the introduction of protective tariffs in Germany was preceded by tariff revisions in Russia and Spain in 1877 and in Italy, Switzerland, Austria-Hungary, and Romania in 1878, it is credited to have signalled the beginning of the protectionist turn in Europe after the 'free-trade interlude' (Bairoch 1989). However, few contemporaries saw the German Customs Act of 1879 as an essential turning point or even a precursor of future developments. Only some historians of the interwar period, among them most notably Gerschenkron (1989), developed such a view. Such a 'turn to protectionism' was viewed as being intimately linked with the other expansive and aggressive policies of the German Empire with far-reaching consequences: 'High tariffs ultimately led to two world wars and to fascism' (Gourevitch 1977: 282).

By contrast, the French conversion to protectionism that came with the enacting of the Méline[1] tariff in January 1892 has been treated more leniently; only Sternhell (1986) has hinted at a link with 'French fascism'. Perhaps the protectionist turn was 'worse than a crime, it was a mistake', as it further strengthened the powerful forces that insulated the French economy from changes in the outside world. Other critics argue that it was yet another instance of building an ineffectual 'Maginot line', which did not prevent the stagnation of the French economy. However, many historians agree that the turn to protectionism heralded the formation of a new conservative consensus similar to that in Germany.

The present study attempts to show that the chronology advocated by this literature is wrong in several respects: In a remarkable chronological parallel, both countries erected protective trade barriers in the 1880s to stem the so-called European grain invasion, which threatened to submerge their domestic markets and damage their food producing sector. It was only in its aftermath

DOI: 10.4324/9781003283430-21

that the Bismarck tariff of 1879 veered towards heavy agricultural protection, while the Méline tariff of 1892 only consolidated the piecemeal measures taken in the previous years and complemented them with tariffs on selected industrial products.

For a long time, historians on the two banks of the Rhine have naturally focussed on the idiosyncrasies of each political setup. German historians of the interwar period, such as Kehr (1928, 1965) and Rosenberg (1943, 1967), considered Bismarck's *Schutzzoll* policy a constitutive element of the German *Sonderweg*. After 1945, the Méline tariff was increasingly regarded as an outgrowth of the 'Malthusian'—meaning adverse to growth—inclinations of French capitalists. With the privilege of hindsight, it is easy today to stress instead the remarkable similarities in the ways the protectionist turn took place both in the two countries as well as in other neighbouring countries. The fact is that analogous political considerations and constraints governed customs policy in many countries. The first guiding principle was the need for new state revenue, which was most easily satisfied by imposing new tariffs (Section 2). It was superseded by the 'globalisation backlash', specifically the need to alleviate the consequences of the deep economic slump in the mid-1870s (Section 3). Also significant was that the most affected sectors of the economy began to organise themselves to influence policy decisions. Section 4 is accordingly devoted to comparing the organisation and strategies of the pressure groups that emerged in these critical years. Procedures of decision-making at the executive level and in the legislatures are examined in Section 5. Both countries were at the time experimenting with some measure of representative democracy, but the exact nature of the relationship between parliaments and the executive differed considerably. However, variations in institutional structure seems to have played a subordinate role. 'Different political systems produced very similar policy outcomes' (Gourevitch 1977: 293).

2 The transition from trade liberalisation to trade protection

2.1 Restraint is called for: preserving the gains from liberalisation

French exporters were among the primary beneficiaries of the initial phase of trade liberalisation. In the two decades before 1870, France recorded the second-fastest growth in foreign trade among European countries (after Denmark), with an average rate of increase of 12 percent per annum. Advances in transport and communication technology mainly drove the growth of international trade. Moreover, this was also supported by a policy shift towards the liberal model of Britain, in which tariffs served only as a source of public revenue rather than a barrier to trade. Specifically, the Cobden–Chevalier Treaty concluded between France and Britain in January 1860 was pivotal in ushering in an era of trade liberalisation in Europe.

The German *Zollverein* was the third largest beneficiary of trade liberalisation in Europe in export growth. The treaty concluded between Prussia and France on 2 August 1862 integrated the *Zollverein* into the emerging Cobden–Chevalier network. Thanks to the most favoured nation clause, Bismarck aimed to preserve access to the markets of important trading partners. It was through prior bi-lateral treaties concluded by France that Germany gained access to the vast network of trade partners of Belgium and the United Kingdom (Henderson 1968: 293, 293). In this way, Germany could hope to substitute France as the hub of the trade network on the Continent—which it largely succeeded in doing in the following decades.

After 1871, the German Empire's government had good reasons to maintain an arrangement that had served German export interests well. The conservative politicians who were in power in France until 1879 acted with restraint on the issue of trade policy as well. As late as February 1877, the French government was considering liberalising foreign trade further. Against this background, the aggregate tariff rate (tariff revenue divided by import value) reached its lowest point in both France and Germany around the middle of the 1870s (Figure 17.1).

2.2 The quest for state revenue

Recent scholarship on late nineteenth-century protectionism has revived the view that fiscal considerations were the driving force behind introducing

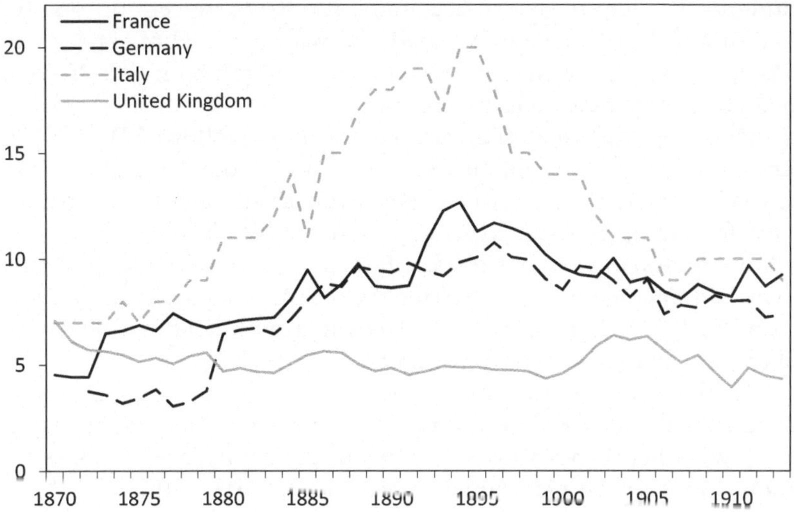

Figure 17.1 Aggregate tariff rates in select European countries 1870–1913 (ratio of tariff revenues to import value).

Source: Dormois (2008).

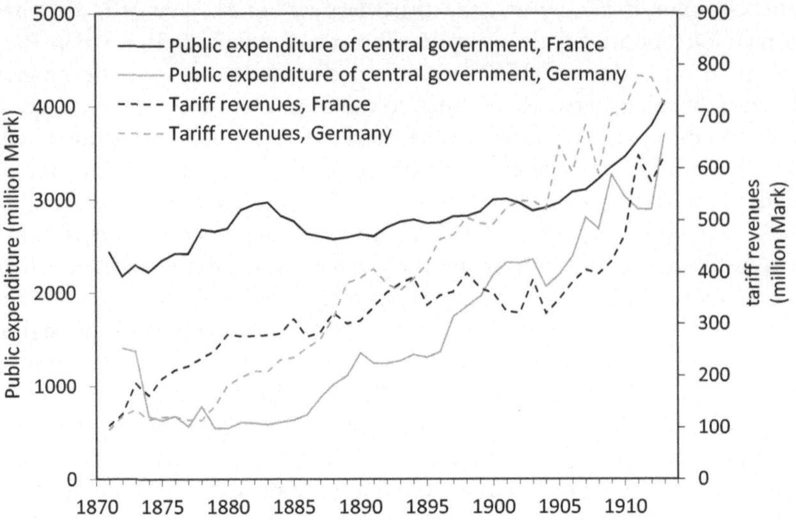

Figure 17.2 Public expenditure of the central government and tariff revenues in France and Germany, 1871–1913.
Source: Dormois (2008).

new tariffs (Pahre 2008: 105–15). New resources had to be found to meet the needs of growing states. Data on expenditures of central government show significant growth for both France and Germany (Figure 17.2). The resources accruing to the Empire, which accounted for 30–35 percent of total public expenditure in Germany, almost caught up with the level of expenditure of the French central government, which comprised the bulk (70–85 percent) of total public expenditure in this country.

In a sense, the expansion of government spending followed Wagner's Law, which states that as per capita income rises, so does the demand for government services. In addition, however, governments also sought to expand state activity, for example, in the areas of education, health, transport, and welfare. More resources were needed for all these tasks. As a result, 'government officials had an interest in restricting free trade for purely fiscal motives' (Meadwell 2002: 632). In this respect, late-nineteenth-century policy-makers faced two challenges and one constraint.

First, in the absence of detailed and accurate data on individuals' resources, government officials faced an information asymmetry, making it expedient to tax flows rather than stocks. This explains the dominance of indirect taxes on transactions in the government revenue structure at the time. Second, with average income levels roughly equivalent to a tenth of what they are today,[2] the tax base was necessarily very narrow and concentrated on the small group of recipients of high incomes. As this group corresponded with the ruling class, any expansion of their tax burden met with great resistance. Thus, in France, more than in Germany, the introduction of a nationwide income tax was fiercely opposed. Léon Say (1826–96),[3] when he was Minister of Finance, introduced a bill for an income tax in 1891, which met with fierce opposition in the Chamber of Deputies and had to be abandoned. In the German Empire, direct taxation fell under the authority of the states, which levied an income tax in one form or another. In Prussia, the Minister of Finance Johannes Miquel (1828–1901) succeeded in 1891 in reforming the system of direct taxation and introducing progressive taxation, which more than doubled tax revenue the following year (Spoerer 2004). In such circumstances, indirect taxation appeared to politicians the easiest way to raise state revenue, and customs duties represented France's fastest-growing government revenue during the three decades after 1880 (Figure 17.3).

2.3 The first step is the hardest: the challenge of forging political alliances

Although it was presented as a 'protective tariff' (*Schutzzoll*), the law of 15 July 1879 appears retrospectively as merely a timid step in this direction. The French tariff of 7 May 1881 shares many of its features but was instead branded as too conservative, too free-trade oriented. 'We have obtained a new version of the 1860 treaty', protested Jules Méline, who later contributed significantly to the 1892 Customs Act and was then a mere backbencher in the Chamber of Deputies.

In 1878, the *Association de l'Industrie française* held a congress in Paris chaired by Augustin Pouyer-Quertier, a textile manufacturer and former Minister of Finance, to launch a campaign for a protectionist tariff. In its aftermath, its

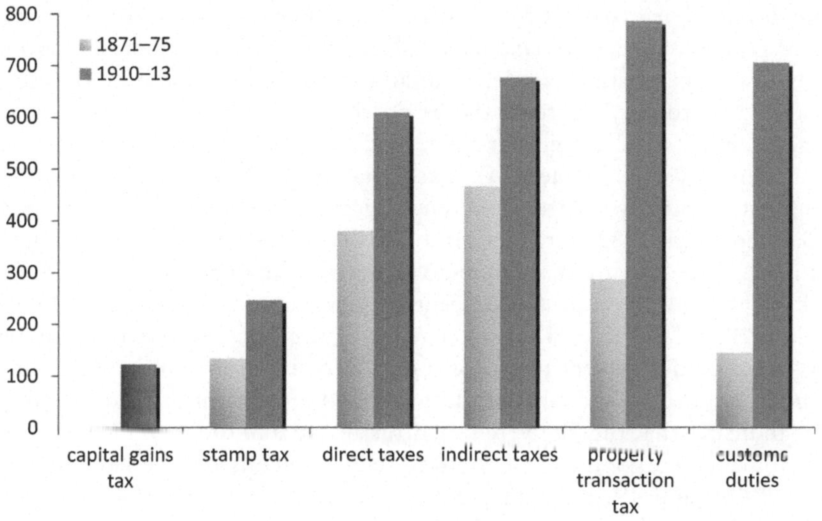

Figure 17.3 Government revenue by tax category in France, 1871–1913.
Source: Annuaire Statistique de la France, several years.

members succeeded to form a coalition with agricultural interests. However, the cooperation foundered in 1881, first in the Chamber, where the supporters of protective tariffs for industry failed to vote for the protection of agriculture, then in the Senate, where the agrarians broke ranks by voting against tariffs on textile imports. As a result, the changes fell short of the protectionists' expectations: The general tariff on manufactured goods was raised by an average of 24 percent, but it only applied to a minority of France's trade partners (seven out of 68). The only gains for the protectionist camp were that specific tariffs levied by quantity were replaced by ad valorem tariffs (computed on the basis of value). This ensured that tariffs on foodstuffs could not be reduced in any future commercial treaty.

In its basic features, the so-called 'Iron and Rye Tariff' of the German Empire enacted in 1879 differed only marginally from its French counterpart of 1881. It led to an increase in tariff revenues from 130 million Mark in 1880 to 200 million in 1884; by 1891, they reached 400 million Mark. While imports of raw materials remained duty-free and the rates for 44 dutiable products were left unchanged, the rates for 14 goods were increased. These included consumer goods such as spirits, wine, coffee, tea, and tobacco, and four classes of already taxed products, namely petroleum, scientific instruments, vehicles, and lamps, were newly added to the list of taxable imports. These were primarily grain and milling products. Imports of live animals (horses, oxen, and sheep), pig iron and semi-finished iron products, machinery and railway equipment, as well as timber and lumber were also affected. An amendment published on 25 July also made imports of flour, artificial wine, oil and fats, and cattle subject to tariffs.

As was common practice, the German and French tariff laws of 1879/81 were designed primarily as fiscal instruments. They mainly weighed on consumer goods, which were characterised by extensive consumption and relatively low price elasticity of demand, and for which no domestic substitutes existed. Accordingly, customs duties on these imports—coffee, tea, cocoa, tobacco, spices, and tropical fruit—accounted for a disproportionate share of customs revenue (Table 17.1). Excluding tropical commodities from the computation wholly reduces the French aggregate duty rate by half (from 6.7 to 3.3 percent in 1882), a reduction that also obtains for the Bismarck tariff.

In 1882, the ten most remunerative dutiable imports accounted for the bulk of customs revenue (60 percent in Germany, 47.5 percent in France; Table 17.1), while 45 and 23 percent of all imports respectively remained duty-free. Goods subject to customs duty accounted for only 20 percent of German imports, while customs duty covered 68 percent of French imports. This indicates that the Zollverein had further liberalised its trade, especially in manufactured goods, prior to 1877 than France had. The later tariffs of 1892, 1906, and 1910 would preserve the features of the compromise of 1879/81: Essentially conceived as revenue-raising instruments, import tariffs were intended to provide sometimes superficial but in some cases effective

Table 17.1 Imported products most heavily taxed in 1881/82

	Germany				France		
	Amount revenue (Mm)	*Duty rate (%)*	*Share of revenue (%)*		*Amount revenue (Fm)*	*Duty rate (%)*	*Share of revenue (%)*
Coffee and tea	43.2	30.8	22.5	Coffee	67.6	68.3	19.5
Breadstuffs	19.7	5.7	10.2	Colonial sugar	37.5	73.1	10.8
Tobacco	19.4	52.9	10.1	Foreign sugar	31.9	53.9	9.2
Wine	10.8	20.0	5.6	Mineral oils	12.4	72.5	3.6
Tropical fruit	5.9	16.4	3.1	Cotton tissues	6.1	12.8	1.8
Cattle	4.4	2.3	2.3	Cotton yarn	2.6	12.0	0.8
Cotton yarn	4.0	4.4	2.1	Tools and machinery	2.8	7.7	0.8
Timber	2.8	3.3	1.4	Linen from flax	1.3	10.0	0.4
Pig iron	2.5	4.7	1.3	Pig iron	1.1	16.2	0.3
Spices	2.2	17.5	1.2	Manufactured tobacco	0.8	22.9	0.2
10 products			59.8				47.5

Sources: Own computation based on Statistisches Jahrbuch für das Deutsche Reich 1884; Tableaux du commerce de la France 1882.

protection for some sectors, but not to the extent of excluding imports and/or drying up revenue.

2.4 Stepping up protectionist measures, 1885–1892

The provisions in the laws of 1879 and 1881 soon proved utterly inadequate to stem the continuous fall in agricultural prices and stop the grain invasion. 'In Germany as in France [...] it was cheap grain that triggered the return to protection' (O'Rourke and Williamson 1999: 101). In a remarkable parallel, both countries significantly increased taxation on agricultural imports in 1885, with further increases following in 1887/88. By this time, German tariffs, except for those on barley and sheep, were higher than French tariffs, but the Méline tariff of 1892 and further increases in 1894 reversed this situation, following tariff reductions for Romania and Russia under German chancellor Caprivi.

It is uncertain whether the increased tariffs actually protected French agriculture from import competition. There is evidence that they did mitigate the fall in prices to some extent. But as France was not self-sufficient in many commodities, the country still had to rely on imports after poor harvests. In May 1898, Méline, who had become Prime Minister, suspended the 1892 wheat duty named after him for a month to allow urgently needed grain imports into the country quickly. Over the whole period until the early twentieth century, the tariff on grain imports hardly proved to be an effective defence against import competition. While it insulated domestic prices to some extent, it could not influence the level of imports and their change from year to year. The variations in the implicit tariff rate (measured by the ex post ad valorem equivalent, the ratio between the collected tariff revenue and import value) suggest that there were loopholes and that in years of plenty, a portion of the tariff was indeed paid by foreign suppliers (who had to lower their selling price in order to be able to sell their products). In this respect, the German tariff scheme seems to have been more efficient, especially in the case of rye, not least thanks to a system of transferable import certificates (*Einfuhrscheine*; see Gerschenkron 1989: 68–70). While the ratio of customs revenue to import value ('nominal protection') for wheat fluctuated between 15 and 25 percent in France during the 1890s, this figure was more stable in Germany (between 22 and 27 percent; compare also the last rows in Table 17.2 with the 'ex ante' rows).

Political scientists have therefore probably exaggerated the differences between French and German tariff policies. On paper, it seems that the German tariff protected agriculture from import competition better than its French counterpart. In 1894, the cost of protection on consumables was estimated at 7.3 Mark and 10.5 Francs (8.4 Mark) per person, respectively (Rosenbaum 1908: 343). However, the greater reliance of German tariff revenues on staple imports had the same result as the French tendency to rely on purely fiscal tariffs, namely those on colonial goods.

Table 17.2 Changes in the French and German tariffs, 1885–94 (ad valorem equivalents, in percent)

	1885		*1887/88*		*1892/94*	
ex ante	*France*	*Germany*	*France*	*Germany*	*France*	*Germany*
Wheat	13.4	21.6	23.1	37.0	42.4	32.4
Rye	9.5	25.0	22.2	41.0	18.8	30.1
Barley	9.0	9.5	17.8	14.1	18.2	13.7
Oats	8.8	12.6	16.8	35.3	17.6	25.7
Maize	0.0	6.0	0.0	9.0	20.0	7.5
Flour	19.1	33.0	25.1	41.2	48.0	34.1
Meat, salted	4.0	18.9	3.3	18.9	17.9	14.7
Oxen	5.6	32.1	8.8	33.3	9.3	23.2
Sheep	6.7	1.1	12.2	1.1	39.7	1.0
Pigs	5.7	6.4	6.3	7.0	7.0	5.5
actual (ex post)	*1886*		*1888*		*1894*	
Breadstuffs	7.1	18.1	15.8	29.6	16.9	23.1
Live animals	4.3	1.5	5.8	1.7	4.8	1.6

Source: Own computation based on Statistik des Deutschen Reichs and Annuaire Statistique de la France, various years.
Note: 'Ex ante' refers to the statutory tariff rates in relation to import prices at the time of the enactment of a law. 'Ex post' refers to the ratio between customs revenue and import value in relation to the respective category of goods.

3 Globalisation backlash: the impact of the slump

The economic slump of the second half of the 1870s provided the catalyst for the reintroduction of protectionist legislation. This crisis, which shook the internal fabric of both economies and their external balance, resulted from the forces driving the first wave of globalisation. The dramatic fall in transport costs had intensified international trade competition, which in turn gradually undermined the dominance of many industries in their domestic markets. Through the price mechanism, its effects permeated the entire supply chain and affected relative rates of return in agriculture and industry—hence the *Leutenot* (shortage of farmhands) much lamented by German and French farmers alike.

Historical research, however, has put the pessimistic perception of the economic situation by contemporaries into perspective. Despite their inherent tentativeness, existing reconstructions of national accounts justify Hans Rosenberg's appraisal of Germany that between 1875 and 1882, 'total output, commercial turnover and national wealth continued to increase, though at a distinctly lower rate' (Rosenberg 1943: 60). Thereafter, the German economy experienced a rapid upswing, interrupted only by a recession in 1890–92. By contrast, in the decade after the war with Germany, the French economy developed in an erratic up-and-down fashion—hardly surprising for a country that had been amputated of three relatively prosperous departments and had

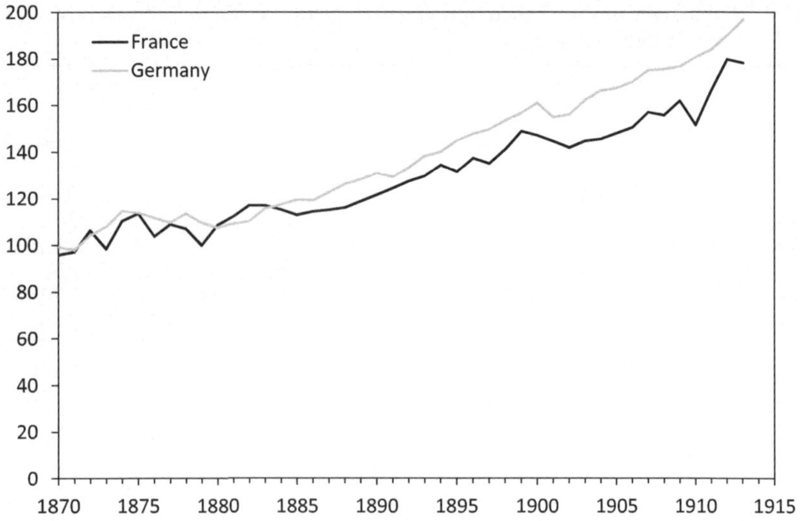

Figure 17.4 Real gross domestic product per capita in Germany and France (index, 1868–70 = 100).

Source: Maddison Project Database 2013.

paid a tribute equivalent to one-sixth of its pre-war GDP. Like Germany, France recovered at the beginning of the 1880s but continued on a much slower growth path (Figure 17.4).

3.1 The threat of the grain invasion

In the twenty years after 1848, agricultural output in both countries had expanded in an unprecedented fashion. Prussia and France had become net exporters of bread grains—France intermittently (1848–52, 1858–60, 1864–66) and Germany continuously, in the case of wheat, until 1872. After around 1870, however, both countries became increasingly dependent on imports of foodstuffs due to growing urban populations and the associated structural change (Table 17.3).

This so-called European grain invasion materialised more quickly in Germany, where wheat imports came to represent 58 percent of domestic consumption in the last decade of the nineteenth century. By contrast, domestic rye production withstood foreign competition well, and rye became an important export commodity in the first decade of the new century thanks to the import certificate system. In France, the grain invasion was limited to years following poor harvests, as in 1891 (the same year the Méline tariff was debated in the Chamber), when wheat imports reached a quarter of domestic consumption. Overall the shortfall in production was only 13 percent of consumption between 1871 and 1900.

Table 17.3 Output and imports of breadstuffs in France and Germany, annual averages in million quintals (q.m)

	France			*Germany*					
	Wheat and wheat flour			*Wheat and wheat flour*			*Rye*		
(Mq)	*Production*	*Foreign imports*		*Production*	*Foreign imports*		*Production*	*Foreign imports*	
	q.m	*q.m*	*%*	*q.m*	*q.m*	*%*	*q.m*	*q.m*	*%*
1871–74	76.0	7.0	9	–	−0.6	–	–	5.3	–
1875–79	70.6	9.7	14	–	2.3	–	–	7.3	–
1880–84	89.5	13.8	15	21.5	6.1	28	55.7	7.3	13.1
1885–89	81.6	9.4	12	24.0	4.7	20	58.3	7.4	12.7
1890–94	78.6	14.8	19	26.7	9.8	37	69.4	6.3	9.1
1895–99	104.7	6.9	7	29.2	14.6	50	82.5	8.1	9.8
1900–04	–	–	–	33.1	19.3	58	89.50	8.1	9.1

Source: Own computation based on Statistisches Jahrbuch für das Deutsche Reich and Annuaire Statistique de la France, various years.

What was most worrying for contemporaries was not so much the worsening prospects of self-sufficiency as the shrinking monetary value of domestic production. In this way, international market forces had a strong influence on politically influential groups in both countries: Through the decline in commodity prices, they reduced the profitability of farms and the market value of the land, with accompanying downward pressure on money rents.

3.2 Industries under pressure

The price deflation that accelerated around 1875 also hit the now mature industries of the first phase of industrialisation, which were confronted with the exhaustion of demand in their domestic markets and fierce competition in international markets. The railway companies were among the first victims of the downturn.

Partially due to diminishing orders from the railway industry, iron and steel manufacturers faced falling prices, unsold inventories, and consequent overcapacity. Between 1870 and 1876, the output of iron and steel had doubled in France and Germany (Nitzsche 1905: 46), but in 1874 exports began to fall. In France, the price of pig iron dropped by 40 percent between 1873 and 1879. Within a few years, the crisis wiped out the traditional foundries of the Massif Central and the Pyrenees and put 20 percent of all puddling furnaces out of business nationwide, as their technology had now become obsolete. In Germany, excessive stocks fuelled a merciless price war, which prompted the *Verein deutscher Eisen- und Stahlindustrieller* to lobby to repeal the decision taken in 1873 to make pig iron imports duty-free from 1 January 1877.

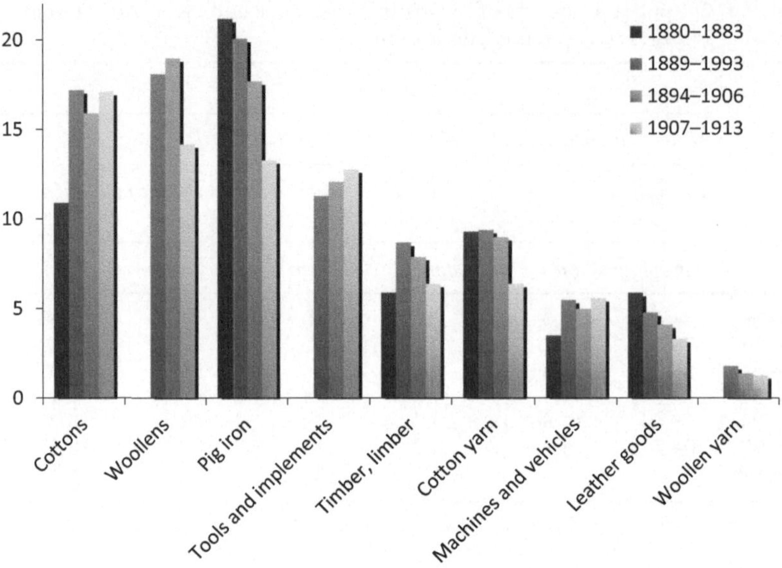

Figure 17.5 Tariffs on imports of important industrial goods in Germany, 1880–1913.
Source: Statistisches Jahrbuch für das Deutsche Reich, various years.

The situation was similarly alarming in the textile trades, as producers faced a glut both in domestic and international markets. In France, 105 weaving mills (probably a tenth of the total capacity) were either inactive or closed by 1877; in Roubaix, a centre of the woollen industry, close to a third of all looms, was out of operation at that time. A similar contraction was reported across the Rhine in Wuppertal. Unemployment became a serious problem, especially in large cities like Paris, and was included in the census nomenclature for the first time.

In the original Cobden–Chevalier agreement of 1860, provisions had been made to maintain a safety net for the traditional woollen and linen industries and the emerging cotton industry: previous outright import bans had been replaced by high tariffs for many products of these industries to protect domestic producers. In the customs regulations of 1865 issued in both France and the Zollverein, the highest rates had been reserved in each case for the finished products of the various textile industries (Nos. 49–54 of the German customs nomenclature; Figure 17.5). This was the area in which the British government had mistakenly hoped for overtures from its continental partners.

The two statesmen responsible for drafting the tariff bills in 1878 and 1891, Arnold Lohren (1836–1901) and Jules Méline, both owned spinning mills and thus knew the difficult situation of the textile industry very well. Like the iron and steel industrialists, they lobbied to maintain existing trade barriers and for increased protection against competing imports. However, to win support for their strategy, they had to consider demands from other industries. Protectionist interests had to be organised to influence political decisions effectively.

4 The logic of collective action: the role of interest groups

In comparison to the situation in the contemporary United States (see Irwin 1998), France, and Germany in the late nineteenth century offer an insight into rent-seeking strategies, especially the *log-rolling* that often accompanied them in political systems that were only partially democratic.

4.1 Industry moves first

With the relaxation of legal constraints on the formation of economic coalitions, the last decades of the nineteenth century witnessed the emergence of collective action by interest groups. In 1864, a French law had legalised industrial action and lifted the ban on so-called coalitions, allowing the creation of professional associations. Thus, the *Comité des forges*, the most important federation of the iron and steel industry, was founded on 19 February of that year on the initiative of two iron and steel magnates, Charles de Wendel and Eugène Schneider, with the avowed aim of checking the dismantling of tariff barriers initiated with the Cobden–Chevalier treaty. The founding of the *Comité* inspired W. T. Mulvany (1806–85), a German mining entrepreneur, to launch the Langnam-Verein[4] in 1871, which aimed at bringing together the interests of the Rhenish and Westphalian textile and heavy industries to influence the future trade policy of the Empire. In 1874 Karl Richter and Henry Axel Bueck sponsored an Empire-wide umbrella organisation, the *Verein Deutscher Eisen- und Stahlindustrieller*, which brought iron smelters outside Rhineland-Westphalia into the fold, especially those from Silesia and Saxony. Finally, 1876 saw the formation of the *Centralverband Deutscher Industrieller* (CDI), which also represented mostly the interests of heavy industry.

The textile industry—the other dominant industry of the time—was much more fragmented in its structure and interests across different branches (wool, worsted, cotton, flax and hemp, silk) and stages of production (spinning, weaving, finishing, garment production) with very few vertically integrated firms. Typically, the production branches at the end of the production chain (finished textiles, garments) had stakes in the export trade and were reluctant to support protection of their inputs. By contrast, producers of intermediate goods (spinning mills and some weaving mills) favoured protection for their goods and free imports of their raw materials and intermediate products. The fact that some textile fibres—specifically flax, hemp, and silk—were also produced domestically further complicated a unified strategy. This explains that no attempt was made to create an umbrella organisation for the textile industry similar to the *Verein Deutscher Eisen- und Stahlindustrieller* or the *Comité des Forges* before the protectionist campaign was already underway.

In the face of foreign competition, especially from manufacturers in Britain, the textile industry had the same handicap as the iron and steel industry, namely technological backwardness. Therefore, organisations were founded early on to protect domestic producers against import competition starting from this industry. Specifically, Auguste Mimerel, a cotton spinner and mayor of the northern city of Roubaix, founded a *Comité de l'industrie in* 1842, which was renamed the *Association de l'industrie pour la défense du travail national in* 1846. Although it was dissolved in 1863, it was revived in 1878 to attract industrial entrepreneurs keen on strengthening the protection of their markets.

To win the *Association* over to their crusade, the iron and steel industrialists had first to gloss over divergences of interest and convince them that a well-designed tariff could take care of differences between different industrial branches with respect to their need for protection. Once the two main players had agreed on a protectionist platform, many firms in smaller industries were eager to join the platform—on a 'first come, first served' basis—in an endless log-rolling process. 'In order to attract followers, the bait of drag-net tariffs was necessary: every faction was promised a share of the spoil' (Dietzel 1903: 380). Some industries—especially wood processing, chemicals, and leather processing—were able to assert their interests better than others in this process.

4.2 Building the solidarity bloc

The greatest challenge to building a powerful political base was to forge an alliance with the agrarians. Commercially oriented large landowners had organised themselves in France in the *Société des Agriculteurs de France* (1871) and in Germany in the *Kongress der Landwirte* (1868). Neither of the associations were particularly representative of the agricultural sector as a whole, and their strategy was still unclear when the consequences of the economic crisis were felt. Having previously produced exportable surpluses, the large landowners initially favoured a policy oriented toward free trade. The transition to a protectionist orientation necessitated the creation of new associations: the *Vereinigung der Steuer- und Wirtschaftsreformer* in 1876 and the *Société Nationale des Agriculteurs de France* (SNAF) in 1879. In Germany, the forging of a broad alliance progressed quickly thanks to the connections that Wilhelm von Kardorff (leading representative of the CDI) had in agrarian circles and Bismarck. In March 1878, the CDI pledged support for agricultural tariffs. Six months later, immediately after the election of the new Reichstag, a

Table 17.4 Main interest groups of the protectionist camp in Germany and France

	Germany	*France*
Iron and steel syndicate	Verein Deutscher Eisen- und Stahlindustrieller (1874)	Comité des forges (1864)
Umbrella organisation	Centralverband Deutscher Industrieller (1876)	Association de l'Industrie française (1878)
Landowners' interest group	Kongress deutscher Landwirte (1868)	Société de l'Agriculture Française (1871)
(wheat and rye)	Vereinigung der Steuer- und Wirtschaftsreform (1876)	Société Nationale des Agriculteurs de France (1879)
alliance	1878	1888

protectionist lobby group was constituted, the *Freie Wirtschaftliche Vereinigung*, which collectively petitioned Bismarck for a tariff bill. This petition was supported by 204 of the 397 Reichstag members.

Once the French protectionists had finally organised their interests, their leader, Jules Méline, followed a similar strategy: first, the unification of industrial and agrarian interests, a common platform (with the endorsement of bona fide candidates), and finally, a voting coalition of sympathetic members in the new Chamber elected in October 1889, supported by 301 signatories out of 578 deputies (Table 17.4).

Subsequently, the two peak organisations of the agrarian sector in France sought to build a network of local farmers' unions (*syndicats agricoles*) securely placed under their control. The national government lent a helping hand by extending its patronage and subsidising credit facilities. By 1910 one in five farmers was a member of a *syndicat*. In Germany, such mobilisation had not been necessary after the adoption of the tariff of 1879. Rather, it developed after the Caprivi treaties, which motivated the formation of the *Bund der Landwirte* in 1893. Its initiator Karl von Riepenhausen-Crangen (1852–1929), was allegedly inspired by the lobbying and tactics of the French agrarians of the SNAF. He promoted the foundation of numerous *Bauernvereine* (farmers' associations) and cooperatives, especially in the southern and central states (Hesse, Bavaria, Württemberg). By this time, lobbying members of parliament and advertising campaigns in newspapers had become routine.

5 The political stage

In Gallarotti's (1985) 'business model' of the protectionist turn, 'tariff legislation is sold by governments and purchased by interest groups'. Despite their growing influence, protectionist interest groups had to enter into at least an informal contract with politicians. Economic rents were to be divided among various groups in return for political support. As in the contemporary United States, the tariff debates of the late nineteenth century offer an example of 'pork-barrel' politics in action. In 1891, Guyot[5] opined that one could name the individual firm intended to be the beneficiary of the tariff provisions under discussion for a specific industry. In 1902, Schmoller—although being a supporter of protective tariffs—complained that the proposed law 'looked like the work of cartels'. While the Imperial constitution of 1871 contained distinctly authoritarian features, the French Third Republic after 1879 moved towards a purely parliamentary regime. However, as Gourevitch (1977) and others have pointed out, these differences in constitutional arrangements did not make any difference with respect to the policy outcome.

5.1 The dispute over the control of trade policy

Before 1848, customs laws were decided by oligarchic regimes. The introduction of constitutions with popular representation—the *Reichstag* in Germany and the Chamber of Deputies in France—changed the rules of the game. Policy decisions taken by the executive had now to be sanctioned by a majority of elected representatives while retaining the right of initiative of the executive. Thus, Bismarck's 'conversion' to tariff reform in 1877/78 certainly played a decisive role in its successful completion in 1879. Legend has it that he planned, should the bill face opposition in the Reichstag, to request permission from Wilhelm I to ask for a vote of confidence, which would have pushed the bill through. Similarly, Caprivi used the full weight of the executive in 1892 and 1894 to obtain ratification of the customs treaties with Romania and Russia.

During the economic crisis and as part of a change in the political constitution, France embarked on a different path, as the Assembly gained control over trade policy. First, Napoleon III had, by 'plotting' the Cobden–Chevalier treaty of 1860 without consultation, entirely bypassing the legislature, given 'fast-track' legislation a bad name. Under the constitutional laws of 1875, the prerogative over foreign policy—which included foreign trade—remained a prerogative of the president as the head of the state. However, in 1877, President MacMahon (1873–79) was unable to impose a cabinet of his choice without a parliamentary majority, which led to a shift of power to the lower chamber. Henceforward the Chamber of Deputies was de facto responsible for designating the head of government who assumed the powers previously reserved for the head of state. Prime ministers now had to cooperate with the Assembly and, in particular, with the Chambers' standing committees. After the defeat of the protectionist camp in 1881, Méline realised that 'he was no Bismarck' (Gourevitch 1977). He had to take the helm of the parliamentary Customs commission as soon as the 1889 elected assembly convened if he were to win the next fight.

5.2 Political allegiances and the making of a non-partisan platform

For the protectionist tariff reform to succeed, the balance in the assemblies had to swing in favour of protectionism. Until 1876, the French conservatives, who had held an absolute majority in the Chamber, had tended towards free trade. Like the Junkers in Germany, many were estate owners and lived off the land rent. Ideologically, the French mainstream conservatives of the 1870s were close to Bismarck's supporters, the National Liberals. Not only in Germany but also in France, 'the slump of 1873–1879 transformed political parties and ideologies' (Rosenberg 1943: 61) and led to a realignment of allegiances along with economic interests (Smith 1980). From 1880 onwards, the French conservatives, still hopelessly divided over the question of the constitutional changes they wanted, gradually lost more and more seats. They were gradually marginalised by their republican opponents, who came to control both chambers and thus the executive. In the 1889 elections to the Chamber of Deputies, the Conservatives still obtained 200 seats (out of 578), but their priorities differed from a decade earlier. After the constitutional amendments, they had demanded were postponed indefinitely, the tariff issue offered them

Table 17.5 Outcomes of the final vote on tariff laws in the German *Reichstag* (1879) and in the French Chamber of Deputies (1892)

	Germany		France		
Party affiliation	*Yes*	*No*		*Yes or abstention*	*No*
SPD	0	7	Socialists	0	12
Freisinnige Partei	1	23	Radical left	53	47
Partikularisten	0	10	Republican left	193	23
Zentrum	77	0	Moderate Republicans	32	6
Nationalliberale	20	65			
Konservative	99	0	Conservatives	202	8
Other	20	12			
Total	217	117	Total	370/88[a]	96

Source: Dormois (2012); Schonhardt-Bailey (1998: 308).
a Abstained.

an opportunity to re-enter the political debate and forge a new conservative alliance with like-minded republicans. Just like all members of the *Zentrum* switched sides shortly after the end of the *Kulturkampf* to join Bismarck's conservatives and vote for the 1879 tariff bill, in 1891, French conservatives joined forces with their hitherto staunchest enemies to carry the Méline tariff bill (Table 17.5). In both countries, the new tariff laws were adopted with a two-thirds majority.

To account for the incongruity of a bi-partisan alliance 'against nature', their defenders and later historians have claimed that the move was necessary to win over the still undecided peasant vote to the new regime, thereby consolidating a 'republican consensus' in France. In spirit, this was very similar to the defection of the Catholic *Centrum* to the conservatives in Germany.

While the voting behaviour of members of parliament on the margins of the political spectrum was closely correlated with the interests of their respective constituencies, the real puzzle concerns the middle ground: why did Republicans and Radicals vote for a measure which would undoubtedly harm their constituents? While industrial workers did not bite the bait of their employer capitalists—tariff protection in exchange for higher wages—and opposed a protectionist trade policy, why did the peasant population believe that large landowners would defend their interests?

5.3 Popular consensus and the peasant vote

Two schools of thought have approached this conundrum from different angles. A traditionalist camp has maintained that the tariff bill was essentially a con, that voters and demagogic legislators were led down the protectionist path by what would qualify today as cognitive bias. Voters remained unimpressed by the free trade sermons preached by Lujo Brentano, Yves Guyot, and others who stood up to convince society of the harmful effects of protectionism on their living standards and economic prospects.

A revisionist school, by contrast, has pointed to the inherent fragility of the protectionist coalition and pursued the hypothesis that farmers and their workers may have been rational in endorsing a programme that only prima facie seemed harmful (for a similar analysis regarding Germany, see Lehmann 2010). Many owners of family farms identified themselves first and foremost as self-sufficient producers and viewed the tariff as a step in the right direction. Perhaps it would not create benefits for them in the short term, but its introduction opened up the prospect that their livelihoods would also be protected in the future. And to some extent, they were right: the list of beneficiaries of the tariff grew longer in the following decades, and rates rose over time. Moreover, as Gerschenkron (1989), Kehr (1928, 1965), and others have pointed out, the tariff debates took on a class-struggle dimension, and the transition to protectionist trade policies was perceived in both countries as a victory of the countryside over the menacing cities and socialism or social democracy. In the French case, the pattern is obvious: opposition to the tariff in 1891 was concentrated among the deputies elected in large urban centres such as Paris, Lyon, Lille, Marseille, Nice, and Bordeaux (Dormois 2012).

Even more than the *Reichstag* election campaign of 1878, the French general election of 1889 was dominated by customs issue. Support for the much-vaunted tariff reform became a litmus test of good sense and decency. Voter turnout in 1889 was particularly high at 76.5 percent, while in the German *Reichstag* elections of 1878, this proportion was the highest of the whole decade (63.3 percent). The protectionist propagandists had succeeded in making their cause a national one.

6 Conclusion

Funck-Brentano (1896) noted that it was inevitable that protective tariffs would give the impression of a declaration of war to trading partners. Ironically, in August 1914, tariffs were suspended immediately: Actual war now ruled out trade war. Leaving aside the question of whether the 'protectionist rearmament' of the 1880s and 1890s actually anticipated the military conflagration of 1914, a century of scholarship has come to a balanced judgement on the defining features, causes, and effects of the introduction of neo-mercantilist policies in the late nineteenth century.

First, 'the primacy of domestic politics' (Kehr 1965) needs to be reasserted: A policy instrument with international repercussions was chosen as the preferred option to alleviate or divert domestic problems and tensions of an economic, social and political nature, and in this way maximise government support. Bismarck's strategy in this regard has been analysed in great detail, but the Republicans in power in France after 1880 also used 'the regime's resources to maximise support and minimise counter-mobilisation by their opponents' (Verdier 1994: 128). From a fiscal policy perspective, no alternative to increased revenues was as readily available or practical as raising import tariffs. Economically, protectionism offered the path of least resistance: maintaining past practices behind tariff walls. Moreover, most politicians indulged in the comfortable thought that the country they governed was a great power capable of shifting foreign trade patterns in its favour.

Second, for all their unavoidability, late nineteenth-century tariffs were flawed policy instruments. It is doubtful whether they affected the trade flows of the two countries under consideration here more than marginally. Even without them, French foreign trade would have stagnated, and protection played little or no part in the spectacular forays of German exports into world markets. It represented an uneasy, suboptimal compromise: 'No group favoured the actual policy outcome—high tariffs on both industrial and agricultural goods' (Frieden and Lake 2000: 42). As mostly left-wing observers pointed out, protectionist tariffs implied a form of highly regressive taxation. They involved 'readjustments without end' (L. Brentano), and the 'seamless fabric of equal protection' (J. Méline) was a deceitful ploy. Much time and energy were spent setting rates for individual goods in the general or maximum tariff schedules, which concerned only a tiny fraction of the two countries' total trade but gave the illusion of a 'tariff wall'. Actual protection was instead granted to a handful of privileged branches: The complexity of tariff schedules acted as a smokescreen to conceal preferential treatment. 'A policy of protection of national labour had the effect of protecting a small minority' (Lotz 1904: 522).

Finally, even if the direction of the correlation is difficult to ascertain, the protectionist revival coincided with a surge in xenophobia in the two countries. The openly anti-Semitic *Deutsche Reformpartei* and its allies had 16 deputies in the *Reichstag* elected in 1893, and anti-Semitism was rampant among General Boulanger supporters, 30 of whom were elected to Parliament in 1889. In August 1893, a pogrom against Italian salt farm workers took place in Aigues-Mortes, and the antisemitic campaign against Captain Dreyfus began in the following year. As was observed when comparing the McKinley tariff of the United States with its German counterpart: 'Tout comme chez nous' (Dietzel 1903: 389).

Notes

1 Jules Méline (1838–1925) had one of the longest political careers during the Third Republic. A lawyer from the Vosges and representative of the Republican opposition in the Second Empire, he was a member of the Chamber of Deputies from 1872 to 1903 and a member of the Senate from 1903 to 1925; he was also Prime Minister in 1896–1898. As Minister of Agriculture (1883–85), Méline was praised as the 'saviour of French agriculture'.

2 Calculated on the basis of the Maddison Project Database 2013.

3 Together with Guyot, he led the opposition to the Méline tariff in the Chamber of Deputies; he was the grandson of the famous liberal economist Jean-Baptiste Say (1767–1832).
4 The *Verein zur Wahrung der gemeinsamen wirtschaftlichen Interessen in Rheinland und Westfalen* allegedly received this nickname ("the association with the long name") from Bismarck himself.
5 Yves Guyot (1843–1928) was one of the main advocates of free trade in the tariff debates of 1891. Out of government loyalty (he was Minister of Public Works), however, he voted in favour of the tariff in the last ballot (January 11, 1892).

References

Bairoch, P. (1989) 'European trade policy, 1815–1914' in P. Mathias and S. Pollard (eds), *The Cambridge Economic History of Europe*, Vol. 8, Cambridge: Cambridge University Press, pp. 1–160.

Dietzel, H. (1903) 'The German tariff controversy', *Quarterly Journal of Economics*, Vol. 17 (3): 365–416.

Dormois, J.-P. (2008) *La défense du travail national: L'incidence du protectionnisme sur l'industrie en Europe (1870–1914)*, Paris: PUPS.

Dormois, J.-P. (2012) 'The best of intentions? Determinants of members' vote in the adoption of the Méline tariff (1892)', *Annual Conference of the Economic History Society*, University of Oxford, 30 March–2 April 2012.

Frieden, J. A. and Lake, D. A. (2000) *International: Political Economy: Perspectives on Global Power and Wealth*, London: Routledge.

Funck-Brentano, T. and Dupuis, C. (1896) *Les tarifs douaniers et les traités de commerce*, Paris: Arthur Rousseau.

Gallarotti, G. M. (1985) 'Toward a business cycle model of tariffs', *International Organization*, Vol. 39 (1): 155–87.

Gerschenkron, A. (1989) *Bread and Democracy in Germany*, 3rd ed., Ithaca, NY: Cornell University Press.

Gourevitch, P. A. (1977) 'International trade, domestic coalitions and liberty: comparative response to the crisis of 1873–96', *Journal of Interdisciplinary History*, Vol. 8 (2): 281–313.

Henderson, W. O. (1968) *The Zollverein*, 2nd ed., London: Frank Cass.

Irwin, D. (1998) 'Higher tariffs, lower revenues? Analysing the fiscal aspects of 'the great tariff debate of 1888', *Journal of Economic History*, Vol. 58 (1): 59–72.

Kehr, E. (1928) 'Englandhass und Weltpolitik', *Zeitschrift für Politik*, Vol. 17: 500–26.

Kehr, E. (1965) 'Das soziale System der Reaktion in Preußen unter dem Ministerium Puttkamer' in H.-U. Wehler (ed), *Der Primat der Innenpolitik: Gesammelte Aufsätze zur preußisch-deutschen Sozialgeschichte im 19. und 20. Jahrhundert*, Berlin: De Gruyter.

Lehmann, S. H. (2010) 'The German elections in the 1870s: why Germany turned from liberalism to protectionism', *Journal of Economic History*, Vol. 70 (1): 146–78.

Lotz, W. (1904) 'The effect of protection on some German industries', *Economic Journal*, Vol. 14 (56): 515–26.

Meadwell, H. (2002) 'The political economy of tariffs in late nineteenth-century Europe: reconsidering Republican France', *Theory and Society*, Vol. 31 (5): 623–51.

Nitzsche, M. (1905) *Die handelspolitische Reaktion in Deutschland: Eine historisch-politische Studie*, Stuttgart: Cotta.

O'Rourke, K. H. and Williamson, J. G. (1999) *Globalization and History: The Evolution of a Nineteenth-Century Atlantic Economy*, Cambridge, MA: MIT Press.

Pahre, R. (2008) *Politics and Trade Cooperation in the Nineteenth Century*, Cambridge: Cambridge University Press.

Rosenbaum, S. (1908) 'Food taxation in the United Kingdom, France, Germany and the United States', *Journal of the Royal Statistical Society*, Vol. 71 (2): 319–60.

Rosenberg, H. (1943) 'Political and social consequences of the Great Depression of 1873–1896 in Central Europe', *Economic History Review*, Vol. 13 (1): 58–73.

Rosenberg, H. (1967) *Große Depression und Bismarck Zeit: Wirtschaftsablauf, Gesellschaft, und Politik in Mitteleuropa*, Berlin: Walter de Gruyter.

Schonhardt-Bailey, C. (1998) 'Parties and interests in the 'marriage of iron and rye'', *British Journal of Political Science*, Vol. 28 (2): 291–332.

Smith, M. S. (1980) *Tariff Reform in France 1860–1900: The Politics of Economic Interest*, Ithaca, NY: Cornell University Press.

Spoerer, M. (2004) *Steuerlast, Steuerinzidenz und Steuerwettbewerb: Verteilungswirkungen der Besteuerung in Preußen und Württemberg*, Berlin: Akademie.

Sternhell, Z. (1986) *Neither Right nor Left: Fascist Ideology in France*, Princeton, NJ: Princeton University Press.

Verdier, D. (1994) *Democracy and International Trade: Britain, France and the United States, 1860–1990*, Princeton, NJ: Princeton University Press.

18 The economics of the Italian unification

Giovanni Federico

1 Introduction

In 1861, Italy was a poor country with a glorious past. In the middle ages, the Centre-North of Italy had been the richest area in Europe, jointly with the Southern Low countries, and one of the richest in the world. It remained quite rich and prosperous until the late seventeenth century or the early eighteenth century (Malanima 2013). Afterwards, the combination of a fast decline in manufacturing and the rise of population in a land-scarce country resulted in declining GDP per capita. The trend continued until the mid-1850s, with an ephemeral recovery during the Napoleonic period and its immediate aftermath. By then, the GDP per capita of the Centre-North was about 1360 1990 Geary–Khamis dollars—that is, 10 percent lower than the German GDP per capita, 15 percent lower than the French, and less than half the British.

Actually, Italy had not existed as a polity since the fall of the Roman Empire. The number of independent polities had shrunk from hundreds at the heyday of the *comuni* in the tenth and eleventh century to seven after the Congress of Vienna—the Kingdom of Sardinia (which consisted mostly of Piedmont and Liguria), the Duchies of Parma and Modena, the Grand Duchy of Tuscany, the Papal States (including most of Emilia, Marche, Umbria, and Latium) and the Kingdom of Two Sicilies (i.e. Sicily proper and the continental South). Also, Lombardy and Venetia were formally independent, under the name of Regno Lombardo-Veneto. However, in practice, they were Austrian provinces. The Habsburg monarchy exerted a strong hegemony on the peninsula, as the Austrian army frequently had intervened to prop up rulers. Only the Kingdom of Sardinia had an independent foreign policy, which continued the traditional policy of the Savoy dynasty. It had expanded from its original duchy in the Alps towards the Po valley by deftly siding with the winning side in all European wars, with quite a few changes of alliances (e.g. during the war for Spanish succession). The penultimate step in its century-old ascent had been the annexation of Liguria, with the rich port-town of Genoa in 1815. The final one was the solemn proclamation of

DOI: 10.4324/9781003283430-22

Vittorio Emanuele II as king of Italy on March 17 1861 in the first session of the Italian parliament.

The unification was the final act of a process (officially known in Italy as *Risorgimento* or renaissance) that had started just after the end of the Congress of Wien, which had re-instated the pre-Napoleonic dynasties.[1] Small groups of *patrioti* had been plotting since the 1820s to overturn the rulers and get rid of Austrian hegemony, with many failures and few ephemeral successes. As in Germany, the revolution seemed to have won in 1848. Most rulers were forced to grant constitutions and join in a war against Austria, under the leadership of Carlo Alberto, the Sardinian king. However, the war ended in a crushing military defeat, which was replicated in the subsequent year when Piedmont re-started the war without allies.

Nevertheless, these events marked a watershed in the *Risorgimento*. In 1848, the Savoy dynasty was still widely mistrusted by *patrioti* because it had adopted a strict reactionary policy after the restoration in 1815. After the defeat, the king, Carlo Alberto, abdicated, but his successor, Vittorio Emanuele II, did not abolish the constitution as other Italian rulers, probably out of fear of an insurrection in Genoa. Sardinia was a constitutional monarchy, which greatly enhanced its standing in the pro-independence movement, while the economic and social conditions of the kingdom were improved by a far-reaching plan of modernisation, liberalisation, and construction of infrastructures, under the leadership of Cavour, by far the best politician in Italy and probably in Europe in the nineteenth century.

Thus, after 1848, Piedmont maintained a leading role in unification, which has drawn many comparisons with the Prussian role in German unification. There are of course similarities (the 1848 revolution, a towering prime minister, wars with Austria), but they must not be over-emphasised. Prussia was one of the great powers of Europe, with 18.5 million inhabitants in 1860. In 1861, the Kingdom of Sardinia had about 3.2 million inhabitants and arguably had been able to pursue an independent foreign policy only because France and Austria preferred a buffer state over another big European power at their border. The Piedmontese army was not a match for the Austrian one, and in 1859 it succeeded to win only with the support of the French, which Cavour had gained with a series of shrewd political moves and with the promise to surrender Savoy and Nice. His initial plan was to extend the kingdom to Lombardy and to other Northern and possibly Central regions, but Garibaldi thought otherwise. With a small army of volunteers, he invaded and defeated the Southern Kingdom and Cavour had to rush sending the Sardinian army to prevent him to march on Rome and overthrow the pope's regime. By October 1860, the Piedmontese army controlled the whole peninsula, except Veneto (still under Austria) and the rump of Papal States around Rome. A series of plebiscites, from August 1859 to October 1860, sanctioned the unification to the Kingdom of Sardinia, and in January 1861, a very small, all-male constituency (less than a half-million voters out of a population of 22 million) elected the first Italian parliament. Veneto was annexed in 1866, after another war with Austria, where Italy was badly defeated by land and by sea, and rescued only by the Prussian victory. Latium was annexed in November 1870, when the defeat against the Prussians left the pope without French protection.

This chapter starts with a description of the economic conditions of Italy in the 1860s (Section 2) and then discusses the economic motivations for Unification (Section 3). Section 4 outlines the creation of 'Italian' institutions, which in most (but not all) cases consisted of an extension of the Sardinian ones to the rest of the country. Section 5 deals with the macroeconomic conditions and the policy choices of the early 1860s, while Section 6 focuses on the economic effects of the Unification. Section 7 concludes.

2 Italy in 1861

In 1861, Italy was a backward country according to all economic and social indicators (Vecchi 2017). The mortality rate was approximately 30 per 1000, and infant mortality was approximately 230 (ISTAT 1958 and Serie storiche, Table 2.3). The nationwide literacy rate was as low as 41.4 percent for males and 22.1 percent for females (Ciccarelli and Weisdorf 2019). Out of over six million boys and girls aged 5 to 19, only one million were attending primary school, less than 20,000 high school and less than 10,000 university (ISTAT Serie storiche, Table 7.3).

Agriculture, forestry, and fishing accounted for 45 percent of GDP (Baffigi et al. 2013) and employed two-thirds of the workforce (Giordano and Zollino 2015). Agricultural experts, slavishly echoed by historians, described it as hopelessly backward, with some island of good practice in the Po Valley. They unfavourably compared the Italian cereal yields (i.e. land productivity) and the number of livestock with the British ones. This harsh assessment may be excessive (Federico 2009b). Italy was not Britain. British high farming was considered the most advanced agricultural technology, but it had been perfected for a specific environment (rainy summers) and factor endowment (abundant capital and scarce labour). In Italy, summers were hot and dry and in the South land was rather abundant. Thus, tree crops and wine all over the country, and oil in the Centre-South accounted for a much higher share of output than in Great Britain. Moreover, in many Southern regions, extensive cultivation in large estates (latifundia) was likely to be the rational choice Furthermore, Italians were also unlucky. In the 1850s, the production of wine and silk cocoons was hit by devastating diseases, the mildew, and the pébrine. The former could be cured with the spraying of sulphur, whereas the latter was uncurable. The only solution was to hatch uninfected silkworm eggs, which producers started to import from Japan.

Italy was not lucky with natural resources either. There were no coal mines (Sardinian coal was to be exploited in the 1930s), and the endowment of other minerals was limited to iron in Tuscany, lead, and zinc in Sardinia, was limited. The only relevant resource was Sicilian sulphur, a key raw material for the traditional chemical industry.

Manufacturing contributed to less than a quarter of the Italian GDP and most of it was traditional urban artisanal production. There were few modern factories, almost exclusively located in the North-West (Piedmont, Liguria, Lombardy), which was later re-named industrial triangle. The most important industrial sector was silk reeling—that is, the processing of cocoons to extract raw silk. At the time of unification, it was undergoing a massive process of modernisation because the dearth of raw materials forced many small factories to close. Only the most advanced steam-powered plants survived, and Italy gained a technological lead over its competitors, China and Japan, which lasted until the 1920s (Federico 1997). However, in 1891 (no earlier estimate is available), industrial processing accounted for less than 2 percent of value added in manufacturing and the whole silk complex, including the production of cocoons, for the same percentage of Italian GDP (Federico 2005).

Italy now features huge regional differences in GDP per capita, the largest in Europe. At the time of the Unification, the industrial triangle was in all likelihood richer than the South, but the gap was still fairly small and within the limits of the statistical error. The earliest regional estimates refer to 1871, when the GDP per capita was about 25 percent higher in the Centre-North than in the whole South (Felice 2014). The gap with the most advanced areas of the *Mezzogiorno* was clearly smaller. The available figures, possibly overestimated, imply that Campania (the region around Naples) was only 5 percent less productive than Lombardy. Furthermore, one might argue that the 1871 gaps were not representative of the situation ten years earlier. The only available data for the early 1860s refer to real wages. Wages for unskilled workers in the North-West were 28 percent higher than in the South and 39 percent higher than in the centre (Federico et al. 2019). In contrast, wages for skilled workers were over a fifth higher in the South, possibly because the supply of skills was scarcer than in the North (Federico et al. 2021).

Even if the interregional income gaps around 1860 were not that large, the North had greater potential for development. First, it had more rivers with a more regular flow across seasons. This was a very relevant advantage in a country without coal, where water was an essential source of energy (Bardini 1997). Second, the North had more human capital (Ciccarelli and Weisdorf 2019). Its literacy rates were double for males and four times higher for females and the gaps were respectively 3.5 and 9 times between the provinces of Turin (78 percent for men and 54 percent for women) and Caltanissetta in Sicily (respectively 23 percent and 6 percent). The conventional wisdom also suggests that Centre-North had greater social capital, even if proxies are, as it often happens, questionable (Cappelli 2017). Lastly, as argued by Cafagna among others, the proximity to North Europe may have offered the North a greater market potential. However, this advantage could be exploited only with railway connections, and the first tunnel under the Alps, the Frejus to France, was opened only in 1871. Some recent econometric tests on the causes of the North-South divide fail to reach conclusive results on the role of foreign as opposed to domestic, market potential in the Northern development (Missiaia 2016; Ciccarelli and Fachin 2017; Daniele et al. 2018).

3 Economic motivations for the unification?

Until the late 1950s, economic motivations loomed large in the conventional wisdom about the causes of the *Risorgimento*. The seminal works by Ciasca (1916) and Greenfield (1934) had argued that the *patrioti* were aware of the benefits of free trade and market integration and that they blamed the old political order for the failure to reap them. First, they stressed the lack of infrastructure. In 1859, there were only 2236 km of railways in the whole peninsula, and almost all of them were in Piedmont and Tuscany, plus the Austrian line connecting Venice to Milan and Turin (Ciccarelli and Groote 2017). The Papal States and the South had only respectively 131 and 101 km of railways because the Pope and the Neapolitan king had rejected a lot of proposals for investment in new lines.

Second, all pre-unitary states, with the remarkable exception of the tiny Tuscany, raised barriers to trade. Lombardy and Venetia were protected against foreign manufactures by the Austrian duties (27 percent on average on manufactures [Lampe 2020]) and from the competition by other provinces of the Habsburg Empire by poor communications. Papal States and the Kingdom of the Two Sicilies allegedly imposed heavy duties on manufactures, letting imports of agricultural products free. Under absolutism, Piedmont had been the most protectionist country in the peninsula as it heavily protected both manufacturing (37 percent on average in 1846; Lampe 2020) and, unlike other countries, wheat-growing (39 percent on average from 1819 to 1846; Federico 2012). The liberal turn of the late 1840s brought about a change in trade policy (Di Gianfrancesco 1974). Cavour was an ardent supporter of free trade (Romeo 1977–1984) and his government altogether abolished the duty on wheat and slashed duties on manufactures to 8 percent in 1859. In the 1830s and 1840s, there had been a lot of discussion and dozens of projects for a customs union on the model of the German *Zollverein*, which failed because of the opposition of Austria (Pichler 2001). Eventually, even the most moderate members of the (agricultural) elite came to the conclusion that annexation to the Kingdom of Sardinia was the only solution to get the benefits of free trade. The policies after Unification fulfilled their dream.

This interpretation of the *Risorgimento*, inspired, at least in part, by economic considerations, is no longer accepted. The conventional wisdom considers it as a purely political and ideological movement (Banti 2000, 2004; Riall 2009) by a small minority who cared little for the economic gains.

The economic underpinning for this view has been provided by Cafagna in several papers of the 1960s, later collected in a book (Cafagna 1989). He argued that political division before 1861 had not been a major hindrance to development because economic relations between Italian polities were limited. There was no potential for a fruitful division of labour among Italian states as they were all similarly poor and backward. In spite of their glorious economic past, they specialised in the production of primary commodities for the industrialising countries of Northern Europe. The three regions of the 'industrial triangle' in North-West Italy (Piedmont, Lombardy, and Liguria) were more successful than the rest of the country in exploiting this opportunity, and their early growth opened a gap with the rest of the peninsula ('dualism'). Therefore, the potential gains from Unification were small and the economic motivations for Unification were weak. Only long-run growth could change the factor endowment and create opportunities for nation-wide division of labour and profitable trade.

In theory, these two views are testable, with a massive research effort to collect data on trade and its costs. The partial attempts so far have yielded mixed results. On the one hand, Federico and Tena (2014) have confirmed that the inter-Italian trade was modest. They estimate, quite crudely, that in the 1850s it accounted for less than a fifth of total trade (17 percent of imports and 18.4 percent of exports) and most of it within the North. The authors run a simple gravity model, proxying economic size with population, transportation costs with distance, and adding a dummy for flows between the Kingdom of Two Sicilies and all other polities. The coefficients for distance and the Southern dummy are negative and significant as expected. On the other hand, Federico (2007) finds a strong convergence of wheat and corn prices (but not for olive oil) before the Unification. His econometric analysis highlights the (small) contribution of the abolition of Piedmontese duty on wheat and the (quite substantial) effect of the decline in freights, which was brought about by technical and organisational progress in shipping (Di Gianfrancesco 1979). A substantial part of the overall convergence is explained by a time trend, which captures unaccounted developments in the market (e.g. in the circulation of information). These results might be cautiously interpreted as consistent with the traditional, pre-Cafagna, view of the expected gains from trade as one of the motivations of the *Risorgimento*. On the other hand, wheat or agricultural commodities may not be representative of the overall integration of the market. Furthermore, the relation between actual gains (or lack thereof), expected gains, ideology, and political action appears hugely complex. It is impossible to deal with this issue here.

4 Creating Italian institutions

The fast unfolding of military events and the flight of the previous rulers caught the Sardinian government and the local *patrioti* by surprise. Most interim governments opted for the simplest solution, the extension of the Sardinian legislation. They abolished all barriers to domestic trade and immediately adopted the liberal Piedmontese tariff. They adopted the Piedmontese economic legislation in the former Papal States, while in other regions, such as Lombardy, Tuscany, and the South the interim governments kept the existing laws. After the Unification, Cavour and, after his sudden death (6 June 1861), his successors (collectively known as the *Destra Storica*) faced the huge task of building a new state. They adopted a strong-arm approach, which earned the sobriquet of *unificazione a vapore* (steamrolling Unification).

It is evidently not feasible to describe the sweeping reforms of the early 1860s in detail. We will focus on the measures with the greatest impact on the economy but it is nevertheless worth quoting some key decisions. First and foremost, Italy adopted a very centralised organisation from the 1847 Piedmontese law, which was largely inspired by the French model. The parliament extended it to Lombardy (*legge Rattazzi*) in October 1859 and to the whole Kingdom in March 1861. The new kingdom was divided into 69 provinces (the French *départements*), each managed by a *prefetto*. The local authorities were given only very limited autonomy. The municipal councils were elected, but the mayor was chosen among them by the *prefetto*. This solution was intended as a temporary one, pending the approval of more organic legislation. Minghetti, *ministro degli interni* (Home Secretary) introduced a bill in March 1861 that increased the autonomy of the municipalities (with an elective mayor), gave extensive powers to the provinces, and suggested experimenting with larger territorial units (*regioni*) as an aggregation of provinces. The project faced strong opposition from the civil service and many members of parliament, who feared that federalism could splinter the state. The project was bogged down in endless discussions regarding the boundaries of the *regioni* and eventually abandoned in 1864 (Candeloro 1968).

In May 1861, the armed forces of the pre-unitary polities were merged into the Piedmontese ones, whereas the Garibaldi army was disbanded. The negative impact of this decision was compounded by the generalised adoption of a two-year compulsory draft in all regions. In November 1861, the government extended the *legge Casati*, which mandated two years of compulsory primary school for boys and girls (interestingly, four years for city dwellers) and, thus, was one of the most advanced in the world (Cappelli 2015). The re-organisation of the Italian state was completed in the early months of 1865 with the approval of new legislation on several issues. The law on local authorities re-asserted the key provisions of the Rattazzi law and put paid to any hope of a federal Italy. The parliament approved a comprehensive set of Italian laws, after a preparatory work that had started before the unification. The economic legislation, the *Codice civile* (tort law), the *Codice di Commercio* (commercial law), and the *Codice della Navigazione* (maritime law), were inspired by a strong protection of property rights with no intermediate agent between the individual and the state.

The steamrolling approach was also adopted for most economic decisions. All barriers to domestic trade had already been abolished by the interim governments and in June 1861 Italy took over all debts of pre-unification polities. The sum was not really large in proportion to Italian GDP (Figure 18.2) but its geographical distribution was highly unbalanced. About 55 percent of the total had been issued by the Piedmontese government and a further 15 percent by the interim governments (Corbino 1931–1936, Vol. 1: 210), while the debt of the Kingdom of the Two Sicilies was comparatively small. In May 1861, Italy started to issue its own currency, the lira (equal to the Sardinian lira and the French franc) and in August of the following year, it withdrew from circulation the currencies of the pre-unification states.

The economic unification was much more cautious in two key areas, the banks of issue and taxation, which directly affected the economic interests of the elites. In the nineteenth century, the banks of issues were private institutions at the top end of local credit markets and thus the local elites were loath to relinquish control. In 1859, six banks had issuing rights—the *Banca Nazionale* in the Kingdom of Sardinia, the *Banca Romana* in Papal States, the *Banca Nazionale Toscana* and the *Banca Toscana di Credito* in Tuscany, the *Banco di Napoli* and *Banco di Sicilia* in the South. The *Banca Nazionale* pushed very hard to get an exclusive right to issue but it failed (Sannucci 1989). The topic was resumed more than thirty years later, in 1892/93, when the *Banca Romana* collapsed for its imprudent lending during the housing boom in Rome and Naples. It was rescued by the *Banca Nazionale* and merged with the two Tuscan banks into the *Banca d'Italia*. The two Southern banks lost their right to issue only in 1926.

The fiscal systems of pre-unification states differed substantially in the total amount of revenues and to some extent also in their distribution by source (e.g. direct tax, consumption taxes, and custom duties). Taxation was traditionally higher in the Kingdom of Sardinia, which spent between two and three times more than other states on its military and had to fund its investments in infrastructures in the 1850s (Dincecco et al. 2011, Table 4). On the eve of Unification, the total taxation per capita was double the Southern one, while the income gap did not exceed 10–15 percent. An immediate extension of the Sardinian system to the whole country would have been politically difficult and thus in the early 1860s, the Italian government adopted a piecemeal strategy (Parravicini 1958; Marongiu 1995; Federico 2009a). Given its pressing financial needs (cf. section 5), it aligned the rates to the highest levels and increased them further in the following years. The Piedmontese taxation on business was extended to the whole country in April 1862, with a modest reduction in rates. The government waited a bit longer to re-order the jungle of taxation on consumption (July 1864), but it succeeded to double its revenues, partly by squeezing the local authorities, which traditionally got most of the revenues. Before the Unification, direct taxation was heavily unbalanced across polities. Rents on land and buildings were taxed in all states, but rates differed and, in most states, the taxable value of estates was based on obsolete and/or imperfect cadastres. Lombard landowners paid twice the Sicilian ones. Non-agricultural incomes were not taxed at all in the South and Papal States and were subject to specific taxes in Piedmont and other states. In 1864, the government introduced a new unified tax, the *ricchezza mobile*, setting a national target of double the pre-unification revenue. The sum was to be divided between provinces with a complex formula and then among taxpayers according to their income. A similar partition system was applied to the land tax in the same year: the parliament set a target for revenue, to be divided between regions according to a crude assessment of the value of land (*conguaglio*). This was to be a temporary solution, waiting for the completion of a new cadastre which would have made it possible to redistribute the tax burden according to the real rents (*perequazione*). The parliament earmarked funds for the new cadastre twenty-two years later, and its results were made available in 1956, when the land tax had long become irrelevant.

5 The spending spree of the early 1860s

While the institutional unification was still going on, the new government took two far-reaching decisions. First, it positioned itself firmly in the spaghetti bowl of trade treaties and international relations of the post-Cobden-Chevalier era by signing a new trade treaty with France in January 1863 (Lampe 2011). Italy got cuts on French duties on her exports of primary products in exchange for lower duties on manufactures, which were extended to imports from Britain and all major trading partners under the most favoured nation clause. By nineteenth-century (and current) standards, Italian trade after the Unification was free. The average nominal protection remained approximately 5–7 percent throughout the 1860s and early 1870s and the Trade Restrictiveness Index, which takes into account the downward bias from trade restrictions, was hardly higher (Federico and Vasta 2015).[2] Two years later, in 1865, Italy reaffirmed its strong and somewhat unequal link with France by joining the Latin Monetary Union, which also included Belgium, Switzerland, and Spain. All countries adopted the same (bimetallic) standard and coinage, ensuring the free circulation of coins (Timini 2018).

Second, the government decided to invest massively in infrastructures, especially in railways, which were deemed indispensable for the development of a truly national economy and, in general, a powerful sign of modernity (Schram 1997). The length of the network doubled in five years, and it continued to rise by about 5 percent per year until the mid-1870s. At the end of this first wave of construction, in 1876 the network totalled 8422 km (i.e. about half the length in 1913), with 1215 km in former Papal States and 2351 in the South (Ciccarelli and Fenoaltea 2009; Ciccarelli and Groote 2017). These early investments concentrated on the building of long-run North-South lines, while local railways were built in the second wave of the 1880s and 1890s. The financial effort was huge: In 1861–1865, investment

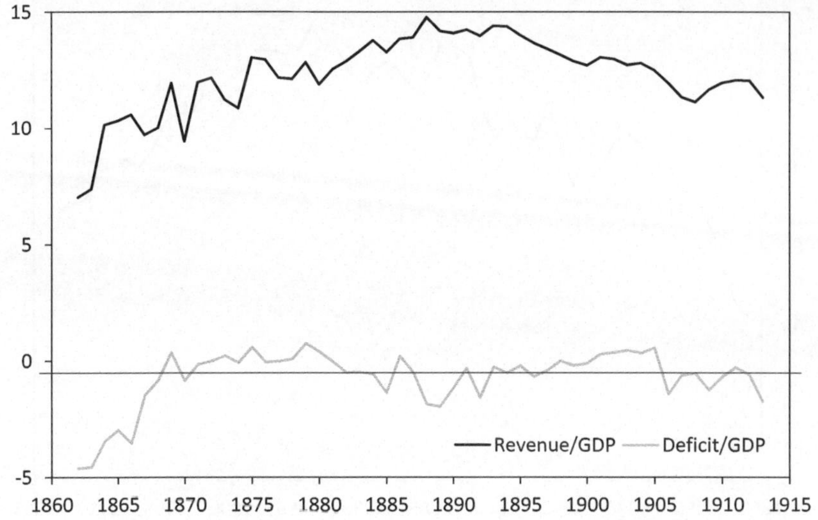

Figure 18.1 Revenues and deficit as percentage of GDP, 1861–1913.
Sources: Deficit and revenues: RGS (1969); GDP: Baffigi et al. (2013).

in railway construction accounted for 58 percent of all investments in social overhead capital, 18 percent of all fixed investments, and 1.9 percent of GDP (Fenoaltea 1988, 2020).

These investments and the sharp increase in current expenditures (including the military, to get ready for another war with Austria) resulted in a severe strain on the budget (Figure 18.1). In 1862, revenues covered only about 60 percent of expenditures, and, despite the howls for the crushing tax burden, they remained quite low, as a proportion of Italian GDP. The government tried to rake up additional resources by farming out the tobacco and salt monopoly (causing the first big scandal in the history of the Kingdom) and by selling the land owned by the state and local authorities and the remainder of the church properties after the massive sales in the French years. These sales were decided as early as 1861/62 (1866 for the church land) but the process took years and most of the land was sold at low prices with long extension, so revenues were substantially smaller than expected.

The gap between expenditures and revenues was filled with debt. As early as July 1861, Italy issued over 700 million lira of *rendita* (perpetual consols), equivalent to about a tenth of GDP at the very attractive rate of 7.1 percent. In the next four years, Italy succeeded to sell vast amounts of *rendita* and other bonds, and the debt/GDP ratio rose correspondingly from 43 to 74 percent of GDP (Figure 18.2). In April 1866, the international financial crisis and the imminent start of the new war with Austria caused the price of the *rendita* to collapse and Italy was forced to let the lira float against gold (*corso forzoso*).

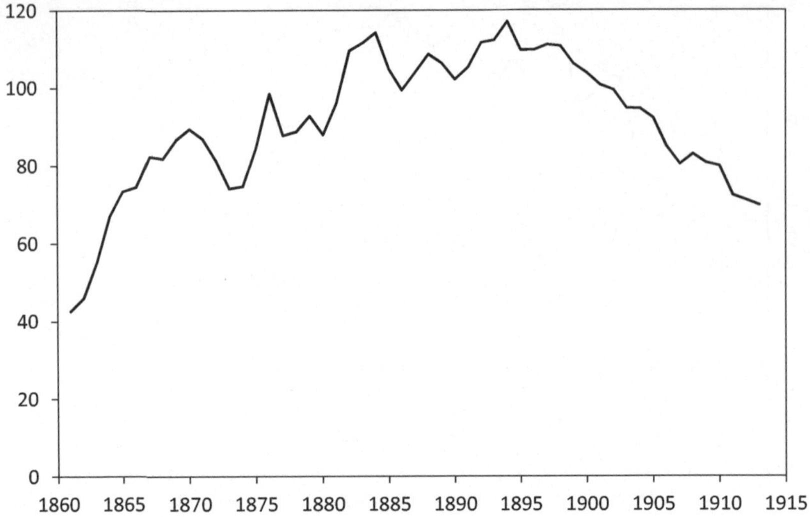

Figure 18.2 Debt/GDP ratio, 1861–1913.
Sources: Debt: Zamagni (1998); GDP: Baffigi et al. (2013).

The government had to intensify efforts to balance the budget. In the second half of the 1860s, expenditures remained roughly constant as a proportion of GDP, but revenues increased by three further points. The key measure was the introduction of a tax on milling in 1869, which in the mid-1870s yielded 7–8 percent of revenues (0.7–0.8 percent of GDP). Thus, many historians labelled the policy of the *Destra Storica* as deeply reactionary (Sereni 1968). However, to be fair, the ruling elites paid their dues, in spite of all dithering. The share of direct taxation on revenues increased from about 28 percent in 1862 to 34 percent in 1871—from 1.7 percent to 3.3 percent of GDP (Repaci 1962). This policy succeeded to rebalance the budget, but it did not prevent a further rise in the debt/GDP ratio as prices started to decrease in the 1870s (Figure 18.2). The financial situation of the Kingdom was restored only by the growth of real GDP and prices in the early twentieth century.

6 The long-term economic effects of the unification

The abolition of trade barriers and the construction of railways were instrumental in the creation of a national market, which was the main aim of the economic agenda of the *Destra*. The results were not impressive. In the 1860s and 1870s, wheat prices show no further convergence (Federico 2007). For quite a long time, railways were used for short-range traffic, especially in the North, including the movements of exports and imports to and from main harbours, while they did not substitute coastal shipping in the North-South trade. To some extent, railways were not competitive because the government set quite high fares in order to increase its revenues (a third of the gross total) and to attract private investors (Fenoaltea 1983). However, the demand for long-range transportation was not large. According to Zamagni (1983: 1648), as late as 1911, 'exchanges were intensive in the industrial triangle and there was a sizeable trade between it and the North-East and Central regions, while trade between the South and the rest of the country, and within the South was extremely modest'.

Arguably, this definition of the effect of Unification is too narrow, as it misses the impact of the institutional change as described in Section 4. A more comprehensive definition should take into account the steamrolling unification and the measures and policies of the early 1860s, which conceivably would not have been adopted had Italy not become unified. One might surmise that institutional change had a substantially greater long-run impact than the decline in domestic trade costs. However, measuring its effects is extremely difficult. In some cases, such as the changes in administration or legislation, it is impossible to define meaningful counterfactuals. In others, such as trade policy, tests can be designed but data are scarce.

Waiting for proper analytical work, one has to resort to the traditional post hoc propter hoc approach, that is, to draw inferences from economic growth. The performance of the Italian economy was undoubtedly better after than before the Unification, but this was not really a challenging yardstick. There is anecdotal evidence of industrial growth, a 'first coat of paint' according to the felicitous expression by Cafagna (1989). Ciccarelli and Fenoaltea (2013) find some positive effects on industrial value added in some Southern provinces and Rueda and A'Hearn (2020) argue that municipalities close to abolished borders grew faster than the rest of the peninsula. The (uncertain) data of national GDP per head shows some fluctuation but almost no permanent growth until the 1880s. That decade featured a mini-growth spurt, which concluded in a bad financial and economic crisis, triggered by the housing boom in Rome and Naples. Yet, just before the crisis, GDP per capita was only about 15 percent higher than twenty-five years earlier, with a paltry growth rate of 0.5 percent per year (Figure 18.3). One can conclude tentatively that the post-Unification institutional shock changed little, in contrast with the hopes of the *patrioti* and the investors in Italian bonds. This hypothesis would need a lot of work to be confirmed, but, if true, would raise an intriguing question: Why was the impact of these massive institutional changes so small?

In some cases, the potential benefits were reduced by poor implementation. For instance, the Italian army performed poorly in the 1866 war against Austria because of the antagonism between officers from different provenances. The primary school system developed very slowly because it had to be funded by local authorities, which in many regions were uninterested or cash-strapped (Cappelli 2015). Thus, the literacy rate increased slowly—in 1881 it was only about 12 points higher than at the time of the unification. In other cases, the institutional change was not as large as it may seem on

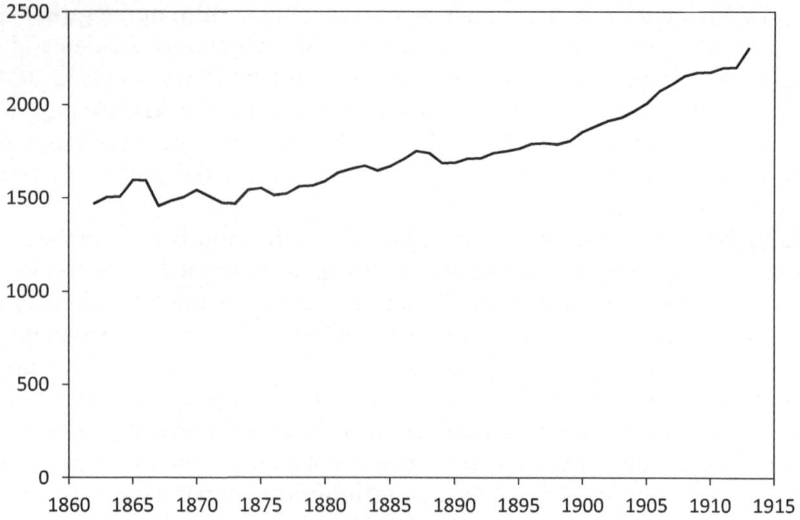

Figure 18.3 Italian GDP per capita, 1990 Geary–Khamis dollars.
Source: Baffigi et al. (2013).

paper because the differences before the Unification were fairly limited. The adaptation to the Italian business laws was fairly easy because they were quite similar among pre-unification polities. All French-dominated states (i.e. the whole of continental Italy) had adopted the Napoleonic legislation in the early nineteenth century. Upon their return to power after 1815, the old/new rulers formally abolished the French laws and replaced them with new legislation, which in most cases reproduced all the key provisions of the French laws (e.g. the Two Sicilies in 1819, Sardinia in 1837). Lastly, the adoption of the lira was relatively simple because circulation in all pre-unitary states consisted mostly of coins, which could be converted according to their metal content. The use of 'Italian' paper currency remained limited to the wealthy for long after the unification.

One might surmise that the trade and fiscal policy of the new state had a major impact on the South, which was used to a high-duty/low-taxation regime. After the Unification, the manufacturers had to face competition both from North Italian products, without any barrier, and from foreign products, which were subject to low duties, especially after the 1863 treaty with France. This was a major shock for the Southern industry, but ultimately most companies, including the Swiss-owned cotton factories in Southern Campania, survived. The short-term macroeconomic effects of the industrial crisis were limited because manufactures accounted for a small share of Southern GDP. The potential effects of the fiscal policies could have been even larger. The revenue/GDP ratio was fairly low, but even low taxation had a large impact on the poor, who constituted the majority of the Italian population (Vecchi 2017). The milling tax caused countrywide riots, with dozens of deaths (Cammelli 1984). In the South, just after Unification large swathes of the population were hostile to the new government. They resented the compulsory military draft, the increase in indirect taxation, and the announced sale of common and church land, which supplied the poor peasants with a much-needed integration to their meagre incomes. The outcome was widespread banditry (*brigantaggio*), which was fuelled by the money of the deposed Bourbon king, exiled in Rome, and by an influx of legitimist volunteers from all over Europe. In the beginning, the bandits had substantial success and gained control of some areas, but the movement was eventually repressed by the army and by the National Guard, which was recruited from the local elite. Thus, the *brigantaggio* was more a war within the Southern elite and between landowners and peasants, rather than a North-South issue.

7 Conclusion

The performance of the Italian economy was undoubtedly better after the Unification than before it, but in absolute terms, it can be characterised as modest at best. The gap with fast-growing European countries widened: in the early 1890s, the Italian GDP per capita was about two-thirds of the German and French one, and less than half the British one. Since the late 1890s, the performance improved markedly, with fast and wide-ranging industrial growth in the North-West, and massive wage-raising emigration from the South. In the fifteen years before World War One, Italian GDP per capita grew at 1.6 percent per year and the North-South gap widened sizeably. Attributing this growth to the delayed effects of the Unification stretches credulity. The economic effects of Unification were comparatively modest.

This is not the case of political effects. Unification arrived as a sudden and unexpected shock, rather than a long and consensual process, as in Germany. Some contemporaries defined the steamrolling unification as Piedmontese conquest, and this idea has resurfaced in very recent years as the rallying cry of neo-Bourbonic political movements, which claim further subsidies to the South. This idea has no historical foundation. All the measures were approved by the Italian parliament, where the South was proportionally represented. The *Destra Storica* had to build a new state out of a motley collection of very different polities and managed the task rather successfully, admittedly without much consideration of the political and social consequences of its policies. Furthermore, state-building was not completed in some key functions, such as central banking, and state capacity remained weak in others, such as tax collection. Prominent *patrioti*, intellectuals such as Cattaneo, and politicians, such as Minghetti, argued that a federal structure would have been more suited to such a diverse country and would have increased the consensus around the new state. The Minghetti project failed and the idea of a federal structure remained the reserve of few intellectuals. The constitution of the Italian Republic, which replaced, at last, the *Statuto Albertino* in 1947, did include a clause for devolution, but the *regioni* were created only in 1970, more than one century after the Unification.

Notes

1 For a detailed account of the political and military events, see Candeloro (1958, 1960, 1964, 1968). For more concise outlines, see Woolf (1969) and Riall (2009). In the following, we will use Piedmont and Ancient provinces, as well as Sardinia, to refer to the Kingdom, and South to refer to the Kingdom of Two Sicilies.

2 The Trade Restrictiveness Index (TRI) is defined as 'the uniform tariff which, if applied to all goods, would yield the same welfare as the existing tariff structure'. The TRI of the European Union in 2002 was 40.6% (Kee et al. 2009: Table 3).

References

Baffigi, A., Broadberry, S., Giordano, C. and Zollino, F. (2013) 'Data Appendix—Italy's national accounts (1861–2010)', in G. Toniolo (ed), *The Oxford Handbook of the Italian Economy Since Unification*, Oxford: Oxford University Press, pp. 631–712.

Banti, A. M. (2000) *La nazione del Risorgimento*, Turin: Einaudi.

Banti, A. M. (2004) *Il Risorgimento italiano*, Bari: Laterza.

Bardini C. (1997) 'Without coal in the age of steam: a factor-endowment explanation of the Italian industrial lag before World War I', *Journal of Economic History*, Vol. 7: 633–53.

Cafagna, L. (1989) *Dualismo e sviluppo nella storia d'Italia*, Padova: Marsilio.

Cammelli, S. (1984) *Al suono delle campane: Indagine su una rivolta contadina: i moti del macinato (1869),* Milan: Franco Angeli.

Candeloro, G. (1958) *Storia dell'Italia moderna*, Vol. 2, *Dalla Restaurazione alla Rivoluzione Nazionale 1815–1846*, Milano: Feltrinelli.

Candeloro, G. (1960) *Storia dell'Italia moderna*, Vol. 3, *La Rivoluzione Nazionale 1846–1849*, (2nd ed., 1974), Milano: Feltrinelli.

Candeloro, G. (1964) *Storia dell'Italia moderna*, Vol. 4, *Dalla Rivoluzione nazionale all'Unità 1849–1860*, Milano: Feltrinelli.

Candeloro, G. (1968) *Storia dell'Italia moderna*: *La costruzione dello stato unitario 1860–1871*, (2nd ed., 1974), Milano: Feltrinelli.

Cappelli, G. (2015) 'Escaping from a human Capital Trap? Italy's Regions and the Move to centralized primary Schooling, 1861–1936', *European Review of Economic History*, Vol. 20 (1): 46–65.

Cappelli, G. (2017) 'The missing link? Trust, cooperative norms and industrial growth in Italy', *Journal of Interdisciplinary History*, Vol. 47 (3): 333–58.

Ciasca, R. (1916) *L'origine del 'Programma per l'opinione nazionale italiana' del 1847–48*, Milano-Roma-Napoli: Dante Alighieri.

Ciccarelli, C. and Fachin, S. (2017) 'Regional growth with spatial dependence: a case study on early Italian industrialization', *Papers in Regional Science*, Vol. 96 (4): 675–95.

Ciccarelli, C. and Fenoaltea, S. (2009) 'Social overhead constructions in Italy's regions: 1861–1913', *Research in Economic History*, Vol. 26: 1–80.

Ciccarelli, C. and Fenoaltea, S. (2013) 'Through the magnifying glass: provincial aspects of industrial growth in post-Unification Italy', *Economic History Review*, Vol. 66 (1): 57–85.

Ciccarelli, C. and Groote, P. (2017) 'Railway endowment in Italy's provinces, 1839–1913', *Rivista di Storia Economica*, Vol. 33 (1): 45–88.

Ciccarelli, C. and Weisdorf, J. (2019) 'Pioneering into the past: regional literacy developments in Italy before Italy', *European Review of Economic History*, Vol. 23 (3): 329–64.

Corbino, E. (1931) *Annali dell'economia italiana*, vol. 5, Città di Castello: Tipografia Leonardo da Vinci.

Daniele, V., Malanima, P. and Ostuni, N. (2018) 'Geography, market potential and industrialization in Italy 1861–2011', *Papers in Regional Science*, Vol. 97 (3): 639–62.

Di Gianfrancesco, M. (1974) 'La politica commerciale degli stati sardi dal 1814 al 1859', *Rassegna storica del Risorgimento*, Vol. 61: 3–36.

Di Gianfrancesco, M. (1979) *La rivoluzione dei trasporti in Italia nell'età risorgimentale*, L'Aquila: Japadre.

Dincecco, M., Federico, G. and Vindigni, A. (2011) 'Warfare, taxation, and political change: evidence from the Italian Risorgimento', *Journal of Economic History*, Vol. 71 (4): 887–914.

Felice, E. (2014) 'Il Mezzogiorno fra storia e pubblicistica: Una replica a Daniele-Malanima', *Rivista di storia Economica*, Vol. 32 (2): 197–242.

Federico, G. (1997) *An Economic History of Silk Industry 1830–1930*, Cambridge: Cambridge University Press.

Federico, G. (2005) 'Seta, agricoltura e sviluppo economico in Italia', *Rivista di Storia Economica*, Vol. 21 (3): 117–49.

Federico, G. (2007) 'Market integration and market efficiency: the case of 19th century Italy', *Explorations in Economic History*, Vol. 44 (2): 293–316.

Federico, G. (2009a) 'Always on the brink: Italy, 1861–1914', in J. L Cardoso and P. Lains (eds), *Paying for the Liberal State: The Rise of Public Finance in Nineteenth-Century Europe*, Cambridge: Cambridge University Press, pp.186–213.

Federico, G. (2009b) 'Agriculture and economic development in Italy 1861–1939', in P. Lains and V. Pinilla (eds) *Agriculture and Economic Development in Europe Since 1870*, London: Routledge, pp. 234–54.

Federico, G. (2012) 'The Corn Laws in continental perspective', *European Review of Economic History*, Vol. 16 (2): 166–87.

Federico, G. and Tena-Junguito, A. (2014) 'The ripples of the industrial revolution: exports, economic growth and regional integration in Italy in the early 19th century', *European Review of Economic History*, Vol. 18 (3): 349–69.

Federico, G. and Vasta, M. (2015) 'What do we really know about protection before the Great Depression: evidence from Italy', *Journal of Economic History*, Vol. 75 (4): 993–1029.

Federico, G., Nuvolari, A. and Vasta, M. (2019) 'The origins of the Italian regional divide: evidence from real wages, 1861–1913', *Journal of Economic History*, Vol. 79 (1): 63–98.

Federico, G., Nuvolari, A., Ridolfi, L. and Vasta, M. (2021) 'The race between the snail and the tortoise: skill premium and early industrialization in Italy (1861–1913)', *Cliometrica*, Vol. 15 (1): 1–42.

Fenoaltea, S. (1983) 'Italy', in P.K. O'Brien (ed), *Railways and the Economic Development of Western Europe, 1830–1914*, Oxford: Macmillan, pp. 49–120.

Fenoaltea, S. (1988) 'International resource flows and construction movements in the Atlantic economy: the Kuznets cycle in Italy', *Journal of Economic History*, Vol. 48 (3): 605–37.

Fenoaltea, S. (2020) 'Reconstructing the past: the new expenditure-side and composition-of-investment estimates for Italy: 1861–1913', *MPRA Paper* 99432.

Giordano, C. and Zollino, F. (2015) 'A historical reconstruction of capital and labour in Italy: 1861–2013', *Rivista di Storia Economica*, Vol. 31 (2): 155–223.

Greenfield, R. K. (1934) *Economics and Liberalism in the Risorgimento*. Baltimore: John Hopkins University Press (revised version 1965).

ISTAT (1958) *Sommario di statistiche storiche 1861–1955*, Rome: ISTAT.

ISTAT *Serie storiche*, https://seriestoriche.istat.it/ (accessed 26 January 2021).

Kee, H. L., Nicita, A. and Olarreaga, M. (2009) 'Estimating trade restrictiveness indices', *Economic Journal*, Vol. 119 (534): 172–99.

Lampe, M. (2011) 'Explaining nineteenth-century bilateralism: economic and political determinants of the Cobden-Chevalier network', *Economic History Review*, Vol. 64 (2): 644–68.

Lampe, M. (2020) 'European trade policy in the 19th century', *Oxford Research Encyclopedia of Economics and Finance*, https://doi.org/10.1093/acrefore/9780190625979.013.551.

Malanima, P. (2013) 'When did England overtake Italy? Medieval and early modern divergence in prices and wages', *European Review of Economic History*, Vol. 17 (1): 45–70.

Marongiu, G. (1995) *Storia del fisco in Italia: La politica fiscale della Destra Storica*, Vol. 1, Turin: Einaudi.

Missiaia, A. (2016) 'Where do we go from here? Market access and regional development in Italy (1871–1911)' *European Review of Economic History*, Vol. 20 (2): 215–41.

Parravicini, G. (1958) *La politica fiscale e le entrate effettive del Regno d'Italia 1860–1890*, Turin: ILTE.

Pichler, R. (2001) *L'economia lombarda e l'Austria: Politica commerciale e sviluppo industriale 1815–1859*, Milan: Franco Angeli.

Ragioneria, Generale dello Stato (1969) *Il bilancio dello Stato italiano dal 1862 al 1967*, Rome: Poligrafico dello Stato.

Repaci, F. A. (1962) *La finanza pubblica italiana nel secolo 1861–1960*, Bologna: Zanichelli.

Riall, L. (1994) *The Italian Risorgimento: State, Society and National Unification*, London: Routledge.

Romeo, R. (1977–1984), *Cavour e il suo tempo*, Vol. 3, Bari: Laterza.

Rueda, V. and A'Hearn, B. (2020) 'Internal borders and population geography in the unification of Italy', *CEPR Discussion Papers* 14604.

Sannucci, V. (1989) 'The establishment of a central bank: Italy in the 19th century', in M. De Cecco and A. Giovannini (eds) *A European Central Bank?* Cambridge: Cambridge University Press, pp. 224–47.

Schram, A. (1997) *Railways and the Formation of the Italian State in the Nineteenth Century*, Cambridge: Cambridge University Press.

Sereni, E. (1968) *Il capitalismo nelle campagne (1860–1900)*, (1st ed., 1947), Turin: Einaudi.

Timini, J. (2018) 'Currency unions and heterogeneous trade effects: the case of the Latin Monetary Union', *European Review of Economic history*, Vol. 22 (2): 322–48.

Vecchi, G. (2017) *Measuring Well-Being: A History of Italian Living Standards*. Oxford: Oxford University Press.

Woolf, S. (1969) *The Italian Risorgimento,* London: Barnes and Nobles.

Zamagni, V. (1983) 'Ferrovie ed integrazione del mercato nell'Italia post-unitaria', *Studi in onore di G. Barbieri*, Vol. 3: 1635–49.

Zamagni, V. (1998) 'Il debito pubblico italiano 1861–1946: ricostruzione della serie storica', *Rivista di Storia Economica*, Vol. 14 (3): 207–42.

19 After exit

The Habsburg economy since 1870

Max-Stephan Schulze

1 Introduction

Austria's defeat at the hands of Prussia in the 1866 war settled the long-running struggle for supremacy in German-speaking Central Europe. It concluded a process that saw Austria shift out of and Prussia 'grow into' Germany since the end of the Napoleonic Wars. Unification of the separate states of the German Confederation in a new nation-state was attained on Prussian terms after the Franco-Prussian War of 1870/71. The new German Empire excluded Austria—once the leading power in the Holy Roman Empire and, at least nominally, the most senior member state of the Confederation.

However, the main challenge for the multi-national Habsburg Empire was not its exclusion from the new German nation-state. For a range of both domestic and external reasons, it had not been part of the German customs union, the *Zollverein*, and its early precursors either. Rather, the immediate issue was the political and economic integrity of the Habsburg state itself. Austria had lost Lombardy after the 1859 war against France and Sardinia. Interrupted by yet another war (against Denmark and on Prussia's side), the following period of around five years was characterised by rapidly mounting government debt, currency problems, economic stagnation, and political instability (Matis 1972: 128–52; Okey 2001: 157–90). It is against this background that the broader impact of the military defeats of 1866, not just against Prussia but also Italy, must be considered. Austria had to cede Venetia in the aftermath of this conflict, the *Third Italian War of Independence*. The double defeat exposed Austria's decline as a European power. It triggered a re-orientation in the Monarchy's internal and external policies to enhance intra-empire cohesion and to arrest and reverse this decline.

The constitutional Compromise of 1867, effective from 1868, established Austria-Hungary (or the *Dual Monarchy*) in place of the former *Austrian* Empire, where Hungary gained 'full internal autonomy and most of the status of an independent country, but remained united with Austria in the person of the common monarch (...)' (Eddie 1989: 814).[1] It was an attempt to reduce intra-empire nationality conflict and bridge the differences between the two politically and economically dominant nationality groups—the

DOI: 10.4324/9781003283430-23

Germans in Austria and the Magyars in Hungary.[2] This altered both the institutional framework within which policies, economic or otherwise, would be made and the distribution of power within the Empire. Budapest rather than Vienna would henceforth direct government economic policy in Hungary. Two strands of policy were established under the Compromise. *Common affairs* included foreign policy and the (joint) military, managed under the authority of common administrations in Vienna.[3] *Dualistic affairs* were conducted by passing identical legislation in each of the two separate state parliaments. They included tariff and commercial policy, consumption taxes, the common currency, the central bank (initially the pre-existing Austrian National Bank and later the Austro-Hungarian Bank), state debt, and railway issues to the extent that they affected the interests of both parts of the Empire (Good 1984: 97–98; Eddie 1989: 814–15). Common expenditures were covered by tariff revenues and any shortfalls would be met out of the two states' budgets in accordance with the so-called quota—70 percent to be contributed by Austria, and 30 percent by Hungary. In effect confirming the customs union of 1850, the economic parts of the Compromise had provisions for a common tariff and customs territory. They also stipulated the continued operation of the common currency that was under the authority of a shared single bank of issue from 1878 and provided for the free movement of the factors of production across the Empire. The economic arrangements of the Compromise were to be renewed or renegotiated every ten years (cf. Eddie 1989: 815). Whatever its shortcomings, and minor modifications notwithstanding, for half a century the Compromise formed the basic institutional structure within which economic relations between the two constituent Habsburg states evolved. Without making causal claims, the observation that economic growth in both Austria and Hungary was significantly faster in the years after the Compromise than in the half-century before would suggest that it was, at least, not a major impediment to economic change.

This chapter examines the economic development of the Habsburg Empire within this new, post-1866 setting. It seeks to address two questions. First, how did Austria-Hungary's macro-economic performance up to the First World War compare with that of its regional neighbours, especially Germany? Second, to what extent was this performance shaped by the geographical location of the Empire and its regions?

2 Austria-Hungary's economic growth in regional context

One of the largest European economies before the First World War, the multinational Habsburg Empire had a population of more than 50 million people (1913) and a territorial expanse spanning from the borders with Switzerland in the west to Russia in the east, and from a northern border with Germany to the Mediterranean. Similar to other regions in Europe, the origins of *modern economic growth* and industrialisation in the Habsburg lands date back to the eighteenth century (Good 1984; Komlos 1983, 1989).

The Empire's geographical position, straddling the boundaries between Europe's west and east meant that the temporal and spatial diffusion of growth mirrored many characteristics of the European experience in general, including pronounced *regional* variations in income and economic structure. In other words, the European developmental gradient from the northwest to the southeast passed right through the Habsburg domains. The signs of modern economic growth and the transition to modern industry first emerged in the regions closest to western Europe such as Alpine Austria and the Czech lands during the late eighteenth and early nineteenth centuries (Good 1984: 15). In contrast, the Empire's large and populous east had hardly begun to industrialise before the First World War. In the first few decades after the Napoleonic Wars, the Austrian *Hereditary Lands* were economically at par with or even ahead of the countries that were, collectively, to form the new German nation-state (Freudenberger 2003).[4] In 1830, per capita product in these core Habsburg regions was about 10 percent above the German average, if our numbers are about right. Forty years later, the gap had been closed and the German economies had caught up with the western, economically most advanced areas of the Empire.[5] By that time, they were already well ahead of Cisleithania's other regions.

Over the period 1870 to 1913, GDP per capita in Austria-Hungary grew by 1.12 percent per annum compared to 1.52 percent in Germany.[6] The Habsburg Empire was falling behind as its GDP per capita declined from 67 percent of the German level in 1870 to about 56 percent on the eve of the First World War. There were, however, significant performance differentials between the two halves of the Empire. Starting from far lower initial levels of output, economic growth in Hungary was markedly faster than in Austria. *Within* the Empire, Hungary was catching up (proportionally) so that by 1913 its product per head was just above three-quarters of the Austrian level (Table 19.1).

Austria's relative income position weakened as her economic fortunes diverged not just from those of Germany but also much of western Europe (Schulze 2000, 2007a). Yet, given the Empire's specific locus on the European map, comparisons with Germany or western Europe may not necessarily be the only relevant or most apt ones. The comparative performance of the Austrian and, more broadly, Habsburg economy appears in a more benign light when viewed in comparison with its other immediate neighbours such as Italy, Romania, and Russia. The relative decline vis-à-vis Italy was far less pronounced than in comparison with Germany (Table 19.1). Further, the Empire maintained or even enhanced its status as the richest, most advanced economy in central, eastern, and south-eastern Europe (Kopsidis and Schulze 2020). Growth in Romania, eastern Europe's most rapidly expanding economy at the time, proceeded from such low initial levels that it was insufficient to narrow the per capita income gap in absolute terms. Growth in Russia was

Table 19.1 GDP per capita (1990 international $)

	1850	*1860*	*1870*	*1890*	*1913*	*Δ (% p.a.)* *1870–1913*
Habsburg Empire	1216	1301	1364	1620	2202	1.12
Austria	*1390*	*1504*	*1585*	*1798*	*2443*	*1.01*
Hungary	*986*	*1034*	*1071*	*1377*	*1875*	*1.31*
Germany	1629[a]	1877	2041	2726	3902	1.52
Italy	1516	1501	1635	1902	2749	1.22
Romania		792[b]	890	1269	1705	1.52
Russia		1051[c]	1118	1042	1472	0.64

Sources: Austria, Hungary (Habsburg Empire): 1870–1913: Schulze (2000) with minor corrections; 1850–1860: Own calculations based on Kausel (1979) and Komlos (1983). Germany: Hoffmann (1965), Burhop and Wolff (2005). Italy: Malanima (2011). Romania: Axenciuc (2012). Russia: Own calculations based on Allen (2003), Goldsmith (1961), Gregory (1982) and Suhara (2006).

a 1851.

b 1862.

c 1861.

extensive and driven by an exceptionally fast rise in population—its per capita output growth was little more than half the Habsburg rate.

To what extent were the differences in Habsburg and German per capita product growth an outcome of differences in labour productivity growth? We use basic growth accounting to measure the contribution of the different factor inputs labour, human capital, and physical capital to growth in aggregate output and to derive the contribution of total factor productivity as a residual. Total factor productivity, in turn, captures the residual output growth that cannot be explained by growth in factor inputs (i.e. labour, human, and physical capital). Table 19.2 documents alternative calculations to address this issue.[7] Once couched in terms of output per worker rather than output per head of population, the perceived performance gap between Austria-Hungary and Germany largely disappears. This reflects, in part, a rising overall labour force participation rate in Germany and a declining participation rate from a higher level in the Habsburg Empire (Hoffmann 1965; Schulze 2007a).[8] Output per worker rose by 1.19 percent per annum in Austria, 1.44 percent in Hungary, and 1.20 percent in Germany over the period 1870–1910 (Table 19.2, Panel A).[9] Excluding residential housing may be more appropriate for productivity comparisons. This leads to some modest changes in estimated comparative productivity growth, raising the rates of change for both Austria and Hungary in absolute terms and relative to Germany (Table 19.2, Panel B). The number of workers, though, is a fairly crude measure of labour input that fails to take account of changes in the days and hours of work. Hence, the growth accounting results in Table 19.2 also include labour productivity measures based on hours worked. However, for Austria

Table 19.2 Sources of labour productivity growth (percent per annum)

	Output per worker				*Output per hour worked*			
	Δ Q/L	*Δ K/L*	*Δ H/L*	*Δ TFP*	*Δ Q/L*	*Δ K/L*	*Δ H/L*	*Δ TFP*
A. GDP								
Austria								
1870–1910	1.19	0.57	0.36	0.25	1.43	0.64	0.45	0.34
1870–1890	0.80	0.56	0.29	−0.06	1.00	0.62	0.36	0.01
1890–1910	1.59	0.58	0.44	0.57	1.86	0.67	0.53	0.66
Hungary								
1870–1910	1.44	1.02	0.34	0.08	1.68	1.09	0.43	0.17
Germany								
1871–1910	1.20	0.57	0.05	0.59	1.62	0.69	0.19	0.73
1871–1890	0.94	0.51	0.04	0.38	1.23	0.60	0.14	0.49
1890–1910	1.46	0.62	0.05	0.78	1.99	0.78	0.25	0.96
1871–1913	*1.26*	*0.56*	*0.04*	*0.66*	*1.72*	*0.69*	*0.20*	*0.82*
B. GDP excluding housing								
Austria								
1870–1910	1.33	0.56	0.36	0.41	1.57	0.63	0.45	0.49
1870–1890	0.92	0.55	0.29	0.08	1.12	0.61	0.36	0.15
1890–1910	1.75	0.57	0.44	0.74	2.02	0.65	0.53	0.83
Hungary								
1870–1910	1.63	1.00	0.34	0.29	1.87	1.08	0.43	0.37
Germany								
1871–1910	1.15	0.50	0.05	0.60	1.57	0.63	0.19	0.75
1871–1890	0.88	0.42	0.04	0.42	1.17	0.51	0.14	0.52
1890–1910	1.41	0.58	0.05	0.78	1.94	0.74	0.24	0.97
1871–1913	*1.22*	*0.49*	*0.04*	*0.68*	*1.67*	*0.63*	*0.20*	*0.84*

Sources: See Table 19.A1 for output, physical capital, and human capital (schooling); average annual hours worked from Huberman and Minns (2007), for Austria and Hungary weighted average of European countries.

and Hungary no estimates of average annual hours worked are available and Huberman and Minns' (2007) weighted average for Europe has been used instead.[10] The results should, therefore, be treated with some caution. Finally, the average years of schooling of the age cohorts represented in the labour force have been included as a basic approximation of improvements in labour quality due to education.

The key result here is that in terms of aggregate labour productivity *growth*, the Habsburg Empire does not appear to have been lagging behind the rising German economic powerhouse. On the contrary, three out of the four different measures documented in Table 19.2 suggest that, if anything, growth in labour productivity was slightly faster in Austria-Hungary than in Germany during the period from 1870 to 1910.[11] However, despite catching up proportionally, the Habsburg domains failed to reduce the (absolute) gap in productivity *levels* that had emerged because of the loss of 'momentum' in the first half of the nineteenth century (cf. Freudenberger 2003). Whilst inter-economy productivity comparisons are fraught with substantial conceptual problems (Broadberry 1998; Broadberry and Burhop 2007), the magnitudes are such that large *level* differences in aggregate output per worker (and per hour) seem highly likely: According to the revised estimates, German labour productivity was about twice the level prevailing in the Austro-Hungarian economy by 1870.

Growth in capital per worker (or per hour worked) made a distinctly larger contribution to the increase in labour productivity in the Habsburg Empire than in Germany (Table 19.2). This was an outcome of the particularly rapid expansion of the capital stock in Hungary (at 4 percent on annual average over 1870–1910 compared to 3 percent in Germany) combined with labour inputs that were growing at less than half the German rate. Capital deepening in Austria was considerably slower than in Hungary and contributed about as much to labour productivity growth at the aggregate level as in Germany.

The impact of improvements in human capital varied considerably between Austria-Hungary and Germany. Approximated by the educational experience of the labour force, the contribution to productivity growth over 1870–1910 ranged between 0.34 (Hungary, output per worker) and 0.45 percent per annum (Austria, output per hour) in the Empire. This contrasts with Germany where changes in the stock of human capital made far less of a difference to productivity growth. Here, educational attainment accounted for between 3 and 13 percentage points of the increase in labour productivity. This reflects relatively high German levels of schooling in 1870, which implied only limited scope for further increments in the period 1870–1910. By contrast, average years of schooling in the Habsburg Empire in the 1870s were far below those in Germany and remained so throughout the next four decades, though differentials declined over time (Schulze 2007a).

As a measure of residual output growth that is not accounted for by growth in factor inputs, TFP growth reflects a host of factors; most frequently it is associated with the impact of technological progress, organisational advance, structural change (i.e. the shift of resources from one sector to another) and the forces that make for such changes. The growth accounting results reported in Table 19.2 suggest that the TFP contribution to labour productivity growth was smaller in the Habsburg Empire than in Germany. This holds across all four measures employed here and across almost all sub-periods.[12] In some instances, the difference is substantial, ranging between 4 and 38 percentage points (Panel B, Table 19.2). However, Austrian TFP growth accelerated substantially in the post-1890 recovery from the *Great Depression* (Good 1978; Komlos 1983; Schulze 2000). The evidence would suggest that in the Habsburg lands a significantly larger proportion of TFP growth than in

Germany can be attributed to the impact of structural change—that is, first, a shift of labour from sectors with lower productivity *levels* to higher productivity sectors (static shift) and, second, from lower productivity growth to higher productivity *growth* activities (dynamic shift) (Table 19.3).

There are three main findings thus far. First, in the decades after German unification, the Habsburg Empire was falling behind in terms of per capita output. However, it was at least keeping pace with its northern neighbour in terms of labour productivity growth. This result offers some qualification to the more pessimistic assessments of economic development in post-*Ausgleich* Austria-Hungary (Gerschenkron 1977) and earlier comparative estimates of productivity growth (Schulze 2007a). It is not the outcome of significant changes in the evidence of the Habsburg economy, minor corrections notwithstanding. Rather it reflects the impact of revisions to the German national product data that are part of the present labour productivity approximations. On the output side, it is especially Burhop and Wolff's (2005) re-estimation of industrial production that implies a substantial reduction in aggregate growth over 1851–1913 and far higher initial output levels compared to the original Hoffmann (1965) estimates. Second, the contribution of TFP growth in the Habsburg Empire was markedly lower than in Germany and a far larger proportion can be accounted for by the effects

Table 19.3 Structural change and growth in output per worker (percent per annum)

	Δ Q/L (% p.a.)	*intra-sector*	*static shift*	*dynamic shift*
Habsburg Empire				
1870–1910	1.44	0.96	0.33	0.15
1870–1890	1.15	0.86	0.21	0.07
1890–1910	1.73	1.17	0.47	0.08
Austria				
1870–1910	1.33	0.81	0.37	0.15
1870–1890	0.92	0.60	0.60	0.06
1890–1910	1.75	1.13	0.52	0.09
Hungary				
1870–1910	1.63	1.24	0.21	0.18
1870–1890	1.57	1.35	0.08	0.13
1890–1910	1.70	1.26	0.40	0.05
Germany				
1871–1910	1.15	0.84	0.23	0.08
1871–1890	0.88	0.59	0.29	0.00
1890–1910	1.41	1.16	0.21	0.04

Sources: Schulze (2007a) revised; Table 19.A1.
Note: growth in output per worker excluding housing.

of structural change. Technical and organisational progress, then, made a markedly smaller contribution to labour productivity growth in the Empire compared to Germany. Third, Hungary, the least developed of the three economies, exhibited significantly faster rates of output and labour productivity growth in agriculture and industry than either of its customs union partner Austria or Germany (Table 19A.1). Here, some of the characteristics typically associated with poor economies catching up with the rich were on display (Abramovitz 1986). Hungary did not face as rapidly diminishing returns to capital as high-income and capital-rich economies. Hence, its aggregate growth was associated with particularly rapid increases in capital–labour ratios and strong *intra*-sectoral productivity growth. Note that this process of capital-deepening was not confined to the emerging industrial sector but, in stark contrast to Austria, constituted a prominent feature of a fast-growing agricultural sector (cf. Komlos 1983; Good 1984; Eddie 1989; Kopsidis and Schulze 2020).

3 Spatial dimensions of economic change in the Habsburg Empire

Industrialisation as well as the timing and pace of modern economic growth in late eighteenth- and nineteenth-century Europe were profoundly regional phenomena (Pollard 1986). The Habsburg Empire was no exception to this broader European experience. This section explores the extent to which Austria-Hungary's aggregate performance was shaped by its regions' geographical location, that is, its 'unique position—being both close to and at the same time far away from the European industrial core' (Klein et al. 2017: 64).

Even a glance at a map of Europe before the First World War would indicate that most of the lands under Habsburg rule were geographically distant from the economically most advanced western and north-western parts of the Continent, except Germany. Austria-Hungary's immediate neighbours in the east and south-east were poor in European comparison. This, the following discussion suggests, had far-reaching economic implications. Krugman (1991), Redding and Venables (2004), Head and Mayer (2011) and others writing in the spirit of the *New Economic Geography* have argued that the geography of a region (or country) determines not just its own physical characteristics but, importantly, also its location *relative* to other regions. This relative position can exert strong effects on a given country or region's access to markets, the location of economic activity, and income. Indeed, market access as a 'second nature' (as distinct from physical, 'first nature') geography measure—and indicator of economic centrality—has been identified as one of the major determinants of cross-country income differences and regional income differentials *within* countries (Redding and Venables 2004; Mayer 2009; Head and Mayer 2011; Martinez-Gallaraga et al. 2015; Jacks and Novy 2018).

It is a key insight of New Economic Geography that the spatial structure of economies and the location of activity—at regional, national, and international levels—are to a large extent determined by the interplay between trade costs and increasing returns to scale. If trade costs are very high or very low, economic activity tends to be spatially dispersed. In contrast, if trade costs fall into an intermediate range, industries subject to increasing returns to scale (in the production of final and intermediate goods) will be attracted to locations close to large and growing markets and associated gains from region-specific external economies of scale. Proximity to suppliers of capital goods and intermediate inputs lowers the production costs of firms. The 'pull of centrality' leads to economic activity intensifying in some regions and declining in others, at least in relative terms. The implication is that even with perfect institutions everywhere, trade and the integration of markets brought about by falling trade costs may lead to income divergence between regions or whole 'national' economies as economic activity becomes more concentrated spatially (Krugman 1991).

The question to be addressed now is whether and to what extent differences in market access (or market potential) can account for differences in economic activity across the regions of the Habsburg Empire over the late nineteenth century. Further, what are the implications of differential regional economic development for the assessment of the Empire's aggregate performance?

The data required to align with the recent literature and derive measures of market access that are grounded explicitly in theory are not (yet) available at the level of the individual regions of the Habsburg Empire. The analysis, therefore, relies on an earlier, pioneering approach that first introduced the notion of market potential (Harris 1954). In this setting, a region's market potential is measured as the sum of trade cost-weighted GDP in that region and in other adjacent or distant regions. Changes in market potential are the outcome of changes in income—regions' own as well as that of other regions—and/or changes in the distance-related costs of accessing this income. A reduction or rise in transport (or, more broadly, trade) costs will, therefore, affect regions' access to markets.

Approximating market potential requires data on the GDP of domestic regions and foreign countries, transport costs over land and across the sea as well as other trade costs such as tariffs. With these data in place, market potential was estimated for a balanced sample of all 22 Habsburg regions and at decadal intervals from 1870 to 1910, taking into account the least-cost routes and modes of accessing domestic purchasing power (DMP) and the GDP of the Empire's fifteen main trading partners—Belgium, France, Denmark, Germany, India, Italy, the Netherlands, Portugal, Russia, Spain, Sweden, Switzerland, Turkey, United Kingdom, and the United States.[13] Note that almost three-quarters of the Empire's total foreign trade was conducted with continental Europe and more than half of that was with Germany alone (Eddie 1977, 1989; Tessner 1989).

The discussion builds on a simple panel regression framework and the balanced sample of 22 regional economies across the Habsburg Empire. The variable of interest here is regional market potential which captures 'the changing costs of economic interactions across distance' (Crafts and Venables 2003). What have been its effects on per capita regional income and manufacturing output? Some specifications include controls for time-invariant, 'exogenous' physical geography characteristics—access to the sea, terrain ruggedness, soil quality, area size, natural endowments with mineral resources, and climate—which may confer different geographic advantages or disadvantages for economic activity across different regions.[14] For example, being landlocked or faced with very rugged terrain raises transport costs, while poor soil quality lowers (agricultural) productivity. The specifications with region-fixed effects also include time-variant measures of regions' primary resource endowments as controls (cf. Redding and Venables 2004): the proportion of arable land and access to energy, the latter captured here by a calorific content-weighted measure of regional lignite, anthracite and oil production per capita.[15]

By construction, the market potential measure includes regions' own GDP and that of other regions and countries. With GDP per capita as the dependent variable, this raises potential reverse causation and endogeneity problems. These issues are addressed by drawing on two-stage least-squares estimation and instrumenting market potential with the sum of the inverted distances to *all* nodes in domestic regions and foreign countries in the relevant sample. This is to avoid the explicit imposition of a centre (cf. Head and Mayer 2006). Table 19.4 documents the main results, referring throughout—for simplicity of exposition—to the same measure of market potential, that is, combined access to both DMP and European purchasing power (EMP). This maps best onto the actual foreign trade relationships of the Empire in the late nineteenth century. Note, that it makes no material difference to the argument if, instead of EMP, the broader measure including also access to India, Turkey, and the United States (foreign market potential, FMP) were used.[16]

In terms of the relationship between GDP per capita and market potential, the estimated coefficients on market potential are stable across different specifications and significant throughout. They are fully within the range observed in other recent studies, indicating an elastic response of real GDP per head to changes in market access. While area size has no discernible effect, the controls for terrain ruggedness and soil quality have the expected signs and are significant. The coefficient on the intercept dummy for coastal access is negative and significant due to the disproportionately large and growing FMP, especially in Dalmatia and the Littoral. At the same time, for reasons that are beyond the scope of the present analysis, these regions were not able to benefit from good market access. The coefficient on the dummy for within-region sources of energy is positive but insignificant, likely reflecting that domestic inter-regional trade in coal mitigates the disadvantages of lacking local resources. The outcomes of the region fixed effect regressions, with

Table 19.4 Market potential and per capita output (second stage regression coefficients of 2SLS regression, robust standard errors in parentheses)

Dependent variable:	*(1)*	*(2)*	*(3)*	*(4)*	*(5)*
	GDP p. c.	*GDP p. c.*	*GDP p. c.*	*GDP p. c.*	*Industrial output p. c.*
Ln(market potential)	0.312**	0.358**	0.332**	0.336**	0.688**
	(0.023)	(0.085)	(0.060)	(0.060)	(0.167)
Area	0.000	0.000			
	(0.000)	(0.000)			
Slope	−0.049$^+$	−0.050$^+$			
	(0.029)	(0.029)			
Soil quality	0.426$^+$	0.447$^+$			
	(0.254)	(0.260)			
Longitude	−0.026	−0.023			
	(0.018)	(0.019)			
Latitude	−0.018	0.017			
	(0.040)	(0.040)			
Coast	−0.485*	−0.492*			
	(0.193)	(0.196)			
Mineral deposits	0.027	0.025			
	(0.131)	(0.132)			
Constant	3.997*	3.653*	5.133**	5.244**	0.709
	(1.876)	(2.016)	(0.465)	(0.484)	(1.585)
Ln(share arable area)				0.247$^+$	0.180
				(0.135)	(0.664)
Ln(energy output p. c.)				−0.015	0.012
				(0.011)	(0.048)
N	110	110	110	110	110
Region FE	No	No	Yes	Yes	Yes
Period dummies	No	Yes	Yes	Yes	Yes
Adjusted R^2	0.694	0.689	0.939	0.941	0.902
F statistic	31.83	25.63	45.81	42.62	29.03
p (F)	0.000	0.000	0.000	0.000	0.000

Sources: See text, especially endnotes 13, 14, and 15.
Notes: ** $p < 0.01$, * $p < 0.05$, <0.10. The table reports the second-stage results of 2SLS regressions. Instrument is ln(sum of inverted distance to all sample cities)*time.

or without geography controls (Table 19.4, columns (3) and (4)), confirm the role of market potential. As expected on theoretical grounds, the impact of changes in market potential is particularly strong in the case of manufacturing output per head (column 5 in Table 19.4). The estimated elasticity of response to changes in access to markets is about twice as high as for aggregate output per capita and equally significant.

These results support the argument that geography played a critical role in the economic development of the Habsburg Empire and its regions. In the absence of major differences in institutional quality at the region level,[17] and controlling for key characteristics of the physical environment ('first nature' geography), 'second nature' geography forces accounted for much of the substantial regional differentials in output and income in the forty or so years before the First World War (cf. Klein et al. 2017: 73, Table 4.6). Proximity mattered: regions enjoying better access to markets performed much better in terms of per capita income. Even so, many of Austria-Hungary's regions were physically and economically far removed from domestic and international markets. This had far-reaching consequences for the performance of the aggregate economy and its fortunes relative to those of its German neighbour.

4 Conclusion

While Austria-Hungary maintained—and in some ways even enhanced—its status as the leading economy of central and eastern Europe, its position vis-à-vis the newly united Germany eroded over time. The income and productivity gap that had emerged in the decades before 1870 was not to be closed in the years thereafter, despite respectable *growth* in labour productivity that was at par with that of Germany. In absolute terms, this gap widened. This was not an outcome of misguided economic policy but rather a result of geographical fundamentals—the very location of the country, which limited comparative access to markets and so left little room for effective policy in the first place. In that sense, it is misplaced to view the Habsburg economy as a 'failure' (Gerschenkron 1977).

The limited comparative evidence that is currently available suggests that economic agents in Germany and its regions enjoyed far better access to markets than the Habsburg Empire. If recent estimates of access to domestic and international markets are about right, producers in the Habsburg regions faced a very substantial disadvantage with an average market potential in 1860 that was approximately half the size of Germany's. Initial exploratory estimates for the post-1870 decades point to a somewhat smaller gap of 25 to 30 percent (cf. Caruana-Galizia et al. 2021). These are large differentials even after considering a fair dose of measurement error. At the level of the typical elasticities such as those obtained here, these differences are substantial enough to support the point that aggregate and industrial growth in Germany was underpinned by productivity gains derived from market size—*inter alia* through the exploitation of economies of scale, specialisation and agglomeration—to an extent that was not possible in the Habsburg realms. It is here, then, where at least part of the gap in total factor productivity growth likely originated. In short, too many of its regions were too far away from purchasing power to keep up with the northern neighbour. For the populous eastern parts of the Empire, in particular, being on the geographical periphery of Austria-Hungary meant being on the economic periphery of Europe.

Appendix

Table 19.A1 Output and factor input growth, 1870–1910 (percent per annum)

	Output		*Capital*[e]		*Labour*	*Schooling*
Agriculture						
Austria	1.39		1.08		0.28	
Hungary	2.15		2.86		0.50	
Germany[a]	1.63		1.16		0.54	
Industry						
Austria	2.40		4.74		1.26	
Hungary	3.81		4.62		2.25	
Germany[a]	2.94		4.72		2.01	
Total Economy	GDP	*GDP*[b]	total	non-residential[d]		
Austria	1.84	*1.98*	2.55	*2.52*	0.65	1.69
Hungary	2.10	*2.29*	4.05	*4.01*[c]	0.66	1.64
Germany[a]	2.55	*2.50*	3.21	*3.02*	1.35	1.48

Sources: Schulze (2007a) revised. Output: Table 19.1. Schooling: Schulze and Fernandes (2009).

a 1871–1910.

b Excluding rent.

c 1867–1913.

d Excludes non-agricultural residential dwellings.

e Information on capital formation excludes livestock.

Notes

1 In the following, 'Austria' in her post-1867 guise refers to all *Kingdoms and Lands Represented in the Imperial Council* (or, in contemporary usage, *Cisleithania*, i.e. this side of the river Leitha that ran between the two halves of the Empire). 'Hungary' (or *Transleithania*) refers to all territories of the Hungarian crown (Hungary proper, Fiume, Croatia-Slavonia).

2 The settlement, however, largely ignored the political and economic aspirations of the Slavs in both halves of the Empire. See Okey (2001) for a general treatment of the nationality problem and Schulze and Wolf (2012) for an exploration of intra-Empire *economic* nationalism.

3 Specifically, this entailed a common foreign office, a common war office and a common finance ministry for the purpose of dealing with the financial aspects of foreign policy, the common army and navy. Note that the much smaller armed forces of the Austrian *Landwehr* and Hungarian *Honvéd* remained under the separate authorities of the two national governments.

4 In the narrow definition, used here, the Austrian Hereditary Lands included the regions of modern-day Austria (excluding Salzburg) in their pre-1918 borders and Carniola (nowadays part of Slovenia). In the broader definition, they also included the lands of the Bohemian crown.

5 These comparisons are based on the following data: first, a backward projection for the Hereditary Lands derived from 1870 GDP per capita of the Empire's

regions (fully revised estimates based on sources set out in Schulze 2007b, 2019) using the index for modern Austria from Maddison Project Database (2013); second, a backward projection of Cisleithania's 1870 GDP per capita (Schulze 2000) drawing on Kausel (1979) and Komlos (1983); and, third, Pfister's (2011) baseline estimates of German GDP per capita for 1800 and 1850.

6 Both the Habsburg and the German series are estimates from the output side. The German rate of per capita growth reported here is only marginally higher than Pfister's (2020) income side revision of earlier 'compromise' estimates of national product (Burhop and Wolf 2005).

7 This growth accounting exercise is based on a standard Cobb-Douglas production function with constant returns to scale, augmented to allow for human capital to feature as a third factor of production: $\Delta(Q/L)/(Q/L) = \alpha(\Delta K/L)/(K/L) + \beta(\Delta H/L)/(H/L) + \Delta(A/A)$ where Q is real GDP, K is physical capital, L are labour inputs, H is human capital and A is total factor productivity, assuming factor shares in value-added of 70 percent for labour (half of which is taken to accrue to human capital) and 30 percent to physical capital.

8 Here, the participation rate is taken as the simple ratio of the total labour force to population.

9 In all variants discussed here, the growth rates for labour productivity in Germany are slightly higher if measured over the period 1871–1913 rather than 1871–1910. The choice of 1910 is for ease of comparison (as no post-1910 labour force data are available for Austria-Hungary) and makes no material difference to the argument. However, the 1871–1913 rates are reported in Table 19.2 for completeness.

10 Note that the results are not materially affected if, as a robustness check, one were to use the annual working hours for Germany in the labour input estimate for Austria-Hungary.

11 Across the Empire as a whole and during 1870–1910, output per worker rose by 1.28 percent per annum (GDP) and 1.44 percent (GDP excluding residential housing). For output per hour worked, the corresponding rates are 1.51 and 1.67 percent per annum.

12 When any advances in schooling are subsumed into a broader, 'crude' TFP measure, much of the difference between Austria-Hungary and Germany disappears.

13 See Schulze (2007b) for details on sources and methods used. The regional GDP estimates reported there have since been revised comprehensively. In particular, the new estimates for Hungary are now based on the same approach used for Austria, where regional GDPs have been built up from sector level estimates, drawing mostly on procedures akin to those used in the construction of state-wide aggregates (Schulze 2000).

14 Table 19.4 includes the following variables: *Area* is a control for a region's surface size; *Slope* is the mean slope ordinal value for each region based on United Nations Food and Agriculture Organisation (FAO) global raster maps of slopes (FAO 2015b); regional *Soil quality* is based on data from the global raster map on soil nutrient availability produced by the United Nations Food and Agriculture Organisation (FAO) (FAO 2015a); *Coast* is a dummy taking the value of 1 if a region has direct access to the sea; *Mineral deposits* is a dummy taking the value of 1 if a region has coal (anthracite, lignite) and/or oil deposits as documented in the official Austrian and Hungarian statistical publications; *Longitude* and *Latitude* serve as a proxy for climatic conditions.

15 The relevant data are documented extensively and in detail in the official Austrian and Hungarian statistical publications. Neither of the two measures is exogenous to income activity. Both the expansion of arable land and the prospecting for and subsequent exploitation of natural resources such as coal or oil require human effort, incentives and investment.

16 Using alternative market potential measures but otherwise the same specification (3) as in Table 19.4 yields the following coefficients on market potential: 0.392 (EMP), 0.369 (FMP), 0.284 (DMP), 0.313 (FMP+DMP), all significant at the 1 percent level.

17 The regions *within* each of the two Habsburg states shared a common institutional and legal framework. Economically relevant institutional differences *between* Austria and Hungary in the post-*Ausgleich* period were distinctly limited. Hungary was granted autonomy in government policy under the terms of the 1867 *Dual Settlement,* a privilege not extended to Austrian provinces run from Vienna (notwithstanding some limited measure of autonomy given to Galicia in 1869). Nevertheless, the extent to which constitutionally and institutionally established self-governance could make for systematic, far-reaching policy differences between the two parts of the customs and monetary union, was seriously constrained by the *Dual Settlement* itself. All dualistic affairs (including tariff and commercial policy, consumption taxes, the common currency, the central bank, state debt and railway issues affecting both sides) were subject to identical legislation in Budapest and Vienna. Different policy emphases between the two governments notwithstanding (cf. Good 1984: 156–61), by the 1870s the two halves of the Habsburg Empire were institutionally closely aligned.

References

Abramovitz, M. (1986) 'Catching-up, forging ahead and falling behind', *Journal of Economic History*, Vol. 46 (2): 385–406.

Allen, R.C. (2003) *Farm to Factory: A Reinterpretation of the Soviet Industrial Revolution*, Princeton NJ: Princeton University Press.

Axenciuc, V. (2012) *Produsul Intern Brut al Românieri 1862–2000: Serii Statistice Seculare şi Argumente Metodologice*, Vols. 1, 2, Bucarest: Editura Economicâ.

Broadberry, S. (1998) 'How did the United States and Germany overtake Britain? A sectoral analysis of comparative productivity levels, 1870–1910', *Journal of Economic History*, Vol. 58: 375–407.

Broadberry, S. and Burhop, C. (2007) 'Comparative productivity in British and German manufacturing before World War II: reconciling direct benchmark estimates and time series projections', *Journal of Economic History*, Vol. 67: 315–49.

Burhop, C. and Wolff, G. (2005) 'A compromise estimate of net national product and the business cycle in Germany, 1851–1913', *Journal of Economic History*, Vol. 65 (4): 613–57.

Caruana-Galizia, P., Hashino, T. and Schulze, M. S. (2021) 'Underlying sources of growth: first and second nature geography', in S. Broadberry and K. Fukao (eds), *Cambridge Economic History of the Modern World*, Vol. 1: *1700 to 1870*, Cambridge: Cambridge University Press, pp. 339–68.

Crafts, N. F. R. and Venables, A. (2003) 'Globalisation in history: a geographical perspective', in M. D. Bordo, A. M. Taylor and J. G. Williamson (eds.), *Globalisation in historical perspective*, Chicago: Chicago University Press, pp. 323–70.

Eddie, S. M. (1977) 'The terms and patterns of Hungarian foreign trade, 1882–1913', *Journal of Economic History*, Vol. 37: 329–58.

Eddie, S. M. (1989) 'Economic policy and economic development in Austria-Hungary, 1867–1913', in P. Mathias and S. Pollard (eds), *The Cambridge Economic History of Europe*, Vol. 8., Cambridge: Cambridge University Press, pp. 814–86.

Freudenberger, H. (2003) *Lost Momentum: Austrian Economic Development 1750s–1830s*, Vienna: Böhlau.

Gerschenkron, A. (1977) *An Economic Spurt that Failed; Four Lectures in Austrian History*, Princeton: Princeton University Press.

Goldsmith, R. W. (1961) 'The economic growth of Tsarist Russia 1860–1913', *Economic Development and Cultural Change*, Vol. 9 (3): 441–75.

Good, D. F. (1978) 'The great depression and Austrian growth after 1873', *Economic History Review*, Vol. 31 (2): 290–294.

Good, D. F. (1984) *The Economic Rise of the Habsburg Empire 1750–1914*, Berkeley: University of California Press.

Gregory, P. R. (1982) *Russian National Income 1885–1913*, Cambridge: Cambridge University Press.

Harris, C. (1954) 'The market as a factor in the localization of industry in the United States', *Annals of the American Geographers*, Vol. 64: 315–48.

Head, K. and Mayer, T. (2011) 'Gravity, market potential and economic development', *Journal of Economic Geography*, Vol. 11: 281–94.

Hoffmann, W. G. (1965) *Das Wachstum der deutschen Wirtschaft seit der Mitte des 19. Jahrhunderts*, Berlin: Springer.

Huberman, M. and Minns, C. (2007) "The times they are not changin': days and hours of work in the Old and New Worlds, 1870–2000', *Explorations in Economic History*, Vol. 44 (4): 538–67.

Jacks, D. S. and Novy, D. (2018) 'Market potential and global growth over the long twentieth century', *Journal of International Economics*, Vol. 114: 221–237.

Kausel, A. (1979) 'Österreichs Volkseinkommen 1830–1913', in Österreichisches Statistisches Zentralamt (ed), *Geschichte und Ergebnisse der zentralen amtlichen Statistik in Österreich 1829–1979*, Vienna: Österreichisches Statistisches Zentralamt, pp. 689–720.

Klein, A., Schulze, M. S. and Vonyo, T. (2017) 'How peripheral was the periphery? Industrialization in East Central Europe since 1870', in K. H. O'Rourke and J. G. Williamson (eds), *The Spread of Modern Industry to the Periphery Since 1871*, Oxford: Oxford University Press, pp. 63–90.

Komlos, J. (1983) *The Habsburg Monarchy as a Customs Union: Economic Development in Austria-Hungary in the Nineteenth Century*, Princeton, NJ: Princeton University Press.

Komlos, J. (1989) *Stature, Nutrition, and Economic Development in the Eighteenth Century Habsburg Monarchy: The 'Austrian' Model of the Industrial Revolution*, Princeton, NJ: Princeton University Press.

Kopsidis, M. and Schulze, M. S. (2020) 'The long 19th century (1800–1914): economic growth and sectoral developments', in M. Morys (ed), *The Economic History of Central, East and South-East Europe: 1800 to the Present*, London: Routledge, pp. 39–68.

Krugman, P. (1991) *Geography and Trade*, Cambridge, MA: MIT Press.

Maddison Project Database (2013). https://www.rug.nl/ggdc/historicaldevelopment/maddison/releases/maddison-project-database-2013

Malanima, P. (2011) 'The long decline of a leading economy: GDP in central and northern Italy, 1300–1913', *European Review of Economic History*, Vol. 15: 169–219.

Martinez-Gallaraga, J., Tirado, D. A. and González-Val, R. (2015) 'Market potential and regional economic growth in Spain (1860–1930)', *European Review of Economic History*, Vol. 19 (4): 335–58.

Matis, H. (1972) *Oesterreichs Wirtschaft 1848–1913: Konjunkturelle Dynamik und gesellschaftlicher Wandel im Zeitalter Franz Josephs I*, Berlin: Duncker & Humblot.

Mayer, T. (2009) 'Market potential and development', *Centre d'Études Prospective et d'Information Internationales, Document de Travail* 24.

Okey, R. (2001) *The Habsburg Monarchy c. 1765–1918*, London: Macmillan.

Pfister, U. (2011) 'Economic growth in Germany, 1500–1850', *Contribution to the Quantifying long run economic development conference, University of Warwick in Venice, 22–24 March 2011.*

Pfister, U. (2020) 'The Crafts-Harley view of German industrialization: an independent estimate of the income side of net national product, 1851–1913', *European Review of Economic History*, Vol. 24 (3): 502–21.

Pollard, S. (1986) *Peaceful Conquest: The Industrialization of Europe 1760–1970*, Oxford: Oxford University Press.

Redding, S. and Venables, A. J. (2004) 'Economic geography and international inequality', *Journal of International Economics*, Vol. 62: 53–82.

Schulze, M. S. (2000) 'Patterns of growth and stagnation in the late nineteenth century Habsburg economy', *European Review of Economic History*, Vol. 4 (3): 311–40.

Schulze, M. S. (2007a) 'Origins of catch-up failure: comparative productivity growth in the Habsburg Empire, 1870–1910', *European Review of Economic History*, Vol. 11 (2): 189–218.

Schulze, M. S. (2007b) 'Regional income dispersion and market potential in the late nineteenth century Habsburg Empire', *LSE Working Papers in Economic History* 106/07.

Schulze, M. S. (2019) 'From empire to republic: regional inequality in Austria, 1870–2010', in J. Roses and N. Wolf (eds), *The Economic Development of Europe's Regions*, London: Routledge, pp. 42–68.

Schulze, M. S. and Fernandes, F. T. (2009) 'Human capital formation in Austria-Hungary and Germany: time series estimates of educational attainment, 1860–1910', in K. Halmos et al. (eds), *A felhalmozás Míve: Történeti Tanulmányok Kövér György Tiszteletére*, Budapest: Századvég Kiadó, pp. 275–89.

Schulze, M. S. and Wolf, N. (2012) 'Economic nationalism and economic integration: the Austro-Hungarian Empire in the late 19th century', *Economic History Review*, Vol. 65 (2): 652–73.

Suhara, M. (2006) 'Russian industrial growth: an estimation of a production index, 1860–1913', *Nihon University, College of Economics, Working Paper* 05–03.

Tessner, M. (1989) *Der Aussenhandel Oesterreich-Ungarns von 1867 bis 1913*, Cologne: Mueller Boltermann.

United Nations Food and Agriculture Organisation (FAO 2015a) Harmonized World Soil Database v 1.2: Soil Qualities for Crop Production, Nutrient availability. Online: http://www.fao.org/soils-portal/soil-survey/soil-maps-and-databases/harmonized-world-soil-database-v12/en/

United Nations Food and Agriculture Organisation (FAO 2015b) Harmonized World Soil Database v 1.2: Global Terrain Slope and Aspect Data. Online: http://www.fao.org/soils-portal/soil-survey/soil-maps-and-databases/harmonized-world-soil-database-v12/en/

20 British relative economic decline in the aftermath of German unification

Nicholas Crafts

1 Introduction

Between 1871 and 1913, economic growth in the UK was considerably slower than in Germany. The UK was overtaken by the United States in terms of real GDP per capita. Whereas labour productivity growth in the UK slowed down quite markedly in the 1870s and failed to pick up as the second industrial revolution gathered pace, the opposite unfolded in Germany. By 1913, Germany had reduced the gap in its real GDP per capita with the UK quite considerably and had established a lead in terms of productivity in the industrial sector. Evidently, the relative economic decline of the UK, which was to continue through much of the twentieth century, had already begun.

There is a strong tradition in British economic history that alleges that late Victorian (and Edwardian) Britain 'failed' and that, as a result, economic growth was retarded. This claim was vigorously disputed by the early cliometricians. However, it cannot be considered completely refuted, especially with the advent of endogenous growth economics. The suggestion of failure typically entails the hypothesis that British institutions and/or government policies compared unfavourably with those of other countries, notably including Germany, and needed reform. It has been suggested that the UK could have benefited from a German-style banking system, that German policies to promote scientific and technological education were superior during the second industrial revolution, and that the UK was ill-advised to maintain free trade when its main rivals, including Germany, were being protectionist.

A prominent feature of the decades before World War I, especially for contemporaries, was the growing Anglo-German trade rivalry. The populist idea of 'Made in Germany' (Williams 1896) reflected a widespread angst that German prowess in manufacturing was undermining Britain's position in the world economy and advocated an end to free trade. The UK share of global exports of manufactures fell while that of Germany increased. Germany, rather than the UK, established a comparative advantage in several new industries. If there were direct adverse effects of the development of the German economy on British economic growth, the trade channel has been seen by some as the obvious possibility.

DOI: 10.4324/9781003283430-24

In what follows, I start in Section 2 by setting out the details of comparative growth and productivity performance for Germany and the UK in the period 1871–1913. In Section 3, I review the extensive literature on a possible growth failure in Britain during these years and highlight some areas of concern but conclude that there was no massive growth failure. In Section 4, I examine the implications of Anglo-German trade rivalry for UK growth performance and find that there is no strong evidence that this had serious implications.

2 Comparative growth and productivity performance

Over the period 1871–1913, the growth of real GDP per capita was 1.48 percent per year in Germany when compared with 0.81 percent per year in the UK. Faster German growth came in the context of an initially much lower level of real income and entailed catching up with the UK such that real GDP per capita rose from 56.2 percent of the UK level in 1871 to 74.1 percent by 1913 (Table 20.1).

As might be expected, Table 20.2 shows that faster growth of real GDP per capita is accounted for by superior growth of labour productivity in Germany, which averaged 1.75 percent per year over the period 1871–1913 compared with 1.06 percent per year in the UK during 1873–1913. Table 20.2 also reports that labour productivity growth in Germany sped up after 1871, whereas in the UK, the opposite unfolded. An econometric analysis of UK labour productivity growth based on output per hour worked finds that trend growth declined from 2.15 percent per year in 1869 to 0.84 percent per year in 1890 such that the so-called 'climacteric' was in the 1870s, and not after 1899 as is sometimes claimed (Crafts and Mills 2020).

According to the growth accounting exercise which is implemented in Table 20.2, both capital deepening and crude total factor productivity (TFP) contributions to labour productivity growth were larger in Germany than in the UK with the latter accounting for a substantial share (64 percent) of German outperformance over the entire period. The gap in TFP growth between both countries is quite considerable (0.68 percentage points) between the late nineteenth century and World War I, at which point German

Table 20.1 Growth of real GDP per capita, 1871–1913 (% per year)

Germany	1.48
UK	0.81
Memorandum item	
Real GDP/Person, Germany/UK ($1990GK)	
1871	56.2
1913	74.1

Sources: Maddison (2010), Pfister (2020), Thomas and Dimsdale (2017).

Table 20.2 Growth accounting estimates (% per year)

	Capital deepening	*Crude TFP Growth*	Y/HW *Growth*
Germany			
1851–1871	0.39	0.39	0.78
1871–1898	0.55	1.13	1.68
1898–1913	0.79	1.10	1.89
1871–1913	0.63	1.12	1.75
UK			
1856–1873	0.72	1.34	2.06
1873–1899	0.37	0.81	1.18
1899–1913	0.42	0.42	0.84
1873–1913	0.38	0.68	1.06

Sources: Germany based on output growth from Pfister (2020), capital stock growth from Burhop and Wolff (2005), labour force growth from Hoffmann (1965), and hours worked per year from Huberman and Minns (2007). UK from Crafts (2021).

Notes: Derived using a standard neoclassical methodology that imposes the identity $\ln(Y/HW) = \ln(K/HW) + \ln(A)$ where K is capital, HW is hours worked, Y is real output and A is (crude) total factor productivity (*TFP*). Crude *TFP* indicates that labour quality is not separately accounted for, but rather subsumed into *TFP*. Labour productivity growth for Germany in 1851–1871 is the growth of real output per worker.

TFP growth was sustained, but UK TFP growth weakened appreciably. A sizeable part of the excess of TFP growth in Germany compared with the UK came from a structural shift associated with a decline in the share of low-productivity employment in agriculture, which was an important component of catch-up growth. Schulze (2007) estimated that structural shift contributed 0.36 percentage points per year to German productivity growth between 1871 and 1910, whereas the discussion by Matthews et al. (1982: 266) implies that it accounted for only 0.06 percentage points per year in the UK between 1873 and 1913.

Ideally, a contribution from labour quality should be included in the accounting, but a full treatment of this is not feasible. However, a crude allowance for the impact of education can be attempted. This suggests that rising years of schooling added a bit more to productivity growth (captured in Table 20.2 by TFP) in the UK where it increased from 4.13 years in 1870 to 6.35 years in 1910 than in Germany where it increased from 5.25 years in 1879 to 6.92 years in 1910 (Morrisson and Murtin 2009). If an additional year of schooling is assumed to raise labour quality by 6 percent, the contribution to labour productivity growth would have been 0.17 percent per year in Germany and 0.22 percent per year in the UK over the 40-year period.

Capital deepening contributed more to labour productivity growth in Germany than in the UK (0.25 percentage points per year) according to the estimates in Table 20.2. To some extent, this may be expected as a corollary of faster TFP growth, but also reflects a significant difference in the decisions made by investors in both countries, as reported in Table 20.3. Over

Table 20.3 Savings and Investment (% of GDP)

	Domestic investment	*Foreign investment*	*Savings*
Germany			
1871–1898	11.7	2.2	13.9
1898–1913	14.8	1.6	16.4
1871–1913	12.8	2.0	14.8
UK			
1873–1899	7.9	4.3	12.2
1899–1913	8.4	5.4	13.8
1873–1913	8.0	4.7	12.7
Memorandum item			
Foreign capital stock, 1913 ($bn.)			
Germany	6.7		
UK	19.5		

Sources: Jorda et al. (2019), Obstfeld and Taylor (2004).
Note: Foreign investment equals balance of payments current account surplus.

the entire period, Germany invested 12.8 percent of GDP at home and 2.0 percent abroad compared with 8.0 and 4.7 percent, respectively, for the UK. Savings constituted a larger share of GDP in Germany, but more importantly, a much higher proportion of savings were invested at home. Accordingly, the UK had a much larger stock of foreign assets in 1913, and net property income from abroad was a much greater proportion of GDP (8.6 percent versus 1.9 percent).[1]

A complementary analysis of contributions to the difference in labour productivity levels (based on output per worker) is reported in Table 20.4. This shows that the gap between the two countries in 1910 is almost all due to higher TFP in the UK. Although the UK was investing abroad rather heavily at this point, the contribution of capital per worker was similar in Germany and the UK. Despite common preconceptions to the contrary, there is little difference in the contribution of labour quality. Slightly more German workers had intermediate skills (9.7 versus 7.5 percent) but slightly more British workers had higher skills (0.9 versus 0.6 percent) (Broadberry 2003). The lower level of TFP in Germany may well largely reflect inefficiency in the use of factor inputs rather than an inferior level of technology. However, this awaits further analysis. It tends to support the suggestion that faster German TFP growth in the preceding decades was largely based on catch-up rather than superior technological progress.

It is interesting to look at comparative productivity levels at the sectoral level as seen in Table 20.5. Germany performed very well in industry but was slow to catch up in agriculture and services. In 1911, a large low-productivity agricultural sector was a major reason for Germany's labour

Table 20.4 Contributions to Germany/UK labour productivity gap, 1910

	Labour quality	*Capital*	*TFP*	*Total*
Agriculture	0.0	-5.8	-26.9	-32.7
Industry	1.6	18.9	1.5	22.0
Services	0.5	-2.3	-16.9	-18.7
GDP	−0.1	0.2	-24.6	-24.5

Source: Broadberry (2003).
Note: These estimates are derived using the standard neoclassical formula for levels accounting: $\ln(Y/L)_G - \ln(Y/L)_{UK} = \alpha(\ln(K/L)_G - \ln(K/L)_{UK}) + \beta(\ln(HK/L)_G - \ln(HK/L)_{UK}) + (\ln(A_G) - \ln(A_{UK}))$. This is implemented using labour quality (*HK*) estimates based on shares of the labour force with no skills, intermediate skills, and higher skills weighted by their relative wages. Labour productivity is measured per worker (*Y/L*). For other symbols, see Table 20.2. $\alpha = 0.4$ and $\beta = 0.6$.

Table 20.5 Relative productivity in Germany at the sectoral level (UK = 100)

	Agriculture	*Industry*	*Services*	*GDP*
Y/L				
1871	55.7	91.7	62.8	59.5
1881	54.7	93.7	61.3	57.3
1891	53.7	99.3	64.4	60.5
1901	67.2	105.0	71.9	68.4
1911	67.3	127.7	73.4	75.5
TFP				
1871	58.3	86.0	69.7	61.6
1891	59.8	86.1	71.9	63.2
1911	71.4	102.6	83.2	75.3
Memorandum item: *Shares of employment (%)*				
Germany				
1871	49.5	29.1	21.4	
1913	34.5	37.9	27.6	
UK				
1871	22.2	42.4	35.4	
1911	11.8	44.1	44.1	

Source: Broadberry (2006).
Note: Labour productivity is measured per worker.

and TFP productivity gaps with the UK with the services sector making a somewhat smaller contribution. German industrial labour productivity was already ahead of that of the UK by 1901. As Table 20.6 shows, relative productivity levels within manufacturing varied a great deal in the early twentieth century with a marked German superiority in cement, chemicals, iron and steel, and non-ferrous metals, but a British lead in the other activities that can be quantified.

Table 20.6 Relative labour productivity in manufacturing c. 1907 (UK = 100)

General chemicals	126.6
Coke	98.9
Iron and steel	137.8
Nonferrous metals	157.9
Motor vehicles	89.7
Cotton	87.3
Silk	74.9
Leather	67.8
Brewing	90.5
Tobacco	28.3
Sugar	47.3
Cement	124.1
Total manufacturing	108.4

Source: Broadberry and Burhop (2008).

3 Did Victorian Britain fail?

The heading of this section is also the title of a famous article written by McCloskey. In it he claimed that in the pre-First World War period, the British economy was 'growing as rapidly as permitted by the growth of its resources and the effective exploitation of the available technology' (McCloskey 1970a: 451). This conclusion was based on three neoclassical arguments. First, using the insights of the traditional growth model, he argued that devoting more resources to home investment would have run into diminishing returns. Second, he claimed that the technical choices made by British firms were efficient and that the highly competitive market environment ensured that there would be no serious and persistent errors at the industry level while the capital market operated to equalise returns at the margin to different types of investment. Third, he maintained that British productivity growth was similar to that in the United States, aside from an inconsequential slowdown in the Edwardian era, and in any case could not have been any higher as would be the case with exogenous technological progress. At the same time, in another paper (McCloskey 1970b) he calculated that any loss to UK national income from German industrialisation was trivial—no more than 0.2 percent in 1913—and concluded that technology, rather than exports, was the key to British prosperity.

If McCloskey is right, then faster German productivity growth before World War I was to be expected since it had considerable scope for catch-up, was inevitable once Germany embarked on modern economic growth, and did not have any adverse consequences for the UK. Allegations of a growth failure continued after McCloskey's intervention including entrepreneurial failure leading to sluggish development and adoption of new technology (Landes 1998), capital market failure with excessive foreign investment and too little finance for domestic industry (Kennedy 1987), and an inadequate national innovation system with sub-optimal investment in human capital and R&D (Pollard 1989).

Some parts of McCloskey's defence of British growth performance stand up well to scrutiny. It is a staple of the literature that the only well-established failure to adopt cost-effective new technology, namely not to switch from the Leblanc to the Solvay process in soda manufacturing, was in a cartelised activity; this is seen as underlining the point that competition was an antidote to entrepreneurial failure (Magee 2004). In the most-studied choices of technology, the evidence seems clear that the British industry was rational to stick with mule spinning for the vast majority of its cotton textile production (Leunig 2001; Ciliberto 2010) and that the delay in adopting the basic process for steelmaking was justified (Wengenroth 1994; Broadberry 1997).

Although the new economic history has largely succeeded in rejecting claims of managerial failure in the pre-1914 British economy, complete exoneration would be going too far. For example, Crafts et al. (2008) quantified the excess of actual over minimum feasible costs for a sample of 14 major railway companies and concluded that median cost inefficiency was 10.2 percent in 1900, equivalent to about 1 percent of GDP. Two salient features of the railway sector were that competition was weak, as were the shareholders in companies that were notable for the separation of ownership and control. This entailed significant principal-agent problems as railway managers had considerable scope to pursue their own objectives and to fail to minimise costs at least while profits remained 'acceptable'.

There was no major capital market failure. Foreign investment accounted for about a third of all British savings, but this was justified by the returns available and the diversification of risk that was achieved (cf. Goetzman and Ukhov 2006; Chabot and Kurz 2010). British investors would not have been well served by switching out of foreign assets into new domestic industries (Edelstein 1982; Chabot and Kurz 2010). The financial system was not markedly inferior to that of Germany, despite oft-repeated claims to that effect. In a specialised capital market, the clearing banks provided valuable support to industry through financing working capital while longer term finance could be obtained through corporate bonds and equities and through retained earnings (Chambers 2014). The market value of corporations was 256 percent of GDP in 1910 (Hannah 2015) and the stock of corporate bonds had grown to 22 percent of GDP in 1909, compared with only 0.5 percent 50 years earlier (Coyle and Turner 2013). Universal banks in Germany did not make a significant difference to the performance of firms with which they had close relationships or supply major amounts of finance for industrialisation (Edwards and Ogilvie 1996; Fohlin 2007).

Clearly, improvements were necessary, but perhaps not in the direction of adopting a German-style banking system. For example, company law was inadequate in various respects which meant company accounts did not present adequate information (Edwards 1989) and that the market for new issues was inefficient (Foreman-Peck 1990). Accordingly, an adequate market for corporate control through takeovers did not exist (Hannah 1974).

McCloskey's claims that British productivity performance was on par with that of the United States are not borne out by the estimates that are now available. As was reported in Table 20.2, labour productivity growth in the UK fell from 2.06 percent per year in 1856–73 to 1.18 percent in 1873–99 and 0.84 percent in 1899–1913, whereas the United States recorded 2.11 percent per year in 1874–99 and 1.72 percent in 1899–1913 (Kendrick 1961: 333–34). A critic of UK performance may look at Table 20.1 and emphasise the failure of productivity growth to accelerate in the early twentieth century and to match the much faster TFP growth achieved by the United States (1.7 percent per year in 1899–1929 and 2.3 percent per year in 1929–41) as the second industrial revolution took hold.

The estimates in Table 20.7 suggest that the United States had attained a higher TFP level than the UK by 1911, except in the service sector. The large TFP gap in manufacturing is especially striking and at first sight, this may seem to connote British failure. However, this is rather misleading as these estimates reflect the direct impacts of scale economies and natural resources and of technologies that were developed in the American environment to exploit scale and cheap energy (Abramovitz and David 2001) but were not appropriate for British conditions. Cain and Paterson (1986) found that from 1850 to 1920, technological changes in American manufacturing generated economies of scale and entailed pervasive materials- and capital-using and labour-saving biases. The network of cumulative technological learning was a national one at this time (Nelson and Wright 1992).[2] In the second industrial revolution, this underwrote clear American advantages in much cheaper electricity (Ristuccia and Solomou 2014), which promoted the diffusion of electric motors and the associated transformation of American factories, and in the mass production of cars, which was not viable in the much smaller (and more working-class) British market (Bowden 1991).

McCloskey's argument was fundamentally based on an exogenous growth model and the proposition that faster UK TFP growth was not possible. The subsequent development of endogenous growth economics complicated matters. An analysis of this kind may explain the unmatched acceleration of American TFP growth as unavoidable given an economic environment that was more conducive to innovative effort and that tended to produce

Table 20.7 USA/UK Productivity levels in 1911 (UK = 100)

	Labour productivity	*TFP*
Agriculture	181	208
Industry	206	161
Manufacturing	214	185
Services	119	79
GDP	138	106

Sources: Broadberry (2006) revised in accordance with Woltjer (2013).

innovations that were unsuited to British conditions. It may also point to policy interventions (perhaps by rivals like Germany and the United States) that could have raised British TFP growth but were not pursued.

In the early twentieth century, the United States had several obvious advantages that endogenous innovation theories may emphasise because they influenced the expected profitability of expensive innovative effort. These included a much larger domestic market and capital stock, and greater availability of engineers and science/technology graduates. Large markets encouraged independent inventors (Nicholas 2010) and partly explain the higher R&D spending of firms in the United States, perhaps 0.25 percent of GDP (in a much bigger economy) compared with 0.02 percent. American factor endowments encouraged 'directed technical change', which was often not appropriate for use in British conditions but increased the transatlantic TFP and income gaps. Labour scarcity in the United States may have increased the rate of technological change (Acemoglu 2010). These arguments go against the notion of an avoidable failure.

However, the UK's national innovation system left a good deal to be desired, compared unfavourably with that of Germany, and would have benefited from a more proactive government policy to boost technological progress. This is where an approach based on endogenous growth might undermine McCloskey's position, especially in the context of the second industrial revolution as technological progress became increasingly science-based. The UK's technological performance was mediocre as highlighted by the patenting data (Nicholas 2014). In 1883, the UK's share of foreign patents in the United States was 34.6 percent as against 18.7 percent for Germany; by 1913, the UK's share was 23.3 percent compared with Germany's 34.0 percent (Pavitt and Soete 1982).

Although small beginnings were made to promote scientific research, for example, through the National Physical Laboratory (1899) and the Medical Research Council (1913), public expenditure on science and technology was only 0.06 percent of GDP in 1914. This implied that there was too little government support for R&D, a pro-growth activity where social returns exceed private returns. There was a rapid expansion of scientific and technical education that began in the late nineteenth century with significant investments in municipal technical colleges, polytechnics, and red-brick universities. However, in 1910, there were only 3000 science and technology students in UK universities compared with 25,000 in Germany (Pollard 1989). The responsiveness of the German university system may have been a key factor behind the success of synthetic dyes in particular and the chemical industry, in general, a sector where German outperformance of the UK was very clear both in global market share (Brenner and Murmann 2016) and patenting (Cantwell 1991). The build-up of knowledge stocks reflected in patenting was a significant factor in the export success of German mechanical engineering (Labuske and Streb 2008). German foreign direct investment in the UK revealed strong ownership advantages in the science-based industries of the second industrial revolution (Hagen 1999).

Overall, it still seems reasonable to conclude that there was no massive growth failure in the pre-1914 UK economy. American outperformance may have had its roots in unique American advantages based on a favourable configuration of factor prices and market size rather than serious errors by British businesses or governments. That said, McCloskey (1970a) certainly went too far and glossed over weaknesses in productivity performance.

4 Economic implications of Anglo-German trade rivalry

From 1880 to 1913, Germany overtook the UK in terms of its share of world manufacturing production, which increased from 4.9 to 14.8 percent, whereas that of the UK fell from 22.9 percent to 13.6 percent (Bairoch 1982). This was accompanied by a narrowing of the gap in the shares of world manufacturing exports, which rose for Germany from 22.4 percent in 1899 to 26.6 percent in 1913, compared with 33.2 and 30.2 percent, respectively, for the UK. Losses in the market share reduced UK exports by $0.36 billion (about 18 percent) and raised German exports by $0.33 billion over the same period (Maizels 1963). In the early twentieth century, the revealed comparative advantage of the UK remained in the old export staples of the industrial-revolution era, especially textiles, whereas that of Germany included new industries such as chemicals and electricals (Crafts 1989; Varian 2020).

The industrialisation of Germany was understood by many at the time as a threat to British economic prospects. It provoked demands for the imposition of tariffs on German imports (Hoffman 1933) and intensified demands for protection from groups like the Tariff Reform League. A more sophisticated version of the case for intervention was presented by Richardson (1965) who argued that the UK economy was 'over-committed to its old industries' and needed infant-industry trade policies to encourage the growth of new industries. In fact, the proponents of tariffs were badly defeated in the 1906 elections. The UK remained a 'free-trade' economy until World War I, and only became seriously protectionist in 1932.

Both Germany and (much more so) the United States employed protectionist policies. In 1913, the average German and American tariffs on manufactured imports were 13 and 44 percent, respectively (Bairoch 1993). It has often been claimed that protection was highly favourable for American economic growth and was central to the ascent of the United States to world economic leadership (Chang 2003). By implication, the UK's free trade stance was a mistake. However, detailed analysis suggests otherwise. Crafts (2018) noted that slower productivity growth in UK manufacturing compared with the United States was intra-sectoral and not a result of having too small a new-industry sector.[3] Irwin (2001) pointed out that faster productivity growth in the United States mainly accrued in non-traded sectors that did not benefit from protection and that American policies did not add up to a successful infant-industry strategy.

Germany was less protectionist than the average of western European countries (see Chapter 16 of this volume) but it did protect agriculture more than manufacturing. Lehmann and O'Rourke (2011) estimate average tariff rates of 12 percent and 5 percent, respectively, on the eve of World War I. This suggests both that the imposition of tariffs was not a successful infant industry policy and that structural change (an important part of catch-up growth in Germany) was retarded.[4] Protectionist policies contributed toward trade as a share of GDP being lower in Germany (41 percent in 1913) than in the UK (56 percent). This can be expected to have had a cost to Germany in terms of lower income and productivity—amounting to about 7 percent of GDP using the elasticity of 0.2 estimated by Feyrer (2009).[5]

Careful econometric analysis of cross-country evidence does not support the hypothesis that higher tariffs raised growth rates in this period—if anything, it points to the opposite conclusion (Schularick and Solomou 2011). This may reflect the tendency for protection not to be tightly focused on a few selected sectors with excellent growth prospects or positive externalities for the rest of the economy (Tena-Junguito 2010).

Similar problems would have undermined any British attempt to use protectionism to promote faster growth. The political economy of tariff protection was such that the proposals that had the most political support such as those made by Joseph Chamberlain would have actually tended to divert employment towards traditional sectors like agriculture and textiles, which were relatively labour-intensive rather than new growth industries (Thomas 1984).[6] A general tariff policy may have weakened competition in product markets with potentially adverse effects on productivity performance. If the real problem was market failure, which implied too little investment in human capital and R&D, then the right response was policy intervention by the government to address these failures directly.

Although there are endogenous growth models in which the protection of manufacturing could improve productivity performance in the long run, it seems unlikely that this would have been the outcome for the late-Victorian UK economy. American overtaking was not down to protectionism. The adoption of protection in the face of German economic advances would have been an adverse impact of German economic development on Britain but it did not happen.

A traditional explanation for slower UK economic growth from the 1870s is that it resulted from a slowdown in export growth (Meyer 1955; Coppock 1956). The volume of British exports grew at 5.9 percent per year from 1831 to 1857, 3.5 percent from 1857 to 1873, but only 2.6 percent per year from 1873 to 1913. To a considerable extent, this reflected a weakening of exports to industrial countries, especially in Europe whose share of UK exports fell from 35 percent in 1865–74 to 24 percent in 1905–13 (Feinstein 1996). It may be reasonable to consider this an exogenous shock that could have had adverse consequences, but a causal link from this shock to weaker UK productivity growth has not been established (cf. Feinstein 1996).

McCloskey (1970b) made an admittedly crude estimate of the impact of foreign industrialisation on British national income. The methodology was partial equilibrium comparative statics with intelligent guesses at relevant elasticities of demand and supply for manufactured exports (treated as a composite commodity). The result was that, if the manufacturing output of the rest of the world was reduced to the 1870 level in 1913, the UK loss of producer surplus minus gains to consumers and output from the redeployment of resources used in exporting manufactures would amount at most to 3.9 and probably less than 2 percent of national income. The loss from just reducing German manufacturing output to the 1870 level would have been about one-eighth of the total. This exercise may be improved upon using modern computable general equilibrium modelling.

5 Conclusion

Economic growth in Germany was considerably faster than in the UK after 1871. To a large extent, this represents successful catch-up growth at a time when UK productivity growth had slowed down from its mid-nineteenth-century peak. Nevertheless, in 1913, real GDP per capita and labour productivity in Germany were still well below the UK level. At that point, Germany was held back by a relatively large and low-productivity agricultural sector. Germany overtook the UK in industrial labour productivity around the turn of the twentieth century and was more successful than was the UK in developing new industries like chemicals.

The claim that relatively slow growth connotes a British failure has been hotly disputed. Whereas the complete exoneration of British performance would definitely be going too far, it is fair to say that a number of well-known criticisms have been refuted including capital market failure, slowness to adopt new technology, and retention of free trade. The UK's main weakness was its national innovation system, where more proactive government policies to address market failures would have been appropriate. That said, in any case, it was probably not possible to match the big advance in productivity growth achieved by the United States in the early twentieth century.

There is no strong reason to think that Germany's successful economic development had important adverse effects on the British economy even though by the early twentieth century, Germany's industrial strength was increasingly considered a threat by British commentators and politicians. The most obvious way in which the UK may have suffered is through international trade and the loss of economic rents obtained by its exporters. However, the only attempt to quantify this loss found that its impact was very small.

Notes

1 This implies that German GNP per person was 69.6 percent of the UK level in 1913, compared with 74.1 percent on a GDP basis as in Table 20.1.
2 This amounts to an argument that technology was not universal. Using this as a defence of McCloskey is somewhat ironic because it is not the standard neoclassical assumption.

3 If the sectoral composition of American manufacturing had been the same as that in the UK, in 1899–1909, its total manufacturing labour productivity growth would have *increased* from 1.65 to 1.73 percent per year.

4 Dedinger (2006) explored the impact of protection on changes in Germany's comparative advantage in exports and concluded that it was negligible. However, Webb (1980) asserted that the elimination of competition through tariff protection and cartels encouraged investment in technologies that were capital and scale intensive, thus raising productivity in the German steel industry.

5 This is smaller than the oft-cited estimate of 0.5 to 0.75 in Feyrer (2019). However, this is seen by the author as more applicable to a case in which trade in goods is the main channel of influence.

6 Thomas estimated that employment in agriculture and textiles would have risen by 45441 and 149851, respectively, whereas employment in chemicals, motor and cycle, and engineering would have risen by 241, 3102, and 10619, respectively, had a Chamberlain tariff been introduced in 1907, reflecting the pattern of effective protection that this would have entailed.

References

Abramovitz, M. and David, P. A. (2001) 'Two centuries of American macroeconomic growth: from exploitation of resource abundance to knowledge-driven development', *Stanford Institute for Economic Policy Research Discussion Paper 01–05.*

Acemoglu, D. (2010) 'When does labor scarcity encourage innovation?', *Journal of Political Economy*, Vol. 118 (6): 1037–76.

Bairoch, P. (1982) 'International industrialisation levels from 1750 to 1980', *Journal of European Economic History*, Vol. 11 (2): 269–331.

Bairoch, P. (1993) *Economics and World History: Myths and Paradoxes*, Brighton: Wheatsheaf.

Bowden, S. M. (1991) 'Demand and supply constraints in the interwar UK car industry: did the manufacturers get it right?', *Business History*, Vol. 33 (2): 241–67.

Brenner, T. and Murmann, J. P. (2016) 'Using simulation experiments to test historical explanations: the development of the German dye industry, 1857–1913', *Journal of Evolutionary Economics*, Vol. 26: 907–32.

Broadberry, S. N. (1997) *The Productivity Race*, Cambridge: Cambridge University Press.

Broadberry, S. N. (2003) 'Human capital and productivity performance: Britain, the United States and Germany, 1870–1990', in P. A. David and M. Thomas (eds), *The Economic Future in Historical Perspective*, Oxford: Oxford University Press, pp. 103–33.

Broadberry, S. (2006) *Market Services and the Productivity Race, 1850–2000*, Cambridge: Cambridge University Press.

Burhop, C. and Wolff, G. B. (2005) 'A compromise estimate of German net national product, 1851–1913, and its implications for growth and business cycles', *Journal of Economic History*, Vol. 65 (3): 613–57.

Broadberry, S. and Burhop, C. (2008) 'Resolving the Anglo-German industrial productivity puzzle, 1895–1935: a response to professor Ritschl', *Journal of Economic History*, Vol. 68 (3): 930–34.

Cain, L. P. and Paterson, D. G. (1986) 'Biased technical change, scale, and factor proportions in American industry, 1850–1919', *Journal of Economic History*, Vol. 46 (1): 153–64.

Cantwell, J. (1991) 'Historical trends in international patterns of technological Innovation', in J. Foreman-Peck (ed), *New Perspectives on the Late-Victorian Economy*, Cambridge: Cambridge University Press, pp. 37–72.

Chabot, B. R. and Kurz, C. J. (2010) 'That's where the money was: foreign bias and English investment abroad, 1866–1907', *Economic Journal*, Vol. 120 (547): 1056–79.

Chambers, D. (2014) 'The city and the corporate economy since 1870', in R. Floud, J. Humphries and P. Johnson (eds), *The Cambridge Economic History of Modern Britain*, Vol. 2., Cambridge: Cambridge University Press, pp. 255–78.

Chang, H.-J. (2003) 'Kicking away the ladder: infant industry promotion in historical perspective', *Oxford Development Studies*, Vol. 31 (1): 21–32.

Ciliberto, F. (2010) 'Were British cotton entrepreneurs technologically backward? Firm-based evidence on the adoption of ring spinning', *Explorations in Economic History*, Vol. 47 (4): 487–504.

Coppock, D. J. (1956) 'The climacteric of the 1890s: a critical note', *The Manchester School*, Vol. 24 (1): 1–31.

Coyle, C. and Turner, J. D. (2013) 'Law, politics, and financial development: the great reversal of the UK corporate debt market', *Journal of Economic History*, Vol. 73 (3): 810–46.

Crafts, N. (1989) 'Revealed comparative advantage in manufacturing, 1899–1950', *Journal of European Economic History*, Vol. 18 (1): 127–37.

Crafts, N. (2018) *Forging Ahead, Falling Behind and Fighting Back: British Economic Growth from the Industrial Revolution to the Financial Crisis*, Cambridge: Cambridge University Press.

Crafts, N. (2021) 'The sources of British economic growth since the Industrial Revolution: not the same old story', *Journal of Economic Surveys*, Vol. 35 (3): 697–709.

Crafts, N., Leunig, T. and Mulatu, A. (2008) 'Were British railway companies well-managed in the early twentieth century?', *Economic History Review*, Vol. 61 (4): 842–66.

Crafts, N. and Mills, T.C. (2020) 'Sooner than you think: the pre-1914 UK productivity slowdown was Victorian not Edwardian', *European Review of Economic History*, Vol. 20 (4): 736–48.

Dedinger, B. (2006) 'From virtual free trade to virtual protectionism, or, did protection have any part in Germany's rise to commercial power, 1850 to 1913?', in J.-P. Dormois and P. Lains (eds), *Classical Trade Protectionism, 1815–1914*. London: Routledge, pp. 227–49.

Edelstein, M. (1982) *Overseas Investment in the Age of High Imperialism: The United Kingdom, 1850–1914*, New York: Columbia University Press.

Edwards, J. R. (1989) *A History of Financial Accounting*. London: Routledge.

Edwards, J. and Ogilvie, S. (1996) 'Universal banks and German industrialization: a reappraisal', *Economic History Review*, Vol. 49 (4): 427–46.

Feinstein, C. H. (1996) 'Exports and British economic growth (1850–1914)', in P. Mathias and J.A. Davis (eds), *International Trade and British Economic Growth*, Oxford: Blackwell, pp. 76–95.

Feyrer, J. (2009) 'Distance, trade and income: the 1967 to 1975 closing of the Suez Canal as a natural experiment', *NBER Working Paper* 15557.

Feyrer, J. (2019) 'Trade and income: exploiting time series in geography', *American Economic Journal: Applied Economics*, Vol. 11 (4): 1–35.

Fohlin, C. (2007) *Finance Capitalism and Germany's Rise to Industrial Power*, Cambridge: Cambridge University Press.

Foreman-Peck, J. (1990) 'The 1856 companies act and the birth and death of firms', in P. Jobert and M. Moss (eds), *The Birth and Death of Companies: An Historical Perspective*, Carnforth: Parthenon, pp. 33–46.

Goetzmann, W. N. and Ukhov, A. D. (2006) 'British investment overseas 1870–1913: a modern portfolio theory approach', *Review of Finance*, Vol. 10 (2): 261–300.

Hagen, A. (1999) 'German direct investment in the UK, 1871–1918', *Business History*, Vol. 41 (2): 37–68.

Hannah, L. (1974) 'Takeover bids in Britain before 1950: an exercise in business pre-history', *Business History*, Vol. 16 (1): 65–77.

Hannah, L. (2015) 'A global corporate census: publicly traded and close companies in 1910', *Economic History Review*, Vol. 68 (2): 548–73.

Hoffman, R. J. S. (1933) *Great Britain and the German Trade Rivalry, 1875–1914*, Philadelphia: University of Pennsylvania Press.

Hoffmann, W. G. (1965) *Das Wachstum der deutschen Wirtschaft seit der Mitte des 19. Jahrhunderts*, Berlin: Springer.

Huberman, M. and Minns, C. (2007) 'The times they are not changin': days and hours of work in the old and new worlds, 1870–2000', *Explorations in Economic History*, Vol. 44 (4): 538–67.

Irwin, D. A. (2001) 'Tariffs and Growth in Late Nineteenth-Century America', *The World Economy*, Vol. 24 (1): 15–30.

Jorda, P., Schularick, M. and Taylor, A. M. (2019) *Jorda-Schularick-Taylor Macrohistory Database* http://www.macrohistory.net/data/

Kendrick, J. W. (1961) *Productivity Trends in the United States*, Princeton, NJ: Princeton University Press.

Kennedy, W. P. (1987) *Industrial Structure, Capital Markets and the Origins of British Industrial Decline*, Cambridge: Cambridge University Press.

Labuske, K. and Streb, J. (2008) 'Technological creativity and cheap labour? Explaining the growing international competitiveness of German mechanical engineering before World War I', *German Economic Review*, Vol. 9 (1): 65–86.

Landes, D. S. (1998) *The Wealth and Poverty of Nations*, London: Little Brown.

Lehmann, S. H. and O'Rourke, K. H. (2011) 'The structure of protection and growth in the late nineteenth century', *Review of Economics and Statistics*, Vol. 93 (2): 606–16.

Leunig, T. (2001) 'New answers to old questions: explaining the slow adoption of ring spinning in Lancashire, 1890–1913', *Journal of Economic History*, Vol. 61 (2): 439–66.

Maddison, A. (2010) *Historical Statistics of the World Economy, 1-2008AD*. http://www.ggdc.net/maddison.

Magee, G. (2004) 'Manufacturing and technological change', in R. Floud and P. Johnson (eds), *The Cambridge Economic History of Modern Britain*, Vol. 2, Cambridge: Cambridge University Press, pp. 74–98.

Maizels, A. (1963) *Industrial Growth and World Trade: An Empirical Study of Trends in Production, Consumption and Trade in Manufactures from 1899–1959 with a Discussion of Probable Future Trends*, Cambridge: Cambridge University Press.

Matthews, R. C. O., Feinstein, C. H. and Odling-Smee, J. C. (1982) *British Economic Growth 1856–1973*, Stanford: Stanford University Press.

McCloskey, D. N. (1970a) 'Did Victorian Britain fail?', *Economic History Review*, Vol. 23 (3): 446–59.

McCloskey, D. N. (1970b) 'Britain's loss from foreign industrialization: a provisional estimate', *Explorations in Economic History*, Vol. 8 (2): 141–52.

Meyer, J. R. (1955) 'An input-output approach to evaluating the influence of exports on Britain's industrial production in the late nineteenth century', *Explorations in Entrepreneurial History*, Vol. 8 (1): 12–34.

Morrisson, C. and Murtin, F. (2009) 'The century of education', *Journal of Human Capital*, Vol. 3 (1): 1–42.

Nelson, R. R. and Wright, G. (1992) 'The rise and fall of American technological leadership: the postwar era in historical perspective', *Journal of Economic Literature*, Vol. 30 (4): 1931–1964.

Nicholas, T. (2010) 'The role of independent invention in U. S. technological development, 1880–1930', *Journal of Economic History*, Vol. 70 (1): 57–82.

Nicholas, T. (2014) 'Technology, innovation and economic growth in Britain since 1870', in R. Floud, J. Humphries and P. Johnson (eds), *The Cambridge Economic History of Modern Britain*, Vol. 2., Cambridge: Cambridge University Press, pp. 181–204.

Obstfeld, M. and Taylor, A. M. (2004) *Global Capital Markets: Integration, Crisis, and Growth*, Cambridge: Cambridge University Press.

Pavitt, K. and Soete, L. (1982) 'International differences in economic growth and the international location of innovation', in H. Giersch (ed), *Emerging Technologies*, Tübingen: Mohr Siebeck, pp. 105–33.

Pfister, U. (2020) 'The Crafts-Harley view of German industrialization: an independent estimate of the income side of net national product, 1851–1913', *European Review of Economic History*, Vol. 24 (3): 502–21.

Pollard, S. (1989) *Britain's Prime and Britain's Decline: the British Economy 1870–1914*, London: Edward Arnold.

Richardson, H. W. (1965) 'Over-commitment in Britain before 1930', *Oxford Economic Papers*, Vol. 17 (2): 237–62.

Ristuccia, C. A. and Solomou, S. (2014) 'Can general purpose technology theory explain economic growth? Electrical power as a case study', *European Review of Economic History*, Vol. 18 (3): 227–47.

Schularick, M. and Solomou, S. (2011) 'Tariffs and economic growth in the first era of globalization', *Journal of Economic Growth*, Vol. 16 (1): 33–70.

Schulze, M. S. (2007) 'Origins of catch-up failure: comparative productivity growth in the Habsburg Empire, 1870–1910', *European Review of Economic History*, Vol. 11 (2): 189–218.

Tena-Junguito, A. (2010) 'Bairoch revisited: tariff structure and growth in the late nineteenth century', *European Review of Economic History*, Vol. 14 (1): 111–43.

Thomas, M. (1984) *An Input-Output Approach to the British Economy, 1890–1914*, Ph.D. thesis, University of Oxford.

Thomas, R. and Dimsdale, N. (2017) 'A millennium of UK data', *Bank of England OBRA Dataset*. http://www.bankofengland.co.uk/research/Pages/onebank/threecenturies.aspx.

Varian, B. D. (2020) 'The manufacturing comparative advantages of late-Victorian Britain', *Cliometrica*, Vol. 14 (3): 479–506.

Webb, S. B. (1980) 'Tariffs, cartels, technology, and growth in the German steel industry, 1879 to 1914', *Journal of Economic History*, Vol. 40 (2): 309–29.

Wengenroth, U. (1994) *Enterprise and Technology: the German and British Steel Industries, 1865–1895*, Cambridge: Cambridge University Press.

Williams, E. E. (1896) *Made in Germany*, London: William Heinemann.

Woltjer, P. J. (2013) 'Taking over: a new US/UK productivity benchmark and the nature of American leadership c. 1910', *Groningen Growth and Development Centre Research Memorandum* 140.

Index

Note: **Bold** page numbers refer to tables; *italic* page numbers refer to figures and page numbers followed by "n" denote endnotes.